THE
CANADIAN
FINANCIAL
SYSTEM

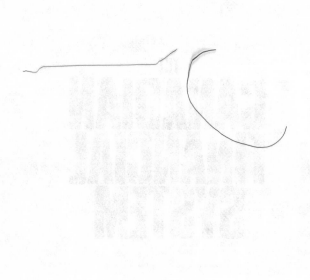

THE
CANADIAN FINANCIAL SYSTEM

Warren J. Blackman

Associate Professor of Economics
University of Calgary

McGRAW-HILL RYERSON LIMITED

Toronto   Montreal   New York   St. Louis   San Francisco
Auckland   Bogotá   Guatemala   Hamburg   Johannesburg
Lisbon   London   Madrid   Mexico   New Delhi   Panama
Paris   San Juan   São Paulo   Singapore   Sydney   Tokyo

THE CANADIAN FINANCIAL SYSTEM

ISBN 0-07-082987-X

1 2 3 4 5 6 7 8 9 10 D 9 8 7 6 5 4 3 2 1 0

Printed and bound in Canada

Care has been taken to trace ownership of copyright material contained in this
text. The publishers will gladly take any information that will enable them to
rectify any reference or credit in subsequent editions.

Canadian Cataloguing in Publication Data

Blackman, Warren, date
The Canadian financial system

Includes index.

ISBN 0-07-082987-X

1. Finance – Canada. 2. Banks and banking –
Canada. 3. Money – Canada. I. Title.

HG153.B53   332'.0971   C79-094742-0

Contents

Preface

Customarily, a statement as to why a book has been written and what it proposes to accomplish is included at its beginning, and this book is no exception. To put it simply, it has been written for two reasons: first, there is a lack of published Canadian textbook material on the subject of monetary economics, and second, there is very little in published material generally as to what monetary economics is all about. In much of the literature currently being published, the subject of monetary economics has almost been drowned in a flood of continuous dialogue between "monetarists" and "non-monetarists" on the question of the importance of money in a modern economy. The focus of this debate seems to centre on a single idea – the fact that money matters does or does not mean that money is *all* that matters. In other words, the monetarists interpret economic phenomena, particularly inflation and unemployment, as the consequence of changes in the supply of money. The non-monetarists (sometimes referred to as the "income expenditure school") consider the causation chain as the other way round: changes in variables within the structure of the economy bring forth changes in the supply of money.

For many of us as instructors of monetary economics, it has been difficult to deal adequately with a topic that is current enough but that is also a subject of debate. What *is* this particular subject that is so controversial? Is it macroeconomics with a money and banking emphasis, or, is it distinct enough to warrant treatment on its own? It is the conviction that the answer to the latter question is affirmative which served as the motivation to undertake this somewhat lengthy project in the first place.

It is true that monetary economics as a separate study embraces aspects of both micro and macroeconomics. Yet, when seen as an analysis of how money is integrated into our economic lives, the never-ending controversy concerning monetary policy is an issue of importance, certainly, but only an issue and not the major subject. For instance, it is true that countries which have been most successful in controlling their money supply have had the least rates of inflation and unemployment, but this does not mean that monetary economics should be concerned entirely with the supply of money and how it is generated. Similarly, if monetary authorities devote their attention to maintaining a fixed rate of interest, they must ensure that the money supply will be adequate to meet the demand. Again this does not warrant confining the subject of monetary economics to the macroeconomic factors which produce that demand.

Money is, of course, an essential ingredient in the modern economy. Scarcely anyone disputes this, but there are few who can identify its function and show how it renders its service. This is what this book attempts to accomplish.

The principal argument is that money is really no more than a mechanism by which liquidity is transmitted from person to person, and liquidity, in its turn, is the necessary ingredient in the process of exchange. Furthermore, we as individuals in a modern economy have a demand for this liquidity which derives from the very necessity for exchange, both current and future. Contrary to the more common interpretation, however, we do not "bid up" the price level with our extra funds; no one actually participates in an auction in this way. All we really do is finance general price increase with our excess liquidity.

It is unfortunately true that very few students in Canada are familiar with the work of Professor Friederich Hayek and the Austrian School of which he is the greatest living proponent; on the other hand it is impossible for a student to pass a Principles of Economics course without becoming thoroughly immersed in Keynes and post-Keynesian economics. Yet it must be apparent by now that macroeconomics as we have known it does not give us all the answers we seek. It is to correct this apparent "imbalance" in our economics that the contributions of Professor Hayek, particularly his development of capital theory, are included in Part 2, with the emphasis placed on their relationship to the structure of liquidity which the public chooses to hold. Indeed, it might just be true that in developing our economic policies for Canada over the past two decades, we have neglected a very important aspect of economics, viz., long-term consequences, for in the long-run, we are not *all* dead and many of us are forced to live with the results of short-run policy measures.

To justify writing and publishing another book in monetary economics for the reason that everything else currently being published is just not adequate, may sound presumptuous. Nevertheless, this is precisely the rationale underlying this book. The book itself has grown over very many years of teaching Money and Banking as well as experiencing the sense of unease that what ought to have been included in the course material was just not available to students in the current literature. If there are others in the profession who have shared a similar frustration, they are invited to participate in the development of a truly Canadian point of view in the subject of monetary economics, and, hopefully, in the course of time, assist in the shaping of a genuinely Canadian discipline appropriate for Canadian students. In the final analysis, this is the objective of the many years of hard work and effort which have gone into these pages.

W.J.B.

Acknowledgements

Very many people have contributed to this book; so many that the author has occasionally felt like a scribe setting forth the knowledge and experience of others. Much of the material of Part 3 would not have been possible without the assistance of the Bank of Nova Scotia and its European branches. Certainly the descriptive material on foreign banks is due to their kind assistance as well as the cooperation and guidance of friends in British and Swiss banks. The Canada Council was very helpful with its generous assistance which made the necessary beginnings of research possible. To Professor Hayek, Nobel prize-winner, and probably the greatest living economist, is owed a great debt. Any errors committed in the presentation of his principles are purely my own. Also, a great debt is owed to my many students who graciously put up with initial drafts through the years and contributed their own measure of helpful comments and criticisms. Particular thanks goes to the Killam Foundation for financing the writing of the final draft and to my wonderful typist who made the manuscript legible.

Finally, to my loving wife and family who did without a husband and father during the many months of work, a very special acknowledgement.

Introduction

The late Sir Dennis Robertson in his delightful classic, *Money,* said, "A monetary system is like a liver: it does not take up very much of our thoughts when it goes right, but it attracts a great deal of attention when it goes wrong."* Even though he wrote these words a long time ago, they are as true today as then; in fact, considering the pace of economic change as well as the recent turmoils in foreign money markets, it is likely that even a liver would no longer serve as a useful figure.

Indeed, even though money has been the subject of serious thought and study for several hundred years, there is still no general agreement on what a monetary system is, how it works, and what it accomplishes. The trouble is that of all the inventions of the human mind, money is the most flexible; ever-changing and adaptable, it adjusts to the economic system in much the same way as water fills the shape of its vessel. As the economic system changes, so does the monetary system which makes it work.

The analogy of water isn't precisely apt, however, because water adjusts instantly to its container. Not so money. Always there are time lags between the changing economy and the monetary adjustment necessary for adaptation, and it is during these time lags and the accompanying maladjustments that things are likely to go wrong. Like the liver, we try an economic medicine to cure an ever-changing malfunction.

On the other hand, it is precisely because of economic change that it is so difficult to derive valid conclusions which are true for all time. Like a slippery eel, once we *think* we have it, it eludes our grasp. So in beginning a study of money, as this book purports to do, we must avoid the complacency of arriving at final conclusions and considering the task as finished. "Pride goeth before a fall" as many economists have learned from experience.

But what are the objectives in a study of money? What gain of knowledge is to be expected? In the first part of this book, money, or, more precisely, monetary assets, are considered particularly in relation to economic activity. From this, one would expect to find out how best to organize his own economic life in accordance with the ever-changing economic scene. Or, even more important, one may interpret and assess the actions of the government in terms of monetary policy.

In the second part, the capital market is explored. Here we find what is probably the most interesting and least understood of all our economic activities – stock markets, bonds, and other forms of investments. That is, when *should* we buy stocks or bonds? Is land really a better form of investment? Rarely can

---

Cambridge Economic Handbooks, 1948, p. 2.

we find answers to questions such as these from even so-called "experts." In fact, it is often difficult to identify a rational behaviour pattern in most stock and bond price movements.

Part 3 is concerned with international money, and, more specifically, how Canada fits within an international flow of capital. What are Eurodollars and why do they exist? Are we really independent in a monetary sense, or do we rely more on U.S. capital than we need? These are questions we should all ask ourselves, particularly since we, as a nation, are a member of an international community, and the value of our dollar abroad is important to us.

In the last analysis, no single book can hope to provide answers to questions or solutions to problems as they arise. The best that can be expected is that the reader may find himself equipped to arrive at his own rational solutions and answers to a host of problems and questions which are certain to arise throughout the economic lives of all of us. This is precisely what this book is all about.

PART 1

Money in the Process of Exchange

In our society the era of exchanging goods and services by means of barter belongs to the past—the days of our pioneer forefathers. There is a reason for this: our society which uses money and financial institutions which accompany money is vastly more efficient than the simple economy of early Canada. This is not to suggest that direct exchange without the use of money is impossible; it is just more convenient to use a separate "commodity," money, as a *numeraire* against which all other goods and services can be measured in terms of value. This is the central thrust of Part I. It explores the reasons for money, its purposes, and its accomplishments.

Chapter One considers the demand for money, why it is needed, and why it has a value. As a background to this interesting and somewhat abstract concept, it introduces the Quantity Theory of Money as developed by Fisher, Pigou, and, later, Friedman. In addition, and more important for the analyses of later chapters, it introduces the process of monetization.

Chapter Two continues this analysis to show why money is required (or "demanded") by our payments process. It also looks at our Canadian money supply statistics in the light of a Quantity Theory analysis, sometimes referred to as a "crude Quantity Theory." More fundamental, however, is the introduction of a theoretical model relating demand for money and the level of prices which is somewhat different from the more typical Quantity Theory. In this analysis, sellers are not suppliers of goods and services at all but "demanders" of money. Similarly, buyers and potential buyers are actually suppliers and potential suppliers of money. Examining our economy in this way not only helps to understand the direct relationship between the amount of money and the price level, but also helps to shed more light on the inflation/unemployment processes of our recent past.

Chapter Three, the "Genesis of Money," analyzes the process of money manufacturing by the banking system. Each bank is considered as a manufacturing firm which produces a specific commodity, money, in response to profit maximization principles. In this sense, banks are no different from any other firm, and hence can be treated in the same way in terms of theory.

In Chapter Four, the very important concept of liquidity is introduced. Of the "commodities" which range through the spectrum of monetary assets, money is unique in that it represents 100% liquidity — a quality which derives from its exchange media function. At the same time it is the overall structure of liquidity which the public desires, both as creditors and debtors, which makes possible the functioning of the banking system as intermediaries between creditors and debtors. In this way the banks act as dealers in liquidity. The money manu-facturing function of chartered banks, while it derives from this intermediary function, is really subordinate to the intermediary function.

The Central Bank, its function as a money "creator" (as opposed to a money manufacturer) is discussed in Chapter Five. The Bank of Canada, its origins and development, is considered along with the important aspects of monetary policy and techniques which have been developed through the years. The relationship and function of the Bank of Canada within the entire money and payments system is also considered in the light of the decennial revisions of the Bank Act both past and present.

Finally, Chapter Six concludes Part I with a brief examination of other banking systems of which some, notably German and Swiss, are quite different from the Canadian. The objective of such a cursory glance at other countries is for the purpose of comparing and contrasting common characteristics of our joint bank-ing systems. In some instances, we have much to learn from the experience of others; in others, the opposite is true, for our system, and the British and Ameri-can systems from which it springs, does have much in its favour. In view of our recent history of unemployment and inflation, however, it would appear that Canada can learn a great deal.

CHAPTER 1

Demand for Money

I. THE NATURE OF ASSETS

A. Financial Assets

All of us as humans possess some kind of assets which constitute our "wealth." Such assets may assume a number of varied shapes and forms, as, for example, clothing, automobiles, houses, etc. Ordinarily we think of these as consumer durables and do not consider them as part of our wealth. In a modern western society hardly anyone would rationally consider accumulating great stores of clothing as a means of accumulating wealth. However, in many societies, clothing is an important asset which can be sold in the second-hand markets. As long as some wearable quality remains, clothing can be truly considered a financial asset.

Probably no difficulty exists in reconciling, say, automobiles and houses as both consumer durables and assets. These items simply require a longer time to wear out. Furthermore, a well-developed market exists for the sale of both automobiles and houses so that the value of these as assets may actually increase, depending upon the original price paid and the market price received.

It follows, then, that almost anything may be considered a financial asset so long as it can be a store of value. The particular form the asset takes is quite arbitrary and is dependent upon the cultural and economic system which prevails. This is particularly true of physical commodities which embrace a whole range of items from diamonds to factories. The only requirement for a commodity to be an asset is that society places a value upon it.

What about other forms of assets which may be non-material? Can there be assets other than purely physical ones? Of course, one may consider Elizabeth Taylor's beauty, the late Sir Harry Lauder's Aberdonian accent, the skill and artistry of Menuhin, or the talent of Tom Jones as assets.

In many cases the individual performer was endowed at birth with a talent, in which case he is as fortunate as are the children of the Rockefellers. As will be shown presently, all these may be better assets to a banker than some physical things including, at the extreme, the man-made mountains of slag of England and Wales, which litter the coal fields. Indeed, one can imagine a situation in which a person might even say to himself "My greatest asset is that I am a Canadian!" though it is doubtful that his banker would agree.

In sum, then, a financial asset is a store of value which may or may not be physical; in fact, when financial assets are considered in the broadest context, they may be neither physical nor non-physical but something in between, viz., merely claims to wealth. If one asks the question, why store value in the first place, one must seek the answer in the most fundamental nature of every human. Value may be useful in the sense that it *represents* future consumption, i.e., the asset may be useful because it can be exchanged for consumption in the future. In any case, the "future" is involved in a "store" since the genius of man seeks various means by which value may be most successfully stored. These assets may have future value in the sense that they may be consumed by either the actual owners or his heirs or they may be exchanged today for current consumption.

Another rather interesting use of an asset which is automatically possessed by everyone is the guarantee by the State of certain basic services. Pension rights, universal education, medical attention, protection from an "enemy," etc., are all assets which accompany one's entry into this world. Indeed, a minimum living standard guaranteed to all through our welfare system is a similar asset. Again, these somewhat unusual forms of assets are really stored values to be utilized at some time in the future. They are basically no different from assets which a person might provide for himself by individual saving, but the state itself provides them instead through public saving. One can conceive of socialist countries in which all individual assets are public and awarded to people entirely in accordance with need.

In sum, our assets are a measure of "how well off we are." The fortunate individual who has stores of value, counting up all his assets in all shapes and forms, greater than someone else's, is wealthier both in the ordinary sense of the word and in an economic sense as well.

B. Monetary Assets

Of the greatest importance for the subject of Money and Banking are monetary assets which are simply stores of value in their most liquid form, i.e., money. Of itself, money is a receipt for wealth (not to be confused with wealth) which is a claim against a portion of society's production and which enables the possessor to consume an amount equal to the dollar value of his money divided by the price level of the goods. In a real sense, therefore, monetary assets merely represent real assets, for money itself has no intrinsic value.

This store of value function is indeed useful quite apart from the fact that the value of money, to be realized, must be exchanged for goods. Thus, *even though money is not actually being spent*, the fact that it *can* be spent is sufficient to endow it with utility as a store of value.

In many countries people may prefer to store their value in the form of gold, especially if there is a general distrust in the capacity of a currency to maintain its value over long periods. Gold has a distinct advantage over pure cash in that it is universally recognized as a substitute for money, in the first place, and, in the second, it often enjoys a rising price level. Further, in some societies, gold serves as a mark of prestige, displaying to all and sundry the degree of wealth and social status attained by the owner. In the final analysis, however, for the value of monetary assets to be realized, whether gold or paper currency, a process of exchange is required, i.e., the store of value must be converted into real, consumable goods. This means that a market and price system is necessary in order for monetary assets to be exchanged.

It is not difficult to understand that monetary assets possess a distinct advantage over real as-

sets as value stores. Monetary assets are flexible in that, as long as the marketplace exists, they can be converted into any form of real asset the owner may choose. Real assets, on the other hand, are fixed in form and should an owner decide to change the form of his store of value, he would, of necessity, have to find a buyer, viz., someone who is willing to pay the required price for that specific commodity.

In our modern capitalistic market economies, this is by no means the severe problem it would be in less developed economies which do not possess highly organized markets. The market itself is an agency which brings seller and buyer together; hence, the problem of searching for an appropriate buyer is greatly reduced. In our North American society, for example, the purchase of real assets as value stores is made quite simple through the existence of a market in commodity futures. These are actually real assets such as wheat, potatoes, etc., which are not yet in existence. Since they do not exist, there is no problem of cost of storage so that all one need do is make the purchase to sell it, hopefully at a profit, to a buyer who will be ultimately the individuals or firms that want the commodity for its own intrinsic value. This is not true in countries which do not possess such markets. A particular owner of a fixed asset may find it quite difficult to sell his store of value; indeed, the risk for the enterprising capitalist in countries without adequate markets is high.

Even with a market, the owner who decides to sell his real asset can never be sure of the price he will get. This, too, is a risk, and the fixed asset is just as likely to fall in value as it is to rise. Here, monetary assets share a common fault with real assets for the value of money is subject to change just as the value of real assets. The relationship, however, is an inverse one, i.e., as real asset prices rise (real assets increase in value), monetary assets decline in value. Nevertheless, monetary assets do have a distinct advantage over real assets since they possess a flexibility in that, given a particular market situation, they can be converted into any other type of asset more easily than any single fixed asset. Since money is only a *claim* to wealth rather than wealth itself, and so long as society continues to recognize it as a claim, it is readily exchangeable for any number of wealth forms.

As an asset, money is by no means the *best* form

which a store of value can take. Indeed, our modern economy has developed other more efficient methods of value stores which depend upon rather complex market structures and which are major subjects of study in themselves. Such is the genius of modern capitalism. However, in less developed economies, people have much less choice. They are oftentimes forced to accept monetary assets alone as a store of value as alternatives to real assets. Therein lies the reason for the popularity of gold as the only asset other than currency which enjoys flexibility, (readily convertible into real assets) and at the same time, helps to overcome the one major difficulty of monetary assets as stores of value. Money is frequently subject to the risk of value depreciation (through rising prices) and this risk often increases with time, i.e., the longer the time period during which a monetary asset is held, the greater the risk of a loss of value due to rising prices. This great disadvantage of money arises from the fact that it is just a claim to wealth and, in the final analysis, must be converted into real assets at some market price. It is this future conversion which determines its efficiency as a value store today.

To be sure, no one will wish to hold money as a store of value if expectations of rising prices are generally strong. This is the essence of the "inflation psychology" of which one hears a great deal. Under such conditions, people may even try to convert their monetary assets into real assets even to the point of converting future expected monetary assets into current real assets. This they can do by incurring consumer debt.

In summary, anything can be an asset so long as it serves as a store of value. The particular form of the asset depends to a great degree upon the society in which we happen to be living; the fact that some types of assets may be more efficient than others is entirely the result of the peculiar economic environment and circumstances which prevail. In all cases, however, monetary assets enjoy a quality not shared by real assets, i.e., they are only claims to wealth rather than wealth itself and, hence, are endowed with a flexibility not shared by other assets. However, as claims to wealth rather than wealth, monetary assets *per se* have the distinct *disadvantage* in that their value depends upon their ultimate and inevitable measure against the real assets they can command.

II. PROCESSES OF MONETIZATION

Just as monetary assets derive their current value from ultimate exchange for real assets, it follows that money has as its second important function the facilitating of exchange of real assets. In effect, the distinction between money or monetary assets as stores of value and money as a medium of exchange is simply one of money at rest and money in circulation. Yet, it must not be forgotten that monetary assets only serve as value stores so long as the *expectation* of their being put into circulation exists. Thus, while the distinction between the two functions of money is important, in reality one function derives from the other.

To understand the monetization process, we should begin with those countries and economic systems which are less developed than our western societies. These regions have problems, of course, quite different from ours, yet they reflect the same basic process of monetary development. In all cases, they are characterized by poverty and a general low standard of living for the majority of the population.

We may conceive of a typical primitive economic system as consisting of two sectors, an exchange sector, and, for want of any other descriptive term, a self-sufficient sector. The self-sufficient sector is characterized largely by agricultural pursuits, food production being the first basic, and essential, economic activity, and also by subsistence agriculture which involves the production of food for direct consumption by the farmer and his family. It does not involve any sale or exchange of the product for money. In some poor countries as much as 90% of the working time of subsistence farmers may be occupied with just such production of food for direct consumption. The remaining 10% would be devoted to producing items for sale, i.e., folk artifacts or fruits such as grapes, melons, etc., which are purely "cash crops." With the proceeds of these sales, the farmer may purchase from the market the few additional items which he cannot produce by himself.[1]

---

[1]These observations are not new. A. C. Pigou quotes from a paper entitled "Industrial Organization of an Indian Province," by Sir Theodore Morison as follows: "A very large number of exchanges were in old days effected by means of barter. Rents were paid in kind, and debts between the cultivator and the money-lender, tho reckoned in terms of money, were usually settled in

In many cases this becomes the "traditional" way of life with the same pattern having been followed for a thousand years without much alteration for each succeeding generation. Social customs tend to reinforce the economic pattern, hence avoiding the problem of keeping up with the neighbours which we have in western, consumer oriented, societies. In recent years, however, the traditional subsistence economic system has been subject to continuous stress as the "have-not" nations become aware of the widening gap between themselves and the wealthy "have" countries. The governments of these countries in particular lay emphasis upon economic development, growth rates and capital-output ratios; five-year plans have become the fashion with certain economic targets and goals to be achieved.

This process of economic development and change necessarily involves contact with an already existing exchange sector. The reason for this can be readily seen. Economic growth and development involve an expansion of an industrial labour force which must, in turn, be dependent upon the agricultural sector for its basic necessities. This requires an increase in the efficiency of the agricultural sector so as to produce both a redundancy of labour and a "cash crop" for sale in the market. In this way a growing secondary industry is manned by a population shift from rural to urban areas, on the one hand, and the means of sustenance furnished by a more efficient agricultural sector on the other. The speed of transformation from the self-sufficient to the exchange sector will depend upon a combination of both the value of the marginal products of labour in industry as compared to agriculture and the degree of resistance to change on the part of a traditional way of life. Ultimately, as urban eco-

nomic life becomes the more attractive alternative in terms of living standards, the process of population shift accelerates and the exchange sector predominates as the normal. Farmers sell their produce for money and all their crops become "cash crops" as they enter the exchange sector to be consumed.

When this hitherto self-subsistent sector of the farming population thus sells its product for money instead of consuming it directly, a money requirement is born. Of course, a direct barter system could be used instead of money, in which case the benefits of exchange without a money requirement could, theoretically, exist. But, for the rather obvious reasons of inconvenience and difficulty of arriving at an agreed exchange ratio, barter is, quite simply, not successful. Money is a much more efficient method of valuation by means of price and its use is universal throughout most countries of the world.

When the production of a self-subsistence sector enters the exchange sector, we may say that monetization, which may be defined as the satisfaction of a demand for money, has taken place. Money in some form must now be provided by a central authority (government, central bank, etc.) before any exchange is possible. It is important to make this concept clear at the outset, for it is this principle which underlies the functional relationship between money and income, on the one hand, and the possibility of control of the price level and economic activity on the other. Money is so fundamental to any economic system beyond the most primitive self-subsistence/barter stage of development that it may almost be considered a factor of production along with labour and capital.

Monetization is a never-ending process. It is the genius of the money and banking system that new and better methods of facilitating exchange are forever being developed. In fact, the monetary system itself evolves just as fast as new techniques of production of goods and services develop; indeed, taking production in the broadest sense to include all the processing stages from raw material to consumer, it is easily seen that pure cash alone is entirely too cumbersome as a medium of exchange in 1978. We have already passed through the era of cash.

Furthermore, monetization affects everyone. One can imagine the plight of a traditional Asian housewife confronted with the prospect of

---

grain. The wages of field laborers and of the village artisans were paid almost entirely in grain, and it was, therefore, possible for the cultivator in former days to make a large number of transactions in the year without employing money at all. Now that the self-sufficiency of the village is being impaired, the occasions for the use of money are largely increased. The tenant usually pays his rent in money; he also employs money, along with bundles of corn, to pay his laborers; a few articles of foreign manufacture are coming into common use, which are purchased at fairs, and for them money is the only payment accepted." Pigou, "The Value of Money," *Quarterly Journal of Economics*, November, 1917. Reprinted in *Readings in Monetary Theory*, Lutz and Mints, eds. Allen and Unwin, London, 1952, p. 168-169.

purchasing bread with cash instead of baking it with her own home-grown wheat, something she has never done before, as similar to a western housewife making a purchase at the local supermarket with a card which automatically deducts her bank balance, an experience equally new to her. The transition in the one case is to a cash society, in the other, to a cash*less* society, both equally difficult for a conservative public to accept.

By implication, then, the economy never reaches a state of *complete* monetization, for the reason that technological change in terms of production and marketing requires corresponding changes in the techniques of making payments. Both, of course, require adjustments on the part of the general public. In our western societies, these changes have generally been in the manner of speeding up the payments process, for just as production is accelerated, so is the pressure exerted on the exchange system to speed up payments to the same extent. Computerized banking services are the technological revolution in our payments system which correspond to similar changes in production technology, and acceptance by the general public is necessary for both.

A. Stages of Production and Money Requirements

For the purpose of monetary analysis, it is helpful to conceive of the process of production as a continuous flow of goods and services through all producers to ultimate consumers. In the case of the self-sufficient sector, which in less developed countries tends to be rather large, the producer *is* the consumer and the production/consumption process is complete within just one stage of the productive process. Here, no monetary requirement exists, but the moment a *second* stage is introduced into the process, a requirement for money arises. This second productive stage would be, say, the grinding of wheat into flour, or some other manufacturing process which utilizes the output of the first stage. The monetary requirement appears because some method of valuing the product as well as paying for services rendered is required.

As further stages in the productive processes are added, still more money is needed, but in this and subsequent stages, the increase in the monetary requirement will probably not be so great as in the case of the second stage. This fact arises from a "leakage" principle. Not all money, that is, passes directly from one stage to another. Some will recirculate back to the originating, or consuming, stage. For example, very much of our modern economic activity consists of the production and consumption of services. Here, we have a simple two-stage economy not unlike the more primitive agricultural/exchange sector relationship. The consumer purchases a service, say a haircut, hands the money to the barber, who, in turn, may purchase another service, etc. Each producer of the service becomes in this way a consumer of another service so that 100% of the money recirculates directly back to a consuming stage as soon as his specific service is rendered.

For consumer goods, on the other hand, only a portion, perhaps 10%, of the money received at a modern retailing stage may be returned to the consuming sector as income for the owners and employees of the retailing establishments. The balance, 90%, will then be passed on to a wholesaling stage for the discharge of debt. The wholesaler will pass on a large portion to the fabricating stage, etc., until the last stage of production, the initial stage, has been paid for its part in the productive process. In the first case, services only, no "leakage" at all occurs as each payment is made, whereas in the second, a retail outlet, the leakage equals 10%. Of course, the degree of leakage will vary considerably depending upon the nature of the productive process performed by each stage. In national income terms, the value added at each particular stage is the counterpart of the value of the leakage of money to the consuming stage and is made for payment of productive factors used.

It is important here to understand the precise nature of these "stages" in addition to their contributions to the productive process. Most of us, as members of an economic society, are part of some productive stage since we all perform some productive service. The exceptions are the unemployed, the pensioners and welfare recipients, who are not included in production but, since they are consumers, are part of the consuming stage. Corporations, as legal "persons," business enterprises and governments also exist within the circle of payments, and, like the rest of us, are either a complete stage of production within themselves or part of a larger stage. At the same time, all of us, without exception, are part of an ultimate consuming stage. Thus, excluding nonproducers in our modern society, the balance of our population exists within two stages, a producing and a consuming stage, simultaneously.

The counterpart of the productive and consuming stage within the production process is the monetary stage in the cycle of payments. The monetary stage arises because each productive stage must make payments for productive services received before it receives payments for its own productive service. If receipts and payments were perfectly coordinated, the need for holding money would be nil, but, unfortunately, life is not so simple and a money balance must be held stationary for a period of time. Conceiving the cycle of production and payments as a series of stationary stages as opposed to the more orthodox continuous flow process gives considerable insight into the working of a monetary system, and for this reason, a more formal definition may be attempted. *A monetary stage is any point in the flow of payments at which money pauses.* It is possible to visualize this idea of stages as the frames of a never-ending motion picture. The classical circular concept of the Gross National Product involves a movement of money in the opposite direction from the flow of goods and services. At each stage (or frame) the money pauses for a period of time, then is passed on to the next frame to discharge another obligation. Generally, a transfer of goods or services accompanies the money movement, but this need not necessarily be the case.

In a modern capitalistic economy, such as Canada, there is, in addition to those monetary stages directly involved with production, an additional number of monetary stages which exist for the purpose of the transfer of ownership of securities, stocks, bonds, etc. Corporations specialized in such activities are now well-known household names—Merril Lynch Royal, Greenshields, etc., and are not at all concerned with the production of goods and services in the ordinary sense, but act as brokers to assist the general public in its relations with the capital market. These are purely financial transactions which require rather large sums of money and which increase the total number of monetary stages in our economy. Thus, in general, the more "developed" our economy becomes, in terms of financial sophistication, the greater the number of monetary stages which will be required. Of course, this is not to deny the possibility of a consolidation of stages in the interest of efficiency so that the total number of stages, and the corresponding monetary requirement, may sometimes decline, but the general trend appears to be an increasing number.

In recent years, the pace of technology has accelerated to such a remarkable degree that productive processes themselves have considerably lengthened to incorporate many new, hitherto unknown monetary stages. Under a more simple, labour oriented type of production, payments would be made directly to workers for services rendered and the "leakages" would be nearly 100% complete with a single payment. However, as the productive process becomes less labour intensive and more capital equipment is utilized, the stages of production and the corresponding monetary stages increase in number until somewhere at the very end of the process, a small number of final payments are made for services rendered. As an example, consider the purchase on the part of a consumer of a haircut. This is a two stage production process requiring money for exchange. A single stage production process would be the consumer cutting his own hair. In contrast, a consumer's purchase of an automobile will involve stages anywhere from two to very many, the salesman's commission representing the second stage, and the various types of steel, plastics, glass, etc., involved in manufacturing the car, being the many. Thus leakages occur in the flow of money from the moment of purchase to the last stage of mining of iron ore, etc. In all cases, the larger the number of stages in the productive system, the larger the number of monetary stages and the greater is the monetary requirement.

B. The Monetization of Stages

The process just described can be expressed more neatly in the form of a diagram (see Diagram 1–1A). At the outset a small monetary requirement exists for the reason that humans cannot be *completely* self-sufficient in their economic activity. The exchange sector itself, however, is small and rudimentary with relatively little service to be performed. Though small, its importance must not be overlooked, for whatever requirements the self-sufficient sector cannot meet by itself must be provided through the exchange

Diagram 1-1

**MONETARY REQUIREMENTS—
HORIZONTAL MONETIZATION**

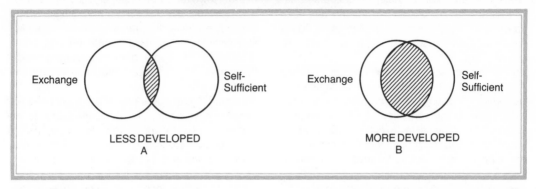

Exchange — Self-Sufficient
LESS DEVELOPED
A

Exchange — Self-Sufficient
MORE DEVELOPED
B

sector. It can be visualized as simple bazaars consisting of merchants who spend much of their time haggling over prices. Since there are so few transactions during a single day, it is profitable to spend much time in establishing individual prices for each transaction. The goods purchased in this way (handwork, carpets, etc.) will likely find their way into exports to earn precious foreign exchange. At the same time, imports will be channeled through the same exchange sector to meet those requirements the self-sufficient sector is unable to meet itself. The intersection of both the exchange and self-sufficient sectors represents this activity.

The increased reliance on the cash crop, the specialization of agriculture in a few specific areas both mean that it is no longer possible for farmers to be as self-sufficient as they once were. The two sectors are merging as in Diagram 1-1B. It is this process of merging which is referred to as "horizontal monetization" and is characterized by a growing monetary requirement. Perhaps most significant, the consumption pattern of the formerly self-sufficient sector has changed completely. Agriculture is now, as in Canada, dependent upon manufacturing, trade, and even banking, to such an extent that anything approaching self-sufficiency is no longer possible, and, of course, farmers enjoy a much higher living standard than before and likely have no desire to return to their original status if given the choice. To be sure, there will likely be the occasional romantic "back to nature" movement, but this will most likely be short-lived once harsh realities are experienced. So the process of merging continues until the two

sectors are almost completely united as in Diagram 1-1B. The rather small area of "single stage sector" remaining even in more developed economies, such as Canada, consists of that portion of our economic activity which the public performs for itself. "Do-it-yourself" activity such as property repair and maintenance by the house owner who contributes his own labour, housewives' contributions to their own families without which some paid service would be required, and, of course, whatever is left of frontier existence, would be the last, lingering, representatives of the single stage or self-sufficient economy which still requires no money.

From what has been discussed to this point, it should be clear that economic growth and development and monetization (or the use of cash or cash substitute to expedite trade) are essential partners. This means that at some time or other during the process of economic growth, existing institutions will be strained to their capacities to provide the necessary funds for continued monetization. Complaints by businessmen will be heard regarding the inadequate and conservative nature of bankers, and banks, in their turn, will find it necessary to adjust to changing conditions as they develop new techniques and seek alternative and more efficient methods to their existing payments procedures. This occurs because of the "absorption" of money by the hitherto self-sufficient sector which finds itself relying more heavily on a means of exchange. Processes of production are passing from one monetary stage to two or more, and a steady stream of increasing amounts of means of payment is required to keep the process of growth in motion. Should this stream fail, for any reason, shortages of the means of payment, particularly credit facilities, will in all likelihood become translated into a failure of demand for the output of producers. Growth requires monetization and a failure of monetization will mean a slowing of growth.

An interesting example of the contact between the two sectors in less-developed countries can be found in the form of loans, and the interest rates charged thereon, made by the exchange to the single stage sector. Frequently, due to personal difficulties, accidental weather conditions, etc., it becomes necessary for peasant farmers to seek a loan. In such circumstances, interest rates assume fantastic proportions and are secured by signing over the ownership of property. The lender in such a case is not a bank, such loans being not "bankable" because of high risk, but a private money lender. This individual, frequently the object of severe social criticism, is not simply avaricious by nature, but is "forced" to require high interest because so many of his loans can never be repaid.

The root of the problem lies in the still dual nature of the system. The self-sufficient sector when forced to use the credit facilities of the exchange sector cannot earn the necessary cash for repayment. The market facilities do not exist within the farmer's range of activity. He will, therefore, repay his loan in kind at even more exorbitant rates. The farmer is a victim, not of the avarice of money lenders, but of the system itself.

There is probably no other more important contribution of the exchange sector to the process of growth and development than credit, or the granting of the right to consume in advance of earnings. While it lies at the very heart of our productive system on the one hand, it may prove a disaster for many unfortunates whose capacity to acquire money income is limited. After all, a money loan must be repaid with money, and should there exist no feasible method of acquiring funds, the debtor becomes a victim of his own miscalculation. In less-developed societies, a farmer may lose his property to the local money lender; in our modern economy an individual may misjudge his earning power as he succumbs to the temptations of consumer loans. "He who goes a-borrowing goes a-sorrowing" expresses the folk wisdom of such situations.

Within the exchange sector itself, the rate of interest is a most important price for credit which is determined by market forces of supply and demand. However, when credit crosses the boundary between the exchange and single stage sectors, hardship frequently prevails. The self-sufficient sector by itself cannot provide credit facilities for its people, nor can it alone produce the wherewithal to repay the cash to the exchange sector.

As development takes place, the authorities attempt to convert the self-sufficient sector to an exchange basis by encouraging the production of cash crops. To further this end, agricultural banks, sponsored by the governments themselves and their central banks, attempt to loan money to farmers for productive purposes at reasonable rates of interest; but, even here, the banks frequently have to write off loans because farmers cannot repay.

In our western "developed" economies, on the other hand, nearly all forms of production are for money. The exchange sector is almost in complete control; however, this is not to suggest that the process of horizontal monetization is complete — far from it. What was started in North America during the early settlement days is continuing still. Indeed, with the pace of modern technology, the demands made upon our monetary system grow ever greater, and the exchange sector itself, while firmly in the saddle in western countries, may give way to still further changes such as the "cashless society" for the reason that the ordinary methods of exchange are entirely too cumbersome a method of discharging obligations.

C. Monetization Processes—Vertical

The absorption of the single stage sector into the exchange sector can be considered as horizontal monetization. While the process continues, the central authorities must provide increasing amounts of cash or other means of effecting exchange. It should be noted that this cash is not necessarily accompanied by an increasing amount of production, but rather by an absorption of existing production within the framework of a market structure which requires money for its successful operation. In this sense, a horizontal monetization process occurs.

The monetization process also turns vertically as the volume of production increases through utilization of additional stages of production. New and more efficient techniques of production require more machinery and involve the sale or transfer of semi-finished goods from intermediate production stages to later stages; hence, a money requirement arises from this source. This simply means that as the real output of goods increases, the supply of money must likewise increase to enable the goods to be sold, ultimately, to the final consumer. How much increase in the money supply is required to facilitate this vertical monetization process is still one of the most interesting subjects of research and study to this day and one upon which there is still no general agreement.

The process may be illustrated in Diagram 1-2. Stage 1, the consuming stage, is completely monetized through horizontal monetization which occurs without any increased flow of goods and services. Additional stages, 2 through *N*, are added vertically and do require additional

amounts of money as the flow of output increases. Production flows, of course, move toward consumption (Stage 1) at the same time that money moves in the opposite direction; thus, production stages are simply the producing counterpart of monetary stages.

Discerning readers may recognize in Diagram 1-2 a familiar flow chart which only requires a circular relationship to unite the consuming sector (Stage 1) with the various producing stages to develop the familiar Gross National Product analysis. Actually, all that has been done thus far is to work out the money flows which must accompany the flow of production, of course, always in the opposite direction. As productive stages are added vertically to the producing economy, new monetary stages are automatically created, and, since a monetary stage is any point at which money pauses in its circulatory flow, a demand for money is generated. If the question be raised — why *should* additional productive stages be added vertically to the GNP flow process — the answer would be purely to increase the size of the flow of goods and services.

Just to fix more precisely the ideas involved, we can consider a simple example. Let us start with a single stage economy which has a stationary population level and which produces 1000 units of consumer goods. Suppose that a division of labour becomes possible so that half the population specializes in what it can do best. The result is an increase in total output to 2000 units. In the first case, the monetary requirement is exactly zero, and in the second, assuming that money makes a complete revolution during a producing time period, 1000 units of money (1 unit of money equals 1 unit of goods) would now be required to generate a total of 2000 units of income.

Now let us add a third stage by removing some workers from the original two stages and put them to work making machinery to increase the output of the first two stages. Greater output, that is, is attained from Stages 1 and 2 with the aid of more capital goods and less labour; otherwise it would not have been worthwhile to initiate Stage 3 in the first place. If the output should reach the level of 3000 units, and, assuming that money continues its same speed of travel, the demand for money would now reach 1500 units. We may add further that unless the amount of money reached this 1500 mark, *the price level would have to fall*. This is a process of vertical monetiza-

Diagram 1-2

MONETARY REQUIREMENT WITH HORIZONTAL AND VERTICAL MONETIZATION

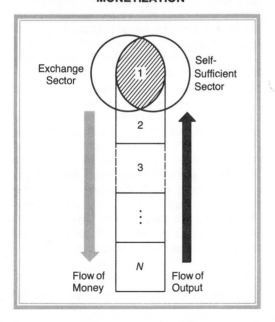

tion which develops because of a deepening of the production process, i.e., first, machines are produced which are used for further production of consumer goods, etc. Just how "deep" and why the machines are developed in the first place is a complex subject of capital and interest theory to be developed in later chapters. At the moment, it is important to recognize how a monetary requirement (demand for money) is created by means of an increased flow of goods alone. The increase in the monetary requirement stems from the additional flow of goods which results from the higher productivity of a more capital intensive process of production. It does *not* (note carefully) derive from the fact that the machinery must be paid for before it is put into place. This is quite a different matter.

The same increase in monetary requirement will occur in the event of an increase in the size of the monetary stages. In our simple example, we only need to let the population and labour force increase and we have a greater size of, firstly, the consuming stage, and secondly, some producing stage somewhere within the system. Again, the monetary requirement (demand for money) will rise as the new workers demand their pay for productive services rendered.

In the two-stage example involving only specialization of labour, 1000 units of money generated 2000 units of income (1000 units per stage) during one complete return journey. Money could be conceived, like a bird, as flying back and forth to bestow extra income upon the fortunate recipient whenever it comes to rest, but such shuttling in this way would only be possible if each stage has something to sell to the other. This means that as much as a production period must lapse before the money can complete its return journey. The production period may be as long as a harvest season or as short as the production of a single service, but the speed of movement between stages, or velocity of circulation, is always limited by the period of production, however long or short it may be. In our simple case, the velocity of circulation would be measured as GNP/M = 2. The addition of a third stage which resulted in an increased output did not alter the production period nor the velocity of circulation; hence the demand for money itself increased.

There is a curious anomaly in this definition of velocity. The ratio GNP/M (Gross National Product divided by the money supply) suggests that each single unit of money will produce a certain amount of "GNP units" during a time period. This follows from the definition of GNP as the total value of incomes earned during one year. The ratio could be very much larger had the time period been selected as a decade, or, conversely, much smaller had the time period been one month. In either case, velocity of circulation is actually the same, only the unit of measurement has changed. The time period of one year is purely arbitrary and bears no relation to the production period which is the real determinant of velocity in our simple example.

D. Financial Monetization

A third type of monetization which has occurred more recently in our more highly developed capitalistic economic system results from the generation of a demand for money for the purpose of effecting the exchange of financial assets — stocks, bonds, and, more recently, property. J. M. Keynes noted the existence of such a money requirement for the "business of holding and exchanging existing titles to wealth ..."[2] and that money used for this purpose generally had a higher velocity of circulation than "ordinary" money. The significance to Keynes of this money requirement was that money could be drawn from other uses (both horizontal and vertical monetization in our analysis) to finance speculative activities on the stock exchanges. Thus, despite an extraordinary variability in the velocity of circulation of money in the financial circuit, which stems from the capacity of the market to develop money substitutes during periods when competition for limited funds becomes severe, financial markets can, and do, use funds from banks which would ordinarily have been put to other uses. This was certainly the case during the great stock market speculative boom in 1929 when funds became locked up in speculative ventures. It was also true in Great Britain during the early 1970s when property speculation drew considerable amounts of funds from other more productive uses. British secondary banks faced near collapse as a consequence of unwise lending to speculators.

---

[2]J. M. Keynes, *A Treatise on Money*, Vol.I., Macmillan, London, 1958, p. 243.

It would, however, be incorrect to lay too much emphasis upon what is the exception rather than the rule. In point of fact, financial monetization has been very important in the growth and development of the capital markets. It is not a coincidence that well-developed financial sectors are to be found in only a few countries, those, incidentally, in Western Europe, North America, and Japan, which are also world leaders in production, trade, and economic activity in general. Those of us who are fortunate to be living in these areas tend to forget that primitive economies with successful exchange systems are under a severe handicap without a developed capital market and a domestic financial sector to accompany it. Many of us in western countries are so accustomed to our banking and financial institutions that we accept them as matter-of-fact.

However, they have not always been so commonplace. The financial sector has grown through years of evolutionary development to the highly efficient state in which it exists today. Precisely how and why it has grown and how we as individuals may use it to our advantage will be examined in Part II. At the moment, it is sufficient to conclude our diagram analysis with Diagram 1-3, which relates the financial sector to the other two sectors in terms of our monetization analysis.

E. Demand for Capital (Money)

To this point our concept of monetization has been simple— the satisfaction of a demand for money. This money demand arose, in the first instance, with the so-called union of the self-sufficient sector with the exchange sector. Once the merging process is completed, the former distinction is really superfluous; it is more convenient to simply consider the producing sector and the exchange sector within the framework of a market economy. This new market economy has considerably greater productive capacity than the old self-sufficient sector, the consequence of specialization, economies of scale, etc., all made possible by the use of money as a medium of exchange. A demand for money, then, arises precisely from this increase in productive efficiency which is itself desirable and requires money to effect.

It remains now to examine more closely the concept, "demand for money," and the processes of monetization which satisfy this demand. The precise details of how money is supplied will be postponed until an examination of the Canadian banking system has been completed.

If we were to ask the question what exactly *is* demand for money, the answer would be more easily approached from the standpoint of what demand for money is *not*. It is not, for example, the desire for a higher living standard which additional money could bring, nor is it a demand for a living wage which pushes us into the job market. Even the delinquent whose desire for the pleasures that money can bring is great enough to overcome the risks entailed in robbing a bank, does not have a "demand for money" in the sense that we are using the term.

Demand for money in our terminology refers to a negatively-sloped demand function relating quantity and price in the same way as any other economic commodity. Money, that is, has a price and those of us who are part of this demand function must be willing to pay this price. The

Diagram 1-3

MONETARY REQUIREMENT WITH HORIZONTAL, VERTICAL, AND FINANCIAL MONETIZATION

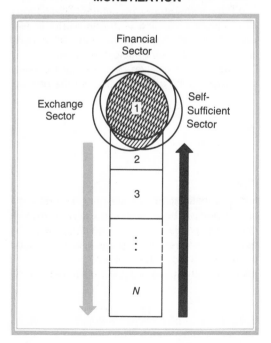

"price" in this sense is an interest rate which individuals, businessmen, etc., are willing to pay for a loan. Business enterprises must pass on this cost as part of their marginal efficiency of capital to society as a whole; hence, the entire community pays the price for money. This is exactly as it should be, for it is the economic community itself which benefits from monetization processes. Note carefully that the fact that a businessman "borrows" money from a lending institution (bank) and pays interest to the bank directly is quite incidental and merely happens to be the institutional mechanism through which society acquires the money for which it has a demand.

In the sense we are discussing it here, demand for money is really a part of the larger demand for capital which a business enterprise requires for purposes of production. Entrepreneurs can acquire this capital from either source, the savings of the public or new money loaned by banks, and when the capital consists of new money, a monetization process takes place with society acquiring the new money. For businessmen, the source of funds, savings or new money, is immaterial, but for society as a whole, it matters a great deal, as will be shown in subsequent chapters.

In our free market economy, the profitability criteria is generally the method by which society's wishes are made known to producers. This means that two basic principles common to all alternative uses of resources must obtain: (1) an increased flow of consumer goods and services both in the present and in the future, and/or (2) an increased price of consumer goods and services. Suppose, by way of illustration, that the first prin-

pressed in terms of both prices and costs, lie in the "roundabout" or long-term method of production. Similarly, when higher market prices prevail for specific items for consumption as well as higher interest rates, businessmen will be encouraged to produce for the short-term, more direct methods of production for the reason that profits are greater that way. Society prefers those consumer goods which are more labour intensive in the "now" area of production. It thus becomes a combination of both market prices and interest rates (the cost of capital and monetization) which act as signals to entrepreneurs in their decision-making process as to what to produce, how much to produce, and the method of production.

In order to make this principle quite clear, (it is of fundamental importance in our analysis of the demand for money and capital) we may extract a simple Table from one of Professor F. Hayek's works.[3] He uses this Table to demonstrate what he terms the "Ricardo Effect." The Ricardo Effect refers to the well-known Ricardian principle that as the wages of labour rise, machinery will be substituted for labour; conversely, as the wages of labour fall, labour will be substituted for machinery. Of course, it is also true that as the cost of capital equipment falls (the interest rate declines), machinery will also be substituted for labour.

The Table below shows five different time periods for production, ranging from one month to two years. The one month production period uses only labour with capital equipment being minimal. The two year production period is capital intensive requiring the additional time for the produc-

Time for Investment (years)	2	1	1/2	1/4	1/12
Profit %	12.36	6	3	1 1/2	1/2
Plus 2%	14.36	8	5	3 1/2	2 1/2
Annual rate (%)	6.9	8	10.0	14.0	30.0

ciple is dominant. Businessmen would likely find that interest rates are low, especially long-term rates, at the same time that market demand, as reflected in current prices of specific consumer goods, is not increasing. There is little opportunity to raise prices so as to increase profits in the immediate future. The encouragement, therefore, is to put into place capital equipment, thereby increasing the long-term output of a specific commodity. The greater profits, as ex-

tion and installation of machinery. The different time periods in between these extremes involve different quantities of labour and machinery. The question we are concerned with is which method of production would be chosen?

We begin with a state of equilibrium in which it is a

[3]F. A. Hayek, *Profits, Interest and Investment*, A. M. Kelley, New York, 1969, p. 9.

matter of indifference as to which method of production to use, for the reason that the rate of profit is exactly the same, 6% *per annum*. Further, we make the simplifying assumption that these profit rates all coincidentally equal the rate of interest, also 6%. Suppose, now, a price increase occurs, or, to express the same thing in a different way, real costs decline. This means an increase of profits by 2% for all productive techniques. It is now no longer a matter of indifference which productive method is used, for using all labour and no machinery yields a return of 30% per year. This is preferable (and more profitable) because the annual turnover is 12 times, as opposed to the 2-year turnover period for the capital intensive technique.

The Ricardo Effect, in this case, results in the substitution of labour for capital because even though a price increase lowers real interest cost just as much as real wages, the shorter production time makes the labour intensive technique more profitable. Similarly, a lowering of the rate of interest from 6% to 4% without changing prices will increase the profit for the capital intensive method from 6% to 8% per year, a greater annual rate than the $1/2$% per month for the labour intensive method. This will encourage a switch to more machinery as a substitute for labour.

This leads to an important conclusion regarding the demand for capital which must be clear at this stage. In general, business enterprise will increase its demand for capital as the rate of interest falls and decrease its demand for capital as the price level rises. This is in accordance with Professor Hayek's Ricardo Effect and derives from the fact that rising prices mean lower real wage costs. We can show this demand for capital as a negatively-sloped function relating interest and capital as shown in Diagram 1-4. To the extent that demand for capital for investment purposes is met by new money, the demand for money is being satisfied. This new money moves into the entire economy via the capital investment route and will be absorbed by the monetization processes both vertical and financial, as well as through an increase in the size of the stages. To the extent that the money is absorbed by means of an increased flow of goods and services, it is vertical monetization; to the extent that the new money satisfies an asset holding desire on the part of the public, it is financial monetization. Finally, to the extent that it satisfies the require-

Diagram 1-4

DEMAND FOR CAPITAL

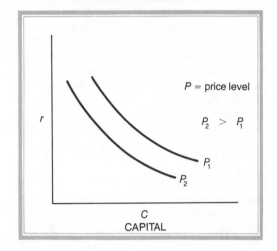

ments of an increased population, it is satisfying an increased size in the producing and consuming stages.

The money requirement of the economy (or society's demand for money) need not only be met through the capital investment route, though, to be sure, this is likely to be the most important. The general public itself borrows from the banking system for the purpose of direct consumption and, thus, satisfies a demand for money in that way. Once again, the finance of consumption may be satisfied by way of the savings of the public or by new money and, to the extent it is the latter, anyone who borrows on the strength of a personal loan for the purchase of, say, a new car, is contributing to the satisfaction of society's demand for money. The price for money, interest on the loan, is paid by the individual borrower as a member of society to be met from his future expected income. Society, as expressed in the actions of an individual consumer, has purchased money by paying a price for it; monetization has taken place.

A personal consumer loan, then, is one additional channel (or route) through which new money can satisfy demand; there are, of course, others such as loans for speculative purposes or even government loans. If we define economic efficiency as the degree to which the flow of goods and services matches society's desire for them, it is clear that some routes of monetization may be more economically efficient than others. In fact, perfect efficiency would be a rare achievement indeed, for it is not just a matter of the size of the flow of consumer goods equalling the size of demand, but the *structure* of these goods matching the structure of demand. Furthermore, it is also a matter of the savings of consumers matching the capital investment of business enterprise both in quantity and length of time involved, but this is a topic which will occupy a great deal of attention in later chapters.

III. THE QUANTITY THEORY OF MONEY

It is not the purpose of this section to simply retrace the steps of others. There are already excellent commentaries, both historical and analytical, on the Quantity Theory of Money, tracing its development through the centuries to our own day, some with original contributions of the writers.[4] It would serve a useful purpose, however, to include an in-depth discussion of the three principal versions of the Quantity Theory so as to integrate our own discussion of monetization with the work of other monetary theorists both past and present.

Certainly the Quantity Theory of Money in some form must be the oldest continuous piece of analysis in the history of economics, but for all practical purposes, the modern version really begins with David Hume.

Hume, a philosopher, as was his close friend Adam Smith, was principally concerned with why some nations were wealthy and others poor, in a word, the causes of the wealth of nations. He concluded that it was not the existence of money, credit, or precious metal, but the industry ("men

and commodities") which constitutes the real strength of a community. To us today this may sound obvious, but we must remember, in interpreting Hume, that both he and Smith were directing the force of their logic against the Mercantilist school of thought which was prevalent at the time and which had argued that trade, commerce, and, of course, money (gold) were the real sources of wealth. Mercantilist philosophy was reflected in the legislation of the day, particularly the Navigation Acts, which proved to have more of a nuisance than a constructive value.

We do not find in Hume, therefore, a strict logical development of a theory. He wished to show that money itself has no value, but that "... prices of everything depend on the proportion betwixt commodities and money"[5] — an excellent and precise statement of the simple Quantity Theory of Money. Note carefully that money, in order to have the property of determining prices in this way, must be "neutral" in the sense that it has no effect on either relative prices or real values, only money values.

At the same time, Hume was very conscious of the impact of an *increase* in the amount of money on the community. Theoretically, a continuous increase could influence real values, thus:

> From the whole of this reasoning we may conclude, that 'tis of no manner of consequence, with regard to the domestic happiness of a state, whether money be in a greater or less quantity. The good policy of the magistrate consists only in keeping it, if possible, still increasing; because, by that means, he keeps a spirit of industry alive in the nation, and increases the stock of labour, wherein consists all real power and riches.[6]

Here it is the increase in the amount of money which is definitely not neutral and which does impact upon real values as well as a system of relative prices. The difference in Hume's two approaches in modern terminology, would be statics vs. dynamics, and to him, dynamic changes in the money supply (so long as they are positive) have

---

[4]One of the best and most recent is Gail Makinen, *Money, The Price Level, and Interest Rates*, Prentice-Hall, Englewood Cliffs, 1977, Chs. 2, 3, and 4. Another, though with a much broader interpretation of the Quantity Theory, is H. Visser, *The Quantity of Money*, Martin Robertson, 1974, Chs. 5 and 6. K. Wicksell's earlier discussion is also very appropriate, *Lectures on Political Economy*, Routledge and Kegan Paul, London, 1935, Ch. IV. Keynes' very original analysis of the Quantity Theory especially in relation to his earlier "macroeconomics" is best seen in the "Fundamental Equations for the Value of Money," *A Treatise on Money*, Macmillan, London, 1958, Vol. I, pp. 135-156. The list of references could go on endlessly.

---

[5]Hume "Of Money," A. A. Walters, ed., *Money and Banking*, Penguin, 1973, p. 31.
[6]*Ibid*. p. 30.

definite worthwhile effects resulting in increases of the wealth of a nation. He did not consider such questions as optimal rates of increase in the money supply nor the possibility of hyperinflation in his analysis. Once the change in the money supply has been completed, to achieve a higher static level than the former, the strict proportionality rule holds once more.

About a century and a half later, Irving Fisher addressed the Quantity Theory in more precise scientific terms. There is nothing vague or "woolly" about Fisher's thinking as was characteristic of Hume. Fisher was a mathematician as well as an economist, interested in establishing the relation between the supply of money and the price level. Further, the "price level" he had in mind was a general level of prices which he defined as a weighted average of all individual prices, the weights being the quantities of an item purchased in a transaction. Thus, to Fisher, an aggregate (or general) level of prices was a real, definable entity, which could be measured in terms of index numbers, a macroeconomic concept which foreshadowed our Statistics Canada GNE deflator. Once the existence of the general price level was established, it remained only to develop the determinants of this price level as follows:

> Overlooking the influence of deposit currency, or cheques, the price level may be said to depend on only three sets of causes; (1) the quantity of money in circulation; (2) its "efficiency" or velocity of circulation; and (3) the volume of trade.[7]

This led directly to the formulation of his famous equation of exchange as

$$MV = PT \text{ where}$$

M is the quantity of money in circulation, V is velocity or rate of turnover during a time period, P is the general price level, and T is the sum of individual transactions, $PT = \Sigma p\ Q$. To bring into the analysis the effect of chequing accounts, Fisher simply extended his equation of exchange to

$$MV + M'V' + pQ = PT \quad [8]$$

where M' is the level of bank deposits which are proportional to M, the amount of cash, and V' is the velocity of circulation of bank deposits which is different from the velocity of circulation of cash (V). "P is a weighted average of all the p's and T is the sum of all the Q's."[9] If we can measure changes in P by means of an index number of some type with a reasonable degree of accuracy, we have accomplished a great deal toward defining the equation of exchange more closely.

Modern students may be struck with the simplicity (almost naïveté) of the equation of exchange, particularly when the chain of causation is realized. Fisher begins his analysis with the general level of prices and its determination first, *then* proceeds from the general to the specific price, say, of apples. His logic, therefore, can only really make sense if it is considered in a macroeconomic context as a statement of aggregate demand.[10] Fisher was aware of this; in fact, much of his *Purchasing Power of Money* is devoted to precisely an explanation, or justification, of the use of his equation of exchange as a scientific analytical tool.[11] He was aware that his equation was only an identity, but "The greatest generalizations of physical science, such as that forces are proportional to mass and acceleration, are truisms, but, when duly supplemented by specific data, these truisms are the most fruitful sources of useful mechanical knowledge."[12] Furthermore, since it was Fisher's objective to show that control of the money supply could, at the same time, influence the general price level, it was necessary for the equation of exchange to be true in its simplest context, *viz.*, money must be neutral in the sense that real factors, such as velocity of

---

[7]Fisher, *The Purchasing Power of Money*, Kelley, New York, 1971, p. 14.
[8]*Ibid.*, p. 48.

[9]"*P*, then, represents in one magnitude the level of prices and *T* represents in one magnitude the level of trade." *Ibid.*, p. 27.
[10]Samuelson attempts to show the relationship of money supply and aggregate demand in Chapter 17 of his *Economics*. Samuelson and Scott, *Economics*, 3rd Edition, McGraw-Hill Ryerson, Toronto, pp. 407-427.
[11]One cannot avoid being impressed with Fisher's careful and precise treatment of a subject. Not even the minutest detail escaped his attention. In fact, having examined the historical and statistical evidence to verify the Quantity Theory, he proceeded to develop a measure of the general price level P, thus leading directly to one of his greatest contributions to economics and statistics, the theory of index numbers.
[12]Fisher, *op. cit.*, p. 157.

circulation and volume of trade must be unchanged. Fisher assumed that all these real factors were "normal," i.e., determined by custom, population, transportation techniques, etc., and therefore not influenced by the money supply itself. In this sense, money was truly "neutral" so that "...the normal effects of an increase in the quantity of money is an exactly proportional increase in the general level of prices."[13]

All this may sound somewhat "gimmicky" to a more sophisticated generation; it was true that Fisher was somewhat prone to enthusiasm regarding new and different ideas (viz., the compensating dollar, health fads, etc.). Nevertheless, the equation of exchange does go far in explaining the phenomenon of hyperinflation, in the first place, and long-term movements of prices and the money supply in the second. To this extent there is that element of truth in the equation. Further, a careful reading of the *Purchasing Power of Money* will show that the Fisherine Quantity Theory is very much more than a mechanical truism. To the contrary, the relationship between M and M', closely established via the banking mechanism, combined with their appropriate velocities which are determined exogenously, and the value of T also determined by factors outside the equation, mean that a genuine theory of prices is established. It would, in fact, be difficult to refute such a theory especially in view of historical evidence relating price movements with the money supply.

The weakness of the equation of exchange is not that it is a truism (which it certainly is not) but in the assumption that a general price level, Fisher's original premise, does, in fact, exist. It is the transformation of a complex structure of relative prices in a modern economy into a simple statistic, an index number of the "price level," which is the real difficulty. Prices, to Fisher, become purely passive in the equation of exchange; hence, we face the logical dilemma that we cannot accept the market rationing function of prices equating supply and demand and, at the same time, the direct result of the amount of money in circulation. In terms of the equation of exchange, the market rationing function of prices would affect the amount of production within the summation of the

q's and the extent to which the q's are affected depends upon the elasticity of supply. Similarly, the extent to which demand is affected by an increase in the amount of money available depends upon peoples' tastes and desires as to how they wish to spend their increments of income, i.e., the extent to which the demand curves shift. We must proceed, in other words, not in the Fisherine direction from the money supply to the price level, but from the money supply *through* the price structure to everything else in the economic system, *including the general level of prices* as measured by an index number.

Somewhat similar, though different in some important aspects, to Fisher's equation of exchange was the Cambridge version of the Quantity Theory.[14] This version, according to Alfred Marshall, stemmed from several eighteenth century writers, including Adam Smith, and is structured on the propensity of society to hold a certain portion of its wealth in the form of money. Since money is "barren," earning no income, everyone must balance the utility, or advantage, of holding cash against the loss of income in deciding how much of his wealth to hold as money.

This is the starting point for the Cambridge version. It differs from Fisher's equation of exchange in that it is based on what, to the economist, is a more comfortable marginal utility theory than Fisher's velocity of circulation as established by custom and tradition. Equating the marginal utility of a given money stock with foregone interest means that a certain portion of a person's wealth will be held as a money stock. In a pioneering article in 1917, Professor Pigou developed the Cambridge version of the Quantity Theory.[15] In his approach, he uses a proportion, k, of total resources, R, (Pigou used the commodity, wheat, to represent total resources) which is held as claims to legal tender. The equation which determines the price level of money in terms of resources (N.B., the inversion of the more typical

---

[13]*Ibid.*, p. 157.

[14]J. M. Keynes originated the term "Cambridge Quantity Equation" for the reason that it was developed largely by Professors Marshall and Pigou at Cambridge. See J. M. Keynes, *Treatise on Money*, Vol. I. p. 229.

[15]A. C. Pigou, "The Value of Money," *Quarterly Journal of Economics*, Vol. 32, November 1917, reprinted in *Readings in Monetary Theory*, Lutz and Mints, ed., Allen and Unwin, London, 1952.

price level of resources in terms of money) is

$$P = \frac{kR}{M} \text{ or } M = \frac{kR}{P}$$

This is Pigou's demand for money equation which states the simple truism that the price level of money in terms of real resources *at any given moment* is determined by the ratio of resources which people want to hold in monetary form, kR, to the number of units of claims to legal tender, M.

Pigou then proceeded to convert his equation for demand for claims to legal tender to actual legal tender (cash). He was aware that bank deposits are substitutes for cash to the extent that people have the banking habit; hence, the demand for cash will be equal to a certain proportion, c, of the total resources, kR, which people wish to hold as legal tender. This would be

$$kRc$$

The balance of kR, the ratio $1-c$, would be held in the form of bank deposits.

Against these bank deposits, banks must hold reserves of cash. This is a fundamental banking principle so that the proportion, h, of these bank deposits held as reserves would constitute the bank's cash requirements. Thus, to the public's proportion of cash, c, must be added the bank's proportion of cash, $h(1-c)$, which depends directly upon the public's use of cheques. In the final analysis, then, the amount of cash (or legal tender) the public will hold depends upon the decisions of the public. The final version of Pigou's Quantity Theory becomes

$$P = \frac{kR}{M}[c + h(1 - c)],$$

or

$$M = \frac{kR}{P}[c + h(1 - c)]$$

with $M =$ to the amount of legal tender. It is evident from inspection that the amount of resources (kR) which people wish to hold as legal tender (or cash) is now very much less than the "titles to legal tender" expressed in the simple Quantity equation.

It will be obvious that Pigou's Quantity Theory is more sophisticated than Fisher's equation of exchange. In the first place, it rests upon another functional relationship which is implicit, viz., $P = f(M_P + D)$, with D equal to total demand deposits and M_P, the cash in the hands of the public. In the second place, it is really a demand for money function similar in content to our monetization demand discussed above. Thus, the larger the volume of resources available to the community (R), and the more they are monetized (kR), the greater is the money requirement. This is, quite simply, vertical monetization. Finally, Pigou's version suggests distinct areas for empirical research in the form of the three determining coefficients, k, c, and h. These coefficients are, in fact, very much the same as Fisher's external factors which determine velocity of circulation and, as such, probably could have served more efficiently as analytical tools. This was Pigou's objective, to provide a logical machinery which was, he thought " ... more convenient" than Fisher's but, he asserted " ... I am not a hostile critic of Professor Fisher's lucid analysis."[16]

Pigou's demand for money equation is a rectangular hyperbola since $kR[c + h(1 - c)]$ is a constant *at any moment of time*. Further, since the amount of real resources available to the community changes with time, the hyperbola shifts outward as the resources increase; hence, the demand for money function increases as well. (See Diagram 1-5.)

It is unfortunate that the Cambridge version of the Quantity Theory, as developed by Pigou, failed to progress beyond a theoretical statement. The

Diagram 1-5

PRICE OF MONEY IN TERMS OF GOODS

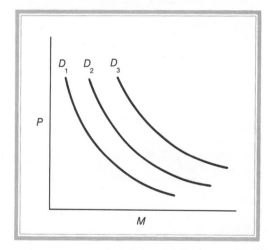

[16]*Ibid.*, p. 163.

fault, it would appear, lies partly with Pigou himself, for in his QJE article in which he developed his demand for money function, instead of stressing the important differences between himself and Fisher, he tried to show how his version was really the same. Consequently, since the Fisherine version was more widely accepted amongst economists at that time, Pigou's humility resulted in much less credit to himself than he deserved.

In demonstrating the close relationship between his work and Fisher's, Pigou used the simplified version, i.e., his claims to legal tender, of his Quantity Theory:

$$P = \frac{kR}{M}$$

Since P is the price of money in terms of "things" and since Fisher's P is the price of "things" in terms of money, let π be Fisher's price so that

$$P = \frac{1}{\pi}$$

Fisher's equation is $\pi = (MV/T)$. It follows that

$$\frac{kR}{M} = \frac{T}{MV} \text{ or } kV = \frac{T}{R}.$$

In Pigou's own words, "Evidently in given conditions of production and trade, T may be taken as constant."[17] This means that the sum of all the q's (the Fisherine T) and the total resources available (Pigovian R) must bear a constant relation to each other. It follows from this that kV must also be constant.[18] In other words, velocity of circulation is merely the reciprocal of the Cambridge k.

Perhaps more important for the failure of the Pigovian version to become a more widely used method of analysis was the fact that Keynes himself in his Treatise rejected both his own version of the Quantity Theory which he had developed in his Tract on Monetary Reform and Pigou's Cambridge version in favour of his own refinements. In the Treatise he segregated the quantity of money, M, into three parts, M_1, income deposits, M_2, business deposits, and M_3, savings deposits. Each of these deposit categories have their own respective velocities of circulation so that a single "k," as in the Cambridge case, cannot embrace all the various uses to which the various deposits would be put. To Keynes, M_1, or income deposits, was the important determinant of the price level. So an analysis of the price and income changes which were characteristic of the early years of the Great Depression (the Treatise was published in 1930) required a corresponding analysis of shifts from M_1 into M_2 or M_3 as well as changes in the value of k.

But most important, neither the Fisher equation of exchange nor the Pigou Quantity Theory, as they existed at the time, were capable of explaining the Depression phenomenon as it developed. Neither could account adequately for the changes in levels of prices and the unprecedented unemployment which was so prevalent during the early 1930s, and, since the central focus of economic thinking and research lay with business cycles, the Quantity Theory of Money and any further refinements fell into the background.

It should be pointed out, however, that Keynes did seriously misinterpret Pigou's R (real resources) in the Quantity Equation. He treated this R as the real income of the community over a period of time.[19] This was not Pigou's intention, as is evidenced by his development of his hyperbolic function, though, admittedly, he was not precise in his definition.[20] This apparent error may be the source of a frequently used statement of the Cambridge Quantity Theory as

$$M = k(PY)$$

where M is demand for money, PY is money income, and k, the "Cambridge k" as defined above.[21] While this particular form most closely resembles Fisher's equation of exchange, it is certainly not the formulation of Pigou in the original QJE article.

---

[17]Ibid., p. 173.
[18]Let $k = 5\%$ and $V = 20$. C (a constant) is, therefore, 100. Doubling k to 10% means halving V to 10; hence,

$$V = \frac{1}{k}.$$

[19]Keynes, op. cit., Vol. I, p. 231, footnote 2.
[20]"Let R be the total resources, expressed in terms of wheat, that are enjoyed by the community (other than bankers) whose position is being investigated." Pigou, op. cit., p. 165.
[21]See, for example, Makinen, Money, The Price Level and Interest Rates, p. 110, or most standard textbooks on Money and Banking. The variables used may vary somewhat from book to book, but the formulation is the same.

While it is easy enough to state the similarities in the two versions of the Quantity Theory, as Pigou himself did, what is really important are the differences which stem from their original starting points. The Cambridge version is a demand for money function which arises from the necessity to have sufficient funds to bridge the gap between incoming and outgoing payments. The Fisher version approaches the matter from the supply of money side. Paraphrasing Harry Johnson, we can outline the Fisher causation as follows: an increase in the money supply causes some people to have more cash balances than they wish to hold (assuming velocity and output are unchanged). They then pass on their problem to someone else and so on until the price level in general has risen to wipe out the difficulty. At that point real cash balances are the same as before.[22]

The Cambridge version is different. It assumes full employment, and any increase in available resources increases money demand without an increase in the price level. In Diagram 1-4, a shift of D to the right occurs, increasing the monetary requirement with the price level constant. On the other hand, any increase in the price of goods in terms of money ($1/P$) without an increase in output will result in a corresponding increase in demand for money, i.e., moving down the D function. The difference, then, between the two versions becomes the emphasis laid upon the direction of causation. To Fisher, the direction is from the money supply to the price level; to Pigou, it is from both real resources and/or the price level of money to commodity prices.

It was unfortunate that the course of events after the crash of 1929 forced the Quantity Theory as a method of economic analysis into the background, as economists concentrated their attention on the business cycle. Public debate, writing, etc., was on the subject of unemployment and the urgency of the matter was such that any other area of economic analysis became subordinate. This was reinforced by the actual experiences of the time, for it was clear that monetary stimuli designed to encourage rising prices and greater employment were not equal to the task. As Professor Williams points out, the emphasis of policy in the United States during the 1920s was via the Federal Reserve System controlling the amount of money; this, in turn, controlled the interest rate, which also controlled investment which, finally, controlled the business cycle. This procedure failed during the Great Depression when, after 1933, bank reserves were high, interest rates were low, and *still* the Depression continued.[23] A kind of "liquidity trap" had apparently been reached so that other measures, viz., deficit finance, were required to stimulate the U.S. economy.

However, instead of fading completely from the scene, the Quantity Theory did remain active in the Chicago University Department of Economics with such people as Professor Henry Simons, Jacob Viner, and others continuing their research and teaching in a monetary tradition. The result was an eventual new formulation of the Quantity Theory under the powerful intellect of Professor Milton Friedman.

It is not possible to discuss this new Quantity Theory in an introductory chapter since most of the material included in it is really the subject-matter of the remainder of this book; hence it is better left to a concluding section. We can, however, discuss some aspects of it by way of a conclusion to this section on the Quantity Theory of Money. The first of these is that the new Quantity Theory, like the Cambridge version, is a demand for money function alone. It relates the demand for money to some seven different independent variables, each of which bears directly on the money requirement of the public with greater or less force depending on the circumstances of the time. Thus, during periods of hyperinflation, actual and expected price increases become dominant. During "normal" periods, a long-term rise in real income seems to be the more significant variable, and in abnormal periods such as wartime other uncertainties, e.g., fear, hysteria, migration, etc., seem to predominate.

[22]H. G. Johnson, *Macroeconomics and Monetary Theory*, Aldine, Chicago, 1972, p. 60.

[23]J. H. Williams, "Deficit Spending" *American Economic Review*, Vol. XXX, Feb. 1941, reprinted in *Readings in Business Cycle Theory*, G. Haberler, ed., Allen and Unwin, London, 1950, p. 273.

It should be pointed out that Friedman's demand for money function is somewhat narrower than our monetization demand for money as discussed above. Friedman is concerned with the factors influencing the public's demand for money as a financial asset, whereas our analysis deals with the requirement of the economy as a whole for money, including both the exchange requirement and the asset requirement. The differences will become clear as the analysis and discussion proceed.

A second aspect is the fact that the Quantity Theory (which is a demand for money function) is not a theory of prices or of output, as is implicit in the Fisher equation of exchange. Supplementary material would be required to develop a theory of prices and output based on the new Quantity Theory. For example, suppose that the money supply should increase, would that result in a corresponding increase in prices? The answer is no for some of the increased money would be channeled into higher output (or employment) and some into increased prices. *How* the additional money would be so divided would require additional information. It is interesting that Keynes himself discussed this point at some length in the *General Theory*.[24]

Finally, is it conceivable that *seven* variables operating on the demand for money with varying force at different times is so many that the Quantity Theory is rendered useless? After all, an indefinite number of variables in any function is tantamount to having no functional relationship at all. This is an open question to which there is no answer. In order for the Quantity Theory to have value as a tool of analysis and policy it must have the capacity for prediction, i.e., to show that a certain cause is likely to result in a specific effect. It is useless, that is, to suggest that some effect will follow from an expansion of the money supply depending upon *everything else* in the economy! *Ceteris paribus* is acceptable for a theory of prices when everything else is indeed equal most of the time. The same cannot be said for the macroeconomic framework within which the Quantity Theory is operative. However to repeat,

further discussion of the question must be postponed until much more territory has been thoroughly explored.

CONCLUSION

The objective of this introductory chapter has been two-fold: first, to outline a general analytical framework within which our monetary system can be examined and, second, to consider the more orthodox monetary analysis known as the Quantity Theory of Money. In the first section, the concept of assets was introduced with the emphasis laid on their store of value function. All assets can be stores of value, though some may be more efficient than others. Money, of course, is one of these assets which derives its asset value purely from its ultimate exchange value.

The exchange value of money, then, highlights the very important function of money within our modern economy as a medium of exchange. Monetization is the process of absorbing this medium within the economy and means that we have a demand for money which must be met by a supply. The mechanism by which the money is "manufactured" is the subject of later chapters; hence, our analysis of monetization simply assumes that such a money manufacturing process exists. Demand for money is generated by the monetization process itself and means that a price must be paid for money, in this case, the bank interest rate.

An important part of the monetization demand for money is producers who find that the lower the interest rate (the cost of capital), the less expensive is the roundabout or machine-type productive process. Their demand for capital will, therefore, increase. That portion of capital they desire which consists of new money will be part, indeed an important part, of the demand for money function. Similarly, consumer loans which require new money will also be included within the demand function. All this means that the monetization demand for money function will be negatively sloped relating the rate of interest to the quantity of money.

In the discussion of the Quantity Theory of Money in Section III, no attempt was made to be exhaustive or complete for the reason that other excel-

---

[24]J. M. Keynes, *General Theory of Employment Interest, and Money*, Macmillan, London, 1949, ch. 21.

lent material on the subject has already been published. It is, of course, a very old theory which has been particularly appropriate during times past, say, in Hume's time. Our society and economic system today are simply too complex to accept a simple, even Fisherine, relation between quantity of money and prices.

The modern version of the Quantity Theory is really an asset demand for money function. It is a demand for money because the public "demands" money to hold as a store of value. In doing so, it pays a price, in this case interest foregone, so that, in general, the lower the price the more money will be demanded. This is the same general shape of our monetization demand though it is not the same. In monetization demand, a price is paid directly in the form of bank interest which is likely to be passed on through the price mechanism eventually to consumers. An asset demand for money is the desire people have to hold money as a monetary asset, the price being interest foregone.

In Part II we examine very closely the nature of assets both financial and monetary and consider them as alternatives. Our analysis, in fact, is in much greater detail than that included in the Quantity Theory as developed by Friedman. However, it must be made clear that our total demand for money represents the demand of the entire economy for money both for exchange purposes (or monetization) and for holding (asset value); hence, it is considerably greater than the more orthodox demand for money.

An introductory chapter necessarily brings ideas and concepts "out of the blue." Very much of what is introduced here will be considered in depth at more appropriate points in subsequent chapters. This is not repetition, but development.

ADDITIONAL READINGS

Artis, M.J. and M.K. Lewis, "The Demand for Money—Stable or Unstable," *The Banker*, March, 1974, p. 239.

Fisher, Irving, *The Purchasing Power of Money*, A.M. Kelley, New York, 1971, ch. XI.

Friedman, Milton, "The Quantity Theory of Money — A Restatement," *Studies in the Quantity Theory of Money*, University of Chicago Press, Chicago, 1956, p. 3.

————, "The Demand for Money: Some Theo-

retical and Empirical Results," *The Optimum Quantity of Money and Other Essays*, Aldine, Chicago, 1970, ch. 6.

Laidler, David E.W., *The Demand for Money, Theories and Evidence*, International, Scranton, Pa., 1969.

Renshaw, Edward F., "Money Prices and Output," *Journal of Finance*, June, 1976, p. 956.

Selden, Richard T., "Monetary Velocity in the United States," *Studies in the Quantity Theory of Money*, University of Chicago Press, Chicago, 1956, p. 179.

Visser, H., *The Quantity of Money*, Pitman, Bath, England, 1974, chs. 3 and 4.

Recent Econometric and Mathematical Studies

Clower, Robert W. and Peter W. Howitt, "The Transactions Theory of the Demand for Money: A Reconsideration," *Journal of Political Economy*, June, 1978, p. 449.

Miller, M.H., J.P. Gould, and C.R. Nelson, "The Stochastic Properties of Velocity and the Quantity Theory of Money," *Journal of Monetary Economics*, April, 1978, p. 229.

For an excellent more broadly based analysis of demand for money, see Harry G. Johnson, *Macroeconomics and Monetary Theory*, Aldine, Chicago, 1972, Part II.

APPENDIX

Conceptually, the idea of "demand for money" is more difficult than demand for commodities. Demand for money is really a by-product of economic activity and it is through economic activity that a demand for money develops in the first instance.

Considerable effort has been expended by economists in attempts to quantify money demand as well as to identify the specific economic variables to which demand for money might be related. But this has not been easy. There is, firstly, an identification problem. After all, the only measure of money, however defined, is what actually exists in the form of bank deposits and cash. But is this money demanded or money supplied? We cannot say because the quantity of money in the published statistics is a specific amount and precisely that amount was demanded by the public in the course of economic activity. It is possible that less money could have been supplied without any effect on either prices or real income.

One of the better known monetary economists who has attempted to distinguish between the demand and supply of money is Professor Ronald Teigen.[1] He recognizes that a supply of money function does indeed exist and that commercial banks (Chartered banks in Canada) do respond to interest rate incentives in the process of increasing the supply of money. Identification of the supply elasticities of these responses, therefore, is essential for the development of an effective monetary policy. When the supply of money function is combined with a demand for money function, an equilibrium solution relating the significant economic variables to the amount of money in circulation is possible.

Pursuing this same line of research, equating demand and supply, Stephen Goldfeld developed some bank portfolio equations using econometric estimating techniques.[2] Consumption and investment equations were developed from the side of demand with the result that a 32 equation model of the U.S. economy was built. The advantage of a model of this type (and complexity) is that it makes possible an analysis of the impact of monetary policy on the economy, particularly as it affects the banks which are the transmitting agents of policy through their supply functions. The significant variables are the interest rates which are the incentives for banks to increase the supply of money and consumption and investment from the side of demand.

---

[1]R. Teigen, "The Demand for and Supply of Money," *Readings in Money, Income, and Stabilization Policy*, Irwin, Inc., Homewood, Ill., 1974, p. 68.

[2]Stephen Goldfeld, *Commercial Bank Behaviour and Economic Activity*, North Holland Publishing Co., Amsterdam, 1966.

CHAPTER 2

Money and Prices

I. MONEY AS A MEANS OF PAYMENT

The use of money to facilitate exchange is really nothing more than a mechanical necessity simply because of the impracticability of barter. In fact, were there no money in existence, man would very quickly invent something equivalent. Such an invention would probably consist of a commodity of some agreed universal worth, such as cigarettes among smokers, against which all other commodities could be compared. This form of "commodity money" is what Sir John Hicks would refer to as "indirect barter," and it serves as money for the reason that "it can be spent in the shops."[1]

However, our current form of money, both paper and bank deposits, is actually much more efficient than indirect barter. It is not only more efficient in a physical sense, that is, more readily divisible into smaller units, has greater durability, is easily transferred, etc., but it is also more efficient in the sense that it can be spent at a future time, as opposed to the present, without an intrinsic deterioration in value. In fact, it is this efficiency of money as a store of value which gives rise to the monetary asset function of money and, hence, money *itself* becomes a commodity which has a demand of its own.

A. The Monetary Stage— The Saver and the Spendthrift and Their Demand for Money

We shall begin the analysis of money in exchange by recalling the definition of a monetary stage as — any point in the flow of payments at which money pauses. There are two key words here — "flow," implying a movement not unlike a river, and "pause," or a break in the flow process. A motion picture may be a more apt figure in that the movement of the film between frames is a flow, while the frame itself is a pause. Of course, this definition is an all-embracing one and refers to private individuals, corporations, business enterprises, and governments — in fact, to any institution, human or otherwise which receives money and holds it until the moment of disbursement arrives. But this is a rather large and heterogeneous agglomeration in any country, especially in a highly developed economy such as ours. In fact, not only will the time lapse of the pause vary among institutions, but also the motives for the pause will vary. Corporations and governments, for example, will have very different motives for holding funds, and, certainly, the timing and amounts of disbursements will bear little or no relation to the amounts which are actually available.

But, as in many cases of immense complexity, it often helps to begin with the analysis of the simplest of cases, the smallest of the monetary stages, and yet by far the largest group, individual household income earners. Once certain principles are established, the task of approaching the more complex becomes very much easier. As a further simplification, we shall assume in the first instance that credit facilities are not available so that expenditures will not exceed income.

Money payments are received into our bank accounts or into our pocketbooks to rest there safely until the moment of expenditure arrives. As individuals receiving money we constitute a monetary stage, and with our expenditures, we endow money with its flow properties. In this way, our income/expenditure process becomes a monetary pause/flow process in more or less

---

[1]Hicks, "The Two Triads—Lecture I," *Critical Essays in Monetary Theory*, Oxford University Press, 1967, pp. 4 and 5.

rapid succession. Of course, a portion of the money we receive as income may pause for a considerable length of time; indeed, it may even earn interest in a bank savings account in the process of pausing. However, most of our money will ultimately be passed on to another stage or stages where the same procedure of pause-flow will be repeated.

Sometimes, simple diagrams are helpful in visualizing an abstract process. Suppose an individual income earner is paid an amount of money, M, either in the form of cash or an addition to his bank account, on a monthly basis, and he spends all of it before receiving the next pay packet. His balance of monetary assets (money during the "pause") through time would appear approximately as shown in Diagram 2-1. Of course, many of us may not spend our money balances in this precise, regular way throughout the month, but it is likely that taken altogether, individuals will spend an amount in one day which is just about the same as any other day.

The important thing here is that a requirement for money *as money* exists in this simplest case. To be sure, this requirement for money is for the purpose of spending before the end of the month and derives from the fact that we all must ration our spending on a daily basis. That is, being sensible, we don't spend all our money balances

at the beginning of the month because we expect further necessary expenditures before we receive our next pay. Nevertheless, the requirement for a monetary asset is there, for whatever reason, and income earners *must* have this requirement satisfied.

A simple example may help to make this point clear. Suppose a household receives an income of $600 per month (instead of M in Diagram 2-1) and decides to spend it in a sensible fashion, that is, at a rate of $20 per day. The balance of monetary assets would be $600 on the first day of the month, $580 on the second day, $560 on the third, etc., until on the very last day the balance is only $20 to be spent just prior to receiving the next month's pay cheque. The arithmetic average of monetary balances on any day throughout that particular month, or, for that matter, *any* month during the year, is the sum of all daily balances divided by 30 days.

Of course, any household may elect to spend all of its income in one grand burst during the first day, but that would be irrational behaviour since there are 29 days of starvation to follow. Anyway, we know that households as a whole do not behave in this way though there may be a few deviations on either side of the norm. Thus, while some households may desire to spend all or most of their incomes during early weeks of a month,

Diagram 2-1

**MONTHLY BALANCE, ASSUMING EQUAL
DAILY EXPENDITURE, NO SAVING**

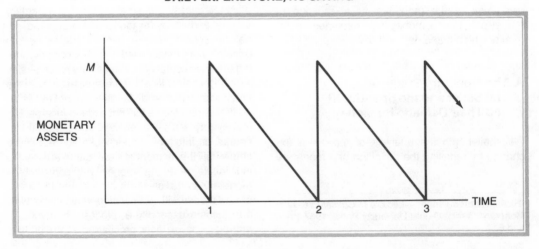

others may postpone their expenditures until later, hence serving to cancel each other.

The interesting feature of this example is the fact that the amount of the money requirement at any time throughout a 12-month period will be equal to the average balance of monetary assets which, as a little arithmetic will show, will be equal to one-half the value of the monthly payment ($\frac{1}{2}$ M).[2]

The requirement for a balance of monetary assets in this and all other similar cases is referred to as a *transactions demand* for money. This demand, like a demand for any commodity, food, clothing, etc., derives from the fact that we must all have the minimum daily necessities of life at the least, and money is needed in our modern society to acquire them. Since the flow of income never coincides with the flow of expenditures, we must all hold money in some form or another until the moment of spending arrives.

To repeat, a monetary requirement (or demand) arises from the fact that monetary assets must be held during the interval between income receipts, and the amount of this demand is equal to one-half the income payment. Thus, the relationship between money requirements and income is obvious — in this case the money requirement equals one-half the monthly income.

Yet another principle emerges in this simple case which must be carefully noted. Each individual income earner is, of course, a monetary stage, but he is, by no means, a stage in isolation. As money is disbursed by reducing a monetary balance it *builds up* a money balance for the next stage. This it does by adding to the income of the next stage, so that by the time the month is completed, *two* incomes will have been generated, one at the beginning and one at the end. Since the end of one month is always the begin-

ning of the next, the process is an endless one of income generation through time by the disbursement of funds received by each monetary stage. In one year, for example, a given money balance would generate 24 incomes, each equal to the size of the money balance.

In this way the money received and disbursed during a time period (one month) makes possible *two* incomes during the same time period. For example, suppose the household which is, of course, a monetary stage in miniature, with a $600 inflow of income spends all of it by the end of the month. That self-same expenditure will be an income for the next monetary stage before the end of the same month! The total of incomes generated during the month, therefore, will be $1200, and this income generation is accomplished by a single monetary balance of $600. We say, in effect, that this money has a monthly income velocity of circulation of 2 since it "turns over" twice during a month. We recall also that the amount of monetary assets, on the average, was equal to $\frac{1}{2}$ the income; hence we reach the significant conclusion that income velocity of circulation is merely the *reciprocal of the proportion of income held as monetary assets*. This was the conclusion, mentioned in Chapter 1, which Pigou had reached to show that his Cambridge k was actually the reciprocal of Fisher's velocity of circulation. It is really a matter of two different ways of looking at the same thing; while velocity measures flow, the proportion of income held as monetary assets measures the pause for each monetary stage.

Before leaving the simplest case for an analysis of the more general, we should first consider what both saving and excess spending does to the demand for monetary assets. After all, there is no reason to assume that all money earned from economic activity need be spent; on the other hand there is no reason to assume that spending in excess of income need not occur. Suppose, then, that our hypothetical income earner (who is really a composite of all of us) begins a saving program and sets aside a certain amount, S, of his monetary assets, M, on a monthly basis. For convenience, we will consider that the program of savings lasts for only one year. The balance of monetary assets would appear as shown in Diagram 2-2. The requirement for monetary assets has now increased from $\frac{1}{2}M$, as in the

---

[2]The need, or demand, for money would be equal to the monetary asset requirement on the average throughout the month; hence with 30 days per month, this would be

$$\frac{M + M\text{-}d + M\text{-}2d \ldots + M\text{-}30d}{30}$$

with d being the amount spent per day. Using the formula for an arithmetic progression, this reduces to

$$\frac{30(M/2)}{30} = M/2.$$

Diagram 2-2

MONTHLY BALANCE, ASSUMING EQUAL
DAILY EXPENDITURE, SAVING

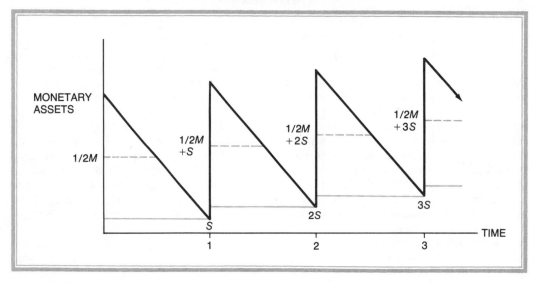

former case without saving, to $1/2M + 11/2S$.[3] Of course, since the volume of monetary assets is growing on a monthly basis because of saving, the ratio of these assets relative to the monthly income is growing. This means that the income velocity of circulation, the inverse of this ratio, is becoming less.

It is easy to see just why and how this occurs. An income equal to a money value M is being earned, but only an amount of money equal to

$M - S$ is being disbursed. The second monetary stage is being "cheated," as it were, out of its money income, which is of course the consequence of a slower velocity of circulation.

Now, no single rational individual will continue to save in this way forever for the reason that savings accumulate month after month. Savings are a stock, whereas income is a flow. Ultimately, the marginal utility of an addition to a savings stock will just equate the marginal disutility of consumption foregone so that the savings process will cease for that individual. However, this does not violate our analysis for the reason that as one individual ceases his saving from his income flow, another individual will certainly replace him, etc., through the succeeding generations. The saving process for the community is an endless one, growing larger, we might add, with increasing real income which lowers the marginal utility of present consumption relative to the marginal utility of saving.

Now let us consider the opposite case, the disbursement of money in *excess* of income earned. Here, the second monetary stage is receiving more income than was earned by the first stage. This *of itself* constitutes an increase in velocity of circulation, since the subsequent

---

[3]The assumption of a 1-year's saving plan is purely for convenience. We may just as easily assume a lifetime equal to t months. In such a case, the money balance M would be

$$\bar{M} = \frac{1/2M + 1/2M + S + 2S \ldots 1/2M + (t-1)S}{t}$$

Once again this is only the monthly average of the money balance M required to sustain a given income as well as its savings component.

Using the formula for the sum of an arithmetic progression with a difference of S, the money balance in total is

$$\Sigma_M = \frac{t[M + (t-1)S]}{2}$$

which becomes an average of

$$\bar{M} = 1/2M + 1/2(t-1)S$$

throughout a lifetime of t months.

Diagram 2-3

MONTHLY BALANCE, ASSUMING EQUAL
DAILY EXPENDITURE IN EXCESS
(−S) OF INCOME

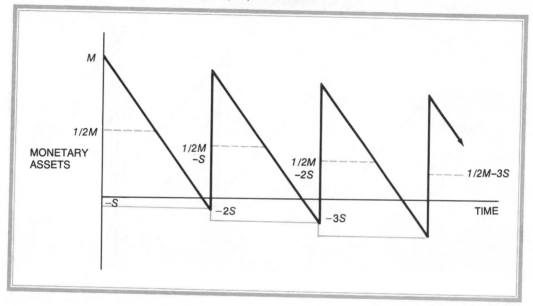

monetary stage is receiving *more* income than was earned by the first stage and would result in a lowering of the amount of monthly monetary balances, or, conversely, an increase in the velocity of circulation.

Let us see, precisely, how this would work. Suppose a specific monetary stage (or individual income earner) were to spend in excess of his income. This he can only do by going into debt. We will assume for the sake of simplicity that the amount of the debt exactly equals the amount saved, S, by the saver. The balance of monetary assets would appear as in Diagram 2-3. We note that the average monthly balance required is steadily declining since a debt repayment is involved each month (again on the average) so that as soon as the hyper-spending income earner receives his pay packet (equal to M) his balance of monetary assets declines at once. Theoretically there is a limit to such a spending pattern with debt mounting higher and higher, but practically, of course, the ability to repay would be questioned by creditors. Just as for savers, the marginal utility of consumption by increased debt

must equal the marginal disutility of non-debt consumption foregone because of debt repayment. For the individual rational debtor, therefore, there is a limit to excessive spending, but this again is largely academic because there are always additional potential debtors waiting in the wings.

Let us now superimpose the monetary balance of the spendthrift upon the monetary balance of the "virtuous" saver. It may be quickly seen that the spending patterns of the spender exactly cancel the savings pattern of the saver so that when the two patterns are combined in this way, average monetary balances of both the spender and saver are exactly as in Diagram 2-1. Of course, mathematically, the result is obtained by combining the two average balances of monetary assets which for the spendthrift would be $\frac{1}{2}M - 11/2S$, assuming that the spending program lasts for only one year,[4] for the saver, $\frac{1}{2}M +$

---

[4]Just as before the average money balance is as follows:

Diagram 2-4

COMBINED MONEY BALANCES OF BOTH SAVERS AND SPENDTHRIFTS

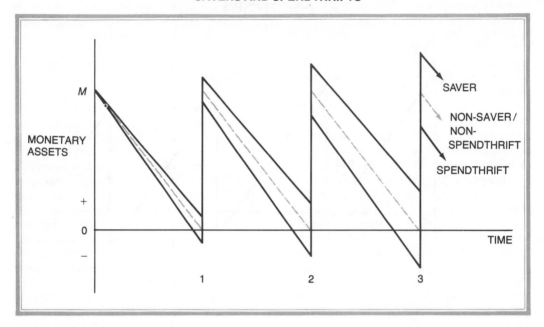

11/2S, and for both, $\frac{1}{2}M$ + 11/2S + $\frac{1}{2}M$ − 11/2S = M. For the average of the two, monetary balances equals $\frac{1}{2}M$, the same result as in Diagram 2-4.

We have now reached some conclusions of major importance, all of which will yield considerable insight into the workings of a modern monetary system. The first of these is the fact that the money of which the second monetary stage was deprived by the saver has been restored by the spendthrift. That is, the spender, far from being without virtue is, in fact, performing a useful and

$$\overline{M} = \frac{\frac{1}{2}M + \frac{1}{2}M - S + \frac{1}{2}M - 2S \ldots \frac{1}{2}M - (t-)1S}{t}$$

which again is the sum of an arithmetic progression with a difference of S. This reduces to

$$\Sigma_M = \frac{t[M - (t-1)S]}{2},$$

and the average is therefore

$$M = \frac{1}{2}M - \frac{1}{2}(t-1)S.$$

Combining this with the saver's balance of monetary assets (see footnote 3, above) we have

$$2\overline{M} = \frac{1}{2}M + \frac{(t-1)S}{2} + \frac{1}{2}M - \frac{(t-1)S}{2} = M.$$

important function. He is restoring monetary assets to their correct level; he is, in effect "undoing" the consequences of savings which increases balances of monetary assets to a higher than normal level.

From a purely monetary point of view this is, of course, correct; however, it would be incorrect to consider the restoration of monetary assets (or balances) to their former level purely in isolation from the rest of the economy. In our example, for instance, spending exactly what is saved means that there is no provision for economic growth, no capital accumulation. What is likely to be true, and certainly would be more appropriate from an economic point of view, is that the "spendthrift" is an entrepreneur who wishes to expand his business enterprise by means of investment. He can do so by borrowing the savings of the saver, and in the process of restoring money incomes (or lowering money balances) new capital equipment has come into existence. So it matters a great deal *how* monetary balances are restored.

A second conclusion is implied in the analysis.

The saver could easily have loaned his savings on his own to the spendthrift had they been neighbours, for instance, again assuming the extraordinary coincidence that what the saver wished to save exactly equalled the excess of spending on the part of the spendthrift. Thus, without the intermediation of banks or other financial institutions, a mutual arrangement between the two could have been made such that for one year the spendthrift would borrow from the saver. Naturally, a fee or reward might have been required by the saver for the service rendered, the size of which would be subject to joint agreement. For the present, this may be referred to as interest.

This raises the important question of why the saver should save in the first place unless there is a reward. Unless he is a miser, the accrual of excess money balances purely for their own sake is irrational, but this important question of the reasons for saving is considered in detail in Part II.

Thirdly, the important concept of velocity of circulation, the inverse of the proportion of income held as monetary assets, falls out naturally from the analysis. The spendthrift increases velocity while the saver decreases velocity. It follows that the greater the proportion of saving relative to spending, the less will be the income velocity of circulation.

Fourthly, following directly from the third, there is a direct relationship between income and money for transaction purposes. This relationship is *itself* velocity of circulation and derives from the fact that money is spent after a pause in each monetary stage. Incomes are generated by money which is spent and reduced by money which is saved.

Most important, however, for the purpose at hand is the fact that for the individual monetary stage, money itself serves a most useful function. Neither the saver nor the spendthrift could have indulged his whims and fancies without money. Indeed, even "indirect barter," as referred to at the beginning of this chapter, could hardly serve the purpose as well as cash or demand deposits at the bank.

The reason that nothing else is quite so good as money is that money, for the purposes of transactions, is really a *right to consume*. And it is this that is being saved by the saver and spent in advance of earnings by the spendthrift. The saver simply prefers to postpone a small portion of his total earned right to spend, whereas the spender wishes to advance his right to consume by an amount equal to a small proportion of his total earned right to consume and before he has acquired it through earnings.

It will be observed that even though money is no more than a right to consume, it is required by both savers and spendthrifts for itself alone. The only difference between the two is that the saver has a greater demand for money balances (assets) than the spendthrift, but in both cases a demand for money exists, one for monetary assets and the other for transactions. It exists as a consequence of the necessity for retaining monetary assets until they are replenished as further earnings. In fact, it is just this demand for money *purely as money* which gives rise to the pause, i.e., the monetary stage, itself. Consider, for example, what would be the result of a zero demand for money so that instead of pauses we had a continuous flow. As soon as the money is earned it would be spent, "cashing in," as it were, the right to consume on the consumer goods themselves. It would be clear that an infinite expansion of the value of consumption must take place. Retailers' stocks would vanish from the shelves, and the transportation facilities would be strained to the limit in a mad rush to supply more goods. In fact, since an infinite expansion of output is impossible, retailers and producers all along the line of production would have no choice but to "ration" what resources they had by means of the price mechanism. Prices, therefore, would rise.

Another way of looking at the same thing is velocity of circulation. Velocity, being the reciprocal of the proportion of income held as monetary assets, would approach infinity as the proportion approached zero.[5]

The importance, therefore, of the demand for money cannot be overstressed. Suppose, for in-

---

[5]Of course the classic case of near infinite velocity is the great German inflation of the early 1920s. Money was spent as fast as it was earned since prices were rising at such a rate that monetary assets declined in value daily. The impact of this experience upon the minds of the Germans can be seen even to the present time, as German political leaders scrupulously maintain cautious monetary policies.

stance, that one of the three income earners, the saver, the spendthrift, or the "neutral," were to be granted an increase in income. The saver would likely wish to save more either as the same proportion of a higher income or a higher proportion of his income. Similarly, the spendthrift *might* wish to spend more, or he might prefer to merely maintain his current consumption without going deeper into debt, i.e., he would become "neutral." And, of course, the "neutral" spender would increase his consumption as a consequence of an increase in income. In all three cases the demand for money would rise along with the increases in incomes, but we cannot say how much the demand would go up because we cannot be certain how each individual income earner would react to changes in his income.

It only remains to generalize from these three examples to the many and varied economic agents which make up the producing and consuming stages in our economy to arrive at the description of monetization demand for money introduced in Chapter 1. The money balances requirements of producing and/or consuming agencies must be met to the amount of the requirement with additional money. Is it possible that over-monetization could occur, the consequence of too much money being manufactured? The answer is yes, and the consequence of such a circumstance is discussed in the last section of this chapter.

In our example, the "spendthrift's" additional demand for money happened to be met precisely by the saver. The spendthrift in this case could be business enterprises, individuals, or governments. If the collective savers can meet the needs of the collective spendthrifts in this way, no new money need be supplied. But, suppose they don't. Suppose the requirements for money exceed the amount which is provided by savers and the excess demand is met by newly manufactured money. In this case a process of monetization is again taking place which once more could become over-monetization.

B. Monetary Stages in an Economic System

Remembering the definition of a monetary stage as a pause in the flow of money, we can readily see that any point in the process of production or consumption which accumulates balances of monetary assets is crucial to our analysis. Consumers, of course, are the last link in a lengthy process of production and, at the same time, are an important part of the flow of funds. But, and here is the main point, there are many types of monetary stages with different motives for holding monetary assets. Consumers too have a variety of motives for holding monetary assets, but within the confines of this chapter, we are considering only one, i.e., the spending or transactions motive. It is this which gives rise to a demand for money, or paradoxically, we require money in order to get rid of it at some future moment!

But when we move out of the area of pure consumption, we encounter a different motive, viz., a demand for monetary balances for production purposes. Business enterprises, that is, will require money for the purchase of machinery and equipment, for making payments to labour as wages, for payments to sellers of raw material or semi-finished goods for supplies, etc., entirely for the purpose of engaging in the process of production itself.

It would help to visualize the modern productive process in its elemental form as something like Diagram 1–2, Chapter 1. There the consuming stage, number 1, was the objective toward which the flow of production was directed. Stages 2 through N represent both monetary and production stages, for at the same time that money flows in one direction, goods and services flow in the other. Thus, stage N, the last of the monetary stages, is also the beginning of the productive stages. We may consider stage N as agriculture, mining, or other forms of primary industry. All stages in between stages one and N would represent manufacturing, transportation, processing, etc., all the various levels of the productive process which assist the flow of goods to the consumer.

Some goods and services will involve rather many stages in the flow of production whereas others, notably the provision of services, will involve only two. For most of the goods which we consume, a "roundabout" method of production is involved, that is, value is added from the raw material stage through lengthy manufacturing and processing stages involving machinery and equipment until the ultimate consuming stage is reached. It is this last consumption process which measures the contribution of production to the Gross National Product.[6]

It would also be helpful to visualize the process of production as a series of interlocking exchange circuits, all involving monetary stages. For example, food products will be purchased from agriculture, monetary stage N in this case. A food manufacturing stage would be represented by stage $N - 1$. However, this stage would in the course of its production require machinery and equipment just as would the agricultural stage. The purchase of such machinery would involve an interlock with other exchange circuits which are concerned with the production of both farm machinery and food processing equipment. The process would continue, involving transport to markets of food products, the purchase of trucks for the purpose, until the final consumer is reached. In all cases, machinery manufacturing, truck manufacturing, etc., exchange circuits are involved, with money payments flowing in the opposite direction to the flow of production. Diagram 1-2 in Chapter 1 would now appear as if a series of appendages were attached at various stages, each appendage being a separate exchange circuit on its own.

This entire, immensely complicated system of exchange circuits is, fortunately, simplified by means of the national income analysis which is concerned with the sum of all incomes earned in the process of production. We simply take for granted the complicated process of payment flows which are required to generate a certain level of the Gross National Income (or Product).[7]

There is one feature, however, which cannot be taken for granted. Just as consumers require monetary balances, so do producers. In fact, they are an absolute essential to the process of production and they derive from time differences. Production is a time-consuming process, and the wages of labour in particular must be paid *before* the fruits of production are sold.

To emphasize this point we might consider a single exchange circuit which is involved in production directly for consumption. Suppose that only three monetary stages are involved in the circuit. Stage 1, consumers, have a balance of monetary assets, $600, which they spend entirely by the end of the month. Stage 2 acquires all the $600, pays out $200 to its workers as wages and passes on $400 to Stage 3 which then concludes the circuit by paying all of $400 to its workers to supply Stage 1 with a balance of $600 once more. (See Diagram 2-5.)

If we make the absurd assumption that each stage can wait to receive its money balance until the preceding stage is ready to spend, the requirement for money would be the absolute minimum, which, if we have an efficient banking system, would be zero! All debts would cancel and a simple accounting procedure would be all that is required.[8] However, life is not at all so simple and consumers cannot wait, nor, for that matter, can some producers, so that a money balance is essential. At the maximum this money balance, assuming that all stages must hold their balances at the same time, would be $1600, the total of all the payments.

In reality, the monetary requirement, or demand for money, in a modern economy will lie somewhere between the extremes of zero and the total value of payments. It is quite possible, however, to economize in the use of money and thus lower the money requirement. This would be the case if the monetary stages were able to postpone their expenditures until receipts come in from preceding stages. To the extent that this is possible, the money requirement becomes less. We shall have occasion to use this significant conclusion later. What is most important at this juncture is to see precisely how and why the monetary stages themselves bring about a demand for money purely for the purpose of transactions.

---

[6]The Gross National Product is defined as the total value of final goods and services produced. Of course, this includes *all* production, i.e., consumers goods, machinery and equipment, goods and services for government use, and production for export.

[7]Attempts have been made to estimate the total value of these payment flows. These are the input/output tables of national accounting.

---

[8]Of course, were there no accounting procedure (or banking system) at all and actual cash were required, the absolute minimum would be $600.

Diagram 2-5

FLOW OF PAYMENTS THROUGH THREE STAGES

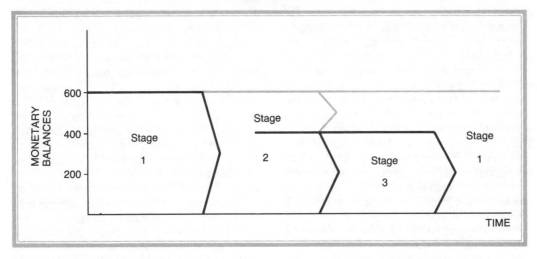

C. The Demand for Money—Real Balances and National Income

It should be clear that an actual demand for money is generated by a production process. However, the converse is also true, that is, money itself is an essential input into the production process. Without some monetary balances, no production can take place. Of course business enterprises may provide credit amongst themselves or, indeed, provide their own monetary balances from retained earnings; in either case, balances of money or credit are required for the reason that production takes time.

Generally, it is the function of the banking system to provide these balances in the form of loans to producers, and this it does especially for smaller businesses which, for various reasons, are unable to provide their own money balances. When, therefore, the banking system is unable or simply refuses to supply these loans, these businessmen can no longer meet payrolls, make payments to preceding stages, or otherwise discharge obligations, all of which arise from production. Faced with such a situation, businessmen will likely seek credit from each other, i.e., request that a preceding stage postpone its payment requirements, or even liquidate personal assets. In the end, however, the result can only be

a halt in the production process with consequent unemployment.

Under any circumstances, it is the responsibility of the banking system to provide this essential ingredient for the entire productive system. Should it fail to discharge this responsibility for any reason, the results can be disastrous. On the whole, the banking system does discharge its responsibilities very well. The exception to this was the earlier years of the decade of the 1930s during the Great Depression at which time bank loans were simply not forthcoming. The banks, using the criteria of risk, refused to make loans and incur consequent losses in the event of default, a strong possibility during those grim years. Some argument still exists as to the lack of effectiveness of the banks in supplying loans for business enterprises in certain regionally depressed areas of Canada. As in the depression years, chronically depressed areas mean greater risk of loan default for business enterprises. In such a case, a kind of feedback of pessimism may exist which could result in further depression.[9]

---

[9]J.M. Culbertson, *Money and Banking*, McGraw-Hill, 1972, ch. 9. The problem of banking pessimism may be much greater in Canada than in the U.S., especially when considered on a regional basis. Very little concrete evidence exists for such regional discrimination

But the task of banks is not so simple. Let us consider once more the monetary stages which make up payments circuits with money flows opposed to production flows. It will be recalled from Chapter 1 that an expansion of the exchange sector into the self-sufficient sector generates a demand for money. The provision of money in this case was referred to as horizontal monetization and is particularly prevalent in less developed countries which have a strong traditional agricultural sector. In Canada, however, horizontal monetization is typified more by an expanding population and labour force.[10] Each new entrant into the labour force, is, of course, a new monetary stage in miniature which requires a balance of monetary assets; hence, the demand for money is now greater than before. With our rapidly growing Canadian labour force, the demand for money which derives from this source is particularly strong and *must* be satisfied through additional supplies of money.

Not only is increased money required to satisfy the demand for horizontal monetization, but the requirements of increased production of goods and services must also be met. This, it will be recalled, is vertical monetization and is characterized by supplying additional funds to act as the monetary counterpart of the increased flow of production (see Diagram 1–2, Chapter 1). Should the monetary authorities responsible for the control of the banking system somehow fail in their responsibility to supply additional finance for this purpose, the flow of goods and services will likely cease to grow. On the other hand, should the monetary authorities increase the money supply faster than the growth of output of goods and

services, the consequence is likely to be rising prices. Precisely how and why the monetary authorities should err in this way will be examined in some detail in Chapters 3 and 4. For the moment, it is enough to grasp the concept that the supply of money is not at all, nor should it be, fixed. Quite the contrary; a considerable degree of flexibility is necessary as monetization requirements result in changes in the demand for money.

But the responsibility of the banking system and the monetary authorities which control it would *still* be relatively simple if this were all there was to it. There is, unfortunately, one other complicating factor which has been the subject of considerable controversy amongst economists over the years and still defies precise analysis. It is known in the economic literature as the "real balance effect" of rising prices.

To understand this extremely interesting phenomenon, we can return once more to our three examples of the savers, the spendthrifts, and the "neutralists." On the assumption that a monetary balance of $600 is received each month and all of it is spent by the end of the month, the average balance of monetary assets is, it will be recalled, $300. This happens to be just enough to enable the income earner to meet his needs and wants. But, to throw in a spanner, suppose the price level of all the monthly purchases were to rise by equal proportions. In terms of goods and services (the *real* value of $300) the balance of monetary assets is worth less than before. Let us consider, then, what is likely to be the reaction of all three of our hypothetical consumers.

The saver would find that the value of both his consumption and his savings stock had declined in real terms. His reaction (by definition he is a saver) would likely be to cut consumption for a few months so as to restore the real value of his savings. He will do so until the marginal utility of his stock of savings is equated with the marginal disutility of consumption foregone; in other words, he will restore his earlier position. But, unless his income rises, the savings stock must be less in real terms than before. This is the consequence of the law of diminishing marginal utility and since there is now less real income than before the price increase, the marginal utilities of the two uses of income, consumption and savings, will be equated faster than before.

---

because of pessimism; however, in the west, it is a source of considerable discontent among businessmen.

It is interesting that the Social Credit Party, with its original concept of expanding the money supply through Central Bank facilities, had its greatest success in the Canadian west during the depression years.

[10]It is an interesting question whether an expanding population is horizontal monetization or simply an increase in the size of the consuming stage and some producing stage. Logic would favour the increased size interpretation since no actual merging of sectors is taking place when population increases. Yet, for all practical purposes, the expansion is developing "horizontally" without a deepening of the productive process through additional productive stages as is characteristic of vertical monetization.

This extra "burst" of savings will result in additional money balances (or a lower velocity of circulation); hence, the next production stage will be deprived of income. Unemployment will be the likely result. This can be avoided, however, if the extra demand for money, which stems from savers' attempts to restore real balances, is met by an increased supply of money. With this additional money, savers are satisfied, producers are producing as much as before, since consumption has not declined, employment has not been reduced and the real stock of savings is restored exactly as before. In other words, nothing has changed in the long run. Money is completely neutral.

The assumption, of course, in this case is a once-for-all price increase, but what happens if prices continue to rise and furthermore, are *expected* to rise? The saver is now caught in a dilemma for now he faces an eternal treadmill in his attempt to equate his marginal utilities of consumption and savings. Moreover, the supply of money must *likewise* continuously rise to satisfy the increased demand; otherwise unemployment will result.

The spendthrift faces quite a different situation. From his current income he must deduct his debt repayment requirement which is, of course, at the expense of non-debt consumption. He will reach equilibrium when the marginal disutility of the non-debt consumption foregone just equals the marginal utility of his total consumption both debt and non-debt. Being rational, his additional spending beyond his income will stop at that point.

A once-for-all price increase reduces the real value of his non-debt consumption alone. He has, in effect, "insured" a portion of his consumption against a loss of real value by means of a contractual obligation for the debt portion of his consumption. Consequently, the loss in real income is less, relatively, than for either the saver or the "neutralist." The spendthrift therefore will be less discouraged than either of his consumer counterparts; nevertheless, he still will find a reduction in his living standard. This reduction will likely have its greatest impact on his propensity to go further into debt since credit buying is that portion of his total consumption which is most discretionary.

There is a leverage effect in all this because for any moment of time a decision *not* to increase debt burden by a certain amount means a corresponding decision not to consume a much *greater* amount in terms of money. Debt repayment involves future time; whereas the decision to purchase through credit is a "now" phenomenon involving a much greater sum of money to be financed by the capital market. All this means that subsequent producing stages which rely on this type of consumption will be deprived of considerable amounts of money. Once again employment will be threatened unless their demand for money is satisfied. In this case the "channel" through which the money is fed to the productive stages which require it is the consuming "spendthrift."

If price increases are continuous and are, consequently, *expected* to increase, the spendthrift has a distinct advantage over the saver. Such continuous price increases must be correspondingly "fed" by growth in the money supply to avoid unemployment; this means that incomes must be rising in money terms along with price increases so that real incomes do not change. The spendthrift now enjoys a continuous "insurance coverage" for his real consumption because of the contractual obligation of his debt repayment; in fact, a transfer of real wealth is taking place from the saver to the spendthrift. Of course, this abstracts from interest payments which partially correct this situation.

The analysis of the hypothetical consumers and their responses to the real balance effect of price increases has served to identify a relationship between prices and the demand for money. One must be careful here, however, to avoid the mistake of using the "general price level" for prices. All prices do not rise together and certainly not proportionately; pocket calculators are a case in point. This means that a substitution of the cheaper items for the more expensive will take place, reducing the impact of the real balance effect. With this caveat we can move into the macro-economic area of national income.

When we speak of the national income in general terms we have in mind all the many alternative measures of incomes such as Gross National Product, Net National Product (GNP less depreciation), National Income (NNP less indirect taxes plus subsidies), etc. The idea behind national income analysis is to ". . .apply the measuring rod of money to the diverse apples, grain, and machines that any society produces with its land, labour, and capital resources."[11] As such, it is an extremely useful statistic, principally because we measure not only the total value of goods and services, but also the value of all the incomes, wages, profits, rent and interest, which make it up. After all, the money payments received in production must go *somewhere*!

For our purposes, the Gross National Product is the most useful measure. It is strictly defined as "the total money value of the flow of final products of the community" (including depreciation allowances).[12] As a statistic, it is available on a quarterly basis both in money terms and in "real terms" (deflated by an index of price change) from Statistics Canada. Conceptually it is the value of the flow of output from the initial stages of production (see Diagram 1-2, Chapter 1) through to the consuming stages and represents *only the value added at each stage*. Of course, the value added to output at each stage is equivalent to the total of incomes earned at that stage.

It follows directly from the twin facts that (1) GNP (Gross National Product) is the statistical measure of all incomes, and (2) incomes earned *necessarily* involve a pause in the flow of money during which balances of monetary assets are held, that there exists some level of GNP which is appropriate to a given money supply and vice versa. What this level is, we just don't know since it depends upon the level of economic development, size of population, corporate structure and degree of integration, etc. (horizontal monetization), the output of goods and services (vertical monetization) and the amount of cash balances the general public wish to hold.

Since this latter is subject to many influences, psychological and otherwise, in addition to the real balances effect, it is next to impossible to relate the money supply and GNP in a precise quantitative form. This is why we merely state

$$M = f(Y) \text{ or } Y = g(M), \text{ with } Y = GNP.$$

We can, however, *observe* the statistical relationship which has prevailed in the past between GNP and the money supply in Canada by simply dividing the GNP by the total quantity of money.[13]

$$\frac{Y}{M} = \text{Income velocity of circulation}$$

This tells us that the total money supply circulates on the average a certain number of times per year during which process of circulation it generates an annual GNP. This makes possible the closest functional relationship we can develop as

$$M = 1/V \, (Y) \text{ or } Y = V(M).$$

Of course, just as Statistics Canada deflates current GNP with a price level index, we may express the current money value of Y and the real value Q (in terms of goods and services) of GNP multiplied by the price level P. Thus

$$PQ = VM$$

which is the well-known relationship between money and national income.

Remembering that velocity of circulation is merely the reciprocal of the proportion of total income held as monetary assets, we may quite simply convert this last version of the Quantity Theory of Money into the form used at the conclusion of Chapter 1.

Since $V = 1/k$, with k as the proportion of total income held as balances of monetary assets,

$$PQ = \frac{1}{k}M \text{ or } M = kPQ.$$

Of course, to repeat the same word of caution as before, this applies only to money used for the purpose of generating national income and not to money used for facilitating the exchange of bonds, stocks, used cars, houses, etc., all of which constitute financial assets in some form or another.

D. Canadian Demand for Money

Analytical techniques are sterile without a practical application. In this section the theoretical tools developed will be applied to the Canadian economy with the hope that conclusions of some significance may be drawn. Of course, we must

---

[11]Paul A. Samuelson and Anthony Scott, *Economics, Fourth Canadian Edition*, McGraw-Hill Ryerson Limited, Toronto, 1975, p. 160.
[12]*Ibid.*, p. 161.

[13]The total quantity of money in Canada is defined as "currency outside banks and chartered bank deposits." It is a fairly universal definition, though in some countries, savings deposits are excluded from the money supply.

always avoid the temptation of attributing greater degrees of precision to the results than is warranted.

1. Canadian Money Supply

The sophisticated monetary and banking system that exists in Canada is characterized by a degree of efficiency almost unmatched by any but the most highly developed countries. This arises from the fact that the banking system continuously grows and adjusts to satisfy the demade upon it. That is, a high consumer standard of living combined with an extremely efficient productive system means that the institution of banking must become correspondingly efficient; otherwise, the high degree of economic development which we enjoy today would be impossible. It is only necessary to compare the Canadian banking system with those of less developed countries to realize the significance and importance of our banks.[14] Payments are made with speed and accuracy by simply transferring the ownership of demand deposits upon the order of a cheque. With the aid of computers, this important monetary function is performed through clearing houses in staggering volume as well as speed. Indeed, it *must* be this way since how else could the enormous level of transactions required in an economy such as ours take place? Cash transfers are cumbersome, suitable only for personal day-to-day expenditures. Because of this, we find that the largest portion, by far, of our money supply consists of bank deposits. Our money takes that particular form that serves the greatest efficiency.

At the beginning of 1968 (see Chart 2-1) currency outside the banks, in our pockets in other words, amounted to $2,671,000,000. From this level it rose steadily, but surely, to $3.6 billion by June, 1971. It is interesting, however, to observe the monthly "sawtooth" effect of the graph which reflects the general pattern of Canadian income earners receiving their monthly paycheques and withdrawing sufficient cash from their bank balances to serve as balances of monetary assets

until the end of the month. As these balances are spent, they are returned to the banks once more for the reason that retailers prefer not to maintain such large cash balances in their tills. If in Diagrams 2-1, 2-2, 2-3, and 2-4, *M* were to represent cash in circulation, the graph of currency in circulation would be the exact statistical counterparts of the diagrams. It will be noted that the "tooth of the saw" assumes a much larger dimension at Christmas time for the obvious reason that cash purchases become very much larger at that time.

Looking at Currency and Demand Deposits combined, it will be observed that this quantum climbed from about $8.2 billion to about $11.3 billion by June, 1971. Demand deposits are, of course, the substitute for cash in circulation since the general public prefers to write cheques against their deposits, especially for large purchases, rather than carry cash. It is the combined total of cash outside the banks plus demand deposits, therefore, which constitute our money supply for transactions purposes only. Everything we buy, that is, must be purchased sooner or later with cash or a cheque.

Again the interesting feature of the graph is its purely seasonal fluctuations. Around tax paying time, demand deposits owned by the general public decline rather sharply. In addition, there is a fairly regular, and mysterious, quarterly pattern of peaks and troughs which, presumably, are seasonal.[15]

Personal Savings Deposits are, in all likelihood, the most familiar to us all. They are precisely as the title suggests, a form of saving for individual Canadians and are particularly useful because they can be readily transferred, in most cases, into demand deposits or cash. They are, in a real sense, "liquid" but also have the advantage that they earn interest on the monthly balance.

Savings deposits exist for the reason that the individual income earners have a positive balance of monetary assets (Diagram 2-2) at the end of each month. Savers could, of course, hold these balances as cash or demand deposits,

---

[14]In the author's experience, the banks of land-locked Afghanistan are an excellent example of banking institutions in early stages of development. Cheques are virtually unheard of in that country, with cash the only significant means of carrying on trade and commerce.

[15]At the time of writing, these quarterly fluctuations in demand deposits are a mystery. The Bank of Canada does "de-seasonalize" these figures, however, using the U.S. Bureau of Census system of moving averages. The rationale behind this is known to the Bank of Canada.

but being rational, they prefer to earn some interest. Accordingly, the steady climb of savings deposits indicates the savings habits of those many Canadians who elect this form of saving.

The increase in savings deposits from $11.8 billion in January, 1968, to $17.5 billion in June, 1971, which amounts to almost 12% per year, indicates that savers are, indeed, a significant and growing part of our population. In fact, were it not for the spenders who restore the incomes of subsequent stages (those with negative monthly balances of monetary assets as per Diagram 2-3) declining incomes would result. In actual fact, however, remarkable as the saving record appears, it is *still* not enough to counter the effect of all spenders in our economy with the result that a net expansion of our money income occurs.

Another interesting feature of the Personal Savings Deposit graph is the annual competition with the Canada Savings Bonds campaign which is launched every autumn. This is reflected in the annual dip and indicates quite clearly how chartered banks must compete with *all* institutions, not just Canada Savings Bonds, which offer an equal degree of liquidity, i.e., can be readily converted into cash or demand deposits. Chartered banks' interest rates on savings accounts must be sufficiently high to encourage income earners to use this form of savings rather than others; otherwise an important source of funds will be lost to them.

The impact of the annual competition for savings can also be seen in the Government of Canada deposits held in chartered banks which, conversely, increase each autumn. In effect, the ownership of these savings deposits is simply transferred from a private individual's account to the Government's account, the individual, meantime, receiving a Savings Bond in exchange for the transfer.

The governments of Canada, both federal and provincial, use the facilities of chartered banks despite the fact that the central bank itself is the Federal Government's bank. This is a matter of both convenience and policy, the precise details of which will follow in a subsequent chapter. At the moment it is essential to note that deposits owned by the government are *not* available for spending by the private sector — until, that is, they are actually spent by the government itself.

This is why the total of currency and chartered bank deposits is shown both with and without government deposits. "True" active money supply would be the total money supply less government deposits.

Under any circumstances, government deposits are fairly steady throughout the period embraced by Chart 2-1 with only seasonal peaks at both the Savings Bond season and income tax collecting time. These deposits are transferred to the Central Bank for expenditure purposes as each year progresses.

Perhaps the most interesting graph of all on Chart 2-1 is Non-personal Term and Notice Deposits. These are interesting for two reasons: (1) their behaviour during 1969 and 1970, and (2) the fact that they are owned not by ordinary individuals but generally by very large companies. They are, as the title suggests, deposits for a fixed term and of very large denominations of 100,000 to 500,000 blocks. Interest rates paid by the banks are highly competitive with other rates in the money market, though an "informal ceiling" does exist on the rates chartered banks pay.[16] This is why only corporations with large amounts of liquid funds will take advantage of this banking facility. Such funds are much better utilized when earning interest than when remaining idle.

2. *Impact of Changes in the Money Supply*

The reason that Chart 2-1 is included for analysis is that it spans a very interesting period. It was during the year 1969 that the government embarked upon a tight monetary policy. Details of how and why this was done will be discussed at considerable length later, but the significant feature of this period was that business enterprises were unable to receive the loans they ordinarily require. In a word, the central authorities, which mean the central bank and the Minister of Finance, had decided to restrict the growth of the money supply. Precisely how this is done is the subject of Chapter 3, but for the moment it is sufficient to recognize that the money supply in any modern banking system is directly under the control of the central authority.

---

[16]J.A. Galbraith, *Canadian Banking*, The Ryerson Press, Toronto, 1970, p. 87.
[17]Mathematically, the relationship is *linear homogeneous*.

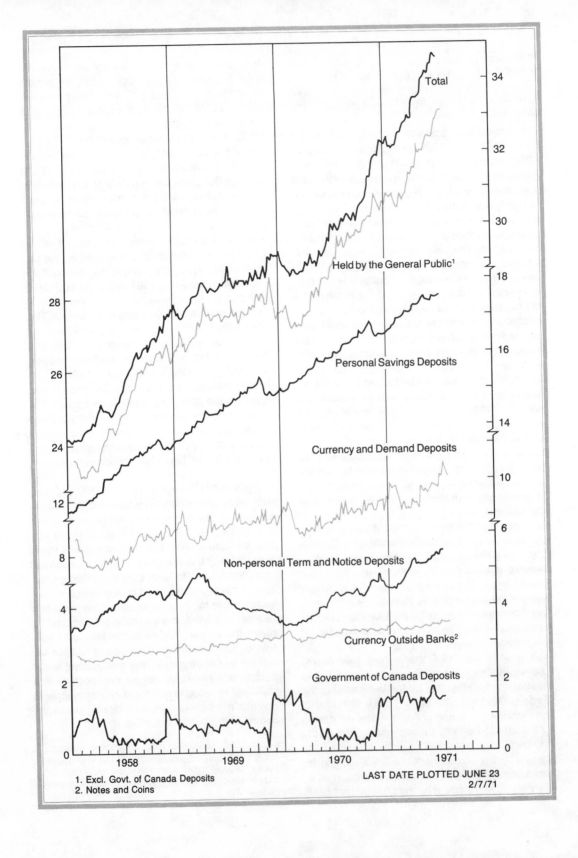

Total

Held by the General Public[1]

Personal Savings Deposits

Currency and Demand Deposits

Non-personal Term and Notice Deposits

Currency Outside Banks[2]

Government of Canada Deposits

1958   1969   1970   1971

1. Excl. Govt. of Canada Deposits
2. Notes and Coins

LAST DATE PLOTTED JUNE 23
2/7/71

◀ **Chart 2-1**

CURRENCY OUTSIDE BANKS AND CHARTERED BANK DEPOSITS
(Wednesdays—Billions of Dollars)

It has been argued in the first chapter that monetization processes require an increasing amount of money as means of payment. Exactly how much, of course, we do not know; all we can do is observe past behaviour. But of the three sources of demand for money, one, vertical monetization, is related directly to the output of goods and services, i.e., the real Gross National Product. Furthermore, this relationship is most likely to be direct in the sense that a given proportionate increase in the GNP will require the same proportionate increase in the money supply to satisfy the needs of vertical monetization.[17]

But what about the other two sources of demand for money, i.e., horizontal monetization and the important real balances? The money supply must increase by *more* than the absolute minimum required by the growth in output; otherwise we will find ourselves with a shortage of monetary assets purely for the purpose of spending.

This was precisely what was happening during the year 1969. The growth of the money supply had been restricted to the absolute minimum with an almost 4% increase over the year. The real GNP, on the other hand, grew by about 5% over the same time period. Now in view of the fact that the later 1960s were a period of generally rising prices (around 4 or 5% per year) it is likely that people were indeed holding extra funds as monetary assets because of rising prices. Furthermore, the growth of population and the formation of new companies and expansion of old (horizontal monetization) could only add a further pressure of demand for money as against an already strained supply.[18] It is not surprising, then, that the pressure of total demand for money for transactions purposes would be considerable

with the consequence that corporations liquidated some term and notice deposits in 1969 in order to finance their business activities. There simply was not enough money available to satisfy all the demand, and corporate businesses used the only source of ready funds they had available. When this fact is combined with the drying up of funds from the U.S. which, as will be discussed in Part III, are ordinarily available in some considerable quantity, it is hardly surprising that a slowdown in business activity with consequent unemployment would result.

The second period (see Chart 2-2) for the Canadian money supply and its growth begins with March, 1970. At that time, a complete reversal of the attitude of the central authority took place. Instead of restricting the money supply so as to inhibit monetization, a deliberate expansionary policy was begun. Loans became easy at the banks, interest rates on savings deposits began to decline as the process of money expansion developed.[19] Almost immediately the total money supply chart began its sharp upward trend. Unfortunately, however, once business becomes slack and unemployment high, it is not so easy to generate the optimism necessary to restore the confidence of businessmen. The new funds found their way at first into Non-personal Term and Notice Deposits to restore the lost liquidity of corporations, there to remain until needed for business expenses. Demand deposits also rose rather substantially during 1971, as income earners found themselves with increasing amounts of monetary assets.

The expansive posture of the government was reflected in the low level of government deposits in the months following March, 1970. That is, not only was the money supply to rise, but it must

---

[18]The growth of population during the year 1969 was about 1½%. Increases in new corporations and corporate growth, using net new issues of stocks as an indicator, reached their highest level in recent years with net new stocks at $994 million, a peak not achieved since.

[19]Savings Deposit interest rates began their decline in June, 1970 to reach 4% in November, 1971. Chartered banks were simply no longer interested in Savings Deposits since other sources of funds for lending were available. For a complete discussion of this important point, see Chapter 3.

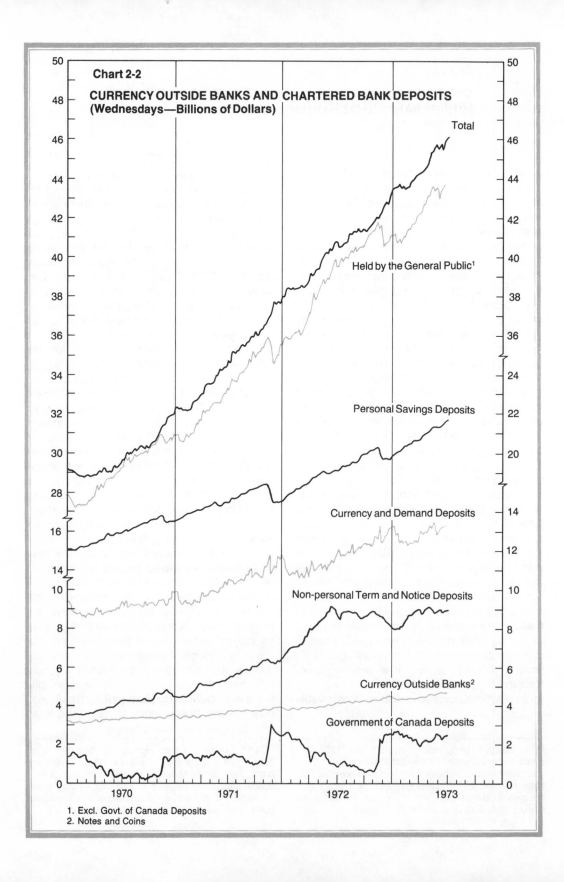

Chart 2-2

CURRENCY OUTSIDE BANKS AND CHARTERED BANK DEPOSITS
(Wednesdays—Billions of Dollars)

Total

Held by the General Public[1]

Personal Savings Deposits

Currency and Demand Deposits

Non-personal Term and Notice Deposits

Currency Outside Banks[2]

Government of Canada Deposits

1970   1971   1972   1973

1. Excl. Govt. of Canada Deposits
2. Notes and Coins

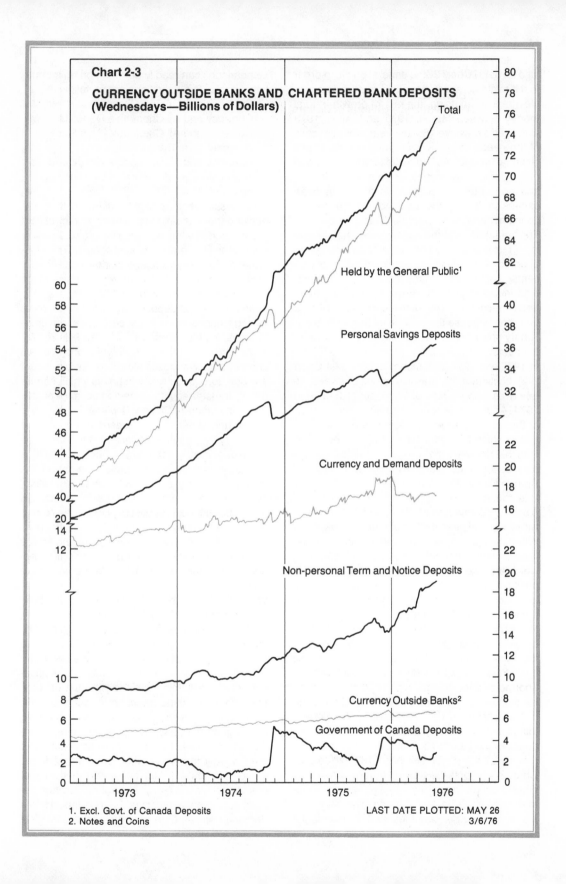

Chart 2-3

CURRENCY OUTSIDE BANKS AND CHARTERED BANK DEPOSITS
(Wednesdays—Billions of Dollars)

Total

Held by the General Public[1]

Personal Savings Deposits

Currency and Demand Deposits

Non-personal Term and Notice Deposits

Currency Outside Banks[2]

Government of Canada Deposits

1973   1974   1975   1976

1. Excl. Govt. of Canada Deposits
2. Notes and Coins

LAST DATE PLOTTED: MAY 26
3/6/76

also be held largely by the general public in order that it might be spent, hopefully, to stimulate employment. In so doing, the rate of growth in total money between March, 1970 and June, 1973 averaged a massive 15% per year, well in excess of the needs of purely real growth in the Gross National Product. As if to make up for that portion of the demand for money for both real balances and horizontal monetization in 1969, an over-expansion took place designed to encourage consumer and investment demand.

The contribution of the expansive monetary policy in stimulating employment can hardly be doubted since, finally, unemployment as a percentage of the labour force (seasonally adjusted) did turn down in 1973. However, as might have been forecast, the cost of this contribution was a dear one because the price level began its inflationary upward trend even more strongly than in the past.

In 1973 and 1974 total money supply (see Chart 2-3) continued its massive upward sweep to reach an annual rate of increase of 24.8% in 1974. As will be recognized from the chart, much of the increase went into Personal Savings Deposits which rose by 21% in 1974 at the same time that Non-personal Term and Notice Deposits also reached a comparable 20.7%. Currency and Demand Deposits, on the other hand, rose very little during that year.

A careful examination of Charts 2-1, 2-2, and 2-3 will reveal a distinct pattern of money expansion. When the total money supply increases at a rate greater than "normal," i.e., greater than that which prevailed earlier, it flows into the two deposit categories which act as a "storage" to await an opportunity for spending. This means that the public's demand for money is not sufficient to use the increased money for expenditure purposes; consequently, surplus funds tend to be stored in the form of interest bearing deposits. All this means that the extra funds required to finance the enormous price increase of 1974/5, the peak inflation years, were already "in place," requiring only a transfer into demand deposits. We can see this in the growth of currency and demand deposits for the year 1975. In that year, this category rose by 21.6% ($15.5 billion to $18.8 billion).

Chart 2-4 reflects the new and more convenient classification of monetary aggregates recently introduced by the Bank of Canada. This brings us into line with other countries so that meaningful comparisons can readily be made on an international basis. The definitions are as follows:

Currency and Demand Deposits	M_1
Currency and All Chequable Deposits	M_{1_B}
Currency and All Chequable, Notice and Personal Term Deposits	M_2
Currency and All Chequable Notice and Term Deposits *plus* Foreign Currency Deposits of Residents	M_3

This classification is slightly different from the earlier deposit breakdown; it does, in fact, reflect more accurately the monetary nature of deposits, hence, the title "monetary aggregates." The classification M_{1_B}, for example, includes those chequable savings deposits of chartered banks which are still being used by the public along with the ordinary demand deposit. M_2 includes personal savings deposits, savings certificates in chartered banks, etc., along with M_{1_B}, and, finally, M_3 is the largest category of all which includes all chartered bank deposits plus, and this is a recent addition, foreign currency deposits which can be readily transferred into Canadian dollar deposits. An examination of Chart 2-4 will reveal both the nature and size of the increases in our various monetary aggregates. M_3 grew from 70.9 billion at the beginning of 1976 to $121 billion in 1979, a 72% increase! During the same time period, M_1 increased by only 22% ($18 billion to $22 billion) reflecting the growth of demand for money for purely transactions purposes. Under the former deposits breakdown personal savings deposits rose by 66% and Non-personal Term and Notice deposits precisely doubled during this time period, once again making possible the finance of future price increases.

We can draw some interesting conclusions from this brief survey of the Canadian money supply which is not only useful for practical applications but important for the analysis which follows. We note, in the first place, that any increase in the total money supply (M_3 in the current classification) must go *somewhere*, i.e., it must become the property of some members of our economic community—governments, business enterprise, or the general public. As these spending agencies acquire these funds, they are entitled to hold them in any form they wish, only one of these being "spendable," i.e., chequable deposits or cash in circulation (M_{1_B}). A personal savings deposit, for instance, must first be transferred into a demand deposit, then used to discharge a debt

Chart 2-4

MONETARY AGGREGATES
(Wednesdays—Billions of Dollars)

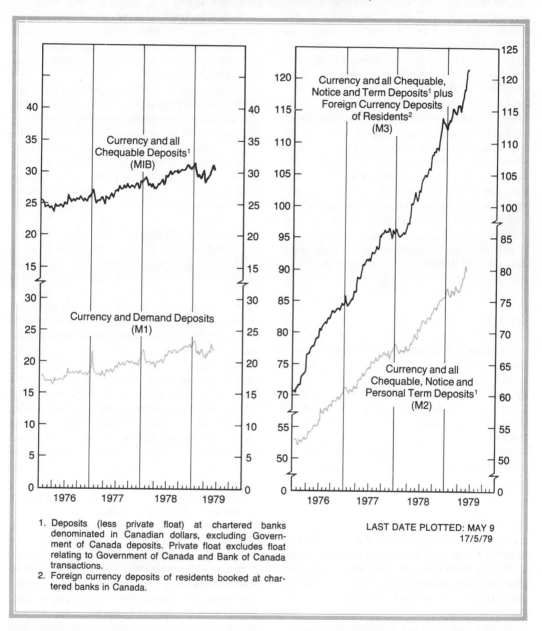

Currency and all Chequable Deposits[1] (MIB)

Currency and Demand Deposits (M1)

Currency and all Chequable, Notice and Term Deposits[1] plus Foreign Currency Deposits of Residents[2] (M3)

Currency and all Chequable, Notice and Personal Term Deposits[1] (M2)

1. Deposits (less private float) at chartered banks denominated in Canadian dollars, excluding Government of Canada deposits. Private float excludes float relating to Government of Canada and Bank of Canada transactions.
2. Foreign currency deposits of residents booked at chartered banks in Canada.

LAST DATE PLOTTED: MAY 9
17/5/79

by transferring the ownership to a second individual. The latter may elect to re-transfer his newly acquired deposit into another personal savings deposit once more. If he does so, we can consider, from a statistical point of view, that the personal savings deposit has a "velocity of circulation."

This velocity of the savings deposit would be less

than the demand deposit which, in turn, is less than cash in circulation. Most of us, of course, discharge our obligations first by cash, then by cheque, and, lastly, by withdrawals from savings accounts. In this way velocity of circulation decreases as the form of our money becomes less "liquid." After all, interest is earned on savings accounts and this is an incentive not to dip into them for transactions purposes any more than necessary.

Secondly, it follows that our Canadian money supply (M_3 in the new classification) is not at all fixed in form or structure. It is fluid, continuously shifting from one type of deposit to another, only one of which (M_1) is suitable for spending. It is not easy, therefore, to decide on what *is* our true supply of money, M_1, M_{1_a}, M_2, or M_3. Currently the government and the Bank of Canada focus attention on M_1 noting that the growth of this category is within a specific "target" range. The other categories, on the other hand, have been showing considerably greater growth rates (see Table 2-1).

Table 2-1
ANNUAL RATES OF GROWTH (%)

	M_1	M_2	M_3
1974	9.5	20.1	24.8
1975	13.8	15.0	14.7
1976	8.0	12.6	18.4
1977	8.5	14.0	15.8
1978			
I Qtr	5.8	8.9	8.6

Source: Table 1, *Bank of Canada Review*, June, 1978.

Since it is entirely the decision of the public which form our money supply takes, it is not unlikely that shifts from the other categories into M_1 will take place in the near future to reflect the pattern of the years 1968, 1971/72, and 1974/75.

3. Money Supply and the Price Level

The computation of the Gross National Product involves the estimates of total output (or incomes) using the common measuring rod of money. Estimates of the real value, exclusive of price change, of the GNP necessarily involve

some quantitative measure of price changes. This is done with the use of price index numbers of various categories of expenditures which make up Gross National Expenditure, the same as GNP, but from the side of expenditure rather than production. Statistics Canada's publication "National Income and Expenditure Accounts" presents these "implicit price deflators" in considerable detail.

Currently, the price deflators are based upon the Gross National Expenditure for the year 1971 as 100. For example, a price deflator for the GNE of 170.9 for 1977 says that the level of prices is 70.9% higher than 1971. Or, similarly, dividing the GNP for 1977 by 170.9 gives the measure in real terms (goods and services at 1971 prices) of the GNP for 1977.

($ MILLIONS)

1971	1977
$\dfrac{94,450}{1.00} = 94,450$	$\dfrac{207,714}{1.709} = 121,566$

Thus, a comparison in real terms of the Gross National Expenditure (Product) reveals only a 28.7% increase, whereas in money terms the increase is 120%.

An expansion of the money supply of the magnitude which we have seen since March, 1970 must, of necessity, satisfy all the demand for money. In fact, to proceed one step further, not only are real balances and horizontal monetization requirements satisfied, but there is still more than sufficient funds for transactions. The consequence of this is that the general public as consumers and business enterprises as producers have on hand sufficient funds to pay higher prices once they appear in the market.

We cannot argue, that is, that excessive amounts of money *cause* higher prices; quite the contrary — by removing the resistance to higher market prices, the excess money permits all the other actual causes to act unrestrained. Such causes, of course, are always there in greater or less strength, for the very nature of the free market is one of an equilibrium between forces of demand and supply. This is why world shortages of food or raw material, for example, result in prices which are much higher when money is plentiful than when it is not. Prices rise because we are willing to pay them with our excess money balances.

Some measure of this excess of money may be had by means of income velocity of circulation. This, it will be recalled, is simply the functional relationship between the money supply and the GNP in money terms and it does, of course, encompass all three facets of the demand for money. From observation of the past we may infer that currently a "normal" level of income velocity is something like 2.6, having increased from the years following World War II when the money supply was extremely high. However, the recent expansion of the money supply since 1970 has produced a rather lower than normal income velocity, suggesting that the money value of the GNP will likely rise further as velocity approaches normal once more.

the GNP to grow in real terms sufficiently to account, in some measure, for the increased velocity. This would be particularly true if the "cost push" effect is slow in forthcoming. However, given the economic climate these days which leans somewhat heavily toward inflation, it is likely that price levels in general will indeed increase as a normal income velocity is restored.

II. A THEORETICAL RELATIONSHIP BETWEEN MONEY AND PRICES

In Section I,C of this chapter a relation between prices and money was established through the Real Balance Effect. The argument was that a

Table 2-2
INCOME VELOCITY OF MONEY IN CANADA

	GNP (Y) (millions of dollars)	Money Supply (M)* (millions of dollars)	Income Velocity* Y/M
1947	13,744	7,236	1.899
1952	24,640	9,307	2.647
1957	33,513	11,923	2.666
1962	42,927	15,683	2.641
1967	66,409	24,242	2.595
1969	79,815	29,155	2.829
1970	85,685	32,066	2.720
1971	94,450	37,886	2.550
1972	105,234	43,437	2.422
1973	123,560	48,412	2.552
1974	147,175	56,521	2.604
1975	165,445	66,696	2.481
1976	190,027	78,510	2.420
1977	207,714	89,103	2.331

Source: G.F. Boreham et al, *Money and Banking: Analysis and Policy in a Canadian Context,* Holt, Rinehart and Winston of Canada, First Edition, 1969, pp. 820-821.
*Currency plus privately-held Canadian dollar deposits.

Of course, if it is not possible for the GNP to grow in real terms quickly enough, it follows that the price level *must* rise. *When* prices will rise, however, we cannot tell since these depend upon market forces of demand and supply. Some increase in cost or an abnormal shortage which results in higher market prices will likely restore normal velocity for the reason that all the demand for money is satisfied and resistance to higher prices on the part of the buying public is weak.

On the other hand, it would be quite possible for

rising price level caused an increase in the demand for money. The supply of money, in turn, increased because the consequence of not permitting the money supply to grow was unemployment. The monetary authorities, in other words, see to it that the money supply rises for the reason that they choose the lesser of two evils, inflation. It is now time to reverse the causation, i.e., permit the money supply to rise first. This is in accordance with the standard Quantity Theory approach which does indeed make this assumption.

Most standard expositions of the Quantity Theory of Money conclude with a formulation such as

$$PQ = \frac{1}{k}(M)$$

which relates (see Section I,D) prices and the quantity of real output to money by way of some measure of velocity of circulation. The function is, of course, velocity itself. But in this form, velocity is like the statistician's famous "little black box." A crank is turned, a number (income velocity) falls out, and we really know little more than we did before. Being economists, we are not satisfied. We must, therefore, try to determine the workings of the box, not merely for curiosity's sake, but to deduce why some measures of velocity vary from one time to the next, how institutions affect velocity, and the nature and impact of "inflationary expectations" upon velocity. These are just some of the important questions which require careful analysis.

A. Market Equilibrium

We begin, therefore, at the beginning with a brief, but necessary, exposition of market equilibrium from a monetary viewpoint. Marshallian equilibrium (as conventionally taught in the textbooks) suggests a static concept of "rest." That is, when supply and demand are equated at a certain price, a stable equilibrium exists. Any departure from this equilibrium would automatically call forth market forces which would restore the equilibrium price and quantity, and this is how price stability in general can be shown to exist in the marketplace.

But this is not a correct picture, especially during our own times of inflationary *in*stability of prices. If we accept, for instance, the existence of market equilibrium, we are forced to conclude that there must be a continuous shift of market demand and supply curves through time as prices rise. But this is an awkward concept which must involve an explanation of *why* there is a shift in the first place. Thus, it would seem better to conceive of equilibrium not as a static, rest situation, but, more realistically, as a dynamic equilibrium of forces. One might imagine an aspiring "Mr. Canada" developing his biceps by pulling against a spring-loaded device. Equilibrium exists when movement ceases, but to maintain this equilibrium requires an expenditure of energy. Eventu-

ally, the muscle tires and the spring overcomes, gradually at first, but progressively faster, depending upon the degree of muscular fatigue. There is, note carefully, no "rest" for Mr. Canada at equilibrium.

For our purposes, market equilibrium may be conceived not as the demand and supply of a commodity, as in the Marshall case, but as the demand for and supply of money. As we have seen, a demand for money exists which derives, basically, from the "bridging service" provided by money balances. Similarly, a seller of goods has a demand for the same money for income purposes. When the buyer's demand for money is overcome and he makes his purchase, he *supplies* (or offers) the money to satisfy the seller's demand. In some cases, food, shelter, etc., the natural human drives are certain to overcome consumers' demand for money in the end, so the seller need only wait patiently. In others, demand for money must be overcome by skillful advertising, cajoling, "sales" (real or imaginary), etc. Clothing stores and automobile retailing are both cases in point. Ultimately, the success of the seller is determined by wearing away consumer's resistance so that the consumer's demand for money is at last overcome.

We can describe this situation more analytically. We will assume that consumers' demands for money rest upon two principal foundations, ignoring, for simplicity, other less important sources of demand. These are (1) the amount of money available to consumers at any one time, and (2) the price level of commodities. In the first case, the greater the amount of money any single consumer has (given the price level of goods and services), the less will be his demand for the marginal money unit. This follows directly from the Law of Diminishing Marginal Utility and results in a negative relationship between demand for money on the part of buyers and the amount of money available to them. This is illustrated in Diagram 2-6. D_b (buyers' demand for money), given a specific price level, is negatively sloped relative to the amount of money available. Should prices, for any reason, rise to P_2, demand for money, given a specific amount of available money (M), will rise (D_{b_1} to D_{b_2}).

The second relationship can be similarly expressed (see Diagram 2-7), though this time the function is positive.

Diagram 2-6

BUYERS' DEMAND FOR MONEY (1)

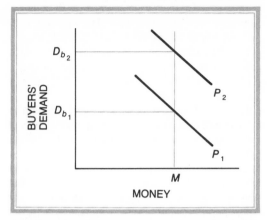

As the price level rises (given the available money, M,) buyers' demand for money will increase. This is, of course, the consequence of the rather obvious result that it is the amount of money in *real* terms (money divided by the price level) which will determine consumers' demand for money. Given the buyers' demand for money D_b, any increase in available money (M_1 to M_2) will result in a higher price, P_1 to P_2.

It remains to combine these two relationships into a form which is most useful for analytical purposes. This is shown in Diagram 2-8. This diagram results from holding buyers' demand (D_b) constant as in Diagram 2-7 and plotting prices against available money. As is apparent, there is a positive relationship between money and prices

Diagram 2-7

BUYERS' DEMAND FOR MONEY (2)

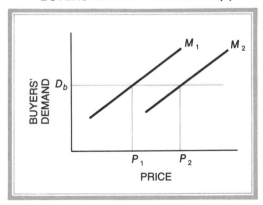

suggesting that, given the buyers' demand for money, an increase in the money supply will result in higher prices.[20]

But this is still fairly obvious and does not take us much further than the Quantity Theory itself; certainly it does not get to the heart of market equilibrium. Still, however, it may be intuitively obvious that the more money becomes available to satisfy the demand for money, the more is available for spending. Thus, the supply of money for the market at any one time varies inversely with the strength of demand for money.

There is another factor, however, which must be considered and that is the elasticity of buyers' demand curve for money (D_b) in Diagram 2-8. As will be readily noted, the function intersects the Price axis indicating an elasticity greater than unity.[21] The reason for this stems from the ordinary substitution effect and the Real Balance Effect discussed earlier and means that any price increase with which a consumer is presented will result in a greater than proportionate increase in demand for money. The reason for this is twofold: (1) If the price increase happens to be for a single commodity, the rational consumer will likely seek a substitute, therefore increasing his demand for money to infinity as far as the specific single transaction is concerned; in other words, the consumer refuses to buy. The (D_b) function in Diagram 2-8 is horizontal. (2) Suppose price increases are general so that prices of substitutes are rising as well. In this case the Real Balance

---

[20]Mathematically, the diagrams can be expressed as the following:

$D_b = f(M,P)$ with $\frac{\partial f}{\partial M} < 0$ and $\frac{\partial f}{\partial P} > 0$.

It follows that

$$dD_b = \frac{\partial f}{\partial M} dM + \frac{\partial f}{\partial P} dP.$$

Dividing all three terms by $(\partial f/\partial M)\, dM$ and setting dD_b equal to zero (*ex hypothesi*) gives

$$-1 = \frac{\frac{\partial f}{\partial P} dP}{\frac{\partial f}{\partial M} dM}, \text{ or } -1\,(-)\frac{\partial M}{\partial f} \cdot \frac{\partial f}{\partial P} = \frac{dP}{dM}.$$

Since $\partial m/\partial f$ is negative in sign, it follows that dP/dM, the slope of the function Diagram 2-7, is positive.

---

[21]Calculation of elasticity in this case is the same as for the ordinary market supply function of microeconomics:

$$\varepsilon = \frac{dM}{dP}\frac{(P)}{M}.$$

Diagram 2-8

BUYERS' DEMAND FOR MONEY (COMBINED)

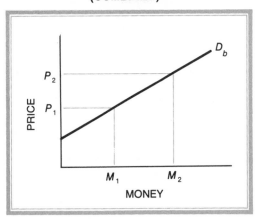

mand for money is satisfied with an amount, m, the residual, O, is available for offering in the market.

Suppose, first, that m is constant, i.e., it does not increase with the price level. The increase in O will exactly equal the increase in M and the slope of the O function will be 45°. But this is not likely to be the case. Demand for money *will* increase with the price level (see Diagram 2-8) leaving *less* for offering on the market. Thus, just as the elasticity of the demand for money function in Diagram 2-8 is greater than unity, the elasticity of the offer curve in Diagram 2-9 is less than unity. This is a most important point to grasp.

Let us consider now the sellers' demand curve for money. Purely for the convenience of analysis, we will assume that only a given stock of inventory of goods will be sold, the time being too short to permit any increase in stocks through the production process. This assumption is relaxed later, but at present it is easier to consider the realistic case of retailers who desire to exhaust seasonal inventories, and can only do so by adjustment of their selling prices. So, assuming that no increase in stocks of inventory can take place, the sellers' demand for money would precisely equal the price level, i.e., the sellers' demand for money, D_s, has a slope of exactly 45°. We are, now, ready to consider market equilibrium purely in terms of demand and supply of money.

Suppose a price P_1 should be tried in the market. The amount of money forthcoming from buyers' offers, the offer curve, would exceed the sellers' demand for money. This stock of inventory would be exhausted and, at the same time, the stock of money would be less than what it could have been. This, however, is unlikely in practice since sellers want to maximize revenues and profits. What is more likely to be true is a price P_2 which represents a first attempt by sellers to gain maximum revenue. But at this price, the amount of money offered falls short of the sellers' demand with the consequence that additional advertising, sales offering "discounts," or other gimmicks must be resorted to which will, ultimately, equate the sellers' demand with the buyers' offer. This would be the equilibrium price P_o. This equilibrium price would be either a *bona fide* reduction in the sellers' demand for money or an increase in the buyers' offer curve as a result of persuasion or a combination of the two. However, the "equi-

Effect will force consumers to increase their demands for money by a greater percentage than prices rise unless, of course, incomes are rising by precisely the same proportion as prices (real income is constant). In this latter case, the D_b function would intersect the origin of the graph (elasticity equals unity) and there would be no Real Balance Effect at all. While such a circumstance would be an unlikely coincidence, we must remember that during the inflationary periods we have been experiencing recently, many incomes do indeed keep pace with price increases so that the same demand for money functions will be close to unity elasticity.

To see precisely how a market equilibrium in terms of money comes about, we require a final step — the development of consumers' "offer curve." As might be guessed, the consumers' offer curve of money is complementary to the demand curve for money. Thus, if we subtract from total available money, M, the amount of money, m, to satisfy demand, the residual, O, is the amount offered in the market. Diagram 2-9 illustrates this. On the diagram are indicated three levels of money, M_1, M_2, and M_3 available to consumers. Where does the money come from? It can come from past savings locked up with varying degrees of liquidity (discussed in detail in Part II), from increased salaries and wages, or, indeed, from borrowing if buyers' credit is good. From whatever source, after de-

Diagram 2-9

MARKET EQUILIBRIUM

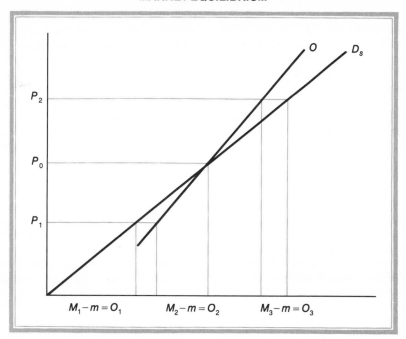

librium price" is not what sellers would have preferred. They are *forced* (market equilibrium is an equilibrium of forces) to accept the facts of the market. Similarly, buyers would have been happier with a price, P_1, but they too are forced to adjust their plans and expectations and compromise with the price P_o.

We are now in a position to examine more closely the nature of market equilibrium under our assumptions. Suppose, first, the slope of the offer curve in Diagram 2-9 is less, i.e., approaching 45°. This, it will be recalled, is the complement of the buyers' demand for money in Diagram 2-8 which approaches 45° *from the other side*, increasing its slope. The equilibrium price level of goods and services would, as a consequence, be much more susceptible to upward adjustments. Such upward movements in equilibrium prices must, of course, be accompanied by greater amounts of money available to consumers; there is no other alternative.

Now suppose that in some way (how, precisely, is the subject of the next chapter) the money supply *in general* should increase. Does this mean an automatic and corresponding increase in the

amount of money available to consumers? No! Consider, for example, Chart 2-2 which breaks down the Canadian money supply into its component parts. During the year-and-a-half span from early 1971 to mid-1972, the money supply increased, but the increments took the form of increased Non-personal Term and Notice Deposits. Non-personal deposits are those deposits owned by "non-humans," firms, agencies, organizations, etc., generally spent for specific reasons and not for the purchase of consumer goods. Fixed term deposits are large sums of money (generally $500,000) placed with banks at interest rates competitive with other rates obtainable elsewhere. They are generally "locked up" (redeemable only at penalty) for a fixed term and again are not available to consumers for the obvious reason of size. Only corporations or firms with large amounts of idle funds are in a position to own such deposits.

After mid-1972, the increased money began to "filter down" to persons to take the form of both currency and demand deposits and personal savings deposits. Thus, the amount of money *available* to consumers increased in late 1972 and 1973. We can imagine this increased availability as a reduction in the slope of the offer curve in Diagram 2-9 as a consequence of satisfying the demand for money. Slowly, gradually at first, sellers' money demand rises, moving up the D_s curve in response to the profit motive. In some cases, such as food prices, a shortage of supply because of poor harvests, etc., may be responsible for the initial upward thrust of sellers' demand for money. Obviously buyers are not about to go hungry since additional money is now available to them. Other items, housing, durable goods, etc. follow, again in response to upward thrusts by sellers which meet little (or less than before) resistance from consumers. "Mr. Canada" is weakening and the springs are compressing. After all, why not? The muscles are becoming flabby and further resistance is more difficult. The demand for money on the part of consumers is now more satisfied than before.

Ultimately, the last of the resistors, old-age pensioners and the like, succumb by being forced to locate more money through asset liquidation or additional public assistance. Lady Churchill sells her husband's paintings; others, less fortunate, seek welfare. However one looks at it, it is these unfortunates who bear the greatest burden in times of rising prices.

During the initial period of monetary expansion, such as 1971–72, income velocity of money (Y/M) declines (see above, page 30). New money, in other words, is not yet available for spending by consumers to generate additional income. How long it will take (the time lag between money expansion and price increases) for this new money to become available to consumers we cannot tell. It depends upon the spending and investment decisions of, generally, corporations and business enterprises which first receive the new money. In the end, of course, it must be spent to generate additional personal income. This could be the consequences of higher wage contracts negotiated by trade unions, additional workers on the payroll in response to decisions to expand the enterprise, overtime payments, etc.; ultimately, inevitably, the money finds its way into personal ownership. *Still*, however all the money is not spent as soon as it is received. People tend to spend by habit, all "money illusion," by allocating specific amounts of money for various purposes. Any additional amounts of funds are left either as idle balances

in chequing accounts or placed into personal savings. In the end, the sellers' demand for money is satisfied by drawing forth even the most reluctant of moneys into circulation through the stream of income generation as normal income velocity is restored at higher levels of prices.

Is there any way that the tendency for prices to rise may be checked under these circumstances? If the sellers' demand for money is satisfied not by price increases but by increases in output of goods and services, and the buyers' demand for money is satisfied in the first place, so that they are willing to make additional purchases, the new money will be spent for the increased output. In other words, the initial assumption of a fixed inventory of goods may now be relaxed. In this case, the analysis of Diagram 2-9 does not strictly apply and the monetary inflation, with consequent rising prices, will be considerably less. The analysis of the effect of increased output on the sellers' demand for money is included in Chapter 5 below.

B. General Market Equilibrium

It would not be correct to conclude a theoretical analysis involving buyers' offer curves and sellers' demand curves for money as if all sellers were in collusion to push up their money demand curves just to the points of equilibrium with buyers' offer curves. The implication is that a vast monopsony confronts buyers' collective offer curves, hardly a true representation of the economy.

Few of us, as consumers, are faced with pure monopsony. Quite the contrary; many sellers in certain defined urban areas, well within the reach of the family car, means that several alternatives are available to us from which we must choose only one seller. We do indeed have a choice in a competitive market, and this means that we can distribute our total funds for expenditures amongst several sellers in accordance with a variety of inducements, not the least of which is the lower price. Sellers, then, have a demand for buyers' money, to be sure, but the existence of competition between dealers who sell the same or similar products generally involves considerable advertising expense, discounts, prizes, premiums, or even outright price competition (probably a last resort!) especially in the business of retailing. The less rational are consumers in their decision as to their choice of seller, the less related to the purchasing process are the seller's inducements. Automobile buyers, for instance, may prefer a remote chance to win a colour TV to an actual reduction in the cost of their new car, so dealers take advantage of our irrational gambling instincts.

All this is accepted and justified as an integral part of a free market system. We might question the economic efficiency of such a system and ultimately conclude that what is fundamentally wrong is that sellers are not interested in giving buyers the best product value for their money, but rather in coaxing money from buyers by whatever means at their disposal including outright deception. This is not merely the upper and nether blades of Marshall's famous scissors.

To be more precise, analytically, let us consider two competing department stores which sell "everything" (or nearly so) and are identical in size, inventory, etc. Let us also suppose that two buyers, a and b, confront these two department stores. Now it so happens that each store has a demand for money exactly equal to $10 ($20 between them). The buyers, on the other hand, have only $7.07 each ($14.14 between them), but, of course, the sellers are not aware of this. The sellers must now offer their inducements and encouragements so as to compete for the buyers' money. In doing so, seller 1 is successful. He manages to draw $5 from each buyer while seller 2 is forced, therefore, to console himself with the remainder, a total of only $4.14. Seller 2 is the unsuccessful loser of one round in an endless "sparring match" of competition for the consumers' dollar.

We can depict this situation in a more analytical fashion by borrowing the concept of force vectors from elementary physics. In Diagram 2-10, the two sellers are represented as having a demand for $10 as indicated by the length of their vectors, Ds_1 and Ds_2. For the first department store, the money demand (Ds_1) is satisfied by both buyers, a and b, spending $5 each and is represented by $\cos \alpha_1$ ($7.07) + $\cos \beta_1$ ($7.07) = $10. The balance of the $7.07 is available for spending by both buyers and accrues to department store #2 [$\cos \alpha_2$ (7.07) + $\cos \beta_2$ (7.07) = $4.14]. In both cases, the length of the diagonals of the parallelograms are the buyers' offer curves and represent

the amount of money being offered. It is obvious that store #2 is disappointed; he has lost his hoped-for sales to his competitor.

But this is only one round. Seller 2 may regain his lost sales, perhaps by lowering prices (scaling his demand for money downward) and seller 1 may retaliate in a similar fashion. In this way, an endless series of adjustments will result in lowered prices (lowered sellers' demand for money) until the demand for money on the part of both sellers is exactly $14.14 to be equally divided between them precisely equal to the buyers' combined offer curve. This is equilibrium. In terms of the parallelograms, the cosines of both α and β would equal $1/2$ (the angles α and β are exactly 60°). Equilibrium would appear as in Diagram 2-11.

Of course, the equilibrium represented in Diagram 2-11 is for both department stores, each having now the same parallelogram. In competitive terms, they are equals. Were this not the case, a smaller department store might be content with something less than 50% of the buyers' offer curve. The only condition, therefore, for equilibrium is that the sellers' combined money demand equals the buyers' combined offer curves. For the two seller case just examined,

(1) $\cos \alpha_1 \, a_1 + \cos \beta_1 \, b_1 = Ds_1$
                    and
         $\cos \alpha_2 \, a_2 + \cos \beta_2 \, b_2 = Ds_2$

where a_1 and a_2 represent buyer a's money offer to sellers 1 and 2 respectively, b_1 and b_2 represent buyer b's offer of money to sellers 1 and 2, and Ds_1 and Ds_2 are the money demands of sellers 1 and 2. The cosine coefficients, as indicated in Diagrams 2-10 and 2-11, determine how much of each buyer's money offer will go to each seller.

We can generalize these equations for the entire economy as follows:

(2) $\cos \alpha_1 \, a_1 + \cos \beta_1 \, b_1 + \ldots \cos \gamma_1 \, N_1 = Ds_1$
    $\cos \alpha_2 \, a_2 + \cos \beta_2 \, b_2 + \ldots \cos \gamma_2 \, N_2 = Ds_2$
                    $\vdots$
$\cos \alpha_m \, a_m + \cos \beta_m \, b_m + \ldots \cos \gamma_m \, N_m = Ds_m$

The set of equations, which appear "Walrasian" but are much less complex, relates the demand for and the supply of money in all the markets of Canada. As such, they are really the component parts of the money demand curve of sellers and the offer curve of buyers as depicted in Diagram 2-9. It is useful to set forth the offer and demand

Diagram 2-10

TWO DEPARTMENT STORES

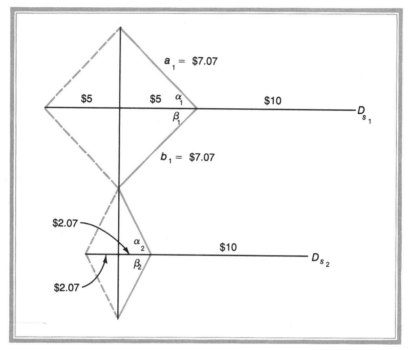

curves in this way because not only can we see the complex nature of both curves but also the complicated process involved in moving up (or down) the sellers' demand for money curve. A shift in either direction really means an alteration of the coefficients in favour of some sellers and against others. It is the values of these coefficients which are in a continuous state of adjustment, a monetary version of the Walrasian "*tatonnement*" process. In other words, markets are in a continuous state of groping toward an equilibrium in which the demand for money exactly equals the supply.

Another aspect of the equations is that they apply to very much more than just retail markets. In fact, the entire system of equations must include all markets for intermediate goods as well as final goods, from the last consuming stage back to the initial producing stage. Seen in this light, we can readily understand why the process of inflation, once begun, is so difficult to stop. A continuous *tatonnement* in the upward direction is taking place with sellers always attempting to push up

their demand for money functions. This they do, in some cases, just to stay ahead of their costs, and in others, to gain additional profits, all of which can be rationalized on moralistic grounds as "just." In such circumstances, it is only the power of the federal government which can halt the upward *tatonnement* with price/income controls.

Now suppose that, for reasons to be examined in detail later, the buyers should simply run out of money. They could be either final buyers or businessmen in intermediate stages. The system would at once become "tight" in the sense that *some* seller, or group of sellers, would be forced to revise his expectations of money demand. During inflation, it would be a downward revision of an *upward* expectation. There would likely be, at first, attempts to collect past debts, obtain credit from suppliers, etc., or otherwise try to increase the velocity of circulation of existing money, but eventually, as in musical chairs, the unfortunate seller must drop out of the system. This means, of course, unemploy-

Diagram 2-11

TWO DEPARTMENT STORES (CONT'D.)

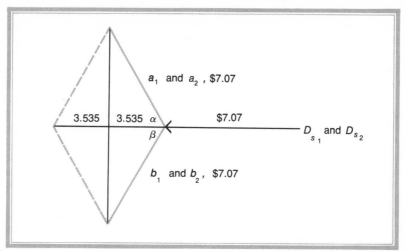

a_1 and a_2, $7.07

3.535 | 3.535 α

$7.07

D_{s_1} and D_{s_2}

β

b_1 and b_2, $7.07

ment for his staff of employees, hardly a pleasant prospect.

There is another feature of the equations which is worth careful consideration at this point. Generally speaking, the lower the value of the cosine coefficients, the greater the degree of competition and the less easy would it be for sellers to revise their demands for money upward through increased prices. Consumers can more readily shift their offers of money from one seller to another when the alternatives are close at hand. We, thus, appear to have an argument for greater degrees of competition to serve the objective of price stability, but the argument is based not on traditional microeconomic grounds but purely on the demand for money.

Probably just as obvious is the desire on the part of sellers to increase the value of the cosine coefficients. This assures them of a supply of funds from buyers' offer curves. It is to the sellers' advantage, therefore, to limit competition since in this way sellers can quite readily pass on increased costs or gain additional profits virtually at will. The decision to raise prices can safely be taken in the board rooms of corporate administration.

However, even with lower cosine coefficients, there does appear to be a national tendency toward raising prices by businessmen which can be accomplished by all sellers moving jointly. It is a kind of common reaction to national economic events amongst businessmen in general, and it is not so much the result of conscious collusion, as of the dissemination of common ideas through professional journals. Professional organizations, involving as they do the exchange of ideas, also help to ensure joint reactions to national economic events which impact upon everyone. Federal budgets, oil price increases, the Anti-Inflation Board, and massive and disruptive labour stoppages are cases in point.

But there is at least one equation in the entire set which is unaffected by such events; this is the import sector. When imports are such a large proportion of our Canadian GNP, the cosine coefficients of dealers in imports will be relatively large. The domestic sellers, then, face their stiffest competition from this source whenever attempts to increase their demands for money are made. Obviously, the solution is to impose a tariff structure sufficiently high to permit upward shifts in prices without the risk of consumers shifting their offers of funds to imported products. The protective tariff is quite simply an insurance against the risk of being caught between the millstones of rising costs and prices which are difficult to raise.

CONCLUSION

There *is* a relationship between money and prices — of that there is no doubt. The fact that economists have been unable to identify precisely this relationship does not deny its existence. The real difficulty appears to lie in the complexity of the relationship, on the one hand, and its variability on the other. Thus, even if some past relationship were identified it would not necessarily hold for the present or the future. To refer to Friedman's demand for money function once more, there are seven variables only two of which have been discussed in this chapter — the price level and the rate of change of prices. This chapter, therefore, is by no means exhaustive; we cannot encompass the complexity of economic life within either the limits of a single book or a macroeconomic model. All we can hope to accomplish is to lay the foundation for the analysis of demand for money on a firmer ground than the various versions of the Quantity Theory mentioned in Chapter 1.

The first fundamental requirement for money is for bridging the gaps between income receipts. Since expenditures occur continuously and incomes are periodic (e.g., monthly) a balance is required. This is the first and most fundamental cause for money demand and gives rise to a monetization process within each of the stages in our economy.

The impact of the Real Balance Effect on demand for money as it affects both savers and debtors is particularly interesting. The saver is penalized by rising prices and must reduce his consumption in order to restore real balances. The debtor, however, has "insured" his purchases by means of a contractual obligation against future price increases. His greatest advantage arises from an inflationary spiral of rising prices and incomes because so long as he can be granted credit, he is able to continue to fix the real value of his debt consumption. The greater the proportion of this debt consumption to total consumption, the greater is his advantage. In both cases, however, savers and debtors, the Real Balance Effect can be disastrous for employment levels. Unless the increased demand for money is satisfied by means of an increased supply, unemployment is likely to rise.

The opposite relationship, increases in the money supply causing higher prices, was also considered. Here the result is to break down resistance to rising prices so that sellers have no difficulty satisfying their demand for money by setting higher prices for their products. When this is combined with the Real Balance Effect, there is a distinct possibility of a circular action taking place, i.e., in one segment of the economy the direction of causation is money to prices, in another, the reverse. Some evidence of a money to price causation seems to appear in the structural pattern of money supply expansion in Canada during recent years. The "storage" deposits appear to have filled up first in three instances during the past decade, suggesting this relationship. Evidence of an opposite causation is more difficult to detect, but it is certainly there.

It can hardly be overemphasized, therefore, that any conclusions drawn on the basis of the analysis, both statistical and theoretical, which relates changes in the money supply and the price level should always be interpreted with caution. One fact should have emerged clearly from the discussion — the demand for money is not at all a clear, precise functional relationship between the Gross National Product and the money supply. Certainly, any demand for money function is not stable through time, but varies considerably with the particular economic circumstances. This is why statistical observation, even using refined econometric analysis, can do very little by way of forecasting the behaviour of our economy strictly on the basis of money supply alone. Income velocity of circulation as is commonly measured is not a precise measure of human behaviour. Therefore, to apply any past observations and relationships to future conditions is very wrong.

Despite these words of caution, there does remain something to be learned from past experience. We can say what we can *expect* to occur given certain circumstances. Thus, when an overexpansion of the money supply occurs, we may look forward to some enhancement of inflationary tendencies. This is not to say that prices *will* rise, but rather will likely show rising tendencies. Similarly, when a restriction of the growth of the money supply occurs, we may expect tendencies toward unemployment due to the failure of the money supply to grow sufficiently to accommodate the monetary demand of producing stages.

If this chapter were written even ten years ago, it would have been necessary to qualify the relationship between money and prices with the *caveat*, "given full employment." This would have been the result of our Keynesian tradition and background. Such, however, is no longer the case, for rising prices and unemployment can and do co-exist and will likely continue to do so in the future. It is becoming more clear that inflation and unemployment are really the consequence of different sets of causes. The fact that the two sets may have one cause, the money supply, in common, may be true today but may not be true in the future. Thus, to attempt to cure unemployment by means of money supply expansion may be not only futile but may also result in only more inflation.

Whatever the future, it may be hoped that this chapter has lent some insight into the operation of our economy, especially in relation to the supply of money.

ADDITIONAL READINGS

Section I of this chapter is really concerned with velocity of circulation of money and the influences which determine it rather than money itself. In the past, there have been two analytical approaches to this topic, both stemming from the Quantity Theory of Money, particularly the Cambridge version. The Cambridge *k* is (see Chapter 1) the reciprocal of velocity of circulation and represents the proportion of income held as money balances.

An analysis of velocity based upon "income-expenditure periods" and "payments intervals" originates with Professor Angell and Professor Ellis during the decade of the 1930s. The underlying principle is that efficiency in the use of money can increase with the result that less money need be held as idle balances. The consequence is, of course, an increase in the velocity of circulation of money.

Alternatively, velocity can be viewed quite simply as the ratio between national income and the money supply; furthermore, if this ratio is determined by exogenous factors, custom, tradition, efficiency, etc., the relationship between money and the national income becomes a functional one instead of being a mere identity. The disadvantage of defining velocity in this way is that we know nothing of the determinants of its value. It becomes a statistician's "little black box" which turns out a number but says little of why the number is what it is. For further reading using both these approaches the following will be found helpful:

Ellis, Howard S., "Some Fundamentals in the Theory of Velocity," *Readings in Monetary Theory,* Allen & Unwin, London, 1952, p. 89.

Fisher, Irving, *Purchasing Power of Money*, A.M. Kelley, New York, 1971, ch. IV.

Keynes, J.M., *A Treatise on Money*, Macmillan, London, 1958, Vol. I, ch. 14, also Vol. II, ch. 24.

Newlyn, Walter T., *Theory of Money*, Clarendon Press, Oxford, 1964.

Pigou, A.C., "The Value of Money," *Readings in Monetary Theory*, Allen & Unwin, London, p. 162.

Selden, R.T., "Monetary Velocity in the United States," *Studies in the Quantity Theory of Money*, Friedman (ed.), University of Chicago Press, 1958, p. 179.

CHAPTER 3

The Genesis of Money

I. PRODUCTION OF MONEY

No one in Canada today, with the possible exception of children, can be unaware of the fact that money exists in forms other than pure cash. It is simply not possible to avoid contact with banks in some form of daily business. So complete is the integration of banks in our lives that bank savings books, cheques, credit cards, deposit accounts, etc., are part of our basic vocabulary. The banking counterpart of all this is records of deposits, entries in ledgers or computers, etc., which are maintained by the banks themselves. As far as the general public is concerned, the central focus of the system is the fact that funds may be withdrawn by means of the simple expedient of subtracting a certain amount from the book entry and withdrawing cash to that same amount. A pay cheque, for instance, may be deposited and cash withdrawals occur throughout the month in response to a demand for money which arises, in this case, from a demand for goods and services.

It is an inescapable fact that money, whether cash or computer entries, must be "manufactured," i.e., it must come into existence in some way. Furthermore, it is manufactured in response to a demand in much the same way as any other commodity through a price mechanism. The particular form which money takes, gold, paper, bank entries, etc., is really immaterial, purely the result of the choice of society at a specific time. A hundred and fifty years ago, gold would have been the popular choice; seventy-five years ago paper money would have served; and today, bank deposit entries (or computer data) are perfectly acceptable to the public.

Aside from the obvious differences in costs, the really fundamental distinction between the manufacture of gold, paper, and bank entries as money is time. Gold requires a more lengthy period of production (it must be mined) and any increase in

the demand for money must be sufficiently slow so as not to outpace the increase in supply. Paper money is more quickly produced and, consequently, can accommodate correspondingly faster increases in the demand for money. Finally, computer data can be virtually instantaneously produced to satisfy even the most rapid changes in demand for money which can be conceived.

Time appears also in the matter of money transmission, i.e., the change of ownership of money quite apart from the manufacturing requirement. Modern banking systems, of which Canadian chartered banks are typical, can transmit payments in larger quantities and with speeds undreamed of in the mid-nineteenth century. In fact, the sheer convenience of bank entries, as opposed to either gold or cash, guarantees the existence of a modern banking system in today's world of high technology and sophisticated business finance.

Most commentaries and analyses of money and the money supply which originate from banks, including the central bank, implicitly accept money and its existence as already determined. The assumption is that money is really part of a larger financial system within which banks operate purely as transmitters of payments. To a certain degree, this interpretation is correct. It is especially correct when the financial system as a whole is viewed as a structure of liquidity of which money (both cash and bank deposits) is representative. Nevertheless, money, *of itself*, (apart from liquidity) must have an origin, and to the economist the concept of an automatic existence of money is simply not satisfactory. It is not that bankers are wrong; it is what appears to be a confusion between liquidity and money which is the source of difficulty. Liquidity, its definitions and concepts, is considered in Chapter 4 and subsequent chapters, and, as the analysis proceeds, it will become more obvious that liquidity is actually more important than money itself.

A. Banks and Money

We will consider money firstly as M_1, i.e., demand deposits plus cash in circulation owned by the general public as follows:

M_1, 26 JULY, 1978
(MILLIONS OF DOLLARS)

Currency	Demand Deposits (excluding float)	Total
8,245	13,507	21,752

Source: Bank of Canada, *Weekly Financial Statistics*, August 31, 1978

Currency, the $8.2 billion, causes no difficulty. It consists largely of bank notes which are carefully tucked away in the public's wallets. As to their origin, it is clearly stated on the bank note itself: it is legal tender (exchangeable for goods and services) and bears the signatures of both the governor and deputy governor of the Bank of Canada. The bank note is, therefore, a liability or claim against the Bank of Canada.

But, what about the other $13.5 billion of demand deposits which are the liabilities of chartered banks? These represent some 62% of M_1 and must be accounted for as to their origin. In fact, if we were to extend the monetary aggregate to the level of M_3 (Currency and all Chequable, Notice and Term Deposits plus Foreign Currency Deposits of Residents) the total for the end of July, 1978, would be $104,802 millions, and of this total, currency would represent only about 7.9%. It should be pointed out here that only deposits at chartered banks are considered in the monetary aggregates, M_1 through M_3. This happens to be a characteristic of the Canadian banking system which is unique to Canada and which stems from the fact that our chartered banks engage a great deal in the business of attracting savings deposits; in many other countries the equivalents of our chartered banks (commercial banks in European countries and clearing banks in Great Britain) do not compete for such deposits, preferring to leave such business to other banking institutions.

The origins of the money manufacturing function of banks make a fascinating account and, at the same time, serve to press home the fundamentals underlying the banking process. What we take for granted today really has its ancestral roots in seventeenth century England. At that time, it appears that the goldsmiths of the City of London had lost a great deal of their ordinary business of supplying works of art, tableware, etc., to the wealthy classes for the reason that the nobility and gentry preferred the "melting of their old plate rather than buying new."[1] (We may speculate that rising costs and prices were the true cause of this "change of taste.") As a substitute for this lost trade, they turned to the business of accepting the gold of merchants for safekeeping, and, indeed, some goldsmiths with the best reputations actually collected rents for landlords in addition to their ordinary business of accepting deposits of gold. These goldsmiths began to assume a greater importance in financial affairs than the early bankers, or "scriveners" as they were called, who were active long before the goldsmiths appeared on the scene.

By the end of the Civil War and the period of the Commonwealth, the whole process of accepting gold deposits became much more common. Prior to that time, only a service of safe-keeping in the strong rooms of goldsmiths served as a sufficient incentive for customers, but, as both the activities and numbers of goldsmiths grew, competition for deposits forced them into the practice of paying interest to their depositors. By the time of the Restoration of Charles II, interest as high as 6% was being offered.

The banking habit became so complete during this period that Roger North in *The Lives of the Norths* mentioned that his brother, Sir Dudley, having returned to England from Turkey during the latter years of Charles II, was appalled at the laziness of businessmen who relied on goldsmiths (or bankers) for so much of their routine affairs. To him it was a "foolish, lazy method, and obnoxious to great accidents."[2]

The technique the goldsmiths followed was to issue two kinds of notes in exchange for deposits of gold. One was a "running cash note" (the equivalent of a modern bank book) and the other a promissory note obligating the particular goldsmith to pay a certain amount of money in gold.

---

[1] E. Lipson, *The Economic History of England*, Vol. III, p. 229. The quotation is from an original source entitled, *The Mystery of the New Fashioned Goldsmith or Banker*, 1676.
[2] *Ibid.*, p. 230.

This latter note was transferable, and hence could be used for the discharge of an obligation. At the same time, the goldsmith who issued such promissory notes, even though they were payable at sight, did not keep the gold which he received on deposit but loaned it to merchants, etc., at interest. Frequently, the goldsmiths supplied gold to merchants in exchange for bills of exchange "discounting sometimes double, perhaps treble interest for the time as they found the merchant more or less pinched."[3] Lipson, in a footnote, notes that Sir Dudley North found a banker who owed £10,000, "seldom kept £1,000 in specie."[4]

For all practical purposes, this early banker, even though he lived and functioned during the reign of Charles II, was as modern as our nineteenth century Canadian banks which also issued their own bank notes in a similar fashion. The difference between the two lay in the degree of individual trust involved; while the early banker depended entirely upon the confidence of the public, the bank notes issued by our early Canadian banks were regulated by law. Once confidence in the ability of a specific goldsmith/banker to redeem his promissory notes in specie was lost, a run on his bank was inevitable. Just as one might have expected during those early years of banking history, such runs were very common. In the same way our early Canadian banking history was characterized by many bank failures despite the legal regulations, albeit somewhat lax by our standards today, imposed by governments for the protection of the public.

It is interesting that the evolution of any modern banking system always seems to include a bank note issue stage in its process of development. The fact is that banks can only reflect the level of development of the public which they serve. Thus, if the public will only accept gold as money, the banking system must supply it. Similarly, if the public is prepared to accept bank notes, banks must likewise be ready to supply them. Finally, the last stage of evolution, deposit ownership, requiring payment by cheque instead of notes, must also have public acceptance before it can be developed by the banks. Banks merely reflect the degree of sophistication of the public in its

payments system, and can develop no faster than society permits.

Walter Bagehot himself recognized the importance of bank note issue in the development of banking, and, of course, the provision, or "manufacture" of a much needed circulating medium of exchange.

> A system of note issue is therefore the best introduction to a large system of deposit banking. As yet, historically, it is the only introduction. No nation as yet has arrived at a great system of deposit banking without going first through the preliminary stage of note issue, and of such note issue, the quickest and most efficient in this way is one made by individuals resident in the district and conversant with it.[5]

Today, the right of note issue is restricted to the central bank in Canada just as in most countries. This is why our bank notes bear the signature of the Governor of the Bank of Canada — they are the liabilities of the central bank. Commercial banks (chartered banks in Canada) must confine their money manufacturing to the demand deposits only. The difference between bank notes and demand deposits is not so great as would appear at first sight; it lies purely in the transmission mechanism — bank notes are passed from hand to hand whereas cheques are cleared through a clearing house mechanism. Again the question of which method is used depends entirely upon the preference of the public.

B. The Manufacturing of Money (Bank Notes)

Any analysis of banks and banking must always include the balance sheet, for the balance sheet is really the exposure to public scrutiny of banking processes. It tells us two things: (1) from where the resources have come, and (2) where they are going. The liabilities of a bank are the public's claims against the bank and these constitute its sole resources; the assets are the bank's claims against the public and tell us the uses to

---

[3] *Ibid.*, p. 232.
[4] *Ibid.*, footnote 2, p. 232.

[5] Walter Bagehot, *Lombard Street*, John Murray, London, 1919, p. 94.

which the resources have been put. Of course, liabilities and assets must balance for the simple reason that all resources so acquired must be accounted for in some way.

In our analysis, a simplified system of balance sheets is used. This abstracts from unnecessary details such as a bank's capital, building and equipment, etc., and permits concentration on the important concepts. Suppose, then, we have a balance sheet which looks something like the following:

T table 3-1

Assets		Liabilities	
Cash	1,000	Deposits	1,000
TOTAL	1,000	TOTAL	1,000

The entry "cash" would consist of gold or some other official "coin of the realm" which is held by this bank for a customer. Suppose further that within the particular district a businessman wishes to borrow the sum of 1,000. The banker need only issue his own bank note as a claim against himself. Thus,

is willing to borrow and the public *in general* is willing to accept the promissory notes of the bank. However, the time must come when "ultimately," says Bagehot, "a private person begins to possess a great heap of bank notes, it will soon strike him that he is trusting the banker very much."[6] The public, therefore, aware of an excessive and perhaps unwarranted trust will return the bank notes in exchange for either (1) gold in the case of early goldsmith/bankers or Dominion notes in nineteenth century Canada, or (2) actual deposits which were required by law in Canada to be available as alternatives to a bank's notes. If the former, the cash entry on the assets side would run down to the danger point forcing the bank to cut back its notes issued or suffer the consequence of a genuine run on the bank—the result of a complete loss of confidence. For the latter, the bank would quickly discover its deposits entry rising as the bank notes entry falls. In such a case, the substitution of interest paying deposits for interest-free bank notes increases the cost of operation of the bank causing it to

T table 3-2

	Assets			Liabilities	
	A	B		A	B
Cash	1,000	1,000	Deposits	1,000	1,000
Loan	1,000	10,000	Notes	1,000	10,000
TOTAL	2,000	11,000	TOTAL	2,000	11,000

The borrower who receives the bank note purchases goods, if, say, he happens to be a merchant, from a supplier who accepts the note as payment, i.e., money. He, the supplier, can retain the note as his own monetary asset or send it on its way in exchange for some goods or services which he might require.

At first sight, it might appear that a "fraud" has been perpetrated. After all, a promissory note (the bank promises to pay) to the value of 1,000 has been handed over to a borrower without any cost or effort on the banker's part, and, furthermore, the banker is earning interest. Of course, the banker must be prepared to honour his promissory note to its full value in the event it is presented to him for payment. But as long as the notes are *not* returned for payment, the process of loaning by note issue has no end. Thus, the totals in column B in T table 3-2 can assume any magnitude so long as some member of the public

reduce its bank note issue or be forced into liquidation.

In Canada, the first Bank Act of 1871 permitted the issuance of bank notes in "denominations of $4 or upwards."[7] There were no reserve requirements at all against these notes *per se,* the only stipulation being that 30% of the bank's cash reserves should be in Dominion notes—the original currency of the new Dominion, as provided for in the Dominion Notes Act of 1868. Subsequent Bank Act revisions increased this requirement to 40%. After some rather unfortunate experiences with bank failures, the revisions of the Bank Act in 1880 and 1890 provided for a

[6]Ibid., p. 85. Bagehot also cites the case of the Bank of Dundee which for 25 years after its foundation in 1763 "subsisted mostly on its note issue and a little on its business." Thereafter, it began to gain deposits, p. 83.
[7]Banking and Currency in Canada, *Report of the Royal Commission*, Ottawa, 1933, p. 15.

Bank Circulation Redemption Fund (an early version of the Canadian Deposit Insurance Corporation) to protect holders of bank notes from the failure of banks to redeem their notes.

C. Deposits

But the uniquely Canadian development was the founding of the Canadian Bankers Association in 1892 which voluntarily policed its membership to avoid excessive note issue. The consequence of this *and* a tax of one per cent on the amount of bank notes issued *plus* an absolute restriction of issuance to the amount of paid-up capital was a decline in the notes issued. The rate of decline can be seen from the ratio of demand deposits to bank notes in circulation which rose from 2.7 to one in 1871 to 17.1 to one in 1931. Thus, Bagehot's logic, combined with the official discouragement of bank notes, took their toll so that by the time the Bank of Canada was established in 1935, the process of phasing out chartered bank notes after 1935 was a simple matter.[8]

It is not difficult to appreciate the problem. Any country which is characterized by purely regional economic activity such as early Canada or seventeenth century Britain will find that money which is a satisfactory substitute for gold (the only universally acceptable money) and which can readily increase in supply along with economic activity, is most useful. But, since this money is founded purely on confidence, it can only be used within a specific region, the boundaries of which are defined by the extent of the bank's reputation. The system can work very well initially since certain regions may enjoy greater economic growth, hence a greater money requirement, than others, but once trade and commerce cross regional boundaries, the reputation of the bank and the confidence it enjoys begin to weaken. This is why the Bank of Canada is now the only bank permitted to issue notes and the chartered banks are dependent entirely on their capacity to

attract and hold deposit liabilities for most of their assets. The difference between the two types of operation, bank notes and deposits, is that the banks must now seek many depositors in competition with each other—the more the deposits the greater the loan assets and the higher the profits. In the bank note case, no depositors need be attracted at all, only borrowers. The difference, of course, is crucial as will be shown in subsequent pages.

Suppose, in our T tables, the entries were as follows:

T table 3-3

Assets		Liabilities	
Cash	1,000	Deposits$_1$	1,000
Loans	900	Deposits$_2$	900
TOTAL	1,900	TOTAL	1,900

T table 3-3 is substantially different in appearance from T table 3-2. The difference lies in the substitution of a Deposit$_2$ entry for "Notes" and the much smaller, 900, loaned than the 10,000 in column B of T table 3-2. The initial entries, Cash under Assets and Deposits$_1$ under Liabilities, are the same. In both cases the bank has received 1,000 in cash and credits the depositor with that amount as Deposit$_1$, but in the second case a loan is made by further crediting a borrower with a new deposit, Deposit$_2$; furthermore, this new deposit must, in accordance with the law, be less than the first deposit. Or, to put it slightly differently, the bank has loaned just 90% (with 10% for reserves) of its original deposit and in doing so it has created a *claim against itself* of 900 in the form of additional demand deposits instead of bank notes. From a money manufacturing standpoint there is no difference between the bank note case and this deposit creation since purchasing power is now in the hands of the borrower. (There is a subtle difference in the meaning of the words "manufacture" and "creation" used here. If the bank did not require an initial deposit, a new deposit could truly be created from nothing. However since an initial deposit is necessary, the word "manufacture" seems more appropriate because the new deposit is manufactured from the "raw material" of the initial deposit. Thus, the term "manufacture" refers to the entire process of deposit acquisition and the creation of a new deposit.)

---

[8]Actually the chartered banks were permitted to continue issuing notes after 1935 but the issues were gradually reduced to 25% of their paid-up capital. After January 1, 1945, the Bank of Canada was given a legal monopoly of note issue.

The "cost of production" of these claims is precisely the cost necessary to acquire the initial deposit, i.e., variable costs such as the interest paid to depositors, the cost of advertising, services made available to the public, etc., in addition to the fixed costs of salaries of staff, lease of building, etc. In general, variable costs are those costs which vary with the amount of money manufactured; fixed costs are those which are constant. In combination, total costs will rise as the amount of initial deposits acquired, and the amount of money manufactured therefrom, is pressed to the limit.

In Canada, our oligopolistic banking system faces sharply rising variable costs in competing for savings deposits. This competition is particularly intense with other financial institutions (often referred to as "non-bank financial intermediaries") such as trust companies, credit unions, etc. Such savings deposits to the chartered banks are part of the "initial deposits" and therefore can be very important in the money manufacturing process. They are also important, as we shall see in detail later, to these other financial institutions; hence, a fiercely competitive situation can develop between the two groups. *Among* chartered banks, however, the interest/cost of savings deposits does not vary to any great extent. Competition, as in any other oligopoly, tends to manifest itself in advertising, services rendered, etc., rather than directly through prices.

D. Costs and Revenues

Diagrams are always helpful in developing the degree of precision essential to an analysis, and these we can supply quite easily. We shall consider first the situation facing the nineteenth century Canadian bank which manufactured its own bank notes. On the horizontal axis, we have quantity of money manufactured, and on the vertical costs/revenue (see Diagram 3-1).

For the earlier banks, the only significant costs were the wages of employees, the rent of buildings, equipment costs, etc., all of which must be paid regardless of the amount of business activity of the banks. In other words, such costs are fixed as indicated by the horizontal line (functionally unrelated to the Money axis). There are no variable costs in this case, with the possible exception

Diagram 3-1

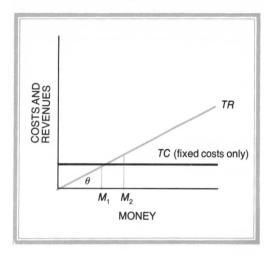

of paper for bank notes, ledgers, etc., so that marginal costs are zero. Revenue, to the bank, consists of loan interest which increases in the same proportion as money is manufactured, the slope of the Total Revenue function being the rate of interest.

The break-even point occurs at the intersection of the TC and TR functions at a point M_1 on the Money axis; thereafter, any further bank note manufacture, to the amount of M_2, for example, means additional profit. Is there any limit to a bank's activity and resulting profit? There are two checks to a bank's growth: (1) for every loan made, a borrower must be found who is both willing and able to pay the interest to the bank, and (2) the public must be willing to accept the bank notes as money. Once these two conditions are satisfied the bank can grow and prosper.

Both these checks are "outside" the system; therefore they cannot be included on the diagram. The system is open-ended in the sense that there is no built-in limit to increases in the money supply. Nevertheless it is easy to see why such a system, instead of being inflationary, could be successful during the years of early Canadian growth and development, especially between 1871 and 1883. Processes of monetization were continuously absorbing bank notes, and continuous economic expansion during the railway construction years of 1888-90 meant an ever growing monetary requirement. An "open-ended" cost/revenue structure for banks was precisely what was required at the time.

Despite this, bank failures and withdrawals from business were considerable. Between 1867 and 1899, 19 banks disappeared with heavy losses to shareholders.[9] In fact it was these failures which led to the Bank Circulation Redemption Fund, included in the Bank Act of 1890, which became a further important limitation to the banks' manufacturing capacity since 5% of a bank's average yearly note circulation was to be deposited with the Fund. The fact that this amount was in "legal tender" (gold or Dominion bank notes) made it a *de facto* reserve requirement.

Deposit creation, on the other hand, exercises some limitation on the bank's manufacturing powers. The cost of acquiring initial deposits rises with the amount of additional deposits created, and this cost increases rather sharply when interest must be paid for more savings deposits.

In Diagram 3-2, the cost/revenue structure of a modern chartered bank is laid out. Just as before, on the horizontal axis is Money (now deposits) in the form of liabilities or claims against itself the bank can manufacture. On the vertical axis are the cost and revenue derived from this manufacture. Thus, a bank which manufactures no claims has zero revenue, but fixed costs. As it competes for initial deposits, the "raw material" for new deposits, its total costs rise, gently at first, but more sharply as it reaches the point of resistance from competitors. Money becomes tighter at this point.

In a similar fashion, total revenues increase as the claims produced are increased, only in this case there is no end to the function since the total revenue function has a constant slope throughout its length. It is this slope (angle Θ) which is the significant feature here. The slope represents a weighted average of interest rates charged on all types of loans. If a bank's assets were heavily structured toward high interest consumer loans, for example, the angle Θ would be greater than if it were mostly prime rate business loans.

It will be apparent on careful inspection that a certain point exists on the horizontal axis at which the distance between the total revenue and total cost functions is the greatest. This is the point of profit maximization. Banks will strive to reach this point, *M*, in their claims manufacturing process

and will compete in terms of interest to depositors, advertising, services, etc., until that point is reached. This competition is often at the expense of other deposit-taking institutions as well as other claims creating banks, and is keenest when the limit of the manufacturing capacity of the banks is reached as represented by the sharp upturn of the total cost function. It is this limit which is the subject of analysis of the next section.

II. THE BANKING CONSTRAINT

Returning once more to the last hypothetical "balance sheet" (T table 3-3) we note that an original deposit was made of 1,000 along with a corresponding entry of cash on the assets side. This cash represents what economists refer to as "base money," "high-powered money," "outside money," or "primary money." Originally it took the form of Dominion bank notes and gold; now it is simply legal reserves. Whatever it is called it is very important to the operation of a modern banking system.

It is the borrower's prerogative to take his money in either cash or deposits. Let us suppose he should request cash. The bank's balance sheet would appear as:

T table 3–4

Assets		Liabilities	
Cash	100	Deposits	1,000
Loans	900		
TOTAL	1,000	TOTAL	1,000

But the crux of the matter is that in Canada and other similarly advanced countries the borrower accepts claims against the bank as the same thing as cash, i.e., a chequebook with the right to write cheques to the amount of 900. This is why the balance sheet in T table 3-3 is more like the balance sheets we know today.

Assuming the borrower is rational, he will purchase something which has an asset value to him (after all he must pay interest on his loan). The seller of the item has now a cheque drawn against the borrower's account which he transfers to his own bank. His bank has now acquired the right to collect 900 of high-powered money from the first bank since the cheque is a *claim against the first bank*. It proceeds to do so by way

Diagram 3-2

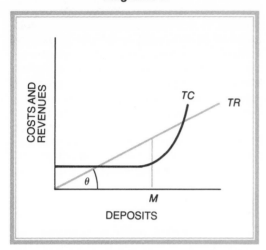

of the Central Bank clearing houses located in various centres throughout Canada, and is now in a position to manufacture claims against *itself*.

T table 3-5 (second bank)

Assets		Liabilities	
Cash	900	Deposits$_1$	900
Loan	810	Deposits$_2$	810
TOTAL	1,710	TOTAL	1,710

The first bank has now lost 900 of its original high-powered asset (the deposit liability remains) and the first bank is in the same position as T table 3-4, i.e., just as if it had lost its cash to the original borrower. Of course, therein lies the essence of the structure of modern banking—very little cash is lost to the bank's customers; most of it goes to other banks in the system. Thus, what would appear to be a matter of indifference to an individual bank, whether or not the borrower requests his loan in cash, is a matter of considerable importance to the country as a whole. Cash lost to another bank means that more deposits can be manufactured, whereas cash lost to a customer means the end.

This brings us very close to the original question posed at the outset. How did the Canadian money supply develop its predominantly deposit characteristics? For the present, we assume that 90% of high-powered money can be "loaned out" by means of loans which are made as new deposits or claims against each bank. The process of deposit manufacture will go on indefinitely un-

til, theoretically, the high-powered money approaches zero. Thus,

$$900 + 810 + \ldots 0 = 9,000^{10}$$

The total amount of money manufactured is the sum of each bank's portion and since the borrowing and redepositing process is endless, it continues until the deposit expansion on a base of high-powered money is

$$D = \frac{a}{1 - d} - a,$$

with a as the base and d the ratio of manufactured deposits to the high-powered base. At that point, the deposit manufacturing process ceases and the banking constraint is complete.

Even though the constraint exists, we must not lose sight of the important fact that money is being manufactured by private institutions which, like other producing firms, desire to maximize their profits. Whether this money is bank notes, as in the past, or demand deposits as at present, purchasing power which can command goods and services is being created. This is an awesome privilege and not to be considered lightly. In fact, the responsibility to society of any money manufacturing agency must be considerable for the basic reason that the relationship between the quantity of money manufactured and demand for money in its broadest context is extremely complex and at best imperfectly understood. If we knew, for example, precisely how changes in the money supply would affect prices or how much new money could accommodate productivity changes, it would be an easy matter to regulate banks by means of an exact formula to be included in the Bank Act. But, since we cannot be so precise, we must be content with a much less complete understanding of the relationship between the supply of money and the demand for money of which only a glimpse of the barest outlines has been suggested in the preceding chapters.

---

[10]This results from the formula for the sum of a geometric progression, viz.
$D = ar + ar^2 + \ldots ar^n$ with r the proportion of each high-powered deposit loaned as claims against each bank and a the high-powered deposit itself. We know that $D = (a/1 - d)$, and for the manufactured deposits alone, $D = (a/1 - d) - a$. In the simple case used here,
$$D = \frac{1,000}{1 - .9} - 1,000 = 9,000$$
of created deposits.

It is for this reason that banks are chartered by law under rather stringent provisions of operation. Further, these charters expire every ten years and a new revision of the law must be prepared. The first law enacted in 1871, the Dominion Bank Act, laid down the rules of operation, such as the legal liability of shareholders, minimum capitalization, the issuance of bank notes, etc. But it did not include what is of much greater importance for our purposes, the reserve requirement. This came much later.

Originally the Canadian banking system had no specific reserve requirement, the only specification being that 40% of cash reserves be in Dominion Bank Notes. These cash reserves, following the British system, were held in two categories, cash assets and "quickly realizable assets," such as short term securities and call and short (30 day) loans. Later revisions of the Bank Act stipulated an 8% cash reserve against an average of all deposits, and currently (The Bank Act of 1967) a 12% reserve against demand deposits and 4% reserve against notice (saving) deposits is required.

It is this cash reserve, determined by the specified ratio of deposits, which is subtracted from each high-powered initial deposit first before the balance is loaned. In the T table examples used above, a 10% reserve ratio was used with 90% of initial deposits being loaned. In reality, it is 12% of demand deposits (88% loaned) and 4% of notice deposits (96% loaned). This is why, incidentally, notice deposits are so important to chartered banks and why they are willing to encourage them with the reward of interest. In the formula for deposit expansion developed above, $(1 - d)$ would become r, the reserve ratio, which in turn would be a weighted average of 12% and 4% with the proportions of demand deposits and notice deposits to total deposits as the respective weights. Thus:

$$D = \frac{a}{r} - a$$

Sufficient has been shown thus far to indicate how it has been possible to have, in Canada, amounts of bank deposits which are some 92% of the total money supply. Many economists, particularly Americans, build money supply functions based on this sum of the geometric progression. A rather complex "money multiplier" is thereby developed which relates high-powered money (or bank reserves) to total money supply defined either as M_1 or M_3, including drains of cash from the banks. Such a supply function tends to create an illusion of precision which is not warranted by the facts, especially in Canada. While it is possible to show a relationship between deposits and reserves, it is not possible to show how *changes* in reserves will be reflected in *changes* in total deposits within any reasonable time span. Our banking system, dominated by five large banks, has enormous resources with a great potential for accommodating any tightening of reserves, a, without any appreciable effect on D until after a considerable time lag. Deposits (and the loans which generate them) are the source of greatest profit and are always the last to be affected.

A. Supply of Money under Constraint

The complex nature of the money supply function and its operation via the chartered banks can be glimpsed with the aid of the diagram analysis developed further in Diagram 3-3. The slope of the total revenue function is the interest rate charged by banks for new money manufactured; thus, if R is the revenue of the bank and M, the money manufactured,

$$\frac{R}{M} = r^{11}$$

on the assumption that all loans, and money manufactured therefrom, are made for one year only and reloaned as soon as the year is over.

It should be clear by now that given a TC function and a TR function, the amount of money manufactured will be M_1 where the spread between the TR and TC functions, or profits, is greatest. But suppose the bank wishes to increase its revenue (at the expense of greater risk). It can do so through a restructuring of its asset portfolio by concentrating its loans in those areas where interest rewards are greater, e.g., mortgages or

---

[11]Strictly speaking, R, revenue, would be equal to the difference between the actual money loaned, M, and the total repayment plus interest, i.e.,

$$R = M (1 + r)^t - M, \text{ or } \frac{R}{M} = (1 + r)^t - 1,$$

with time, t, equal to time in years. Diagram 3-3 abstracts from time.

Diagram 3-3

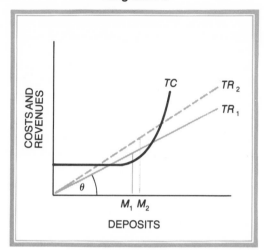

consumer loans, and less in business loans at prime rate. In this situation, the *TR* function increases its slope, say, to TR_2, and profits are now higher than before. Note that a slight increase in the amount of money manufactured occurs because the point of profit maximization has changed; also, of the two profit maxima, the maximum at TR_2 is greater than at TR_1.

At the same time, it is quite possible for loan interest rates in general (prime rate and all other rates) to rise. Such a situation could be the result of rising market rates which have the effect of encouraging borrowers to switch from the market to the banks. Again this would be shown by a shift in the *TR* function to TR_2 with correspondingly higher profits.

Prior to the Bank Act of 1967, a 6% ceiling on loan rates existed making shifts of the *TR* function more difficult. This rate was supplemented, of course, by additional "fees" so that the ceiling was circumvented to a considerable degree. Nevertheless it did have an effect in actual practice so that bank rates for money were always less than those of other market lenders. This was tantamount to fixing the price of money being sold to the community and forcing the total revenue curve to have a constant slope.

During periods of tight money supply or when the demand was great, banks were forced to resort to rationing their output to individual borrowers, at best an arbitrary method.[12] Of course, it was also not feasible to try to increase the volume of their notice deposits because it would necessitate increasing their costs and shrinking their profits. The situation can be seen in Diagram 3-3 which shows a rising cost function and a revenue function which has a constant slope. Profits would shrink if the money supply were increased beyond M_1 to M_2. With the passage of the Bank Act of 1967, the 6% ceiling on interest charged was removed so that banks are now in a position to adjust the slope of their *TR* functions.

Without the banking constraint, since the banking system as a whole manufactures deposits (one bank's deposits production is another bank's raw material), there would be no limit to the deposit production process. The limit imposed by law upon the banking system's capacity to produce money is the legal reserve requirement. This reserve is that proportion of total deposits which must be held in high-powered money, as legal reserves. When the balance is loaned, as in T table 3-4 above, it becomes a claim against the bank, and in this way when all the process of creating claims has been completed, with the last claim approaching zero, the limit of expansion is reached. At that point, the Total Cost curve turns sharply upward as competition for a now limited amount of deposits becomes considerably greater.

The Bank Act of 1967, currently in effect, provides for cash reserves (cash and deposits at the Central Bank) of 12% of demand deposits and 4% of notice deposits. This is a substantial difference from the fixed 8% of all deposits in effect prior to the Bank Act revision. The differential between the 4% and 12% means that the actual reserve ratio against total deposits varies depending upon the relative amounts of each type of deposit a bank happens to have in its liabilities. For example, in January, 1978, statutory demand deposits were $19,300 million, and notice deposits $67,228 million. Twelve per cent of demand deposits are $2,316 million and 4% of notice deposits are $2,689.1 million. The total required reserves are therefore $5,005.1 million which is 5.78% of total deposits. Actual holdings of reserves for that month were notes, $1,186 million

---

[12] *Report of the Royal Commission on Banking and Finance*, 1964, p. 365.

plus Bank of Canada deposits of $3,874 million or a total of $5,060 million; there was, therefore, a slight excess of reserves.[13]

It is the reserve requirement which effectively "brakes" deposit manufacture. In the geometric progression discussed above, the reserve ratio, r, is equal to $1 - d$. Thus

$$D = \frac{a}{r} - a = \frac{a(1-r)}{r}$$

is the maximum amount of deposits banks can manufacture. This last expression is the simplest version of the Bank Act constraint. The term a, high-powered money, is actually the Bank of Canada notes held by the chartered banks plus the deposits at the Bank of Canada in favour of the chartered banks.

There is an additional restraint on banks which acts in a similar fashion. This is the drain of cash from the banks into the hands of the public, and it is just as effective as is the legal reserve ratio. In fact, this was the only effective constraint on banks during the early years when bank notes were common. The effect of the drain of cash within the Canadian system is to reduce the amount of cash the banks have on hand; hence, the value of a, high-powered money, becomes less. But since the drain is generally amenable to forecasting during normal times it is a simple matter to provide extra Bank of Canada deposits or otherwise to prepare to meet the drain. Christmas time is an excellent example of a foreseeable cash drain.

B. Bank Adjustments to Changes in Reserves

The point on the TC function (see Diagram 3-4) where the function turns upward is the beginning of "tight" money. Up to this point, initial deposits have been demand deposits which involve no cost to the bank (marginal costs of money manufacture are zero). Any further expansion of the supply of money must occur by way of attracting notice deposits which have a lower reserve ratio. But, since these involve an interest cost, marginal costs are no longer zero, but positive. Still, how-

---

Diagram 3-4

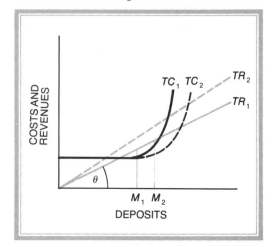

ever, profits can increase so long as the slope of the TR function (marginal revenue) exceeds the slope of the TC function (marginal costs) —

$$\frac{dTR}{dM} > \frac{dTC}{dM}.$$

The money supply will still increase with a growing degree of "tightness" until

$$\frac{dTR}{dM} = \frac{dTC}{dM}.$$

This point of profit maximization can be extended by two methods: (1) a lowering of the reserve ratio, or (2) an increase in the quantity of reserves. The latter means an increase in the initial deposit (Deposit 1 in T table 3-4) so that the quantity of manufactured money, M, can increase in response to profit maximization incentives. In Diagram 3-4, the TC function has shifted to TC_2. In Canada, method 1, the lowering of the cash reserve ratio, is not possible without changing the Bank Act. There is, however, a secondary reserve ratio which can be adjusted with similar results, but this is discussed in a later chapter.

Banks then have every incentive to expand the money supply as profits increase, but the question is what happens when money becomes "tight" more quickly, i.e., the slope of the TC function increases faster than before? This is the equivalent of a shift back from TC_2 to TC_1 and is accompanied by a decrease in profits. In this case banks will not restrict the money supply (the opposite of easy money) but will restore profits by increasing the slope of the TR function so as to equal the greater slope of the new *TC* function, i.e., raise interest rates.

The nature of the money supply function should now be emerging. We note, in the first place, that the function is not symmetrical, i.e., the consequence of easy money is a money supply expansion, but the consequence of tight money is not contraction, but an increase in loan interest rates. In part this is the result of an oligopolistic banking system which operates very much within ample safety margins and with a great capacity to adjust to changing conditions. A more highly competitive banking system with many more banks, such as in the United States, would likely mean a sharper reaction of the money supply to negative changes in reserves since profit margins would not be so secure due to the force of competition. At the same time, interest rates on loans would likely not rise so fast.

In the second place, our analysis has proceeded along static lines on the basis that a bank can increase or decrease its money production on the horizontal axis. This is not necessarily correct; in fact, a more realistic, but more complex, analysis might be to measure changes in the money manufactured *(ΔM)* instead of money itself. In reality, it is the increase in the growth of a bank's money production which responds to easy money, and, conversely, restrictions in the growth of money are more difficult to achieve since higher interest rates respond more readily to tight money. Such an analysis would require a dynamic time framework and would not be appropriate for the single bank, microeconomic approach, which is being used here.

In the third place, there is nothing automatic about the reactions to tight or easy money on the part of the banks. Banks must seek borrowers in order to increase their money production and may indeed find that the price, or interest rate, on their loans will have to be reduced. Competition to expand *M* may encourage a general lowering of interest on loans so that the *TR* function will assume a smaller slope with a corresponding increase in *M*. This is likely to be true at first when the banks are seeking new borrowers. "Gimmicks" such as paying the first year's registration on a new car to entice auto loans, etc., may be resorted to. Ultimately, however, unless the reserves are increased once more, it is likely that the demand for loans will increase sufficiently to restore the original slope of the *TR* function.

Finally, the encouraging of notice deposits has an advantage in addition to the relief of pressure on tight reserves. (This, it will be recalled, stems from the 4% reserve requirement against 12% for demand deposits.) Notice deposits have greater "sticking power" (or stickability) than demand deposits in the sense that their ownership is not so likely to be transferred. This permits chartered banks to make longer-term, and more profitable, investments similar to trust companies, credit unions, etc., in mortgages, bonds, or similar long-term debt. The notice deposit is particularly suited to this purpose because in practice, the longer the deposit remains without withdrawal, the longer and more lucrative can the corresponding investment be. At the same time, therefore, that the *TC* function turns upward as banks bid vigorously for sticky notice deposits, the *TR* function is likely to assume a steeper slope as the longer-term higher interest loans are made possible.

SUMMARY AND CONCLUSION

The purpose of this chapter has been to accomplish more than just explain how our money supply comes into existence. This is important enough, but in addition an attempt has been made to develop a method of analysis which will help to explain the behaviour of banks in their day-to-day affairs. This is why there has been a rather significant departure from the usual treatment of the subject of money supply. The traditional approach followed by some writers is to consider high-powered money as a base upon which deposit, or bank, money is created by means of a bank "multiplier." Even though these writers are careful to assert that a money stock, as opposed to a flow, is being created, this method of approach obscures what is likely to be the most interesting aspect of the banking business. At best it is an equilibrium approach — a kind of long-term money production function which serves only to show how our modern money supply can exist.

What is really important is the behaviour of banks to various stimuli in the short term. Banks do behave just as the profit maximizing business enterprises that they are— probably never reaching long-run equilibrium. As such they produce almost to their capacity, almost (but not quite) to the maximum permitted by the legal reserve ratio. This is a constraint, not a multiplier, which establishes by law an equilibrium of the banking system which would otherwise not exist other than in a weak form.

In the final analysis, money is a commodity just like any other commodity. Banks are producers of this commodity, and they exact a payment for their output. They sell deposit money (some 92% of our total money supply in Canada) to society which finds money so useful and so important that it is willing to pay the price. At the same time, banks are willing to incur costs in the form of interest on notice deposits, advertising, etc., which are additional to their high fixed costs. The difference between their revenue and costs is, of course, profit.

It is the deposit money which is manufactured by banks and sold to society which is essential to the processes of production and exchange. In particular, it is this deposit money which finances the various stages in our economy during the interval between payments and receipts, thereby giving rise to society's demand for money.

If the demand for money is insufficient to absorb the supply at a particular interest rate, monetary expansion to the limit of the constraint will not take place. In this case, the price of money (interest) would fall so as to induce the public to "purchase" the money. How much of a price drop would be required would depend upon the price elasticity of demand for money for transactions purposes.

ADDITIONAL READINGS

Anon., "The Goldsmith Banker," *Money and Finance*, D. Carson (ed.), John Wiley & Sons, New York, 1966, p. 61. A most interesting historical account.

Galbraith, J.A., *Canadian Banking*, Ryerson, Toronto, 1970, chs. 32, and 33.

Pesek, Boris P. and Thomas R. Soving, *The Foundations of Money and Banking*, Macmillan, New York, 1968, ch. 12.

Rosengren, E.M., "Creation of Credit," *Readings in Money and Banking*, University of Toronto Press, 1947, p. 3.

Tobin, James, "Commercial Banks as Creators of 'Money,'" Smith, Teigen (eds.), *Readings in National Income and Stabilization Policy*, 1974, p. 224.

CHAPTER 4

Liquidity

INTRODUCTION

It would be incorrect to lay too much emphasis on the money manufacturing function of chartered banks; after all, if the banks did not supply money some other institution in our society would have to. Both money production and its transmission existed long before our banking system, and the fact that banks have taken over this particular activity simply happens to be what our North American society prefers. We should not, therefore, judge the overall efficiency of a banking system by the quality of either its money manufacturing function or its money transmission. Other banking systems, as we shall argue, are highly successful, perhaps more so than our own, and have very little to do with money production or transmission.

What is really important is the position of the chartered banks within a very much larger framework of liquidity. In this the chartered banks share a market with every other financial institution; indeed, they are sometimes in direct competition. However, the fact that the chartered banks have been granted what amounts to a statutory monopoly of money manufacture is an added source of profit and prestige. The extra profit derives from the production of money which takes place before the total cost function turns upward. Marginal costs of money manufacture are zero up to that point because demand deposits, the raw material of money manufacture, require no interest payment.

We can gain a concept of the relative importance of this monopoly "bonus" by considering that in January, 1978, 22% of total deposits were statutory demand deposits; the balance, 78%, require an interest payment to depositors, and, hence, represent a cost to the banks. Nevertheless, even though demand deposits are only about one-fifth of the total deposit manufacture, the advantage to chartered banks over other financial institutions in terms of profit and prestige is substantial.

In this chapter, we begin the analysis of the very much larger concept of liquidity. In doing so, we are, in effect, looking at "things" from the bankers' point of view, i.e., as if money itself were either already in existence or really doesn't matter. The truth of the matter is that money, per se, and its manufacturing process are really quite unimportant within the entire economic scheme of things. The bankers, in other words, have been quite correct in their approach all along.

I. CHARTERED BANKS

In the previous chapter a total revenue function was developed which related the money creation process of individual banks to the revenue derived therefrom. This function was linear, positive, and may be expressed simply as

$$TR = rM$$

with r as a coefficient which relates the money manufactured to the revenue of the bank. This rate is in terms of a percentage of total assets, just as the cost function is a percentage of total liabilities. Since liabilities and assets are equal, both cost and revenue functions can be measured against the same axis.

The slope of the TR function, as represented by r, is the result of a specific interest rate structure, i.e., the more money that is manufactured at higher rates of interest, the greater is the value of r. This raises immediately the question: Why should not the banks maximize the value of r, i.e., *always* gain the highest rate possible? The answer lies in the existence of another constraint, liquidity, which is an essential ingredient of the operation of all deposit-taking institutions.

Like so many concepts, liquidity does not lend itself to easy, precise definition. In fact, it will have different meanings to different individuals and institutions. However, for our purposes, we will consider liquidity as the *capacity of a financial asset to be converted into a monetary asset without capital loss and without a lapse of time*. From the individual person's point of view liquidity has relevance to his own store of value, a topic considered in Part II. From the standpoint of a bank, liquidity means a protection against embarrassment or inconvenience associated with being unable to honour its commitments, legal or otherwise.

A. The Creation of Deposits and Asset Monetization

In the last chapter, the function of chartered banks was discussed in terms of the generation of deposits which constitute most of our money. Money (or deposits) is sold to the community for a price. This does not mean, however, that bankers should simply hand over cash or cheque books to those who can afford to pay the price in the form of interest. This process of deposit manufacture is an important one and certainly carries with it a degree of responsibility. Thus, an indiscriminate creation of purchasing power, the right to purchase goods and services, could, after the analysis of Chapter 1, lead to rising prices and inflation. This is why it is imperative that some extra goods and services be forthcoming to meet the extra funds created. We can best ensure that this stream will indeed be forthcoming by being certain that the assets which are related directly to the extra deposits are productive in that they themselves contribute to generating a stream of goods and services. Of course some assets may be extremely productive while others may prove to be complete failures, but if, on the average, the value (at the current price level) of these new goods equals the amount of new deposits which the public wishes to spend on them, the equilibrium, as expressed either by the Quantity Theory of Money or in an income-expenditure sense, is not disturbed.

One might imagine a perfect market system in which a producer who wants a loan and a banker who has perfect knowledge are performing their respective functions exactly as the free market dictates. In this way consumers would want to purchase precisely what is produced and in exactly the right amounts—a kind of Paretian equilibrium. Of course, such is not the case in the world of reality; in fact, the interests of the banker frequently coincide neither with those of producers nor with those of consumers. It would be a remarkable coincidence if the banker's performance was exactly what society wants.

Consider the situation. The banks will create deposits, but in so doing, they will also *monetize* assets. (By "monetize," we mean the creation of purchasing power as a counterpart of a particular asset.) This is why assets and liabilities equate in value terms on the balance sheet, and, in terms of the economic significance, the flows of goods and services generated by these assets must correspond in value to the flow of money.

Let us examine the situation more precisely. Suppose a factory is planned for a community. The corporation responsible proposes to finance the factory with a bank loan from a chartered bank. (Such loans, incidentally, are not traditionally appropriate for chartered banks. We shall see why presently.) When the loan is made, deposits are credited to the corporation's account in the usual manner to be spent for the purpose of paying construction costs, etc., for the plant. These deposits will be demand deposits which, according to our definition of liquidity, are purely monetary assets (100% liquidity). Suppose the recipients of these deposits (carpenters, plumbers, etc.) proceed to spend them *while* the factory is being built. New, additional money (or monetary assets) will be in circulation without a corresponding increased flow of goods and services (the factory is not yet in production) and a disturbance of economic equilibrium occurs.

Now suppose that the payroll recipients do not spend their money but decide to reduce their newly acquired liquidity to zero by saving in some particular form. Suppose, further, that the zero liquidity holds until (remarkable coincidence) the factory begins production. On that date the new output of goods and services happens to exactly equal the reconversion to 100% liquidity. In other words economic equilibrium is maintained since the increased flow of production just equals the increased supply of liquidity in circulation.

Of course, such a coincidence will not be true for an individual bank nor would it likely be true for all chartered banks as a group; this is why such loans are not considered appropriate for chartered banks in the first place. Other instruments such as bonds sold in the market automatically reduce the liquidity of the purchaser until the maturity date when they are repaid from the proceeds of sales of the factory's production. In this way liquidity is restored to 100% when total output of goods and services increases.

From the banking point of view, assets to the banks are liabilities of the public, and, by the same token, liabilities to the bank are assets to the public. Further, these assets of the public can assume a whole range of liquidities from highly monetary assets to whatever degree of illiquidity individuals may wish. They can be as good as cash with 100% liquidity, as in the case of demand deposits, or they may be deposit certificates with many years to maturity. Similarly, from the banks' point of view, their assets (liabilities of the public) can be pure cash (100% liquidity) or complete illiquidity as in the case of loans which are absolute write-offs with no possibility of collecting any portion whatsoever.

In some instances, the bank's assets may be transformed into cash without loss of value but only after a time lapse. In this case, the asset is not completely liquid because the true value of an asset today is *greater* than the value of an asset which will be liquidated after a time period even if it is worth the same amount of money. The reason is that the future value must be discounted at the current interest rate to the present, and the longer the time period to liquidation of the asset, the less is its *current* value.[1]

The assets of our Canadian banks range in liquidity from cash (Bank of Canada notes) through day-to-day loans, 90-day loans such as Treasury Bills, short term bonds, loans to business enterprises, loans to consumers, 20-30 year mortgages, etc.; in other words, a structure of liquidity from highest to lowest. This is what constitutes the total revenue curve of the banks. Occasionally the shorter term, more liquid asset may yield the greatest returns; at other times, more usually,

the longer term, less liquid assets have the greatest yield. Whichever structure of liquidity the bank follows is the responsibility of each banker, for he is the one who maximizes the bank's profits consonant with the least risk.

Coming back to the important point of the creation of deposits against assets once more, we can draw some significant conclusions. Since a good portion of a bank's profits derive from monetizing assets, it is in the bank's interest to make loans which bear the minimum of risk. In some cases the profit to the bank from this monetizing process may have little or no relation to the social desirability of the asset. For example, a loan granted to Hell's Angels for the purchase of noisy motorcycles may be quite profitable to a banker if he is convinced of the certainty of repayment. The cycles are purchased with new money which is passed on to the cycle manufacturer who in turn pays his labour, materials, etc.

On the other hand, a violinist may be granted a loan for the purchase of a rare instrument to enthrall millions of concert-goers. The banker may be sure of his assets in both cases but the music created by Hell's Angels is different from the violinist. Or again, consider an asset in the form of a factory, on the one hand, or a palace for an oil sheik on the other. The factory may be more economically desirable from the standpoint of the citizens of the sheikdom, but the palace is likely to be both more profitable and pose less risk as a banker's asset. In a word, it does not follow that the objectives of the banker will always coincide with the objectives of society.

B. Asset Liquidity

The banker faces problems of liquidity from another aspect — other than purely profit. Remember that the banker is liable to his creditors (i.e., his liabilities) and must consider the desire for liquidity on the part of his depositors. This means that some of his assets must be readily turned into cash either in the form of loans due for repayment in the near future or bonds which can be readily sold in the capital market. This he will be able to do since in most cases the markets are quite prepared to purchase securities of various types. However, the banker must be extremely careful that when he sells, or liquidates, assets

---

[1]This may require some clarification. Suppose the nominal value of an asset equals $100 but cannot be realized until after a time lapse. The true present value of a future asset of 100 is, therefore,

$$V = \frac{100}{(1 + r)^t}$$

with r as the current rate of interest appropriate to that asset and t, the time lapse in years. But if the nominal present value is also just $100, it follows that the real present value, V, must be greater than 100, i.e.,

$$V = 100(1 + r)^t > 100.$$

for cash, he does not suffer a loss of capital from being forced to accept a market price less than what he expects.

Consider the structure of the liquid assets of Canadian chartered banks as presented in official statistics:

they serve as a source of funds to replenish the pools of legal liquidity when they run dry. Thus, should a bank find itself short of cash reserves (the cash reserve ratio must average on a half-monthly basis) it can secure the necessary cash it

Table 4-1
CHARTERED BANK LIQUID ASSETS
(millions of dollars) Average 1.6—
31 August 1978
Total Major Assets—100,704

Reserves			Free Liquid Assets (as of 30 Aug. 1978)	
	Cash	Secondary		
Legal Reserves	5,343	5,415	Excess Secondary	962
Legal Minimum	5,282	4,639	Other Liquid*	5,589
Excess	61	777	TOTAL	6,551

*Holdings of government bonds, call loans, and excess of Bank of Canada Notes.
Source: Bank of Canada Weekly Financial Statistics, September 7, 1978.

The first set of liquid assets, Cash and Secondary Reserves, are the consequences of the legal requirement of the Bank Act of 1967. These are the legal constraints on the banks which prevent an infinite expansion of the money supply. The cash reserves of 12% of demand deposits and 4% of notice deposits are indicated as slightly over $5.3 billion as of the last two weeks of August, 1978. These are held in the form of Bank of Canada notes and deposits at the Bank of Canada. The actual legal reserves exceeded the legal minimum by $61 million — banks never run their reserves down to the absolute minimum; they prefer a "cushion" of safety.

In addition to the purely cash reserve, the Bank Act stipulates a secondary reserve of "not-quite-but-almost" liquid assets. These are Treasury bills, day-to-day loans to the money market, and excess deposits at the Bank of Canada. The amount of secondary reserves which chartered banks are required to hold is variable in the range of 0 to 12% of Canadian dollar deposit liabilities (irrespective of type) with the Bank of Canada having the power (section 18[2] of the 1967 revision of the Bank of Canada Act) to set the requirement. At the present time, since February, 1977, the required secondary reserve ratio is 5%, a rather low figure compared to the past.

On the right side of Table 4-1 are the "free" liquid assets. These are likely the most important in that

needs very quickly from its secondary reserves. The secondary reserves in turn (this reserve ratio must average on a monthly basis) will be replenished from the free reserves which are the least liquid of all of the liquid assets. There is no statutory requirement on these free reserves, the level being entirely the responsibility of the banks.

Changes in the amounts through time of these reserves can be readily seen in Charts 4-1 and 4-2. From these charts we can analyze the state of liquidity of the banking system, i.e., is it "tight" or "easy"? We recall that the most liquid of the reserves, cash and deposits at the Bank of Canada, are statutory, 12% of demand deposits and 4% of notice (or other) deposits. As a consequence of the relative proportions of these two categories of deposits, the overall legal reserve ratio is generally around 6%. There has, incidentally, been a steadily declining trend in this ratio from about $6\frac{1}{4}$% during the latter 1960s to the current $5\frac{3}{4}$% as chartered banks learn the art of persuading the public to hold more of its deposits as less liquid notice deposits instead of the 100% liquidity of demand deposits.

Because of the statutory nature of cash reserves, the rising trend of these reserves from 1972 through 1974 reflects the corresponding increase in total deposits during that period which, incidentally, averaged about 15% per year. From what

Chart 4-1

CHARTERED BANKS — LIQUID ASSETS
(Billions of Dollars)

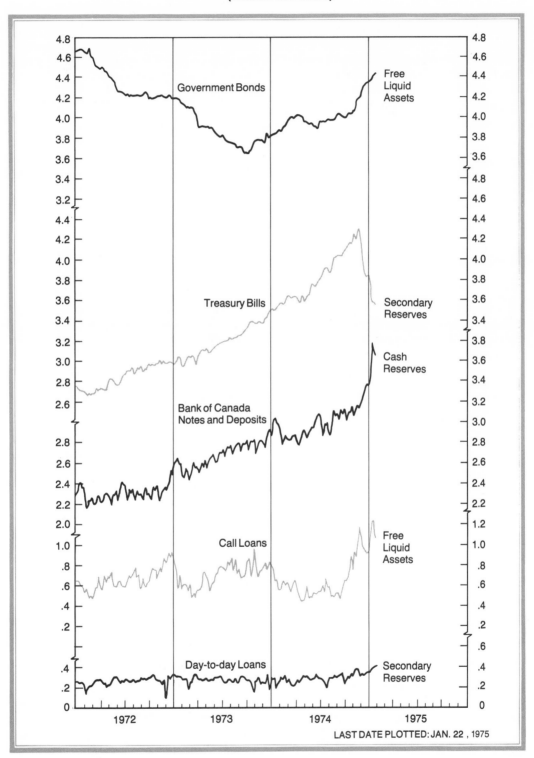

LAST DATE PLOTTED: JAN. 22 , 1975

Source : Bank of Canada

Chart 4-2

CHARTERED BANKS—LIQUID ASSETS
(Wednesdays—Billions of Dollars)

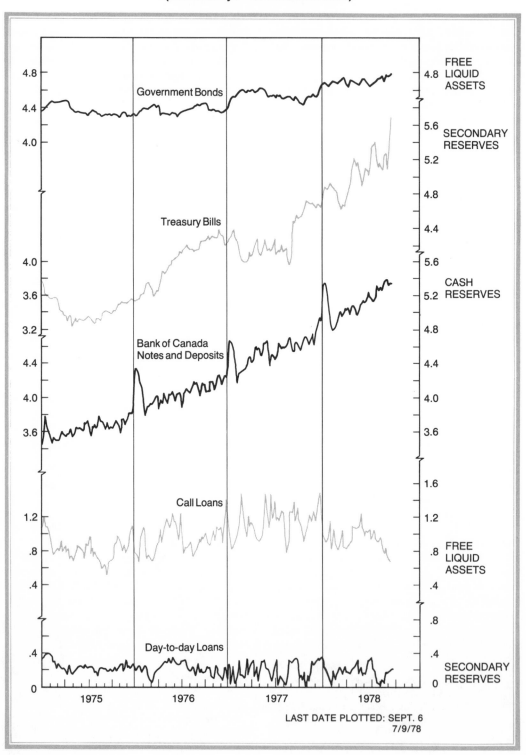

FREE LIQUID ASSETS

SECONDARY RESERVES

CASH RESERVES

FREE LIQUID ASSETS

SECONDARY RESERVES

Government Bonds

Treasury Bills

Bank of Canada Notes and Deposits

Call Loans

Day-to-day Loans

LAST DATE PLOTTED: SEPT. 6
7/9/78

Source : Bank of Canada

source did the cash reserves come? They came, first, from secondary reserves (Treasury Bills, and day-to-day loans to the money market). But this will not be apparent in the respective graphs in Chart 4–1 either because these are *also* statutory, 8% of total deposits from January, 1972 to November, 1974. The question, therefore, is still unanswered until we look at the top graph of Chart 4–1. Here there is a decline in government bonds held by the banking system through 1972 to the last quarter of 1973. Since bonds are the major portion of free liquid assets (see Table 4–1 for the components) and the principal source of liquidity to meet the statutory requirements, their decline during the $1\frac{3}{4}$ year period in 1972 and 1973 tells us that bank liquidity was becoming sharply tighter (referred to generally as "tight money").

A more general ease of liquidity returned in the last quarter of 1973 permitting a partial restoration of free liquid assets, but most of the extra liquidity was used as statutory reserves to make possible an enormous increase in the money supply, 20.1%, in M_2 and a still greater increase, 24.8%, in M_3 in one year, 1974. The lowering of the secondary reserve ratio from 8% to 7% in December, 1974, is apparent in the abrupt decline of treasury bill holdings as banks liquidated their holdings through sales and maturing bills and transferred the proceeds into their tight cash reserves. Thereafter, the secondary reserve ratio was reduced by the Bank of Canada month by month to a level of $5\frac{1}{2}$% in March, 1975, permitting a further divesting of treasury bill holdings for still more liquidity for statutory cash reserves.

From 1975 to the present, free reserves (government bonds) have shown a slight tendency to increase (see Chart 4–2) at the same time that total deposits (M_3) continue to grow at close to 16% per year. This tells us that liquid assets needed to fulfill statutory reserve requirements are being made available from a source *outside* the chartered banks themselves; the exact source is discussed in Chapter 5 along with the techniques of monetary policy implemented by the Bank of Canada.

The development which is important for our immediate purpose is not these statutory reserves at all but the decline in asset liquidity of the banks over the years. We can measure this change in terms of a liquid asset ratio which measures the proportion of all liquid assets to total assets. (Liq-

uid assets are defined as the total of government bonds, call and short loans to the capital markets, Treasury Bills, day-to-day loans to the money market, and Bank of Canada notes and deposits.) The liquid assets are those which can be readily turned into cash or demand deposits so as to meet the requirements of depositors whenever the need arises. The degree of tightness of asset liquidity can be seen from the liquid asset ratio which has currently (mid-1978) reached a low of $16\frac{1}{2}$% compared to 31% in 1967. The fairly steady decline in this ratio over the 11-year span indicates how the chartered banks have become less and less liquid over the long term, changing their overall asset structure from higher to lower liquidity.

From this discussion, two facets of liquidity will have emerged:

(1) Firstly, there are the ratios of liquid assets to total deposits (liabilities) of the banking system. These are legal ratios defined by the Bank Act and exist purely for the purpose of establishing a control by the Bank of Canada over the money manufacturing function of the chartered banks. How this is done is discussed in detail in the next chapter.

(2) The second is the asset liquidity of the chartered banks which is measured by means of the liquid asset ratio. It is this aspect of liquidity, how readily the banking system's asset structure may be turned into cash, which is both the most interesting and the most important, and to the analysis of which we turn next.

C. Bank Liquidity

Historically, the problem of liquidity, in the sense that a bank's debts must be honoured when necessary, is as old as banking history itself. It was from the experience of banks with the consequences of insufficient liquidity that the long-standing tradition of "bankable" loans being only highly liquid commercial loans grew. Early Canadian banks, rooted in this tradition, concentrated their activity in the discounting of commercial paper, secured, of course, by the goods themselves. But this type of lending was clearly inadequate for a young country expanding both geographically and industrially. Farmers in particular were hard put to it to finance their normal operations since their credit requirements could not be shorter than a crop season—too long for the ordinary bank.[2] Even so, a rather interesting by-product of a perhaps excessive liquidity and the restraint it imposed upon an overextension of credit was a sound and stable currency which did, during the early years, help to maintain flows of payments from foreign importers of Canadian products.

However, even with this emphasis upon liquidity, banks did overextend themselves in their note issue. There were two bank failures of importance in pre-Confederation years, the Bank of Upper Canada and the Commercial Bank. The Bank of Upper Canada had been in a state of decline for many years before its final collapse in 1866, and the Commercial Bank had simply made a "single" large, unfortunate, loan.[3] These experiences, combined with the Anglo-Saxon banking tradition of lending only for commercial purposes, must have had considerable influence on the thinking of politicians and bankers alike.

After Confederation, the measures taken by the government in the Provincial Notes Act of 1866 and the Bank Act of 1871 effectively ensured liquidity by tying the notes to gold and limiting the amount that could be issued.[4] However, the economic expansion of the country, following the railway construction, was so great that a *shortage* of currency became the problem. Like so many of our economic difficulties even to this day,

by the time the politicians arrive at a solution, the problem has changed and the solution is out of date. While a superfluity of bank notes issued by many banks without sufficient means of absorbing them within the early Canadian economy was the problem before Confederation, a shortage of money existed after Confederation; hence, the early banking legislation simply contributed to the problem rather than helping to solve it.

The problem of a shortage of money then as now translates itself readily into the more serious problem of a shortage of liquidity for the banks. Everything can run smoothly with banks increasing their non-liquid assets until the unfortunate day that borrowers find themselves with insufficient funds to repay their loans. Banks, in their turn, discover that non-liquid assets are converted into complete illiquidity with little or no cash for honouring their liabilities.

In the earlier years of Confederation, our money and banking system was dominated by two laws, the Provincial Bank Notes Act of 1866 and the Bank Act of 1871. The first restricted the notes issued to a maximum of $8 million with a 20% gold reserve for the first $5 million and a 25% gold reserve for the balance. After Confederation these became Dominion bank notes. The second, the first of the series of Bank Acts, limited the note issuing powers of the banks to the amount of paid up capital and, in addition, required a one-third cover of Dominion bank notes. The combined result of both was that as far as the public was concerned, bank notes issued by the banks were actually money since demand deposits and cheques were only rarely used during this early period. The system worked well during the prosperous times, but with the onset of the depression years of the latter 1870s, the inevitable bank failures resulted from the inability of bank creditors to honour their debts.

The rigid control over the issue of bank notes exercised by the Bank Act of 1871 and subsequent Bank Act measures effectively discouraged the use of bank notes as money and encouraged the growth of the demand deposits and cheques. The money supply, then, became elastic upward; however, a truly flexible currency system without gold was not achieved until the Finance Act of 1914. This was accomplished by issuing Dominion bank notes against railway securities as well as "uncovered issues" to finance

---

[2]W.T. Easterbrook and H.G.J. Aitken, *Canadian Economic History*, Macmillan Company Limited, Toronto, 1956, p. 455.

[3]Easterbrook, *op. cit.*, p. 460. It would be interesting to know to whom and for what this loan was made. Innis attributes the downfall of the old banking structure to the dependence upon land and railroads for assets, and when these moved west eastern banks withered. M.Q. Innis, *An Economic History of Canada*, Ryerson, Toronto, p. 216.

[4]The Act of 1868 stipulated a maximum issue of $8 million, 5 million of which required a 20% gold cover and 3 million a 25% gold cover. From the beginning of Confederation, Provincial notes became Dominion notes. The first Bank Act of the new Dominion (that of 1871) limited the issue of bank notes to the absolute amount of paid-up capital. C.A. Curtis points out that it was the requirement of the new federal government for funds which prompted the Dominion bank note issue. Requiring banks to accept these simply guaranteed their acceptance by the public. C.A. Curtis, "History of Canadian Banking," *Readings in Money and Banking*, Rosengren (ed.), University of Toronto Press, 1947.

war purchases. In effect, it amounted to a suspension of the gold standard, a measure made necessary by the heavy gold withdrawals in August, 1914. Prior to that time, gold withdrawals were accommodated by the conversion of call loans into gold by the banks in New York, Canadian banks having been lending in the New York Money market. It was a simple matter to convert these loans into gold to accommodate the moderate gold withdrawals by their customers, but with the advent of World War I this short-term lending was sharply reduced.

The significance of the Finance Act of 1914 and the Finance Act of 1923 which made the provisions of the former Act permanent lay in the fact that the liquidity of the banking system no longer rested on the availability of gold, but on the Minister of Finance who could make advances to chartered banks against "approved securities." These advances were for one year with interest rates determined by the Treasury Board. Of course, these advances took the form of Dominion notes, furnishing a ready facility for transforming certain securities into cash. In this way, liquidity storms could be weathered.

That the system worked is evidenced by the statement of Mr. Fielding, the Minister of Finance. "...It may be said that the war being over we no longer have any need for the Act [the Finance Act of 1914], but experience has shown that the Act is still required; indeed I am inclined to think that something of the kind will have to become almost a permanent part of our financial system."[5] We may add, using our hindsight, that the reason it worked was that a flexible credit base for the banking system was essential to satisfy the monetary requirements of a rising Gross National Product. Gold could no longer perform this important task, making a return to the gold standard an impossibility. When the attempt was made in 1926 to return to gold, it was doomed not only by the requirements for liquidity but also by world conditions since Canada's problem was shared by all other countries with which trade was maintained.[6]

---

[5]Macmillan, *op. cit.*, pp. 22-23.
[6]In effect, banks were no longer under an obligation to maintain a gold standard in their process of credit expansion (or money creation). *Ibid.*, p. 59.

D. The Collapse of Liquidity

Under any circumstances, the Great Depression would assuredly have destroyed any attempts to hold fast to a gold standard under the conditions of the Finance Act of 1923. The weakness of the Act was the absence of control by a central authority (in this case, the Department of Finance) over the liquidity of the banking system. Reserves could not be increased, or decreased, at the discretion of the authority. It was rather up to the banks themselves to increase their own credit base, hence their liquidity, and, for this reason, centralized discretionary control was not possible.

In fact, it was the Depression itself which demonstrated the weakness of the structure of banking and finance in Canada and led to the appointment of the Macmillan Committee in 1933. The report of this Committee and its recommendations led further to the establishment of the Bank of Canada in 1935. It was the Depression also which accentuated the problems of liquidity which the banks experienced, particularly in the west.

Before examining the situation in detail, it would be worthwhile to review once more our banking theory up to this point. It will be recalled that by making loans to individuals, businessmen, corporations, etc., bankers are performing a very important function, that of creating purchasing power in order to help in bringing to fruition real assets of various kinds. In this way, the community becomes wealthier than it was before. We say that assets are monetized. The important thing to keep in mind is that bankers can monetize a whole series of assets ranging in quality from extremely poor to excellent. In this case "quality" would be measured by the ability to repay the loan plus interest within the agreed period, hence not necessarily in agreement with society's measure of quality.

The following T table shows that a bank has acquired 1,000 in notice deposits, the first entry of liabilities, and, consequently, an additional cash reserve by the same amount. Assuming a reserve ratio of 10%, 900 can be loaned by means of the deposit manufacturing process, in other words, an asset is monetized. The borrower proceeds to spend the loan, drawing down his deposit to zero (the vertical arrow). The bank then loses 900 of cash reserves to another bank

Assets		Liabilities	
Cash reserve	1,000 ↓	Notice Deposits	1,000
	100	Demand Deposits	900 ↓
Loan (repayable			0
in one year)	900		
TOTAL	1,900 ↓	TOTAL	1,900 ↓
	1,000		1,000
		Reserve ratio:	10%

drawing down reserves of the first bank (the vertical arrow again) to 100.

But this is only half the story. The other half can be explained by seeing, first, what happens when a loan is repaid to a bank. Of course, the mechanism of repayment is exactly the reverse, viz., a cheque for 900, in this case, is drawn on some other bank in the system and is handed over to the borrower who may have sold some products. He then presents the cheque to his bank to wipe out the debt of 900 (the loan entry vanishes), and the cash reserve entry, after a suitable "float" period for cheque collection, goes back once more to 1,000. Therefore, for the banking system as a whole, 900 of purchasing power was manufactured for the period of time that the loan was outstanding (one year). When the loan is repaid, the loan asset of 900 disappears and the cheque for 900 (plus interest) is collected by destroying 900 of deposits.

It is important to grasp this point. Just as a deposit was created by issuing a claim against the bank, so a deposit somewhere in the banking system is destroyed by a bank's acceptance of its own claim against itself as repayment. This is true whether bank notes or demand deposits constitute the money supply. However, this is not to suggest that the money supply actually shrinks permanently. As fast as deposits are "destroyed" they are recreated by monetization of some other asset, for a queue of potential borrowers with a variety of assets to be monetized is always waiting in the outer office.

But suppose the original borrower is just unable to repay his loan, for reasons, say, of miscalculation of his business prospects. The additional borrowers cannot be satisfied; the money manufacturing process ends, for the reason that the first manufactured deposit cannot be "destroyed", and worse still, the bank may not be in a position to honour its liability should the owner of the

original Notice deposit demand payment in cash. The bank has ceased to be liquid. The only way to save the situation is for a "central authority" to provide both additional reserves to satisfy depositors, if required, and the additional borrowers who wish to monetize their own assets. In the first case, the central authority would be supplying additional reserves of cash, but in the second, there is no feasible method of forcing loans upon borrowers any more than water into a horse.

An interruption of the process of deposit manufacture and "destruction" means only that no *further* loans can be made by the original lending bank. After all, deposit destruction is as important as deposit creation in the entire process of business finance. The original cash reserves, however, are still intact in the possession of the bank which *would have lost them had the loan been made*. This second bank now has an *excess* of cash reserves. Now let us imagine this entire process of reserves which do not move from bank to bank and a portfolio of uncollectable loans amongst *all* banks, and we are presented with the extraordinary picture of declining loans, on the one hand, and a high level of reserves on the other, i.e., the *potential* for lending is there but to whom can the banks lend? Only the safest, surest type of lending will take place to compensate for the disastrous decline in asset liquidity.

This is an often misunderstood point. The misunderstanding stems from confusing the liquidities of assets with liquid bank reserves. During the depression years banks were not being deliberately perverse in refusing loan applications; quite the contrary, we can easily visualize the dilemma of a banker during this period. His asset liquidity is very low with a larger than normal group of uncollectable loans, yet at the same time he has ample cash reserves with which to make additional loans. Being rational, his excess reserves are used for short term commercial loans or highly liquid government securities with low risk and high liquidity.

In the early days of the Great Depression, banks, particularly western prairie banks, found themselves in just such a situation. Loans to agriculture were not collectable because of the enormous shrinkage of agricultural income. The depression was particularly hard on the prairie farmers because of the fall in the price of wheat.[7] As a consequence, farm income in the prairie provinces, in terms of gross revenue, dropped from $843.2 million in 1928 to only $273.7 million in 1932.[8] In a word, debt repayment to banks as well as tax payments to the government were virtually impossible since the fall in price of wheat, and the failure of harvest because of dry weather (not to exclude the grasshoppers) conspired against the farmer.

The consequence was a break in the banking chain at its weakest link, with the queue of additional would-be borrowers being turned away. This again had its own disastrous effects since these potential borrowers were interested in acquiring funds for many and varied reasons. Employers, for example, expecting to meet their payrolls on borrowed funds pending receipt of payment for products, suddenly discovered that there was no longer any more money available. This led to further unemployment since producers could not pay their employees, and in this way, the banking system itself added its own contribution to depression conditions.

Chart 4–3 shows clearly the decline in bank loans during the depression years along with the increase in short-term liquid securities which were used by banks as substitutes for loans. At the same time, the relative proportions of loans vs. securities is shown in Chart 4–4. It is interesting that loans show a declining trend long before 1929 (since about 1915) though a cyclical fluctuation does take place with loans increasing during prosperous times and decreasing during recessions. Business enterprises, particularly corporations, were supplying their own working capital requirements not only from retained earnings but also from the capital market which was rapidly developing during the predepression

years.[9] This declining loan trend undoubtedly accentuated a cyclical decline beginning in 1930 by virtue of the fact that a credit machinery from banks to business enterprise had already ceased to be operative.

Of course, one must avoid exaggeration, for not all loans to agriculture and businesses were completely uncollectable. "During the middle thirties," writes Gibson, "the upturn in prices and the expansion of production enabled many firms and individuals to liquidate their hitherto frozen bank loans and to reduce unduly large loans."[10] Also, D.C. McGregor, with reference to the collapse of security values on the stock markets and elsewhere notes, "Notwithstanding this disorganization, the flow of funds from the public into the hands of insurance and trust companies continued, while customers of the banks repaid their loans."[11] But, as McGregor makes clear, as these loans were repaid, the funds did not return to the public as new loans but as investment in government securities. A similar situation developed with the insurance and trust companies which reinvested funds, "without delay," in government bonds which alone were considered safe.

Canada's banking system, operating under the Finance Act of 1923, was just not equal to the task of generating a sufficient flow of liquidity which was so badly needed in depression times. There was no provision for such an increase in liquidity by the central authority. Individual banks could have increased their own asset liquidity on their own initiative and doubtless did, up to a point, but it would be illogical to expect them to continue to make loans in view of the high risk involved! What was needed was a deliberate increase in bank lending so that additional borrowers could be accommodated in spite of the risk of loan defaults, but there existed no mechanism by which this could be accomplished.

Most important was the provision, or lack thereof, of agricultural credit. The situation was so difficult that the Macmillan Committee could note, "The indebtedness of many farmers appears to be such that even a substantial rise of agricultural prices would not be sufficient to warrant the extension of new credit through ordinary commer-

---

[7]Innes, *op. cit.*, p. 296. In Saskatchewan wheat fell from $1.03 per bushel in 1929 to $0.35 per bushel in 1932.
[8]Macmillan, *op. cit.*, p. 70.

[9]Gibson, *op. cit.*, p. 59.
[10]*Ibid.*, p. 55.
[11]D.C. McGregor, "Tendencies in Canadian Investment," *Readings in Money and Banking*, Rosengren (ed.), University of Toronto Press, 1947, p. 69.

Chart 4-3

DEPOSITS, LOANS, INVESTMENTS AND CASH OF THE CANADIAN CHARTERED BANKS

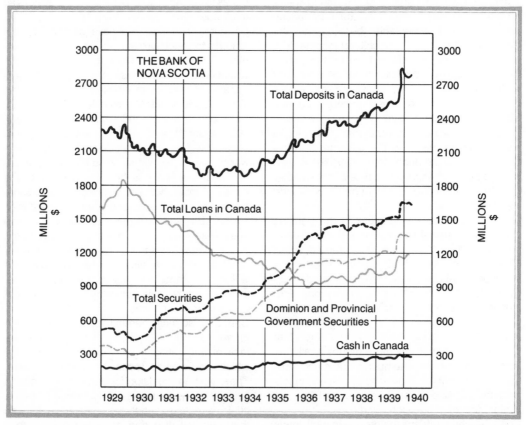

J. Douglas Gibson, "The Trend of Bank Loans and Investments in Canada," *Canadian Investment and Foreign Exchange Problems,* J. F. Parkinson, (ed.), University of Toronto Press, 1940, p. 154.

cial channels."[12] In other words, as the Canadian Bankers Association expressed it, ordinary banks were simply not up to the tasks, i.e., the necessary liquidity to warrant long-term farm loans was absent.

E. Social Credit

It was this failure of the banking system to perform its most basic function which, among other reasons, led to the acceptance on the part of Alberta's citizens of the doctrine of Social Credit.[13] This interesting and novel concept was formulated by C.H. Douglas, a British economist, who achieved some popular recognition both in Great Britain and abroad. His writings preceded the great *General Theory* of Keynes, yet, with careful reading of both, one can hardly avoid concluding that if Douglas did not influence Keynes' thinking, they were both influenced by a common strain of economic thought. Douglas was a pro-

---

[12] *Ibid.*, p. 71.

[13] The Social Credit movement had a long historical background rooted deeply in Progressive movements in the western provinces. It can be argued that the establishment of the Bank of Canada in 1935 owed much to the political pressure of these groups. See Professor W.L. Norton, *The Progressive Party in Canada*, University of Toronto Press, 1950.

Chart 4-4

CURRENT LOANS IN CANADA AND TOTAL SECURITIES EXPRESSED IN EACH CASE AS PERCENTAGES OF TOTAL ASSETS

J. Douglas Gibson, "The Trend of Bank Loans and Investments in Canada," *Canadian Investment and Foreign Exchange Problems,* J. F. Parkinson, (ed.), University of Toronto Press, 1940, p. 155.

lific writer and lecturer; nevertheless, his entire thesis can be expressed in the following excerpt:

> A factory or other productive organization has, besides its economic function as a producer of goods, a financial aspect — it may be regarded on the one hand as a device for the distribution of purchasing power to individuals, through the media of wages, salaries, and dividends; and on the other hand, as a manufactory of prices — financial values. From this standpoint, its payments may be divided into two groups:
> A. All Payments made to individuals (wages, salaries, and dividends),
> B. All Payments made to other organizations (raw materials, bank charges, and other external costs).
> Now the rate of flow of purchasing power to individuals is represented by A, but since all payments go into prices, the rate of flow of prices cannot be less than A + B. Since A will not purchase A + B, a proportion of the product at least equivalent to B must be distributed by a form of purchasing power which is not comprised in the description grouped under A.[14]

The crux of the matter, of course, is these "B" payments. One must keep in mind that Douglas wrote before the development of national income

---

[14]C.H. Douglas, *The New and the Old Economics*, Scots Free Press, Edinburgh, p. 9. This pamphlet, of course, is out of print. The author is indebted to Mr. Robert Klinck, Research Director of the National Social Credit Party, for a Xerox copy.

accounting with its identity, Gross National Product ≡ Gross National Income. Incidentally, he categorically denied the existence of this identity, recognizing that it would be disastrous to his thesis.

It is difficult to be certain just what Douglas had in mind by the "B" payments; however, they would appear to represent payments on the part of producers for the use of capital equipment, buildings, etc., which were built long ago and for which wages, profit, etc., ("A" payments) had already been made. Since the price of the product includes the cost of all payments, it follows that consumers cannot purchase what is produced without massive infusions of extra money in the form of bank credit. This would take the form either of an excess of exports over imports or new capital investment.

This, to Douglas, was the reason for the Depression, a failure to supply enough "B" loans to keep the system running. To him, the difficulty lay within the structure of capitalism itself, not in a temporary breakdown of the banking system because of a collapse of liquidity.

The naïveté of his reasoning is so obvious that the gem may escape us. Douglas had (correctly) grasped the concept of money being manufactured by the banking system. However, he saw it as loans *preceding* deposits and being created from nothing; i.e., loans are the chicken, deposits, the egg; or, to put it slightly differently, the deposits *themselves* were de facto loans. As these loans were repaid, the deposits were destroyed so that "B" payments were that portion of the price of everything we buy which marches, lemming like, to its own destruction. Since we only receive "A" payments to spend, a steady expansion of debt is inevitable if we are to avoid collapse. It follows that in some way consumers must acquire extra funds and they could do so in only two ways: (1) an expansion of exports over imports, or (2) a progressively expanding production of capital goods. (Consumer debt did not exist to any extent either in Douglas' time or thinking.)

The fallacy in his logic lay in his failure to recognize the fundamental function of banking. Loans do not precede deposits — nor do deposits precede loans — deposits are the raw material from which additional loans are manufactured. Bankers who receive "B" payments must honour

the debts owed to depositors; hence, these "B" payments are the property of depositors who have, *at the moment*, no use for them and have loaned them to the banks. Thus, even though banks manufacture money they can only do so if the public (the depositors) is willing to accept these new funds.

One can easily underestimate Douglas' contribution to economic science. He did indeed perceive a fundamental disequilibrium in the economic system. Had he, for instance, recognized that "B" payments are made through the medium of banks to savers, he would have likely closed upon the famous Keynesian equation,

$$Y = C + S$$

National Income equals Consumption plus Saving. The disequilibrium which gives rise to underconsumption occurs when savings exceed investment, when deposits in the banking system are not being loaned, i.e., the banks are either excessively liquid, or completely illiquid with no possibility of collecting loans. In the former case, banks are overconservative, in the latter, they are nearly bankrupt; in both cases, legitimate credit requirements will not be met.[15]

Further, the fact that capital goods plus an excess of exports over imports is investment, which must equal savings for equilibrium to exist, shows that Douglas had a grasp of the working of a macroeconomic system which was unusual for his time. Indeed, it would be no exaggeration to argue that, though imperfect, his suggestions for escaping the appalling hardships of depression

---

[15]As an example of Douglas' rather naïve mathematics and the direction of his thinking, the following is an excerpt from his testimony to the Macmillan Committee in 1930.

Let Deposits = D
Let Loans   = L
Let Cash   = C
Let Capital = K
Assets = $L + C$ and Liabilities = $D + K$, so that $L + C = D + K$.
Differentiating with respect to time we have:
$$\frac{dL}{dt} + \frac{dC}{dt} = \frac{dD}{dt},$$
K being fixed. Assuming cash fixed, $(dC/dt) = 0$.
Therefore, $$\frac{dL}{dt} = \frac{dD}{dt}.$$
This latter equality is his "proof" that loans equal deposits.
The Monopoly of Credit, K.R.P. Publications, Belfast, pp. 136-137.

years were not only the earliest, but basically correct. There *was* a shortage of purchasing power, which, as we have already shown, was due to an absence of a flow of liquidity but not for the reason that he argued. The remedy, a distribution of funds to everyone to spend was the application of the solution which can be attributed to the genius of William Aberhart, the leader of the Social Credit government of Alberta. This would have struck directly at the heart of the difficulty which was the absence of an incentive for businessmen to borrow.

It was the coincidence of the depression years which presented the paradox of an abundance of produced goods for sale and a shortage of purchasing power along with the Social Credit analysis which led to the success of the political party in Alberta.[16] In addition, the insistence of the representatives of the banks and financial interests on being paid for loans in full without lowering the interest burden appeared to confirm Douglas' contentions. Further, the semi-religious enthusiasm of Aberhart combined with the circumstances of the time and the Douglas Social Credit analysis, erroneous though it was, generated the momentum of a political movement which continues even to this day, especially in Quebec. Still, it is to the credit of the movement that it recognized the nature of the problem and advanced the only suggestion for a solution. This was the injection of additional liquidity by way of the consumers themselves, who would certainly spend, to generate profit incentives for businessmen. This would encourage them to return to the banks with feasible, *liquid*, loan propositions to increase production and employment.

Unfortunately, the distribution of funds from the "social dividend" never took place in Alberta for the reason that the social dividend really never existed; it was purely imaginary. This solution to the Depression's agony had to await the massive injections of funds through deficit financing of war production; hence, what was accomplished by a war had escaped the wit of men during peacetime.[17]

F. The Banks and the Public— An Interrelationship

History, particularly the years of the 1930s, demonstrates very clearly what can happen when the asset liquidity of banks collapses. The natural reaction, to restructure liquidity by concentrating in the no-risk, highly liquid assets, is exactly what the economic system needs the least. It can be argued that the failure of the banking system to supply additional liquidity when it was most needed was a significant contributory factor to the Depression itself. Some may even go further and insist that the failure of the banking system was the *major* cause of the Depression (Friedman) while others might assert that the banks had nothing to do with the Depression.[18] Be that as it may, our chief concern is our current structure of Canadian banking and to this we must return.

Our banking system today, just as in the 1930s, follows profit maximization principles; hence, asset liquidity will represent a trade-off, i.e., higher profits result from less liquid assets than more liquid assets. Thus, should a bank wish to increase total profits beyond the level earned at M_1 (see Diagram 3-2, Chapter 3) it is necessary to acquire additional deposits so as to invest in less liquid, higher return assets. This means that deposit liquidities must match as nearly as possible the asset liquidities. The more closely they match, the less provision need be made for deposit liabilities when they mature. Consider an example: Suppose a bank has some 25-year loans as part of its asset structure which are scheduled for repayment at 5-year intervals. The bank can finance these by rolling over 5-year savings certificates five times which will ultimately mature on or about the same date as the loans since funds for repayment of the last series of certificates will coincide with the due dates of the loans.

Suppose, instead, ordinary notice deposits were used to finance the mortgages. The liquidities of

---

[16]John A. Irving, *The Social Credit Movement in Alberta,* University of Toronto Press, 1959, p. 335.

[17]This sentiment was expressed by Graham Towers, Governor of the Bank of Canada, in his first post-war Annual Report.

[18]P. Temin, *Did Monetary Forces Cause the Great Depression?*, MIT Press, New York, 1976. The answer, for Temin, is "no." His argument, largely historical and too long to be included in a footnote, seems to show a lack of understanding of the banking principles discussed, i.e., asset liquidity and its importance.

the public's deposits do not match the assets of the bank and some short-term, more liquid assets must be available to meet the notice deposits as they are withdrawn. Since these generally have a lower return in terms of interest, profits will be less. Should chartered banks, then, wish to increase revenues with long-term loans, they must likewise reduce the liquidity requirements of their depositors. This they can do through encouraging savings deposits—deposits which have more "sticking power." An added benefit is the lower cash reserve ratio against these deposits, making it easier to satisfy the legal liquidity requirements.

But at the same time that the savings deposits are encouraged, the *TC* function is bent upward (see Diagram 3-4, Chapter 3). To a degree this is counteracted by a rightward shift in the entire *TC* function through a lower reserve ratio. This strengthens the chartered banks in their capacity to compete with other financial institutions in the field of lending.

The essence of the argument is that banks' liabilities consist of borrowing from the public. Even the early note issue was a kind of "borrowing" since the fact that they were a "first lien on the assets of the issuing bank" and, with the exception of emergencies, were redeemable in legal tender meant that they were just like deposits, bank debts owed to the public.

It is now appropriate to address, for the last time, the question, if the banks are in debt to the general public, how is it possible for them to manufacture deposits, i.e., create their own debt? It is this which is so imperfectly understood by very many people, and it may be added, it is an essential point to be grasped by anyone since it lies at the very root of our monetary system.

Banks cannot expand their debts indefinitely. Even without the legal reserve requirement which restricts debt expansion they still could not do so unless the general public were willing to become bank creditors. There are, thus, two necessary conditions which must be fulfilled before deposits can be manufactured: (1) borrowers must be willing to borrow, and (2) the public must be willing to lend. Once both these conditions are satisfied, a deposit (debt) may be manufactured. But this means further that the essence of the system lies in the fact that some portion of the general public is lending to another portion of the same general public and that the bank is merely the intermediary between the two. In effect the bank brings borrowers and lenders together through intermediation. Since the bank's debts to the public are money, when both borrowers and lenders are willing to borrow and lend, they have the means by which their transaction may take place.

The question remains still, what *precisely* is it that lenders are willing to lend and borrowers desire to borrow? The answer is liquidity, that abstract quality which all assets possess to a varying degree. Lenders have too much and wish to be less liquid. Borrowers have too little and desire more, and this is why borrowers are willing to pay interest to lenders who, in their turn, demand a reward for parting with their liquidity. Money, or deposits, is simply the mechanism (or "wagons" if one prefers a homely figure) by which liquidity is transported. This is the sole function of money in this sense.

Banks, therefore, in their functions as intermediaries, act as a bridge between the desired liquidities of both lenders and borrowers. The bridging action is accomplished by bringing together these two sets of desired liquidities which are otherwise impossible to match. Lenders, who have too much liquidity, are willing to reduce their excess to a certain level but prefer to lend for short periods only or even to have their liquidity in the form of immediately realizable notice deposits. Borrowers who desire additional liquidity cannot alone satisfy these liquidity requirements since they prefer to borrow long, i.e., to have the liquidity as long as possible. The banks make the impossible possible through accepting short-term, liquid deposits and lending to borrowers who prefer long-term illiquid borrowing; this is the bridging function and involves satisfying the different liquidity requirements of both borrowers and lenders at the same time.

The people and institutions that borrow liquidity from banks in this way range from government, large corporations, business enterprises, etc., all the way to individuals who wish personal loans for consumption purposes. The form of these bank loans, or assets to the banks, may be highly liquid securities such as Treasury Bills and 24-hour loans to the money market, or illiquid, medium to long-term loans such as 25 or 30-year mortgages. The short-term highly liquid loans are necessary to satisfy the liquidity requirements of depositors (lenders), and the longer-term loans are appropriate for the investment of funds not required by depositors (highly illiquid).

Of course, banks are human institutions that may make decisions regarding their investments which are different from the liquidity preferences of depositors. Suppose, as an example, that the banking system decides to "intermediate" (or bridge) between lender and borrower somewhat more than borrowers appear to desire, i.e., banks have some extra liquidity in the form of more notice and demand deposits than they consider normal. Banks must entice borrowers, in this case, by lowering their loan interest rates and at the same time, raising deposit rates as rewards for longer-term illiquid deposits. Banks' profit margins will be reduced and they will quickly discover the error in their decision. Suppose a different case, i.e., borrowers wish to borrow but lenders are loathe to accommodate them. Banks, in this case, must raise the deposit rate of interest, and, very likely, raise their loan rates enough to protect or even increase profits. Now suppose that both borrowers and lenders are reluctant! This puts banks in a real dilemma and in order for them to perform their intermediation function, they must raise deposit rates and lower loan rates, squeezing profits severely. This is an unusual circumstance which, if carried to the extreme, can only result in a national calamity such as the Depression of the 1930s.

Lastly, there is one other possibility which may be mentioned at this point to be considered in much greater detail later. It is, in fact, at the very heart of the controversy amongst economists to this day and will require careful analysis in ensuing chapters. This is the matter of "forcing" liquidity on the public by means of the Bank of Canada permitting more deposit money manufacture (hence more liquidity) purely for the purpose of satisfying borrowers. It is precisely this which is not possible during depression conditions for the reason that borrowers refuse to take the extra liquidity even at extremely low cost. But in more normal times, borrowers will accept this "manufactured liquidity" if the interest cost is low enough, but which, in turn, exceeds the requirements of the general public for monetary assets. As we shall argue, such a condition lies at the root of monetary inflation.

The process of intermediation, or accepting deposits and lending, is a continuous one involving a flow of liquidity through time. It may be visualized as a pipe connecting two containers, one with excess liquidity and the other with a shortage of liquidity. The flow from one container to the other may be increased or decreased by the action of the chartered banks and, in particular, the Bank of Canada which, in turn, regulates the chartered banks in their money manufacturing function. Always the precondition of the desire of lenders to lend and borrowers to borrow must be satisfied so that any expansion of the flow must involve the consent of lenders and the willingness of borrowers. This is accomplished through an adjustment of the respective rates of interest on loans and deposits.

The analysis thus far has come a long way from the simple cost/revenue functions discussed in Chapter 3. It would be difficult indeed to show a flow process with a static diagram; to do so would require a series of diagrams showing different positions of both the *TR* and *TC* functions, a difficult task which can be more easily accomplished by imagination than drafting.

II. THE CLEARING FUNCTION

If there is one distinguishing feature which sets chartered banks apart from other financial institutions, it is the money transmission or cheque clearing function. In this our banks are the inheritors of a long tradition in banking which has been characteristically British.[19] In fact, the great London clearing banks, as their name implies, were developed on the basis of cheque clearing through a clearing house and served as both an example and precursor of our own system of chartered bank clearing.

While the clearing or transmission function is quite distinct from intermediation, it must be emphasized that the very process of cheque clearing makes possible the money manufacturing function itself which, in turn, transmits liquidity.

---

[19]To quote from Lipson, "The next step (after the issuance of a promissory note) was to dispense with the personal application of the depositor, and allow him to address an order to the goldsmith to pay the bearer a stated amount: an early example of this, the precursor of the modern cheque, is dated 1675." *Op. cit.*, p. 231-232.

There were earlier examples of such orders to pay found on clay tablets amongst ruins of ancient Babylon; however, for all practical purposes, our system has evolved from the British.

Thus, having access to the clearing house means that our chartered banks occupy an extremely important strategic position in the entire financial structure of Canada. Furthermore, this position is unchallenged by potential competitors for the reason that the Canadian Bankers Association is empowered by law to establish the clearing house and to administer its operation.[20] Since only banks can be members of the CBA *and* the clearing house (but no banks *must* be a member of the clearing house) it follows that the monopoly is complete. It would be no exaggeration to say that the banks are the hub of a financial wheel around which revolves our entire payments system; no payment, except for direct cash, can be made without ultimately passing through the clearing house.

The process of cheque clearing is really quite simple and can be readily understood with an example of a two-bank clearing point. Note carefully that Bank of Canada branches are represented at all clearing points wherever the branch exists and act as the ultimate clearing agent. This is logical for the reason that all banks are required by law to hold deposits with the Bank of Canada. Suppose we have T tables representing the two banks which appear as follows (ignore for the moment the assets side of the tables):

Thursday.

The cheque itself is still a claim which is outstanding against bank X. If this should happen to be the only claim between the two banks it would be settled through the clearing house by means of a transfer of cash or, what amounts to the same thing, an ultimate transfer of ownership of deposits at the Bank of Canada. Bank X would lose 100 and bank Y would gain 100 of Bank of Canada deposits (see assets side of T tables). The interbank deposits would be restored to their former levels and the T tables would balance with bank Y having acquired additional reserves at the expense of bank X.

In contrast to the theory of cheque clearing, the details of the actual process can be quite complex. There are many "subclearingpoints" operated by individual banks at which claims of individual bank branches against each other are settled before the main clearing is reached, thereby forming a vast network of clearing throughout the country. For our purposes, it is sufficient to note that there are nine Bank of Canada clearing points, plus the Quebec City agency of the Bank of Canada, making a total of ten. Outgoing payments for each bank are settled against incoming payments and the difference (net) is settled ultimately through the Bank of

Assets	X	Liabilities		Assets	Y	Liabilities	
Deposits at		Deposit$_A$	100↓	Deposits at		Deposit$_B$	100
Bank of Canada	-100	Deposit$_Y$	100	Bank of Canada	$+100$	Deposit$_X$	100↑

For reasons of convenience, banks X and Y hold deposits in favour of each other. These are interbank deposits which will assist in the cheque clearing process. Suppose a customer of bank X, A, writes a cheque for an item in favour of B. B presents this cheque for payment at his bank Y. His deposit is credited by subtracting from the deposit of bank X and adding to the deposit in favour of B. The cheque now "floats" (it is passed on to the clearing house for collection). The interbank deposit itself, in this case, is purely a convenience, useful only when the clearing process requires a considerable time, say, a weekly clearing on Wednesday and it is now the preceding

Canada deposits in Ottawa.

What is important is that for payments purposes, the entire banking system is an integrated unit with deposits owned by the people and governments of Canada. The integration is so complete that we can combine all the balance sheets of chartered banks into one great balance sheet and study the relationships of the various components just as if it were indeed one great single bank. Within this "great bank" the ownership of deposits is transferred in a vast "whirring" of activity as transactions for goods and services of all kinds take place in a continuous process of flow. It should, however, be emphasized that the integration process is for payments purposes only. Banks are by no means integrated when it comes to their many other activities such as deposit-

[20]J.A. Galbraith, *Canadian Banking*, Ryerson Press, Toronto, 1970, p. 356.

taking and loans.

There is, of course, no apparent end to the possible improvements in efficiency in the clearing process which modern computer technology makes possible. We are all familiar with our personal cheque books designed for computer reading and sorting, but what staggers the imagination is the revolutionary Banks Automated Clearing Services Ltd. (BACS) introduced in Great Britain in 1968. In this system, magnetic tapes are submitted to a computer centre which then authorizes payment from banks' customers' accounts on a credit basis, i.e., a kind of overdraft. These are particularly useful for payroll or other periodic payments. Originally banks (all financial institutions which take deposits are called "banks" in Great Britain) used the facilities of BACS, but now even individual companies find it cheaper and more convenient to prepare their own magnetic tapes.

Something of this kind is probably in Canada's future also. The proposed new decennial revision of the Bank Act includes a separate Canadian Payments Association Act which will require that all chartered banks, the Bank of Canada and Quebec Savings Banks be members of a Canadian Payments Association. All other institutions which accept chequable deposits *may* join the CPA if they so wish and are, at the same time, able to meet the requirements of the Association. With a centrally located computerized operation, it is likely that payments transmission (as opposed to purely cheque clearing) services will not only be speeded up but will also be cheaper. It is expected that very many of the financial institutions other than banks will voluntarily become members for this reason.[21]

It is interesting that banking and financial systems other than those of North America and Great Britain have developed highly efficient payments systems quite separate from the banks. In Continental countries outside the Communist Bloc (East Germany being the exception) a postal Giro system of payments is used. The brainchild of George Koch, an Austrian, it was first put into the Austrian post office in 1883 and has since spread to many other countries.

Actually, the Giro system is (in theory) simpler than cheque clearing. Of course, like a clearing system, it is highly complex in detail but can easily be understood in theory. It actually is a means by which payments in an economic system which relies heavily on cash transactions can be effectively transmitted to other, even the remotest, parts of a country without the awkwardness and risk of physically transporting cash. The underlying principle of a modern postal Giro is that a centrally located computer holds the records of all account holders. Payments are made by simply transferring from one debited account to another credited account upon receipt of the appropriate instructions, generally a simple form to be filled in. In addition, such payments can be made on a continuous basis without further instruction (monthly bills, etc.). Payments to non-account holders are also just as easily made, but in this case the correct authorization, or voucher, is sent through the post rather like a postal money order so that the non-account holder can collect his cash from his local post office. Conversely, cash from a non-account holder can be paid in to the credit of an account holder just as simply.

Since the entire Giro system involves only a cheap and efficient payment transmission service, it does not compete with continental banks which provide all other banking services. The Giro introduced in Great Britain, however, has not proved to be successful for the rather obvious reason that the clearing banks themselves have provided highly competitive services in their own general clearing services. In addition, just as in Canada, the credit card has made possible bank clearings on a credit basis without the use of cheques. Once more the addition of a service rendered by the banking system which complements pure payment transmission assures the dominant position of the banks against a potential competitor.

But there is one other factor which seems to account for the success of the Giro in Continental countries. This was noted by the Radcliffe Com-

[21]Banks' reserves will no longer be held with the Bank of Canada but with the CPA itself. In the proposed legislation, reserves will be (1) 12% of Canadian dollar demand deposits to be reduced gradually to 10%, (2) 2% on the first $500 million of term and notice deposits, (3) 4% on the remainder of term and notice deposits except those non-encashable deposits which will be reduced gradually to 3%, and (4) 4% of foreign deposits used domestically— *Financial Post*, May 27, 1978.

mittee report nearly 20 years ago.[22] To the extent that Giro balances accumulate over and above that which is required for transactions purposes, an interest-free loan is being made to the postal service which, in turn, is made available to the government. These funds, invested in short-term government securities, earn an interest which defrays the cost of the Giro operation itself. Of course, since the interest on the debt is paid by the taxpayers, the whole operation becomes one of paying for the Giro service through taxation, but the fact remains that governments do have a ready source of funds without resorting to a capital market which is non-existent in many cases. It is not being cynical to argue that this is the real reason for governments encouraging the use of the postal Giro in the first instance.[23]

It is unlikely that the Giro system would ever succeed in North America for the same reason that it has not generally "caught on" in Great Britain — competition from banks is too severe. One might imagine a further, more practical reason. Suppose we in Canada *did* have an ongoing postal Giro system on the same scale as Continental countries. With our penchant for postal strikes, our entire payments system would be subject to frequent and complete collapse, with consequences too appalling to imagine. We can do without our mail, but we cannot survive without a payments system!

III. COMPETITION IN BANKING—
FINANCIAL INTERMEDIARIES

It would be an exaggeration to argue that a large measure of competition exists among the chartered banks themselves. One would describe them as oligopolistic, showing all the signs of oligopolistic market behaviour. This is why bank interest rates, both deposits and loans, not only move together but are also at very much the same levels. The same is true for charges on

cheque clearings. On the other hand, banking services offered to the public may vary among banks as each oligopolist strives to attract customers from the others.

But oligopoly certainly does not hold true when it comes to the other deposit-taking institutions, sometimes referred to as "near banks," but which will here be conveniently referred to as financial intermediaries (FI's). In fact, in recent years a great deal of attention has been paid in the literature to this important segment of our financial system. Indeed, for all practical purposes the distinction between chartered banks and these other intermediaries is no longer quite so clear.

By financial intermediaries, we mean those institutions which appear to most people as banks. They encourage deposits, cash cheques, offer cheque clearing services and generally behave as banks. Most important, they offer long-term deposit certificates at rather attractive interest rates, generally more attractive than chartered banks. Specific examples are trust companies, mortgage loan companies, and credit unions, branch offices of which are located in cities, towns and shopping centres across Canada. This does not exhaust the list of financial intermediaries by any means; these few examples are selected for analysis because they are the almost-but-not-quite banks. "Almost-but-not-quite" implies a distinction which can be made between financial intermediaries and chartered banks, yet, at the same time, this distinction must not be overstressed. In the final analysis, both types of financial institutions act as intermediaries which bridge the desired liquidity of lenders and borrowers in our society, and this is their most important function which they both have in common. The difference, which is less significant, will become apparent in the analysis which follows.

We will once more use the same cost/revenue diagram of the previous chapter with the only difference being the horizontal axis (Diagram 4-1). Instead of money being manufactured, we have simply assets/liabilities. A cost function rises from the fixed cost "floor," gently at first, then progressively steeper as assets/liabilities increase. In order for these FI's to expand their assets, they must attract liabilities, and the more liabilities they attract, the greater the cost *per liability*.

---

[22]Committee on the Working of the Monetary System, Cmnd. 827, August, 1959, para. 962.
[23]The British government even offers loan facilities to account holders through the finance house, Mercantile Credit Co. Ltd., and arranges repayment through easy deductions from a Giro account. See "National Giro, What's in it For You?", a pamphlet distributed by the British postal service.

Diagram 4-1

COSTS/REVENUE FUNCTIONS, FINANCIAL INTERMEDIARIES

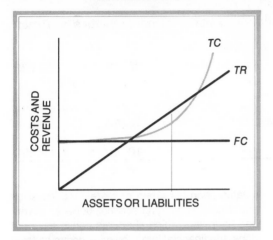

Similarly, the total revenue function, linear as in the case of chartered banks, has its origin at the zero point, rising with the same slope, r, throughout its length. The slope is variable, of course, depending upon the asset structure of the intermediaries. As interest rates earned by FI's rise, so does the angle r increase.

Just as in the case of banks, the amount of assets/liabilities the FI will generate will depend upon the spread between the TR and the TC functions, the profit function. The objective of the company will be to maximize profits and this they will do to the best of their ability.

It is the difference in the horizontal axis between FI's and chartered banks which marks the fundamental distinction between the two types of institutions. The FI is not a bank in the sense that it can issue claims against itself when it makes loans. The reason for this lies in the fact that the FI's do not have clearing privileges in the same way as chartered banks. Not having these privileges means that they must have accounts in their favour just as any other depositor with chartered banks. In fact, the so-called "chequing accounts" which may be offered by FI's are, strictly speaking, not cheques at all, but orders. These orders direct a chartered bank to transfer a sum on behalf of the FI from its own account with the chartered banks to some other account in the system; similarly, cheques drawn on some other chartered bank are cleared in favour of

the FI account.[24] In a real sense, FI's "ride on the backs" of the chartered banks through the clearing house in order to have their "cheques" cleared.

This leads directly to the second distinction between FI's and banks—the deposits at the central bank. These the FI's need not have. Of course, these deposits are the ultimate clearing and constitute the base of the total money supply, and by not having the right to issue claims against themselves and having these cleared via the clearing mechanism through accounts at the Bank of Canada, the "chequing accounts" are not technically money, *even though the general public may treat these accounts as cash for transactions purposes*. The orders of the FI's actually result in the existing money supply in chartered banks spinning faster, i.e., an increased velocity of circulation. How this is accomplished will be clear in the next few paragraphs.

But the so-called "chequing accounts" are by no means the important function of the FI's nor are they their major source of funds. Consider Table 4-2 (page 92).

"Other liabilities" in this case include shareholders' equity, some debentures, sundry debts, etc. Most of the liabilities, or sources of funds, of the FI's, about 70%, are in the form of deposits of varying terms up to the 5 years and over. Only a small portion of these, between 4 and 6%, are "chequable" in the sense that they are used by the public for transactions. This is why the TC function turns up rather sharply, because in order to secure these funds, FI's must compete directly with chartered banks' personal savings deposits. Furthermore, this competition is likely to be quite severe with the FI's gaining a substantial portion of savings deposits for themselves.

The fact that FI's do not have reserve requirements in the same way as chartered banks does have its advantage in the sense that the FI's are free to match the liquidities of both their borrowers (assets) and their lenders (liabilities). At the same time some highly liquid assets must be at hand to honour the cash requirements of their depositors. This liquidity matching has a great advantage in that as 5-year certificates, for example, fall due for payment, the FI's can prepare

---

[24]Galbraith, *op. cit.*, pp. 349-350.

Table 4–2
LIABILITY STRUCTURE OF FINANCIAL INTERMEDIARIES
(millions of dollars)
June 30, 1974

	Chequable	Deposits	Other	Other Liabilities	Total
Trust and Mortgage Loans Companies	949		25,976	5,713	32,633
Credit Unions and Caisse Populaires		15,134		4,484	19,618
Total FI's		42,054		10,197	52,251

Source: Bank of Canada Review, July, 1978.

their asset liquidity positions with enough cash on hand to meet their obligations. This is not the same for notice deposits of chartered banks. These must be honoured with a maximum 2-week notice, but in practice they are readily transferable into cash so that liquid assets must always be readily available.

It was this characteristic, the capacity to match long-term loans with long-term liabilities, which made possible the growth of financial intermediaries in the first place. Chartered banks, being commercial banks, have generally followed a long tradition of maintaining asset liquidity; therefore, they have tended to concentrate their loans in the short-term commercial field, the discounting trade bills, loans to brokers and finance houses, first grade bonds, etc. The consequence is that there has been no source of funding for longer term loans such as mortgages, land development, construction, etc.; in other words, a kind of gap existed in the supply of funds for lending for any purpose other than commercial loans and risk-free investment.

At the same time, there has been a similar gap from the savings side. The public is willing enough to part with its surplus liquidity if the rewards are either sufficiently great or take a particular form which the saver might wish. Mortgage loan companies served this function along with trust companies which now have expanded so much in the long-term lending field that their original business, that of executors of wills and estates, is of minor significance. Life insurance and pension plans are also sources of long-term lending which offer the saver more than just interest on his investments; they provide, in addition,

estates upon his death or retirement. Thus, by performing a "bridging service" between savers and borrowers which chartered banks have not done, the financial intermediaries occupy a fairly well-defined position within the complete spectrum of institutions which specialize in the business of channeling savings into investment. Only occasionally is there overlap with chartered banks in the investment process; there is, however, considerable competition for savings deposits which, as we have seen, are extremely useful for chartered banks as well as for financial intermediaries.

Broadly the same situation, filling a gap in the public's requirement for funds, is true for the credit unions and caisses populaires. Small personal loans at moderate interest rates were not available to the general public around the turn of the century, so that the credit needs, often quite legitimate, of the average person had to be supplied by usurious and often unsavoury loan companies. The consequence was the importation of the European concept of co-operative banking (Raiffeisen in Germany, Peoples Banks in France, etc.) by Alphonse Desjardins into Montreal.[25] By acquiring deposits in small amounts from within local or regional areas, they are able to apportion funds for small, medium-term lending to the *same* community from which the funds were drawn. This, in itself, means a high degree of efficiency in the process of intermediation since the borrowers are in close proximity to

[25]E.P. Neufeld, *The Financial System of Canada*, St. Martin's Press, New York, 1972, p. 383.

lenders and can be readily checked for credit worthiness. Risk, therefore, is minimized.

The success of and growth of these financial intermediaries has not been continuous since it depends entirely upon the degree to which each occupies its own non-competitive niche within the overall structure of the savings-investment market. This, in turn, depends on the propensity of the chartered banks to move into the same "spaces" occupied by them. For example, a general movement of the chartered banks into the small personal loan area, as has been the case in recent years, has been at the expense of both finance companies and credit unions. Similarly, the entry of chartered banks into long-term mortgages in the mid-1950s and 60s has cut deeply into the activities of mortgage loan and trust companies. In a real sense the chartered banks, by virtue of their size and monopoly position within the entire intermediation field, are dominant. They are subject only to the legal restraint of the Bank Act.

Competition from chartered banks is the greatest during times of "tight" money. Since the constraint of the chartered banks' cash reserves is tightening, their *TC* function increases more sharply. This is why a tight money policy, which acts on the chartered banks directly, has an initial opposite indirect effect on the financial intermediaries.

An interesting period before the Bank Act of 1967 shows the nature of this competition (Table 4-3).

the necessity for a spread between costs and revenues. This was a period of slow growth for the chartered banks and rapid growth of financial intermediaries. In percentage terms, the FI's increased twice as fast as the chartered banks. After 1967, however, the situation changed. Once the chartered banks were able to compete on more equitable terms with the introduction of the new Personal Savings Deposit and the abandonment of the interest ceiling for loans, the banks' growth rate was about the same as that of the intermediaries.

At this juncture it would be helpful to see precisely the relationship between the FI and the chartered banks in terms of T tables, remembering that the chartered banks, because of their peculiar structure and legal basis, are the only financial institutions equipped to supply money. In the tables on page 94 we assume that there was a demand deposit in favour of an individual who decided to transfer it to a financial intermediary as a savings deposit. It appears, therefore, as a savings deposit on the liabilities side (S Deposit 100) of the FI.

The FI has now acquired the ownership of the chartered bank deposit in exchange for its own savings deposit liability. This is recorded as a demand deposit at chartered banks as assets (D Deposit 100) and again as a demand deposit in favour of the FI on the liabilities side of the chartered bank's balance sheet.

Table 4-3
ASSET GROWTH OF FINANCIAL INTERMEDIARIES
(end of year assets)
Millions of Dollars and Year to Year Change

	Mortgage Loan	%	Trust Companies	%	Credit Unions	%	Canadian Dollar Assets of Chartered Banks	%
1963	1,544	—	2,321	—	NA	—	17,857	—
1967	2,772	80	4,353	88	3,382	—	25,199	41
1971	4,159	50	7,470	72	5,532	64	39,958	59
1974	6,743	62	12,443	67	10,315	86	68,481	71

Source: Bank of Canada Monthly Review.

Prior to the Bank Act of 1967, chartered banks were restricted by the 6% interest rate limitation on their loans. This meant that active bidding for notice deposits was similarly limited because of

Very shortly, i.e., in a continuous operation, a loan, say, a mortgage, will be granted. The borrower may specialize in residential construction in which case he will acquire the ownership of the

| CHARTERED BANK | | FINANCIAL INTERMEDIARY | |
Assets	Liabilities	Assets	Liabilities
	D Deposits$_{FI}$ 100 ↓	D Deposit 100 ↓	S Deposit 100
	D Deposits 100 ↓ (builder)	Loan 100	
	D Deposits 100 (tradesman)		

demand deposit in the chartered bank as indicated by the downward pointing arrow. But this is only temporary, for he will proceed to pay his expenses for labour, materials, etc., in the process of construction and the deposit will change its ownership once more. We note finally, that the original depositor still holds a claim against the financial intermediary (the savings deposit) and that the demand deposit in the chartered bank has changed its ownership several times in the interim.

Now suppose that the original depositor had preferred a savings deposit in the chartered bank itself instead of with the financial intermediary. This would have resulted in a corresponding loan asset of 96 (100 less the reserve ratio of 4%) which would be exactly 8 more than the loan asset of 88 (100 less the reserve ratio of 12% for demand deposits). Since the chartered bank loans are claims against themselves (or deposit money), the total money supply would have increased by 8 as a result of the transfer from demand deposits to notice deposits within the chartered bank itself.

We conclude, therefore, that the real function of the FI has been not to increase the supply of money but to "activate" deposits, i.e., make the turnover faster in the process of payments. This is, quite simply, an increased velocity of circulation. In return for this activation function of the FI a revenue is earned—the difference between the interest cost to the FI of savings deposits and the interest earned on assets. Whereas chartered banks expand the money supply, financial intermediaries speed up its circulation. At the same time that the function of each institution is different, the "raw material" for both is the same; hence, the competition between them for savings deposits can be very keen.

This relationship between chartered banks and financial intermediaries will likely change with the introduction of the new Bank Act—to what extent remains to be seen since some time will elapse before the new conditions of operation will be learned. It is likely, however, that some financial intermediaries will decide to become part of the new Canadian Payments Association. Those that do will be in a position to issue claims against themselves just as chartered banks do at present; hence, they will enjoy the money manufacturing privilege as well. Furthermore, and this may be an awkward point, they will not be under obligation to hold a specified ratio of deposits as cash reserves—only sufficient cash for clearing purposes (see footnote 21 above).

On the assumption that the Canadian Payments Association Act and the Bank Act become law sometime in 1979, at least some financial intermediaries will find themselves no longer with the requirement to "ride on the backs" of the chartered banks for cheque clearing purposes. Furthermore, if a specific financial intermediary happens to be a subsidiary of a chartered bank, when money becomes tight, the financial intermediary may continue its loaning by deposit manufacture even further since there is no specified cash reserve ratio. At first sight, it would appear that a massive escape hatch would be opened should banks wish to avoid reductions in profits due to tight money.

Also, independent financial intermediaries could continue expansion of loans through deposit manufacture without the check of required reserves. The only real constraint to deposit expansion would be that of the necessity to meet demands for liquid funds when they arise. It would still be necessary to finance long-term mortgages with long-term savings and the ever-present threat of insufficient funds when deposits fall due should deter any financial intermediary from excessive illiquid lending. But all this is pure speculation. We cannot foretell institutional behaviour as it adjusts to changing conditions.

CONCLUSION

This chapter has been a difficult one to write for the reason that the topic, liquidity, is difficult. It is not easy to express an abstract concept in concrete terms in such a way that a reader will perceive the subject-matter in the same way as the writer. Difficult though it may be, liquidity is none the less important — more important than money itself. Money is, at best, only a proxy for liquidity.

We may conceive of liquidity as a framework within which financial institutions operate to move liquidity where it is in surplus to those areas where it is in deficit. In this sense, the chartered banks occupy the centre of the picture doing three things: (1) intermediation, (2) manufacturing money, and (3) transmitting payments. Other financial institutions are confined in their activities to the first function only. It is the concentration of the three functions in a small number of chartered banks that characterizes the Canadian financial system and makes it unique in the western world. This is also why the decennial revision of the Bank Act is so important to all Canadians.

The institutions within the liquidity framework have evolved since Confederation through several stages from the issuance of bank notes through chequable demand deposits to the highly sophisticated level of specialized deposits appropriate to a modern economy. Still, however, the importance of bank liquidity as distinct from the entire liquidity framework must not be overlooked. Banks in their liquidity transmission function have their own liquidity ratios to consider.

Broadly, bank liquidity is conceived as being of two types: (1) deposit liquidity, and (2) asset liquidity. The first is something of a hangover from the past and means that all deposits must be backed with sufficient cash to be paid when required. Now, it is purely a policy mechanism by which the money manufacturing function may be controlled. The second relates to the capacity of borrowers to repay loans, be they businessmen, individuals, or government securities. Traditionally a liquidity ratio of 30% of total assets for chartered banks was considered correct (the ratio was 30.5% in 1971), but currently banks are operating at very much lower levels (17.2% in 1977). Under ordinary conditions the rate of loan

defaulting would be considerable in the event of depression (or recession) conditions and would lead to bankruptcy, but it is unlikely that the government and the Bank of Canada today would be willing to permit any one of our major chartered banks to become insolvent. The danger inherent in a collapse of liquidity would be too great.

Financial intermediaries play an important role in the liquidity framework as well, yet one cannot but be impressed with the fact that they exist largely on the sufferance of the chartered banks. Should profit margins and risk levels warrant, chartered banks appear to be able to move into any area of intermediation they wish so that in the last analysis, the chartered banks rule the roost. Undoubtedly this enormous power stems in a large measure from the money manufacturing and transmission functions.

In all likelihood, the new Bank Act will mean some changes in this situation. For one thing, foreign banks, though limited in size, will be permitted in Canada and we will assuredly be seeing many of the great banking names of the world, Chase Manhattan, Barclay's, Citibank, etc., operating subsidiaries all over Canada. (Actual branches of foreign banks are excluded). Apparently these subsidiaries will have access to the Canadian Payments Association just as any other Canadian institution. In addition, new banks will likely be formed as some financial intermediaries become complete banks. All this means considerably more competition for existing chartered banks. Whether or not this will bring greater efficiency to banking services or, more important, improvements in bank control measures remains to be seen. Certainly the chartered banks' statutory monopoly of money transmission services (function 3 above) will be brought to an end as the Bank of Canada clearing points become obsolete.

ADDITIONAL READINGS

Curtis, C.A., "Creation of Credit," *Readings in Money and Banking*, E.M. Rosengren (ed.), University of Toronto Press, Toronto, 1947, p. 3.

Federal Reserve Bank of Chicago, "Mystery of Credit Creation," *Money and Banking, Theory, Analysis, and Policy,* S. Mittra (ed.), Random House, New York, 1970, p. 56.

Galbraith, J.A., *Canadian Banking*, Ryerson Press, Toronto, 1970, ch. 34.

Gibson, J.D., "The Trend of Bank Loans and Investments in Canada," *Readings in Money and Banking*, E.M. Rosengren (ed.), University of Toronto Press, Toronto, 1949, p. 52.

McGregor, D.C., "Tendencies in Canadian Investment," *Readings in Money and Banking*, E.M. Rosengren (ed.), University of Toronto Press, Toronto, 1947, p. 66.

Neufeld, E.P., *Money and Banking In Canada*, McClelland & Stewart, Ltd., Toronto, 1964. Very interesting historical material.

Report of the Royal Commission on Banking and Finance, Queens Printer, Ottawa, 1965, ch. 19.

CHAPTER 5

The Central Bank

Introduction

To this point, the argument has developed through the money creation process to the analysis of the framework of liquidity. Money is really the means by which liquidity is transferred from creditors (depositors) to debtors (borrowers). The function of banks in this process is to make this transfer possible by the creation of money.

There is something paradoxical here. Lenders have excessive current liquidity and are willing to become less liquid, *but* not without payment. They do not press their liquidity onto borrowers. The active agent is the borrower who seeks out the lender, offering him the reward of interest for the lender's liquidity foregone.

It is the genius of banking that the liquidity is transferred in such a way that both borrowers and lenders are satisfied. Lenders can reclaim their liquidity at any time they wish at the same time that borrowers are under no obligation to repay their loans until maturity — an amazing achievement to say the least. It is made possible by the banks maintaining a liquidity "cushion" which will satisfy those few lenders who wish the return of their liquidity momentarily. This liquidity cushion can be less if the bank's assets are so structured as to be close to maturity and depositors can be persuaded to assume less liquidity in their deposits. Conversely, the banks' liquidity cushion must be more if depositors refuse to be less liquid and the banks' assets are further from maturity.

The point is that banks are not free agents. The size of their liquidity cushions is determined by the general public, both borrowers and lenders. All the money in the treasury of Croesus will be refused by borrowers unless the terms of lending are such that repayment of principal and interest is a feasible proposition. Further, the longer the term for borrowing the more feasible (or attractive) does the loan become; similarly, the less the interest to be paid the more attractive is the loan. From the banks' point of view, the less liquid (longer term to maturity) its loans are the greater must be the liquidity cushion.

A major factor, to be sure, in the liquidity cushion can be cash reserves, but this is not all. Liquid assets are also important and banks can compensate for a weak cash position with more liquid assets. This was the case during the earlier years prior to the Bank of Canada Act when chartered banks used the New York money market for their purchases of liquid assets. A purely Canadian market for the sale of similar securities to banks had to await the development of a central bank.

I. THE BANK OF CANADA

As central banks go, the Bank of Canada is relatively young, having been established by the Bank of Canada Act of 1934, just about the worst possible moment in history for the establishment of a central bank. The nation was in the depth of the greatest depression it had ever experienced with prices and production falling and unemployment rising. To make matters worse, the Depression was world-wide, resulting in a collapse of demand for Canadian agricultural exports.

Caught in the midst of economic chaos and confusion, politicians and economists alike were unable to agree on consistent rational suggestions for possible solutions. Certainly it was clear that Canada's monetary and banking system, like a house of cards in a wind, was unequal to the demands made upon it, so that the one single outcome of the debates of the early 1930s which could be considered constructive and on which there was general agreement was the establishment of a Royal Commission to consider the matter of a central bank in Canada.

There were two statutes which were the "underpinning" of our money and banking system at the time. The first was a Dominion Bank Notes Act which, aside from the original issues of the original $50 million with a gold cover of 25% and a $26 million of wartime issue, required a dollar for dollar banking of gold. This meant that to increase the issue of these notes, gold from external sources (there were no feasible internal sources at the time) had to be forthcoming. This, in turn, required either a surplus of exports over imports or an import of capital. The second statute was the Finance Act of 1923 which was supposed to lend a degree of flexibility to our monetary system because banks could borrow Dominion Bank Notes from the Minister of Finance with appropriate securities and at appropriate rates set by the Treasury Board.

But even before the onset of the Great Depression, in 1928 and 1929 the Canadian financial system was showing strains. In both those years the investment boom was at its height, and chartered bank loans were at their peak. In 1928, even though exports exceeded imports, the current account balance of payments was unfavourable because of a negative balance of trade in securities, symptomatic of the speculative boom on Wall Street. In 1929, another and larger current account deficit appeared, this time enhanced by a genuine deficit in the balance of trade. The consequence of both these circumstances was substantial outflows of monetary gold, so much so that the government suspended payments of gold to protect the dwindling gold reserve. This was necessary, in turn, to avoid the deflationary impact of a restriction of the Dominion Bank Note supply which would certainly follow. As it turned out, this was the true end of the gold standard in Canada — the suspension of gold payments in 1929.

It is curious that in taking this action, the government was deliberately frustrating the automatic regulatory function of the Quantity Theory of Money in either the Fisherine or Pigovian version. The excessive activity which accompanies boom periods and leads to overheating of the economy (and rising prices) can, according to orthodox Quantity Theory, be checked by the export of gold. In a real sense, therefore, the Canadian government itself contributed to the weakness of its own monetary system by its refusal to permit the Bank Notes Act to work itself through to its logical conclusion. At the same time, chartered banks were protecting their cash reserves

through borrowing from the Minister of Finance under the provisions of the Finance Act of 1923. This had an additional effect of frustrating the deflationary impact which the pure Quantity Theory of Money would have imposed just when it was most needed, in a speculative boom.

By 1930, the decline of Canada's exports again resulted in a deficit in the balance of trade, and this deficit combined with the necessity for payment of interest and dividends to service past foreign capital imports, produced a balance on current account of −$267 million, an exceptionally large figure at the time.[1] The coincidence of the government's borrowing $100 million from the New York market to provide funds in Canadian dollars for railway improvement and for public works helped the situation by providing additional foreign exchange to support the Canadian dollar.[2] In providing the much needed foreign exchange, it did postpone the inevitable collapse which was to come later.

What seems incredible now, in reviewing those early depression years, is the lack of awareness on the part of the government not only of the nature of the collapse of liquidity but also of the magnitude of the idle capacity which was developing within the economy itself. To be sure there was a lack of statistical material (the Dominion Bureau of Statistics was small and barely able to cope with the demands made upon it) which we take for granted today. Nevertheless, the attention of the government was concentrated upon the narrower problem of how to maintain the inflows of foreign capital rather than the enormously broader scope of depressed business activity and unemployment within the country. Traditionally wedded to a sound currency so that foreign borrowing could be sustained, the government could not bring itself to the conclusion that to stimulate business and employment, very much more money (or, rather, liquidity) was required. During the special session of the House of Commons following the election of 1930, some independent western MP's did suggest that

---

[1] F. A. Knox, Dominion Monetary Policy, 1929-34, Ottawa, 1939, Table 11, p. 10.
[2] Support of the Canadian dollar was not yet the objective of the government, but the effect was to maintain the dollar at par with the U.S. dollar. Ibid., p. 14.

monetary measures could be useful in reducing unemployment by amending the Dominion Bank Notes Act to provide more notes to finance public works. This, they argued, would be preferable to either taxing or borrowing from the public which would reduce consumer purchasing power. In reply to this the Prime Minister stated:

> ... The suggestion which my honourable friend has made is one of which I was not enamoured when first it was proposed and which at this moment I do not think is sound. Unless the paper money of this country has behind it an adequate reserve of the only commodity that passes in the settlement of international exchanges namely, gold, I would suggest that it is of very little value; and to the extent to which the reserve may be depleted or the ratio decreased by the issue of legal tender or of Dominion of Canada bills, to that extent is there a possibility of the money of this country becoming debased and not of par value in the countries of the world... (the use of the printing press) ... would hardly serve as a palliative in the present situation.
> ... Insofar as the question of the emission of paper money by this country without reference to the gold reserve is concerned I certainly am not prepared to take any action at the moment..., so far as the present moment is concerned, having regard to the position that this country must take amongst the countries of the world, I certainly would not be prepared to ask parliament to agree to the emission of legal tenders by the Dominion without having behind it the ratio of gold reserve which is essential to give it value in the market places of the world.[3]

A better example of monetary conservatism can hardly be imagined especially in view of the fact that Canada was *already off the gold standard*.

Parliament's failure to comprehend the gravity of the situation was shown again in 1931 when both the government and the opposition condemned the western MP's for suggesting that the Canadian dollar ought to depreciate. Such a deprecia-

tion would restore the Canadian wheat farmer's competitive position vis-à-vis Argentina and Australia whose currencies had already depreciated. Once more a fear of inflation was expressed by the government. It was, in fact, not until the Ottawa conference of the British Empire countries recommended an "easy money" situation (carefully to avoid inflation, of course) that the Canadian government finally raised the issue of Dominion Bank Notes by $35 million. This had the effect of easing the pressure on the banks' reserves of cash which had been reduced by their earlier gold exports, but it was too late to increase the liquidity of the economy through business loans. Businessmen already were pessimistic about the future and banks were not prepared to assume the risks of lending. Too little too late, but at any rate, the banks were able to assist by purchasing Treasury Bills so as to provide the funds for new public works with the extra $35 million.

Just about the only constructive action, from a monetary point of view, during the early depression years was the setting up of the Royal Commission and the ultimate passage of the Bank of Canada Act in 1934. Pending the establishment of the Bank of Canada, Parliament in the 1934 session passed legislation authorizing an additional $52½ million in Dominion Bank Notes to finance greater treasury requirements and to increase bank reserves. Carefully pointing out that this did not constitute a departure from gold, the Prime Minister justified this action on the grounds that world opinion was swinging toward a smaller (25%) gold cover as opposed to 35 or 40%. It was not, he argued, "... unorthodox or a departure from the accepted canons of sound monetary practice."[4]

In maintaining this monetary orthodoxy until the Bank of Canada could take over, the government was not just acting in a perverse manner. Canada as a nation had been (and is very much to this day) dependent upon foreign capital and anything which jeopardized the nation's credit in foreign bond markets could lead to disaster. Foreign lenders must be assured of the value of their investments in terms of some accepted international means of payment so that when the time

---

[3]House of Commons Debates, Special Session 1930, p. 78 and p. 114, quoted in Knox, *op. cit.*, p. 19.

[4]House of Commons Debates, Session 1934, Vol. IV, p. 4085, quoted in Knox, *op. cit.*, p. 45.

comes to repatriate their capital there will be no loss of value. A depreciating Canadian dollar relative to gold meant that the dollar would likely be worth correspondingly less in terms of the lender's own currency; hence, the risk of capital loss in purchasing Canadian securities would be too great.

Actually, it is not likely under the conditions of the time that the government could have done anything very much toward restoring reasonably full employment via the monetary route alone. The task was simply too enormous, so much so that only a World War could accomplish it. At any rate the Royal Commission was appointed and began its work at once.

In an incredibly short time, (it was appointed on July 31, 1933 and reported on September 27, 1933), the Commission not only studied the "facilities now afforded by the Finance Act and a careful consideration of the advisability of establishing in Canada a Central Banking Institution ... " but also included " ... a study of the entire monetary system of Canada, including credit, currency, and coinage... "[5] Even for Lord Macmillan, whose experience included chairing the famous Macmillan Committee in Great Britain, which had enquired into the British banking and financial system, this was an incredibly short time. Nevertheless, with a majority of three to two, the Committee recommended the establishment of a central bank forthwith.

The Committee's philosophy and thinking can be best expressed by the three rhetorical questions posed at the beginning of Chapter V of its Report. "To what extent and through what organization should the volume of credit and of currency be regulated? On what body should be the primary responsibility for maintaining the external stability of the country's currency? To what institution may the Government of the day most suitably turn for informed and impartial advice on matters of financial policy?"[6] Of course, the single answer to all three questions was a central bank; specifically, one similar to the Bank of England.

In fact, there was nothing at all unique about Canada's experience. Central banks were blossoming forth on a world-wide scale with a total of 48 new central banks established in a variety of

countries between the years 1921, when the South African Bank was established, and 1954, with the Bank of Israel.[7] It was not only a general recognition of the need for controlling the money and credit policy which led to the setting up of these banks, but, rather cynically, a means by which governments might find ready cash for their needs. It was also the success of the Bank of England in handling the financial crises of 1873 and 1890 which stimulated the growth of central banking in other countries.[8]

Despite all these factors, there were two dissenting voices on the Commission, Mr. Beaudry Leman and Sir Thomas White. Both these gentlemen expressed the view that such times as depression are not suitable for the introduction of a new central bank with all the power and influence on the economy which it entails. Government, in their opinion, was more suitable for dealing with the economic problems of the time. Taken out of a depression context, such argument may seem strange to us today, and certainly, the formation of the new Bank of Canada did have a minimal impact upon the depression economy. To this extent, the critics were correct; however, there was little doubt that the Bank of Canada would be established. The Prime Minister had already declared himself to be in favour even before the report of the Commission. The only objection to the Act was one of detail; the Opposition preferred public to private ownership. (The Bank was later nationalized.) Within the provisions of the Act was a 25% gold reserve against all liabilities, a concession to monetary orthodoxy once again.[9] The other provisions were typical of central banks throughout the world — a monopoly of the note issue, the government's bank, custodian of the nation's gold and foreign exchange reserve, management of the public debt, and a provision for a 5% cash to deposit ratio for chartered banks to keep as bank notes or on deposit with the Bank.

---

[7]M. H. de Kock, *Central Banking*, Staples Press, London, 1960, pp. 19-20. One might add further that central banks for all countries were considered as advisable by the International Financial Conference in Brussels in 1920 and the World Monetary and Economic Conference of 1933.

[8]*Ibid.*, p. 13.

[9]The Exchange Fund Order of May 1, 1940 provided for "temporary" suspension of the 25% gold reserve. The gold reserve has never been reinstated.

---

[5]Macmillan, *op. cit.*, p. 5, Order in Council, P.C., 1562

[6]*Ibid.*, p. 62.

The organization of the Bank was begun immediately after passage of the Act with Graham Towers as the first Governor and a general recruitment of some of the best people in the country for its staff. It opened its doors for business on March 11, 1935, and at once assumed responsibility for the redemption of all Dominion Bank Notes and the repayment of all borrowings under the Finance Act—the necessary process of transition to the new system.

The transition stage from the Finance Act to the Bank of Canada was accomplished with relative ease. The chartered banks were required to repay their Finance Act borrowings (about $35 million) in Dominion Notes. To avoid the potential loss of reserves which this would entail, the new Bank of Canada purchased Treasury Bills to the same value, the proceeds of which were used to repurchase by the government *other* Treasury Bills owned by banks to the same amount. The result of this transaction was to leave the chartered banks with the same amount of reserves as before, but their structure had been changed. Instead of Dominion Bank Notes, bank reserves consisted of Bank of Canada notes and deposits.[10] The transition was completed in short order. Canada's money supply now rested on a structure of Bank of Canada notes and deposits at the Central Bank rather than on Dominion Notes and gold. But having accomplished this much, then what? The fact of the matter was that the Bank and its staff had to prove itself to be more than just a "fifth wheel to the coach" (Governor Towers' words in his first annual report to the shareholders), yet no one in Canada really knew from experience what central banking was all about. Consider the situation. It was well known that a central bank should control the money supply by manipulating the reserves of the banking system, but when depression conditions call for the easiest monetary policy possible and reserves are already ample and interest rates low, what *else* can the central bank do? The difficulty was that it could not influence the liquidity structure of the economy and that, precisely, was what was required. Businessmen, in a word, did not desire additional liquidity and banks were not willing to accept the risk involved in assuming illiquid positions for their assets; consequently no new employment could be generated. Under the circumstances, the best the Bank of Canada could do was to avoid any possible roadblocks of tight money.

From a theoretical viewpoint it was clear that Graham Towers saw the most important function of the Bank of Canada as acting upon the volume of chartered banks' reserves. "When a country is not on the gold standard, the central bank can do more than affect the commercial banks' cash reserves; it *determines* them." Hence, "An expansion of cash reserves tends to produce an increase in the commercial banks' loans and investments; a contraction of reserves tends to produce a curtailment of these assets."[11]

Far from the actual implementation of these principles, the Bank spent its initial "formative" years in laying the foundation, developing the expertise, and, generally, gaining the experience appropriate to the art of central banking. A great deal of consultation with other government departments (Ottawa was a small town then), particularly finance, took place. After all, the Depression was a new experience and no one had the answers to the problems it posed, and certainly no one had the statistics to evaluate and quantify either the magnitudes of the problems or the effects of policy measures.

With the outbreak of war came the necessity to finance the expenditures for war so that once more easy money was essential. Chartered banks had to purchase government securities through the deposit manufacturing mechanism and thereby provide the funds. In order to make these purchases possible, reserves had to be

---

[10]The comparison between the two structures can be seen by the following:

March 10, 1935		Dec. 31, 1935	
Dominion Bank Notes in circulation and at the Banks	$220 million	Bank of Canada Notes in circulation and at the Banks	$99.7 million
Gold in Chartered Banks	37 million	Deposits at the Central Bank	181.6 million
TOTAL	$257 million	TOTAL	$281.6 million

G. F. Towers, *First Annual General Meeting of Shareholders, Bank of Canada,* 25 February, 1936, pp. 8–9.

[11]*Ibid.,* p. 11.

ample, and once more the Bank of Canada had to continue its easy money policy. The result was that security holdings of the chartered banking system increased by three times during the seven years 1939 to 1946.[12] During the same period, total money supply, defined as the bank notes held by the public plus all chartered bank deposits, rose from $3.2 billion to $7.5 billion.[13]

A rather interesting and prophetic observation by Governor Towers was included in the Annual Report for 1943. It shows the extent to which the Bank of Canada was becoming aware of the immensity of the surplus capacity in Canada during the Depression.

> . . .In terms of employment and, to a smaller degree, standards of living, the contrast with the depressed years before the war was striking. In the later stages, of course, war expenditure has increased more rapidly than national production and average living standards are therefore declining. But the experience of the last four years has shown that Government war expenditure on a sufficient scale can produce full employment.
>
> These developments undoubtedly have made a deep impression upon the public mind. There may be a tendency to conclude that Government expenditure for other purposes, at a high enough level, is all that is required to prevent depression in peace time.[14]

A. Central Banking and the Chartered Banks

Governor Towers' statement regarding the function of a central bank is interesting on two counts. It is not, strictly speaking, correct in the sense that the Bank of Canada alone does not and cannot determine the level of reserve of chartered banks. Secondly, the statement is also only partially correct with reference to the absence of the gold standard since it depends entirely upon how "gold standard" is defined. In the Canadian interpretation, it means the sale or purchase of monetary gold by the government. The United States was on the "gold standard" in this sense until relatively recent times since it purchased and sold gold at $35 (U.S.)/oz. At the same time, the Federal Reserve Board did affect member banks' reserves rather successfully. Yet, from another point of view the U.S. was *off* the gold standard in the sense that gold coin and bullion could not be used for domestic money supply.

Assuming what Mr. Towers had in mind was the gold reserve as a determinant of the money supply, when did Canada go *off* the gold standard? We do not know, for obviously Mr. Bennett, the Prime Minister, in his statement to the House of Commons during the 1930 special session still clung to a gold "backing" of the Canadian dollar. Sometime between 1930 and the Order in Council of 1940 the "fiction" of remaining on a gold standard was quietly dropped.

But this is precisely what the western Social Credit MP's had in mind when they first requested that the issue of Dominion Notes be increased by statutory means. In this way they had hoped to eliminate the obstacle of an absence of liquidity which was hindering the expansion of production and employment. What neither they nor the government understood however was that easy money, whether by an expansion of Dominion Bank Notes or by ample reserves in the Bank of Canada, was not enough. It is a necessary but not sufficient condition for restoring economic activity via the monetary route and, to be effective, must be accompanied by an increase in the desire of borrowers to become more liquid as well as the willingness of banks to correspondingly reduce their asset liquidity. This, borrowers were not prepared to do.

1. Cash Reserve Requirement

The best way to define the relationship between the Bank of Canada and the chartered banks is by way of a balance sheet (or T table). In the analysis which follows, the approximate rates of percentage used to develop a hypothetical balance sheet are fairly typical of the proportions

---

[12]E. M. Rosengren, *Readings in Money and Banking*, University of Toronto Press, 1947, p. 57.

[13]Appendix A, Annual Report of the Governor of the Bank of Canada, 1946.

[14]Annual Report to Minister of Finance, February 9, 1942, p. 11. Mr. Towers has in mind, of course, fiscal measures as distinct from monetary policy.

BANK OF CANADA (IN PERCENTAGES)

Assets		Liabilities		
Government Securities	75	Bank of Canada Notes	60	
		Deposits		
		Government of Canada	5	10↑
		Chartered Banks	30	25↓
Other	25	Other	5	
TOTAL	100	TOTAL	100	

which actually exist today. An exception to this is made for the deposits of the Government of Canada which are, in reality, a miniscule percentage of the total but for convenience are represented as 5%.

About 75% of the total assets/liabilities of the Bank of Canada consists of government (federal government only) securities, i.e., Treasury Bills and bonds of varying maturity. Were we still on a gold standard, this entry would be gold, or if our Central Bank and monetary system were modeled after the Continental countries, the entry would be gold *plus* foreign exchange. The differences are important and will be discussed in greater detail in the next chapter.

At any rate, the only significant assets held by the Bank of Canada are government securities. It is by means of these securities that the Bank makes loans to the Government; thus, when the Bank purchases Bonds or Treasury Bills, it does so by the simple expedient of increasing the Government of Canada deposit on the liabilities side by the amount of the purchase. In a real sense a deposit has been created merely by means of an accounting entry.

This may appear somewhat strange at first sight — the fact of deposit creation. For chartered banks the term "deposit manufacture" is more appropriate since a raw material deposit is first required, but not for the Bank of Canada. Here it is a genuine *creation*. The "backing" against these created deposits is simply Federal debt. At one time it would have been gold, and, presumably, this would have inspired confidence in our currency and our credit-worthiness abroad; but no longer. The world is more sophisticated, aware that other things—natural resources, real growth rates of the Gross National Product, etc., are more important than gold.

On the liabilities side are Bank of Canada notes which constitute the cash in circulation and in the tills of the chartered banks. These notes, liabilities of the Bank of Canada, are the approximate equivalent of the old Dominion Bank Notes which were the liabilities of the Ministry of Finance. We know that whenever the public wishes, it can withdraw these notes from the chartered banks (or through a financial intermediary first, then a chartered bank) by substituting them for its deposit entries at the chartered banks. In this case, the amount of notes in the hands of the public rises as the notes in banks' tills go down, leaving total bank notes issued as Bank of Canada liabilities unchanged.

The next item, Deposits, particularly those of the chartered banks, is the most important for our purpose. These deposits are the major portion of the cash reserves of the chartered banks and all transactions between the chartered banks and the Bank of Canada take place by means of these deposits. Payments into the Bank of Canada are affected by reducing these deposits while payments to the chartered banks from the Bank of Canada increase these deposits. It only remains to develop some logical mechanism whereby these deposits may be increased (or decreased) to justify Governor Towers' somewhat strong assertion that the central bank determines reserves. Again a question may arise, when chartered bank deposits decline, where do they go? The answer is, quite simply, they are "de-created" (destroyed). This is the converse of deposit creation and in the process either some other liability must increase or an asset be reduced.

As an example of the operation of the mechanism, suppose that both corporate and personal income taxes are to be collected by the Receiver General on behalf of the Government of Canada. These taxes will first appear in the Government accounts in the chartered banks, but since the central bank is the Government's banker, the tax revenues must appear, before they can be disbursed, in the Government account at the central bank. Assuming that an amount of 5 is to be transferred to the Bank of Canada, this is accomplished by merely lowering the value of chartered bank deposits from 30 to 25 and increasing the Government's deposits from 5 to 10 (see arrows). Of course, the appropriate accounting adjustments are made by the chartered banks as well, but the final adjustment, the one that matters, is that of payments to the central bank from the chartered banks which are made by transferring from chartered bank accounts to the Government account. The consequence is that chartered bank deposits, which are the major portion of their reserves, are now less than before. Unless the Bank of Canada takes appropriate action to increase the chartered bank deposits, the banks themselves will have to find additional deposits by selling some liquid assets; otherwise, their liquid asset ratio may be too low.

One of the more common techniques of affecting banks' reserves is through open market operations. When we speak of the "open market" in this sense, we mean, quite simply, a group of dealers who purchase and sell securities in the course of their normal daily business. They often act as underwriters taking up securities, including government bonds, ultimately to place them with final purchasers. They also purchase securities for their own account with the expectation of selling at a profit, and, of course, sell when the opportunity arises.

These dealers, incidentally, are a very important part of our Canadian capital market; indeed, it is through them that much of our savings is channeled into investment. Through their many branch offices throughout Canada and the world, securities are sold to the general public at a market price dictated purely by the market forces of supply and demand. Thus the function of the dealers, as far as the Bank of Canada's open market operation is concerned, is quite incidental, i.e., their business from which their profits derive has nothing to do with the Bank of Canada's operations in the money market. They happen to be the instrument by which the Bank's open market operations are affected.[15]

Referring once more to the assets side of the T

table, the Government Securities included therein constitute the Bank of Canada's major thrust in terms of influencing the banking and financial system. The Bank is continuously buying and selling securities in the market both on its own account, and, sometimes, to give support to market prices. It also has a third objective, that of affecting chartered bank deposits. Suppose that the Bank is a net seller of securities, i.e., it reduces its portfolio of assets, by the end of a single day. Someone, a dealer in the bond market referred to above, will write a cheque payable to the Bank of Canada drawn against his own account with a chartered bank. The Bank of Canada will collect by subtracting from the chartered bank deposit on the liabilities side of the T table, hence reducing some specific chartered bank's reserves. Of course, the precise opposite happens should the Bank of Canada be a net buyer of government securities, thereby increasing its portfolio. The cheque would be presented to the Bank for collection by crediting the relevant chartered bank's deposit to the value of the cheque and total reserves would therefore increase.

As far as the chartered banks are concerned, what happens as reserves increase is that banks would find their reserves in surplus. The entry "Cash and Deposits at the Bank of Canada" would be larger than necessary for meeting the statutory reserve requirement plus a slight margin of safety. Banks would likely proceed to make more loans, purchase additional securities, or otherwise attempt to expand assets until the excess reserves are exhausted. The exhaustion would occur because deposits have expanded. Conversely, if the reserves are less than the statutory requirement, the banks must find additional deposits by selling liquid assets so as to transfer the extra deposits so acquired to their accounts at the Bank of Canada. In this way statutory reserve requirements are met.

2. Secondary Reserve Requirement

In any banking system, Canada's included, some provision must be made for liquid funds which are readily available when the immediate cash requirement is insufficient. Banks traditionally like

---

[15] The word "dealers" actually means very large and

successful corporations, names of which are so well-known as to be almost household words. McLeod, Young, and Weir; Pitfield, McKay, Ross, and Greenshields are a few examples.

to have such liquid funds on hand, but, at the same time, do not want to lose the opportunity of interest earned. Since cash and deposits at the Bank of Canada do not earn interest, it is convenient and profitable to have available some assets which can be readily converted into cash, yet earn some interest.

During the years prior to the Bank of Canada, i.e., under the regime of the Finance Act, the "secondary reserves" (assets which earn interest but are close to cash) of Canadian banks were largely call loans and bankers' acceptances in New York. The success of this system hinged on the existence of the agencies of the Canadian banks in New York itself; hence, very many call loans were made during the great bull market on Wall Street during the 1920s.[16] Bank acceptances are similar to bills of exchange but are drawn against a bank which accepts them. Banks acquire ready short-term deposits in this way, and once accepted, they can be sold by the drawer on the money market. Being of highest quality, the acceptance is risk-free and is an excellent method of holding secondary reserves.

The most interesting feature of this type of market for secondary reserves was that liquid investments were in foreign exchange; hence, in the event that ready deposits in Canadian dollars were required for cash reserves, it was necessary to use the foreign exchange market at the same time that call loans or acceptances were liquidated. During the early depression years, the fluctuating exchange rate of the Canadian dollar made the New York market a much more risky proposition than before. For this reason, it was considered to be important that a Canadian market be established to replace New York and the development of that market became a primary concern of the Bank of Canada during its earlier years under the governorship of Mr. Towers.

The essential point of a money market from a banker's point of view is that short-term, highly liquid loans can be made and just as readily recalled. This can be done through the instrument of a trade bill. (The term "trade bill" is used in its broadest sense to cover all types of bills of

exchange, both commercial and short-term debt instruments.) Such bills are drawn by a creditor against a debtor, and orders the debtor to pay a certain sum of money on a specified date. When the debtor accepts the bill, he signs it with his acceptance and the bill then becomes an instrument to be sold on the market. The purchaser of the bill, say the chartered banks, will pay something less than the bill's value — the difference being the discount. When banks acquire short-term funds in this way and honour their own obligations with their own signatures, the bill becomes a banker's acceptance. Banks, of course, may purchase other bankers' acceptances as a high quality, low risk, short-term investment.

The highest quality and most risk-free of such bills are Government Treasury Bills. Generally issued for 91 days, Treasury Bills have been useful instruments through which governments may acquire ready cash at the lowest rate. At the same time, they have been useful for banks as liquid assets since they could purchase these, suitably discounted, and hold them to maturity. After the money market was established in Canada in 1954, the Bills could become a ready source of cash simply by selling them on the market. The cheque, so acquired, could then be turned over directly to the Bank of Canada for additional cash reserves if required. But such a market did not exist in Canada in the 1930s and it was to the establishment of this market that Mr. Towers and the Bank of Canada expected to make important contributions.

The money market itself became a reality by the end of Mr. Towers' 20-year tenure as Governor. In 1953, the Bank of Canada established the purchase and resale agreement with those dealers in the market who undertook jobbing responsibilities. These dealers, pledged to bid for Treasury Bills at the offering, are able to sell Bills from their portfolio to the Bank of Canada so as to raise additional funds whenever they happen to be short. At the same time, the agreement is made to repurchase the Bills at a stated price over a short time span, about $2^1/_2$ days on the average. In the following year, 1954, day-to-day loans were introduced. Through this method, chartered banks make available funds to the jobbers themselves for the purchase of Treasury Bills at the weekly tender. These loans are callable, as the name implies, on a daily basis, and hence, are particularly useful for secondary re-

---

[16]A call loan is money loaned to brokers or stock dealers which must be repaid within 24 hours after call. The stock itself is the security for the loan and in a declining market, additional securities must be pledged to maintain the correct ratio of loans to market value of securities.

serves; by presenting the borrowers' cheques to the Bank of Canada for clearing, reserves may be adjusted the following day.

The question may arise, what happens when the 91 day Treasury Bill matures? The government must, of course, honour its obligation and does so by running down its balances at the banks. These balances, in turn, are built up either by taxation or by borrowing through the sale of additional Treasury Bills or by the sale of longer term bonds to the public. In this last eventuality the debt of the government is "funded." The Bank of Canada as fiscal agent for the government manages such sales when the obligations of the government, both Treasury Bills and long-term bonds, fall due.

The institution of the money market in Canada meant not only a cheap supply of funds, always available to the government, but also a domestic secondary reserve for banks. It was now possible for banks to supplement their legal cash reserves at any time by calling in day-to-day loans or selling Treasury Bills from their own assets on the market itself. At first, this was a source of concern to Mr. James Coyne, the second Governor of the Bank of Canada. In 1955, after some considerable discussion with chartered banks, an agreement was reached to the effect that a 15% ratio of liquid assets (cash, Treasury Bills, day-to-day loans) would be maintained as of May 31, 1956. Considering that the Bank Act revision of 1954 had raised the cash reserve ratio to 8% and an amendment to the Bank of Canada Act gave the Bank the power to raise the liquid asset ratio to a total of only 12% of deposits; this agreement was something of an achievement. Now, of course, the Bank of Canada under the 1967 revision of the Bank of Canada Act has the power to establish a secondary reserve ratio varying between 0 and 12%. This replaces the voluntary agreement of 7% (15% less the compulsory 8% cash reserve ratio) reached in 1955.

3. Monetary Policy

Whereas it is desirable to establish a central bank in Canada to regulate credit and currency in the best interests of the economic life of the nation, to control and protect the external value of the national monetary unit and to mitigate its influence, fluctuations in the general level of production, trade, prices, and employment, so far as may be possible within the scope of monetary action and generally to promote the economic and financial welfare of the Dominion...[17]

A masterpiece of generality! Practically any policy or action may be undertaken by the Bank of Canada without violating either the word or spirit of the Preamble. Yet, if the Bank is to be effective at all, it must have the freedom within some such sweeping phrases as these to conduct a definitive, rational policy. Such a policy, presumably, would be worked out in joint consultation with the government of the day. Then, implementation of the policy would involve just two basic control mechanisms — the cash reserves of the chartered banks and the secondary reserves, both of which are statutory.

Using these two mechanisms alone, to what extent *does* the Bank of Canada influence the supply of "credit and currency in the best interests of the nation, etc., etc."? In other words, is there such an instrument known as "monetary policy" which can be used to influence economic activity through the banking system? This question may seem surprising in that it has always been assumed that monetary policy does exist and does indeed influence the economy, but the fact is that attempts to control the economy do appear to be quite different from actual results.

In the last chapter, the banking system was seen as an intermediator between the saving sector and the borrowing sector, or, more specifically, equating the marginal utilities of two different sets of liquidities. Consider the T table on page 107 representing the combined assets and liabilities of the chartered banks:

The savers, or lenders, have an ordered structure of liquidity as represented by the amounts in each of the categories on the liabilities side. The borrowers, on the other hand, structure their liquidity in accordance with what the banks can offer and what they can afford to pay. The central bank tries to affect what liquidity the banks can offer by altering the first category of assets with the consequence as outlined in the following chain of events:

(1) The deposits at the Bank of Canada, we will assume, are reduced by any of the methods dis-

---

[17]Preamble to the Bank of Canada Act.

CHARTERED BANKS

Assets	Liabilities
1. Cash and deposits at Bank of Canada	1. Demand deposits
2. Day/day loans and Treasury Bills	2. Personal savings deposits
3. Government securities	3. Non-personal term and notice deposits
4. General loans	4. Government of Canada deposits

cussed above. Chartered banks will have to restore these reserves to an appropriate percentage (12% of demand deposits and 4% of savings deposits) before the current half-monthly period has expired, i.e., the *daily average* during the two-week period must be restored.

(2) The banks will likely have no alternative but to call in their day-to-day loans from the money market. This they may do with 24 hours notice. If necessary they may even sell Treasury Bills or permit those nearest to maturity to run out without replacing them. Funds in either case will become available for replenishing their Bank of Canada deposits.

(3) Should there happen to be neither excess cash reserves nor excess secondary reserves, some replenishing of both these categories must take place. In the secondary reserve case, the banks have a month to bring their reserves up to the statutory level (5% of total deposits as of February, 1977). Their next move will be to sell short-term government securities from within category 3 and acquire the necessary funds to replenish their secondary reserves. Short-term securities will be sold because this they can do with the minimum risk of capital loss; hence, these will certainly be run down before longer-term securities are sold.

Before continuing the sequential pattern of events, we should pause long enough to see just what is happening to the cost/revenue structure of the banks. In the first place, the calling in of day-to-day loans to replenish reserves means a loss of revenue because Bank of Canada deposits pay no interest. Of course, a similar revenue loss will occur from the liquidation of Treasury Bills because the yields on these are generally higher than on day-to-day loans. In the second place, a sale of short-term government bonds (category 3 of chartered bank assets) also involves a loss of revenue because the yields on these bonds, short term though they may be, is generally higher than either the day-to-day rates or the Treasury Bill rates. The consequence of

this is the slope of the total revenue function of the banks will become less. Should it become necessary to sell long-term bonds (longer term to maturity) the loss of revenue could conceivably be quite severe.

Faced with this situation, banks have a very effective means of protecting their profits, but before considering this, we should look once more at the nature of the two different sets of liquidity with which banks are concerned. Depositors, as we have seen, have an automatic preference for 100% liquidity. They are the non-spenders who were discussed in Chapter 2. Borrowers constitute another set of individuals who desire to increase their current liquidity, i.e., they already have too little, and when they borrow they acquire an increment of current liquidity to the amount of the loan. In the process of acquiring additional current liquidity there is a sacrifice (or "trade-off") of future liquidity which must be made as loan repayment. The amount of future liquidity foregone in this way depends entirely upon the current liquidity borrowed plus an amount determined by the rate of interest.

Now the banks as intermediaries act as a bridge between the two *desired* and very different liquidities. If it is possible to shorten the span, the bridge becomes likewise shorter. This the banks can do by encouraging depositors to part with some of their 100% liquidity by transferring some of their demand deposits into savings deposits (from category 1 to category 2 in the liabilities). Banks can do this by offering a reward in the form of interest for savings deposits. But as they do so they push their cost curves upward. Does this not increase their costs at the same time that revenues are declining?

The answer to this puzzle lies in the quality of "stickability" which savings deposits possess and demand deposits do not. Surrendering liquidity by depositors means that banks not only need keep less cash reserves (now 4% as against 12%) but also that longer term loans can be made at the higher interest rates that these loans command without having to meet all their depositors' liquidity requirements. This is how the gap between the two sets of liquidities can be narrowed — through the quality of stickability. So at the same time that the total costs of the banks rise, the revenue function will increase its slope, thereby compensating for the initial loss of revenue, as longer term, less liquid loans can be accommodated. Of course, a general round of higher interest rates on all loans will likely occur as the shorter-term, day-to-day loans seek to reassert themselves within the asset structure of the banks. Competition for *all* loans, in other words, becomes more severe.

(4) This brings us to our final point in the sequence of events—tight money. The quantity of credit has become less than the requirements for credit with the results that the *cost* of money has risen. From the chartered banks' point of view, a rationing process takes place since the raw material required for manufacturing deposits is in short supply. Banks find it difficult to accommodate all the borrowers because the reserves are just not great enough and the necessary bank liquidity is absent. But what about the fourth category of assets, general loans? These are the last to be restricted because they are both the most profitable and the longest term of all the assets. Banks will protect these to the end, even to the point of offering new and more varied means of increasing the stickability of their deposits.

Now, the interesting feature of the entire sequential analysis is that monetary policy was in the first place probably aimed at restricting an excess of effective demand which was generating inflationary pressures. This can be done by reducing the availability of loans and is, in fact, what "regulation of credit" in the Preamble to the Bank of Canada Act means. We are, thus, presented with the curious anomaly that while the central bank may aim at loan restriction, the chartered banks do all in their power to deflect the aim; indeed, to postpone hitting the target, for only at the last resort will the chartered banks restrict their most profitable assets, general loans.

A Case in Point:

Chart 5-1 (see pages 110 and 111) extracted from the Monthly Bulletin of the Bank of Canada, offers an excellent opportunity to observe a tight monetary policy in action during the latter 1960s and early 1970s. On the right are the different categories of liquid assets plotted against time — 1968 through 1972. The first of the series, statutory, primary and secondary reserves, is a "step function" indicating the result of calculating secondary reserves on a monthly basis. There is, therefore, a series of 12 "steps" for each year. (If primary, or cash, reserves were shown separately there would be 24 steps per year for the reason that these are calculated on a half-monthly basis.) Occasionally the steps become jumps, e.g., June, 1969 and July, 1970. These jumps were the consequence of upward adjustments in the required secondary reserve ratio — 8% in June, 1969 and 9% in July, 1970.

The next series is the free Canadian dollar liquid assets. These are very sensitive in their reaction; consequently, the best way, and probably the *only* way, to identify changes in the monetary policy of the Bank of Canada is to observe the behaviour of these "free" reserves as published weekly by the Bank of Canada. They include any excess secondary reserves, government bonds, call loans (loans subject to call extended to investment dealers and brokers) and any excess Bank of Canada notes. It is these free reserves which are the source of immediate liquidity and are used as a reservoir from which statutory cash and secondary reserves are replenished at a moment's notice.

The third series, net foreign assets, are another source of liquid assets. These are "hangovers" from the old Finance Act days when investments in the New York money market were common as the only feasible store of liquidity which, at the same time, offered some interest on investments. Even today they are still used for that purpose, utilizing the facilities of the forward markets in foreign exchange to overcome the problems posed by exchange fluctuation.

The last two series are simply ratios which relate free Canadian dollar liquid assets to total assets and "total liquid assets" (as opposed to the *excess* of actual vs. statutory which are used in calculating free assets) to the total of all assets. With the aid of these ratios we can at a glance determine the liquidity of chartered banks; in other words, the effectiveness of the current monetary policy of the Bank of Canada.

On the left are most of the non-liquid assets, general loans and two sub-classifications, business and personal loans. It is these at which the thrust of a typical tight monetary policy is directed during periods when the economy becomes "overheated" through excess demand. (Currently, as will be shown later, the target of monetary policy has become the money supply instead of loans.) The objective of the policy is to curb these loans until the productive capacity of the economy has grown sufficiently to accommodate any excess demand.

In the autumn of 1968, the Federal Government initiated its policy of tight money with the avowed purpose of fighting inflation and rising prices. Consumer prices had been rising at a level of $3\frac{1}{2}$ to $4\frac{1}{2}$% per annum which was considered at that time to be an excessive rate of increase. The consequence was that free reserves started their steep decline both in absolute terms and in terms of percentage of major assets. This was accompanied by corresponding declines in both the "free" liquid asset ratio and the liquid asset ratio showing that banks were becoming less liquid during the period.

We recall that the target of the policy was a restriction of loans and credit which were swelling total effective demand beyond the capacity of the Canadian economy to produce. However, as is shown in the charts, neither business nor personal loans moderated their general upward growth trends (n.b., the graphs are semi-logarithmic indicating rates of growth by the slope) until about the mid-point of 1969—a lag of some 6 to 9 months. Banks were finally forced to moderate their loan expansion only after their liquidity positions had run to dangerously low levels.

Meantime, the causes of the recession of the early 1970s were gaining momentum. Unemployment during the first quarter of 1970 had reached 5.1%, seasonally adjusted, of the labour force to close the year at 6.5%. At the same time, the consumer price level continued its upward trend at 4.6% per year in 1969 and 1970. Keeping in mind the stated objective of the tight monetary policy of 1969, to moderate inflationary tendencies in that year, it can be argued that: (1) the shot took far too long to reach the target, and (2) it hit the *wrong* target. The result was that the various producing industries in the economy experienced a *shortage* of funds so that unemployment rose. (The reasons for this have already been discussed in Chapter 2.) By the time tight monetary policy had become sufficiently effective to

moderate inflation, it succeeded in deepening unemployment.

In March, 1970 a complete reversal of monetary policy took place. Reserves were eased, with the result that ample opportunity for loan expansion existed. Unfortunately, however, only personal loans seem to have responded to the easier credit conditions; for business enterprise, confidence was shaken and there was no method of forcing businessmen back to borrow, or, more accurately, incur the risk of future liquidity foregone (we cannot push on a string). The deposit manufacturing mechanism of the chartered banks took the alternative form of restoring bank liquidity to what it had been before through the purchase by the banking system of government debt, call loans, day-to-day loans, etc., assets which are not only liquid but involve the creation of deposits for the financial sector of the community as opposed to the producing sector. The consequence of this was a general collapse of short-term interest rates as the supply of short-term money expanded relative to demand.

The period of monetary ease lasted throughout the year 1970, as is clearly evidenced by the restoration of the banks' former high liquidity positions. Business loans, however, did not resume their upward trend until 1971, yet the "target" in this case was the reduction of unemployment which was over 6% of the labour force, seasonally adjusted. Here, of course, the Bank of Canada is at its weakest with the string analogy as most apt. The best that could be done, so it seemed at the time, was to permit a massive expansion of bank liquidity in anticipation of rising business loans, and this was the Bank of Canada's reaction to the enormous public pressure to take whatever action it could to reduce unemployment.

With the onset of "hyper-inflation" (two-digit inflation) the central bank moved once more to a policy of tight money, but this time to a more "gentle squeeze." Free Canadian dollar liquid assets were gradually reduced in absolute value, but as a percentage of total major assets, they fell to below 10%, considerably lower than in March, 1970 (see Chart 2). Banks were once again "dry" and were forced into high deposit rates of interest in order to reduce the liquidity requirements of depositors. (It is interesting also that banks found that they could protect their domestic liquidity positions by running down their foreign currency

Chart 5-1

CHARTERED BANKS   CANADIAN DOLLAR LOANS
SEASONALLY ADJUSTED-MONTHLY

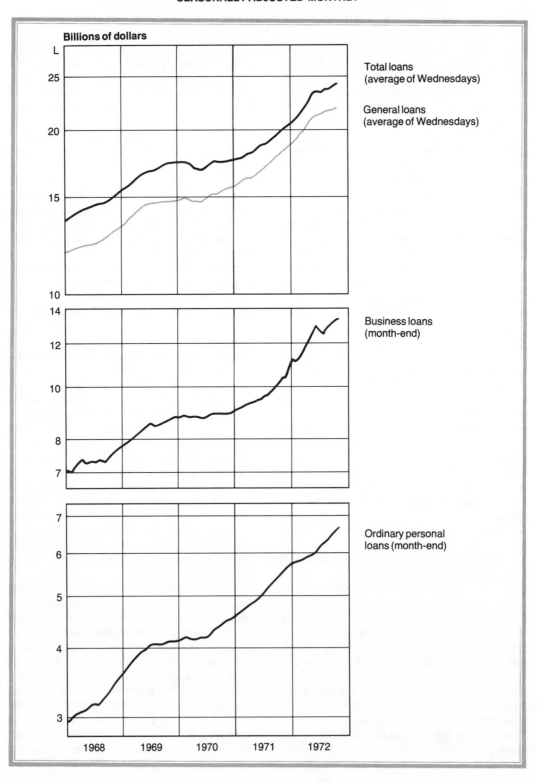

Billions of dollars

Total loans
(average of Wednesdays)

General loans
(average of Wednesdays)

Business loans
(month-end)

Ordinary personal
loans (month-end)

1968   1969   1970   1971   1972

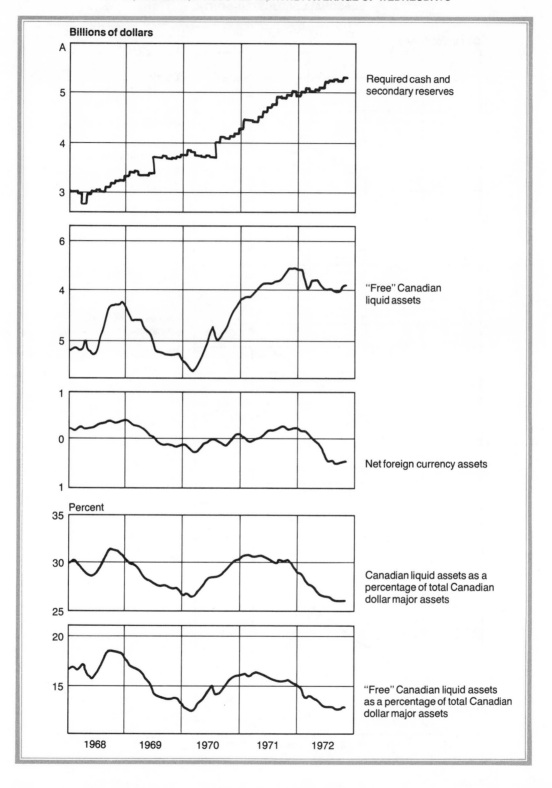

Chart 5-2

**CHARTERED BANKS   CANADIAN DOLLAR LOANS
SEASONALLY ADJUSTED-MONTHLY**

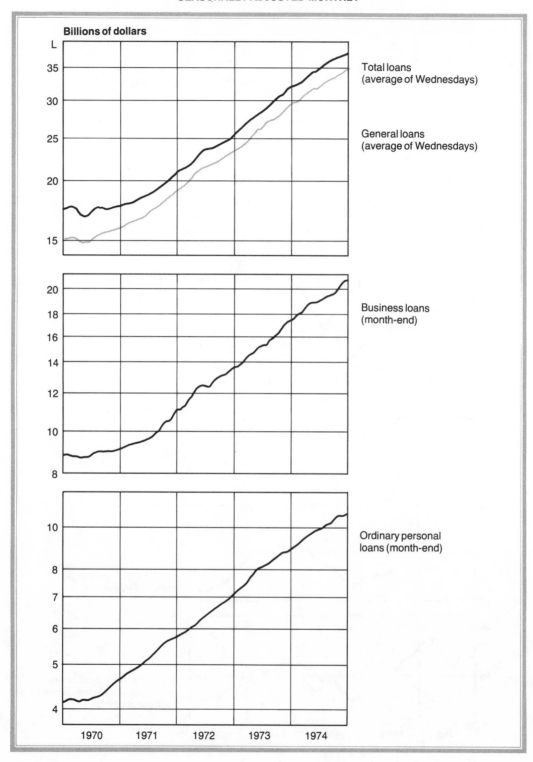

CANADIAN LIQUID ASSETS AND NET FOREIGN ASSETS
NOT SEASONALLY ADJUSTED-MONTHLY AVERAGE OF WEDNESDAYS

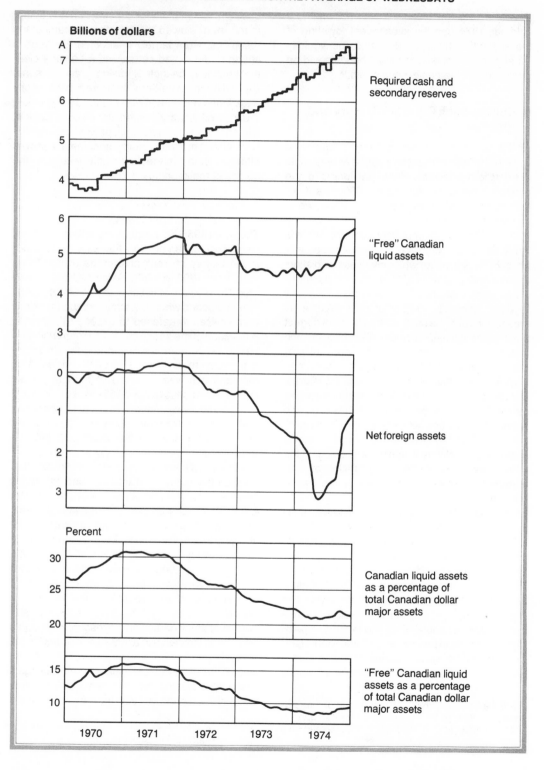

Billions of dollars

Required cash and secondary reserves

"Free" Canadian liquid assets

Net foreign assets

Percent

Canadian liquid assets as a percentage of total Canadian dollar major assets

"Free" Canadian liquid assets as a percentage of total Canadian dollar major assets

1970   1971   1972   1973   1974

assets to very low levels.) It was not until late summer, 1974 and the subsequent lowering of the secondary reserve ratios that the liquidity situation eased and government bonds could be purchased by the banks once again.[18]

B. Central Bank Control—Theory and Practice

All this raises the question as to the efficacy and appropriateness of monetary policy, at least in its extreme forms. In terms of the "fine tuning" of the economy that was intended in 1969, it is likely that the economic problems to be resolved were, instead, accentuated.

It also raises another important question: What is it that should be controlled, the money supply or loans? This is a matter which involves two distinct and conflicting schools of thought. At first blush it would seem that since loans and deposits move together, generally, control of one necessarily means control of the other. In theory this is correct but in practice it means conducting policy in such a way that, to influence loan demand, interest rates must rise or fall to encourage or discourage borrowing. The bank in this case uses the interest rate structure and the capital market as a barometer in its conduct of policy. Emphasis on the supply of money and deposits, on the other hand, means a Quantity Theory interpretation which uses the total volume of money as its guide. In the former case a Keynesian interpretation of economics is involved; in the latter, a Monetarist approach.

For the Bank of Canada this question never really appeared until some years after World War II. Until that time, the depression and wartime finance meant that monetary policy must be one of continuous ease—simply a projection of the old Finance Act. About the middle of the 1950s, it became apparent that all was not quite well. The fear of a massive post-war depression reminiscent of 1929 was subsiding, and in 1954, a post-Korean recession had developed attendant upon the winding down of defence expenditures. Some sectors of the Canadian economy, particularly

business expenditure for construction and equipment, had slowed while others, particularly resources, were largely unaffected. By 1955 a strong rebound had set in, and it became clear that continued finance of business and personal expenditures (long-term chartered bank mortgage loans had already been introduced) would likely be inflationary. For the first time the Bank of Canada saw fit to exercise its powers as a central bank in that monetary policy became active with attempts being made to directly influence the course of the economy.

1. Monetary Policy— "Leaning Against the Wind"

The years 1955-56, perhaps more than any other single period, can be identified as a "watershed" in the history of Bank of Canada policy. To be sure, from 1950 to 1953, policy had been operated "to prevent excessive expansion of credit during a period when the total demand for goods and services threatened to exceed the growing production of the economy."[19] The reference here was to the Korean War boom and the unusually high pressure of demand for commodities. And, following this was a period of monetary ease during the recession of 1953-54, but by 1955 it became very clear to most observers that the productive capacity of Canada was being strained to the point that inflation threatened.

There were a number of economic indicators that showed the strength of this demand for goods and services. The first of these was the achievement of full employment of the labour force. Keeping in mind that these were years of considerable labour force *expansion* (in 1955 the labour force grew by 2.1% over 1954 and 3% in 1956 over 1955), an unemployment rate of 3.4% for 1955 was very low indeed. In fact, during spring and summer of that year, seasonal activity reduced the rate to only 1.7%. The second indicator was investment particularly in resource industries which was indicative of a massive resource boom which began in 1956 and continued well into the end of the decade. The expenditure on oil, gas, and hydro-electric development projects was about 60% higher in 1956 than in 1955. Along

---

[18]See the Bank of Canada Annual Report of the Governor for 1974, p. 31. For the first time the Bank of Canada transactions in securities was presented on a month-by-month basis in this Report.

[19]Annual Report of the Governor, 1954, p. 9.

with this development in resources, business investment in manufacturing and services was higher by some 20% in 1956 over 1955. Government expenditures, particularly provincial, were also rising.[20]

All of this was accompanied by rising consumer expenditures, the third indicator of threatened inflation. This was reflected in a rising consumer price index which during the year 1956 began an upward trend to reach an annual rate of 3.2%. Other indexes were also showing the results of excessive pressure of demand, particularly the investment goods sector. Finally, the fourth indicator of excessive demand, the balance of payments deficit on current account, reached $1.4 billion in 1956 as opposed to $700 million in 1955.

It was clear to the Bank that Canada was balanced on the edge of a classic inflation resulting from an excess of domestic demand. The Bank of Canada, therefore, proceeded to take the appropriate monetary action to restrain the growth of bank credit which was clearly excessive relative to savings in the economy. Its actions involved a number of measures including specific requests that the chartered banks restrain their term lending. Another was an encouragement of the Canadian stock exchanges to reduce their lending on margins, and a third was an attempt, though unsuccessful, to gain the cooperation of lenders within the consumer credit field in curbing their loans. All this is referred to as "moral suasion" in the literature of monetary policy.

At the same time, throughout 1956, the Bank of Canada maintained its operations so as to keep chartered bank reserves continuously tight; in fact, statutory reserves increased by only $27 million ($863 to $890 million)[21] with the result that total assets and liabilities of chartered banks could not grow appreciably. What happened was that an increasing amount of bank loans was financed through the sale of government bonds which also, incidentally, were the source of funds for the secondary reserves banks had agreed to maintain at a 7% level.

In its "holding operation" as far as the supply of money and credit were concerned, the Bank was

doing precisely what would have been done had Canada been on a purely gold standard except that gold is a sterner disciplinarian than a central bank. There is no "moral suasion" with gold; its operation is automatic. There is one other advantage in gold—no one can blame any one individual or institution for what happens. This quality could easily have been appreciated because immediately following the boom years of 1956 and the tight policy of the Bank, a business recession ensued in 1957.

While the Bank did move toward monetary ease in 1957, there was clear evidence of a slackening of demand in the export sector in particular and unemployment rose from 4.6% of the labour force in 1957 to 7% in 1958.

Now the dilemma arises. What should the policy of the Bank be? Obviously the tight restraint of 1956 should have been, and was, released. The consequence was an expansion of chartered bank assets by some $483 million in just 6 months. But, at the same time, this expansion did not move into business loans but into more liquid assets such as government bonds. It was not until 1959 that loans increased so abruptly that they actually became a cause for concern.

In 1960, unemployment reached 7% of the labour force, up from 5.6% in 1959 and 6.6% in 1958. At the same time, consumer price increases in 1960 were minimal, 1.2% over 1959 and 1% in 1959 over 1958. One could hardly argue, therefore, that inflation, as expressed in terms of a rising price level, was a threat. Nevertheless, to Mr. Coyne and the Bank of Canada, it was not correct to try to raise employment by means of increased spending.

The reason for the position of the Bank of Canada was still the underlying pressure of excessive demand which was mostly apparent in the huge deficits in the balance of payments on current account. These, in turn, were financed by corresponding imports of capital.

> It seems clear that the recent high levels of unemployment in Canada do not arise from a deficiency of total spending by Canadians, or of spending for capital purposes. A relatively very large fraction of our gross national expenditure has, however, been spent directly or indirectly on balance for imported goods and services, and has

---

[20] Annual Report of the Governor, 1956, pp. 37–38.
[21] Ibid., p. 42.

to that extent failed to provide employment in Canada.[22]

and even though price increases were minimal, Canada appeared to be balanced on a kind of razor's edge between price stability and inflationary price increases. Rising prices, therefore, which were the consequence of excessive expansion of the money supply, were an everpresent danger to be avoided. Certainly it was the responsibility of the Bank of Canada not to permit the money supply to expand too rapidly under such circumstances.

In retrospect, the Bank was not following a "tight" policy at all, certainly not so tight as a gold standard would have imposed. Chartered bank liabilities (the supply of money) did grow in 1960. The question was, ought the money supply to grow *faster* by means of lower interest rates to encourage loans and investments and thereby reduce unemployment? Again one should note that in 1960 short-term interest rates did fall from a 1959 peak of 6% to a low of about 3% in September. Thus the question really was one of a longer-term, easier monetary policy with an emphasis on lower interest rates in the longer term rather than a policy of "leaning against the wind" which produced fluctuating interest rates and a "not so slack" control of the banks—Mr. Coyne's general philosophy. Certainly unemployment which persisted through the years 1958 through 1961 was in Coyne's view the consequence of a tight monetary policy.

If unemployment was not caused by a deficiency in demand, what then *was* the cause? To Mr. Coyne,

> Undoubtedly one important reason for the slow rise of employment in goods-producing industries, and the decrease in the case of agriculture, has been the great input of capital in the form of machinery and equipment — mechanization and automation. Unfortunately for employment in Canada, a very high proportion of such machinery and equipment has been imported from other countries, instead of being researched, developed and produced in Canada providing a "growth industry" for

Canada in terms of employment and technological progress.[23]

in other words, what we know today as *structural* unemployment.

The conflict between Mr. Coyne's views and those of economists and politicians who followed a Keynesian approach was inevitable. This latter school of thought posited that unemployment was the consequence of a lack of effective demand. Unemployment meant unused capacity, in this case labour, and could be overcome by greater economic growth. Monetary policy, therefore, could play a major role in increasing demand and generating greater output since idle capacity existed in the economy.

2. An Active Policy Through Interest Rates

The use of monetary policy to relieve unemployment stems from the economic thinking of the post-Keynesian era following World War II. During the years of the Great Depression of the 1930s, Lord Keynes had published his great *General Theory of Employment, Interest and Money*. In this, and in the works which followed, it was developed somewhat rigorously that lowering interest rates, given a schedule of the marginal efficiency of capital, generally increases investment and, in turn, employment and national income via the investment multiplier mechanism. Furthermore, given a liquidity preference function on the part of the public, an expansion of the money supply will lower interest rates; hence, it follows that an expansive (easy) monetary policy will reduce unemployment.

While this is not the place to enter into a lengthy discussion of the endless argument which has developed on this particular issue, it would be appropriate to include a passage from the *General Theory* itself — a passage often overlooked by followers of Keynesian thinking.

> We have now introduced money into our *causal nexus* for the first time, and we are able to catch a first glimpse of the way in which changes in the quantity of money work their way into the economic system. If however, we are tempted to assert that money is the drink which stimulates the system to activity, we must remind our-

---

[22]J.E. Coyne, Annual Report of the Governor of the Bank of Canada, 1960, p. 14.

[23] *Ibid.*, p. 9.

selves that there may be several slips between the cup and the lip. For whilst an increase in the quantity of money may be expected, *cet. par.,* to reduce the rate of interest, this will not happen if the liquidity-preferences of the public are increasing more than the quantity of money; and whilst a decline in the rate of interest may be expected, *cet. par.*, to increase the volume of investment, this will not happen if the schedule of the marginal efficiency of capital is falling more rapidly than the rate of interest; and whilst an increase in the volume of investment may be expected, *cet. par.*, to increase employment, this may not happen if the propensity to consume is falling off. Finally, if employment increases, prices will rise in a degree partly governed by the shapes of the physical supply functions, and partly by the liability of the wage-unit to rise in terms of money. And when output has increased and prices have risen, the effect of this on liquidity-preference will be to increase the quantity of money necessary to maintain a given rate of interest.[24]

The last two sentences of the quoted passage are significant. The first of these anticipates a Phillips Curve relationship between employment and rising prices and the second shows the spiralling effect of a money supply increase since ever-increasing amounts of money will have to be produced by the banking system to keep interest rates low enough to maintain full employment. Nevertheless, it was the general consensus among politicians and economists alike that monetary policy should indeed be used as a device to stimulate employment. This, it would appear, is more of a convenience than fiscal policy because even though Keynes advocated deficit financing as a means of generating employment, politicians have consistently found it more difficult to implement than monetary policy. Mr. Coyne's refusal to accede to the pressures of the time culminated in his resignation and the appointment of Mr. Rasminsky as his successor. The following two passages from Mr. Rasminsky's first annual report indicate the abrupt change in policy and contrast sharply with Mr. Coyne's statement in the 1960 Annual Report quoted above.

> I believe that it is essential that the responsibilities in relation to monetary policy should be clarified in the public mind and in the legislation. I do not suggest a precise formula but have in mind two main principles to be established: (1) in the ordinary course of events, the Bank has the responsibility for monetary policy, and (2) if the Government disapproves of the monetary policy being carried out by the Bank it has the right and the responsibility to direct the Bank as to the policy which the Bank is to carry out.[25]

And again on the next page of the same report, the first for Mr. Rasminsky, we find the change in economic philosophy.

> The Central Bank has an important part to play in influencing the trend of interest rates in a direction appropriate to the economic situation. But an attempt on its part to impose a level of interest rates which appeared unrealistic to the market would impair confidence in the value of currency and present a serious obstacle to the orderly flow of funds through the market.[26]

Despite the *caveat* regarding the "value of currency" the thrust of the statement is directed toward interest rates, and this means the *assets* side of the balance sheets of the chartered banks, as opposed to the liabilities (deposits, etc.). It is in the assets of the banks that loans and other credit instruments are used to make available funds to borrowers at low rates of interest. Deposit creation becomes secondary to the primary objective of low interest rates.

Mr. Rasminsky left no doubt as to either his economic philosophy or his policies. To him adequate supplies of credit were important to sustain economic growth and expansion. The justification for this particular policy lay in the fact that " . . . so long as there was a considerable amount of slack in the economy, the policy of the central bank was to allow the increasing demand

---

[24]J.M. Keynes, *General Theory of Employment, Interest, and Money,* Macmillan and Co. Ltd., London, 1949, p. 173, by permission of the International Economic Association and Macmillan, London and Basingstoke.

[25]L. Rasminsky, Annual Report of the Governor of the Bank of Canada 1961, p. 3.

[26]*Ibid*., p. 4.

for credit to be met *without a tightening of credit conditions.*"[27]

Again the Keynesian doctrine finds its expression in this key sentence of Rasminsky: "...I have found it useful to regard the central bank as exerting its greatest influence through its impact on credit conditions generally—that is on the *cost* and availability of money."[28] Note the emphasis of the central bank's action on *cost* and *availability* of money. This is another way, of course, of concentrating upon the rate of interest charged by banks, financial intermediaries, etc., and maintaining a level appropriate, in the opinion of the Minister of Finance and the Governor of the central bank, to the economic conditions of the time. It is obvious, especially with the benefit of hindsight, that any monetary policy which concentrates on credit conditions alone has a fundamental premise that the control of lending activity is *at the same time* the control of the price level. That is, an excessive level of investment will result in rising prices only at full employment, and a deficiency of investment will result in unemployment. This is the essence of Keynesian theory. But what if *both* rising prices and unemployment exist at the same time? A monetary policy based upon credit control alone is helpless. Checking credit to halt inflation creates unemployment, and this may be, in the opinion of the general public, worse than the inflation.

This is precisely the situation which existed in 1969. The following quote from Mr. Rasminsky will sound very strange to us now.

> For five years now, the Consumer Price Index has been rising at a rate in excess of 3 per cent per year and for the past two years at rates of 4 to 4½ per cent. The need for stringent monetary policies to help contain and combat this erosion in the purchasing power of money has been

widely accepted in Canada, mainly, I believe, because of a growing appreciation, based on concrete experience, of the dangers of inflation.[29]

In this case, the Governor is clearly conceding to the wishes of the government which had made its anti-inflation stance quite clear. In fact, Mr. Rasminsky had already embarked upon the tight credit policy discussed earlier, attempting to restrict the chartered banks' ability to make loans, hence, cutting back business loans and generating unemployment—and, we might add, driving up interest rates by about 1½ percentage points. The time lag between its inception in the autumn of 1968 and the end of 1969 was noticed by Mr. Rasminsky.

> The restrictive monetary policy was slow in having a substantial impact on the availability of bank credit because at the beginning of the present period of severe restraint the banks *were quite liquid* and because under the pressure of the heavy loan demand which developed, they turned out to be willing to see their liquidity run down to considerably lower levels than they had in the past.[30]

But even more interesting is the fact that Mr. Rasminsky apparently did not question the existence of liquidity, that is, how and why did it get into the banking system in the first place, and in the second place, he ignored the fact that the general public of Canada was "awash" with liquidity with more money than it could possibly spend on existing supplies of goods and services at existing prices. There were two basic causes for this excessive liquidity in the economy. The first was the policy of the central bank itself, and the second was the Bank Act of 1967.

C. Banks as Profit Maximizers

A major (if not *the* major) thrust of the argument of these chapters is that banks are really profit

---

[27]Quoted from an address by L. Rasminsky at Kingston, Ontario, in T.J. Courchene, "Recent Canadian Monetary Policy" reprinted in Cairns, Binhammer and Boadway, eds., *Canadian Banking and Monetary Policy*, 2d ed., McGraw-Hill Ryerson Limited, 1972, p. 211.

[28]L. Rasminsky, "The Role of the Central Bank Today," Per Jacobsson Memorial Lecture, Rome, November 9, 1966. Reprinted in Cairns, Binhammer and Boadway, eds., *op. cit.*, p. 182.

[29]L. Rasminsky, Annual Report of the Governor, 1969, p. 6.

[30]*Ibid.*, p. 11.

maximizers. This fact has been borne out in the past, as, for instance, when Sir John Rose, Minister of Finance in 1870, proposed that a bond-secured currency issued by a national bank (this would have been the Bank of Montreal) would replace the bank notes issued by banks at that time. The banks protested vigorously — bank notes were highly profitable, involving no cost. Or again, when Sir Francis Hincks (the successor to Rose) favoured a compulsory reserve ratio for the final version of the Bank Act in 1871, he was forced to abandon the idea. Compulsory reserves are the equivalent of a tax, i.e., a proportion of assets are sterilized and earn no interest. The 5% reserve ratio which had been in effect since the inception of the Bank of Canada until the Bank Act of 1954 was really no tax at all since cash reserves were actually something like 10% during the years of the Great Depression and in the post-War years; nor, for that matter, was there any possibility of control of the money supply via the reserve ratio. It was not until the 8% ratio was introduced and the maintenance of reserves close to this ratio that control of banks through tight money could exist.

But the question really is, how *effective* is this control under the circumstances of profit maximization? Our chartered banks are unique in the western world in that they combine both commercial banking and savings banking in one institution. The result has been that since World War II, banks have learned that term (long-term) lending is not only possible but profitable. This has been made possible by the greater "stickability" of savings deposits over demand deposits. Statutory recognition of this function of the banks was included in the Bank Act of 1954 which permitted lending under government insured mortgages. *Still* the chartered banks found themselves severely hampered in their competitive lending activity, so much so that their relative position in terms of total assets of all deposit-taking institutions declined from 86% in 1950 to 82% in 1955 and to 70% in 1964.[31]

1. The Bank Act of 1967

The Royal Commission on Banking and Finance in its report in 1964 recommended more competition in the entire field of finance. It did not recognize, however, any distinction between chartered banks and other intermediaries:

> Banks cannot "create" credit in some mysteriously different way from the others. . .all institutions play an essentially similar role in the flow of credit from lenders to borrowers. What differentiates the banking institutions is the nature of the liabilities they offer — short-term and demand claims which serve as a means of payment or a close substitute for it.[32]

What is curious is that the Commissioners did not attach any significance to the "demand claims which serve as a means of payment" and those claims which do not; hence, they overlooked the fact that some institutions can lend at zero marginal cost whereas others cannot. However, what was important to them was the existence of "credit" (liquidity as defined in the preceding chapter), and recognition of this led them to conclude that a lower cash reserve ratio for notice deposits than for demand deposits was appropriate, and that these ratios should apply to *all* "banking institutions" (trust, loan companies, etc.) which would, in turn, come under the umbrella of an extended Bank Act. This would have the effect of extending competition more equitably to all and thereby make possible equal treatment within the framework of monetary control, a unique and novel idea which was excluded from our own Bank Act but which was "imported" by the British to their policy of Competition and Credit Control introduced in 1970.

Unquestionably, the Bank Act of 1967 brought in the most sweeping changes and reforms since the first Bank Act of 1871. The following excerpt from Professor Reuber's analysis summarizes the main provisions and outlines the conditions under which our banking system currently operates:

---

[31]G.L. Reuber, "Recent Revisions in Canada's Banking Legislation," reprinted in Cairns, Binhammer and Boadway, eds., *Canadian Banking and Monetary Policy*, 2d ed., McGraw-Hill Ryerson Limited, 1972, p. 259 by permission of the author.

[32]*Report of the Royal Commission on Banking and Finance*, Queen's Printer, Ottawa, 1965, p. 563. Reproduced by permission of the Minister of Supply and Services Canada.

1. The 6 per cent interest ceiling on bank loans was removed as of January 1, 1968.

2. Chartered banks are permitted to engage freely in mortgage lending of all types, constrained only by the prescribed limits set on the loan/value ratio and on the ratio of total conventional residential mortgages held/total deposits and debentures.* Under the previous legislation, the banks were permitted to hold residential mortgages guaranteed under the National Housing Act and a limited range of other mortgages on specified assets, but were barred from most of the conventional mortgage market.

*The ratio of mortgages to deposits plus debentures is 10%.

3. Agreements among banks on interest rates on deposits and on interest rates and charges on loans are prohibited.

4. Banks are restricted from owning more than 10 per cent of the shares of a near-bank institution accepting deposits and some limitations are prescribed on bank ownership of other companies as well. In addition, the Act prohibits interlocking directorships among banks and between banks and near-banks; and the number of bank directors on the board of any other company is restricted to a fifth of the company's total board. At least three-quarters of the directors of a chartered bank must be Canadian citizens.

5. The ownership of shares in a Canadian bank by a single person, whether resident or non-resident, is limited to 10 per cent. In addition, total non-resident holding of bank shares is restricted to 25 per cent. In the case of the Mercantile Bank, which was bought out by the First National City Bank of the U.S. several years ago, arrangements were made for the share of ownership to be brought down to the 25 per cent prescribed limit over a period of several years. No provision is made for foreign banks to engage directly in banking operations in Canada.

6. A new cash reserve ratio is established which, for the first time, distinguishes between time and demand deposits. After a transition period, the new reserve ratio for demand deposits will be 12 per cent and for time deposits it will be 4 per cent. In effect, this reduces the comprehensive reserve ratio of the banks to about $6\frac{1}{2}$ per cent compared with the present common ratio of 8 per cent for all deposits, which under the old Act the Bank of Canada, at its discretion, could (but never did) raise to 12 per cent. At the same time, under the new Act, the Bank of Canada may require the banks to hold a secondary reserve ranging from 0 to 12 per cent of Canadian dollar deposit liabilities. Prior to this change, secondary reserves were held "voluntarily" by the banks. The cash reserve ratio under the new Act is calculated on a fortnightly basis, instead of monthly as under the old Act, and the secondary reserve ratio is calculated on a monthly basis.

7. More detailed reporting is required of the banks. The most important change in this connection is the inclusion in the Act of a provision requiring the banks to report inner reserves as well as loss experience in relation to reserves.

8. Under the new Act banks are permitted to issue debentures with a term of at least five years and restricted in amount.

9. Provision is made for informing borrowers in writing of the cost of loans.[33]

Items 1 and 2 make it possible for chartered banks to move freely into the loan market to compete with near-bank lending. The effect of this is not only to enhance competition but also to reduce interest rates of all lending institutions to a somewhat lower level than what they would otherwise have been. We cannot prove such a "what might have been" statement, but it is likely to be true that the enormous capacity of the chartered banks for intermediation in competition with near-banks must have lowered interest rates on mortgages to some degree.

Items 3 and 4 simply encourage greater competition in the whole area of intermediation and finance. Item 5, however, *restricts* competition by effectively removing foreign banks from Canadian domestic banking activity. It is interesting that chartered banks do have their own branches in foreign countries where they are permitted. (Switzerland insists upon reciprocity; hence Canadian banks are not in that country.)

[33]Grant L. Reuber, "Recent Revisions in Canada's Banking Legislation," reprinted in Cairns, Binhammer and Boadway, eds., *Canadian Banking and Monetary Policy*, 2d ed., McGraw-Hill Ryerson Limited, 1972, p. 255, by permission of the author.

Item 6, of course, is major. We can readily see the result of the reduction of the overall reserve ratio from 8% to $6\frac{1}{2}$%. Suppose a bank wishes to increase its loans by $125 million under the former ratio. An additional $10 million would be required in cash reserves. Under the $6\frac{1}{2}$% comprehensive ratio, only $7.8 million is required. Further, suppose the comprehensive ratio is lowered even further as banks learn to operate with the minimum excess reserves (as of mid-1978, the required minimum average was 5.65%). In this case, 5.65%, only $7.06 million is required.

In terms of monetary control, i.e., tight vs. easy monetary policy, the lower the reserve ratio, the greater the "leverage" effect on total deposits; for instance, a Bank of Canada increase of reserves by $1 million will have an impact of $12.5 million on deposits with an 8% reserve ratio as opposed to $17.7 million with a 5.65% ratio. The result does not necessarily mean a tighter control of the money supply at all but a narrower fluctuation of market interest rates. We can readily see this by looking at the situation the other way round. Suppose a decision by the Bank of Canada is made to tighten money and it wishes to do so by applying sufficient pressure to reduce $12.5 million of deposits. With a 5.65% reserve, a shrinkage of only $.71 million of deposits at the Bank of Canada is required; whereas a $1.0 million reduction is necessary with an 8% reserve ratio. In terms of open market operation, only $710,000 worth of Treasury Bills need be sold as opposed to one million. This means that since the amount sold is less, the price of Treasury Bills is not likely to fall so far on the market and the rate, correspondingly, need not rise so high. Of course, all this depends upon the size of the market in Treasury Bills and its capacity to absorb shocks of sales and purchase without significant impact on the rates. In Canada, the market is likely to be more vulnerable in this way than in the U.S. or Great Britain.

Chartered banks, in their turn, must restore their statutory reserves, both cash and secondary, to protect their deposits which are in danger of shrinking by $12.5 million. In their turn they must sell only $710,000 of short-term liquid assets so as to provide the necessary cash. Once more this is easier for the market to absorb than if the ratio were higher.

Items 7, 8, and 9 are not important for our immediate purpose. Debentures and the right to issue them simply mean that banks now have access to the long-term money market as an additional source of funds for their longer term assets, again, as in items 1 and 2, placing chartered banks in a stronger position vis-à-vis their intermediary competition.

We can identify, therefore, two distinct consequences of the Bank Act of 1967 which result in a weakening of control via a monetary mechanism. The first is the tendency for interest rates (particularly short-term Treasury Bill rates) not to react so sharply to changes in monetary policy. As will be examined in detail in Part II, the short-term rates do impact on longer term rates with the result that the overall structure of liquidity in the economy is affected, i.e., higher rates due to tight money reduce liquidity whereas lower rates because of easy money increase liquidity. This consequence of the Bank Act of 1967 was reinforced during the early 1960s by the policy of the Bank of Canada which was stated (see above) to be one of lower interest rates.

The second was a further removal of constraints to profit maximization. Chartered banks now have greater flexibility in their resistance to monetary control. During inflationary periods when overheating of the economy takes place, loans to business enterprises, which are likely to be the primary "target" of policy, will not be restricted until all else fails. Loans are the most profitable of all assets, and the greater the opportunity available to banks to protect their profits, the longer will be the lag time between the inception of tight money and the ultimate objective.

On the other hand, encouragement of loans during periods of *surplus* capacity in the economy becomes more difficult. Business enterprises will not borrow (increase current liquidity) unless the cost is sufficiently low to offset the expense of future liquidity foregone. This means that interest rates as a cost of borrowing must be relatively low. Banks, however, will not (following profit maximization principles) offer loans at rates less than those obtainable through the purchase of bonds since these are both liquid and involve less risk than business loans.

A careful examination of Chart 5-1 will reveal the extent of this lag. In March, 1970, (see series "free liquid assets") monetary policy shifted abruptly from tight to easy. This did not affect business loans until the beginning of 1971, about 9 months later. Personal loans, however, reacted much more quickly with only a 3 month lag.

If the target of monetary policy is money supply (cash plus deposits at chartered banks) there is virtually no lag at all. As is apparent in Chart 5-3, deposit growth was checked quickly enough in 1969 and responded to easy money promptly in 1970. Money, in this latter case, was taking the form of additional notice deposits, etc., in response to the expansion of banks' liquid assets. But a target of money *alone* is useless; it is liquidity in the economy that matters. Money, in other words, must carry liquidity to those sectors in the economy which can use it effectively for employment generating activity.

2. The Next Bank Act

From all indications at the present time, there will likely be no significant improvements in the efficiency of monetary policy when the new Bank Act revision of 1979 comes into effect. The exception to this is the introduction of foreign banking which must increase competition for existing domestic institutions. This will reduce somewhat the profit maximizing opportunities which chartered banks have enjoyed hitherto.

It is, however, clear that the Bank Act appears to

Chart 5-3

MONETARY AGGREGATES

SEASONALLY ADJUSTED-MONTHLY AVERAGE OF WEDNESDAYS

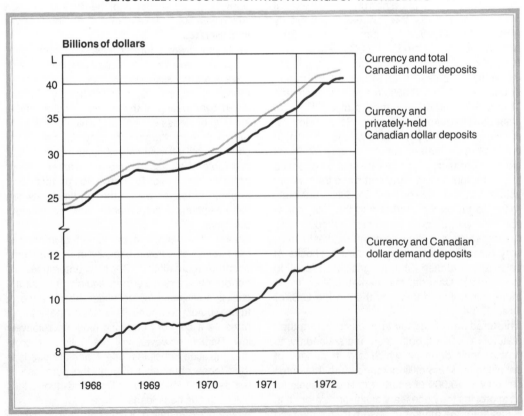

Source: Bank of Canada

be anticipating a capital and management shortage for the future in Canada which banks can at least partially fill. This is apparent from the widening of banks' activities into more diverse areas of investment and the more active participation in industry, including non-financial companies. The outstanding examples are leasing and factoring, both of which have become quite common in the United States. A lease contract permits a business enterprise to acquire capital equipment on a lease basis without outright purchase. A bank (in this case a Canadian bank) will purchase the property, then lease or rent it to the business enterprise. This is precisely the same if a business borrowed the money from the bank, purchased the equipment, then repaid the bank from both business proceeds and the ultimate sale of the equipment. Credit is involved in both cases, but with the lease contract the business is free of the responsibility of buying and selling. As long as leasing is the equivalent of credit, banks will be permitted to participate under the new Bank Act.

Factoring is somewhat different. Banks will purchase accounts receivable from business enterprises which otherwise find it difficult to finance their activities on a short-term credit basis. The proceeds of the sale are then used as capital by the firm for further production. Sometimes loans may be made directly on the basis of accounts receivable; otherwise, direct participation in the management, paperwork, etc., of small businesses is involved. This is again a form of credit and will be permitted by the new Bank Act.

Additional extensions of banking activities are also expected. In the first place, the 10% ratio of residential mortgages to total debentures plus deposits will be removed and no limits are prescribed; the obvious result of this will be a considerable expansion of banks' assets in this highly profitable lending activity. In the second place, there will likely be (we cannot be certain until the new Act is more precisely defined) a further extension of banks' investments in corporate securities, subject again to regulation as they have been under the current Bank Act.

The extension of banks into these areas, with their opportunities for additional profit, may indeed result in less response to monetary policy than has been true in the past. On the other hand, the participation of banks in business enterprise through leasing and factoring as well as more direct involvement may make possible a greater improvement in the overall structure of business liquidity. Thus, a solvent, going concern with a promising future may through factoring with its local bank, have access to the liquidity which it requires but would otherwise not have had. Similarly the inefficient enterprise may be denied the liquidity it ought not to have because a factoring bank could not assume the risk. In this way there may be a more efficient distribution of scarce liquidity throughout the economy. We cannot be certain of our forecasts, but we may be at least optimistic for the future.

II. A LIQUIDITY ANALYSIS

More traditional work in monetary economics has stressed not liquidity but velocity of circulation of money along the lines of either (1) Fisher's V, (2) the Cambridge 1/k, or (3) the modern Friedman velocity function which is considerably more complex in detail but, in principle, the same as both 1 and 2. The advantage of a velocity analysis of this type is that it is measurable from available statistics; hence, more sophisticated econometric analysis is possible. In a liquidity discussion there is very little that can be measured—a Quantity Theory of Liquidity has yet to be developed.

It is possible, however, to gain some insight into the liquidity of our economy by observing the behaviour of income velocity, but this would only be the liquidity of lenders, i.e., those with surplus current liquidity. The liquidity of borrowers, those who are willing to pay the price (interest) for current liquidity, must still remain unknown until some appropriate indicator is devised. In terms of supply/demand analysis, we can identify only supply and the price, but we do not know the demand function. The best we can do is infer something about borrowers' demand for liquidity by observing both interest rates and the indicators of liquidity supply.

Generally, when income velocity is falling (negative changes from year to year), the supply of liquidity is rising. The "supply of liquidity" in this case is simply the deposits of the chartered banks, both notice and demand deposits. We can readily identify notice deposits which are literally liquidity stores to be used with the minimum of "notice" and conclude that the larger the amount of notice deposits, the greater is liquidity. Demand deposits which are idle, however, cannot be so identified. This is why M_2 is used for income velocity of circulation ($\frac{Y}{M_2}$) and a proxy for liquidity. We can do this because a demand deposit which is totally idle (zero income velocity) has the maximum liquidity for the individual; conversely, the highest income velocity has the lowest liquidity. This follows from our original definition of liquidity set out in Chapter 4 — the capacity of a financial asset to be turned into a monetary asset without loss of value. Financial assets are monetary assets at "rest" and the greater the amount of "resting assets" the greater is corresponding liquidity.

We must emphasize that income velocity is only a *proxy* (i.e., it represents liquidity) not a measure of the huge sums of deposits in financial intermediaries, short-term bonds, Canada Savings Bonds, etc., etc., which people may elect to hold. All we can say is that liquidity is likely to be increasing with a decreasing velocity of circulation and decreasing with increasing velocity. In the table which follows, changes in income velocity are calculated with the objective of identifying periods of both increasing and decreasing liquidity.

There are some interesting patterns which can be identified in the annual changes of Quantity Theory variables which may help to identify corresponding changes in liquidity. Column 1, annual percentage changes in the Gross National Expenditure price deflator, shows three distinct periods: 1961–66 when rates of price increases grew from almost zero to around 4%, 1966–72 with annual rates of change fairly stable at about 4½%, and 1972–77 with more rapid rates of inflation peaking in 1974. The next column, growth rates of the Canadian Gross National Product at constant prices, is more stable throughout the decade of the 1960s at about 6½%, on the average, and with occasional lapses during recession years. In the 1970s, these growth rates have proven to be more difficult to sustain at the previous high levels, especially after 1973 when productivity (output per man-hour) growth rates were particularly sluggish.

Column 3, the growth rate of money supply, M_2, (all Canadian dollar deposits at chartered banks except government of Canada deposits) seems to display a three-year cycle beginning with 1963

though the general trend is upward. The peaks of each of these cycles corresponds with negative growth rates of income velocity of circulation (Column 4). The exception occurs during the latter 1960s when most velocity growth rates were negative.

These negative growth rates in velocity follow, of course, from the arithmetic of subtracting Column 3 from the sum of Columns 1 and 2. There is nothing "wonderful" or significant about the behaviour of velocity alone in this case. What is interesting are the questions that are raised, particularly, if money is not being spent at the same rate as prices and output change and it is growing faster than both prices and output combined, what *is* happening to it? One explanation is that some goes into financial circulation. This is borne out by rising equity prices in the stock markets and falling interest rates on bonds during the mid and later 60s. This would account for apparently "idle" demand deposits (idle only in terms of current income). There are, in addition, notice deposits which are included in the total money supply, M_2, and which also increased during this period, and it is these which have contributed directly to total liquidity. Additional deposits at financial intermediaries would also increase liquidity.

The point is that it is likely to be true (we cannot say for sure) that the greater growth rate in the supply of money (and corresponding liquidity) exceeded the requirements of borrowers at a specific rate of loan interest; hence, rates were at their lowest in 1967. All we can say is that this was a contributing factor because Euro-dollar rates were also low during that year.

A second and more important question raised by the negative growth of velocity is, Why did M_2 increase its rate of growth in the first place to produce the negative change in velocity? This directly involves the banking system and the particular policy followed by the Bank of Canada. The expansion of the money supply by the banks carried with it an increased liquidity which was "pushed" into deposits of the public whether the public required them for purchasing additional goods and services or not. Finding this additional liquidity on its hands, the public proceeded to store it in some form to await the opportunity to increase its expenditures.

Table 5-1

ANNUAL PERCENTAGE CHANGES IN QUANTITY THEORY VARIABLES

	1 GNE Price Deflator	2 GNP Constant Prices	3 M_2	4 Income Velocity of Circulation
1960	1.2	2.9	0.5	3.6
1961	0.6	2.9	6.6	−3.1
1962	1.4	6.9	7.4	0.9
1963	1.9	5.3	5.1	2.2
1964	2.4	6.9	7.6	1.7
1965	3.5	6.6	10.4	−0.3
1966	4.6	7.0	7.6	4.0
1967	3.9	3.3	11.9	−4.7
1968	3.3	5.8	12.5*	−3.4
1969	4.4	5.3	10.4	−0.7
1970	4.7	2.5	6.8	0.4
1971	3.1	6.9	12.3	−2.3
1972	5.0	6.1	10.5	0.6
1973	9.2	7.5	14.2	2.5
1974	14.3	3.7	20.1	−2.1
1975	10.7	1.1	15.0	−3.2
1976	9.5	4.9	12.6	1.8
1977	6.5	2.6	14.0	−4.9

*The series 1961 through 1968 is not strictly comparable with the definition of M_2.
Source: Columns 1, 2, and 3 are taken from Table 1, Columns 14, 10, and 3, *Bank of Canada Review*. Column 4 is computed by subtracting Column 3 from the total of Columns 1 and 2. This, for those interested in the mathematics, is in accordance with the following:

$$V = \frac{PQ}{M}$$

$$dV = dP\left(\frac{Q}{M}\right) + dQ\left(\frac{P}{M}\right) - dM\left(\frac{PQ}{M^2}\right)$$

$$\frac{dV}{V} = \frac{dP}{P} + \frac{dQ}{Q} - \frac{dM}{M}$$

The piling up of the excess liquidity (excess to the transactions requirement of the GNP) meant that an ample source of ready funds was on hand to finance the massive inflation of the 1970s. It was only a matter of transforming financial assets into cash, by selling stocks and bonds in the market and by transferring savings certificates in financial intermediaries, etc., into deposits, so that rising prices could be financed.

III. MONEY SUPPLY, OUTPUT, AND PRICES—A THEORETICAL RELATIONSHIP

In Chapter 2 a theoretical relationship between the money supply and the price level was set forth based purely on the demand for money. It is now time to develop this further to include increases in the output of all goods and services. Like all hypotheses, the substance of the argument lies purely in logic. Fundamentally, the argument is a hypothetical explanation of the statistical facts—no more—for it is not possible to develop simple cause/effect sequences relating money supply changes to price changes.

The important years of the early 1970s are cases in point. Canada was not the only country with excessive liquidity. We cannot argue that the excessive supplies of money *caused* rising prices and inflation — oil price rises due to the OPEC decisions were also important. It is likely, however, that the excess money pumped into the economies of the western world during 1970-3 made possible the rising prices of 1973–5. Yet, as will be shown below, unemployment could indeed have resulted from the OPEC price rises had there been no additional supplies of money to finance the price increases.

What happened in Canada, therefore, occurred elsewhere as well. The inflation was international in a kind of "lock step" relationship of domestic prices in all the major western industrial countries. The very closeness in timing suggests that something like the set of equations (2) in Chapter 2 applied, i.e., rising prices in a strategically important import sector made possible domestic market price increases. Ultimately, a devaluation of the domestic currency of the exporting country, as occurred in Great Britain, would restore the competitive position of the exporting country within the Canadian economy.

On the other hand, the years of the 1960s were characterized by rather large annual rates of increase in productivity (output per man hour). These years were also years of relatively stable prices. This suggests that there is indeed a relationship between productivity and prices which ought to be explored in more and greater detail than the Quantity Theory of Money alone can provide for us.

For this purpose, we shall return to the demand for money analysis of Chapter 2 with one precautionary note. For the sake of convenience, and convenience alone, we retain the use of the concept money just as it was used in Chapter 2; however, it should be clear by now that sellers and buyers demand money not for the sake of money alone but for the property of current liquidity which it carries. That is to say, buyers do not "demand money"; they, in fact *part* with money when purchasing goods or services. The reason that buyers demand money temporarily is that only in that way can they have current liquidity which is really what they demand. Only coin collectors, etc., will demand money for its own sake. The same logic applies to sellers; they too want current liquidity and, hence, must have money to part with, ultimately, when the time comes to meet expenses. This distinction between money and its property, current liquidity, is more than mere polemics. It is real and will be applied in Part II. For the present analysis only, we can consider demand for current liquidity the same as demand for money.

With this qualification in mind, we can set forth a series of steps in accordance with the following:

Assumption #1. An increase in productivity without a corresponding increase in the offers of money.

There will be, at first, an accumulation of inventories at the particular stage (or stages) in the production process where productivity is increasing. This could be within the manufacturing sector, for example, which would attempt to pass on the increased inventories to sellers at later stages. This in turn would mean that sellers' *total* demand for money must rise as they attempt to encourage more, and greater, buyers' offer curves. We might see, as a result, a more than usual number of "sales," amounts of advertising, etc.

The increased sellers' demands for money may or may not be met by corresponding increases in buyers' offers of money. In other words, the inventory may still not decline. It follows that sellers' demand for money per unit of inventory (i.e., prices) must fall.

(i) If buyers' demands for goods are price inelastic, they will find that their demand for money is *more* than satisfied and will maintain approximately the same rate of consumption even though at lower prices. Idle money balances will accumulate with the consequence that sellers will likely reduce inventory by cutting orders from manufacturers which, in turn, will result in unemployment but which would be preferable to a reduction in the amount of money sellers are able to acquire. In macroeconomic terms, savings are excessive and a recession results.

(ii) If buyers' demand is price elastic (price elasticity of unity or above), sellers will find that excessive inventories *can* be run down by lowering prices. There will be no change in idle monetary balances with unit elasticity.

We can express these relationships using the market demand for money concepts developed in Chapter 2. At that point, the convenient assumption of a fixed quantity of goods constrained the sellers' demand for money and the buyers' offer curves as functions of the price level alone. To include changes in quantity of output in this analytical framework makes it necessary to shift the functional relationships between money and the price level because both prices and quantities are now variable.[34]

---

[34]Thus, $M = f(PQ)$ with Q, the quantity of goods on the

A second feature of the demand for money functions is that both sellers' demand and buyers' demand for goods have been implicit up to this point, but now must be more carefully defined. Sellers' demand for money is a macroeconomic concept which is the counterpart of the *supply* of all goods and services including capital equipment, intermediate goods, and final consumer goods. (N.B., In this sense, the "supply" of goods is not the same as the Gross National Product since the latter excludes intermediate goods.) Similarly, buyers' offer curves of money are the counterpart of demand for all goods. It follows that the demand for money analysis is, in reality, a monetary counterpart of macroeconomic aggregate demand and aggregate supply.

In Diagram 5-1, the axes are just as before, price, P, and money, M, remembering that M is really current liquidity until the moment of purchase. An equilibrium price P_1 exists where sellers and buyers are both satisfied and the amount of money, M_1, passes from buyers to sellers. In accordance with our assumption, a productivity increase alters the slope of the sellers' demand function from Sd_1 to Sd_2 indicating a greater amount of goods to be sold. Note that sellers' demand for money has shifted to Sd_2, a slope less than Sd_1 (elasticity, however, is still unity). This is the consequence of greater quantities of goods which can be sold at the same price P_1 with greater amounts of money (M_2) to satisfy their demand. If buyers' demand for money does not change appreciably, a qualification equivalent to saying that price elasticity of demand for goods and services is less than unity, in order to exhaust their inventory, sellers must revise their demand for money downward by lowering prices to P_2. But note that the amount of money forthcoming from buyers at that price level is less than before. Sellers will, therefore, return to the former Sd_1 curve, or something like it, and the price level P_1 higher than P_2 to reduce their surplus inventory. In returning to Sd_1 sellers are, in effect, returning to the same quantity of goods as before. How is

Diagram 5-1

OUTPUT INCREASES AND DEMAND FOR MONEY

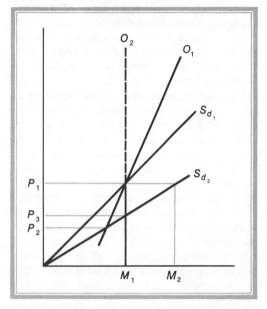

this possible with higher productivity levels? By simply reducing the numbers of employed workers (increasing unemployment as per (i) above). There is no other way to reduce inventory, yet such a situation could introduce a depression sequence if unemployed workers reduce their offers of money and shift the offer curve back to a lower level. Unemployment insurance, of course, mitigates this possibility.

Suppose, however, that buyers' price elasticity of demand were unity, i.e., the same amount of money would be forthcoming as offers from buyers at lower prices. The offer curve O_2, *vertical downward*, would apply and a price level of P_3 would exhaust inventories with the same amount of money as before. This is the analytical equivalent of (ii) above.

Assumption #2. Increases in productivity with corresponding increases in offers of money from buyers.

Sellers' inventory would increase just as before, with the same efforts (sales, etc.) to encourage increased outlays on the part of buyers.

Such increased offers of money would be made possible by increases in the supply of money for the reason that buyers' demand for money is

---

market. Holding Q constant means that
$$M_{pq} = \frac{\partial f}{\partial P}$$
Introducing Q as a variable results in
$$M_{pq}\dot{} = \frac{\partial f}{\partial P}Q + \frac{\partial f}{\partial Q}P$$

satisfied. In addition, it is likely that the increased offer of money would be spent either on the same goods at higher prices or more goods at the same prices. This follows from the fact that consumers' wants generally do not reach the point of satiety in ordinary times. During depression periods, additional supplies of money would likely flow into idle balances (i) above), but as a general rule, sellers' new demands could be met without having to raise prices appreciably.

We can see this using the analytical technique as before. There will be two distinct effects upon the buyers' offer curve of money, the first being a shift of the buyers' offer curve to the right indicating that more money will be offered at the same price for more goods (see Diagram 5-2). In that case a simultaneous increase in the amount of goods offered (a shift to Sd_2 due to higher productivity) will simply increase the amount of money offered at the same price level to M_3 as indicated by the intersection of O_2 and Sd_2. We may imagine such a situation occurring, say, in 1960-62 (see Table 5-1, above) when price levels were fairly stable at the same time that real output and money increased.

Now suppose the offer curve shifts first, or, more realistically, faster than the sellers' demand for money decreases its slope due to productivity increases. This would be typical of the years

Diagram 5-2

EFFECTS OF OUTPUT INCREASES ON PRICES

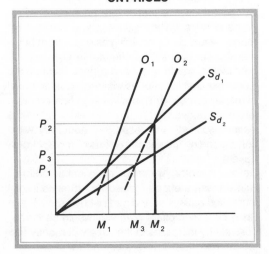

1967-70 when rising liquidity (lower income velocity) was taking place. Sellers will, initially, be satisfied with higher amounts of money but must eventually move up the buyers' offer curve to something approaching P_2. This movement upward would be typical of the years 1970-77 when annual increases in productivity were limited at the same time that the demands for current liquidity were being satisfied by rapidly growing supplies of money.

Having reached P_2 is it possible for prices to fall to P_3 due to a vertical (downward) portion (elasticity of demand equal to or greater than unity) of the buyers' offer curve? Theoretically yes, if no further rightward shift in the offer curve takes place. In practice, falling prices are generally not encountered except in isolated circumstances; technological improvements have been able to produce the combination of high productivity and lower costs and sufficiently high elasticity of demand to produce lower prices without a decreased flow of money (the electronics industry is a case in point). In agriculture, on the other hand, low elasticity of demand combined with falling prices produces a declining farm income (decreased M).

In most cases, however, prices do not fall; quite the contrary, if offer curves do not shift far enough to sustain existing prices, unemployment results as sellers remain on curve Sd_1 instead of shifting to Sd_2. Especially in manufactured goods it is difficult, if not impossible, to reduce prices and costs for the reason that wage costs are always involved, and these are notoriously sticky downward.

In Diagram 5-2 a shift in the offer curve occurs from O_1 to O_2, the consequence of an increase in the amount of money available to buyers. This could, as was discussed in Chapter 2, generate a monetary inflation with all the increased money being used to finance a price level of P_2, up from P_1 by the amount of the increase in money, M_1 to M_2. On the other hand, greater productivity results in more goods. This decreases the slope of Sd_1 to Sd_2 which, in turn, intersects the vertical portion of offer curve, O_2. The result is a price, P_3, which is less than P_2, and is the consequence of a constant expenditure of money, M_2, on a greater quantity of goods than before. Sellers' demand for money is satisfied by both price and production increases.

The analysis is similar if output increases are due to increases in employment rather than to productivity gains. The sequence of events would be reversed, however, with the possibility of an increased money flow to sellers encouraging greater employment, hence, a shift *first* of Sd_1 to Sd_2. If buyers' offer curves of money move to O_2, an increase of money available to sellers would be shown by M_3, determined by the intersection of the dashed O_2 and Sd_2 at the same price level, P_1.

Thus, the difference between productivity gains and employment increases lies essentially in the amount of money buyers are willing to offer. If buyers make available an amount, M_2, and thereby satisfy sellers' demand at a price P_2, any productivity gains will result in a movement down the inelastic offer curve to a lower price. On the other hand, if increased employment generates more output *and* a corresponding increased offer of money from buyers to an amount M_3, the approximate price level, P_1 can hold. It is a matter, essentially, of which comes first, the offer of money or the increased output.

With the aid of the theoretical analysis of offer curves and sellers' demand curves, and remembering that force equilibrium between these curves is unstable, always subject to change and revision, we can now interpret the variables of the Quantity Theory with something more than the automatic relationships of a mathematical identity. To return once more to Table 5-1, we can easily recognize that the money supply in Canada has been subject to continuous changes in annual rates of growth since the early 1960s. This money supply has been available for use by buyers, always at hand for conversion into offer curves. In general, such changes in offer curves would be indicated as changes in M_1 (demand deposits plus cash in circulation) since money in this form represents the medium of exchange.

What we do *not* know, however, is what level of M_1 would have satisfied *both* buyers and sellers. Consider once more the analysis as shown in Diagram 5-3. If we select an arbitrary price, P_1, we can locate the amount of money which would satisfy sellers (given a specific level of real output), M_d, and the amount of money which buyers would offer, M_o. But there is only one statistical figure of M_1 available, so which of the two, M_d or M_o, are we identifying? We have, of course, no

Diagram 5-3

PRICE LEVEL, MONEY, AND EQUILIBRIUM

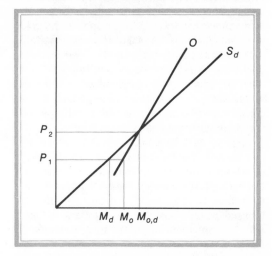

way of knowing. What we *can* say is that if prices are relatively stable, and M_1 is also relatively stable, we are likely to be at something close to an equilibrium level of prices and money supply, i.e., P_2 and $M_{o,d}$.

At the same time, substantial growth of the money supply M_2 means that buyers will have an increasing potential source of additional M_1 whenever it may be required. This means that sellers may push up their demand curves for money by raising prices and at the same time find their inventories depleting just as normally. Buyers will switch from M_2 to M_1 and thereby shift their offer curves rightward. As they do this, velocity of circulation (Column 4, Table 5-1) increases.

All this presents the Bank of Canada and the government with what is likely the most severe dilemma of our time. We know that loans and investments by chartered banks must result in deposit expansion. If the monetary authorities wish to increase loans and investments so as to encourage economic growth, they will manufacture new deposits which are likely to shift buyers' offer curves. The only escape from the dilemma is to discourage the growth of M_1, the medium of exchange portion of total money at the same time that M_2 grows. In other words, a lower velocity of circulation will indicate that buyers' offer curves are also relatively low.

CONCLUSION

Any monetary system which substitutes institutional control of the supply of money and credit for an automatic control mechanism such as the gold standard, becomes the victim of human imperfections as well as the beneficiary of human wisdom. Therefore, in order for the system to work, error must be reduced, knowledge substituted for ignorance, etc., and, even more important, some consensus must be reached as to what is the correct policy for the national economy.

Occupying, as it does, the center of the monetary mechanism, the Bank of Canada wields enormous power. In terms of our economic welfare, the Bank is just as powerful as the federal government itself. The Minister of Finance is responsible for fiscal policy in his budgets; the Bank of Canada develops monetary policy and, therefore, a close coordination of both is very important for our economic well-being.

Just as might have been expected, the Bank of Canada has come a long way from the years of the 1930s to the present in terms of growth and maturity. Many lessons have been learned from experience. But perhaps the greatest source of satisfaction to a researcher in the area is not so much the actual policy actions taken by the Bank in the past, but the fact that the personnel and staff members of the Bank are amongst the most highly qualified in the nation. Certainly, without exaggeration, they earn the degree of trust we place upon them. This is most important because the one aspect of the Bank's history which stands out above all others is the element of continuous change which requires constant revision of decisions, both in substance and in timing. No two situations are alike. The tight money policy of 1955-56, for instance, existed within a very different context than the tight money policy of 1969, yet the methods of constraint were essentially the same. The first anticipated an inflation whereas the second attempted to halt an inflation once it had begun.

In the last analysis, the efficiency of any central bank must be judged not on its capacity to impose tight or easy money as conditions dictate, but on its influence on the overall liquidity position in the economy. Ever since the concept of liquidity first appeared in the Radcliffe Committee Report in Great Britain, there has been no agreement upon measures which would have an impact on liquidity and which could be undertaken within the context of a banking system. Considerably more knowledge and experience are required before practical policy measures can be devised to serve this objective. Actually, since the banks themselves merely intermediate between two liquidities, interposing their own bridging mechanism between them, control of the banks' liquidity through tight or easy monetary policies is really a rather small objective when seen within a much larger context.

Perhaps, indeed, the ultimate stage in the development of monetary policy is the actual manipulation of the liquidity structure of the public so as to bring it more into line with the objectives of the government of the day. But this is a frightening prospect to those who may believe in individual freedom and who might prefer the converse, i.e., the government's objectives be made to conform to the liquidity structure of the public.

This raises an all-important question to which we have as yet no answer. *Ought* we to attempt a control of the money supply at all since instead of promoting the public good we may well cause harm? Suppose we devised a monetary system which was somehow capable of automatically increasing the supply of money just enough to accommodate any increased production of goods and services and satisfy any additional monetization requirements. This would avoid the arbitrary and inflexible constraint of monetary gold on the one hand and the errors and mistakes characteristic of human decision-making on the other. In this situation the Bank of Canada would likely have no place within the overall scheme of things—it could simply wither away. If this is the true direction toward which our monetary system is evolving, the Bank as an administrator of monetary policy is only a temporary stage in our development. "Temporary" though it may be, the Bank and its decisions are still realities in the lives of all of us in this generation.

ADDITIONAL READINGS

There are very many excellent discussions of central banks and monetary policy. The following are just a representative few which are most interesting.

Annual Reports of the Governor of the Bank of Canada, Ottawa.

Coyne, J.E., Testimony to Senate Committee on Manpower and Employment, April, 1961, reprinted in *Money and Banking in Canada*, E.P. Neufeld (ed.), McClelland & Stewart, Ltd., Toronto, 1964.

Culbertson, J.M., *Money and Banking*, McGraw-Hill, New York, 1977, Part 5.

Friedman, Milton, "Current Monetary Policy," *Dollars and Deficits*, Prentice-Hall, Englewood, New Jersey, 1968, ch. 5.

————, "Monetary and Fiscal Framework for Economic Stability," *American Economic Review*, June, 1948, p. 245, reprinted in *Readings in Macroeconomics*, G. Mueller (ed.), Holt, Rinehart & Winston, New York, 1966, p. 337.

————, "The Role of Monetary Policy," *American Economic Review*, March, 1968, pp. 1-17, reprinted in *Money and Banking, Theory, Analysis, and Policy*, S. Mittra (ed.), Random House, New York, 1970, p. 425.

Johnson, H.G., *Essays in Monetary Economics*, Allen & Unwin, Ltd., London, 1969.
  ch. 1, "Monetary Theory and Policy."
  ch. 6, "Monetary Policy in Canada."
  ch. 7, "Monetary and Fiscal Policy in the U.S."

————, "Current Issues in Monetary Policy," Paper presented to 15th Annual Monetary Conference, Puerto Rico, May 24, 1968, reprinted in *Money and Banking, Theory, Analysis, and Policy*, S. Mittra (ed.), Random House, New York, 1970, p. 437.

Knox, F.A., *Dominion Monetary Policy, 1929-1934*, Ottawa, 1939. An interesting historical account of the Canadian government's struggles with the Great Depression before the Bank of Canada.

Maisel, Sherman H., *Managing the Dollar*, W.W. Norton & Co., Inc., New York, 1973. A fascinating account of how the U.S. dollar is managed by a former Governor of the Federal Reserve Board.

Report of the Royal Commission on Banking and Finance (Macmillan Report), Ottawa, 1933. The report which led to the founding of the Bank of Canada.

CHAPTER 6

Banking Systems

INTRODUCTION

Canada's banking system is not the best in the world even though it might possibly be the best that Canada can produce. It should be no surprise to anyone that ours does have weaknesses, and, indeed, deficiencies. We can say this for the obvious reason that *no* system is perfect, yet, to the credit of our banks, to prove or even point out specific examples of deficiencies, is not easy.

There is another reason why it is difficult to be both critical and precise in one's criticism. It is impossible to say, in the social sciences, what might have been, i.e., how much better off we could have been had certain characteristics of our system been otherwise. For example, suppose Canada had not adhered to the "sound money" principle which underlay the gold standard at the beginning of the Great Depression. Could the Depression have been avoided by a money supply expansion sufficient to, possibly, "push" liquidity onto potential borrowers? Probably not, for the reason that the United States was undergoing a liquidity collapse during the early 1930s largely due to the inadequacies (and failures) of the Federal Reserve System in performing *its* task. The world, unfortunately, is not a laboratory with controlled conditions for experiments which make sound scientific conclusions possible. Nevertheless, the assumption underlying this chapter is precisely that we are not perfect and can, therefore, learn from the experience of others even though other banking systems in their turn are not perfect.

There is a second objective in this brief, analytical survey of other systems. Canada does not live in isolation in the modern world. This obvious truism has its strongest application in the field of banking, yet the most surprising feature of our Bank Act Revision of 1967 is the nationalism which manifests itself in the restriction of foreign banks in Canada at the same time that Canadian banks enjoy banking privileges in other countries. This absurd anomaly persists, the cynic might observe, primarily for the protection of a banking monopoly in the domestic field rather than simply to shelter Canada from the classic bogey of foreign domination and control.

Statutory recognition of the fact that twentieth century banking actually does cross national boundaries is to be included in the new revision of the Bank Act; Canadians must deal with non-Canadians in business and commerce, and the more we are aware of other systems and other points of view within the context of their own systems, the greater is our advantage.

Obviously, a description and analysis of other banking systems is a task appropriate for a set of volumes as opposed to a single chapter. The objective here, however, is much more modest— one of broadening the scope of awareness of money and banking systems in general so that further study of any particular banking system becomes that much easier. Volumes already have been written on the various banking systems in different countries and are available to all.

I. THE GOLD STANDARD

A. Great Britain

The logical starting point for our analysis is the one characteristic common to all western banking systems—the gold standard. For our purposes, it began with the early years of the nineteenth century when Great Britain was in the process of developing its own banking system along with its industrial growth. As so often happens, an experience with wartime inflation had resulted in a long controversy, in this case between two schools of thought. During the Napoleonic wars, a temporary Order in Council had suspended gold payments by the Bank of England in exchange for paper pounds. This led to an over-issue of paper money for the purpose of meeting the necessary wartime government expenditures with the result that not only did domestic prices rise but the paper pound came to be priced at a substantial discount vis-à-vis the gold sovereign in terms of foreign currencies.

Distrust in the value of paper currency became so widespread that even landlords refused to accept rent payments in paper pounds and considerable hardship followed. David Ricardo, humanitarian and leader of his contemporaries in the field of political economy, was very conscious of the hardship and suffering around him. He argued in his famous pamphlet, "The High Price of Bullion" published in 1809 that an excessive issue of paper currency was the cause of high prices and the corresponding depreciation of the paper pound. So convincing was his argument, along with that of his colleague, Henry Thornton, that his logic and principles were included in the Bank Acts of 1821 and 1844 which directly tied the paper pound to a one-to-one ratio with gold except for £15,000,000 of issue based on government debt and other securities.[1]

But Ricardo was not without his opponents. Other economists, basing their argument on no less an authority than Adam Smith, asserted that an excess of paper currency was impossible for the reason that if an overissue should occur, the bank notes would tend to be mistrusted and be returned to the bank of issue in exchange for gold. Bank notes, therefore, were useful since they freed gold from the task of being a domestic circulating medium and could be used for foreign trade instead. But how *much* paper currency could be issued? This depended upon the demand for bank notes, i.e., the requirements of commerce and trade. Banks could not overissue bank notes since a surplus would always be returned to the banks for gold. This would necessitate a greater quantity of gold reserve; hence, the more bank notes issued, the greater the quantity of gold required.

Since the only source of gold was through foreign imports (few countries were fortunate in possessing gold mines) the only way that additional gold could flow into a country was through an excess of exports over imports, for most countries, or raising the Bank of England bank rate for Great Britain. Banks, therefore, were effectively prevented from overissue because unless a surplus of bank notes were issued only during periods of great business activity when exports exceeded imports and gold was flowing into the country, their loss of gold reserve could mean bankruptcy.

Despite such a fairly sophisticated argument as this, the "Currency School," as the followers of Ricardo came to be known, won the day. So successful were they that their ideas, even in Canada, were incorporated in the Dominion Bank Notes Act which required a dollar for dollar backing by gold over specifically stated amounts of bank notes issued. This was the gold standard, the consequence of which was that should it be necessary to expand the money supply for whatever reason either additional gold would have to be forthcoming or the laws would be suspended or altered permanently.[2]

The necessity for the use of gold as the "backing" for bank notes profoundly influenced the course of development of British banking. During the earlier years, particularly during the nineteenth century, the so-called "country banks" (those outside the city of London) had already evolved into a rather complex network of correspondent banking between themselves and the London banks. The purpose of these networks was to remit to their London counterparts any cash in excess of

---

[1]As an example, in 1869, 29 December, there were £33,288,640 of notes issued, £18,288,640 of which were in excess of the 15 million, hence backed fully by gold. W. Bagehot, *Lombard Street*, London, 1919, p. 24.

[2]The Currency School ideas arrived in Canada by way of Lord Sydenham who came as Governor General to Upper Canada in 1839. The Union of Upper and Lower Canada in 1841 apparently gave him the opportunity to work toward a single bank of note issue, not only as a means of implementing the principles of the Currency School, but also as a source of easy revenue (printing notes) for the country. While his efforts were not directly rewarded during his lifetime, his influence through his followers continued with the ultimate passage of the Provincial Bank Notes Act. H.T. Davoud, "Lord Sydenham's Proposal for a Provincial Bank of Issue," *Canadian Banker*, Vol. 45, 1937-38, pp. 289-98, reprinted in E.P. Neufeld, *Money and Banking in Canada*, Carleton Library #17, McClelland and Stewart, 1964, p. 95.

their daily requirements for the purpose of short-term lending in the London money market which in those days meant discounting commercial bills of exchange. This they did so long as the interest rate on these short-term funds exceeded the cost of remittance. This excess cash could be either bank of England notes or gold; it mattered little because, as it happened in the former case, the notes found their way to the Bank of England, and in the latter, an actual flow of gold took place in response to the higher interest reward. When bank notes were offered in exchange for short-term securities which the Bank was selling, the Bank of England, by acquiring its own liabilities, was freeing some of its own gold reserve from the responsibility of backing its notes. So whether or not bank notes or gold flowed to the money market, the Bank was "acquiring" gold. This it was able to do by selling from its own portfolio short-term securities at such a cheap price (high yield) that country bankers could not resist. This yield was the Bank of England's Bank Rate which forced the general market rate to the same level simply through the pressure of competition.

The important development in the evolutionary process of banking was the fact that the Bank of England learned how to influence short-term interest rates, and, by this process, attract gold. During the latter years of the nineteenth century, this practice was re-inforced by the growing importance of foreign lending by the London market. Foreign borrowers, that is, would refrain from selling bonds at high interest rates, preferring periods of cheaper money. This had the effect of easing the pressure on existing gold reserves, since once the sterling proceeds of the loans were acquired, they were exchanged for gold or the borrower's own currency.

Another important development at this time was the rise of the London Gold Market. While this market was actually in existence even before the Royal Charter of the Bank of England, it did not achieve eminence until the discoveries of gold in Australia and South Africa assured a growing supply.[3] As a marketing centre for the purchasing and selling of gold by continental countries, the

proximity and ease of transfer between the gold market and the money market meant that the Bank of England could tap short-term supplies of gold merely by making it profitable for the market, i.e., by raising its bank rate. In this way, long before a strain on the balance of payments was felt, the Bank of England was able to acquire supplies of gold to overcome deficits in its balance of trade simply by raising bank rate and thereby acquiring the necessary extra gold in its reserves. Of course, lowering bank rate had the opposite effect on the occasion of excessive gold reserves. To make the system work, it was necessary to establish the important link between bank rate and the rate on the money market; once this link was established and accepted by the banking and financial communities, the mechanism by which gold reserves could be increased or decreased by means of bank rate was complete. So perfect did the mechanism eventually become that the Governor of the Bank of England stated before a U.S. National Monetary Commission prior to establishing the Federal Reserve System that the "bank rate was the most effective measure to protect the bank's reserves." During the crisis of 1907, a rise in the rate to 7% attracted gold from 24 countries.[4]

There was, as is often the case, a trade-off. Raising the bank rate, while it did attract gold from other countries, had an impact on domestic interest rates including rates for clearing banks' loans. The precise mechanism by which the structure of interest rates was affected by bank rate is not at all clear. Certainly raising the bank rate, by offering commercial paper on the market at a lower price, encouraged buyers of that paper (the banks) and as long as the Bank of England continued to sell at a low price, all sellers of commercial paper by reasons of competition would be forced to equal the Bank's offering. This, in turn, would discourage businessmen who relied on this form of credit to finance their stocks of inventory.

But, it is the relationship between bank rate and the rates charged by banks for their *deposits* which is not quite so obvious. We can speculate that banks would use bank rate as an indicator of what the future would bring if they were able to

---

[3]The firm of Mocatta and Goldsmid, one of the current five members of the London Gold Market, was founded in 1684. "The London Gold Market," Bank of England Quarterly Bulletin, March, 1964, p. 16.

[4]R.S. Sayers, *Central Banking After Bagehot*, Clarendon Press, Oxford, 1957, p. 62.

detect a correlation between bank rate and subsequent events. Or, since the investing of excess reserves in London was directly competitive with loans, raising the bank rate could push up loan rates through competition and this, in turn, would somehow react on deposit rates. However, we know that by the beginning of the twentieth century, the flow of excess reserves from country banks to London had disappeared, and the impact of the bank rate was confined to the foreign sector only. Yet, the custom which had long been established of fixing time deposit rates at 2% under bank rate persisted. Similarly, loan rates were generally set at the level of bank rate with a minimum of 5%.

Fortunately, the periods of boom in the British economy were mostly accompanied by import surpluses and corresponding deficits in the balance of payments so that rarely did a conflict occur between the credit requirements of the domestic sector and the necessity to attract gold. Nevertheless, during the period of the 1920s, when Britain was attempting to bring back convertibility of the pound at the old ($4.86 = £1) rate, the bank rate was kept at generally high levels (5%). This was damaging to the British economy not only because of high domestic interest rates but also because of the high cost of British exports which discouraged buyers in overseas markets. So the consequence of the desire to remain on the gold standard at the old rate forced the bank rate to be higher than the requirements of the domestic economy would have dictated. Actually, Britain left the gold standard in 1931 — meaning that the pound was no longer convertible into gold — making one wonder in retrospect if all the hardships of a forced domestic deflation were worth it.

B. The United States

Another legacy of the gold standard and the rigid monetary structure of the Bank Act of 1844, as well as the Dominion Bank Notes Act in Canada, was the development of money "substitutes," i.e., chequebook or demand deposits which in the end were not substitutes at all but a larger part of the money supply. In the United States, this took a slightly different turn. In that country, an inflationary experience similar to that of Great Britain had

taken place during the Civil War when a note issue of $450 million of "Greenbacks" was declared legal tender by Congress to be used to finance the war effort. This declaration of "legal tender," assuming the public will accept such a declaration, means that a substantial source of government finance exists outside the normal taxing powers of a government. As it turned out, the U.S. did not require all this money, only about $430 million were issued, but the New York gold market at one point quoted the Greenback at just 44 cents in relation to the gold dollar when the fortunes of war looked particularly bad for the U.S. government.[5]

Following the war, the Resumption Act was passed in 1875 requiring the re-purchase of all Greenbacks at par with pre-war dollars of the same gold content. This had the effect of holding the money supply constant over a long period of time instead of permitting a money expansion which post-war economic growth and development would have ordinarily required. The consequence was prolonged depression periods — probably the greatest deflation ever experienced in modern times.

Another curious development in the United States was the National Bank Act of 1863 which authorized the issue of bank notes by National Banks, private banks chartered by the federal government. These banks were permitted to issue notes against specific government securities which were supposed to become the principal circulating bank note. At the same time, the troublesome state bank notes were declared illegal, hence eliminating once and for all the practice of bank note issue by many banks scattered throughout the country. This rather curious development was a deviation from the more normal practice of setting up a central bank, similar to the Bank of England, with a monopoly of the note issue. While the rationale is difficult enough to grasp, the result was certainly quite different from the intent, for by eliminating state bank notes and "wildcat banking," state banks proceeded to de-

---

[5]J.M. Culbertson, *Money and Banking*, 2nd ed., McGraw-Hill, 1977, p. 516. Undoubtedly the use of the "legal tender" method of finance has given rise to the expression referring to the printing press as a method of inflation. Governments do not use the printing press any more; their methods are more sophisticated now.

velop the chequebook as a substitute.[6] As it turned out, the chequing account became not only a large portion of the money supply in the U.S. but also a greater source of instability than the bank notes themselves.

C. European Banks

Continental banking took a somewhat different turn; the use of chequebook deposits did not develop to the same extent as in Great Britain and North America. We can only speculate as to the reasons for the different development of the payments system, but there does appear to be two fundamental causes: (1) The central bank monopoly of the note issue was granted much earlier in France and Germany than in either Canada or the U.S. (though *later* than in Great Britain). (2) Having the note issue monopoly, continental central banks were not absolutely restricted as to the amount of issue by the availability of gold cover. In France, there was no gold cover at all, only a legislated maximum note issue. In Germany, a $1/3$ gold cover was required with a full cover of gold beyond a stipulated limit, but, curiously, an uncovered issue was also permitted which was subject to a 5% tax paid by the Reichsbank. There was, thus, in both France and Germany a degree of elasticity of the note issue not available in the three "gold-standard countries." In France, it simply meant raising the issue during times of emergency (real or otherwise), and in Germany, the application of the tax principle meant that during the rapid development of the German empire, a too frequent use of the tax provision exceeded the capacity of the Reichsbank to pay so that the ceiling on the note issue had to be raised.

At any rate, the development of the Girozentrale in Germany, a method of "cash payment" *without* the use of cash, effectively eliminated any possibility of competition from a chequebook system. This was also true of Switzerland, Holland and Belgium which all used the post office technique of giro transfers; in France, on the other hand, an apparent French preference for direct cash pay-

ments made both cheque clearing facilities and a Giro system difficult to develop.

II. BANK RATES TODAY

A. Great Britain

Like the institution of chequebook accounts, the interest rates of the central banks did not disappear when the gold standard was abandoned. Quite the contrary, the concept of a central bank rate of interest (sometimes referred to as discount rate or *re*-discount rate) became more firmly locked into the modern monetary and banking systems of the western world, acquiring a greater prestige than under the regime of gold. In Great Britain, the emphasis was no longer on the amount of gold in the Bank of England but rather the volume of foreign exchange reserves. In addition, bank rate became the central focus of monetary policy for the domestic banking system.

British banks had long ago adopted the practice of maintaining deposits with the Bank of England to an amount of 8% of their total deposit liabilities. The purpose of this "reserve," so called, was not to control the money supply, but to provide cheque clearing balances since the Bank of England was, and still is, the ultimate clearing agent. These clearing balances are very important and are the key to the operation of the money market.

In London, there are some twelve members of the London Discount Market Association which always "covers the tender" of Treasury Bills at the same time that it sets the market rate. For its funding it relies heavily on the commercial banks' call loans; hence, any sale of Treasury Bills by the government must draw funds from the bankers' deposits at the Bank of England, the government's bank; therefore, a net transfer of funds from the banks to the government always takes place. If there is a genuine shortage of funds in the sense that more will be transferred to the government than the banks expected, the "special buyer" (the Bank of England's broker) will purchase some of the surplus Treasury Bills. However, if the Bank of England so wishes, it can force the discount houses into the Bank if they cannot find the necessary accommodation at the commercial banks *and* the special buyer is absent. The discount houses would then borrow at

---

[6]Wildcat banking referred to the practice of setting up banks in such a way that the bank note redemption offices were either remote or difficult to locate. It, thus, became easier to spend spurious bank notes than to take the trouble to turn them in.

what is now known as the minimum lending rate (formerly known as the bank rate) which is generally 1/2% higher than the market rate, though it can be still higher depending upon the policy of the Bank of England.

Now suppose the Bank of England wishes to acquire more foreign exchange for the purpose of supporting the value of the pound against foreign currencies. Pushing up the bank rate in the manner just described encourages foreign funds to come to London for short-term investment. These funds will be transferred to London generally through foreign banks which have London branches, exchanged for sterling deposits at the current rate, and then be used for the purchase of Treasury Bills. Just as under the old gold standard, foreign funds instead of gold flow to London.

Again, just as before, there are domestic repercussions. The entire structure of interest rates at the banks moves with the bank rate and all market rates move with the money market rate. In this way the Bank of England, probably the world's most prestigious central bank, actually determines the entire structure of interest rates. It chooses to do so because this happened to be the method by which the economy of the country can be influenced through monetary policy—the *cost* of credit rather than the volume of credit as is the Canadian case. As Professor Sayers put it, "The (banking) system works not by a volume of bank deposits and of cash being determined as desirable, but rather by the Authorities choosing a structure of interest rates and making the cash fit that structure."[7] It was not that the Bank of England could not control the volume of deposits by way of the 8% cash ratio in a manner similar to North American practice; it had elected not to do so. In all likelihood the impression which many Canadians seem to have of the central bank determining interest rates stems in part from this Bank of England technique of operating monetary policy. As is shown below, the bank rate for Canada is slightly different.

The distinction between controlling the money supply directly and the interest rate structure indirectly and the interest rate directly and the money supply indirectly is an important one and

should be clearly understood. It involves, first, the decision as to what is the more important influence in the economy, the interest rate or the money supply. In electing the direct control of interest rates (or the cost of credit) the British had actually departed from the spirit of a strict Ricardian interpretation of the Quantity Theory which laid emphasis on the supply of money as determining price levels. It was a natural evolutionary process which followed from the importance placed on gold as "real" money. By adjusting the interest rate, gold at the Bank of England could be increased or decreased. Once the gold standard was removed, the mechanism for direct control of the interest rate remained.

There is another more practical consideration which developed largely as the result of nationalization of Britain's basic industry. Since World War II the British government has added to its national debt considerably because of the decisions to nationalize the railroads, coal mines, airways, steel, etc.[8] In the process of nationalizing, the original shareholders were given "gilt-edged" (high quality government stock) in exchange for their original shares. (The word "stock" is used purely as a nominal distinction between ordinary short-term national debt and long-term debt which arises from both government borrowing and nationalization. Actually there is no *real* difference at all.) These gilt-edged stocks are marketable and since they are of high quality it was thought that their market prices had to be supported. It was the responsibility, therefore, of the Bank of England to buy gilts when prices were falling, thereby supporting the market at the expense of increasing the money supply.

At the same time, the structure of long-term yields on government debt could be influenced in such a way that buyers might be encouraged to purchase a particular type of stock in accordance

---

[7]"Bank Deposits: England 1955–56," *op. cit.,* p. 103. Of course, as will be shown subsequently, Professor Sayers' excellent essay is already out of date.

[8]In 1972, net total national debt amounted to £36.9 billion as compared to a GNP of £53.2 billion. By comparison, Canada's national debt was $29.9 billion compared to a GNP of $103.5 billion. As an added burden the British gilt-edged market must compete with the debt of other public authorities, particularly local authorities which have been particularly high spenders. The total public sector debt in 1972 was £76.8 billion. Annual Abstract of Statistics, 1973, HMSO, Tables 305. See also, "Official Transactions in the Gilt-Edged Market," *Bank of England Quarterly Bulletin*, June, 1966, p. 146–147.

with the best returns and length of investment. This is, quite simply, the management of government debt and in Great Britain, has been an important part of monetary policy.[9] But such a tool of policy is not without its trade-offs, for the net purchase of stock by the Bank of England increases the supply of money and net selling lowers it. Thus, a process of supporting yields on government stocks *in general* means that sometimes the money supply must become of secondary importance.

With the emphasis placed only on the interest rate, the monetary "reserve" at the Bank of England (8% of clearing banks' deposits) remained always what the banks wished it to be. There was never any doubt of this. It meant that clearing bank customers could always find accommodation at their bank by simply approaching their banker with a feasible proposition; the banker would locate the necessary deposits and present the borrower with the interest cost for the loan (cost of deposit plus the bank's margin). If the cost met with the borrower's approval, the loan would be granted. For short-term lending, the overdraft facility was provided to customers. (This means, quite simply, a drawing down of a bank balance into a negative range.)

The fundamental difference between the British and North American banking systems is most obvious at this point. Money is "tight" or "easy" in Canada. When it is easy, potential borrowers are encouraged by the availability of funds. The price (or interest rate) of loans may have to be low to encourage borrowers, but this is an *indirect* result which follows from the relationship of the supply of deposits and the demand for them. In the British case the deposits were *always* available at a price.

After so many years of developing a monetary policy apparently suited to the monetary and banking structure of Great Britain, the abrupt change in 1971 is all the more remarkable. However, it was the steady erosion in the value of the pound through inflationary price increases at home and the continuous devaluation of the pound in foreign exchange markets which ultimately convinced the authorities that after all, the supply of money might be as important as the interest rate, if not more so. (Pressure from the International Monetary Fund must also have been a deciding factor.) Actually a special deposits scheme had been worked out earlier which was, in effect, an attempt to control the money supply with a variable reserve system since it required that 1% of gross deposits for the London clearing banks and 1/2% of deposits for the Scottish banks were to be deposited with the Bank of England. The effect was to increase the reserve from 8% to 9% for London banks and 8% to 8 1/2% for Scottish banks.[10] By the end of 1962, the special deposits were all repaid to the banks and all restraints on bank lending were removed.

The reappearance of inflationary pressures led to the recalling of special deposits in 1965, but this time, in a more determined effort to reduce deposit expansion, the growth of bank advances was limited to 5% per year. These controls were lifted *again* in early 1967 to be reimposed in November 1967— a kind of futile "stop-go" approach to credit restriction. About all that was accomplished by these measures was an increase in the levels of frustration for the clearing bankers, and, as could have been accurately forecast, an enormous increase in the assets and profits of financial intermediaries — a situation remarkably similar to the Canadian experience before the Bank Act of 1967.

1. Competition and Credit Control

It is apparent that the Bank of England, i.e., the authorities, was at last accepting the idea that money, after all, just *might* matter. This is the philosophical foundation underlying the special deposits scheme which was, in reality, an increase in reserve requirement with consequent higher cost structures for clearing banks. Clearly, though, it was not possible to impose controls upon one group of banking institutions only and have any measure of success in controlling inflationary pressures. For this reason a new policy was conceived, and, after considerable dialogue and discussion, was implemented on September 16, 1971. The important points of this policy were the following:

1. Banks will observe a uniform daily ratio of 12 1/2% reserve of all net sterling deposit

---

[9]"Official Transactions in the Gilt-Edged Market," *Bank of England Quarterly Bulletin,* June, 1966.

[10]"The Procedure of Special Deposits," *Bank of England Quarterly Bulletin*, December, 1960, p. 18.

liabilities of less than two years maturity with interbank transactions only to be used for computing deposits. The reserves to be used will be balances with the Bank of England (excluding special deposits), British government and Northern Ireland Treasury Bills, . . . call money, British government stocks with one year or less to maturity, and local authority and commercial bills eligible for rediscount with the Bank of England.

2. Special deposits, when called, will be a uniform percentage across the entire banking system.

3. The traditional interest rate structure of the clearing and Scottish banks will be abandoned.

4. Finance houses which accept deposits will be considered as "banks" and the above requirements will apply [except that the required minimum reserve assets ratio will be 10%, instead of 12½%]."

Canadian students of Money and Banking will have no difficulty recognizing item #1. This would be the counterpart of the Canadian cash and secondary reserve ratio as stipulated by both the Bank Act and the Bank of Canada Act in 1967. However, the British version applies to *all* banking institutions, not just clearing and Scottish banks, including financial intermediaries, a recommendation, incidentally, of the Porter Commission for Canada. The second item, linked to the first, would be the counterpart of the Canadian variability of the secondary reserve ratio. The third, as it turned out later, laid the groundwork for an oligopolistic type bank interest rate structure similar to that of Canadian chartered banks. Barclay's Bank was the first to break the long-standing tradition of tying bank interest to bank rate in October, 1972 with the other banks following shortly thereafter.

The program, as a whole, was an attempt to introduce direct credit control into the British banking structure, a concession to the monetarist thinking. This is apparent from the abandonment of the long-term gilt-edged market by the Bank of England which was announced May 14, 1971. The Governor stated that the Bank did not "feel obliged to provide, as in the past, outright support for the gilt-edged market in stocks having a matu-

rity of over one year."[12] This meant that banks could no longer be certain of the price they might receive for their long-term securities in the event they should find it necessary to replenish their reserves.

This meant also a somewhat different approach to the interest rate as a control mechanism, for within the constraint of credit control, competition was to reign supreme, and interest rates were to reflect the supply/demand conditions in a free market situation rather more like the North American practice. This was, in fact, why it was necessary for the clearing banks to abandon their long-standing arrangement of interest rates being tied to bank rate, hence, "In future, the authorities would seek to influence the structure of interest rates through a general control over the liquidity of the whole banking system."[13]

The question to be answered, of course, was, Can such a structured "North American type" framework be imposed on a complex banking and finance system and be successful in moderating the growth of credit? The new policy was introduced at a propitious time of slack demand for credit and low interest rates, and, generally, higher unemployment rates than were usual. Nevertheless, the controls imposed upon financial intermediaries (or non-clearing banks) restricted their activities substantially while, at the same time, *releasing* the clearing banks from the former constraints of quantitative controls. Since these banks already had excess reserves, they quickly moved into the more lucrative markets for credit, i.e., consumer loans, loans to companies dealing in property, and loans to finance companies. The authorities permitted this credit expansion because of the unemployment which existed at the time, and the consequence was an increase of deposits of the London and Scottish clearing banks by 28% in the year 1972.[14]

---

[11]"Reserve Ratios and Special Deposits," Bank of England, July 21, 1971.

[12]"Key Issues in Monetary and Credit Policy," An Address to the International Banking Conference in Munich on May 28, 1971.

[13]*Ibid.*

[14]Derek E. Wilde, Vice-Chairman, Barclay's Bank Ltd., "Competition and Credit Control One Year On," in a conference sponsored by Gillett Bros. Discount Co. Ltd., estimated that total deposits including the new finance house banks had grown from 22 to 29 billion in one year, about 32%. Some of this was due to double recording of certificates of deposits, and if this froth is eliminated, total growth would be about 24%.

But the real test of the new policy came during the foreign exchange crisis of June, 1972. As a consequence of the loss of confidence in sterling, the reserves of the banking system simply melted away as foreign deposits were withdrawn. This necessitated the sale by the banks of long-term gilt-edged securities which were no longer supported by the Bank of England, and interest rates rose considerably.

An even more interesting development was the reaction of the so-called "parallel markets" to the crisis in 1972, for it was in these markets that the weakness of the rate of interest as a free market price for credit was most apparent. It was necessary, in the first place, to protect the foreign exchange value of the pound sterling, and this meant that interest rates in Great Britain had to be high enough to attract foreign exchange, or what amounts to the same thing, foreign sterling deposits. But, if interest on bank advances and overdrafts were to reflect these high free market rates, they would have risen to such levels as to be socially and politically unacceptable. After all, interest in house mortgages, hire purchase, etc., is paid by the general public, and the banks, in response to requests from the Bank of England, kept their own rates low. There were, therefore, *two* interest rates, one for the free markets and one for the banks, an impossibility under a freely competitive system.

2. The End of Competition

The consequence of this situation proved to be the "collapse" of the system of competition and credit control — at least temporarily. Companies which had overdraft facilities at their clearing banks found a margin of profit in borrowing from the banks and *relending* in the parallel markets! They were, in other words, intermediating, just as financial intermediaries, between the two. The situation reached the absurd when clearing banks found themselves selling their own certificates of deposit to these same companies who had the overdraft facilities, i.e., *recycling their own deposits*. In order to stop this process of arbitrage, the Bank of England itself had to violate the principles of Competition and Credit Control by forcing up the minimum lending rate to 13% in November, 1973, thus pushing up the clearing bank rates high enough to close the gap.[15]

To answer the question, can a North American type policy succeed in Britain, the conclusion is that it has already failed in the strictest sense of the word. It failed because of the enormous stresses and strains imposed from outside the banking system, and yet which are still felt within it, that is, in one word, inflation. It was, in the final analysis, inflation which forced nominal interest rates to excessive levels with zero or negative real rates. It was inflation also which precipitated the original balance of payments crisis which caused the run against sterling during June, 1972. About $2,500 million of foreign exchange was lost in that month alone.

B. Canadian Bank Rate

The rather considerable detail included in the above analysis of the Bank of England bank rate (or minimum lending rate as it is now known) will serve as a background to the Bank of Canada's bank rate which is really a modification of the British practice appropriate to a North American context. The Bank of Canada, like all central banks, is a lender of last resort, i.e., it is prepared to make loans to chartered banks whenever they are short of funds. The bank rate is the rate charged for these loans.

At the outset, when the Bank of Canada first began operations in 1935, its bank rate was simply an extension of the rate charged for advances under the Finance Act—$2\frac{1}{2}$%. But this rate was purely nominal because borrowing from the Bank of Canada at that time was never done. Only in times of tight money did it become necessary to borrow from the central bank and during the depression years, money was easy. The degree of this monetary ease is apparent from the low Treasury Bill rates at the time. Since 1934, Treasury Bills have been sold by public tender instead of by private arrangements through the banks, and rates on these bills were less than 1% in 1936; rates on short-term government bonds reached a low of 1.32% in September of that year. It was not conceivable, therefore, that chartered bank borrowing at bank rate of $2\frac{1}{2}$% could even take place.

During wartime, there is absolutely nothing that

---

[15]R. G. Baird, "Competition–But What Credit Control?," *The Scottish Bankers' Magazine,* May, 1974, p. 11.

bank rate can do. Wartime restrictions, the necessity for war finance, exchange controls, etc., effectively perform the function of bank rate so that a "retirement" of the rate occurs. There was, however, one curious development in 1944. The Bank of Canada reduced the bank rate to $1\frac{1}{2}$%, down from the $2\frac{1}{2}$% last set in 1935. The purpose of this was to signal to everyone who may have been interested (the war was far from over at that time) that after the war the Bank would continue the "kind of monetary policy which has brought about the current level of interest rates."[16] This meant that the Bank would maintain the easy monetary policy which it had learned in the pre-war depression era — monetary ease and an encouragement of credit. This is a surprising statement even without the benefit of hindsight because historical experience has clearly taught that inflation has been the problem after wars, not depression.

The next change in the bank rate occurred in 1950 when it was raised to 2%. The reason for this was that due to the increased defence expenditure attendant upon the Korean War when there was full employment, inflationary pressures were appearing in the form of substantial price increases—12% in the wholesale price index and 6% in the Cost of Living Index in one year. Now it is true that interest rates (or yields) on short to medium-term bonds had increased to well over 2% in 1950, but apart from the bank rate aligning with these rates, what did the rise in bank rate mean? So long as chartered banks did not borrow from the Bank of Canada, the "lender of last resort," a rise in bank rate could not mean any more than a psychological indicator—moral suasion — which might have been better accomplished by a public announcement of the policy of the Bank by the Governor. Certainly the bank rate by itself could not address the problem of threatened inflation. It is interesting, though, that the Bank of England raised its rate from 2 to $2\frac{1}{2}$% in November, 1951 pretty much for the same psychological reason, but in this case it was a warning to the world from the world's leading financial centre.

It was not until the establishment and development of the money market in Ottawa that the bank

rate began to have some rational basis. In 1954 an agreement was reached with chartered banks to maintain a 15% liquid asset to deposits ratio (8% cash and deposits at the Bank of Canada in accordance with the 1954 Bank Act revision plus an agreed 7% secondary assets ratio). This could only be feasible if the Bank of Canada would make available its loan facilities to the chartered banks. At the same time it made possible a truly effective bank rate policy which works as follows: Suppose that bank rate is lower than the Treasury Bill rate; chartered banks would prefer to borrow at the Bank of Canada rather than sell their Treasury Bills from their liquid asset portfolio should they happen to have less liquid assets than are required. On the other hand, suppose bank rate is above Treasury Bill rate; chartered banks will prefer to sell Treasury Bills, call in day-to-day loans, etc., rather than have recourse to the Bank of Canada when they find themselves short of liquid assets. All the Bank of Canada has to do to implement, say, a tight monetary policy is to see to it that chartered banks are indeed short of liquid assets. This could be done through open market operations, and when this is combined with a bank rate higher than Treasury Bill rate, it effectively tightens the money supply.

Bank rate also appeared in 1954 in the Purchase and Resale Agreements with the money market dealers. These dealers rely on day-to-day loans from the chartered banks to finance their purchases of Treasury Bills at the weekly tender. If chartered banks are unable to satisfy their needs, because of a tight monetary policy, the dealers can acquire additional funds from the Bank of Canada by selling Treasury Bills from their own portfolio with an agreement to repurchase them within a 30-day period. The rate at which these purchase and resale agreements are made (the resale price is always less than the bank's purchase price) is bank rate. Should this rate be high, dealers will be inclined to bid low for Treasury Bills at the weekly tender and the Treasury Bill yield is given a twist upward.

All this was one of Mr. Coyne's greater achievements during his period as Governor of the Bank of Canada, to bring back bank rate and make it an operative tool within the framework of a specific monetary policy. Of course there is a psychological effect in the announcement of a bank rate change for the reason that it prepares the way for a specific monetary policy to follow. It is some-

---

[16] Annual Report of the Governor of the Bank of Canada, 1944, p. 5.

what surprising, therefore, that having "recommissioned" bank rate, the Bank of Canada in November, 1956 proceeded to adopt the sterile policy of *maintaining* it at a level exactly .25% above the last weekly tender of Treasury Bills. This resulted in bank rate only being effective in a tight monetary policy situation, and, of course, the "bonus" psychological impact of the bank rate adjustment was also completely lost.

Fortunately, the experiment was concluded on June 24, 1962 and bank rate became more useful once more. Actually it was split into two parts. The rate for purchase and resale agreements became known as the Purchase and Resale Agreement rate and remained in effect at .25% above the last weekly Treasury Bill rate with the provision that it could not exceed bank rate. The bank rate itself continued as the cost of loans to chartered banks.

The maximum level of the PRA rate was supplemented by a minimum PRA rate defined in November, 1970 as bank rate less .75%, thereby completing a floor to ceiling limit within which the PRA rate may fluctuate depending upon the market forces which happen to arise from week to week. One can readily imagine the situation without such an arrangement. Market rates do fluctuate from week to week around a general trend. Whenever market rates exceed the PRA rate money market dealers might prefer the purchase and resale agreement as a source of funds to the day-to-day loans of the chartered banks. Such weekly movements of the market rate are almost random and should not be used on this basis for what amounts to an injection of new money. Separating the PRA rate from bank rate and defining limits to its movement outside of random fluctuations avoids this complication. The ceiling, or maximum, was increased in 1974 to bank rate plus .5% where it remains to this day.

By the early 1960s another function of bank rate appeared. The Bank of Canada began the process of adjusting bank rate with the objective of encouraging foreign capital, particularly short-term capital. This was another outgrowth of the Canadian money market which made possible the purchase of Canadian Treasury Bills by foreign investors. Through a hedged operation (discussed in Part III) foreigners, particularly Americans, may purchase Treasury Bills with their U.S. dollars which then find their way into the Canadian Exchange Fund Account as part of Canada's foreign exchange reserves. Raising the bank rate encourages higher Treasury Bill rates which, if higher than corresponding U.S. rates, will attract U.S. dollars. This aspect of bank rate is most useful during periods of foreign exchange crises such as that which occurred in the early 1960s and again in the latter 1970s. It suggests that the Canadian bank rate, like the Bank of England rate, has become a fully operational tool of policy with its effectiveness made possible by means of a mature money and capital market.

C. The United States Discount Rate

There is no question that the United States is proof enough of the platitude that the monetary and banking system of a country develops in accordance with the peculiar characteristics of that particular country. This is easy to understand under the circumstances surrounding the evolution of the modern U.S. banking system—a rigid adherence to the gold standard, a post-Civil War deflation resulting from the return to an operational gold standard, and the prohibition of state bank notes which were made illegal by the 1863 Bank Act. But having closed one troublesome door, the federal government discovered that state banks had found another, the chequebook account. Having no constraints on the manufacture of chequebook money, the many state banks chose this method for their profit maximization objective with the consequence that the great deflation of the latter nineteenth and early twentieth centuries was characterized by periodic bank runs and panics leading to considerable hardship for those unfortunates who happened to rely on their bank deposits instead of "sugar bowl" hoards of cash.

Recognition of the existence of the financial chaos within the American system led Congress to establish a National Monetary Commission to examine carefully both the defects and possible alternatives. Of course, the Bank of England, the most successful and prestigious central bank in the world, was the subject of considerable study, and the Governor and Deputy Governor as well as several British banking officials testified before the Commission at considerable length. Despite the obvious advantage of a single central bank the Commission recommended not a central bank at all but a National Reserve Association with several (15) district branches. After an election in 1912, the Congress passed the Federal Reserve Act which established 12 Federal Reserve Banks with a coordinating Board of Governors in Washington.

Mints argues that the Federal Reserve System was "not designed to create a monetary agency with ample powers for controlling the stock of money in accordance with a rational objective."[17] He notes that in the preamble to the Act it is stated that the purpose is to provide for an elastic currency, a re-discount agency, and effective supervision of banking.[18] It is obvious that an "elastic currency" suggests some variation in the supply of money, but it does not mean a certain *quantity* of money to be determined in any other way than by gold. Elasticity was to be provided in each of the districts by the re-discounting of commercial bills at each Federal Reserve Bank ("*Re*-discounting" means that each individual bank had already discounted the bill once in accepting it for credit; the second discount, or re-discount, was to provide additional funds for the bank itself from its regional Federal Reserve bank whenever necessary). Further, the rate of re-discount was designed to be the cost of this borrowing from the Federal Reserve bank. But, why borrow purely on the basis of "bills" and not, as in Canada, on outright loans? The reason here is a concession to the old "Real Bills" doctrine.

The idea that the banks should discount only commercial bills goes back to the pre-Ricardian era in England. In principle, the argument is that banks should only make short-term loans on the basis of *claims* to commodities both in process of production and in process of exchange as opposed to the commodities themselves (in other words, circulating capital). In this way the supply of money would be sufficiently elastic to accommodate the needs of trade yet controlled by the amount of gold. It means, further, that money has an element of "passivity" in it in that it can expand or contract with changing economic activity. Income changes come first, *then* the money is drawn forth to sustain the income; income is the cause, money the result.

In its broadest outline this was the philosophy underlying the Federal Reserve discounting system as it was stated in the early Federal Reserve bulletins. The monetary system was to be self-liquidating and would work automatically if banks were truly "commercial" banks in the sense that they manufactured money only for short-term lending. As it turned out, self-liquidation was a very different thing from self-creation. Banks, once loans are repaid, are not willing to see their earning assets reduced and actively seek new forms of lending purely for the sake of maintaining their profits. Should actual short-term borrowers happen to be scarce, banks will increase loans to whatever borrowers they can find, for example, by purchasing Treasury Bills from the market.

Is it conceivable that something like a Federal Reserve System could be designed for Canada on a regional basis? The answer is no, and the reason is once more the peculiar structure of the U.S. banking system as opposed to the Canadian. American banks are chartered by both state and federal governments. Thus 48 (now 50) separate banking laws plus one federal law means a banking system consisting of thousands of small, independent banks which Canadians would likely describe as not only incomprehensible but chaotic.

To have any chance of successful operation, some kind of order is necessary. Even before the Federal Reserve System existed, the use of larger banks in larger centres as unofficial "mini-central" banks by smaller banks for cheque clearing purposes had become an established practice. These larger banks used *still* larger banks until New York, Chicago, and St. Louis, etc. became very important financial centres. There was, thus, a regional banking system already in existence without a Federal Reserve System. For the many small banks within each district, money could be tight or easy regardless of the conditions within a neighbouring district. In the Canadian system, on the other hand, consisting of twelve chartered banks with branches everywhere, district boundaries can be readily crossed by the transfer of funds from one branch in an "easy" district to another in a "tight" district. This is why it is not possible to attack the Canadian problem of different regional unemployment rates with monetary policies appropriate for each region. It is simply not possible to confine our chartered banks to a single region alone!

---

[17]L. Mints, *A History of Banking Theory*, University of Chicago Press, Chicago, 1945, p. 281.
[18]*Ibid.*, p. 284.

Hardly had the Federal Reserve begun operation (like the Bank of Canada it had to find something to do) when it was used as an engine for cranking out war finance in 1917. This time, unlike the Civil War, there was no printing of Greenbacks. The U.S. government simply sold interest bearing debt instruments to the banking system and the public. When the Federal Reserve banks bought additional government securities, either new Federal Reserve notes or bank reserves in the form of chequebook money were created. This expanded the money manufacturing powers of the U.S. banking system with the inevitable result that by the end of the war the money supply, prices, and interest rates were rising.

Since rising interest rates mean falling bond prices, the Federal Reserve was obliged to support bond prices by buying more bonds after the war. Of course, this continued the inflation and to curb it, the Federal Reserve raised re-discount rates to make bank borrowing more expensive. To the surprise of the Board of Governors, money supply declined by mid-1921 and a short, sharp recession set in. Prices were reduced, and gold flowed into the country. There were many bank failures (506 in 1921) but (to adopt the moralistic tone appropriate to the time) they *ought* to have failed because of unsound loan practices. At any rate, the whole process laid the groundwork for the unprecedented period of prosperity of the 1920s.

Like the Bank of Canada bank rate, the Federal Reserve discount rate is the cost to members of the Federal Reserve System (all national banks must be members of the System whereas state bank memberships are voluntary) of reserve funds which may be borrowed from the Reserve banks. "Each Reserve bank must establish its own discount rate, subject to review and determination by the Board of Governors in Washington, every 14 days."[19] There is a curious contradiction here in the words "establish" (for each Reserve bank) and "determination" (for the Board of Governors). The fact of the matter is that at *both* the District and Washington levels the rates are set and if the District decides to establish a rate which the Board of Governors does not approve, the decision of the District is over-

ruled. It doesn't take many incidents of veto to convince District banks that the Washington line must be followed; in fact, the best the Districts can hope for now is to have regional input into a centralized decision-making process.

There is another factor at work here. The operation of the discount rate is such that member banks can either borrow at their Reserve bank or sell liquid assets (now mostly Treasury Bills) on the market. With modern communication and branch offices of market dealers in virtually every city in North America, the "market" is available to every bank within reasonable distance. Just as it is true in Canada, if the discount rate is less than the market rate, banks will prefer to borrow at their Federal Reserve bank; conversely, banks will sell Treasury Bills if the discount rate is above market rate. The implication for monetary policy, then, is clear since borrowing from the Federal Reserve means an injection of new reserve funds. It follows that since the market is now so widespread, a uniform discount rate must be maintained; in addition, the discount rate must not be too far out of line with the market rates so as to avoid excessive "jumps" in rate adjustments.

There is another rate of interest which has come into prominence in recent years — The Federal Funds rate. Banks with surplus reserves make available these reserves on a loan basis to banks with shortages. The rate at which those loans are made to a deficit bank is important and can never be greater than the discount rate. The importance lies in the difference between the two rates; for example, if monetary policy is tight the demand for reserve funds is high and the difference between the two rates is small and, further, any increase in the discount rate at that point suggests that money will likely be even tighter. Banks will, therefore, sell Treasury Bills on the market to replenish their reserves and market rates will rise.

The second tool of an operative money policy which is available to the Federal Reserve System is open market operations. The Federal Open Market Committee (FOMC) consists of the Board of Governors, the President of the Federal Reserve Bank of New York, and four other Reserve Bank Presidents on a rotating basis. This committee directs the open market account at the Federal Reserve Bank of New York to either buy or sell securities from dealers who are regularly in

---

[19] *The Federal Reserve System*, Board of Governors of the Federal Reserve System, Washington, D.C., 1961, p. 46.

the market as middlemen. Just as in Canada, sale of securities by the Reserve involves a cheque drawn against a member bank and shrinks the reserves of that bank. Similarly, purchases of securities increase the reserves. In addition, re-purchase agreements are sometimes made by the Reserve to supply temporary funds to dealers.

When both "tools," open market operations and discount rates, are coordinated in one plan of action a monetary policy can be implemented. For instance, a tight money policy can develop from the sale of securities by the Committee in New York. This forces a tight reserve position for the banks so that member banks may either borrow from their Reserve Bank or sell securities. To complete a tight policy, the discount rate should be higher than market rate, forcing a sale of securities, and, in turn, pushing market rates upward.

Finally, a third tool of policy is the power to adjust reserve *ratios* which the Board of Governors has. In Canada, this ratio is fixed under the Bank Act, but in the U.S. their adjustment can be a powerful tool of monetary policy. For this very reason (being, perhaps, *too* powerful) it is rarely used. Commercial banks are understandably unhappy with changes in reserve ratio requirements since enormous adjustments in deposits are entailed. They can, therefore, opt out of the System altogether, if they are made sufficiently unhappy, by securing a state charter instead; such action as this weakens the entire system.

III. MONETARY POLICIES

A. North America

The tools of monetary policy developed by the Federal Reserve System will be recognized as the model for the Canadian counterpart. This is to be expected. Sheer proximity to the United States would dictate Canadian development along U.S. lines even though Canadians might have preferred otherwise. Even during the early history of banking, Adam Shortt observed, "... I may state categorically that the Canadian banking system was derived in a very direct and literal manner from the United States."[20] The use of

the New York money market which required either branches, agencies, or brokers must also have influenced Canadian banking technique through a necessary familiarity with American habits.[21]

However, even though our monetary tools are very much the same, for the United States the control of money and credit is more of a major undertaking than for Canada for the reason that the system itself is more complex and vastly greater in size. For example, as Canadians we can always blame the Bank of Canada, or the Governor, if things don't go right, but for Americans the decision-making process is so diffuse that no one can be truly blamed. To be sure, the Chairman of the Board of Governors is as important as the Governor of the Bank of Canada, but his task as coordinator, and even as a diplomat having to deal with the Executive and Legislative branches of the government, is very much greater.

Sometimes decisions as to the correct monetary policy appropriate for the times can be as tense as a drama. A former Governor of the Federal Reserve Board, Sherman Maisel, has, fortunately, recorded a very interesting episode in recent U.S. financial history which had escaped the notice of the general public, press, etc. In fact, without Mr. Maisel's account we would know nothing of it.[22] He begins this account by noting that 1969 was the year of the end of a long economic expansion so that until 1970, monetary policy was easy. But on April 30, the Cambodian invasion was announced which was followed firstly by the Kent State massacre and secondly by the bankruptcy in June of the Penn-Central Railroad — three events which shook the financial community to its foundations. The stock market dropped by 25% and interest rates rose. Now, as will be examined carefully in Part II, rising interest rates mean a collapse in capital values; hence, assets of banks, savings and loan companies, mutual

---

[20]A. Shortt, "The Early History of Canadian Banking," *Journal of the Canadian Bankers Association*, 1896, reprinted in E. P. Neufeld, *Money and Banking in Canada*, Carleton Library, #17, McClelland & Stewart Ltd., 1964.

[21]Canadian branches made loans to Americans and were even accused of usury. The suits were dismissed in the court at Albany, New York. *The Monetary Times*, November 4, 1870. *Ibid.*

[22]S. J. Maisel, *Managing the Dollar*, W. W. Norton & Co., New York, 1973, p. 5 ff, "The 1970 Crisis."

funds, and other financial intermediaries suffered enormous declines in their worth. Most important in such circumstances is to avoid a panic, i.e., to maintain liquidity at all costs for, when a panic begins, it can spread quickly.

There was, apparently, considerable debate in the FOMC on the issues which were two-fold: (1) satisfy the enormous demand for liquidity by buying securities on the open market, but (2) this would further expand the money supply which already had been growing faster than was considered to be appropriate to a 4% real growth of GNP. In the first alternative, the Penn-Central situation was most ominous since there was a great deal ($80 million) of Penn-Central's commercial paper outstanding. This type of credit, it should be explained, is the private sector's "Treasury Bill"— short-term, higher interest, and generally sound investment. Banks often assist in lengthening the term of the debt in much the same way that Treasury Bills are paid off, but in this case, banks loan funds to repay the creditors who do not wish to renew. The important issue was, How could banks meet such loan demands from reserves which were already loaned up? Yet, if they could not, there was danger that a panic could develop which could readily spread to other corporations.

The decision was reached (right or wrong, we will never know) to risk further inflation by expanding the liquidity of the banking system. A liquidity crisis was thereby overcome and long-term interest rates fell from their historic peaks. All this was unknown to the general public. Indeed, *had* it been known, a financial panic would likely have been assured. Certainly, if the Bank of Canada was aware of the crisis in the U.S., there was no mention in the Annual Report of the Governor for 1970.

In most cases, Federal Reserve policy is not so dramatic. But, even in the case of the failure of Penn-Central the President's Council of Economic Advisers itself denied that a liquidity crisis had existed.

> The question whether a genuine liquidity crisis existed in mid-1970 in the sense that firms otherwise sound were going bankrupt because of a liquidity squeeze can be answered in the negative.[23]

It is apparent, of course, that this denial is based on a particular definition of liquidity; one might argue that had there been no emergency action to expand bank liquidity by the Federal Reserve a genuine corporate liquidity crisis would have followed. It was the prevention of the former that was seen by the FOMC as a higher priority than anti-inflation policy.

Aside from this exception, it was clear that the thrust of Federal Reserve policy in 1970 was directed more toward control of the money supply aggregates, and discount rates were being adjusted with just that in mind.[24] This policy continued with a concentration of attention on the growth of M_1 and M_2 and less on market rates of interest with the result that an upward trend in interest rates persisted. As it turned out, the Federal Funds interest rate was used as an indicator of the appropriateness of a given money stock at a particular time.[25] Thus a shift in attention from market rates to the Federal Funds rate took place.

It is impossible not to observe that during the period when U.S. short-term interest rates fell, because of the measures to overcome the liquidity crisis, Canadian rates also fell, maintaining a positive spread of about $1/2$ to 1%. (There was no "liquidity crisis" in Canada.) Similarly, when U.S. rates rose to unprecedented levels in the U.S. in 1970 (the only other period of such high rates was during the Civil War) Canadian rates also rose again with about the same spread. Furthermore, when U.S. rates increased during the years subsequent to the liquidity crisis when restrictive monetary policy was restored, Canadian short-term rates also increased to reach the incredibly high levels of almost 12% in 1974. Thereafter, a decline in the short-term rates of both countries began until early 1975. At that point the U.S. rate continued its decline while the Canadian rate moved in the opposite direction. Canadian long-term rates (10 provincial bonds) also rose to widen the differential between the corresponding U.S. rate (utility bonds).

The exceptional rise in 1974 of interest rates in

---

[23]*Economic Report of the President*, February, 1971, p. 69.

[24]*Ibid.*, 1970, pp. 33-34. Total reserves of member banks were held constant in 1969.

[25]*Ibid.*, 1972, pp. 57-58. The higher the Federal Funds rate, the tighter were monetary controls, and *vice versa*.

the U.S. was the consequence of an unusual circumstance of continued unemployment and a rising price level due largely to external causes which combined to produce the steepest recession in the U.S. post-war history. At the same time, the Federal Reserve made the colossal mistake of continuing its tight money policy misinterpreting inflation as enemy #1 — the cause of unemployment. Similar misunderstanding of the situation extended into the executive branch of the U.S. government with President Ford's WIN (Whip Inflation Now) campaign. Not much time elapsed before the information and the facts began to present the true state of the economy to both the President and the Federal Reserve which promptly reversed its policy of tight money. So the result was a steep decline of the U.S. short-term rate from over 12% in 1974 to just 6% in 1975, the consequence of an abrupt change in monetary policy, this time to encourage greater employment.

But why should Canada's interest rate structure move precisely with the U.S. with a ½% to 1% positive spread, i.e., the Canadian rate continuously above the U.S. rate? It appears that the Bank of Canada has been concerned with two fundamental principles in the determination of Canada's interest rate structure.

1. The foreign exchange rate of the Canadian dollar. The Bank of Canada, in 1971, noted that "... the upward movement of interest rates in the U.S. contributed to a tendency for the value of the Canadian dollar to decline from the peak level reached in February. In these circumstances the Bank of Canada shifted to a cash management policy that was designed to contain the growth of bank liquidity." (N.B., The use of cautious words such as "contributed to a tendency," is a characteristic of Bank of Canada Annual Reports in the years following Mr. Coyne.) The Bank continued this policy "stance" "... until August when the new policies announced in the U.S. brought a reversal of the rising trend of interest rates in that country."[26] The "new policy," incidentally, was that brought about by the international monetary crisis which led to the setting aside of the U.S. obligation to sell gold at $35/oz. and Mr. Nixon's wage/price freeze of 90 days to be followed subsequently by Phases II and III.

It is evident from the passages quoted that the thrust of the Bank of Canada's monetary policy was to maintain a positive interest differential to protect the exchange rate of the Canadian dollar. Hence, a decision was made regarding tight or easy money in Canada not with regard to the Canadian price level but to maintain *higher interest rates in Canada than in the U.S.* We find this emphasis on the interest rates maintained until 1974. In the Governor's Annual Report for that year,

> Since changes in the cost of money and in returns on financial assets are the *main channels* through which the impact of monetary policy is transmitted to spending and saving decisions...[27]

we find a continued concern for interest rates which in turn follow the movement of the U.S. rates. The absurdity of the situation is obvious upon reflection. Canada's interest rates move precisely as U.S. rates which are determined by monetary policy in the U.S., and, therefore, have no relationship to the Canadian economy except for the exchange rate.

2. "Targeting" of the money supply. In May, 1975, the U.S. announced its growth rate targets as follows:

M_1—5%-7½%; M_2—7½%-10½%; M_3—9%-12%; Credit Proxy 6%-9%.[28] In 1975 also the Bank of Canada announced *its* money supply target, but instead of including the broader definitions of money within its target analysis, it chose to concentrate on M_1 alone. The rationale for this approach is that there has been a tendency in recent years for M_2 and M_3 to respond to adjustments of interest rates for savings deposits in chartered banks, i.e., a positive interest elasticity relationship. If this tendency holds true for the future, a tight money policy will raise interest rates and reduce M_1 by means of a transfer of funds into M_2. By reducing M_1, an inflation can be effectively checked if the money supply alone is the cause.

Since the objective of both the U.S. and Canada in controlling the money supply is now very much

---

[26]Annual Report of the Governor, 1971, p. 38.

[27]Annual Report of the Governor, 1974, p. 21.
[28]Economic Report of the President, 1976. "Credit Proxy" is defined as total loans and investments of member banks.

the same, it follows that the economic circumstances which prompt monetary policy are likely to be similar in both countries though not necessarily *exactly* the same. The recent recession and the long-term inflation affect both countries, but both unemployment and inflation are more severe in Canada. Interest rates, therefore, can diverge depending on the relative tightness of policies as they are applied in the two countries. A tighter policy in 1975 accompanied by increasing bank rate in Canada forced a rising trend of short-term rates while the opposite was true in the U.S. Similarly, monetary ease and adjustments of bank rate to lower levels in latter 1976 and 1977 brought Canadian rates down at the same time that U.S. rates moved up.

Until fairly recently, the first principle, the flow of capital into Canada for the purpose of sustaining the exchange rate, appeared to have been abandoned in the interest of the second. With some reluctance, perhaps, the Bank of Canada has once more used the bank rate to encourage the inflow of more investment to lend support to a weakened Canadian dollar. Hopefully, its attempts will be successful, but certainly, having attained its objective (if indeed it does) we may also hope that the health of the domestic economy will once more assume top priority in all policy decisions.

The lesson to be learned from both the U.S. experience in 1974 and the earlier Canadian attempt to control inflation in 1969 is, quite simply, the advisability of gradualism. We can apply monetary brakes too strenuously and if price increases prove to be intractable the result must be unemployment. This is often the case when inflation is imported, especially when rising energy prices are a basic cause. Tight money cannot finance rising prices, higher real production and a velocity of circulation which will not change in the short term. Or, to look at it from a more fundamental viewpoint than a simple Quantity Theory, the stages of production find themselves short of liquid funds to finance domestic production since too much existing money supplies are being drained into the import sector (candidly, the huge balance of payments surpluses of OPEC countries). We have seen two experiences with acute shortages of money and the lesson, it appears, has been learned by the Bank of Canada in its policy of a more gradual application of monetary brakes. This policy has been followed by

the Bank since the appointment of the current Governor, Mr. Bouey.

B. Great Britain

While the North American banking systems had their roots in a Ricardian gold standard philosophy, once this common underpinning had been eliminated, there was a distinct divergence from the British system which was the "ancestor." We have already noted that the British policy thrust was directed toward the interest rate structure, and that this resulted in a money supply which became a relatively minor statistic. The device of Competition and Credit Control was to change this direction toward the control of credit (or money) but this new orientation, unfortunately, could not cope with the economic difficulties of an enormous price inflation, the depreciation of the pound sterling, and the necessity to attract foreign exchange to finance a growing deficit on the balance of payments. High price inflation meant that domestic interest rates would also have to be high. At the same time, the minimum lending rate had to rise to attract foreign investment. Once again the policy thrust turned toward interest rates with money becoming secondary; Competition and Credit Control had, in effect, failed.

The result was a return once more to the Supplementary Special Deposits scheme which subjects the banks to a tight reserve control and which continues to this day. As such, it is particularly hard on the clearing banks which still do a great deal of lending by overdraft. Quite simply, the scheme, known as the "corset," means that if the growth of interest bearing eligible liabilities (IBELS, or interest bearing deposits) exceeds a stipulated amount over the past year, up to $1/2$ of the excess must be deposited with the Bank of England as *non*-interest bearing deposits.

We can readily see how this works and why it is referred to as a "corset." Since banks, particularly clearing banks, acquire many deposits by bidding in the wholesale market, and proceed to re-loan them at a profit, the requirement to convert up to one-half into non-interest earning deposits at the Bank of England raises the cost of these deposits by an additional 50%. In a competitive market for loans, it is not possible to pass on the extra cost to the borrower, hence, the money supply is effectively checked by this action on the clearing banks alone.[29] Bankers complain about discrimination and the violation of the spirit of Competition and Credit Control but there still remains the necessity to curb the money manufacturing mechanism.

To Canadians probably the most foreign and most difficult to appreciate of the characteristics of British and European banking is the competition which exists in the industry. This is manifest by the number of banks which operate in Great Britain — over 300 commercial banks, both foreign and domestic, along with the six great clearing banks.[30] In addition to these there are, of course, many financial intermediaries which are included as "banks" in the British definition.

To begin with we should realize the extent to which British banking has changed over the past two decades. Within the clearing banks themselves there have been the greatest changes not only in the form of mergers which have reduced their total number from eleven to six but also in their loan deposit techniques. Twenty years ago the overdraft loan was practically the entire lending activity of the banks; today term lending (longer-term contractual loans) is as much as 40% of all domestic loans.[31] Considering the short-term nature of the deposits which originate from branch offices (referred to as retail deposits), the majority of which are sight or 7-day deposits, this is a remarkable achievement in intermediation.

By far the most interesting of the deposit-taking techniques however is not at the retail or branch level which we, as Canadians, automatically think of as "deposits." Since the early 1960s a highly competitive wholesale market has grown up, generally operated by brokers, which has no counterpart in Canada. Through this market, surplus deposits of a certain bank may be transmitted to another bank which can use them to finance a loan or some other form of asset. These are referred to as interbank deposits and are roughly the equivalent of the U.S. Federal Funds market. In addition to the interbank loans there are deposits in excess of £10,000 received through the branch network from business enterprises, etc., which wish a higher interest than would ordinarily be offered by the branch alone. These too are exchanged through the market. Finally, there are certificates of deposits which are simply promises to pay a certain sum at maturity and which are negotiable, hence, quite liquid, and yet pay a higher interest than the ordinary deposit.

banks is obvious upon reflection. Should the clearing banks, for example, extend their assets beyond the capacity of their highly liquid retail deposits to support, they can be certain of acquiring additional deposits from the wholesale market. This is also why British banks are "asset driven" rather than "deposit driven" as in the Canadian case. Banks in Canada acquire deposits retail *then* use them in the most profit maximizing manner coincident with their liquidity requirements; not so British banks. They identify the assets they wish to finance, *then* locate the deposits from the wholesale market if their retail deposits are insufficient.

The competition in the banking field has been intensified by the influx of the many foreign banks of which there are more than 280 in London alone.[32] While their business is mostly international, concerned with multi-national enterprises generally of the same nationality as the bank, they also compete on the retail and wholesale level for deposits. Foreign branches of Canadian banks, for example, are active in the retail deposit business rendering services to tourists, and, in general, competing for loans just as any other British bank. When these foreign banks are included in the entire banking scene of Great Britain, it is hardly surprising that some of the great clearing banks themselves are looking forward to entry into Canada after the Bank Act revision of 1979, for they consider Canada to be a country which is very much "underbanked."

But competition does not end with just foreign banks. There are very many financial intermediaries in Great Britain which compete for de-

---

[29] *London Clearing Banks*, Committee of London Clearing Bankers, 1978, para. 6.18. It is particularly difficult for clearing banks because the non-clearers can draw on their stand-by credits with clearing banks forcing them to incur the penalty.

[30] Strangely, the simple statistic of the exact numbers of banks is difficult to locate. The figure reported here is from the Committee of London Clearing Bankers. *Ibid.*, p. 13.

[31] *Ibid.*, p. 13.

[32] *Ibid.*, para. 18.7.

posits just as they do in Canada. However, the British have used some differences in banking regulations to enable the intermediaries to have some extra advantages over the clearing banks; for instance, the trustee savings banks are permitted a tax-free interest payment to their depositors of up to £70. Building societies are exempt from the 12½% liquidity requirement which was imposed in 1971 as part of Competition and Credit Control and is still in effect. The purpose here is to encourage the flow of funds into needed housing, but, nevertheless, it does constitute "unfair" competition (using Canadian standards of "fairness").

At the same time the clearing banks still must provide the money transmission service via the clearing centres throughout the country. As such they hold deposits in favour of the intermediaries (interbank deposits). This is still the primary function of the clearing banks (just as it has been for centuries) and which is the service counterpart of the money manufacturing function.

Probably the real test, though, of the efficiency of a banking system, Canadian or British, is the degree to which it can intermediate between the liquidity requirements of both borrowers and lenders without forcing additional liquidity through money supply expansion. It is likely that, from the results of the recent inflationary past, *both* systems would fail the test.

There is, however, an important distinction between the two systems which should perhaps be re-emphasized. This is the "asset driven" motivation of the British banks as opposed to our "deposit driven" Canadian banks. It is likely that the identification *first* of investment projects for loan financing can have advantages for the reason that those assets which are sound and beneficial to the economy are likely to be the most profitable to the banks. Identifying these, then locating the deposits places the decision-making process where it properly belongs, on the investment itself. In the Canadian deposit-driven case, the motivation is to employ extra deposits in whatever opportunity is available at the time for the reason that idle deposits have zero earnings. The likelihood, therefore, of unwise use of scarce resources would appear to be stronger in Canada. However, it must be pointed out that British banking did go through an orgy of financing fruitless land speculation during the mid-seventies. It fell to the lot of the clearing banks to assist their

banking competitors in order to avoid what appeared to be an approaching financial collapse. One cannot, therefore, draw easy conclusions which involve qualitative judgments unsupported by the facts.

C. The German Economic Miracle

Germany's record of economic growth and price stability is enviable even without the miraculous recovery from World War II and the immense task of reconstruction which followed. During the years 1950–55 the annual rate of growth of industrial production (including construction) averaged 14%. Thereafter, the growth rate slowed down to about the same as the rate of growth of the real GNP, about 5% per year. The only exceptions to this growth rate appear to be during cyclical recession years.

What has been nothing short of miraculous, however, is the unflagging growth rate of productivity (real GNP per employed person). Until 1969 this averaged about 5% per year, and only during the 1970s has it showed a tendency to decline to an average of about 3.6%. All during the period since 1960, with the exception of the four-year recession 1974–77, the unemployment rate exceeded 2% of the labour force in only one year. Considering that this was the time of great in-migration of foreign labour, the record is remarkable.

While other countries have been wrestling with unemployment rates of twice that of Germany during the recent recession years, the German rate reached its peak at 4.7% in 1975 (see Table 6-1). Even allowing for declines in the labour force through migrant labour returning to their original homelands, the record is still enviable.

The "miracle" actually began in 1948 when Germany was still under the control of the Allied occupation authorities. Under Professor Erhard, Director of the Department for Economic Affairs for the Allied zones, Germany moved into a free market economy without rationing or price freezes, thereby returning to the profit incentive for German business enterprise. At the same time the Bank deutscher Lander (BdL) was established as a central bank along with a new Deutsche Mark (10 old Reichsmark = 1 Deutsche Mark). It was a completely new and

Table 6-1
WEST GERMANY

SELECTED ECONOMIC STATISTICS	1974	1975	1976	1977
Real GNP/person (growth rate)	2.3	1.7	6.3	2.7
Cost of living (annual rate of change)	7.0	6.0	4.3	3.7
Unemployment rate (1% of labour force)	2.6	4.7	4.6	4.5
Annual rate of change of labour force	−0.7	−1.5	−0.9	−0.3
Unemployment ratio	2.6	4.7	4.6	4.5

Source: Monthly Report of the Deutsche Bundesbank, June, 1978, p. 11.

fresh beginning for the German economy. The result has been that German workers, in terms of real wages per employee, have during the period 1950-77 increased their standard of living by 287% — probably the highest paid workers in Europe.[33]

It would be foolish to attribute this achievement entirely to the banking and financial system; certainly a good deal of the credit must remain with a native German penchant for industry and enterprise along with certain other favourable circumstances. Nevertheless it would be equally wrong not to recognize the achievement of the money and banking institutions which have contributed their own measure toward price stability in particular. This is important because, as most people are aware, Germany had its full measure of experience with hyper inflation after World War I and again in the years between World War II and the currency reform of 1948. One can, therefore, easily appreciate the spirit of the authorities in combatting inflationary tendencies with an almost religious fervour.[34]

This spirit is clearly reflected in the extremely careful watch of the variables of the money and banking system kept by the Bundesbank (the successor to the BdL) and its reporting thereof in its monthly reports. Even the minutest detail is included in the analyses. And yet, in maintaining its scrutiny, it exercises a more nearly complete control over the banking system than either of the North American central banks or the Bank of England, for certainly the Bundesbank must be one of the most powerfully armed central banks in the world.

This control of the banking system has developed over the years from experience. It was extremely difficult for the BdL to contain in Germany the effects of the world-wide inflation of the Korean War. It was difficult because it was a decentralized bank dependent for implementation of its policies upon a second rank of central banks, one for each of the German Länder. Because of this inherent weakness, as soon as it was practicable the BdL, which was actually set up by the occupying powers, was replaced by the Bundesbank in 1957.

It is interesting that the same question of independence and control of the new central bank was a major concern in Germany as elsewhere. Who is to direct the central bank and its policies? Ought it to be truly independent of the government? The conflicts were resolved in the Bundesbank Act itself which assigns the Bank the duty of "safeguarding the currency," but the Bank is also required to "support the economic policy of the Federal Government but within the framework of its (primary) duty of safeguarding the currency."[35] Fortunately, no conflicts have arisen as to the responsibility of the central bank, since both the government and the Bank have always been in substantial agreement regarding the enemy — inflation. This meant that a joint agreement as to the objective of policies has always existed, but

---

[33]This and the other economic statistics quoted have been taken from a speech by Otmar Emminger, President of the Deutsche Bundesbank, "Thirty Years of the Deutsche Mark," reprinted in the *Monthly Report of the Deutsche Bundesbank*, Vol. 30, #6, June, 1978, p. 5 ff.
[34]R. G. Opie, "Western Germany," in *Banking in Western Europe*, R. S. Sayers, ed., Oxford, 1962, p. 114. Prof. Opie uses a quote from the Deutsche Bank AG Economic Review to show the overriding importance of the value of the currency. "If there should ever be an *apparent* conflict between requirements of cyclical and monetary policy...such a conflict can be only apparent, because how could cyclical conditions be helped in the long run by what harms the currency?"

---

[35]Emminger, *op. cit.,* p. 9.

the government's responsibility is fiscal policy whereas monetary stability is the Bundesbank's area. This has been made explicit in the recent inflationary period of the 1970s.

Certainly this joint cooperation between the two separate authorities in the pursuit of a single objective, in this case the avoidance of inflation, has enormously contributed to the record of success of the overall anti-cyclical fiscal policy. During the recessionary period of 1975–76 the Bundesbank had stated, in announcing its monetary growth target:

> The Deutsche Bundesbank will conduct monetary policy in such a way that the rate of price rises will progressively be diminished while at the same time the *requisite monetary margin will be granted for the envisaged real growth of the economy.*[36]

All this raises the question posed at the beginning of this section: How have the Germans managed to achieve their remarkable results, when we, in Canada, cannot? The answer lies in the much greater control exercised by the Bundesbank. That is, where the Bank of Canada has a bank rate for loans to chartered banks as well as a Purchase and Resale Agreement rate related to bank rate, the Bundesbank has three rates: (1) a discount rate at which the Bank will discount eligible paper, (2) a Lombard rate ("Lombard loans" are granted to banks on the strength of eligible paper rather than the paper itself), and (3) a penalty rate imposed on banks which fail to meet reserve requirements. But this is not all. The Bundesbank also has the power to alter reserve ratios with different ratios for different types of liabilities so as to either restrict or enhance directly the liquidity of the banking system. This is particularly important when foreign exchange operations by the Bundesbank affect the liquidity of the banks and the reserve ratio against foreign exchange liabilities can be adjusted. But there is yet another method of mopping up liquidity. Compulsory "mobilization paper" which cannot be returned to the Bundesbank until maturity can be sold to banks. Through these techniques, the German banks can be readily forced into the Bun-

desbank for borrowing additional reserves at rates which the Bank itself can determine.

But this is *still* not all. There are quotas assigned to banks for the amount of eligible paper which may be discounted, thereby placing both the quantity and quality of eligible paper which may be discounted directly under the control of the Bundesbank. Once the quota is exceeded by a bank, it must rely either on Lombard credit or the money market for additional reserves.

Lastly, there are, just as in North America, open market operations which the Bundesbank can conduct and which again influence the market rate of interest as well as the total volume of credit. Such operations involve the purchase or sale of Treasury Bills and such other specific paper which the Bank considers appropriate. Repurchase agreements with banks are also entered into by the Bundesbank.

A careful examination of the following Tables will show how the Bundesbank manages its central bank money which is, of course, the base for the entire monetary system.

In Section A of Table 6–2 are the changes in total central bank money (in billions of DM) for the months of January through May. As can be seen, central bank money fell by DM 4.7 billion in January. The cause of this was two-fold; first, a decrease in central bank money *stock* resulting from a decrease in currency in circulation plus an increase (by a lesser amount) in minimum reserves, and secondly, a decline in free liquid reserves of the banking system from DM 13.6 billion in December to DM 10.6 billion in January, a reduction of DM 3.1 billion (rounding errors are apparent here). This reduction means that all German banks are losing liquidity and if some individual banks happen to be short, they must either provide more on their own or "tighten up" their loan availabilities.

How did the Bundesbank bring this about? The answer is in Part B of Table 6–2. There were, in the first place, some purchases of foreign exchange by the Bundesbank for the purpose of supporting the U.S. dollar, in particular in latter 1977, and still in January, 1978. These resulted in an additional DM 4 billion of the banks' central bank money (or reserves) which the Bundesbank did not want; in fact, it wished to lower free reserves to about DM 10 billion, their level during autumn, 1977. It accomplished this by the sale of mobilization paper of DM 3.5 billion which, when

---

[36]Quoted by Emminger, *op. cit.,* p. 9.

Table 6-2

PROVISION AND REQUIREMENTS OF CENTRAL BANK MONEY
JANUARY TO MAY 1978*

DM billion; based on daily averages of the months

Item	Jan.	Feb.	March	April	May
A. Total change in central bank money stock and free liquid reserves (increase: +)					
I. Central bank money stock	−1.6	−1.1	+1.6	−0.1	+1.6
1. Currency in circulation 1	−2.9	−0.0	3+1.7	+0.5	+1.0
2. Minimum reserves on domestic liabilities 2	+1.3	−1.0	−0.1	−0.6	+0.6
Memorandum item: Seasonally adjusted change in central bank money stock at constant reserve ratios (base: January 1974)	(+2.4)	(+1.4)	3(+0.6)	(+0.6)	(+1.1)
II. Free liquid reserves	−3.1	−0.3	+0.3	−0.5	−0.5
Memorandum item: Level of free liquid reserves	(10.6)	(10.2)	(10.5)	(10.0)	(9.6)
Total (A I plus II = B)	−4.7	−1.4	+1.8	−0.6	+1.1
B. Provision or absorption of central bank money through					
1. Foreign exchange movements	+4.0	+0.5	+2.2	−0.0	−3.0
2. Change in public authorities' net balances with the Bundesbank (increase in balances:−)	−5.1	−0.1	−6.5	+3.2	+2.4
3. Change in minimum reserves	−2.4	+1.5	−0.1	−0.1	−0.0
4. Open market operations	−0.4	−2.8	−0.3	−0.3	+0.7
5. Open market operations under repurchase agreements	−	−	+2.1	+1.4	+0.4
6. Lombard loans	+0.6	+0.2	+4.7	−4.2	+0.8
7. Other factors	−1.3	−0.7	−0.3	−0.6	−0.3
Memorandum Item:					
Level of open market operations under repurchase agreements −	−	−	(2.1)	(3.6)	(4.0)
Level of lombard loans	(1.4)	(1.6)	(6.3)	(2.1)	(2.9)
Total (B = A)	−4.7	−1.4	+1.8	−0.6	+1.1

*Excluding postal giro and postal savings bank offices. — **1** As from March excluding the banks' holdings of domestic notes and coins, which are deductible from the required minimum reserves.—**2** At current reserve ratios (changes in required minimum reserves due to policy measures are included in B 3).— **3** Statistically adjusted. —**p** Provisional.
Discrepancies in the totals are due to rounding.

combined with other cash transactions of the public authorities, Item B,2, reduced reserves by DM 5.1 billion. The balance of the DM 4.7 billion reduction was accomplished by an increase in minimum required reserves for foreign liabilities (Item B,3); a sale of securities on the open market (Item B,4); an increase in Lombard credit from DM .8 billion to DM 1.4 billion, or DM .6 billion (Item B,6); and, of course, the inevitable "other" transactions (Item B,7). Through all of these adjustments at varying times throughout the month of January, the increased holdings of foreign exchange of the Bundesbank were "neutralized" and therefore had no further effect on the money supply of Germany. During the entire 6 month period of the dollar crisis, the Bundesbank purchased some DM 12.5 billion from the foreign exchange markets.

In Table 6–3, we can see the results of the influx of foreign exchange which, when sold to the Bundesbank, has an inevitable "one-time" effect on deposits of banks at which the sellers of foreign exchange hold their accounts. The categories, M_1, M_2, and M_3 which are indicated in Table 6-3 are very similar to the Canadian counterparts. There is, however, an additional category in Germany, monetary capital, which is a less liquid set of bank liabilities, consisting of bonds and deposits beyond four years' maturity. Part of the increased supply of money resulting from the foreign exchange transactions is absorbed in this least liquid of categories.

Of course, relationships between the central bank money and the monetary aggregates are not precise for the reason that the public is free to adjust its holdings amongst all four categories. A tight (relatively) control of the monetary aggregates is maintained by keeping as close as possible to an 8% annual growth rate of central bank money. The Bundesbank does occasionally overshoot its monetary target, generally for good reason, but it has through the years remained remarkably close. The Bundesbank was, incidentally, the first central bank to announce the principle of targeting with its 8% growth objective in December, 1974. The Bank of Canada declared its targeting policy in November, 1975.

The precision implied in Tables 6-2 and 6-3 would approach what the British would refer to as "fine tuning" and what has been virtually abandoned as an impossible objective for the British

banking system. Actually this was only a short-term adjustment for the Bundesbank. In the longer run, since 1977, the Bank has been following an easier course in monetary policy, permitting excess reserves to grow and generally lowering discount and Lombard rates. For the *very* long run, an objective of an annual 8% growth rate of central bank money still remains. The Bank adheres to this growth rate despite the many requests from foreign governments to "reflate" the German economy.

In addition to the highly efficient and powerful Bundesbank there is the important link between the monetary controls of the central bank and the very many banks in Germany which make up the entire monetary system of the country. In Canada the mechanism by which changes in bank reserves are translated into corresponding changes in loans, and, eventually, the money supply is laid down by the Bank Act with its decennial revision. It is the 4% reserve ratio for savings deposits and 12% reserve ratio for demand deposits combined with the secondary reserve requirement as required by the Bank of Canada Act (as amended) which constitute the link between the central bank and the chartered banks. Through compliance with these reserves, the chartered banks are effectively controlled.

As we have seen, however, the Bank of Canada's control of the chartered banks is somewhat like a dog on a rubber leash — a year's time lag is possible between the tug and the dog's return. The German system is quite different. The difference lies, firstly, in the many and varied types of banks which perform different specialized functions, though, to be sure, the traditional division of functions is slowly disappearing. Broadly we can use a triple classification for all the German banks: (1) private commercial banks, (2) savings banks with their central Giro banks, and (3) the industrial and agricultural cooperative banks with their central institutions. In the first category there are the "big" banks (similar to Canada's five great chartered banks) which account for about 25% of the total assets. There are also smaller regional commercial banks which do the same type of business on a smaller scale, and, finally, still smaller private commercial banks involving a close relationship with customers.

With the exception of foreign banks, which are

Table 6-3

MONETARY DEVELOPMENTS

Seasonally adjusted change during period

Item	Nov. 1977/Jan. 1978 DM billion	%[1]	Feb./April 1978 DM billion	%[1]	May 1977/ April 1978 %
Money					
Money stock M_3[2]	+14.3	+10.6	+6.3	+4.4	+10.1
M_2 (M_3 less savings deposits)	+10.2	+13.8	+2.3	+2.9	+10.2
M_1 (currency and sight deposits)	+10.9	+24.2	+3.8	+7.6	+13.7
Currency	+3.1	+20.8	+2.1	+13.3	+14.5
Sight deposits	+7.8	+25.8	+1.7	+4.9	+13.3
Time deposits and funds borrowed for less than four years	−0.8	−2.8	−1.5	−5.3	+3.9
Savings deposits at statutory notice	+4.2	+6.8	+4.0	+6.3	+10.0
Credit					
Volume of credit[3]	+23.1	+9.1	+26.4	+10.2	+9.4
Lending to enterprises and individuals	+11.9	+5.9	+20.2	+10.1	+8.6
Lending to domestic public authorities	+11.2	+21.0	+6.2	+10.7	+12.2
Monetary capital					
Monetary capital, total of which:	+11.1	+7.5	+11.3	+7.5	+7.5
Time deposits and funds borrowed for four years and over	+2.8	+7.1	+3.9	+9.6	+9.3
Savings deposits at agreed notice	+1.9	−4.7	+4.7	+7.2	+0.6
Bank bonds outstanding[4]	+3.6	+9.3	+2.3	+5.6	+6.2
Bank savings bonds	+3.9	+32.5	+1.8	+12.9	+27.0

[1]Expressed as an annual rate. — [2]Currency, sight deposits, time deposits and funds borrowed for less than four years, savings deposits at statutory notice. — [3]Bank lending to domestic non-banks including credit based on the purchase of securities.—[4]Excluding banks' holdings.

Source: Monthly Report of the Deutsche Bundesbank, June, 1978, p. 18.

generally treated as domestic banks,[37] the remainder are not banks at all in the Canadian sense, but financial intermediaries. But, since they fit the legal definition of banks, they are included under the Banking Law. These include the very powerful savings banks, mortgage banks, and specialized credit institutions. As one might expect with such a diverse banking system involving about 6,000 credit institutions with about 44,000 branch offices and including some 170 foreign banks and representative offices, some sort of close supervision is necessary.

A second difference is a precise definition of a bank which brings such diverse credit institutions under the regulation of the Banking Law.[38] This definition is comprehensive and means that all

[37]Foreign banks are not permitted to invest in stock exchanges—this is the only difference.

[38]Banks, or, more exact, credit institutions are defined as follows by the Banking Law:

such institutions are under the direct control of the Bank Supervisory Authority in Berlin which grants licences to all banks before they may operate. Canada has no such definition of a "bank," preferring to apply the word "bank" only to those 12 institutions which are chartered under the Bank Act.

A third difference is of far greater importance than the first two and will be discussed in some detail shortly. Before doing so, we should note a few similarities. German banks, like our chartered banks, have reserve requirements. A cash balance, or rather a Giro balance, is maintained at the Bundesbank in accordance with different classes of liabilities—class 1, deposits over DM 1,000 million, class 2, deposits of DM 100-1,000 million, class 3, deposits of DM 10-100 million, and class 4, deposits of under DM 10 million. Further distinctions in reserve requirements are made, as between banks located where an office of the Bundesbank exists and those that are not, as well as sight deposits, time deposits, and savings deposits. The "free liquid reserves," which is the subject of such careful observation by the Bundesbank, consists of excess cash reserves plus open market paper which the Bundesbank will purchase and unused rediscount quotas. The rough Canadian counterpart of these would be the secondary reserves; for German banks they are the potential for acquiring additional cash from the Bundesbank or the money market whenever the occasion might arise. So, up to this point, there is really no fundamental difference between the German banks and our own, certainly there is nothing that should set them apart

as unique.

The difference that really matters, however, lies in the requirements for liquidity. This involves a fairly complex set of ratios based on three principles set forth in the Banking Law and designed with the express purpose of ensuring adequate liquidity for every credit institution engaged in the business of banking. In broad outline, adequate liquidity means that a bank's credits (loans, etc.) must be sufficiently matched with liquid liabilities in order that a bank's depositors may be satisfied. The three principles are as follows:

I. Loans and investments (i.e., volume of credit) must not exceed 18 times issued capital plus retained earnings.

II. Long-term loans and investments (over four years) must be matched with liabilities either by (a) capital, (b) long-term loans from banks and customers, (c) long-term bonds, or (d) 60% of savings deposits and *only 10%* of deposits of less than four years (medium-term loans) from customers.

III. The remaining deposits may be invested in short and medium-term loans to an amount defined by precise ratios.

It would be impossible to over-emphasize the importance of these guiding ratios and the three principles which set them forth. The first is self-explanatory and effectively limits the growth of a bank's assets without acquiring additional capital. The second means that illiquid loans and investments must be matched by corresponding illiquid liabilities, or if more liquid liabilities are used for financing illiquid assets, *more* of these liabilities must be available to accommodate the liquidity preferences of the depositors. As an example, suppose a long-term loan, say of 100, is contemplated by a bank under principle II savings deposits. The bank must acquire 166.7 of these savings deposits *before* the loan can be accommodated. Of course, the bank has another alternative — sell more shares of stock or float more bonds. In this case only 100 will be required since these liabilities are equally as illiquid as the long-term asset.

Principle III is even more rigorous than principle II. A detailed examination of the guidance ratios is not necessary at this point, but it is sufficient to note here that since the assets under principle III are more liquid (generally under four years) than those of principle II, they can be financed by correspondingly more liquid liabilities; however,

---

Credit institutions are enterprises engaged in banking transactions if the volume of such transactions requires a commercially organized business enterprise. Banking transactions are:

1. The receipt of money from others as deposits irrespective of the payment of interest (deposit business),
2. The granting of money loans and acceptance credits (credit business),
3. The purchase of bills and cheques (discount business),
4. The purchase and sale of securities for the account of others (security business),
5. The custody and administration of securities for the account of others (safe custody business),
6. The transaction designated in paragraph 1 of the Law concerning investment fund companies (investment business),
7. The incurring of the obligation to acquire claims in respect of loans prior to their majority.

prudence and safety dictate that the greater liquidity which is always present for liabilities will mean that correspondingly more of these liabilities will be required to finance the principle II assets. A rough analysis suggests that about twice as many liabilities (or deposits) is necessary to support these assets.

Conforming to these guidance ratios is truly a "headache" for German bankers, but conform they must for the penalty is severe — loss of licence. One may appreciate their plight by considering their British counterparts. Bankers in Great Britain first arrange a loan to a customer, then locate the deposits, generally short-term, from the wholesale market. When the short-term deposits must be repaid, they simply roll over with another short-term deposit from the same market. When the British banks learn, as the clearing banks are now doing, how to vary the loan interest with the short-term deposit interest rate as it moves in the wholesale market, their profit margins are intact. Again one may sympathize with German bankers when comparing them to Canadian bankers. Our Canadian banks perform massive "stretches" of bank liquidity between the desired liquidity (which is generally excessive) of depositors and the illiquid loans which borrowers prefer. Borrowers want to avoid the burden of repayment as long as possible while depositors prefer the liquidity of their deposits. German banks, under the guidance ratios which are really nothing more than sound, conservative banking principles, have no such freedom.

The ratios themselves are the outgrowth of historical events, particularly the banking disaster of 1929. Fearing that this catastrophe might be repeated, the federal government observed that banking practices varied considerably amongst banks; to correct this a standardization of lending procedures was put into effect along with the currency reform. It was, of course, particularly difficult for savings banks which rely heavily on deposits to meet these requirements, and, indeed, it still is, since, after the Herstatt affair in May, 1976, the guidance ratios were tightened still further.

Banking history is full of examples of the ultimate result being different from the original intent, the German guidance ratios being just one. In this case, what was thought to be just sensible banking practice became a means by which the German banking system can be directly controlled by the Bundesbank. There is no "rubber leash" here, for it is difficult enough to meet the guidance ratios under ordinary conditions quite apart from periods of tight money. Suppose the Bundesbank should decide to curb excessive money expansion; it has only to reduce free reserves to a minimum safety level after the manner outlined above. This will force the banks to sell liquid assets in the money market, discount bills from their portfolio, or seek Lombard credit which will, at such times, be very expensive. At the same time the rigid enforcement of the guidance ratios precludes the possibility of adjusting deposits in the Canadian style to an overall lower reserve ratio.

But, aside from the enhanced effect of monetary policy, the guidance ratios force the German public to be almost as illiquid as their investments *before* the investment takes place. In the final analysis it is this which is the genuinely positive outcome of the guidance ratios and prevents an excessive demand for goods and services during the period between the "laying down" of investment and its maturity in terms of an increased flow of goods and services. This is the lesson which North American and British governments must somehow learn if they ever hope to control inflationary pressures through monetary policies.

D. Switzerland

If modern Germany is an economic miracle, the banking system of Switzerland is miraculous from its beginnings to the present time. It is, in fact, virtually impossible for an observer from the outside to completely and objectively *understand* the Swiss banking system which literally runs by itself without the rigorous control and direction of either a Bundesbank or even a Bank of Canada. Unless the observer possesses a "feel" for Swiss history and tradition of freedom and democracy which produces laws not from a centralized parliament but from a decentralized people-participating confederation of Cantons, his knowledge of how and why Swiss institutions operate is not complete. Generalizations, of course, are dangerous, but it does appear to be at least approximately true that tight centralized governments do produce the same type of monetary and banking systems. How *else* can trade and commerce so essential to our economic lives be carried out?

Not so with the Swiss. One has the impression that Switzerland, its people, its government and its institutions are an historical accident. If this is true, it is certainly a most fortunate one, for it would be difficult to imagine a world of international finance, Eurocurrencies, etc., without the Swiss banking system. On the other hand, if not accidental there must be *some* reason, and this, to be sure, may be found in geography. Located, as it is, astride the great Alpine passes, commerce must have flowed through Switzerland since its inception, making possible the growth and development of a merchant class. One might speculate, therefore, that the same geographic feature ensured the success of banking. All we can be sure of is that the banks of Geneva are very old, dating from the beginning of the eighteenth century. They had their origins in the finance of wars, particularly those in which France participated; hence, their fortunes depended to a great extent on the military success of France.

Acting as intermediaries between those who had money to lend and the French king, the Geneva bankers prospered. Of course there were mistakes, the outstanding example being John Law's disastrous Mississippi scheme.[39] But the bankers learned from their experience, and ultimately Swiss banks developed a well-deserved reputation for both integrity and safety in a world in which banking was still a primitive and barely understood art.

---

[39]Law, a clever Scotsman, had organized his Mississippi company (1717-1720) which sold shares to be exchanged for French government debt. At the same time, the Banque Royale, with note issue powers, was established to administer the government debt. This "engine of inflation" was so organized that the sale of shares in the company at ever higher prices was effectively financed by bank notes which were, in turn, claims against the Banque Royale. Eventually, the inescapable fact that banks cannot create wealth by expanding debt was realized by the public. Law escaped to Amsterdam while his accomplices disappeared into the Bastille.

The weakness of this type of inflation lies in the engine itself—a bank. Banks can create a money supply simply enough by printing notes, but these notes are debt due for eventual (and inevitable) liquidation. When the means for liquidation is absent, the bubble bursts. Max Iklé, *Switzerland an International Banking and Finance Centre,* Dowden, Hutchison and Ross, Stroudsburg, Pa., 1972, p. 6.

It is not easy to explain why confidence in Swiss bankers grew over the years, since confidence, the one essential ingredient of banking, is still just a state of mind. Some would argue that the effectiveness of the Swiss military in maintaining independence was a major factor.[40] Certainly there is no doubt that Swiss banks have become a haven for refugee capital in a Europe torn by wars and revolutions (where *else* could such capital have gone?). In this way, thanks to the military, neutrality, or whatever, the banks were the fortunate recipients of funds from sources other than the savings of the Swiss themselves.

But this does not mean that all the funds required by Swiss banks are of foreign origin. The Swiss themselves are thrifty, and their domestic savings makes possible a strong base for the banking industry. Once again, this habit of savings is rooted in tradition. Swiss families who save and build up fortunes do not display their wealth in wasteful ostentation but simply continue their habitual, frugal way of life, thereby increasing the total volume of savings.

Another contributing factor to confidence in Swiss banking is the gold content of the Swiss Franc. This is fixed by law at 0.21759 mg = 1 Swiss franc; however, the Swiss franc has been nonconvertible since 1954. Why, then, should the gold content of the franc be a contributing factor toward confidence? There is an effective and highly efficient gold market in Zurich operated by the three largest banks where individuals may purchase gold bullion and, at their convenience, either remove bullion physically or leave it with the bank on deposit. By association, the currency and the gold market appear to reinforce each other to build a psychological state of confidence in a world of depreciating currencies.

Perhaps the most important, and certainly the most well-known, of all the features of Swiss banking that generate confidence is the element of rigidly enforced secrecy. This means that individuals and corporations (Investors Overseas

---

[40]The fact that universal national service *can* maintain a well-equipped modern army always ready for service is also as puzzling an institution as banking. Those who escape this service are the "unfortunates," the mentally or physically handicapped, in a nation which takes pride in military prowess so formidable that no foreign power dare try it.

Services, a Geneva-based selling and management concern which dealt in mutual funds is a case in point) who wish to evade the tax laws of their own country can deposit their income in the Swiss banks. The amount of the deposit will not be divulged. This does not mean that the Swiss authorities will not cooperate with foreign governments; they do indeed when violations of the Swiss criminal code take place. However, in countries where English common law is the background for the legal system, tax evasion is a criminal offence, but not in Switzerland.

Having received huge amounts of foreign funds, what do the Swiss banks do with them? Here, the enormous experience of overseas banking comes into play. It is obvious that such large sums of money cannot be invested in Switzerland itself, so the banks become a means of simply channeling funds from one country to other countries (perhaps even back to the country of origin!). Because of the world-wide network of Swiss branches, the banks hold accounts in very many currencies—more so by far than, say, Canadian banks. In this way investment within the country of these currencies becomes quite possible. At the same time a risk-spreading process takes place with a level of profits for both the banks and the investor which cannot otherwise be achieved. Of course, any devaluation, or expected devaluation, of a specific currency, can easily destroy profits if funds are not withdrawn before the devaluation takes place; hence, a switch from a currency of threatened devaluation will occur. As will be discussed in Part III, the "gnomes of Zurich" can often bring down the foreign exchange value of a currency by the very *act* of selling it on the market.

The banking activities that are most concerned with investment are largely those of the old, well-known, and highly respected private banks. The surprising feature of these banks is the low profile they maintain both in Switzerland and abroad. There is no advertising nor is there an obvious presence either in Switzerland or in foreign countries. They obtain their funds purely by personal contact, quietly, unobtrusively, by building a clientele over the many years of operation. Oftentimes through generations of families within the same bank, a good-will is built as well as a confidence which is so strong that even in times of stress or panic, funds will not be withdrawn in haste.

But, of course, there is much more to Swiss banking than private banks. There are the three great banks (the big three)[41] which tend to dominate the financial field, a situation repeated continuously in other countries as if there is an efficiency level within the banking industry which dictates that a few large banks must co-exist with very many smaller banks. Just as in Germany, these are "universal" Banks involved in very much more than just accepting deposits and granting loans. They acquire funds through bond issues as well as deposits. From the assets side they deal in the stock exchanges, assist in the formation of companies, and are the major dealers in the foreign exchange market as well as the gold market. Since there is no federal public debt in Switzerland, banks have no assets in government securities.

As in other countries which are "overbanked," there are many smaller regional (or Cantonal) banks, savings banks, foreign banks, loan associations, etc., most of which are considered in Canada as financial intermediaries. Some concept of the density of banking may be had from the statistic that in 1973, a bank office existed for every 1,359 inhabitants. For the United States, the comparable figure is 4,940 inhabitants per bank office.[42] As would be expected, such a high concentration of banking and such a diverse structure require a control mechanism in the form of the Swiss National Bank (the central bank of Switzerland).

But, and this is the surprising feature, the National Bank has very little by way of weapons of control over the banking system. What controls that exist have been by way of agreements reached between the Association of Swiss Banks and the National Bank. Once more we find a peculiar Swiss institution without parallel in any other country; apparently the Swiss banks cooperate in these agreements because they prefer them to some legal compulsion which would certainly follow if they did not cooperate.

Aside from monetary policy, there are legal cash ratios which are laid down by the federal banking law as amended in 1971. (This was the first revision since 1935, the year of its inception.) While

[41]These are the Swiss Bank Corporation, Union Bank of Switzerland, and the Swiss Credit Bank.
[42]Hans J. Bär, *The Banking System of Switzerland*, Schulthess Polygraphischer Verlag, AG, Zurich, 1975, p. 44.

they may appear at first sight to be somewhat stringent, they are really not because they are applicable only to "current liabilities," which can be generally defined as deposits and other liabilities which mature within 30 days.[43] Liquid assets are defined as cash on hand and Giro deposits with the National Bank and the Post Office, and must bear the following ratios to current liabilities:

Liquid Asset Ratio	Percentage of Current Liabilities to Total Liabilities
6%	First 6%—15%
12%	Next 15%—25%
24%	Next 25%—35%
36%	35% plus

Since these ratios apply only to current liabilities, a bank which specializes almost entirely in long-term investments (and corresponding long-term liabilities) need only consider 15% of its liabilities as current liabilities (see footnote below) for reserve purposes. On the other hand, a bank which has *all* current liabilities would have a reserve ratio of exactly 27.9%! This is not so high as it might seem since there is no central bank control of the reserve base as in other countries. The cash ratio is purely for the purpose of satisfying the extraordinarily heavy cash requirement which the Swiss still prefer to hold and which is contrary to the experience of other countries with highly developed banking habits. In Canada, for example, the cash requirement is purely incidental to the deposits, depending upon the time of year, etc. Our cash ratio, while it once was for the purpose of ensuring adequate cash, now exists purely for the purpose of making money "tight" or "easy." Not so in Switzerland. The Swiss, showing a preference for anonymity and the individual freedom of action which the use of bank notes makes possible, not only withdraw and carry

large sums of cash (Swiss National Bank Notes) but make payments with cash and/or Giro which is simply the transmittal of cash by post.[44]

In the final analysis, it is likely to be the heavy drain of cash which constitutes the truly effective check on the banking system in its "deposit expansion" process. Since the Swiss National Bank has a monopoly of the note issue, other types of control are just not necessary. Further, since the Swiss Bank Note is legally tied to gold, the National Bank is itself severely restricted in its note issuing capacity. Finally, since any change in the gold content of the Swiss franc requires a change in the law (laws are difficult to change), a stability is imparted to the currency and the banking system which is absolutely unique.[45] Should any change in monetary policy be considered appropriate, a consultation between the Bankers' Association and the National Bank would take place. One might be accused of cynicism if one argued that, since so much of Swiss banking profits originate via the foreign sector including the activities now within Euro-currency markets, domestic banking is not worth the bankers' attention, yet the "miracle" of Swiss banking still stands, along with the Swiss franc, the world's strongest currency, both a lesson and an example.

CONCLUSION

All five of the banking systems examined have shown characteristics unique to the specific

---

[43]It is better to quote directly from the source which is a translation from the German. "The following are to be considered as current liabilities: Bank creditors at sight as well as those due within one month insofar as there are no offsetting deposits, chequing and other accounts payable within one month has been given, 15% of all savings deposits, 15% of all other deposits on pass books, bonds, and certificates of deposits which mature within 30 days, acceptances which mature within 30 days, and all other liabilities payable within one month." Bär, *op. cit.*, p. 54.

[44]Swiss postmen carry bags of cash for the purpose of discharging Giro orders, a practice which would not only be dangerous but just "unheard of" in a North American system.

[45]In the Swiss Confederation, legislation derives from the people within the Cantons to the federal government, a lengthy process, as contrasted with our own parliamentary system which works from the federal government back to the public for all legislation concerned with federal jurisdiction.

country, yet all have sufficient in common that some rather important lessons can be learned. The Bank of England now, after many years of considering that money does not matter, is attempting to restrain monetary growth through the "corset" mechanism. This results, inevitably, in rising interest rates, but it does appear, see Table 6-4, that inflation rates have come down in recent years. We can never be certain, of course, just how important the corset has been in achieving this result as compared, for example, to an incomes policy, which did help to moderate wage demands.

Nevertheless, it does appear significant that of the five countries, Germany with its tight centralized control of the money supply and Switzerland with its built-in tradition of tight money have shown the greatest success in confining inflation. It is not accidental that Germany's experiences with two great inflations have hardened the determination of the authorities to maintain a tight monetary control with the results for the world to see. Switzerland, on the other hand, while not consciously engaging in a restrictive policy, has been most successful in containing inflation with its "primitive," cash-oriented, gold-based currency. This combined with its extraordinary banking system seems to have produced the right combination for the task.

The three "Anglo-Saxon" countries (Great Britain, the United States, and Canada), have considered full employment to be the primary objective of monetary policy. Yet, even here there is a difference in the approach. The "money does not matter" philosophy was never accepted in either the U.S. or Canada, though in these two countries, money has often been subordinated to interest rate control, i.e., control of inflation is less important than unemployment.

We shall have occasion to return once more to these considerations in the final chapters. For the moment, it is sufficient to recognize the degree of inflationary susceptibility amongst all five countries. External price shocks (oil price increases, etc.) are rather quickly absorbed in Germany and Switzerland, but not so readily in North America. Great Britain actually *enhances* the effects of external price increases both by increasing their immediate effect and prolonging their impact.

Aside from monetary policy alone it is possible to identify in broad outline two significant lessons to be learned by Canada from the experiences of others. There is, firstly, the close dependence upon the United States for capital imports which has resulted in a mirroring of U.S. monetary policy in Canada at the expense of domestic price stability. This is why our interest rates move with those of the United States with just about $1/2$ to 1 percentage points above U.S. rates. Sometimes this differential is greater, sometimes less. To a certain degree, since 1975, we do seem to be breaking this tie. The desire to strengthen the Canadian dollar has certainly been part of this "independence" movement. But, to break completely from dependence upon U.S. capital imports must mean that Canadians will either depend on other countries or themselves for the necessary saving; quite bluntly, it is the latter which must eventually prevail. Canadians *will* provide their own savings when sufficient incentives exist, and this means fiscal incentives as well as interest rewards. A negative real interest rate *after tax* does not encourage savings and investment in Canada at all, but perpetuates the dependence of Canada on capital imports.

Secondly, in terms of the objectives of monetary policy, the Bank of Canada continues its policy of targeting M_1 to the exclusion of the other monetary aggregates. There is of course a substantial difference between this and the Bundesbank's targeting of the central bank money supply which, in turn, affects *all* the monetary aggregates. The

Table 6-4 Rates of Increase of the Consumer Price Index					
	1974	1975	1976	1977	1978 (I)
Great Britain	16	24.2	16	16	9.5
United States	10.9	9.2	5.8	6.5	6.5
Canada	10.9	10.7	7.5	8	8.8
Germany	7.0	5.9	4.5	3.9	3.2
Switzerland	9.7	6.7	1.7	1.3	1.1

Source: International Financial Statistics, June 1978.

Canadian rates of growth of M_2 and M_3 have consistently been well above M_1, sometimes almost double, suggesting that liquidity may be growing substantially faster than the money supply. In Germany, liquidity is restrained by the guidance ratios forcing, as it were, the public to accept lower liquidity along with its investments. Both in Canada and Great Britain the banking system itself bridges this gap of desired liquidity, offering the public the opportunity to spend at any time from its liquid savings. Ultimately, excessive liquidity on the part of the Canadian public must be manifest once more in an inflation rate pattern similar to that shown in Table 6-4. At some time in the future an external shock of price increase will appear and the already excessive liquidity will not only finance the first price increase but will lower the resistance to successive rounds of further price increases in much the same manner as Great Britain has been showing during this decade. Of course this is a longer term consideration, but if we are not to repeat the mistakes of the past, we must prepare for the future now.

ADDITIONAL READINGS

The following represents only a small list of the enormous volume of literature on banking systems other than our own which readers will find useful:

The London Clearing Banks, Evidence by the Committee of London Clearing Bankers to the Committee to Review the Functioning of Financial Institutions, Longman Group, Ltd., London, 1977.

Publications and Papers in the Bank of England Quarterly Bulletin on British institutions, such as,
"Official Transactions in the Gilt-Edged Market," June, 1966.
"Monetary Policy Since Radcliffe," December, 1969.
"Sterling Certificates of Deposit," December, 1972.
"Sterling Certificates of Deposits and the Interbank Market," September, 1973.
"U.K. Banking Sector," 1962-67, June, 1969.

Additional articles published in the Bank of England Quarterly Bulletin are particularly helpful in an up-to-date understanding of the U.K. monetary and banking system.

Sayers, R.S., *Central Banking After Bagehot,* Oxford, 1959.
Wadsworth, J.E., (ed.), *The Banks and the Monetary System in the U.K., 1959-71,* Methuen & Co., London, 1973. These articles selected from the *Midland Bank Review* are excellent as both historical background and contemporary reviews of U.K. banking.
Bär, Hans J., *The Banking System of Switzerland,* Schulthess Polygraphischer Verlag, AG, Zurich, 1975. Very accurate in detail.
Iklé, Max, *Switzerland: An International Banking Center,* Dowden, Hutchinson & Ross, Inc., Strondsburg, Pa., 1972. A very interesting account of Swiss banking.
Sayers, R.S., (ed.), *Banking in Western Europe*, Clarendon Press, Oxford, 1962. The essays in this volume vary in quality. J.S.G. Wilson's "France" is particularly good.

The U.S. banking system has been discussed in detail more than any other in the world. The following are particularly useful:

Hart, A.G., P.B. Kenen & A.D. Entine, *Money, Debt, and Economic Activity,* Prentice-Hall, Englewood Cliffs, 1969, Chapter 5.
Luckett, D.G., *Money and Banking*, McGraw-Hill, New York, 1976, Part 2.
Pesek, B.R., & T.R. Saving, *Foundations of Money and Banking*, Macmillan, New York, 1968, chs. 28-30.

The best and most complete study of Canada's banking and financial system is:

Neufeld, E.P., *The Financial System of Canada*, Macmillan of Canada, Toronto, 1972.

PART 2

Stores of Value

Introduction—SOME CONCEPTS AND DEFINITIONS

To this point our discussion and analysis have been concerned with money as a medium of exchange. This concept, medium of exchange, implies a flow, for it is a flow of goods and services which are exchanged in one direction with money exchanged in the other. The medium is a technical device which overcomes the enormous inconvenience of barter. However, as was argued in Chapter 2, the process of flow is discontinuous, involving pauses with the location of each pause representing a stage. The greater the length of time lapse during a pause, the slower is the velocity of circulation.

Velocity in this case refers to total velocity as opposed to income velocity. Total velocity is a much broader concept than income velocity, involving financial transactions of all kinds as well as a whole range of non-income generating transactions. Unfortunately, at the moment, income velocity is much easier to quantify than total velocity, requiring only a ratio of the Gross National Product to the supply of money (however defined). Our statistical techniques are much more developed in the GNP area than in total transactions; hence, for the time being at least, total velocity must remain an unknown measure.

Part II addresses the very interesting set of ideas involved in what happens to money during the pause. Once more, the use of the word "money" is purely for convenience because as soon as money has entered the pause in a particular stage, the word ceases to have meaning. It has now become an asset, a monetary asset with the property of 100% liquidity in accordance with the definition of liquidity introduced in Chapter 4. A financial asset, on the other hand, does not possess 100% liquidity and cannot enter the stream of payments as a medium of exchange.

The difficulty with the word "money" is the ambiguity of its meaning as between a medium of exchange, a monetary asset, and a financial asset. The international definitions of monetary aggregates, M_1 through M_3, are attempts to avoid confusion of definitions so that meaningful international comparisons may be made. *Still,* some confusion remains. For example, the British definition of M_3 includes all time deposits with banks as well as all monetary assets, but "banks" include what are termed in Canada "near banks" or financial intermediaries.

The Canadian M_3 is different. Our chartered banks, as we have seen, perform the function of financial intermediaries in addition to the normal commercial banking function of supplying the medium of exchange. Since our definition of M_3 includes only savings deposits at chartered banks, to the exclusion of the savings deposits at other financial intermediaries, our M_3 is really less rational than the British definition.

To avoid this confusion, we shall use the term monetary asset to represent 100% liquidity for which M_1 is probably the best proxy—we cannot measure monetary assets directly. All other forms of stores of value, then, are financial assets, and for this we have no adequate measure. M_3 and even the German "monetary capital" are really just a small portion of the total, though the most liquid portion, of all financial assets.

In the definition of liquidity mentioned in Chapter 4, two very important concepts were included. The first pertained to capital loss and the second to lapse of time. It is the second which will concern us at first and lead directly to what we will refer to as a First Principle of Interest—a payment for time. We shall add further to this as the argument progresses, considering additional principles as they are required. But since the entire subject tends to be somewhat complex, there are expositional advantages in breaking it down into its logical components.

CHAPTER 7

Preference for Liquidity and Interest

I. INTEREST, AN EQUILIBRIUM PRICE FOR TIME

In general terms the First Principle of Interest, i.e., time payments, follows Irving Fisher's First Approximation in his great work, *Theory of Interest*. He described his First Approximation as being based upon four assumptions; (1) the income stream is certain and fixed, (2) each income is negligible in a vast, competitive loan market, (3) free access to the market as borrower and lender exists, and (4) the income stream may be only modified by borrowing and lending.[1] In these necessarily abstract and rigid assumptions, the emphasis lies on income, whereas in the analysis which follows, it is liquidity which is the main concern. The difference is fundamental because it avoids, in the first place, the hornet's nest of the relation between income and interest, and in the second place, by substituting the word *liquidity* for Fisher's income the assumptions become much more realistic. In both assumptions 1 and 4 a fixed quantum of current liquidity which must exist at any time would be substituted for "the income stream" and this can be exchanged for a known quantum of future liquidity.

In Chapter 2, the monetary assets structure of an income earner was analyzed. For the individual who spent less than he earned, a balance of monetary assets, or 100% liquidity, was being amassed through time. But, if income is defined in the national income sense as the value of productive services rendered, liquidity balances can be altered by inheritances, pensions, welfare payments (or transfer payments), speculative buying and selling, etc. However, both empirical observation and logical relationships suggest that liquidity is strongly related to real income. The greater is the amount of goods and services which flow through the payments stream the more, generally, will be the monetary asset requirement. This need not altogether be true since a higher velocity of circulation can also accommodate greater real income, especially in the short term.

Keeping in mind that the pause in the flow of monetary assets is the source of liquidity, we can generate a series of "willingness curves" (following Fisher's terminology) which show the willingness of three individuals with three different incomes to forego current liquidity. In Diagram 7-1, the axes are laid out to indicate current liquidity (the property of monetary assets) and future liquidity (the property of financial assets). On the diagram is a 45° line which, when bisected, defines a point of equality between future and current liquidity. A movement along this 45° line means that equal increments of current liquidity can be exchanged for future liquidity, an important limiting factor in the analysis.

We can start from this point of equality between L_c and L_f and identify three willingness curves, Y_1, Y_2, and Y_3 corresponding to three levels of real income. Such willingness curves will be similar to indifference curves, convex to the origin, to show, in accordance with the law of diminishing marginal substitutability, that successively increasing amounts of future liquidity will be required to compensate for the surrender of additional increments of current liquidity. This is the logical starting point of our analysis—we must begin *somewhere* — and is based upon behaviour patterns that are observable both within ourselves as well as in others.

The 45° line is the limiting case of a theoretical income which is so large that the individual is willing to forego increments of current liquidity which are equal to corresponding increments of

---

[1] I. Fisher, *Theory of Interest*, August M. Kelley, New York, 1970, pp. 101–102.

Diagram 7-1

WILLINGNESS CURVES, LENDERS

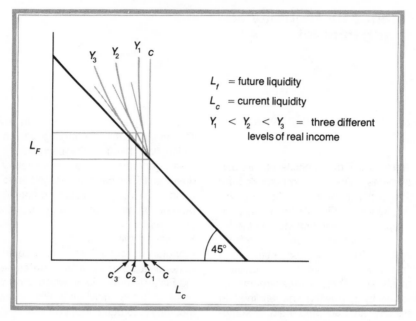

L_f = future liquidity

L_c = current liquidity

$Y_1 < Y_2 < Y_3$ = three different levels of real income

future liquidity, i.e., $(dL_f/dL_c) = 1$[2]. At the other extreme is a theoretically low income defined by the vertical line, C, where an infinitely large amount of future liquidity would be required to compensate for an infinitely small amount of current liquidity foregone, i.e., $(dL_f/dL_c) = \infty$. Between these two extremes are the willingness lines of rational individuals who will refuse to forego current liquidity for the same amount of future liquidity, i.e., at zero interest rate. Furthermore, the slopes of all three willingness lines become greater, $(d^2L_f/dL_c^2) = +$ as we move upward from the point of convergence showing that the ratio of substitution between successive increments of future and current liquidity is becoming greater. As real income increases, the amount of future liquidity necessary to compensate for current liquidity foregone becomes less. Or, alternatively, for a given amount of future liquidity more current liquidity will be surrendered by higher real incomes than lower real incomes. This last statement is just another way of saying that the rate of reward as indicated by the ratio of L_f/L_c must be higher for lower incomes to forego

current liquidity than for higher incomes. The rates of reward are measured by the slope of the tangency lines so that $(L_f/L_c) = (1 + r)$, with r being the rate of interest in percentage terms.

Using the same assumptions and specifications, we can derive willingness curves for borrowers, as in Diagram 7-2, i.e., those for whom their existing current liquidity is inadequate. In this case, however, the willingness lines will be inverted and concave to the origin. The inversion of the willingness curves means that borrowers will forego future liquidity so as to acquire current liquidity. The greater the ratio of incremental future liquidity foregone to incremental current liquidity acquired, $(dL_f/dL_c) = (1 + r)$, the higher is the rate of interest, r. The inversion also means that borrowers are willing to undertake a loan venture because they anticipate a future income stream sufficient to pay off their loan plus interest. Furthermore, the relation between the expected income and interest paid will generally be such that the higher expected income is the greater will be the rate of interest borrowers are willing to pay, i.e.,

$$y_1 > y_2 > y_3$$

where y, now, stands for *expected* real income.

---

[2]Negative signs are ignored for convenience.

Diagram 7-2

WILLINGNESS CURVES, BORROWERS

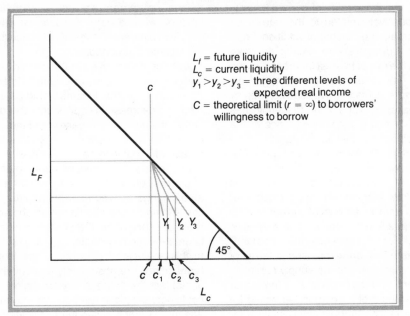

L_f = future liquidity
L_c = current liquidity
$y_1 > y_2 > y_3$ = three different levels of
expected real income
C = theoretical limit ($r = \infty$) to borrowers'
willingness to borrow

Those requiring present liquidity, for which they are willing to sacrifice future liquidity, will offer a reward equal to $(dL_f/dL_c) = (1 + r)$ (with r equal to the rate of interest). Equilibrium between borrowers and lenders will be established when

Lenders	Borrowers

$$\frac{dL_f}{dL_c} = 1 + r = \frac{dL_f}{dL_c}$$

and the quantities of current liquidity transferred from lenders to borrowers are equal.

We can easily show this equilibrium between borrower and lender in Diagram 7-3. In this case, the lender has a low real income, (Y_1), and the borrower has an expected high real income of (y_1). Equilibrium exists where the gain of future liquidity for the lender (indicated by a positive sign on the L_f axis) equals the loss of future liquidity for the borrower (a negative sign). Similarly, in terms of current liquidity, the borrower's gain of current liquidity (a + sign on the L_c axis) equals the lender's loss of current liquidity (a − sign). The slopes of the willingness lines at their points of tangency (the dashed parallel lines) indicate the single rate of reward (1 + r) which will equate the respective gains and losses.

Diagram 7-3

EQUILIBRIUM BETWEEN BORROWERS AND LENDERS

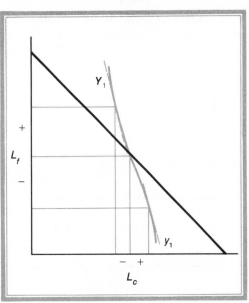

It will be apparent from a careful examination of Diagrams 7-1 and 7-2 that lenders are willing to forego additional current liquidity as the rate of interest rises, i.e., the amount of current liquidity foregone is positively related to the rate of interest. Conversely, the amount of additional current liquidity borrowers are willing to take decreases as the rate of interest increases, or the amount of current liquidity accepted is negatively related to the rate of interest. This can be seen by simply increasing the slope of the tangency lines in Diagram 7-3, and is the consequence of the law of diminishing marginal substitutability of future for current liquidity for lenders and current for future liquidity for borrowers.

With this as the necessary background, we can readily draw Marshallian "supply/demand" curves which relate the amount of current liquidity supplied to the amount demanded at a specific interest rate. For convenience the "demand" curves (Diagram 7-4) are expressed in terms of expected incomes, (y), and the supply curves in terms of current incomes (Y). With an interest rate of zero, the amount of L_c demanded would be infinite for the reason that expected income for the borrower is always greater than present income (tomorrow never comes). With rates higher than zero the amount of L_c demanded decreases. Conversely, a rate of interest of zero means no current liquidity forthcoming from lenders, while a very high interest rate makes very little difference to the supply once the limit of the income is reached.

Equilibrium is achieved in the classic sense that demand equals supply at a specific interest rate. Any increase in real income would be accompanied by a decrease in equilibrium rates of interest unless the demand increases, and the amount of current liquidity foregone by lenders would increase with real income. However, while the concept of equilibrium between demand and supply of current liquidity is perfectly valid, the fact that an exchange *between* current and future liquidities is taking place should not be obscured. This is the essence of the First Principle of the rate of interest—time payments.

In this analysis of equilibrium, the financial intermediaries are absent only for convenience. In actual fact the process of exchanging liquidities could not take place without such intermediation, and in that function lies the justification for their existence. In performing this function, the intermediaries, just like all merchants who buy and sell in the marketplace, charge a spread between the interest rates for the purchaser of current liquidity and the seller; hence, the equilibrium rate of interest must be taken to include a "fair" margin for the intermediary.

But our financial intermediaries do more than merely act as middlemen in a marketplace. Through intermediation, a liquidity level appropriate to a higher real income can be made available to the lender *at the same time that current liquidity is foregone by a lower real income*. This is an important point to grasp and can be best explained by examples.

The British banks, as we saw in Chapter 6, are "asset driven," i.e., they identify specific term loans *then* acquire deposits from the wholesale market to finance them. These deposits are often short-term (7-day) deposits which will require a weekly rollover. The lender(s) is not sacrificing current liquidity to any appreciable extent, yet his funds are being used for long-term lending. Canadian banks also (the chartered banks) have moved into long-term mortgage lending at the same time that savings deposits which finance them can be readily withdrawn by their owners

Diagram 7-4

SUPPLY/DEMAND RELATION

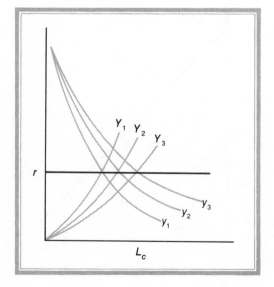

Diagram 7-5

FINANCIAL INTERMEDIATION

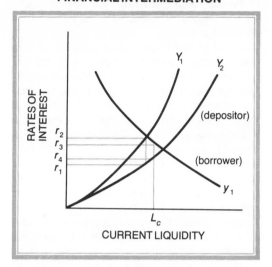

and used as current liquidity. In a real sense we "have our cake and eat it too." We enjoy the fruits of liquidity foregone in the form of additional housing, etc., yet without the sacrifice of current liquidity. Not so the German banks. Guiding ratios effectively preclude such a situation in Germany since the banking law requires a sacrifice of current liquidity *first* before long-term loans can be made.

Suppose in Diagram 7-5 an enhanced supply of current liquidity appropriate to an income Y_2 is granted to a depositor. This makes possible a system of interest rates ranging from a minimum of r_1, the equilibrium rate for Y_1 and y_1 on a "real income" of Y_2, to a maximum of r_2, the equilibrium rate for Y_1 and Y_2. At the two rates, r_3 for the borrower and r_4 for the lender (who has his additional liquidity appropriate to a supply curve Y_2), a profit exists for the intermediary at the amount of lending L_c.

II. THE SUPPLY OF CURRENT LIQUIDITY —TIME

To this point, our discussion has proceeded on the basis that interest is an equilibrium price which equates the forces of supply and demand, which it is. Unfortunately, the equilibrium analysis in its simple form cannot be extended into the more complex functions of both supply and demand for current liquidity, certainly not in the form

of two dimensional diagrams. The supply of liquidity alone is the result of a complex of forces and motives on the part of the general public, and it is this which is the subject of the balance of this chapter.

In analyzing the forces which determine supply, we are, in effect, considering in more detail the nature of liquidity preference in its broadest interpretation. After all, the market supply of current liquidity is no more than a residual, what is left over after preferences for current liquidity are satisfied. The analysis, however, does not assume a Keynesian posture which takes a certain liquidity preference schedule as "given;" quite the contrary, the supply of current liquidity itself is a function of several factors, one of which is time. But time also has two "dimensions," firstly, an unspecified future moment which is different from the present (now) and secondly, a specified future moment which involves an interval of time between now and the future moment — the time lapse.

It is generally true that interest rates as payments for time vary according to the amount of time lapse. To be precise, in a modern financial system such as ours, there is a wide range of alternate future liquidities each of which will become current at different points in future time. As our experience tells us, the longer the time lapse from the present to the future current liquidity, the greater, generally, is the rate of interest. This arises from the necessity of intermediaries to bridge the time differences between the desired liquidities of lenders (those with an excess of current liquidity) and borrowers (those with a shortage of current liquidity). The smaller the span between the two liquidities the easier does this task become. It is worthwhile, therefore, for the intermediary to encourage longer time lapses with higher interest rates as rewards to lenders.

At the same time, the lender with his excess of current liquidity is faced with a "dilemma." The cause of the dilemma originates in the very nature of liquidity as a means of exchange (a flow) and as a store of value (a stock). By performing these two functions, which by their nature are competing, liquidity has alternate uses which involve cost in each case. It is not difficult to understand how this dilemma arises. Any individual may elect to hold all of his funds in the form of current liquidity in which case he gives up the reward of interest entirely. Current liquidity, in this case, incurs a cost to the individual—an opportunity cost — in the form of extra future income foregone. Why, then, should this individual not elect to hold all of his liquidity in the form of interest-earning future liquidity? The answer is there is an inconvenience (hunger, cold, pain, etc.) involved in being unable to meet the exchange requirements which only current liquidity can serve. This again is precisely where the financial intermediary comes into play. The "pain" (or cost) of liquidity foregone can indeed be minimized by offering to depositors a sufficient measure of liquidity to satisfy most foreseen expenditures. Very much of our liquidity is indeed superfluous—a kind of "overcautious" approach to our economic affairs—and can be substantially reduced through careful planning of expenditures. As an example, we might consider the use of the credit card offered by our favourite department store. At the present time there is no price discount for cash payments (perhaps there *should* be). Intelligent planning of expenditures would mean paying for purchases by foreseeable monthly payments and reducing the liquidity of our deposit account by means of the "24-hour" plans which banks now make available. This would be the personal equivalent of the business enterprise which meets its company's monthly payroll not by holding liquid funds for a maximum of four weeks but by purchasing Treasury Bills or such other form of short-term investment which will mature by the month's end.

If all expenditures were perfectly foreseen in this way, current liquidity could be reduced to practically zero, but such, of course, is not the case. In any enterprise, business or household, there are eventualities which must be met and these may arise either as the result of imperfect forecasting or as circumstances which are impossible to foresee. Many of these would arise from an unexpected dislocation in the inflow of payments which can readily occur at random so that at any moment outpayments may exceed inpayments requiring a balance of current liquidity.

In addition, there is a residual of liquidity left in all forms of investment. A 30-day investment is more liquid than a 6-month investment which is more liquid than one year, etc. Hence, even *with* perfect foresight and planning there remains the absolute minimum of residual liquidity which shorter-term investments possess over longer-term. It is this "hard core" of liquidity which financial intermediaries are able to use to their advantage when they satisfy the liquidity needs of their depositors, then use the same deposits for the finance of loans, etc., as part of their illiquid assets.

The total of liquidity, therefore, consists of both this "hard core" residual liquidity plus the liquidity necessary to meet unforeseen circumstances. We might, for convenience, summarize this concept of total liquidity as that which is required to meet foreseen and unforeseen expenditures, and the total cost of this liquidity is the interest reward foregone.

As usual, a diagram may help to make abstract ideas more easily visualized. In Diagram 7-6, time is laid out on the horizontal axis from the present (current liquidity) to the future (the longest possible time lapse). On the left vertical axis, the cost, c, of being unable to meet the expenditure requirements is measured, and on the right is the rate of interest earned by foregoing current liquidity. The rational individual will adjust his overall liquidity balance so that the extra income earned from an increment of interest acquired in exchange for current liquidity will just balance the increment of cost incurred by foregoing current liquidity. This will be functionally related directly to income (Y), and inversely to the price level (P), in other words, real income.

We can see this in Diagram 7-6. Both the rate of interest and the cost, c, are zero if the store of liquidity is held in current form, but they are at their maximum if liquidity is held in the longest possible future form. With a specific income and price structure of (Y/P_1) the rational individual will hold an amount of L_cM of future liquidity with the balance, ML_f, in the form of current liquidity, given a rate of interest, r.[3] Should the rate of interest rise to the average of r', the reward of extra income earned ($r' - r$) must overcome the increment of cost from foregoing current liquidity. If it does, the structure of the liquidity store will shift to M'. An increase in real income to Y/P_2 because of

---

[3]This might appear confusing at first sight. The distance ML_f as measured on the time axis is actually the *equivalent* of a residual of current liquidity. Once a decision is made to hold, say, 10% of total liquidity as future liquidity, it follows that 90% must be current liquidity and since we move along the horizontal axis by an amount equal to one-tenth of the distance, it follows that the balance of the distance, 90%, is the equivalent of current liquidity.

Diagram 7-6

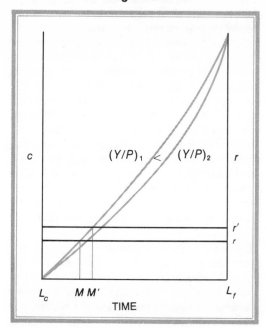

with T = Time
L_c = current liquidity
L_f = future liquidity
r = rate of interest

$$\frac{\partial r}{\partial T} > 0, \; \frac{\partial r}{\partial (L_c + L_f)} > 0 < 1$$

A. Banks and Time Payments

1. Chartered Banks

The sometimes "puzzling" behaviour of chartered banks at various times can be more easily explained with the aid of this functional relationship. We know that these banks manufacture current liquidity for sale at a price which will be acceptable to those willing to make the purchase —the "price" being the rate of interest charged. If an easy monetary policy is being pursued by the Bank of Canada, banks can readily increase total liquidity $(L_c + L_f)$ by increasing L_c alone, with L_f constant. The banks have no need, in other words, to encourage growth in L_f as savings deposits so the rate of interest for L_f will decline and interest rates in general will fall as the ratio $L_f/(L_c + L_f)$ falls.

But bank interest rates apply to loans as well as just deposits. It is quite possible, therefore, that the other member of the equation, T, may grow larger *instead* of interest rates falling. Should banks wish to lengthen the period of their loans to customers during a period of easy money, they could easily do so by means of a readjustment of their portfolio. Of course, since the manufacture of new current liquidity takes place with zero marginal cost, bank profit margins are at least intact if not greater.

A tight monetary policy means less liquidity for the banks which, in turn, will find it less profitable to manufacture additional amounts of L_c. To accommodate their customers, they must increase L_f by reducing the amounts of L_c, sharply raising the value of $L_f/(L_c + L_f)$. From the loan side again, tight money may not result in higher interest rates for borrowers at all but a shortening of the time period of the loan. In this way the loan structure is adjusted to suit the tight money policy. Once more, bank profit margins are not disturbed because a portfolio which is more heavily weighted on the short side means a higher turnover of loans per year.

either a rise in money income or a lowering of the price level, will reduce the cost, c, of current liquidity so that intermediaries will be able to acquire what funds they wish at the old interest rate, r, making a further increase unnecessary.

Whether or not a real income of (Y/P_1) or (Y/P_2) prevails, to increase the time factor of future liquidity, higher rates of interest must be paid to overcome the additional "pain" of liquidity surrendered for longer and longer periods. Since the pain increases rather sharply with increasing amounts of future time for foregone liquidity, incremental pain must be overcome with corresponding sharply increasing interest rates ultimately to the theoretical limit which would compensate for the extreme pain of not spending (or consuming) anything at all.

There are, therefore, two distinct parts to interest as a reward for time payments which have an influence upon the level of interest rates. These are, first, the relative quantity of liquidity foregone, and second, the length of time lapse for which the liquidity is given up. Functionally, we could represent this as

$$(1) \qquad r = f\left(\frac{L_f}{L_c + L_f}, \, T\right)$$

2. Non-Bank Financial Intermediaries

The major competition for chartered banks is, of course, the whole group of bank-type institutions such as trust companies, credit unions, etc., that do not have the legal right to issue claims against themselves which can circulate through the clearing house as money. The important phrase "which can circulate as money" is crucial here because all of the FI's do indeed create claims against themselves (future liquidity) in exchange for the current liquidity manufactured by chartered banks. As they create this future liquidity, they make it impossible for the chartered banks to transfer the *same* current liquidity into future liquidity. Competition, then, becomes keen between the two types of institutions especially during periods of tight money, for additional savings deposits in the FI's will mean less savings deposits in the banks, and customers may choose which financial institution they prefer on the basis of competitive interest rates.

As was argued in Chapter 4, FI's simply spin the same money faster, i.e., the demand deposits within the chartered banking system change ownership more rapidly than they otherwise would. In exchange for this right to increase the velocity of circulation, additional claims against the FI's are issued which carry the promise of future liquidity. In this way *total* liquidity $(L_c + L_f)$ in the economy is increased. It is increased because L_f rises without any change in L_c. However, this increase is accompanied by upward pressure on interest rates, though not so great as in the case of increases in L_f by chartered banks. We can see this in the above equation for interest rate determination, by assuming that the first member applies to financial intermediaries. An additional activity on their part will increase future liquidity, L_f, by an amount ΔL_f without a corresponding decrease in L_c as is the case of the chartered banks. Thus

$$\frac{L_f + \Delta L_f}{L_c + L_f + \Delta L_f} < \frac{L_f + \Delta L_f}{L_c - \Delta L_c + L_f + \Delta L_f}$$

where $\quad |\Delta L_c| = |\Delta L_f|$.

In other words, an increase in future liquidity in chartered banks has a greater impact on interest rates in general than a corresponding increase in future liquidity in FI's because in the former case, it is accompanied by an equivalent *decrease* in current liquidity while in the latter, it is not.

In the time member of the equation there is an other significant difference in the effect of FI's. In fact, it is more of an exception to the general rule regarding interest rates and time. FI's, like chartered banks, generally pay higher rates of interest for longer time periods on their savings accounts, but since FI's have the unique capacity to match maturities (or liquidities) they can make certain loans at, say, particularly high interest rates, *then* secure additional deposits at correspondingly high rates within the time frame of the loans. Thus, shorter time deposits may have higher interest rates than longer-term deposits because it is expected that future loans will be made at lower rates than the current high rates. This factor of expectations is extremely important and will be examined in greater detail in the next section of this chapter.

3. Canada Savings Bonds

The third institutional competitor within this first principle of interest (time payments) is the federal government. Every autumn the government launches its savings bond campaign with the objective of acquiring extra deposits to finance its deficits — a shortfall of tax revenue against spending. Tax collection, of course, is a spring occasion to be balanced by a savings bond campaign in the fall.

Actually, the proceeds of the savings bond drive are for the purpose of funding short-term Treasury Bills, and most important, it makes it unnecessary for the government to go to the market for sales of marketable bonds to the same extent as it would otherwise. The impact of the savings bond campaign on the money supply can be clearly seen in Chart 2-2 of Chapter 2. Government of Canada deposits generally rise substantially in the autumn to be accompanied by corresponding dips in the chartered bank savings deposits.

The effect of the Canada Savings Bond issue is somewhat more complex than in the case of financial intermediaries. When the sale of the bonds is financed by a transfer from chartered bank savings deposits to the government, no change in the public's future liquidity has taken place. A substitution of savings bonds for savings deposits in the hands of the public means no change in the total of future liquidity, L_f. At the same time there is an increase in current liquidity in the government's deposits, but since this is not part of the public's liquidity, no change in interest rates will take place.

However, this transaction is accompanied by a loss of savings deposits to chartered banks. There will, therefore, be pressure on the limited reserves of the banking system because of the loss of deposits which require only a 4% reserve ratio. Any effort on the part of the chartered banks to restore their savings deposits to their former level must result in an increase in the total future liquidity of the public and therefore exert an upward pressure on interest rates. On the other hand, if the Bank of Canada supplies the additional reserves required by the chartered banks, no additional future liquidity is required and there will be no pressure on interest rates at all.

Assuming that the Bank of Canada does oblige in this fashion, when the government spends from its accounts, current liquidity is returned to the public once more. The public, thus, has the same future liquidity as before the sale of bonds and an additional amount of current liquidity as well; hence, a *downward* pressure on interest rates can be exerted. This result may sound surprising at first until it is realized that the Bank of Canada is actually making possible the sale of Canada Savings Bonds by means of its accommodation and involves a joint cooperation between the government and the Bank, a situation which is very likely to develop.

Undoubtedly the growth in recent years of the government sector has contributed to the recent predominance of the Canada Savings Bond in the competition for future liquidity without risk, i.e., interest as payment for time. It is not correct, however, to say that this is always true. Before 1967 the FI's had their greatest growth period, whereas since 1967, the chartered banks have emerged strongly competitive. So it is in this highly competitive environment that the Canadian government currently launches its Canada Savings Bond campaign.

No better example of this can be found than the year 1973 during which time the Bank of Canada was generally following a "less accommodating stance of monetary policy ... "[4] In other words bank liquidity was tight, and deposit manufacturing costs were rising. This policy coincided, unfortunately, with substantial increases in interest rates abroad, particularly in the United States, with the consequence that rates in Canada rose

rather markedly. (See Chart 7-1.) By the end of 1973, especially the last quarter, interest on bank deposits were rising to their peaks of 7 to 10%, with expectations of continued increases in the future. Just at this time the government announced the sale of Canada Savings Bonds to yield a 7.54% to maturity. This was subsequently increased to 9% on May 1, 1974 and 10½% on September 1, 1974, with the addition of cash bonuses. Despite the increases, this bond issue, #28, was a disaster for the reason that the competition was too great. The consequence was a net reduction of savings bonds in the hands of the public from $11.1 billion in December, 1972 to $9.2 billion in October, 1974.

By the last quarter of 1974, interest rates both here and in other countries peaked, to turn downward with the implementation of easier monetary policies. The 1974 issue of Canada Savings Bonds, #29, was brought forward on November 1, 1974 at 9.75% to maturity. The issue was so successful that it was withdrawn at the earliest legally possible moment, November 15. By the end of November, the public had increased its holdings to $13.35 billion and government deposits were replenished once more. Of course, chartered banks savings deposits showed their usual last quarter drop, overwhelmed by the strong competition of government bonds.

The interesting feature of the past decade has been the growing use by the government of the savings bond as a source of finance for public debt. This is apparent from the table on page 175. This enormous growth in the saving bond as a source of debt funding suggests the ease by which government debt may be funded as long as the Bank of Canada maintains its easy monetary policy. These bonds are attractive to the public because the federal government does, after all, carry great prestige, offer security, and does appeal to "patriotic" motives. All this is in addition to attractive interest rates when the bonds are held to maturity. Even so, the 1973 debacle proved the necessity for joint cooperation between the government and the Bank of Canada for the Bond issue to succeed.

B. Interest—The Second Principle

Following Fisher's example, we move to the second principle in interest rate determination, the degree to which a financial asset may be con-

---

[4] *Annual Report of the Governor of the Bank of Canada*, 1973, p. 23.

Chart 7-1

INTEREST RATES (MONTHLY)

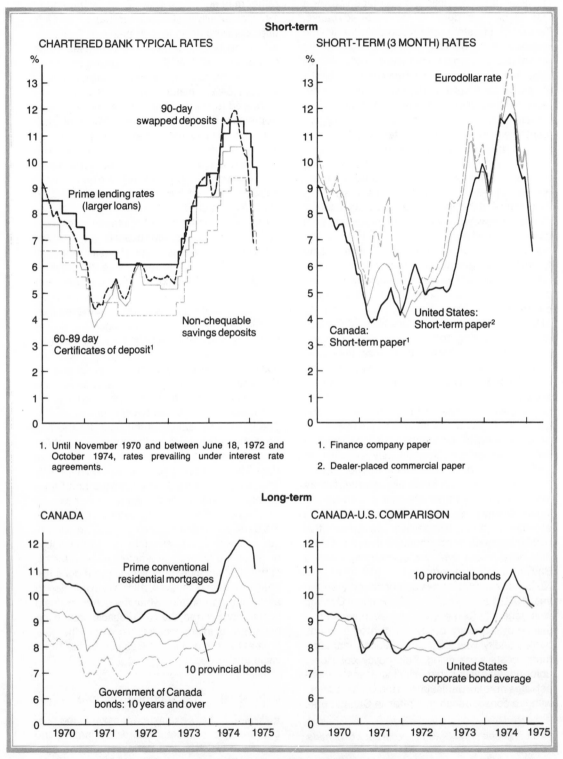

Short-term

CHARTERED BANK TYPICAL RATES

90-day swapped deposits

Prime lending rates (larger loans)

Non-chequable savings deposits

60-89 day Certificates of deposit[1]

1. Until November 1970 and between June 18, 1972 and October 1974, rates prevailing under interest rate agreements.

SHORT-TERM (3 MONTH) RATES

Eurodollar rate

United States: Short-term paper[2]

Canada: Short-term paper[1]

1. Finance company paper

2. Dealer-placed commercial paper

Long-term

CANADA

Prime conventional residential mortgages

10 provincial bonds

Government of Canada bonds: 10 years and over

CANADA-U.S. COMPARISON

10 provincial bonds

United States corporate bond average

Source: Bank of Canada, *Annual Report of the Governor to the Minister of Finance*, 1974, p.22.

DISTRIBUTION OF GOVERNMENT OF CANADA DEBT ($ millions)

	Total Debt	%	Treasury Bills	%	Other	%	Savings Bonds	%
1964	20,733	100	2,140	10.3	12,980	62.6	5,613	27.1
1968	23,556	100	2,825	12.0	14,373	61.0	6,359	27.0
1970	25,746	100	3,625	14.1	14,724	57.2	7,397	28.7
1972	29,873	100	4,160	13.9	14,602	48.9	11,111	37.2
1974	33,952	100	5,630	16.6	15,147	44.6	13,176	38.8
1976	42,152	100	7,845	18.6	17,717	42.0	16,590	39.4
1977	50,172	100	10,315	20.5	21,577	43.0	18,250	36.4

Source: Bank of Canada Review, February, 1975. Table 20.
Bank of Canada Review, August, 1978. Table 21.

verted into a monetary asset without capital loss. This involves a risk factor which is absent from the first principle, i.e., interest as time payments. In practice, however, many of the interest rates we do encounter include a compensation for both time and risk, though it is often not possible to separate one from another so as to identify which of the two is more important at any time.

Until this point, discussion of an organized free market for financial assets has been deliberately avoided, for the reason that first principle interest payments do not require a free market — these assets are nonmarketable. When we move into the sector of marketable assets, however, we must consider the market forces of demand for and supply of financial assets and their interplay which determines both quantity and price. Of course this assumes a perfect market does exist with free competition throughout, and therein lies the advantage of financial assets over other economic commodities. Markets for financial assets are as nearly perfect as can be found anywhere. While it is theoretically possible for monopolies to exist in financial markets, we do have, fortunately, laws and regulations which can be more readily enforced than in the ordinary markets for goods.

The financial assets we are now concerned with are quite different from either Canada Savings Bonds, or ordinary savings deposits. These assets are purchased and sold from dealers, but because of the high degree of perfection of the market, their prices fluctuate considerably in accordance with the forces of demand and supply. The marketable asset, then, has the possibility of a capital gain or loss, for it is quite possible to purchase at one price and sell at another. This is the risk of capital loss which reduces the degree of liquidity from 100% to something less (see

Chapter 4). A portion of the interest rate payment is compensation for this part of liquidity given up, while the other portion is compensation for the foregone time portion of liquidity.

The discussion which follows will be centred, first, on the market for bonds. This is not only a convenient starting point, but it also emphasizes the importance of this market in the entire structure of the market for financial assets. Consider, first, the nature of a bond. It is a debt instrument, a promise to pay, along with interest at a stipulated rate, a certain sum of money within a specific time period. The date at which the time period is exhausted is the date of maturity and may be near or far into the future. This bond constitutes the demand for funds (current liquidity). It is generally turned over to specialist firms for sale to the general public. These firms underwrite, or guarantee, a minimum price at which the bond will be sold, and should the public refuse to purchase at a price above this minimum, the firm will be forced to accept the loss.

It would help to grasp the essential point with an example. Assume, at first, that a long term bond — say 20 years to maturity — promises to pay $1,000 in 20 years plus interest at $4\frac{1}{2}\%$, i.e., $45 per year. What would be the likely price of that bond when sold on the market? The answer to this question resolves itself into another question, what would any rational person pay for a financial asset which assures an income of $45 per year? For the moment, we assume this to be like rent, i.e., $45 in perpetuity. If the market rate of interest for similar investment possibilities were 9%, the price we could expect would be around $500, that is

$$\frac{\$45}{.09} = \$500$$

This important point must be thoroughly understood. Because of the existence of a market rate of interest on *other* financial assets of 9%, the new bond itself must "fall into line" and be sold to *yield* the same rate.[5] The point is also important because it demonstrates the principle that the prices of bonds move *inversely* with their yields.

Canadian bond prices are, in fact, quoted in terms of yields, i.e., a specific bond is priced to yield a certain per cent per year. This, while technically correct, is somewhat confusing because there is a tendency to take the yield itself to be *the* market rate of interest. Actually the bond yield is merely *representative* of market rates. The British practice of quoting a price index for government gilt-edged rather than a yield avoids this confusion.

Actually the price of a $1,000 bond which will mature in 20 years and pays $4\frac{1}{2}$% per year is more than $500. To compute the correct price we would approach the problem in two stages: (1) What is the current value of $45 per year for 20 years if the current rate of interest (yields on alternative assets) is 9%? The situation would be analogous to depositing a certain sum of money in a bank to be worth $45 in one year, a second sum to be worth $45 in two years, etc., until the sum for the 20th year is included. We can find this by discounting as follows:

$$\frac{45}{1.09} + \frac{45}{(1.09)^2} + \frac{45}{(1.09)^3} + \cdots \frac{45}{(1.09)^{20}} = \$410.79.$$

(2) But this is not all. The bond itself is worth $1,000 in 20 years time in addition to the $45 per year. What is this value, i.e., $1,000 in 20 years, today? We can compute this by discounting $1,000 for 20 years as follows:

$$\frac{1000}{(1.09)^{20}} = \$178.43.$$

Thus the price of the bond which yields 9% is
$$\$410.79 + \$178.43 = \$589.22[6]$$
With a little imagination, one may suppose the time to maturity to be infinity so that
$$\frac{1000}{(1+r)}\infty = 0$$
and the first summation of the sequence of terms would approach $500, the limiting value of the summation computed above.

Fortunately all this computation is available in bond tables so that, given the rate and the time to maturity, the price can be readily determined. What is important here, however, is that the relationship between price and yield is purely a mechanical one — if price is determined, the yield automatically follows. Further, the mathematical relationship between the two is such that the longer the term to maturity the greater is the *fluctuation* in price in response to a given change in yield. This can be seen by imagining once more time to maturity at infinity. A change in yield from 9% to 10% would result in a fall in price from $500 to $450. However, if time to maturity is just one year, the price of the bond at 9% is
$$\frac{1,000}{1.09} + \frac{45}{1.09} = \$958.72$$

---

[5]There is a "bootstrap" effect here. To avoid this, we assume that the new bond in question is small relative to the total demand for funds in the market; consequently, the market prices of all bonds are unaffected by the new issue. If it were large, relative to the total demand for funds, the rate of interest would likely rise and the market price be further depressed.

---

[6]In general terms
$$P = \frac{V}{(1+r)^t} + \frac{y}{1+r} + \frac{y}{(1+r)^2} + \cdots \frac{y}{(1+r)^t}$$
where P = Price, V = Value at maturity, y = Annual income and r = Rate of yield.
If the time to maturity of a bond were infinity, its value would be computed according to the sum of a geometric progression as follows.
$$S_N = 0 + y\left(\frac{1}{1+r}\right) + y\left(\frac{1}{1+r}\right)^2 \cdots y\left(\frac{1}{1+r}\right)^N$$
with the first term $V/(1+r)\infty = 0$. Using the accepted techniques of deriving the sum of N terms, we have
$$\left(\frac{t}{1+r}\right)S_N = y\left(\frac{1}{1+r}\right)^2 + y\left(\frac{1}{1+r}\right)^3 \cdots y\left(\frac{1}{1+r}\right)^{N+1},$$
subtracting gives
$$S_N - \left(\frac{1}{1+r}\right)S_N = y\left(\frac{1}{1+r}\right) - y\left(\frac{1}{1+r}\right)^{N+1},$$
$$S_N = \frac{y\left(\frac{1}{1+r}\right) - \left(\frac{1}{1+r}\right)^{N+1}}{1 - \left(\frac{1}{1+r}\right)}, \text{ let } N = \infty$$
$$S_N = \frac{y\left(\frac{1}{1+r}\right) - 0}{1 - \frac{1}{1+r}} \text{ or } \frac{y}{1+r-1} = \frac{y}{r}$$

but at 10%, the price is

$$\frac{1,000}{1.10} + \frac{45}{1.10} = \$950,$$

a decrease of only $8.72. Of course, at zero maturity the bond is worth exactly $1,000 regardless of the interest rate prevailing in the market.

So it follows that the capital value of a bond, determined as it is by demand and supply in the market, is subject to change by a greater amount if the time to maturity is long rather than short. The risk factor, that is, is greater with long-term bonds than short-term bonds. Risk arises here because should it be necessary to sell bonds on the market so as to regain current liquidity, the possibility of capital loss in the event that interest rates in general have risen is much greater with long-term than short-term bonds. In other words, the shorter the period to maturity the closer does the bond approach the first principle of interest—time payments. The longer the period to maturity, the greater is the importance of the risk factor in interest.

Rationally, therefore, long-term yields should be higher than short-term because risk must be compensated, and the greater the risk the higher the rate of yield. Also the greater the risk the less the degree of liquidity, and lenders, before parting with current liquidity must be appropriately rewarded. Put in a slightly different fashion, if one can wait out with certainty the 20 years or so to maturity the risk of capital loss is zero; however, under general market conditions those who can do so are a small minority.

Including the risk factor in interest means an additional variable in our functional relationship. We have now three independent variables instead of two.

(2) $$\left(r = f \left(\frac{L_f}{L_c + L_f} \right) T, R \right)$$

with R = risk and

$$\frac{\partial r}{\partial R} > 0.$$

By "risk" we have reference here to the normal risk of capital loss due partly to the combination of market fluctuations which are the result of random events and the greater sensitivity of longer-term securities to these market fluctuations. This is quite different from the risk of default which

sometimes gives rise to an extra risk premium. It is this additional risk which, incidentally, results in very high rate levels in less developed countries. Similarly, in our own case, the loan shark, the pawnbroker, etc., exist on the same basis — a high risk of default. The same is true of loan companies which make loans on the strength of a signature. Such loans carry the legal limit of interest because of the high risk entailed.

Whether legal or not, these finance agencies can exist only as the result of market imperfections which arise through individual circumstances, ignorance, personal tragedy, or whatever. The free market we are considering here exists without such imperfections, yet, at the same time, maintains a residual risk element consisting of the possibility of capital loss.

It is this risk factor in the market which, under normal circumstances, accounts for about a $1\frac{1}{2}$ to 2 point spread between short-term rates (less than one year) and long-term rates (over ten years). However, as we shall see, the "normal circumstances" often appear less frequently in the market than the abnormal. Life, in a word, is not so simple.

1. Expectations

The fact of the matter is that there are times when short-term rates may equal or exceed long-term rates, apparently violating the principle of liquidity preference as set out above. To see how these "exceptions" can arise, we can return once more to the example which calculated the price of a long-term $4\frac{1}{2}\%$ bond with a 9% yield. In that case the 9% yield was *expected* to be maintained throughout the life of the bond. But suppose the 9% was not expected to remain constant. The problem of computing the price is much more complex, for it involves relating the long-term yield to a series of expected short-term yields. Of course, the situation could be reversed, i.e., the short-term series could be related to the long-term yield depending upon which happens to be the cause or the effect at any time. There is a relationship, however, and it is this which concerns us here.

The approximate long-term yield, for the next 20 years, can be derived by computing an arithmetic average of short-term (say one year) yields which are expected to hold true for each of the next 20 years. This average would then approximate the correct yield to be used as the rate of discount for arriving at the price of the 20-year bond.[7]

As an example, suppose for the next three years short-term rates (one year) are expected to be 5% the first year, 9% the second year, and 3% the third year. The approximate long-term rate for the 3-year period would be the arithmetic average of $5\frac{2}{3}\%$ and this could be used for calculating the price of a 3-year bond when it is first issued. In the second year the long-term rate (just two years now) would rise to 6%, below the short-term rate of 9%.[8] Expectations of future short rates have, in this case, distorted the "normal" liquidity preference pattern of interest rates.

Readers may suspect that this Lutz-Hicks relation between short and long rates is based on an assumption of a "consensus of expectations of interest rates" as far as the market is concerned.[9] This is why the argument is prefaced with "assume that short rates are expected to be..." or in the Hicks case, "assume that forward rates are..." But if we reject this as unrealistic, since crystal balls are inaccurate, expectations must have some other rational way of influencing the

market, for after all, short-term rates *can* be higher than long-term. The analysis which follows is directed toward this problem and its explanation.

We should stress at the outset that in a modern financial market which includes bonds from both the private and public sectors there exists a whole range of degrees of liquidity foregone from the very short, say, one week, to the very long. In the government of Canada case, bonds range from Treasury Bills which are very close to maturity to the October 1, 2003 bonds at the other extreme.

Ideally, a discussion of the bond market should include all bonds, federal, provincial and corporate which are sold on the market. Unfortunately, this is not feasible for the reason that corporate bonds tend to be "sweetened" with additional incentives to purchase such as conversion clauses of various types which distort the correct value of the bond as a pure debt instrument. Only the federal government bonds can offer the necessary combination of "purity" in the sense of absolute freedom from risk of default as well as an undiluted instrument of debt which can serve as a measure of market interest rates. And, it may be added, it is this very quality which is so important in our analysis.

All of us possess a time horizon in the future. For some it may be relatively short depending on life expectancy, proximity to retirement, etc., while for others it may be long. Plans for the future which all of us have in varying degrees will be relevant to our time horizons. At the same time that individual time horizons differ, because of the nature of probability, a *mean* time horizon for the entire population must exist. We shall take this to be a decade beyond which time no one is willing to forecast or expect. Within this horizon we shall assume that there exists a general consensus of opinion that all interest rates (not just short rates) will rise. This could be the result of past experience, i.e., a projection of the past into the future, or any other cause. We can show this with the aid of Diagram 7-7 which relates bond yields (and prices) to the relevant time horizon, assumed to be ten years.

Bond yields are expected to rise because interest rates in general are expected to rise and government bond yields are one of the best indicators of market rates. As we have shown, the price of

---

[7]The correct method of computing the bond price if all annual (short-term) rates are known would be

$$P = \frac{V}{(1+r_1)(1+r_2)\ldots(1+r_{20})} + \frac{1}{1+r_1} + \frac{y}{(1+r_1)(1+r_2)} + \ldots \frac{y}{(1+r_1)(1+r_2)\ldots(1+r_{20})}$$

with specifications as per footnote 6.

[8]The arithmetic mean fails to arrive at the precise long-term average because it does not include the compounding effect. However, since interest payments are assumed to be made annually, the result of compounding is minimized; nevertheless, the correct formula for computing the true long-term rate from a series of short-term rates is as follows:

$$R = \frac{(1+r_1)(1+r_2)\ldots(1+r_n) - 1}{(1+r_2)(1+r_3)\ldots(1+r_n) + (1+r_3)\ldots(1+r_n) + \ldots + (1+r_n) + 1}$$

Friedrich A. Lutz, "The Structure of Interest Rates" reprinted in *Readings in the Theory of Income Distribution*, Allen and Unwin, Ltd., London, 1950, p. 500

[9]Sir John Hicks presented a similar argument regarding the relation between short and long rates shortly before Lutz. He uses a "futures concept" of forward rates, instead of expected short rates, but it all comes to the same thing in the end— expectations. *Value and Capital*, Oxford, Clarendon Press, 1965, p. 144.

Diagram 7-7

EXPECTATION CURVE

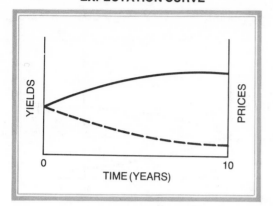

Diagram 7-8

DEMAND AND SUPPLY OF SHORT-TERM LIQUIDITY

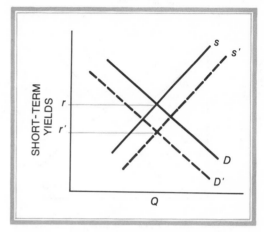

bonds (the dashed line measured against the right-hand axis) is expected also to decline since yields and prices are actually two sides of the same coin. If these expectations within the relevant time horizon are accurate forecasts of the future, the purchase of long-term bonds with rates of maturity over one year would be unwise since loss of capital is certain. The only way to completely avoid this loss is to hold the bonds until maturity, but if it becomes necessary to sell them before the maturity date there is no alternative to accepting the loss. The risk of capital loss is greatest during the earlier years of the decade with a gradual reduction in risk as time passes.

Under the circumstances, therefore, rational buyers of bonds (sellers of current liquidity) will prefer short-term bonds so as to minimize their risk throughout the decade. This will be manifest in a market preference for short dated securities; hence, the supply of short-term liquidity will be greater than normal.

Meantime, those institutions, governments, federal, provincial and civic, corporations, etc., who require current liquidity will prefer to "lock in" their debts at the lowest possible cost to them. They too expect rising interest rates since they are part of the market consensus just as are the sellers of liquidity. Unless they revise their plans for the future, their demand for long-term liquidity (supply of long-term bonds) will increase while their demand for short-term liquidity will fall, within, of course, the relevant time horizon of ten years. The consequence for short-term interest rates

can be shown in Diagram 7-8 with the aid of Marshallian supply/demand curves. Because of the shift in both demand and supply curves, the short-term yields decline to r'.

Meantime, the long-term rate will also react in a specific way. The collapse of demand for short liquidity will likely mean an increase in demand for long-term liquidity, though it need not necessarily follow since the long-term plans may be revised. Certainly there will be a collapse in the supply of long-term liquidity for the reasons discussed above. The consequence will be an upward movement in the long-term rate as per Diagram 7-9. Expectations of rising rates, then, will result in an increasing spread between short and long rates as short rates tend toward the low side and long rates tend to be higher (r').

In a similar fashion, we can analyze the opposite condition, the expectation of falling interest rates, in terms of the expectation curve, Diagram 7-10. Within a 10-year time horizon, interest rates are expected to fall. Using bond yields once more as indicators of market rates, it follows that bond prices are expected to rise making possible additional rewards in the form of capital gain. Now, the longer the term of the bond the better, for long-term bonds tend to increase in value more than short-term bonds. Just as before, a shift in the supply of liquidity occurs, but this time a preference will be shown for long-term bonds. Similarly,

Diagram 7-9

DEMAND AND SUPPLY OF LONG-TERM LIQUIDITY

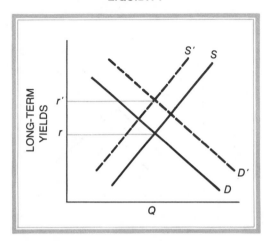

Diagram 7-10

EXPECTATION CURVE

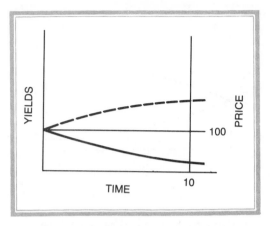

those who require liquidity will prefer short-term funds so as to *avoid* "locking in" their debt at long-term high rates. This shifts the demand for short-term funds to the right as the supply of short-term funds is restricted (see Diagram 7-11). A higher than normal short-term rate, *r'*, is the result.

Of course, the market supply of long-term liquidity will increase as those with an excess seek future capital gain. Similarly the market demand for long-term liquidity will decline for the reasons discussed above so that production plans and expansion activities may tend to be postponed (see Diagram 7-12). A lower than normal long-term rate, *r'*, is the result.

2. Yield Curves

In a perfect world of certainty without differing expectations, it would make no difference whatsoever as to whether a long, medium, or short-term bond were selected by a particular investor. The structure of yields would reflect a Lutz/Hicks averaging process and all expectations would be fulfilled.[10] However, such is not the case. Expectations change and yield structures may be differ-

---

[10]"It is evident that the return on an investment for a given time is the same no matter what form the investment is made. ...An investor who wants, for instance, to invest his money for one year can either invest in the short-term market for one year or buy a bond of any maturity and sell it after a year." Lutz, *op. cit.,* p. 503.

ent from one day to the next. We can learn a great deal from these rate structures and the knowledge gained will prove invaluable in helping to understand the capital market. This is why the yield curve, which expresses rather neatly the relationship of interest rates, can be an important tool of analysis for capital markets.

The yield curve emphasizes the relationship between long and short yields. When short rates are high relative to long rates, expectations are for yields in general to decline; conversely, when short rates are low relative to long rates, market expectations are for rising yields. If we prepare a graph representing time to maturity on the horizontal axis and yields on the vertical, we can plot the points for all the bonds, short to long, beginning with the 91-day Treasury Bill and concluding with the 9$\frac{1}{2}$%, 1994. Such a curve would appear as shown in Chart 7-2.

The bond issues used for plotting are listed at the left of the chart. One issue, that of February 1, 1977, is an extendible bond which may account for its desirability in the market and its low yield. The dates for each issue refer to the date of maturity and by subtracting from these dates the current date (May 7, 1975) we can arrive at the years to maturity which are laid out on the horizontal axis. Once the points are plotted, it is a fairly simple matter to either fit a curve within these points or join them with a smooth curve, "humped" at the beginning.

Diagram 7-11

DEMAND AND SUPPLY OF SHORT-TERM LIQUIDITY

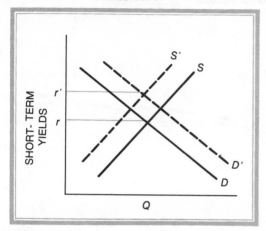

Diagram 7-12

DEMAND AND SUPPLY OF LONG-TERM LIQUIDITY

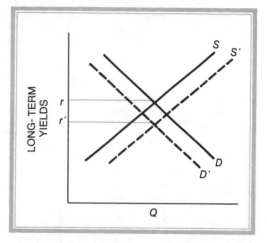

The yield curve thus formed for May 7, 1975, is a "normal" curve showing about a 1½ to 2 percentage point spread between Treasury Bills and other short-term bonds at one end and the longest-term bond at the other. For Canada this appears to be fairly typical of a normal liquidity preference spread. The compensation for both time and risk are accounted for at the long rate of

9%, whereas for shorter rates, the payments, largely for time alone, amount to about 7%.

The yield curve plotted in Chart 7-2, then, tells us that expectations are neutral, i.e., interest rates will likely neither rise nor fall in the collective opinion of the market within the relevant time horizon. This is not to suggest that either bond yields or expectations will not change in the future; we do not live in a world of constant expectations.

Chart 7-2

YIELD CURVE AS OF MAY 7, 1975

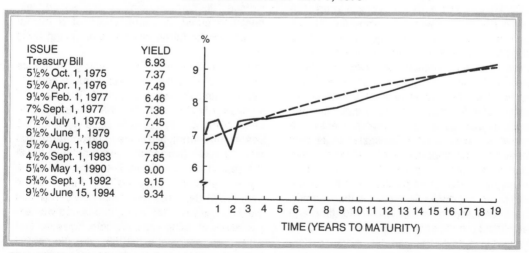

ISSUE	YIELD
Treasury Bill	6.93
5½% Oct. 1, 1975	7.37
5½% Apr. 1, 1976	7.49
9¼% Feb. 1, 1977	6.46
7% Sept. 1, 1977	7.38
7½% July 1, 1978	7.45
6½% June 1, 1979	7.48
5½% Aug. 1, 1980	7.59
4½% Sept. 1, 1983	7.85
5¼% May 1, 1990	9.00
5¾% Sept. 1, 1992	9.15
9½% June 15, 1994	9.34

TIME (YEARS TO MATURITY)

Source: Bank of Canada Weekly Financial Statistics, May 8, 1975, p. 5.

Chart 7-3

**YIELD CURVE AS OF AUGUST 9, 1978,
SELECTED BOND YIELDS**

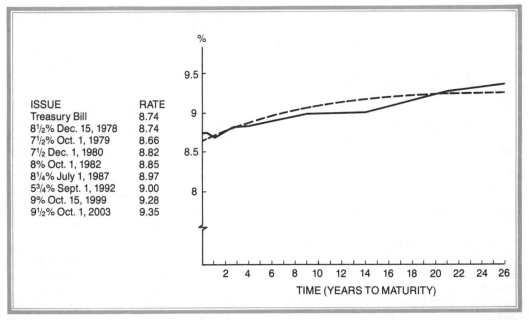

ISSUE	RATE
Treasury Bill	8.74
8¹/₂% Dec. 15, 1978	8.74
7¹/₂% Oct. 1, 1979	8.66
7¹/₂ Dec. 1, 1980	8.82
8% Oct. 1, 1982	8.85
8¹/₄% July 1, 1987	8.97
5³/₄% Sept. 1, 1992	9.00
9% Oct. 15, 1999	9.28
9¹/₂% Oct. 1, 2003	9.35

Source: Bank of Canada Review, August 1978, Table 27.

In Chart 7-3 another yield curve is plotted. It differs rather markedly from that of Chart 7-2 in that short-term yields (90-day Treasury Bills) and the yields of the longest term bond (October 1, 2003) are just 0.61 percentage points apart. The yield curve, in other words, is almost flat. Such a curve tells us that market expectations are for falling rates as opposed to the curve in Chart 7-2 which reflected a market consensus for stable rates. It should be emphasized once more that the fact that the market expects a certain behaviour of rates does not mean that such will occur; in fact, as will be shown presently, the market is indeed a poor forecaster of its own behaviour. The importance of the yield curve does not lie here, but in the adjacent markets.

In Diagram 7-13, three possible shapes of the yield curve are drawn. Number I is the "normal" shape reflecting the compensation for time and risk without the influence of expectations of future changes in rates. More accurately, market expectations are neutralized in that expectations of rising rates are cancelled by expectations of fall-

ing rates. Number II suggests a market consensus in favour of rising interest rates (falling bond prices) with prospects of capital loss. It accords with the first expectation curve discussed above. Number III, corresponding to the second expectation curve, is characteristic of a market consensus for falling interest rates (rising bond prices).

There is another method of identifying the various positions of yield curves which is more convenient though somewhat simplified. The Bank of Canada publishes in its *Monthly Review*, a time series of monthly averages for bond yields for 1–3 years (short-term), 3–5 years (medium-term) and over 10 years (long-term). The graphs of these are reproduced as Chart 7-4. When all three series are closely "bunched" together, as in the years 1968-69, we can be reasonably certain that yield curves were flat during this period with expectations of falling rates. We note, however, that with the exception of mid-1968, rates did *not* fall but continued to rise throughout the 3-year period until the beginning of 1970.

Diagram 7-13

TYPICAL YIELD CURVES

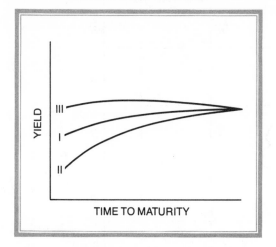

YIELD

III

I

II

TIME TO MATURITY

From 1970 on, bond yields generally fell; however, through 1971 and 1972 a "normal" spread of about $1\frac{1}{2}$ to 2 percentage points prevailed suggesting that the yield structure at the time was about what the market expected it to be without any further change. When bond yields moved to their peaks in 1974, the market again signalled its expectations of declining rates.

The "normal" spread of about 2% did not reappear until mid-1975 with yields having gone through the dip at the end of 1974 and the beginning of 1975. The difference between the rates during the normal spread of the latter 70s and those of the early 70s is that the level of what the market thinks is normal is now some two percentage points higher, about 7 to 9% now as opposed to 5 to 7% in the early 1970s. The market has undergone a substantial change in its expectations.

A careful examination of Chart 7-4 will reveal this pattern of bond yields, bunching together as they rise and spreading apart when they fall. This is in perfect accord with the expectations analysis discussed above for the reason that when rates in general rise the market will expect them to fall (the "what goes up must come down" theorem). This is due to an inertia in economic affairs which projects the immediate past into the future; hence, periods of stability in yields will be expected to return simply because they were stable. Aside from confirming the theory, there is

nothing "startling" about these conclusions; we could hardly expect otherwise.

There is another characteristic about Canada's bond yield structure; short rates rarely exceed long rates, and, if they do, it is only for short periods and by very small amounts. We can see this during periods of rising rates when short-term rates are just about equal to long rates; any further upward movement in the short rates tends to equal the corresponding movement in long rates. When a downtrend begins, the opposite is true. Short rates fall precipitously leaving long rates well behind until the normal spread of $1\frac{1}{2}$ to 2 percentage points is reached. Any further fall in rates means a wider spread, about 2 to $2\frac{1}{2}$ percentage points. The yield curve, in other words, has moved from position III through position I to position II. In the process of moving downward through these positions, short-term rates move much more widely than long rates.

This tendency for short rates to fluctuate more widely than long rates is perfectly in accord with the theory discussed earlier. Bond values, as they approach the maturity date, tend to become fixed by the value at maturity; hence, the yields fluctuate considerably. Longer-term bonds, however, will fluctuate in market value much more, but yields tend to be more static. If, for example, one were interested in the maximum captial gains from bonds, he would purchase long-term bonds when yields are high (prices are low) and market expectations are for falling rates (a flat yield curve). He would sell his long-term bonds, of course, when market expectations are for rising yields (falling prices) as indicated by a yield curve of position II.

Clearly market expectations do not *cause* movements in bond yields; indeed if they did, yields would never move at all. If rates are what they are entirely because they were expected to be what they are, like bootstraps, it is impossible for them to shift themselves. What does cause Canadian yields to change, or, more specifically, what caused the movements in the time series in Chart 7-4? There were two fundamental causes, one of which can be readily identified.

It is not a coincidence that Canada's 10 provincial bond yields tend to follow closely the movements of the U.S. corporate industrial bond yields (always with the usual positive spread). Our provincial bonds are sold in U.S. markets and the price for which they are sold determines their yield.

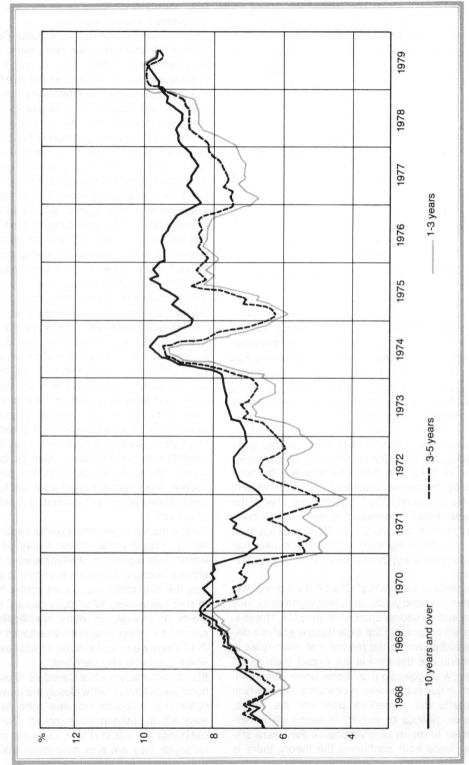

Chart 7-4
Government of Canada bonds   Monthly

1-3 years

3-5 years

10 years and over

Source: Bank of Canada Review, p. 55.

Since to Americans they are not so high in quality as the U.S. industrial bonds, they are sold at a lower price (higher yield). So, the first determinant of Canadian rates is the U.S. rates and in 1967–69 these rose to such high levels because the Federal Reserve Board was following a tight money policy for the purpose of damping the excessive monetary growth of the mid-1960s. The only exception to this appeared during the last half of 1968 when the Federal Reserve Board was confused as to the correct objective of monetary policy in view of the successful revival, earlier in the decade, of fiscal policy. A temporary ease of bank reserves took place as a consequence, but with this exception money remained generally tight until the beginning of 1970.

The second of the fundamental causes of bond yield movements is the Bank of Canada itself which follows its own monetary policy generally "in step" with the U.S. Federal Reserve but occasionally on its own. This accounts for the small deviations in the parallel movements of the U.S. and Canadian series which can be observed particularly in 1970 when the 10 provincial bonds trended downward slightly at the same time that the U.S. corporate bonds were still generally rising (see Chart 7-1). Canada's monetary policy had changed from tight to extreme ease during the early months of 1970. Another example of the same deviation can be observed in 1972.[11]

If one were to ask which has the greater influence on Canadian yields, the U.S. Federal Reserve Board or the Bank of Canada, the answer would have to be the former if one were to judge from past experience. Furthermore, the relationship is so close that it could only be accomplished via the free market since no conscious decision on the part of any human agency could develop such a high correlation.

All this leaves very little as to the influence of market expectations over bond yield movements. Indeed, there *is* very little evidence that expectations cause either downturns or upturns in the bond yields. About all that can be said by way of expectational influences on bond yields is that they are a mechanism through which inflation influences market consensus of what is a "normal"

bond yield. Thus, in order for real bond rates to be at least positive, nominal rates must equal the inflation rate, and it is likely true that the higher normal yield structure in the latter 1970s as opposed to the early 1970s was due precisely to this expected rate of inflation.

It is conceivable also that should either the Bank of Canada or the U.S. Federal Reserve Board attempt to force yields to excessively high levels (low bond prices) the market demand for bonds due to expectations could become so great that any further increase in rates would be impossible. Similarly, yields could be forced to such low levels (high bond prices) that no buyer would be forthcoming; hence, still lower rates would be equally impossible. In this way, expectational market forces could establish a ceiling and a floor which would become effective in the extreme cases.

What is surprising, at least at first sight, is the absence of an elasticity of demand as between real rates and bond holdings by the general public. In the table on page 186, real bond yields (nominal yields less the annual rate of increase in the Consumer Price Index) are compared with marketable bond holding by the general public.

Real bond yields peaked in 1970 at the same time that bond holdings declined substantially. In 1974, on the other hand, bond holdings reached their lowest level at the same time that real bond yields were also the lowest (−2.03%). Undoubtedly the relationship is much more complex than simple elasticity, involving the entire capital market instead of just one segment as we shall see in the next chapter.

CONCLUSION

Of all the subjects of Economics, interest and what determines interest rates are certainly the most interesting, the most controversial, and probably the least understood. In this and subsequent chapters all that is proposed is to shed some light on the subject, particularly in a Canadian context. This is why this chapter began with the preference for liquidity in terms of time—the Fisher contribution. Time preference can be equated as between borrowers and lenders at a price—the interest rate.

Having accomplished this much, it might seem that we have reached the end of the story, i.e., equilibrium has been established. Of course, this

---

[11] This is one example of a statistical relationship which can be readily observed from charts thereby rendering a refined econometric analysis superfluous.

REAL LONG-TERM BOND YIELDS AND
GENERAL PUBLIC HOLDINGS OF LONG-TERM MARKETABLE BONDS

	1967	1968	1969	1970	1971	1972	1973	1974	1975	1976	1977
Yields (%)	2.3	2.63	3.06	4.57	4.15	2.43	−.05	−2.03	−1.08	1.72	.69
Holdings ($ mill.)	6,284	6,498	6,713	6,198	5,433	5,379	4,989	4,702	5,134	6,186	8,308

Source: *Bank of Canada Monthly Review,* August, 1978, Table 1 Col. 33 *less* Col. 36, also Table 21.

is not true because there are many other factors which influence interest aside from time, one being the length of time lapse and the other being risk. When these other factors are brought into the analysis, it is no longer possible to consider a simple supply/demand relationship.

The one aspect of interest which is discernible in the free market is government bond yields. These are equilibrium rates which equate the supply of and demand for bonds on a specific day, but they are *not* interest rates at all. Being the only measure of interest, bond yields are extremely useful for practical analysis. Using these rates, we are forced to the conclusion regarding the determination of interest rates (in terms of bond yields) that Canadian market rates depend more on U.S. rates than on any other single factor. This dependency arises from the need for capital imports from the U.S. on a continuous basis, and, therefore, requires a Canadian rate sufficiently attractive to U.S. investors.

The general tendency appears to be that Canadian market rates maintain an approximate 2% differential above U.S. rates. This differential, it appears, is sufficient to attract U.S. capital. Some variations around this tendency have been apparent and they depend upon Canadian market conditions, particularly the policy being followed by the Bank of Canada at the time.

ADDITIONAL READINGS

Cannan, Edwin, "Application of Supply and Demand to Currency," *Economic Journal,* Vol. 31, 1921, p. 453, reprinted in *Readings in Monetary Theory,* Lutz, Mints (eds.), Allen & Unwin Ltd., London, 1952, p. 3.

Fisher, Irving, *Theory of Interest,* A. M. Kelley, New York, 1970.

Hicks, J. R., *Value and Capital,* Oxford University Press, Oxford, 1939, chs. 11, 12, and 13.

Lutz, F. A., "Structure of Interest Rates," *Quarterly Journal of Economics,* Vol. IV, p. 36, reprinted in *Readings in the Theory of Income Distribution,* Fellner, Haley (eds.), Allen & Unwin Ltd., London, 1950, p. 499.

Newlyn, Walter, *Theory of Money,* Oxford University Press, Oxford, 1964, chs. 9 and 10.

Simmons, Edward C., "The Relative Liquidity of Money and Other Things," *American Economic Review,* Supp. 37, p. 308, reprinted in *Readings in Monetary Theory,* Lutz, Mints (eds.), Allen & Unwin, Ltd., London, 1952, p. 33.

Somers, Harold M., "Monetary Policy and the Theory of Interest," *Quarterly Journal of Economics,* Vol. IV, p. 488, reprinted in *Readings in the Theory of Income Distribution,* Fellner, Haley (eds.), Allen & Unwin Ltd., London, 1950, p. 477. An excellent survey of early interest theories.

CHAPTER 8

Financial Assets

INTRODUCTION

There is no subject which is more fascinating to more people than the capital markets. Millions of people have observed in the past and will likely continue to observe in the future the fluctuations (sometimes wild gyrations) of the stock market, wishing they had purchased stock X instead of stock Y for the reason that X gained 10 points while Y lost 15, etc. Everyone, that is, wants to be rich, hopefully without working.

Neither this chapter nor this book can satisfy *this* desire. There are widely advertised books and "how to" courses which purport to show how everyone can be a millionaire,[1] but this chapter is not one of them. The objective of an academic study is much more modest—it is to identify the rational basis for the behaviour of the capital markets, in other words, to develop some order out of chaos. If the rationale so developed is useful as a tool of analysis and thereby contributes to wise and sensible investing, an important objective will have been served. On the other hand, if it simply contributes to a general understanding of economic phenomena its purpose will also have been well served.

This chapter, and the one which follows, are really extensions of Chapter 7. All three are concerned with the capital market and how it operates; the fact that the subject is broken into three parts is really a matter of analytical convenience, nothing more. Actually, the capital market is a complete entity and to understand any single part requires first a knowledge of the whole.

In the last chapter, the principle of rates of interest in terms of bond yields was introduced. This was

a convenience, because in the whole complex of the market for liquidity, government bond yields are only a small part. They do, however, serve as a concrete introduction to what is a rather difficult subject, and so we may conclude from that discussion that the rate of interest, as far as bonds are concerned, is the rate of discount which equates both future income streams and future values to present value. In the marketable bond case, future income and future values were certain with the only uncertain factor being the current price (yield). If the current price is known, the yield can be directly computed.

The element of risk in interest rate determination enters in the form of the unknown price combined with the mathematical relationship which links time to maturity to price fluctuation. The longer the term to maturity, the less influence does fixed value at maturity exert on the present price and the greater, consequently, is the fluctuation in price.

All this is fairly precise and concrete in conception. It would be quite wrong, however, to apply it directly and entirely to an analysis of the whole financial market. What we can transfer is the principle that future *expected* income and values are equated to present values by means of a discount rate. This gives us a convenient jumping off point into the subject which concerns us in this chapter.

I. LIQUIDITY AND FINANCIAL ASSETS

The idea of liquidity has already been introduced and it is now time to put it to some practical use. We recall that once money enters the "pause" stage, it really ceases to exist except in an accounting sense. In the days when financial markets were more primitive, one might speak of money as both a medium of exchange and a store of value, but today only irrational people

---

[1]It is always a source of wonder, when one reads such advertisements, how any person can believe that he alone can be wealthy to the exclusion of all others who see the same advertisement. Actually, the one who makes a fortune is the seller of the books.

would keep money for both purposes. The store of value function is much better served by holding varying degrees of liquidity.

The key to the whole principle of liquidity is the length of time for a "pause." For a portion of our liquidity the pause may be sufficiently long that to hold it as current liquidity (or money) is simply not rational. In fact, the degree of non-liquidity should vary directly with the length of time involved. We can visualize an individual's complete stock of liquidity ranging from highly liquid (the shortest time span in the pause) to non-liquid (the longest time span) at any moment of time. This stock may be augmented by savings from income flows or by transfer payments, whatever the case may be. As the stock expands we are faced with the problem of how much current liquidity should be maintained and how much future liquidity can be held, always, of course, with the reward of future liquidity exceeding current liquidity by an amount which can be measured by a rate of discount.

The amount of the reward for future liquidity depends upon the strength of the *un*willingness of people to forego their current liquidity (the opposite point of view from the willingness curves in Chapter 7). During the time lapse, certain events can take place — the future is always uncertain. One of these is the possibility of insolvency of a debtor which could mean the complete repudiation of debt in bankruptcy. This possibility varies considerably, of course, depending upon the financial strength of the debtor. Another possibility is the danger of the collapse in value of the financial asset. This may be the consequence of circumstances quite outside the control of the debtor and is generally the result of market evaluation.

We can see this more precisely with the help of a mathematical statement. Liquidity can be considered as a function of three independent variables, time, certainty, and risk.

(1) $L = f(T, C, R)$

with $\dfrac{\partial L}{\partial T} < 0$

$\dfrac{\partial L}{\partial C} > 0$

$\dfrac{\partial L}{\partial R} < 0$

Time, in this case, refers to the lapse of time during which liquidity is foregone. Certainty is the degree to which the value of future liquidity is secure when a financial asset is held to maturity. Risk is the possibility of the loss of value of future liquidity (referred to as capital loss) between the date of acquiring a financial asset through surrendering current liquidity and the maturity date.

In order to make these points quite clear, consider a hypothetical table (Table 8-1). The degree of risk is measured on an inverse scale from zero, complete risk, to 10, no risk at all, while certainty is measured from 10, absolute certainty of success through zero, complete uncertainty, to −10, absolute certainty of failure.

On the scales of both certainty and risk, the savings deposits and Canada Savings Bonds score the highest, while short-term federal marketable bonds are not quite so high because the price on the market is not completely fixed until the date of maturity. Similarly, long-term provincial bonds are not so certain as federal bonds because provincial governments are not so safe as the federal government and are also subject to slightly more price variation than federal bonds, hence, are a little lower on the risk scale. Corporate bonds, those "blue-chip" companies which are well-known, permanent institutions in our industrial and financial lives, enjoy a high degree of certainty but are subject to market price yield fluctuations similar to provincial bonds. However, since these often are "sweetened" with extra privileges to achieve better market performance, they are rated lower on the risk scale than provincial bonds.

Once we move into the equities section, the factor of risk becomes more important. This is the fundamental difference between bonds and stocks—bonds do carry a date of maturity which "locks" them into a degree of surety of value which increases as the date of maturity draws near. Not so with equities. Certainty as far as the company's financial solvency is concerned may be excellent, but there is no way of being sure of the price until the moment of market transaction. As we move down the scale, the factor of risk of loss of capital through price fluctuation becomes greater (the score of risk is less) until "Dry-hole Oils" is close to zero. This is rather typical of such mineral exploratory activity and the consequent possibilities of financial solvency are highly uncertain. To this extent we suggest a zero rating for certainty. The last item on the list, New York City

Table 8-1
RISK AND CERTAINTY

	Risk	Certainty	Total
Savings deposits and Canada Savings Bonds	10	10	20
Short-term federal bonds	9	10	19
Long-term federal bonds	8	10	18
Provincial bonds, long-term	7	8	15
Corporate bonds (blue-chip)	6	8	14
Corporate debentures (blue-chip)	5	8	13
Stocks (blue-chip)	5	7	12
Dry-hole Oils	1	0	1
New York City Bonds	0	−9	−9

bonds, is the one example which, at time of writing, would score the lowest. With costs greatly exceeding revenues from taxation and without any significant credit rating, any purchaser of New York bonds would be practically certain of default. The situation could change, however, if either the U.S. government or the state government of New York does rescue the city from bankruptcy.

The last column of the table would represent a score of "total liquidity." This total attached to each one of the financial assets listed would represent the mental process of liquidity evaluation that each individual would go through before deciding which asset he preferred. Accompanying each liquidity score would be an expected rate of return which would compensate for liquidity foregone — the lower the score the higher the rate of return. The task becomes one of balancing each score with its appropriate rate and deciding which asset is most suitable for each individual circumstance.

A. Liquidity in Terms of Present Value

To avoid confusion, we should really differentiate between a financial asset and liquidity. When any holder of surplus current liquidity decides to exchange some of his surplus for future liquidity, he acquires a financial asset which in turn is a financial liability to a person or institution which happens to have at the moment a shortage of current liquidity. This is not so complicated as it sounds. The financial asset/liability is the equivalent of demand for current liquidity and when acquired, the asset holder has a claim against someone else for liquidity some time in the future.

The problem of what to do with a stock of current liquidity means that holders are faced not only with a bewildering variety of choices but also a growing number. We have, of course, the financial intermediaries and bonds discussed in the previous chapters but, in addition, the possibilities range through equities, insurance, pensions, and even real assets such as land, buildings, or property which can be sold, etc. All of these are financial assets into which liquidity can be stored until the time arrives when they may be "liquidated." All of these financial assets are expected to have a rate of return.

The rate of return is different from the yield discussed in the previous chapter which applies only to bonds. Return is a broader concept than yield and includes an appreciation in value in addition. Equities, for example, may offer both dividends, similar to bond coupons, and appreciation in value which makes the rate of return higher than the yield. Land, on the other hand, may be sold at a higher price to offer only an appreciation in value but which can be sufficiently great to make the rate of return much in excess of any bond yield.

As a broader concept, the rate of return *includes* the yield; hence, the rate of return on bank savings deposits would be the yield (interest) plus zero appreciation. At the other extreme, the rate of return for holding gold for example will include zero yield plus an appreciation in value. It follows that all degrees of liquidity must offer a prospect of *some* rate of return with the exception of purely 100% liquidity, cash itself. This rate of return will be commensurate with the liquidity, as defined in equation (1) above, foregone, i.e., the rate will increase as liquidity decreases. It would be helpful once more to express this in mathematical form as follows:

$$(2) \quad L = L_c + \frac{L_{f_0}}{(1 + r_0)^t} + \frac{L_{f_1}}{(1 + r_1)^t} + \frac{L_{f_2}}{(1 + r_2)^t} + \cdots \frac{L_{f_n}}{(1 + r_n)^t}$$

$$t \leqslant \infty$$

The present value, L, of an individual's liquidity is the discounted *expected* value of his future liquidity with the rate of return, r, being the rate of discount. One might expect that the rates of return would increase with time, but because of the certainty and risk factors this is not necessarily true.

The first term, L_c, is current liquidity required for expenditure without which pain or inconvenience would be suffered. As such it acts as a fulcrum balancing an individual's liquidity structure against his consumption requirements. It is the L_c also which empirical research has shown tends to remain constant in real terms, that is, it increases in money value with rising prices.[2] The second term, $L_{f_0}/(1 + r_0)^t$, is the category of various types of savings deposits with financial intermediaries as well as Canada Savings Bonds which are generally liquid and offer a rate of return, r_0, depending on the amount of time lapse foregone. The future liquidities in this category are always highly competitive. The third category, $L_{f_1}/(1 + r_1)^t$, includes marketable bonds of various types of which the federal government bond more nearly reflects in its yield rate the true interest rate in the market for capital. The rate of return, r_1, in this category includes an allowance for risk. In a similar fashion, the fourth and subsequent terms in the equation represent the balance of future liquidities which would include equities and all the other forms of financial assets, ultimately to include such "real" property as land held for speculative purposes, etc. Generally, the degree of liquidity decreases with the rightward positioning of the terms.

Furthermore, all the terms to the right of the equal sign are *expected* values. Since expectations vary amongst individuals, there must be different structures of future liquidity for each individual,

though, in the aggregate such variations would likely cancel ultimately to reach a liquidity consensus. For instance, the risk-loving millionaire finds his liquidity structure concentrated to the right, whereas the conservative widow will seek left-hand liquidity. Each individual will select his own liquidity structure in accordance with his own criteria such as personal taste, income, proximity to retirement, desire for security, etc.

1. Asset Choice

There is a reasonable amount of literature on the subject of asset choice which has been developed in recent years. It might be helpful to digress briefly, to discuss a few principles of this theory with the twin objectives of showing how a solution (or solutions) to the problem of asset selection may be reached and to relate this theory with that which is being developed in this chapter.

Suppose for the sake of argument and exposition that all the returns from future liquidity (r_1 through r_n) can be collapsed into functions of two criteria, expected earnings and risk. Earnings, in this case, would be a mean value of all possible earnings weighted by their respective probabilities. Risk, in turn, would be defined as the standard deviation of these earnings around the mean. The greater the value of the standard deviation the greater the risk. Clearly, L_{f_0} in equation 2 above possesses zero risk for the reason that all earnings exactly equal the mean.

All individuals, on the basis of this simplification, must trade off risk and earnings, e.g., the greater the risk the greater the earnings, depending upon whether the individual may be a gambler (who loves the risk) or an orphan (who only wants secure earnings). Between these two extremes all of us lie; however, it is likely that a large majority will prefer to avoid as much risk as possible, and we will have an absolute limit of risk tolerance beyond which we will refuse to accept any additional risk. For the timid, anything beyond Canada Savings Bonds, savings deposits, etc., might be this limit; for the venturesome, there are the stock markets with "penny stocks" which may or may not pay dividends and may or may not appreciate in value. But these stocks may offer that pot of gold with a very low probability of occurrence which is the reason for their attractiveness.

We can easily show this situation in Diagram 8-1. The dots on the diagram are a series of assets

---

[2]This means that the demand elasticity for current liquidity (or money in this case) in terms of the price level is unity, a result which empirical research has fairly well established.

D. W. Laidler, *The Demand for Money, Theories and Evidence*, International Textbook Company, Scranton, Pa., 1969, p. 104.

Diagram 8-1

RISK AVERSION AND EARNINGS

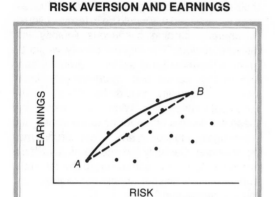

Diagram 8-2

INVESTMENT PORTFOLIOS

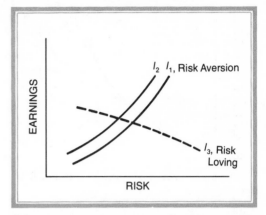

with the appropriate mean earnings and risk which each asset carries. All of these assets are available for inclusion in a portfolio, but only those assets lying on the curve A-B are efficient. Those assets underneath the curve are inefficient for the reason that additional earnings from other assets are possible without incurring additional risk.

We can see this in another way as well by considering the dashed line connecting points A and B. All the assets which lie on this line are perfectly correlated in terms of earnings and risk. By reducing the positive correlation from unity to as close to zero as possible the line A-B (which is really the efficiency frontier) will reach its maximum "bowing."

We can find a solution to the investment portfolio problem by considering an individual's preference as between earnings and risk. A series of utility functions curves may be drawn to suggest how most rational people would behave in the face of both earnings and risk. This would likely be as shown in Diagram 8-2. An upward sloping utility function such as I_1 and I_2 (the real income of I_2 exceeds that of I_1) indicates an aversion to risk and a preference for earnings. Thus, these people would find themselves loathe to accept increasing units of risk (higher standard deviation of earnings) and would require successively greater increments of mean earnings as compensation. Undoubtedly this is typical of most people, though, to be sure, there are the risk-loving millionaires who take pleasure in exposing their portfolios to greater risk at the expense of a lower value of mean earnings. (A lower mean in this

case makes possible a high value for a market "killing." The mean is low because each eventual outcome is weighted by its probability of occurrence.) Such a utility function would slope toward the risk axis — the dashed curve I_3 in Diagram 8-2.

As Prof. Tobin has shown, a very large number of assets can really be considered as a single asset.[3] This "multiple asset" will be represented by a point of tangency between the efficiency frontier and the highest utility function (Diagram 8-3). We may conceive of the efficiency frontier, E, as a range of efficient combinations of assets, L_{f_1} to L_{f_n}. There is, however, only one combination of Earnings and Risk which will satisfy the utility function U. At this point of tangency earnings would be R and risk, S. At the same time there is a "budget line" representing the available funds to be allocated. By substituting cash, or, more rationally, L_{f_0} (savings deposits, CSB's, etc.) for other assets with risk, the individual may slide down this budget line to a point of tangency with U'. On the other hand, he could borrow additional funds and expose himself to both more risk and higher earnings by sliding up the budget line to U''. Borrowing in this interpretation does not increase his available funds since his assets are obligated until payment of the debt. It is actually a

[3]J. Tobin, "Theory of Portfolio Selection," Hahn and Brechling, eds., *Theory of Interest Rates,* Macmillan & Co. Ltd., London, 1965, p. 12, ff., by permission of Macmillan, London and Basingstoke, and the International Economic Association.

Diagram 8-3
EQUILIBRIUM PORTFOLIO

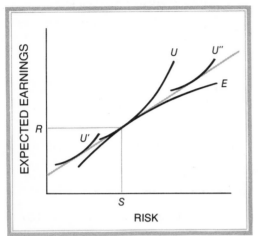

Source: H. Johnson, *Macroeconomics and Monetary Theory*, Aldine Publishing Co., Chicago, 1972, p. 84

form of leverage by which additional assets may be acquired with credit advanced through the medium of brokers.

The combining of all assets into one unique "multiple" asset which can satisfy each individual's utility is ingenious enough; however, in the process we must not forget that mean earnings and risk are the two criteria under which all *other* criteria are subsumed. In equation 1 above, liquidity was expressed as a function of time, certainty, and risk with each of these variables having a precise definition. It is possible to consider certainty and risk of capital loss under the "umbrella" of Tobin's mean earnings and risk. Since capital gain or loss is included in the definition of earnings and certainty, the degree of security of capital value at maturity can be considered as part of risk. However, what do we do with time? Time, or more specifically the amount of time lapse during which current liquidity is foregone, cannot be included in either earnings or risk. Consider, as an example, two assets, a short-term savings deposit and a renewable Canada Savings Bond. The average earnings of both can be precisely computed but without a third axis, time, it is not possible to distinguish between the two. If we did have a third time axis, utility surfaces could be required, which, in turn, would be tangential with portfolio efficiency surfaces.

A more realistic approach would appear to be to consider a series of efficient portfolios each

within a different liquidity sector as defined in equation 2. Rational individuals would likely rank their savings according to the degree of closeness to cash, and this would be in terms of liquidity, thereby dividing continuous liquidity into discrete sectors. The highest priority would be granted the most liquid sector. Thereafter, each succeeding sector with progressively lower values of liquidity would be filled to the individual's satisfaction. Within each sector, and these are defined at the terms to the right of the equal sign in equation 2, an efficient portfolio may be designed. Certainly the criteria of diversification so as to reduce correlation to the minimum and increase efficiency should be followed, and this is only rational.

Perhaps more important from a theoretical standpoint is the fact that the Tobin analysis does show that optimal solutions to liquidity allocations are possible. Efficient portfolios *do* exist and certainly can be found if we have sufficient knowledge. It does not follow that the solution, having been identified, is either the best for all time or static. Inflation, for instance, will alter the optimal distribution of liquidities which, in turn, will likely change the allocation of funds within each liquidity sector, i.e., the utility functions will shift. Thus, this "digression" from the main thread of the argument is not really a digression at all but is complementary to our analysis and is certainly necessary to show that an equilibrium solution to liquidity allocation does exist and is possible of achievement.

2. Liquidity Supply and Interest

The task, therefore, facing the individual is to maximize the values of all future liquidities, consistent with his own criteria, and, at the same time, have sufficient current liquidity to satisfy his exchange requirements. Let us see just how this could be done. In equation 2, the stores of liquidity to the right of the equal sign are ranked, L_{fo}, $L_{f_1} \ldots L_{f_n}$ in accordance with descending liquidity. Those liquidities which are mature *at any time*, L_{fo}, and therefore can be exchanged for current liquidity for a stated amount, have a fixed present value. In other words, we know exactly what the balances in our savings deposits are at the present time because we merely have to ask at the bank. Therefore, any change (say an increase) in the rate of interest, r, must correspondingly increase the value of future liquidity. Thus,

$$L_0 = \frac{\uparrow L_{f_0}}{(1 + \uparrow r_0)^f}$$

Now suppose an asset well to the right in the equation, for example $L_{f_{10}}$, has a fixed asset value not at the present time but at maturity—such as a bond. The result now is very different. Since $L_{f_{10}}$ is fixed, it follows that if the interest rate rises L_{10} will decline, since L_{10} is the current market value of the asset. Thus,

$$\downarrow L_{10} = \frac{L_{f_{10}}}{(1 + \downarrow r_{10})^{10}}$$

There are, therefore, two distinct effects of rising (or falling) interest rates. In the first case the *future* value of the non-marketable asset rises (or falls) and in the second, the marketable asset, the current or market value falls (rises) thereby presenting a risk to the asset holder.

As an example, suppose the rate of return r_0 for the L_{f_0}th asset should rise. This would increase the value of liquidity L_{f_0} in order for the current value $L_{f_0}/(1 + r_0)^f$ to remain constant. The individual, however, may not prefer this increased value, but would, quite rationally, opt for more L_c instead. On the other hand, in view of the rise in r_0 he might prefer to increase further the total value of his future liquidity by reducing the amount of liquidity in any of the other financial assets in favour of the now higher-earnings L_{f_0}. Indeed, he could reduce his L_c in order to increase L_{f_0}, thereby balancing the additional "pain" of insufficient current liquidity against the gain of future liquidity. All three reactions to an increase in r_0 are perfectly rational. In the first instance, liquidity was restructured in favour of more current liquidity. In the second, liquidity was restructured so as to increase the value of future liquidity, and in the third, current liquidity was reduced to achieve the maximum value of future liquidity without restructuring.

In the aggregate, individual reactions such as the first case appear to be swamped by the second and third. Again this appears to be borne out by empirical evidence so that we can be reasonably certain of a supply curve for liquidity which is positively sloped as shown in Diagram 8–4.[4] This

---

[4] . . .there is an overwhelming body of evidence in favour of the proposition that the demand for money is stably and negatively related to the rate of interest." D. Laidler, *op. cit.*, p. 97.

Diagram 8-4

SUPPLY CURVE OF LIQUIDITY

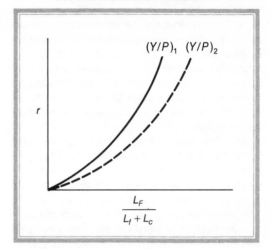

is the equivalent of the supply curve for liquidity developed in the preceding chapter. Generally, higher rates of return are associated with higher ratios of future liquidity to total liquidity.

When real income, money income divided by the price level, rises, an increase in liquidity (L) must occur. This additional liquidity must go someplace to the right of the equal sign. This could be current liquidity (L_c) if the individual desires a higher living standard; however, in the short term the tendency appears to be to maintain the same living standard to which one is accustomed. It is likely, therefore, that one of the assets, L_{f_0} to L_{f_n} will rise. This is why an increase in real income $(Y/P)_1 < (Y/P)_2$ shifts the supply curve to the right; it lowers the rate of return necessary for the same ratio of future liquidity to total liquidity.

We can see more precisely how a shift in real income, $(Y/P)_2$ will affect the supply of future liquidity by reference to equation 2. Any increase in the stock of liquidity would first increase the amount of L_c. However, since bank savings deposits carry a 100% certainty of return without risk, it is irrational to hold unnecessary surpluses of L_c, and savings deposits will therefore rise. The consequent increased amounts of bank savings deposits, L_{f_0}, or other similar highly liquid assets, will cause a "spillover effect" into less liquid forms of assets as individuals restructure their entire patterns of liquidity.

3. Liquidity Supply and Prices

The converse effect can be easily seen in the case of rising prices. Inflation raises the price level, lowering values of real incomes of those whose money incomes rise less than prices. This increases current liquidity requirements so that L_c must rise, *given* the stock of liquidity, L. Of course, L_c would rise at the expense of L_{f_0} since these assets are the most liquid. But, and this is the main point, all the *other* assets, competing as they are for liquidity, must also raise their rates of return as well.

At the same time that rising prices are causing forced transfer into current liquidity, "double digit" inflation (prices rising at 10% or more) forces future liquidity owners to seek more efficient means of protecting the *real* value of their future liquidity. The reason for this is that rates of return on conventional bonds or equities, etc., are generally less than the rate of price increase, so the tendency is to purchase real assets, the rates of return of which are at least equal to their price increase. Land, property, gold, etc., become desirable and a speculative boom in these real assets develops. In this way the "middle ground" of future liquidity is drained in favour of the extreme left (high liquidity) and extreme right (ordinarily low liquidity but in times of inflation quite liquid enough). To acquire the supply of liquidity they require, these "middle assets" would have to offer unheard of rates of return, index their rates to the cost of living, or provide some other sweetening device to make them attractive.

B. Liquidity and Competing Assets

It is the competition for liquidity among the various assets which also transmits the effects of monetary policy throughout the entire equation. Yet, at the same time, there are segments within the equation in which competition is most severe. If we rewrite equation 2 in a schematic form, these segments may be readily identified (see 2' below).

Each segment is defined by its functional definition of liquidity. In the first segment, $L = f(T)$ are the savings deposits of chartered banks and financial intermediaries as well as Canada Savings Bonds. All three of these experience the greatest competition amongst themselves. In the second segment, $L = g(T, R)$, are the marketable bonds including federal, provincial, municipal, and corporate. Once more competition is extremely keen. In the case of corporate bonds, "sweeteners" such as stock warrants, convertibility rights, etc., are included along with the bond issue to enhance its competitive status.

The third segment, equities, is made up of a whole range of corporate stocks, common and preferred, to include the venerable "blue-chip" corporations at one extreme and the high risk, uncertain mining companies at the other. ("Dry-hole Oils Ltd." is a good example.) Here liquidity is a function of both the risk of fluctuating prices and the degree of uncertainty of survival in an uncertain world which can be attributed to the corporation itself. Time, in this case, has no meaning since equities never mature.

Lastly we enter the area of the capital market in which liquidity is a function of certainty alone — pure speculation. In the case of gambling, the risk-lover only will be content— Las Vegas. However, in many areas of pure speculation, land, housing, gold, gems, works of art, or the commodities exchange, rising prices (which have existed in the past and are expected in the future) can develop in those markets which are characterized by inelasticity of supply. The general public learns to expect demand pressures to force up prices and, therefore, buys with the specific intention of selling at a profit. Such "investment" often becomes a better "hedge" against inflation for the reason that the element of certainty is increased. What is extremely risky during periods of falling prices is at best uncertain during stable prices and relatively certain during rising prices.

It is interesting that high inflation, encouraging as it does a concentration of liquidity in the speculative area, also attracts newly manufactured deposits into the same area, i.e., chartered bank loans may be used for financing such speculative ventures. This compounds the difficulty, for in-

$$2'L = L_c + \left| \begin{array}{c} L = f(T) \\ \dfrac{L_0}{(1+r_0)^t} \end{array} \right| \begin{array}{c} L = g(T,R) \\ +\dfrac{L_1}{(1+r_1)^t} \end{array} \left| \begin{array}{c} L = h(R,C) \\ +\dfrac{L_2}{(1+r_2)^t} \end{array} \right| \begin{array}{c} L = k(C) \\ +\cdots\dfrac{L_{f_n}}{(1+r_n)^t} \end{array}$$

stead of alleviating the shortage of funds in the middle segments, it worsens the situation by contributing to a speculative boom. This is why there is likely no other market which feels the distorting impact of inflation more strongly than the financial market.

II. FLOWS AND STOCKS IN THE CAPITAL MARKET

Working with a stock of liquidity (L) should not obscure the fact that our financial structure is a dynamic one in a continuous state of flux. This is implied in the impact of inflation analysis discussed above. Stocks of liquidity in the aggregate increase through time as income earners spend less than they earn in the manner discussed in Chapter 2. Stocks can also increase in the aggregate by means of deposit manufacture by chartered banks. As these stocks increase, a continuous disturbance of equilibrium takes place. This disturbance necessitates a continuous decision-making process as liquidity is required to be disposed of in some way.

In a frictionless financial market, increases in total liquidity would be accompanied by a restructuring process with certain assets gaining more liquidity at the expense of others. However, there are brokerage fees and other costs of transfer which must be overcome by expected earnings before such restructuring will take place. These are, in fact, the only impedimenta to an otherwise perfect market structure. Equilibrium prices for stocks and yields for bonds will be quoted each day in the organized markets, and these prices will always be slightly different from what they would have been in a frictionless market.

Nevertheless, the high degree of efficiency in the financial markets does assure a degree of perfection which is unequalled in other markets. Something very close to the equilibrium price is reached on a daily basis. At the same time, though, tomorrow's equilibrium price may be quite different from today's. This results from a *disequilibrium* in *flows* of liquidity. For example, if the flow of liquidity into a particular market exceeds the available flow of assets, the price of the assets will rise to equate the two flows in value terms. It is only when the flow of liquidity into a market equals the value of the available assets

(at the former equilibrium price) that equilibrium through time, or flow equilibrium, can exist. This is an important point which will be met again very shortly.

A. The Equities Market

In all of capitalism it would be difficult to find a more ingenious institutional invention than the stock market and the limited liability which makes ownership of shares in a corporation possible. As a device for mobilizing and transmitting savings it is, thus far, unequalled, for it accomplishes two things: (1) it "democratizes" the ownership of corporations, permitting many millions of small liquidity owners to participate in profits, and (2) it makes possible the sale of ownership at a moment's notice. In terms of financial intermediation, the equities market makes possible immediate liquidity to owners of these assets. The difference between the equities markets and, say, savings deposits, is two-fold. The market price is not known in advance, and so there exists a degree of risk similar to the bond market. The other factor is certainty, or lack thereof, of success in the corporation's ventures, for few will direct their liquidity toward a company which is approaching certain bankruptcy.

There is, additionally, a degree of perfection in the equities market which is unequalled in ordinary consumers' goods markets. In the first place, there tends to be one dominant market for all equities for a geographic region. This may be a nation like Canada or a continent with the dominant market at Wall Street in New York City. Because of modern telecommunications the barriers of distance are overcome and all prospective purchasers are assured of access to all prospective sellers in one central location. In the second place, there exist no legal barriers to knowledge of the product being traded within the market. Any "wheeling and dealing" such as false rumours, etc., which may take place on the shady side of the law will be outside the market itself. In this way, even though prices are subject to fluctuation because of flow disequilibria, the market assures the buyer and seller of the best possible equilibrium price at any moment of time — an achievement of which no other market can boast. We have, in effect, the closest possible approximation to Marshallian supply/demand curves converging at a central point, say Toronto, and yet reaching all over Canada and the world, thanks to modern telecommunications. This convergence of world-wide supply/demand curves means an equilibrium price which will prevail everywhere at that moment. Consider, as an example, a typical transaction based on the gallery tape from the Toronto Stock Exchange on Bay Street:

A buyer wishes to purchase 100 shares of stock in the XYZ Corporation Ltd. He telephones his broker requesting a quote on XYZ stock. The broker codes XYZ's symbol into The Toronto Stock Exchange's CAN-DAT system. Immediately, current trading information about the stock is flashed onto a screen. Included is a "quote" or the current "bid" and "ask" prices for the stock, for example 10¼ to 10½. By checking the "ask" price, the prospective buyer now knows that the least anyone is willing to sell XYZ stock for at the moment is 10½ dollars per share, and that would-be-seller has learned that the most anyone is willing to pay for XYZ stock is 10¼ dollars. At the same time, the seller is contacting his broker. He already owns 100 shares of XYZ stock and needing more funds for his children's education, he tries to sell his stock. We assume that each, the buyer and seller, instructs his broker to get him the best possible price at the moment. Each broker telephones his client's order to his telephone clerk who sits at one of the elevated desks around the TSE trading floor. Each clerk calls his floor trader by flashing his number on the enunciator board on the wall, by hand signal, or by voice. When each floor trader has been given the client's order he goes to the trading post at which all transactions in XYZ are done. Each trader must exercise his experience, knowledge, and brokerage skill to get the best possible price for his client. The buyer's trader, seeing that someone has already bid 10¼ dollars, and no one will sell at that price, may bid 10⅜. The seller's trader sees that someone has already tried without success to sell at 10½ dollars, hears the other trader bidding at 10⅜ dollars and sells by shouting "Sold! 100 XYZ at 10⅜ dollars." The sale of 100 shares of XYZ is noted on a paper, then flashed via ticker tape to hundreds of TSE members' offices.

An equilibrium price is, thus, achieved which is the actual price for the stock of a particular corporation at that moment. With approximately 1,100 issues of about 800 companies listed on the Toronto Stock Exchange and with selling and buying taking place daily, it is not difficult to imagine the buzz of activity which occurs. In addition, since every transaction must be announced in a clear, loud, voice for all to hear, the din can be nerve-wracking during a busy day.

The hypothetical transaction outlined above represents stock equilibrium for the price of XYZ shares. As we all know from practical experience, the next price quotation of XYZ may be higher or lower, and this is the result of changes in supply and demand. We can consider this in the form of supply and demand curves in Diagram 8-5.

As is true of all market curves, the supply curves represent schedules of how many shares would be sold at particular prices, the higher the price, the more would sellers sell. Similarly, demand curves are schedules of how many shares buyers would buy at particular prices; the lower the price, the more would buyers purchase. Since we have no knowledge of prices other than equilibrium prices, we can only guess at the slopes of these curves, or otherwise deduce the slopes from the

Diagram 8-5

SUPPLY AND DEMAND, XYZ CORP., LTD.

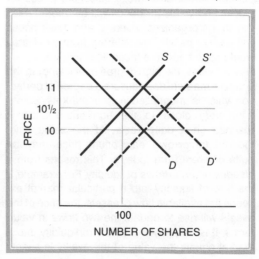

reaction of buyers and sellers to specific price offers, practically an impossible task.

On one particular day, 100 shares of XYZ common were traded at 10½—the equilibrium price which equates supply and demand. The next day it would be reasonable to expect a shift in the demand curve to the right to show an increased desirability (demand) of XYZ shares. We could draw up an entirely new demand schedule if we knew what it was, for example, by conducting a survey amongst prospective buyers. The consequence of this shift in demand is a new equilibrium price of $11 and a new quantity of shares traded, 150. We can see this from the intersection of the new demand curve, *D'*, and the old supply curve. Now suppose that the supply curve shifts to *S'* at the same time that demand shifts. Sellers are, for some reason, willing to sell more shares at the former price. The same price, 10½, prevails, but 200 shares are sold. XYZ shares would experience equilibrium in this case through time (flow equilibrium) since the increased flow of liquidity is matched by an increased flow of XYZ assets. In the former case, disequilibrium through time existed because the increased flow of liquidity was not matched by an increased flow of assets. This distinction between stock and flow equilibrium is important. In general when the market is spoken of as being in equilibrium, it is the flow equilibrium which is referred to so that prices remain unchanged from day to day.

It is obvious from this example why a single location for a stock market is more efficient than many locations. Market efficiency is at its maximum when *all* buyers are aware of *all* sellers, as well as the prices, at the same instant. This objective is more nearly realized with a single location than with many. Of course, it is possible for additional markets to exist in the same area so long as each lists a different set of corporations. It would not be efficient to have a single stock listed in two exchanges simultaneously.

But what is most interesting is the relation between two apparently independent stock exchanges, and how one, the larger, tends to dominate the other. In a kind of tail-dog relationship, the Canadian exchanges tend to follow the New York exchange. This arises because of proximity, ease of communication, common language and background, etc., which makes possible joint investment activity. We can explore this relation-

Diagram 8-6

STOCK MARKET—CANADA

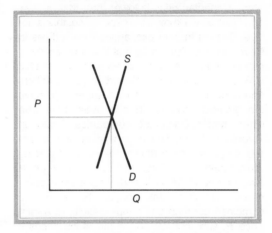

ship more closely with the aid of market diagrams again.

For the Canadian exchange (Diagram 8-6) the supply and demand curves are both drawn to a "Wall Street scale" for both price and quantity. This highlights the fact that we are small relative to New York, trading about 1/6 or 1/7 the volume of shares as on Wall Street, and is the reason for the steeply sloping supply and demand curves.

In a similar fashion (Diagram 8-7) we can draw the supply/demand structure for New York, but using the same Wall Street scale, the slopes are

Diagram 8-7

STOCK MARKET—NEW YORK

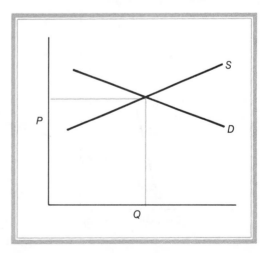

much less steep. Assuming, for the moment, that both markets existed *in isolation*, the price of stocks and quantities traded would be as shown —the Canadian price is lower than that of New York. But, as we know from experience, this is not true. Dealers in both exchanges have offices in New York and Toronto so that it is a very simple matter for an American (Canadian) to convert his U.S. dollar account into Canadian (U.S.) dollars and purchase the stock which appears to have the greatest promise. This is even more true when many Canadian companies listed in Toronto or Montreal have close relationships with a U.S. "parent" corporation. The result of placing the diagrams as in Diagram 8-8, is that the *combined* demand (U.S./Canada) equals the *combined* (U.S./Canada) supply. Equating the combined demand and supply results in a joint price P_j substantially *above* the stock prices if the Canadian market were in isolation, i.e., the price P_c below. This is the consequence (and "benefit") of proximity to a great capital-rich neighbour. It can also be seen in a dynamic sense. Suppose flow equilibrium is disturbed in the U.S. so that the demand curve shifts to D'. This could be due to any cause, real or psychological. The consequence would be a shift in the joint price from P_j to P_j' and Canadians would

note that their stock prices were rising without any apparent justification from the Canadian side.

The close relationship between prices in New York and Toronto is evident from a careful inspection of Chart 8-1. The TSE Industrials end-of-month closing price is plotted along with the Standard and Poor's monthly average of Industrials. Keeping in mind the difference in scales, shown on both vertical axes, and the slight timing difference between average and end of the month, the close correlation between the two exchanges is apparent in the chart. Only rarely do movements not coincide, the outstanding example being the last quarter of 1969 and early 1970 when the New York exchange was already well on the way towards the bottom of the "bear market" with the Toronto exchange holding firm in a general flow equilibrium until March, 1970.

It is also apparent from the chart that flow equilibrium is not the usual state of the markets. In both exchanges an excess flow of supply over demand flows prevailed during the years 1969 and the first half of 1970. This almost continuous shift of the supply curves rightward was indicative of a "bear" market. The second bearish period in the market began during the last quarter of 1973 to reach its termination by the end of 1974.

Diagram 8-8

JOINT U.S./CANADA MARKET

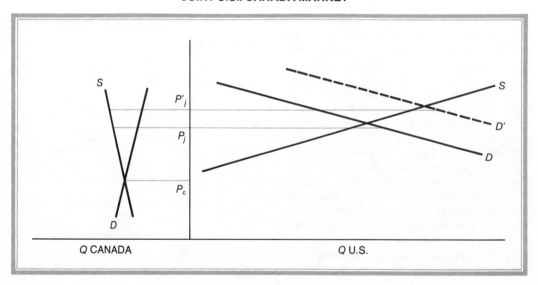

Chart 8-1

INDEX OF STOCK MARKET PRICES, NEW YORK AND TORONTO TSE INDUSTRIALS N.Y. STANDARD AND POOR'S

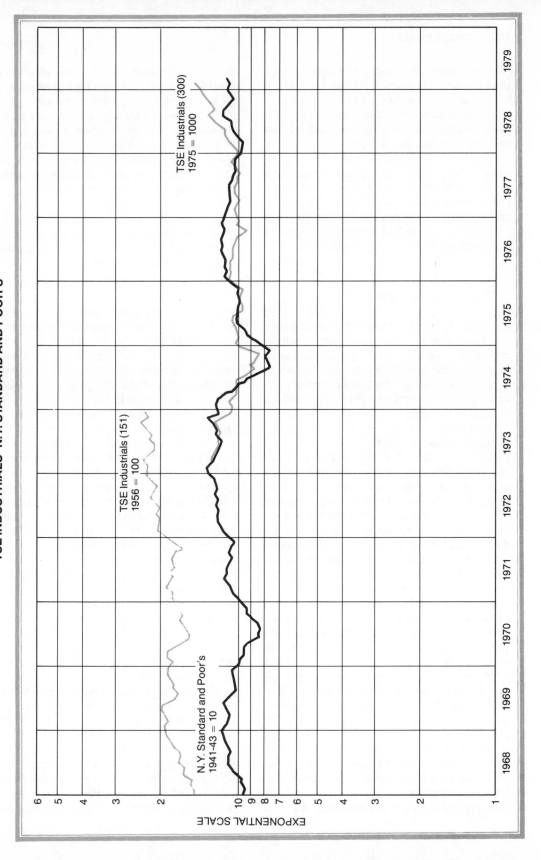

The bear market referred to in this case means a predominance of sellers. A true bear is a profit-taker who sells his shares of stock in anticipation of repurchasing at a later date. When prices in the market are moving down, the expectations of the bear are realized; the real problem facing the bear, though, is *when* to repurchase, for, if he guesses the low point of his stock correctly, he maximizes his profit. At the moment of repurchase, the bear has become a bull. The bull, of course, purchases shares in expectation of rising prices, and again profit is maximized if the bull guesses the market peaks correctly.

B. Price Determination

It is not quite sufficient to note that share prices are determined by stock equilibrium of supply and demand. We still must ask the question, what *determines* the level of demand and supply? In other words, what are the true determinants of flow equilibrium? In the next chapter this difficult and complex question will be considered in more detailed analytical form, but at this point a few principles should be made clear.

As noted in equation 2', shares of stock as financial assets are acquired because their rates of return are sufficiently high to compensate for liquidity foregone. Rates of return are the result of both dividends paid out to shareholders and the capital gain resulting from rising prices. For the dividend portion, the counterpart of the bond yield, the dividend yield can be computed by expressing the dividend expected to be paid over the next 12-month period as a percentage of the current price. This is done for us by the Toronto Stock Exchange and is expressed as the amount of dividends indicated to be paid over the next year divided by the current price. The stock dividend yield for the TSE composite 300 index was 4.65% in April, 1978 at the same time that the Standard and Poor's dividend yield for New York was 5.42%. The fact that the two rates are so close suggests the "sympathetic" movement of the two markets.

As a general rule, the higher the amount of distributed profit in a specific company the greater will be the value of its shares in the market. This follows from the fact that that particular stock will have the higher rate of return, hence, will be a more desirable purchase. The increase in demand will, therefore, result in a higher price. At the same time this increase in demand will be sufficient to exert a leverage effect on prices. For example, suppose an appropriate yield rate for the particular time is 4.65%. Suppose further that a particular stock has a yield rate above this rate. Since the rate is the result of dividing expected dividends by the current price,

$$\frac{d}{P} = r$$

and the particular stock has a rate above the normal, it follows that other things being equal, the price will rise to the level

$$P = \frac{d}{.0465}$$

Still, however, demand for particular stocks can be influenced by psychological factors quite apart from dividend yields. For example, a prospect of corporate growth which carries the promise of future high dividends is often sufficient to generate additional demand. Mergers, new management, etc., are also significant.

An excellent indicator of what to expect by way of future dividends is the stock dividend yield. This is calculated by dividing the indicated dividend to be paid per share of stock over the coming 12 months by the current price of the stock. This is done for us by the Toronto Stock Exchange as a composite yield of a number of stocks, and, as a series through time shows, a fairly normal value for this yield is about 4.5%. For October, 1978, the yield was 4.38%, a rather low figure.

Another index of stock market performance is the price/earnings ratio, a ratio of current price to declared earnings per share over the last fiscal year. The difference between the reciprocal of this ratio and the dividend yield is that the former is concerned only with earnings and the latter dividend distribution; hence, they are not the same thing. In general one might say that a low price/earnings ratio is indicative of likely capital gains as well as distributed dividends so that the reciprocal of the price earnings ratio is representative of the rate of return on stocks which is most comparable with the rate of yield on bonds.

There still remains an enormous potential for pure psychology in the stock market, particularly in speculation, more so than in any other market except, perhaps, commodities. In the last analysis, demand curves are purely psychological and anything rational or irrational which influences demand must impact on stock prices. The famous Keynesian statement

> A conventional valuation which is established as the outcome of the mass psychology of a large number of ignorant individuals is liable to change violently as the result of a sudden fluctuation of opinion due to factors which do not really make much difference to the prospective yield; since there will be no strong roots of conviction to hold it steady. In abnormal times in particular, when the hypothesis of an indefinite continuance of the existing state of affairs is less plausible than usual even though there are not express grounds to anticipate a definite change, the market will be subject to waves of optimistic and pessimistic sentiment, which are unreasoning and yet in a sense legitimate where no solid basis exists for a reasonable calculation.[5]

is as true today as when it was first written. Thus, even though the market may be tightly controlled by not only its directors but provincial laws, it still is subject to fluctuations which are not explained by economic analysis alone.

In addition there is the possibility that individual corporate managers may deliberately engineer the demand for their corporation's stocks with motives other than the best interests of either the corporation or the investor. This can be done through decision-making which results in corporate behaviour which is optimal neither for the corporation itself nor the investor. For example, dividend distributions may be withheld to deliberately undervalue shares for personal reasons.[6] Or the corporation may have a high debt/equity ratio so as to overvalue shares. And, of course, an excessively low debt/equity ratio may not be best for corporate growth.

---

[5]J.M. Keynes, *General Theory of Employment Interest, and Money*, Macmillan, London, 1949, p. 154.

[6]One reason for undervaluation, among others, is the undervaluation of shares to minimize death duties. Another is to permit easy purchase of one corporation by another. D.G. Berry, "Poor Management to Blame for Bargain Price Takeover," *Financial Post*, November 4, 1978, p. 7.

Mr. Berry, a Toronto investor, notes that a working capital in excess of stock market evaluation of debt and equity is indicative of deliberate undervaluation.

III. FINANCIAL ASSETS AND PRICES— AN INTERRELATIONSHIP

A. Current Liquidity and the Offer Curve

It is time to extend the analysis of demand for money which was begun in Chapter 2 and developed further in Chapter 4. The extension will take two forms: firstly, the substitution of current liquidity for money, and, secondly, the aggregation of individuals' preferences for different types of future liquidity and/or current liquidity into a single offer curve which would be characteristic of buyers' offers in the aggregate. The first should cause no difficulty and means, quite simply, the use of current liquidity as a medium of exchange instead of M_1. Actually, M_1 is an excellent proxy for L_c, the only statistical measure available. But, having made this substitution, we will ultimately extend the analysis into a *ratio* of current liquidity to total liquidity.

The second aggregation adjustment is necessary to develop the shapes of aggregate offer curves. While this was implicit in terms of the Real Balance effect in the discussion in Chapter 2, it should now be made explicit in terms of market equilibrium, i.e, what could be true for individual offer curves is impossible in the aggregate. It is because of this that offer curves of buyers, the opposite of buyers' demand curves for money, have restrictions placed upon them. They are sloped positively, in the first place, and have elasticities which vary between zero and unity in the second place ($0 < \epsilon < 1$). This follows from the fact that vertical offer curves of zero elasticity must mean constant offers of money regardless of price levels (the equivalent of unit price elasticity of demand for goods). This could mean a constant money value of gross national expenditure with a declining real value of GNE and is contrary not only to logic but also to empirical observation.

Unit elasticity of offer curves in the aggregate are also impossible for the reason that if the offer curve *should* intercept the origin (hence, an elasticity of unity) and the slope were greater than that of the sellers' demand for money, sellers would experience greater offers of money with increasing prices, hence, would have an incentive to increase prices to infinity. If, on the other hand, the slope were less than the sellers' demand for money, prices would collapse to zero since by lowering prices the sellers more nearly equate their own demands for money with the supply which is forthcoming. Unit elasticity of the aggregate offer curve is, therefore, the upper limit (see Diagram 8-9).

The "explosive" (and "implosive") nature of unit elasticity of an offer curve is obvious. On O_1, the offer of current liquidity of L_2 (price level P_1) exceeds the sellers' demand by $L_2 - L_1$, but at price level P_2, the offer of $L_3 - L_2$ is very much greater than $L_2 - L_1$. Hence, a price "explosion" would take place. At the other extreme (on O_2) the difference between the sellers' demand for money and the buyers' offer declines with falling prices, hence, an "implosion" of prices results. This effectively limits the elasticity of the aggregate offer curve to some value between zero and unity.

Between zero and unity, then, the elasticity can vary, and it is now time to see why and under what conditions the slopes of the offer curves change. In order to do so, we must adjust the concept of "money" to what is more appropriate to the analysis. Instead of "money" (or M_1), we will consider *current liquidity* as represented by demand deposits at both chartered banks and financial intermediaries and cash in circulation, i.e., liquid assets which can be exchanged at any time for goods and services. The diagram analysis would remain unchanged except for the substitution of L_c for M on the horizontal axis as seen in Diagram 8-10.

In equation 2 above, all the expressions to the right of the equality sign express the various forms of future liquidity available to individuals in addition to purely current liquidity. As has been shown, each of these forms of future liquidity has its own unique attractiveness, which can be measured in terms of a rate of return as a reward. When balanced against the degree of risk acceptable to the individual, the rate would be just sufficient to satisfy individuals' aversion to risk. A lottery, for example, offers enormous rates of return at prodigious risk—a satisfactory combination for some people. At the other extreme, a bank savings account, at no risk, is preferable. Purely for the sake of analytical convenience (no more) we shall collapse all of these rates of return (r's) into one great R which will represent a weighted average of all the small r's available to us. This is an abstraction beloved of economists who, following Keynes, prefer to consider bonds as the single form of future liquidity, and then proceed with their analyses toward some significant relationships between the yield on bonds and inflation, national income or whatever. In the process, the reality of the capital market with its enormous potential for switching amongst various forms of future liquidity is generally overlooked.

Diagram 8-9

UNIT ELASTICITY OF OFFER CURVE

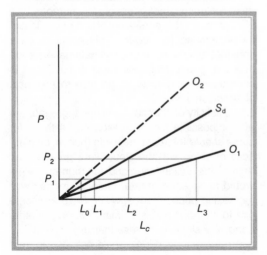

Diagram 8-10

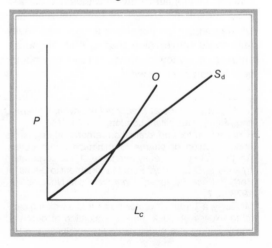

B. Shape of Offer Curves

With a promise, then, of avoiding this trap, we have the following relationship:

$$(3) \qquad L = L_c + \frac{L_F}{(1 + R)^t}$$

remembering that R is some magnificent weighted average of all the r's and L_F is likewise a weighted average of all the L_f's. For analytical convenience, we shall begin with the assumption that the money supply from the banking system is constant and that inflationary expectations are absent. This makes it possible to focus attention on the offer curve alone, with the value of total liquidity being unchanged. Any increase in price, then, is a movement up the offer curve in Diagram 8-10 above. Now the interesting question is, what happens to future liquidity? We know that $L_F/(1 + R)^t$ must decline by the same amount that L_c rises, since the total supply of liquidity is held constant, but suppose that the rate, R, increases rather substantially in the process. It follows that the value of L_F must also rise even though the value of $L_F/(1 + R)^t$ may be less than before.

Just to illustrate the concept, we can substitute numbers for the variables. Let $L = 10$, $L_c = 8$, $R = .05$ (5% per annum), and $t = 10$ years. The value of L_f is, as any pocket calculator will reveal, 3.26. Assume now a price increase which attempts to force a value of 9 on L_c. At the same rate of return, L_f declines to 1.63, a substantial loss. But the rate of return, R, as we shall see presently, will likely not stay the same; quite the contrary, it will likely increase rather sharply. Suppose it rises to 10% per year. This will increase the "pressure" on the public by increasing the opportunity cost of a foregone return, so that individuals may elect to protect the value of their future liquidity by increasing their current liquidity not so high as 9, but to 8.73, in which case L_f would be 3.29, quite close to the original value of L_f. What has happened is that the public has accepted the additional "pain," or embarrassment, of having insufficient current liquidity in exchange for the extra reward of a higher R. The loss of value of L_f, in other words, is unacceptable because with $L_c = 9$, L_f is only 2.59, substantially less than the original 3.26.

We can set forth this illustration more simply with a series of equations as follows:

$$(a) \qquad L = L_c + \frac{L_f}{(1 + R)^t}$$

$$\text{or} \qquad 10 = 8 + \frac{3.26}{(1.05)^{10}}$$

Equilibrium is disturbed with a price increase which results in

$$(b) \qquad 10 = 9 + \frac{1.63}{(1.05)^{10}}.$$

Should the public desire the same future liquidity as before and the rate of return, R, should rise to 10%, the result would be

$$(c) \qquad 10 = 8.73 + \frac{3.29}{(1.10)^{10}}.$$

A *still higher* rate of return, say to 15%, keeping the same value of L_f as in (a) and (c) above, would mean

$$(d) \qquad 10 = 9.19 + \frac{3.26}{(1.15)^{10}}.$$

But, more likely, the public would find the prospect of substantially increased values of L_F very attractive and would prefer to adjust current liquidity downward. For illustration, suppose the public prefers to double its future liquidity at the high rate of 15% per year.

$$(e) \qquad 10 = 8.38 + \frac{6.52}{(1.15)^{10}}.$$

Sellers, under the hypothesis of equation (e), would be forced to accept price levels consistent with a demand for future liquidity of 1.62 and offers of current liquidity of 8.38.

These illustrations, (a) through (e), will indicate how the demand for liquidity, and its counterpart, offers of current liquidity, will be the result of two separate factors: (1) rising commodity price levels which pull more funds into current liquidity, on the one hand, and force the public to provide for future higher spending levels on the other, and (2) higher rates of return which increase the opportunity cost of current liquidity. Thus, while it is quite rational to assume linearity when considering the money offer curve and the demand for money in relation to the price level alone, it is not logical to continue the linearity assumption when the rate of return on future liquidity is included as an independent variable and the offer of current liquidity is the dependent variable. A "two-tier" diagram, Diagram 8-11, shows the approximate relationship among the variables. For analytical convenience, proportions of total liquidity are measured along the horizontal axes. The upper section relates the rate of return, R, to future liquidity (represented as complementary to cur-

Diagram 8-11

PRICE LEVEL, RATES OF RETURN AND THE OFFER CURVE

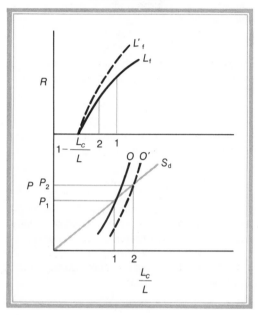

rent liquidity) by way of the demand for liquidity function. The function intersects the horizontal axis at a certain minimum requirement for liquidity after which the slope decreases (elasticity increases) with higher values of R. Correspondingly, the offer curve in the lower section increases its slope (decreases elasticity) as prices increase. The proportion of current liquidity offered in response to price increases is less at higher prices than at lower prices for the reason that demand for future liquidity is strengthened with both higher prices and higher rates of return.

It will be obvious from inspection of the diagram as well as the illustrative equations that high commodity prices requiring large proportions of total liquidity can only be associated with high interest rates and vice versa. Further, an equilibrium, as far as the buyers' offer curve and the sellers' demand for money are concerned, is at the intersection of the O and S_d functions. This could be at, say, a current liquidity ratio, L_c/L, of 70% requiring that $1 - L_c/L$ be only 30%. This might not satisfy the capital market, i.e., equilibrium in the

goods and services market need not mean that the capital needs are met.

C. Monetary Policy

Suppose, now, that a less stringent monetary policy on the part of the Bank of Canada is begun. An easing of chartered bank reserves would be quickly manifest in lower bank loan rates, more advertising for borrowers, and other indications of greater competition for loan customers amongst banks and financial intermediaries. Chartered banks, as institutions which intermediate between that section of the public with surplus liquidity (or savers whose demands for liquidity are relatively satisfied) and those with liquidity in short supply (borrowers), will proceed to satisfy this liquidity demand with what is newly manufactured money. In so doing, they provide borrowers with what they are seeking *without* offering additional outlets for surplus liquidity which the savers have. The banks' interest rates on loans will, of course, decline as they offer additional funds to borrowers – actually a kind of "artificial savings." Lower interest rates will likewise be offered for savings deposits, etc., with the result that the proportion $1 - L_c/L$ will decline.

Correspondingly, the proportion L_c/L will rise. This increase is accomplished by a rightward shift in the Offer Curve as a new equilibrium position is defined, though not yet reached, at $(1 - L_c/L)_2$ and $(L_c/L)_2$. The *dis*equilibrium at price levels P_1 may continue for a considerable time period as long as the monetary policy remains "easy" and until either output increases to shift the S_d curve to S_d', so as to establish a new equilibrium at the same price, or until sellers find their inventories are being depleted with an excess offer of money, and, consequently, raise prices further to approach the new equilibrium level of P_2. The actual price level that will result depends upon the elasticity of the offer curve— the greater the elasticity the higher the equilibrium price and the less the elasticity the lower the equilibrium price. The elasticity of the offer curve, in turn, depends upon the elasticity of the L_f curve itself since it is complementary to the offer curve. To express the idea slightly differently, the new equilibrium price level will depend upon the speed of response of the public's savings to increases in the interest rate.

On the other hand, the disequilibrium may exist for quite some time for the reason that, as the new money is spent, it finds its way into the hands of income earners and they, in turn, discover that their demands for liquidity tend to be satisfied. The offer curve, then, will shift to the right and the demand for liquidity will remain low in a continuous disequilibrium. Ultimately, sellers' demands for money will likely increase either through increased output, higher prices, or a combination of both, and the "semi-permanent" disequilibrium resulting from the excess of buyers' offers over sellers' demands for money will be eliminated by a restoration of equilibrium through higher prices and/or increased output, and, most important, an end to the easy monetary policy of the Bank of Canada.[7]

The new equilibrium will be characterized by a reinstatement of at least the original rates of return, R. These rates will once again equate the demand for liquidity (borrowers in short supply) with the supply of liquidity (lenders with excess supply). It is conceivable, however, that, given a tendency for the central bank to repeat its easy monetary policy more than it restricts monetary growth, the new equilibrium level of R may be higher than the old. Future liquidity (L_F in equations (a) through (e) above) may not be sufficiently attractive at the former level of rates to attract funds for the reason that prices are currently too high and are expected to be even higher in the future. In this case, the central bank may find it necessary to ease the monetary restrictions still further with the objective of lowering what is, politically and socially, an unacceptably high level of R. The consequence, of course, will be instantly recognized as a continuous round of

---

[7]Precisely how this comes about can be easily seen on the diagram. An easy money policy makes possible a "pushing" of additional liquidity on to the public via an increased money supply, M_1. Being current liquidity, the ratio L_c/L is rising. The offer curve is, thus, continuously shifted rightward. This rightward shift, so long as it continues, always makes possible a still higher increase in prices than a simple ratio such as $(\Delta M/M) = (\Delta P/P)$ for the reason that additional current liquidity can always be made available from a store of future liquidity. The tendency to thus transfer into current liquidity would be stronger during periods of high inflationary expectations as the incentive for additional consumer purchasing (before prices rise in the near future) becomes more widespread.

dreary inflation so characteristic of modern western economies (Great Britain is an outstanding example) as offer curves shift rightward and L_F curves move leftward.

We must not forget, in the interest of realism, to drop the convenient abstraction R and consider once more what rates of return for future liquidity really mean. Rising rates would signal, generally, that funds are in short supply, especially toward the longer, less liquid portions of future liquidity so that to attract funds into that area, higher rates of return are necessary. A falling R means, conversely, a surplus of funds. Thus, as we move along the demand for liquidity function accompanied by higher levels of R, it really means that a continuous process of reorganization of portfolios in response to different pressures and stimuli is taking place.

A shift toward the liquid end of the public's store of future liquidity, due to an easy monetary policy, would mean a lower series of short-term returns (r's) relative to longer term returns. This, of course, would result in a declining total R which is really a weighted average of all the r's, yet it must not disguise what is really happening. Actually a *readjustment* of portfolios is taking place with the various categories of liquidity vying for additional funds. A bear stock market, for example, might result from the transfer of funds from equities to other categories of liquidity. Indeed, we may even respond to higher rates of return negatively, i.e., prefer a lower rate with greater liquidity. Hence, the simplification R actually conceals what is in reality a complex of shifts and rearrangements. It is this, of course, which is the logical error committed by economists in using bond yields as "representative" of the entire spectrum of future liquidity. This, as we shall see in the next chapter, by-passes what really is the most important part of the analysis.

CONCLUSION

The discussion in both Chapters 7 and 8 should serve to bring home a very important point, viz., the markets for goods and services and the market for capital must be considered as an integrated whole. This is more than just a truism since before one can accept even a statement such as this, he must have the relationships between the various economic phenomena thoroughly established. This is what the last two chapters and the next two are supposed to accomplish. At the same time, it should be clear by now that these relationships are not at all simple but are an extremely complex interplay of human motives and actions.

The purpose of theory is to bring some order into what would appear to be disorder. This is true in any field of economics including capital markets. In developing the theory, it becomes possible to forecast (or anticipate) what is likely to result from a specific cause. This is what theory is for. The fact that such a result may not develop is not enough to prove the theory wrong; quite the contrary, it means the theory is not sufficiently complete. But, if the theory *were* complete, it would be beyond the human mind to embrace in the first place and not sufficiently static to include in a computer program in the second. Once more this is not the fault of theory but the incapacity of humans and machines to embrace it.

This concluding section, then, is not really a "conclusion" at all but a bridge looking forward to what remains of Part II. It would be comforting to know that, once the contents of these four chapters are read, success in investment in our capital market is assured. Of course this is not the case at all, but if the reader, after having read and understood this chapter, has somewhat reduced the probabilities of failure, the objective is truly served.

ADDITIONAL READINGS

Fisher, Douglas, *Money and Banking*, Irwin-Dorsey, Georgetown, Ontario, 1971, ch. 12. An excellent discussion of portfolio selection.

Goldsmith, Raymond, *Financial Institutions*, Random House, New York, 1968. Good analysis of U.S. institutions.

Moore, Basil J., *An Introduction to the Theory of Finance*, The Free Press, New York, 1968.

Patinkin, Don, *Money, Interest and Prices*, Harper & Row, New York, 1965, ch. 5. A rigorous treatment of the utility of money and financial assets.

CHAPTER 9

Financial Markets

INTRODUCTION

The capital market described in the preceding chapter has been under considerable strain during recent years, especially in the early 1970s. We can see this because of the earlier continuous pessimism within the stock market, on the one hand, and high and rising interest rates on the other. It means that the demand for liquidity is exceeding the supply.

When the question is asked *why* the demand for funds has exceeded supply, the answer must be sought in the producing sector of our Canadian economy which requires funds for investment purposes. It is also to be found in the government sector which requires funds for public expenditure. Such funds are acquired by taxation which reduces disposable income, especially the savings component, and by borrowing from the market itself. It is the latter which competes directly with the private sector for the limited amount of available liquidity.

Canada's capital requirements for investment purposes have been considerable relative to the capacity of the Canadian public to save. This is why we have found it necessary to encourage inflows of foreign capital. So long as foreigners, particularly Americans, have an accrued surplus of savings relative to their own investment requirements and Canadian outlets offer better returns, the savings will flow into Canada. We should experience no real shortage of capital as long as the rates of return are sufficiently high to attract foreign capital.

We can gain some concept of the demand for funds by examining the growth of total real private investment over the years since 1950. A trend line fitted to the logarithms of these data, first deflated by the Gross National Expenditure Implicit Price Index, shows that the growth rate has been about 4.2% per annum. Of course deviations from this growth rate have occurred particu-

larly during the downturn of the business cycle in 1970-71, but on the whole, this high growth of real investment has been maintained throughout the post-war years to the present time. Table 9-1 shows the difference between actual and computed real investment during recent years.

Actual real private expenditure is the difference between total capital expenditure and total government capital expenditure. These are deflated by the appropriate GNP price deflator. (See Tables 16, 51, and 43, *Economic Review*, April, 1978, Department of Finance. Computed expenditures based upon a trendline, $1n\ Y = -73.451 + .04236\ T.\ T = 1950$ through 1977.) Deviations from the trend occur during 1970 through 1972, years of low investment, and in 1973 through 1977. In 1973-77, the actual investment, in real terms, exceeded the computed investment by several billions of dollars. This "burst of investment demand" which was greater than the normal trend puts pressure on the market for liquidity, and, therefore, pulls up interest rates.

But this is not all. The governments of Canada have also been adding their own pressures to the capital markets. This is done both by taxation, which restricts the supply of liquidity flowing into the market in the first place, and in the second place, by entering the market for funds from the demand side to finance deficits. Since the amount of liquidity is not inexhaustible, the upward pressure on interest rates becomes complete. Table 9-2 is the same as Table 9-1, but it computes government expenditure on the basis of a trend line fitted to the logarithms of past *real* government expenditures and compares this with actual *real* expenditures.

During the 6-year period, 1970 through 1975, governments exceeded the long-term expenditure growth trend by substantial amounts as can be recognized in the form of negative differences between computed and actual amounts in Table 9-2.

Table 9-1
ACTUAL VS. COMPUTED REAL PRIVATE CAPITAL EXPENDITURE
(Millions of Dollars)

	1970	1971	1972	1973	1974	1975	1976	1977
Computed	21986.9	22938.2	23930.8	24966.2	26046.5	27173.6	28349.4	29576.0
Actual	21239.5	22530.0	19046.2	27250.9	28920.2	29280.1	31601.8	30972.5
Difference	747.4	408.2	4884.6	−2284.7	−2873.7	−2106.5	−3252.4	−1396.5

Table 9-2
ACTUAL VS. COMPUTED REAL TOTAL EXPENDITURE OF ALL GOVERNMENTS
(millions of dollars)

	1970	1971	1972	1973	1974	1975	1976	1977
Computed	32706.5	34312.3	35996.9	37764.2	39618.3	41563.4	43604.0	45744.8
Actual	33065.8	35205.0	37069.0	38698.5	41561.7	44012.9	43328.8	44726.1
Difference	−359.3	−892.7	−1072.1	−934.3	−1943.4	−2449.5	275.2	1018.7

Source: Table 51, adjusted by the appropriate index on Table 43, *Economic Review*, April, 1978, Department of Finance. The trend line was computed as $1 n Y = -84.0248 + .047929\ T$. $T = 1950$ through 1977.

It is, however, the combination of the demands for capital by the private sector and the finance of greater than normal government expenditure (both by taxation and by borrowing) which puts the strain on the capital markets. This strain can be eased by the manufacture of new money by the chartered banks, and, thus, interest rates are kept from rising; however, there is a limit to this process also if we wish to avoid inflationary pressures.

The "burst" of real demand for liquidity during the early 1970s on the part of the government (exceeding the long-term growth trend) can be likened to a large pig at a feed trough pushing aside smaller pigs to gain more for itself. On the other hand, the subsequent counter burst of private demand for capital (the smaller pigs at the trough in a kind of unified retaliatory action) in excess of the normal long-term growth trend during the latter 1970s adds further upward pressure to interest rates. This pressure is made worse for the reason that the private sector has been using the bond market for about 70% (the sole exception was 1977 with 61%) of its capital financing requirements as opposed to only 30% for the equity markets. The reason for this is that selling stocks does not raise sufficient capital during the depressed state of the equity markets. The governments, of course, rely entirely on the bond markets for their deficit financing.

At the same time, there has been developing in the 1970s a world shortage of liquidity for investment purposes for the reason that other countries have been experiencing similar expansions of investment and government expenditures. In addition, central bank policies have been moving toward tighter monetary policies. This means that our former foreign supplies are likely to dry up, throwing us on our own resources. This is unpleasant enough for our Canadian standard of living, but useful in terms of economic ownership and control of our own production. The only way of relieving this shortage of liquidity is the relatively painless method of lowering the costs of manufacturing deposits, thereby expanding the supply of liquidity and easing the pressure on interest rates.

It is against this background of tightness of the capital market that the analysis that follows is developed. As usual in such an argument, no attempt at "proof" is made. The only proof is, does the analysis fit the facts? If so, the analysis is considered to be an adequate explanation for both theoretical and practical applications.

I. DEMAND FOR FINANCIAL ASSETS

A. Bonds and the Alternative

For the sake of analytical convenience, we will invert the procedure of considering current liquidity as the commodity which is in demand and think in terms of the financial asset as the commodity and the amount of current liquidity as the demand. This is purely a methodological approach and does not change the essential nature of the system; one may argue equally as effectively that apple sellers have a demand for money rather than buyers have a demand for apples. It is only a matter of convention and convenience in the case of financial assets.

Demand for financial assets, on the other hand, involves a slightly greater complexity of analysis than demand for ordinary commodities. In the preceding chapter, the entire market for financial assets (or liquidity which the assets represent) was expressed as an equation and the rates of return equated the values of the assets to the value of a stock of liquidity as measured in money terms. At the same time, the higher the rate of return, expressed as $(1 + r)$, the more desirable was a specific asset. This follows from the fact that the value of the financial asset in terms of future liquidity is greater. Alternatively, if the value of the future liquidity is fixed, as in the case of a bond, the present price will be lower because of the higher rate, r. In the former case, it is the expected future value of the asset which is greater with a higher current and/or expected rate of return which in turn results in an anticipated appreciation of value.

The demand for marketable bonds as financial assets is a convenient starting point. Since bond prices move inversely with yields, there is no difficulty with the concept that the lower the price, the greater the quantity demanded. However, because of the inverse price/yield relationship, the demand curve relating yield to quantity demanded must be positively sloped as in Diagram 9-1. The same, of course, would be true for savings deposits and Canada Savings Bonds — the higher the yield, the greater the amount of the asset demanded. This results directly from the fact that the "pain" of foregoing additional liquidity is overcome by successively higher rates.

The fact that the flow of funds into the market is

Diagram 9-1

DEMAND CURVE FOR MARKETABLE BONDS

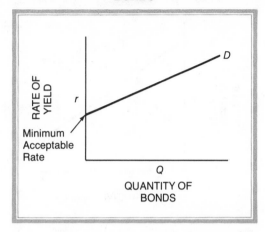

now less able to meet the enormous demand for investment means that funds channeled into the bond market, for example, are not available for the equities market. While this at first sight may sound obvious, the fact is that in the past it really did not matter where specific funds went since there were plenty of funds to meet all requirements at reasonably low rates of return both from domestic and foreign sources. Now this is no longer true. Demand for marketable bonds is *at the expense of* demand for equities and vice versa. It is this plus the fact that financial assets render no service in themselves (automobiles — transport, food — satisfaction of hunger, etc.) which renders the analysis of financial markets more complicated. Demand for specific financial assets stems entirely from future liquidity and this is an expectational phenomenon. It is also the direct consequence of changes in rates of return for competing assets.

Suppose, then, we derive a demand curve for the *alternative* (competing) asset, given a rate of return on a specific asset, on the assumption that rational liquidity owners will continuously adjust their liquidity structures so as to maximize expected returns. (N.B., This excludes the purchase of assets such as Canada Savings Bonds, provincial bonds, etc., for patriotic or other "irrational" motives.) In this case, a demand curve for the alternative asset would appear as in Diagram 9-2. This gives a "normal" shape (downward

Diagram 9-2

DEMAND FOR ALTERNATIVE ASSET

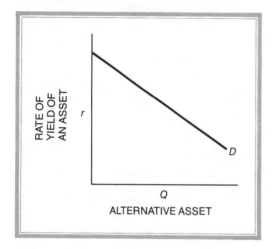

sloping) of a demand curve vis-à-vis the rate of return on a competing asset. The schedule states that as the rate of return on one asset falls, the demand for the *alternative* asset will rise. Because each alternative asset is the competing asset in a "next door" sense, it is a simple matter to sell one asset and purchase another, or more realistically, it is simple to redirect the stream of liquidity to the competing asset. The consequence of this redirection is an increase of flow demand (a shift of the *stock* demand curve to the right) for the competing asset with the consequent fall in the yield of the competing asset.

The relationship of the competing asset is particularly strong in the government bond sector. Chart 9-1 which shows representative bond yields shows this relationship most clearly, for even a cursory glance will reveal that all the Government of Canada bond yields do, in fact, move together. The reason for this can be readily seen in the following analysis of the year 1974: After the first quarter, a strong pressure of short-term interest rates in international markets developed as a consequence of increased demand for funds for the purpose of buying oil from OPEC countries. This led to sharply rising rates in the international markets, particularly Eurodollars

and swapped deposits.[1] (See Chart 9-1, upper left.) The consequence of rising rates in European markets in particular is that large amounts of short-term funds flow into these markets instead of Government of Canada Treasury Bills. Our Treasury Bills, it should be noted, are sound, secure liquid assets with a short-term to maturity which are as attractive as the debt instruments of any other nation. This is why Americans or Europeans are just as interested in Canadian government securities as their own, but when rates are rising in markets for competing assets, our Treasury Bills just cannot compete.

So, the consequence of the flow of liquidity to Europe in response to the sharply increased rate of interest meant a collapse in the quantity demanded of Canadian Treasury Bills, which in this case are the alternative assets in Diagram 9-2 against the Eurodollar rate on the vertical axis. The brokers in Ottawa are obligated to take up these Treasury Bills in the weekly tender and therefore find a surplus of inventory of unsold bills on their hands and in order to reduce it must lower the price (raise the yield) considerably. Finding themselves in a loss position, they must recoup by offering a much lower price (higher yield) in the next weekly tender. The consequence of several weeks of this performance is a sharply rising Treasury Bill rate which can be seen in the second quarter of 1974 (see Chart 9-1).

The interesting feature of the Eurodollar rate is its impact on chartered bank rates only on the high side, i.e., it pulls Canadian bank rates upward but not downward (see years 1975–77). The reason for this assymetry is not difficult to find. Eurodollars are competing assets so long as they maintain rates above our domestic rates. Once they move below domestic rates they cease to be attractive as outlets for short-term investment. Of course, it goes almost without saying that the withdrawal of Canadian banks from the Eurodollar market has no impact at all on Eurodollar rates since Canada's position in the entire market is extremely small relative to other countries. Euro-rates influence Canadian rates but Canadian rates have no effect on Euro-rates.

So the process continues, but now we substitute

---

[1]Both Eurodollars and swapped deposits are discussed

in Part III. For the moment, it is important to recognize that there are strong competitors for Treasury Bills.

the rate (the vertical axis of Diagram 9-2) on 91-day Treasury Bills for the Eurodollar rate. Similarly, the alternative asset is the 1–3 year Government of Canada bonds, the next competing security. Once more the rate adjustment takes place by means of a collapse in demand for these bonds with dealers in Toronto and in branch offices throughout Canada finding a surplus inventory to dispose of by lowering prices (offering higher yields). What we really have is a kind of "domino theory" with quantities demanded of competing assets collapsing in response to rising yields of a specific asset. The last of the Government of Canada bonds to respond are those of 10 years and over.

A reference once more to Chart 9-1 will show the very sharp wide swings in the Eurodollar rate, the shortest-term and the first domino to fall in 1974. The sharpness dulls and the swing moderates with each succeeding and longer-term security. This is the consequence of the mathematical relationship between price and yield discussed in Chapter 7. As time to maturity grows longer, the price of the bond is subject to wider fluctuation and the yield less so. Conversely, the shorter the term to maturity, the more "locked in" is the price and the greater the yield fluctuation.

So the analytical chain is almost complete. An upsurge in demand for oil funds in Europe is transmitted via the Treasury Bill mechanism to marketable bonds which are sold across Canada as the direction of the liquidity stream is altered toward those assets with the higher yields. The shift in demand for those assets causes an upward movement in the rates for competing assets as market equilibrium is restored.

But this is not all as the lower sections of Chart 9-1 make clear. An abrupt upswing in short-term rates, such as that of 1974, has an impact well beyond the marketable bonds category. It is felt in provincial bonds and even in bank savings deposits, ultimately to affect the interest Canadians must pay on their mortgages. In this way the transmission (domino) effect of the demand for oil credits, even though far away from remoter parts of Canada, is certain and sure because of the overall tightness of the market for liquidity. Like ripples on a pond, the impact reverberates on a world-wide basis because the demand and supply of liquidity is world-wide. Canada is a small participant in this market.

B. Demand for Equities

Probably the most interesting result of the analysis is the effect in sectors outside marketable bonds—in the above instance, bank savings deposits. But this is not the end of the matter either, because the impact of shortages of liquidity is felt in equities markets as well. Though equities are a sector quite separate from marketable bonds they are still affected by changes in interest rates. We have all had occasion to read in the financial pages of newspapers of the depressing effect of higher interest rates (or anticipated higher rates) on the equities markets. A traditional Keynesian explanation for this might be as follows: Higher interest rates mean higher cost of borrowed money which discourages investment which in turn affects the national income via the multiplier mechanism, and, hence, lower profits because of a business slump. If anyone questioned this roundabout and lengthy explanation of an *immediate* reaction of equity prices to higher rates of interest, he had good reason to do so. A much more plausible explanation is the logical extension of the bonds argument to the entire capital market. This is possible by means of the analysis of alternative assets.

Equities *do* compete with bonds, particularly marketable bonds; in fact, the "sectorization" of liquidity in the preceding chapter is really more theoretical than practical. Actually there is only a fine distinction between a preferred stock and a convertible bond. Still, though fine, the distinction is there because one is an ownership instrument and the other, debt. But the fineness itself, especially when bonds are sold with stock warrants as "sweeteners," is sufficiently blurred that the equity is truly an alternative asset to the bond. Streams of liquidity can flow into one or the other with the minimum of liquidity loss, but not into both equally. Again, this is the result of an inadequate flow of funds necessary to sustain all markets simultaneously.

There is, however, one important characteristic which distinguishes the equity as an alternative asset. In the analysis above, particularly for Chart 9-1, there is practically no time lag between the rate changes of each of the alternative assets. The competition is very strong and adjustments are only rarely lagged. This is not true when equities are considered as alternative assets.

Chart 9-1 INTEREST RATES

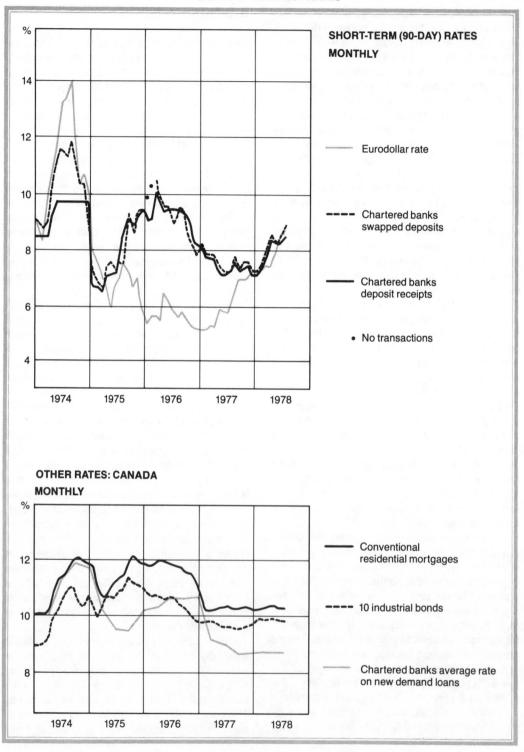

SHORT-TERM (90-DAY) RATES
MONTHLY

——— Eurodollar rate

- - - Chartered banks
swapped deposits

——— Chartered banks
deposit receipts

• No transactions

OTHER RATES: CANADA
MONTHLY

——— Conventional
residential mortgages

- - - 10 industrial bonds

——— Chartered banks average rate
on new demand loans

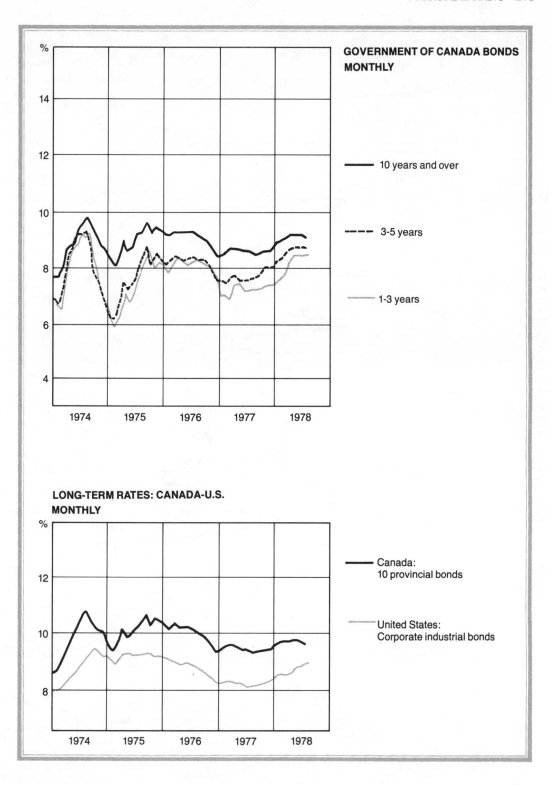

GOVERNMENT OF CANADA BONDS MONTHLY

— 10 years and over

---- 3-5 years

— 1-3 years

LONG-TERM RATES: CANADA-U.S. MONTHLY

— Canada:
10 provincial bonds

— United States:
Corporate industrial bonds

Chart 9-2

BANK OF CANADA BANK RATE AND CHARTERED BANKS' PRIME RATE

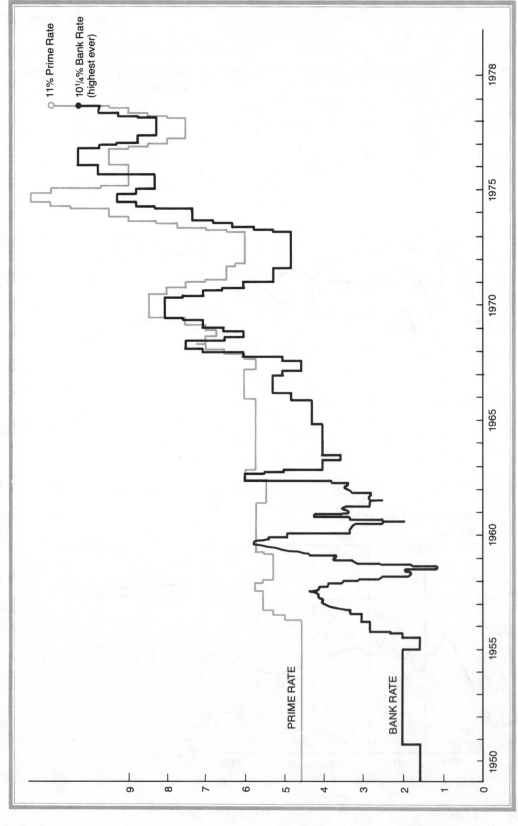

Source: *The Financial Post*, November 4, 1978, p. 18.

Lags in this case may be considerable, and it is the length of the lag which constitutes the most interesting and challenging topic of this chapter. The demand curve for bonds in Diagram 9–2, assuming the alternative asset is just "next door" in terms of time to maturity, is quite likely to be elastic. We can deduce this because of the close and immediate reaction of alternate yields even though we know nothing of the quantity of assets traded. This is likely to be more true within each of the sectors than between sectors; this is why the Canada Savings Bond issues have such a devastating effect on the volume of savings deposits. Between sectors, however, it is likely to be quite different, for sometimes the rate of interest may vary considerably without any appreciable effect on equity prices; on other occasions, only very slight changes in interest rates are necessary for a substantial impact on equity prices. This suggests a demand curve which is sometimes elastic and sometimes inelastic, depending upon the location of the curve itself relative to the interest rate. For example, suppose we have the demand curve (Diagram 9–3) relating bond yields to the quantity of equities.[2] Suppose further that we should happen to be at position a in terms of quantities of equities and bond yields. Position a would be consistent with bond yield r_1. Any increase in bond yields thereafter which is either experienced or anticipated would cause the stock demand for equities to collapse (the flow demand curve is elastic upward) in which case the price of equities would fall. Of course, if the price levels of equities in general are already low, the collapse of demand would likely prevent them from rising, and the financial press would report this as a further depressing effect of rising interest rates on the equities market.

---

[2]No attempt is made in this or the following similar diagrams to attach values to the quantity axis. The closest approximation to reality would be the numbers of shares traded on the stock exchanges which is generally (though not always) excessive during bearish markets as well as in bull markets. Thus, a collapse in demand for equities at point a would be indicated by a large number of shares sold, and an infinite expansion of demand at point b would represent a large number of shares purchased. But this of itself is absurd since every seller has a buyer and every buyer has a seller. The quantity axis, then, measures quantity sold under certain conditions, rising stock prices for point b and falling stock prices for point a.

Diagram 9-3

BOND YIELDS AND EQUITIES

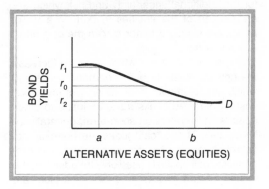

Having examined the bond market and how rising Eurodollar rates were transmitted to all bond yields so quickly and easily, we can readily understand why a suggestion by the Federal Reserve Board or the Bank of Canada that monetary policy would be tighter is sufficient to depress equity prices at once. Like the demand curve for alternative assets as bonds, the equity curve is elastic upward at point a so that only a suggestion is sometimes required for equity holders to sell securities in *anticipation* of rising interest rates. No rational asset holder wishes to be left holding his liquidity store in assets which have fallen in value; hence, he will likely be *overcautious* in protecting himself against such an eventuality by premature selling. A tighter monetary policy means a higher cost of deposit manufacture and this means higher rates on day-to-day loans by means of which the Ottawa dealers finance their weekly purchase of Treasury Bills. This in turn means a recouping of higher costs by bidding lower (higher rates) for Treasury Bills and this will be quickly transmitted to all bond yields. The dominos will eventually fall, including the last one, equity prices.

One final word remains as to why, precisely, the demand curve for equities is elastic upward at point a. This has reference once more to expected rates of return and a recasting of the entire structure of a stock of liquidity in accordance with these expectations. Recognizing the high yield on bonds (low prices), liquidity owners will switch from equities into bonds (or direct their new liquidity flows into bonds) because the yield on bonds either exceeds the rate of return on equities, or at least is sufficiently great that the rate of return on equities no longer compensates for the additional uncertainty and risk which are always part of the equities market. In a word, bonds are simply a better buy, in the opinion of liquidity owners.

There is another factor which tends to increase the upward elasticity of the demand curve and which has its impact from the side of investors' costs. Chartered banks advance loans to stock dealers and brokers on short-term, generally 24 hours' call. These "call" loans are normally not called so long as the account is operating properly; the call option is used only for adjusting the values of the stocks and bonds which are pledged as security for the loan. Security dealers, in turn, pass on this credit to their acceptable clients who wish to purchase more shares of a specific stock than their funds permit. The shares of stock themselves become collateral for the credit. In the event the market value of the pledged shares declines, the dealer will require the client to make up the difference between the current price of the shares and the original "pledged" price. In the same way the chartered banks request payment from the dealers in the form of calls.

This practice of "margin buying" is really quite normal and does give stock purchasers more leverage for speculative purposes.[3] There is, however, the important fact that interest charged on the loans is a cost to the investor and does put pressure on him, forcing him to reconsider his equity position. This pressure is stronger when bullish equity markets are no longer so certain and *static* flow equilibrium with stable stock prices can result in severe losses to the investor.

---

[3]Margin buying means financing additional purchases of stock so as to add leverage to a specific sum of money. Suppose, as an example, yields on stocks, both dividends and capital gains, would amount to 10% per year. One thousand dollars could thereby earn $100; however, with a 50% margin requirement, borrowing additional funds at 8% to purchase $1,000 worth of additional shares to sell at the end of the year could mean $1,100 at year-end less

$1,080 cost of loan equals

$20 profit or $120 profit (12%) on a $1,000 investment. Margin requirements are controlled in the U.S. by the Federal Reserve Board and are, in normal times, 55%.

The interesting feature of margin buying and the stock market is the degree to which the interest rates on the loans are related to all the other rates of interest. In general, yields on short-term bonds will reflect the corresponding yields on Treasury Bills which, in turn, will reflect the degree of ease (or tightness) of money in the money market. Finally, to the extent that bank rate is a close indicator of monetary ease or tightness, the bank rate *itself* will influence the day-to-day loan rate, (which affects the Treasury Bill rate), the call loan rate, and, lastly, the prime rate (see Chart 9-2, page 214).

Chart 9-2 graphically illustrates the growing relationship of the Bank of Canada bank rate to all the other chartered banks' rates of which the prime rate, the lowest rate reserved for banks' best customers, is representative. As can be easily recognized, the bank rate has become much more powerful in its influence in the years since it was put back into genuine service in the latter 1960s. To many people, the close relationship is a mystery since bank rate is generally defined simply as the rate at which the Bank of Canada lends to chartered banks. But, since chartered banks rarely borrow, or borrow in small amounts when they do, why should the bank rate have any impact at all? The answer is that the money market rates and all other short-term rates — Treasury Bill rates, day-to-day loan rates, call loan rates, etc.—are all influenced by the cost of purchase and resale agreements and this complex of short rates itself impacts upon prime rate. From there on the competition for chartered bank loans during a period of tight money forces all loan rates upward as well.

Within this complex of interrelating interest rates or short-term loans, call loan rates are included so that rising bank rate increases the cost of holding equities on the margin and this, when added to expectations of just stable stock prices, increases the pressure for selling from margin accounts. The demand for stocks collapses as both the interest cost of loans and the yield on bonds rises to the point of infinite elasticity on the demand curve for equities.

The impact of selling from margin accounts can be substantially increased when declining stock markets are the general rule. In this case the margin investor is under enormous pressure to sell his stocks to relieve the burden of finding funds to replace the falling market value of pledged securities. Hence, a genuine bear market often characterized by panic selling can result.

Moving to the right from position a (Diagram 9-3) the demand curve is inelastic downward. This suggests a range of bond yields between r_1 and r_2, clustered around r_0, which are less than the yields of competing assets but are not sufficiently low to warrant selling bonds and purchasing equities. This "neutral zone" satisfies the expectations of liquidity holders in that any deviation of r from r_0 is *expected* to result in a return to r_0; it is, therefore, not worth incurring the cost of sale and purchase involved in a transfer of liquidity to alternative assets.

Just as at point a the yield, r_1, is above what is considered an adequate rate of return on equities, so is r_2 at point b *below* the expected rate of return on equities. At least, it is sufficiently low that the rate of return on equities compensates for the added uncertainty and risk of the equities market. This rate of return includes both anticipated capital gain and dividends from stock and can be leveraged by means of margin buying. Precisely the opposite situation applies at point b as opposed to point a, i.e., investors will increase their demand for equities as elasticity of demand becomes infinite.

Between the two points, a and b, is the yield range which constitutes an equilibrium of expectations. Any displacement of bond yields from an equilibrium rate r_0 is expected to be temporary so that no significant change in demand for equities will take place. We can consider how this displacement from equilibrium will automatically call forth a return to equilibrium by analyzing the process of expectations. At rate, r_1, a high rate and low price, expectations are for a return to r_0. Any *further* increase in r will be interpreted by market opinion that bonds are underpriced and profits are to be made in marketable bonds; hence, a flow of liquidity from equities into bonds will occur so long as, to repeat, expectations are for a return to r_0. Point a on the demand curve is the "bear transfer point" for equities and sellers will outnumber buyers (the stock supply curve will shift to the right in the equities market) and equity prices will fall.

Similarly, r_2 will represent a higher than normal price (lower than normal yield) with a strong expectation of a fall in bond prices (rise in yield). Should this expectation become sufficiently gen-

eral, and the bond yield go *still* lower, widespread profit-taking in the bond market will likely occur. At the same time, demand for alternative assets (equities) will increase as buyers substantially outnumber sellers; the stock demand curve will shift to the right in the equities market, and equity prices will rise. This is the "bull transfer point" for equities since bonds, in the opinion of the market, are overpriced and liquidity flows will enter the equities sector. In a word, the liquidity structure is being reordered once more.

C. Flow Equilibrium

Just as in the case of equities, we can construct a demand schedule for marketable bonds given the rate of return on equities. The curve representing this schedule would be approximately the same as that of Diagram 9-3; however, the elasticity would likely be greater except at both extremes where infinite elasticity exists.

On the vertical axis in Diagram 9-4 we would lay out the rate of return on equities. Since this is a rate which includes both the dividend yield and the expected increase in value, it is not so easy to identify in concrete terms as is the case of bonds. As a proxy for this, we can use the reciprocal of the price/earnings ratio. Since the company's earnings are likely to indicate the future possibility of dividends, and consequent future market prices of stock, the inverse of the price/earnings

Diagram 9-4

EQUITY YIELDS AND BONDS

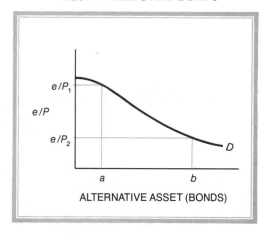

ALTERNATIVE ASSET (BONDS)

ratio is probably the closest approximation to rates of return we can find. The horizontal axis measures bonds in "quantities" though, once more, we have no adequate measure of the numbers of bonds traded. The demand function itself is likely to be less elastic within the "middle range" since by empirical observation we know that wide fluctuations in the price/earnings ratio (or its inverse) can occur with little effect on bond markets.

Broadly, the same analysis applies to the bond market as to the equities market. There will be an expected rate of return, e/P, which a consensus of buyers and sellers will consider as "normal." Departures from normal, say to e/P_1 will generate strong expectations of a return to normal; hence, any *further* increase in e/P will reach a bear transfer point, as shown by a, for bonds and liquidity will flow into the equities market instead of bonds. Conversely, e/P_2, a low expected rate of return, will generate expectations of a restoration of normal rates of return. Any *further* declines in e/P will reach a bull transfer point for bonds. Equilibrium between the two markets is achieved by adjustments of flows. We can readily see the process of restoring equilibrium by placing Diagrams 9-3 and 9-4 together as in Diagram 9-5. We start with an assumption of both stock and flow equilibrium, i.e., the values of both r and e/P lie within the shaded zone. Suppose an increase

in short-term interest rates generated, for example, by a disturbance in the Eurodollar markets in Europe causes bond yields to rise (prices to fall). This is the "domino effect" discussed above. If yields reach the bear transfer point for equities, we can expect, especially if yields rise further, a collapse in demand for equities and an increase in demand for bonds.

Maintaining the assumption that equilibrium had existed prior to the disturbance, we can easily see that the fall in the price of equities will raise the ratio of e/P until the bear transfer point for bonds is reached. At that point the original demand for bonds will collapse and the equity demand will be restored since equities are once more good buys. Both the bond rate and the rate of return on equities will be in equilibrium.

But notice that the bond/equity equilibrium is a "one-way street." Higher bond yields will reduce stock prices, raising the rate of return for equities, but there is no feedback, no built-in device for reducing bond yields automatically. This could only be accomplished by an increase in demand for bonds which would raise the price and lower bond yields, but this can only come from *outside* the system itself. Bond yields, after all, are a concrete measure, not necessarily perfect, of the rate of interest. It is this rate of interest which "rules the roost" and administers the shocks to the capital market, forcing it to readjust and to seek equilibrium again on its own.

Diagram 9-5

FLOW EQUILIBRIUM, EQUITIES AND BONDS

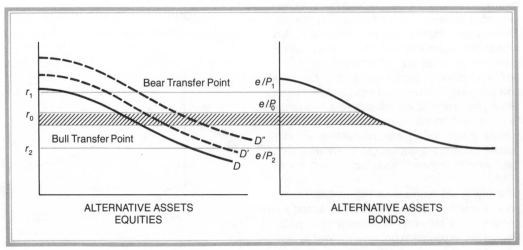

If we ask ourselves what determines the rate of interest which directs the capital market like a *deus ex machina*, we would have to undertake an investigation well outside the scope of this book. We do know, however, that a raising of bank rate which signals an expansion of the volume of deposits by the banking system does indeed lower the rate of interest, and, in turn, bond yields. Conversely, a lowering of bank rate and a restriction of the volume of deposits increase the rate of interest, but that is just about as far as we are prepared to go along these lines. In the next, and last, chapter of Part II, a survey of interest theories and the relationship between interest and economic activity are developed with the objective of clarifying some of these issues.

Suppose, now, that the higher interest rates which resulted from the increased demand for oil credits in the Eurodollar market in 1974 is interpreted as a *permanent* change, i.e., there is a general consensus that interest rates and bond yields will not return to their former levels. This would be the equivalent of shifting to a new demand curve for equities, D'. In this case there would likely be no ensuing bear stock market and the new demand curve for equities and the old demand curve for bonds would represent a new expectational equilibrium. Suppose *further* that an increase in interest rates is expected to be followed by additional increases, i.e., the first increase was not high enough. This would be shown by demand curve D'' and a *bull* market for equities could be precipitated as liquidity holders transfer into equities before the expected fall in bond prices (rise in yields) materializes. Such a bull market would peak out when the bull transfer point for bonds is reached. This latter case, the shift to D'', is rather typical of periods of high inflation when interest rates are expected to be much higher than they are, being held to negative real levels by the expansionary monetary policies of the central bank.

Now all this raises a very important question. When a certain change in interest rates (or bond yields) takes place, how do we know if flow equilibrium is disturbed? In other words, which demand curve are we on, D, D', or D''? This is important, for if a rate r_1 is at a bear transfer point on D, we would do well to sell our stocks and purchase bonds *if further increases are forthcoming*. In other words we are incurring a high risk of capital loss by staying in the stock market.

On the other hand, if r_1 is an equilibrium rate of D', we should make no changes in our portfolios. But if r_1 is on D'', we should seriously consider selling our bonds and purchasing equities because bond prices are likely to fall.

The answer to this important question can be found in the yield curve structure discussed in Chapter 7. In that chapter (see Diagram 7-13) position III was indicative of a market expectation of falling rates. This would represent, for the rate r_1, demand curve D, and we must expect a bear equities market at any time. Position I of the yield curve would be the equivalent of demand curve D' (again assuming rate r_1) since this is the normal position reflecting only liquidity preference. Finally, position II would reflect demand curve D'' and we may expect a bull market for equities.

It is, thus, a *combination* of both the prevailing bond yields and the yield curve itself which is necessary for drawing complete and correct conclusions as to the positions of the demand curve for alternative assets. The yield curve identifies the position of the demand curve by indicating the nature of prevailing market expectations. The rates, in their turn, identify the critical level beyond which the market believes the rate is too high (or too low). When these two pieces of information are combined we have a powerful tool of analysis which can tell us more about the flows of capital from one sector to another.

It may appear strange that we are concerned with the price of one asset (in terms of rates) yet, at the same time, it is the quantity of *another* asset which is demanded — in contrast to a normal Marshallian demand curve. This situation arises because no rational person wants equities *for the sake of equities* or bonds for the sake of bonds, etc., but for the returns which they yield. This is why it is necessary to switch from one asset to another, keeping in mind, of course, that every switch involves a brokerage fee.

II. FLOW ADJUSTMENTS, PROCESSES AND INFLATION

A. Empirical Results

As is always true, the real test of any theory is an empirical one—does it fit the facts? So it is that it is necessary to check the theory of capital flows against statistical evidence to either confirm or deny the theory. We can do this with the aid of interest rates in Charts 7-2 and 7-3. This, it will be recalled, is a time series showing short, medium and long-term interest rates. If these three series are "bunched" closely together, we are identifying a yield curve in position III. If they are spread apart in a "normal" fashion, say 2 or 2½ percentage points apart, we have position I. Finally, a wide spread would indicate position II.

In Chart 9-3 (see page 221), this same time series is repeated with the addition of bull/bear equity market turning points. "Major turning points" are defined roughly as peaks and troughs of the monthly average of the Toronto Stock Exchange Industrials Index which were followed by changes of about 25 or 30 points. "Minor turning points" are defined by any change in the index less than this.

The first "bearish" period in Chart 9-3, the last quarter of 1967 through 1969, was characterized by an upward trend of bond yields, interrupted only once in 1968. This "uptrend" was paced by high short-term rates, largely the response of the market to the tight monetary policy pursued in both the U.S. and Canada. The opinion of the market at the time was clearly that rates were abnormal (on the high side) and that the exogenous disturbance of tight money was contrary to what market forces left to themselves would have dictated. The reaction of the market was precisely what would have been expected—a flight from equities. However, this "flight" was not so abrupt as one might have anticipated. The Industrials Index ceased to rise further in early 1969 but did not begin its actual downtrend until early 1970.

The long time period (2½ years of position III for the yield curve) prior to the actual turning point of the index can be characterized as a long-term speculative boom carried forward by Wall Street and fed by plentiful supplies of liquidity. Ultimately, with the rate of return on equities steadily declining at the same time that bond yield rates were rising, the bear transfer point was reached in early 1970.

From that point forward, the situation in the capital market remained pretty much true to form. During the 3-year period, 1970-73, equities were low in price relative to earnings and the risks of capital loss in equities therefore was minimal. The yield curve was in a "bullish" position with expectation of rising bond yields (falling prices) so that the equities market would be supported by a transfer of funds from bonds to stocks. This situation changed rather dramatically from mid-1973 to the last quarter of 1974 when a bearish period was entered once more. The risk of capital loss in equities became high as a result. Of course, the turning point in the market did not arrive until October, 1973.

By early spring, 1974, the yield curve signalled a bullish period in equities which proved to be short-lived. By mid-1975 the TSE Industrials Index had reached the first of several high points (1055.3 in June with 1975 average = 1000) which has really proved to be a plateau. From that point to the present time (1978) neither the stock market nor the yield curve has shown any significant tendency toward movement up or down.

The relationship between the yield curves as indicated in Chart 9-3 and the Toronto Stock Exchange Industrials Index can be seen by comparing Charts 9-3 and 9-4. In the latter chart there is at least one complete cycle consisting of a bear section (1969 through 1971) and a bull section (1972 through 1974) similar to a sine wave. The twin bear turning points, one in early 1969, the other at the end of that year, were signalled well in advance by the bearish position of the yield curve in 1968 and 1969. Similarly, the bull turning point of the TSE Index in mid-1970 was also forecast with the "bullish" yield curve (in position III) during the years 1971-72. And, finally, the bearish position II of 1973-74 foretold the arrival of a bear market through the year 1974.

During that year, 1974, the index was changed to include a broader base (a composite 300 as opposed to 153 industrials), and, of course, the base was changed to 1975 = 1000. This distorts the series somewhat so that comparability cannot be assured; however, the graph on the lower portion of Chart 9-4 is sufficiently comparable that the almost 1200 (1193.8) in the index reached in July 1978 is roughly the equivalent of 220 for the old index. Does this 1200 mean, then, a bull market in stocks? The answer, based upon yield curve analysis, is *no*. The yield curve has been in neutral position (position I) since mid-1975 and showed no indication of a change at the time of writing (mid-1978).

What we are witnessing during this "neutral" period is a random walk of the TSE Index. This is the response of the stock market to various random

Chart 9-3

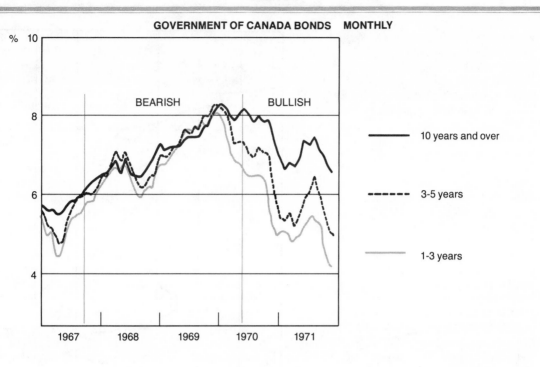

GOVERNMENT OF CANADA BONDS   MONTHLY

BEARISH   BULLISH

10 years and over

3-5 years

1-3 years

1967   1968   1969   1970   1971

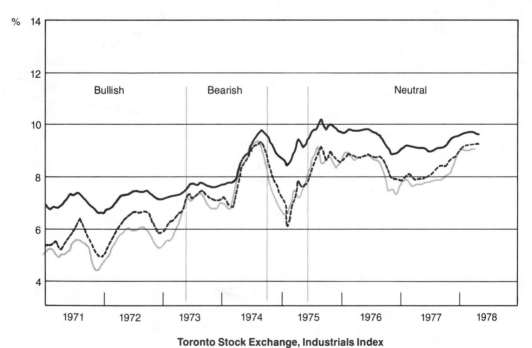

Bullish   Bearish   Neutral

1971   1972   1973   1974   1975   1976   1977   1978

Toronto Stock Exchange, Industrials Index

MAJOR TURNING POINTS
1. March, 1970, downward.
2. June, 1970, upward.
4. October, 1971, upward.

7. October, 1973, downward.
8. November, 1974, upward.

MINOR TURNING POINTS
3. March, 1971, downward.
5. March, 1973, downward.
6. May, 1973, upward.

Chart 9-4

TORONTO STOCK EXCHANGE INDUSTRIALS INDEX
(CLOSING QUOTATIONS, END OF MONTH)

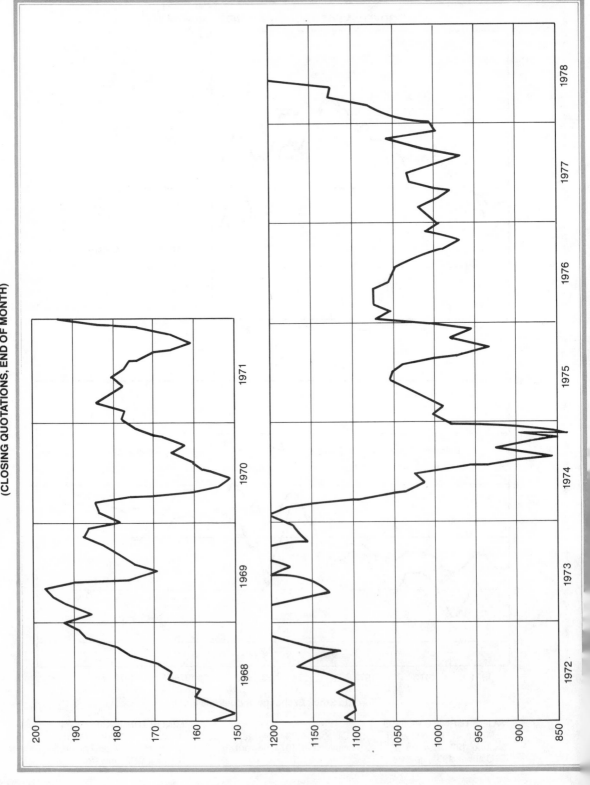

influences and "shocks" which occur from time to time and are completely unpredictable. This is why the various peaks and troughs appear to be showing no consistent movement, precisely what might be expected of the neutral yield curve. Some experts, however, in the investment industry rely on charts of individual stock price movements which, so it is claimed, *do* display some consistent behavioural patterns. These "chartists" as they are referred to, would deny the existence of a random walk, but rightly or wrongly, their work is beyond the scope of this analysis. Anyone interested in pursuing the practice of chartism further would be advised to not only study but master the highly specialized techniques and jargon which chartists have invented to describe movements in stock prices.

When the yield curve positions are laid out in the manner of Chart 9-3, it would appear that one almost has a formula with which it is possible to guide one's investment decisions. A formula it is, but it is not a crystal ball. It is, in fact, but one of many factors which influence the markets for equities. A bull market, for instance, even though interest rates are favourable, will hardly occur against a backdrop of high unemployment, inflation, and poor growth prospects. Similarly, a falling exchange rate of the Canadian dollar will discourage investors until foreign investors become convinced that the rate has reached its low point to turn up once more. It is possible that foreign funds will flow in at that point with the expectation not only of rising stock prices but also a higher exchange rate to increase profits still further. This should help to increase prospects of a bull market.

A careful observer, therefore, will consider all of these influences along with the yield curve and the interest rate, carefully weighing their relative strengths before making his investment decision. Even then the prospective investor is still faced with the decision as to which particular stock to purchase at the time. There are speculative growth stocks (oil and gas) at one extreme as well as the blue chip high quality, but conservative, corporations at the other.

Equity markets undoubtedly continue to occupy a strategic position within the complete structure of the capital market. At least some of the centre of attention has been due to the rather glamourous nature of the market—fortunes have been made

(and lost) in great bull markets which are inevitably followed by the opposing bear market. However, when examined in the context of economic logic, there is really nothing special about Wall Street or Toronto which warrants more attention than any other segment of the capital market.

For many years the stock exchange was considered to be an excellent hedge against inflation. The logic was that as prices in general rose, profits and dividends would rise as well. This would encourage stock purchases until stock prices would rise also, thereby offering a unique protection against inflation. The seemingly endless post-war bull market which came to an end at last in the latter 1960s appeared to bear out this conclusion. Indeed, one expert *still* (1974) has argued that ". . . over the long pull corporate earnings and dividends have risen more rapidly than living costs, and that while the relationship is a very loose one, stock prices too have well outdistanced the rise in consumer prices."[4] However, just to make a point let us select arbitrarily (thereby defying the rules of good statistics) the year 1967 as a base year. Suppose an individual had purchased stock in both Wall Street and Toronto in that particular year and held this stock for ten years. How would he have fared? See Table 9-3, page 224.

During the decade 1967-77 Canadian equity investments would have been worth in real terms just 35 1/2% of their former value. This is hardly a "hedge" against inflation nor does it justify Malkiel's continued optimism regarding the stock market.

> So my advice is that at least some of your funds should be placed in common stocks or other assets that offer a degree of protection against unexpectedly rapid inflation.[5]

An incredible piece of advice!

What, briefly, has happened to the equities market which has eroded its wonderful capacity for anti-inflation protection? The answer is extremely simple. It is true that common stocks do reflect

---

[4]B.G. Malkiel, *A Random Walk Down Wall Street*, New York, W.W. Norton, 1975, p. 222. Unfortunately, Malkiel does not say how long his "long pull" is.

[5]Calculations of real value of stocks excludes dividend distributions over the 10-year period.

Table 9-3

	1967	1977
Wall Street (Dow-Jones) end of year	905.1	831.2
U.S. Cost of Living Index	100	181.5
Stat Can Investors Index end of year	141.9	93.8
Cost of Living Index	86.5	160.8
Wall Street "real" Index (1967 = 100)	100	45.8
Canadian "real" Index (1967 = 100)	100	35.5[5]

corporate profits, but that is the trouble. Wage costs have risen also (faster than the inflation rate) to put a genuine "squeeze" on profits, so, corporate dividends and stock prices have fallen far behind in the race against the cost of living.

Another aspect of equity markets should not be overlooked (or rather forgotten) even though it is obvious enough to any rational individual. Memories are short as 1929 fades into history, but some of the worst practices of stock markets were exemplified in those earlier years. It is possible, for instance, for unscrupulous individuals to form secret pools for the purpose of first buying stocks in a small corporation then, through trading with each other, continuously bidding up the price until the public moves in to buy *all* the stock at grossly inflated prices. Such practices are more easily carried out in small exchanges with smaller companies and require constant vigilance on the part of the directors of the exchange. Generally outside the law, they do no credit to the market and are more easily perpetrated during speculative booms. It is, in fact, just such speculation that the rational investor should avoid.

B. Commodity Markets—Protection Against Inflation?

Perhaps just as objectionable is the other "thief" which also robs effectively, inflation. Savings are destroyed in real terms, and, unfortunately, there is no way of securing police protection. But, if one does seek some measure of protection for his savings, it is clear that equity markets cannot serve the purpose. Quite the contrary; on the basis of the past 10 years, stocks are the poorest possible protection against the rising cost of living.

It is *barely* possible to maintain the real value of one's savings intact by using non-marketable assets such as savings deposits, savings certificates in financial intermediaries or even Canada Savings Bonds so long as the interest earned *net of tax* just equals the inflation rate. However, to increase the real value of one's savings during times of inflation means directing liquidity into areas which are in ordinary times characterized by high risk. Inflation reduces this risk by generating additional (inflationary) demand which expends itself against an inelastic supply. The consequences are rising prices particularly for such assets as land, housing, gold, minerals, agricultural commodities, etc.

For many people the thought of purchasing real assets for speculative reasons is horrifying. To be sure, a great deal of specialized knowledge of an item is necessary for a completely successful speculation; consider, for instance, the purchase of paintings with the expectations of their increasing in market value. Only the art expert is truly qualified for this. Nevertheless there are organized markets in commodities such as barley, wheat, potatoes, rapeseed, etc., and even gold which do not require such a high degree of technical expertise. The Winnipeg Commodity Exchange is one example and the Chicago Mercantile Exchange is another.

It is surprising the extent to which markets such as these are taken for granted by the general public, in the first place, and by many economists in the second. We economists draw our supply/demand curves readily enough so as to explore the logic of demand and supply elasticities without bothering to consider that markets do indeed exist in concrete form. Not only do they exist but they are also the very heart of the capitalistic system, essential to the smooth operation of the entire process of distribution.

Consider the rationale of the market in geographic terms. Producers (potential sellers) wish to contact consumers (potential buyers), a simple enough task on a diagram but virtually impossible in an area the size of Canada without some agreed location for a market. Once the market is established and located, buyers are assured that they can buy at the lowest price possible under the existing circumstances, and sellers, likewise, can sell at the highest price possible. So it is that virtually all the raw materials, basic commodities, etc., reach a processor, or manufacturer, at a certain cost to him; he then proceeds to add further value to the commodity in the form of wages, salaries, etc., until the item is ultimately sold to the consumer.

The final seller, of course, through advertising, attractive display, etc., develops many "mini-markets" between himself and the consumers, but these are by no means so perfect as the original commodity market which was the beginning of the whole process. Consumers' markets are characterized by a high degree of ignorance, misleading advertising, etc., which are in reality the most economically inefficient in the entire production/distribution process. Nevertheless, the fact remains that virtually everything we consume has passed through some commodity exchange somewhere in the world at the very outset of the production process.

In the process of passing through the market, a commodity price is set which becomes the basis for all other prices because production costs (including profit margins) are added to the original market price, to arrive at the final price for the consumer. This is why it is no exaggeration to argue that the commodity exchanges are the heart of our economic body and (to carry the figure one step further) the "pulse-beat" within these markets determines the economic well-being of all of us.

In order to assist in the successful operation of these markets, dealers have invented various devices, the most important of which (for our purposes) is the futures contract. The futures contract arises from the fact that a time lag in the process of production exists. Any manufacturer in planning his production must do so well in advance, hence, must assure himself of a supply of a necessary commodity as raw material perhaps three months to one year before production begins. But the manufacturer is a buyer of an original commodity; therefore, a specific quantity at a specific price to be delivered at a specific time must be arranged. He therefore shops around amongst various "wholesalers" to arrange for delivery at the lowest possible cost to him.

The wholesaler is the one who operates in the market and whose function is to intermediate between buyers and sellers. He is truly a "middle-man," often considered as someone to by-pass through "factory direct to you" type of selling. Sometimes the middlemen and the market can indeed be avoided through vertical integration of production, i.e., the final seller owns all the stages of production from the beginning through to the consumer. Rarely, however, have such types of production/distribution activity been efficient, with the exception of certain rare cases as in the food industry. The market and the middlemen who use its facilities appear in the final analysis to be more efficient than alternative and competing methods of distribution.

The wholesaler, then, obligates himself to supply by means of a cash sale the commodity required by the manufacturer. Having done so he immediately purchases a futures contract from the market. His position now is secure—he has both his own selling price firm by means of a cash contract and his buying price likewise firm by means of a futures contract. But the wholesaler does not stop at this point. He proceeds to locate a still better "deal" by means of a cash purchase when the commodity becomes available from the actual producer, and this is the crux of the matter. The wholesaler sells in advance but cannot buy until the commodity in question is ready for purchase. All he can do is purchase a futures contract at whatever price happens to be available at the time.

We can readily see the importance of the futures contract in seasonal production such as agriculture. A disastrous harvest could result in high prices which could in turn, ruin a wholesaler, but having purchased a futures contract he is safe from danger of ruin by passing the risk of disaster on to someone else. Who this "someone else" is we shall see presently.

Assuming that the wholesaler manages his expected cash purchase with a reasonable margin of profit, he then has to dispose of what could be an "embarrassment"— the obligation to accept and pay for a commodity delivered in accordance with his futures contract. This he can do quite easily because all that is required is that he sell his futures contract on the market and since the price of the futures contract will be fairly close to the cash price, a small loss (or gain) may result.

Who is the ultimate purchaser of this futures contract? Someone else who has sold *another* futures contract of the same quantity and date and must offset his sale with a purchase — in other words, a speculator.

What all this amounts to is simply this. A whole mass of futures contract sales and purchases are changing hands continuously all the time. Suppose, for example, that $10,000 worth of rapeseed is forthcoming from the harvest in 3 months. A hundred thousand dollars worth of paper (futures contracts) might be bought and sold in the meantime. When the time nears for the actual movement of rapeseed from producer to processor, all the paper will "collapse" in an offsetting of purchases against sales at the Commodities Exchange Clearing House. Only the differences (which are really profits or losses) will remain to be settled in cash.

Of course, a single wholesaler in reality is also several dealers within a complete marketing chain, each one buying for cash (to sell future) or selling for cash (to buy future). In all cases, to "hedge" as this process is called, a futures transaction to match an opposite cash transaction is required. Ultimately, to settle the futures transaction, another opposite futures contract must be negotiated. For the middlemen therefore, a total of four transactions is required for one complete hedge (two for cash and two for futures).

The interesting thing about the futures dealing is that since every sale is offset by an equal and opposite purchase, no money is required except for the difference between the two transactions. Thus, to buy and sell futures, one only requires about a 10% deposit with the Exchange Clearing House, and should price differences go beyond this, more funds would be requested. The result of all this is that for a given sum of money, roughly ten times the amount of futures contracts may be purchased; hence, profits may amount to a considerable sum with such enormous leverage. Speculators are those individuals who guess what the futures price will be and those who guess incorrectly pay those who guess correctly. It is, thus, readily seen why speculation in futures is not for the faint-hearted.

But, and this is the main thrust of our argument, when prices in general are rising during inflationary periods, the cash price of the commodity itself is rising so that the "bull" speculation outweighs

"bear" speculation.[6] Those who pay in the end are the ultimate consumers, i.e., all of us who are "robbed" by inflation. Suppose, in Diagram 9-6, an inflationary trend of some 8% per year exists. Price fluctuations around a long-term upward price trend can result in greater return $(c-a) > (a-b)$ than if prices were stable. This is why the markets for commodities can indeed not only protect but increase the value of savings during inflationary periods. In fact, because of their strategic position at the base of our economic system, commodities and commodity markets offer just about the *only* protection from inflation which can be considered as feasible for the large majority.[7]

CONCLUSION

The liquidity structure outlined in the preceding chapters can be compared to a spectrum with each colour merging into the next with no clear delineation between them. From one extreme of liquidity there is a gradual and barely noticeable change from one sector to the other. At the same time that liquidity becomes less, the reward for parting with liquidity rises until the high risk (consequently non-liquid) lottery ticket at the other extreme of the spectrum is reached.

From the standpoint of demand for financial assets, which is the opposite of demand for liquidity, the analysis uses a different approach. No rational individual demands financial assets for their utility alone. Since the financial asset is required purely for its rate of reward, it follows that the amount demanded by liquidity holders will vary with the return of a specific asset relative to the competing assets. This is, of course, impor-

---

[6]The correct term is "long" vs. "short." A short sale would be closed with a later purchase which (hopefully) would result in a buying price less than the selling price. A long position is the opposite, a purchase to be closed out later at a higher selling price.

[7]Anyone interested in commodity speculation need only check the yellow pages of his telephone book for the names of firms who specialize in such investment services. It goes without saying that risk is considerably greater in this investment activity and no one should undertake such ventures without full knowledge of all aspects of the business.

Diagram 9-6

COMMODITY SPECULATION

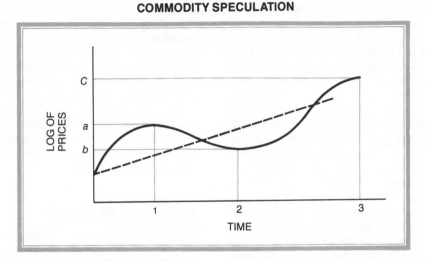

tant because it gives us an understanding of the behaviour of the capital market, particularly the various sectors within the entire structure.

We can identify at least three major factors which have influenced the capital market in recent years. The first of these is inflation. Perhaps nowhere else is the impact of inflation more strongly felt than in capital markets. We know, for instance, that income earners are protected against inflation as long as they can increase their earnings as fast as prices rise. This is made possible by the use of collective bargaining and the threat of the strike weapon for organized labour. For others, the professional classes, the defence against inflation depends upon the monopoly position enjoyed by the particular profession. So it is that inflation is seen by the general public as not so severe an enemy to be wrestled as unemployment. Unemployment, and the threat of unemployment, strike directly and immediately at the wage earner himself.

Because the impact of inflation is not so obvious to the general public, it can be tolerated more readily than unemployment. This is unfortunate because the true effects of inflation can be devastating, especially in the long term. The reason for this is that the capital markets are first to feel the impact of inflation and the consequences are not so immediately apparent in terms of incomes which rise at the same rate as prices. Consider,

for example, housing. Inflation makes speculation in land and housing an attractive alternative to investment in equities as the public learns that house values rise by more than inflation rates because houses are inelastic in supply in the short term. Ultimately, the rising speculative demand results in house prices so high that ordinary income earners are effectively excluded from the market. The impact of inflation, then, though long in arriving, eventually strikes home. In the end, the losers are those who cannot afford the type of housing they had originally wished for.

This is compounded by a second factor which also influences the capital market directly, rising interest rates. In the process of bidding for our savings, both the governments and the private sector will use that particular segment of the capital market which shows the greatest promise for raising necessary capital. For example, corporations have preferred in recent years not to acquire new capital through issuing new shares because stock prices have not been sufficiently high. They prefer to sell bonds at attractive rates, running their debt equity ratios to higher than normal levels. But governments also use the bonds markets extensively for debt financing. This competition for limited funds pushes interest rates still higher until bonds are sufficiently attractive to investors. The point at which investors purchase these bonds, whether Canada Savings Bonds, federal and provincial marketable bonds, or corporate bonds, appears to be when the rate of yield (or interest) just compensates for the anticipated inflation rate.

The shortage of capital for investment purposes is becoming a characteristic of our times. In the past, we have relied upon foreign investment to supplement our own savings, and, hence, have found it necessary to maintain an interest differential between Canadian rates and the U.S. rates so as to make Canadian investment attractive to the foreigner. This is certain to be more true for the future than for the past, and as competition for scarce capital resources becomes greater, world-wide interest rates must necessarily rise. Expansion of the money supply can temporarily relieve this pressure on interest rates but only at the risk of more inflation.

The shortage of capital leads to the third major factor which influences the capital market along with the economy in general — inadequate economic growth. In this case, it is a combination of both output per man-hour and employment which is required to increase. It is, in fact, the failure of economic growth which, when combined with in-flated wage costs, results in insufficient profits and dividend distribution to justify a rising equities market. The consequence is a shift to other areas in the financial asset market, i.e., to the higher risk areas and to the higher liquidity (and consequent low risk). This satisfies the requirements for both the inflated money cost of living and the need for defence of future liquidity against expected inflation. There is a flight, thus, from the centre of the spectrum of financial assets, particularly stock markets, to the extreme ends of high and low liquidity. This is the consequence of inflation combined with low real growth of the GNP and a shortage of capital.

ADDITIONAL READINGS

Fisher, Douglas, *Money and Banking*, Irwin-Dorsey, Ltd., Georgetown, 1971, ch. 13. Note additional References at the end of the chapter.

Loeb, Gerald M., *The Battle for Investment Survival*, Simon & Schuster, New York, 1965.

Malkiel, Burton G., *A Random Walk Down Wall Street*, W.W. Norton, Inc., New York, 1975. A delightful reading experience for the potential investor.

CHAPTER 10

Capital and Interest

INTRODUCTION

The "interest rates" that have been considered in the three chapters preceding are really not interest rates at all but bond yields. As was explained earlier, a bond yield on "pure" bonds (uncontaminated by conversion clauses and other "sweeteners") comes closest to measuring the true cost of borrowed money. Though not perfect, these bonds are the best market indicator of interest that we have. Even the eventual maturity date distorts the true measure of interest because the value of the bond at maturity has nothing to do with the cost of credit at the present time. The British Consuls, which never mature, are really a better measure of the true market rate of interest than government of Canada long-term bonds.

There are a number of aspects of interest and interest rates which have been the subject of considerable research and thought, yet many of us as instructors of economics have never taken the trouble to discuss them in our classes aside from showing how they all fit into a macroeconomic IS-LM model. One is almost reminded of the blind men and the elephant; all of us are familiar with just one facet of interest and capital but we fail to see the complete beast. This is what this chapter is about. Eventually, hopefully, a complete picture will emerge so that not only will interest make sense but we will also be able to better understand the working of a modern economy.

I. SOURCE OF CAPITAL AND INTEREST

A. Productivity of Capital

Institutions grow and develop in a capitalistic, free enterprise system without any central guidance aside from the famous "invisible hand" of Adam Smith. After these institutions have developed, philosophers and thinkers attempt to rationalize their existence. It is a curious inversion which might strike an objective observer as ordering everything the wrong way round. In fact, if one were to assume that a science is for the purpose of finding a better way of doing things, economics as a science should not exist. At least that is the way the early Physiocrats looked at their world; everything is the consequence of a natural order and there is really nothing anyone should do about it.[1] As far as capital and interest were concerned, they, the Physiocrats, were aware of a productivity of capital, hence, it was only "natural" that a portion of the extra output due to capital should return to the individual who provided the capital in the first place. But, if there was no excess of production and no additional income, it was unfair and unjust for the lender to charge interest to a borrower.

Adam Smith also recognized that capital is productive. He reasoned that money capital (or "stock") which was loaned would be put to some productive use for the purpose of maintaining productive labourers who reproduce the value with a profit. The borrower would return the capital with some of this profit (interest) "without encroaching upon any other source of income."[2] Smith recognized that capital increased production and, therefore, was most important in the productive process; he also was aware that capi-

---

[1] Actually the idea of a "natural order" to the Physiocrats was not an existence of mankind in a state of nature but what we might consider today as pure conservatism. Institutions and ways of life which exist are really the best *because* they exist "naturally."
Probably the most objective analytical discussion of Physiocratic principles is that of Charles Gide, Chapter 1, "The Physiocrats" in Gide and Rist, *A History of Economic Doctrines*, Harrap, London, 1948.

[2] A. Smith, *The Wealth of Nations*, McCulloch's Edition, A. and C. Black, Edinburgh, 1889, p. 155.

tal was something other than money because money is "but the deed of assignment, which conveys from one hand to another those capitals which the owners do not care to employ themselves." As such capitals are commonly lent out and paid back in money they constitute what is called the monied interest.[3]

Since capital is used for the employment of labourers, the more capital which exists at any time the higher must wages be and the lower the rate of interest. But the productivity of capital derives not from itself alone but from the fact that workers are employed by the fund of capital, and in their work they produce not only the equivalent of the capital which employed them but an additional amount known as interest. Smith did not recognize that capital and labour were employed jointly in production to produce more than labour by itself. He did, however, observe that agriculture seemed to be more productive as far as the fruits of labour were concerned and reasoned (erroneously) that nature worked along with labour in agriculture whereas in manufacturing it did not. It followed, therefore, that to Smith agriculture was the more fruitful use for capital.[4]

It is natural, then, considering the enormous prestige of Adam Smith, that economists succeeding him would have attributed the payment of interest to some excess of production, (what else *could* it have been?) and since this excess was the residual which accrued to entrepreneurs as profits, interest must be part of profits. The logical explanation for this line of reasoning was that interest was the profit due a capital stock owner which he could have earned had he employed the stock himself.

One of the post-Smith economists was Nassau Senior, a professor at Oxford. He first originated the idea that interest might be the reward of savings or "abstinence," and since abstinence necessarily involved a pain or sacrifice it must be rewarded. Abstinence itself does not create wealth, it merely constitutes a title to wealth. In this, Senior had gone beyond even Ricardo who, like Smith, simply treated interest as a residual. By pinning interest to saving, Senior gave it a

logic, a *raison d'etre* which his contemporaries had failed to recognize.

By the time of mid-nineteenth century, J.S. Mill was able to develop a synthesis of three rewards, to be included in his "gross profits," abstinence, the reward of risk, and the wages of entrepreneurship.[5] Interest, of course, was the reward of abstinence, i.e., that portion of gross profits reserved for that purpose. The other two rewards were simply logical reasons for justifying the existence of profits.

Alfred Marshall also considered interest to be the reward of "waiting." By this he simply meant not consuming what could have been consumed; thus, a rich person who refrains from consumption is as entitled to interest as a poor person since the waiting process is the same. He preferred, incidentally, the term "waiting" to "abstinence" because of the sarcasm of Marx who referred to the "virtuous" abstinence of Rothschild contrasted with the "profligacy" of a labourer who "feeds his family on 7 shillings a week." As an incentive for waiting, then, the higher the rate of interest was, the greater the incentive and the saving.[6]

By way of distinct contrast with the British economists and the Physiocrats, the early French socialists, St. Simon, Fourier, Proudhon, etc. (along with the Scotsman, Robert Owen) attempted to use their political economy not to describe the world in which they lived but to reshape it. For our purposes, it is Pierre-Joseph Proudhon who stands out as the most interesting because of his Exchange Bank Theory, probably the first true attempt at developing a revolutionary theory of exchange.

To Proudhon, interest was a means of exploitation and something to be abolished. Once this had been accomplished, the other means by which workers were exploited, rent, would also disappear. Once capital had become available free of charge, the workers would be able to dispose of it as they saw fit. Of course, since money is merely a medium of exchange, a bank of issue, like the Bank of France, would make bank notes available whenever the needs of commerce and trade required them. For in-

---

[3] *Ibid.*, p. 156.
[4] This conclusion of Smith's has been sharply criticized. However, considering the state of the art of manufacturing in Smith's day, his error is understandable.

[5] J.S. Mill, *Principles of Political Economy*, Longman, Green, London, 1892, p. 156.
[6] A. Marshall, *Principles of Economics*, Macmillan Co. Ltd., London, 1947, p. 234.

stance, suppose an entrepreneur (who is really a "worker" at heart) conceives a scheme for production. He first takes order for his products, then acquires the raw material with promissory notes which are then converted by the exchange bank into paper currency. Along with the necessary raw materials would be the machinery, buildings and equipment, etc., which would also be "converted" into paper currency so that the entire capital requirement for production would be interest free. The responsibility for deciding upon the worthiness of the production scheme and whether capital should be so created for the purpose would rest with the exchange bank itself.

As we can readily identify, what was absent from the thinking of Proudhon was the fact that saving is necessary before capital may be loaned and interest payments are necessary for the generation of these savings. This resulted in the confusion in his mind between capital, the result of saving, and simply money expansion which to him could be a substitute for capital. This confusion, incidentally, has even persisted well into our own day in a more sophisticated era. Nevertheless, there is some logic in the idea of the mutual exchange of credit which seemed to run through the exchange bank. We can see this in the concept of exchange bank notes which are not "backed" by gold at all but by the public's capacity to produce. The public, in effect, loans to itself through the intermediary of the exchange bank, but without the payments of interest. In general terms, this is the principle of the credit union, the cooperative in Great Britain, Raiffaisen in Germany, etc. Eventually, since the borrowers and lenders were *supposed* to be the same people, interest, or discount, would be reduced to low levels and ultimately disappear altogether.[7]

There is, of course, a considerable degree of fascination in an idea such as this. Certainly the concept of issuing notes against commodities and services alone has its counterpart in the Real Bills Doctrine in the U.S. in the 1920s, and the possibility of capital creation without the "pain" of

saving has become a part of our contemporary times. Chartered bank term loans are just such examples of "painless abstinence." There are, however, no examples of interest-free loans, though such proposals have been made. The nearest to this concept we have today would be creation of central bank money—Dominion bank notes prior to 1935 and reserves of chartered banks in the Bank of Canada today. In the former case, interest free loans were made available to the government without term and, in the latter, central bank money (legal reserves of the chartered banks) *could* be interest free since no interest is paid to chartered banks for their deposits at the Bank of Canada.

We can, therefore, identify some aspects of the exchange bank of Proudhon even in contemporary practice. Still, both in his mind as well as in practice today such interest payments have nothing to do with savings or investment. They are purely a "mechanical process," a ritual, as it were, made necessary because of the institutional mechanism of our monetary system. We require *some* form of money in order to facilitate exchange and we must pay for it. Interest in this case is just one small aspect of the much greater concept of Capital and Interest, really no greater than the tail of the blind man's elephant. We must not, therefore, confuse, like Proudhon, the payment of interest for credit manufactured by an exchange bank with the payment of interest as the reward for parting with liquidity or interest as a factor income resulting from the productive service of capital.

1. Böhm-Bawerk

The analysis of capital and interest and the consequences resulting from the use of capital as a productive factor was the great achievement of the Austrian School, the most notable representative being E. von Böhm-Bawerk.[8] Early in his great work, *Positive Theory of Capital* he makes very clear the nature of the "roundabout" method

---

[7]It is interesting that the bank advances in the exchange bank of Proudhon were to take the form of "discount." Not one of his contemporaries seems to have questioned his distinction between discount and the interest which he would have abolished. Gide and Rist, *op. cit.*, p. 317.

[8]The title "Austrian School" applies to a number of economists who were not necessarily Austrian but followed in the tradition of the marginal productivity theory and the capital/interest analysis which followed from it. As to some names, one would suggest von Thünen, Wieser, Menger, Sax, Wicksell (Swedish), Mises, and Hayek, in addition to Böhm-Bawerk. Jevons and Clark (English and American) could also be included.

of production and the contribution to production which capital provides. Using an example (Böhm-Bawerk was fond of examples of which there are almost *too* many in the *Positive Theory*) of his own near-sightedness, he cites his need for eyeglasses, but, unfortunately, nature has provided him with only silicones and iron-ore, both quite useless without the means of conversion into glass and frames. Something else is required and this is the necessary manufacture, the grinding and polishing of lenses, etc., until the finished product is available for sale.[9] The roundabout process of converting nature's original material into eyeglasses involves factories, steel mills, glassworks, etc., all of which are necessary stages in the process of production. But precisely *why* is this method of producing eyeglasses more productive than the direct method? Because, says Böhm-Bawerk, "Every quantum of capital is, so to speak, a container of useful forces of nature."[10]

In a word, factories, glassworks, etc., make possible the use of natural forces which are exceedingly more productive than human physical energy. We might add today that modern scientific computers are much more effective through their use of natural energy than human brain power! But to call this capital into existence means that production in excess of consumption must take place, and this production in excess of consumption "embodies (or encapsulates) the elemental forces of nature and labour." The objective of this production becomes not to produce for consumption at all but to develop something which will harness natural energy and apply it to a useful purpose. This is why saving is necessary for the existence of capital, consisting, as it does, of the two elemental factors, raw material and labour in a stored form. Saving itself is not capital; it makes the creation of capital possible. If no one saves, the demand for consumption goods is so great that all the nation's elemental factors of production are used in the direct production of goods necessary to satisfy this consumption.

If we ask ourselves the question how, or through what mechanism in society this saving is transmitted to the elemental factors in order that they may be employed in capital production, the answer is, firstly, the price mechanism. If no one saved, the price for directly produced consumption goods would be so high that all factors would be employed in their direct production; however, and this is the important point, we would have no eyeglasses to assist our faulty vision. On the other hand, if saving does take place, the demand for directly produced consumption goods is less and the price is *correspondingly* less so that entrepreneurs will reconsider their techniques of production with the objective of lowering costs. In every case this will result in a more "roundabout" method of production, infinitesimal to be sure at first but gradually gaining in "roundaboutness" through time. Ultimately, after many generations of cost cutting entrepreneurs, the degree of roundaboutness is so great that not only eyeglasses but many other items for consumption are produced at costs which are so low that they would astound the entrepreneurs of the earlier generations. Of course, another way of looking at the same thing is that real incomes rise through time so that our living standard is much higher than that of our ancestors.

In the economically advanced countries, such as Canada, the saving is passed on to the enterprising entrepreneurs through the credit mechanism and the capital market which has been the subject of the chapters preceding. This enhances the entrepreneur's purchasing power, enabling him to acquire the capital goods he thinks he needs. Once more, through the price mechanism, this causes the price level of capital goods to rise, thereby encouraging productive factors into their production. The chain, thus, is complete. It is a combination of both relative prices in the market and some institutional mechanism whereby the savings are made available to entrepreneurs. It matters little what sort of mechanism this might be, varying, as it does, from country to country, but it must exist in some form.

Having established why and how the roundabout (or capitalistic) method of production is worthwhile, Böhm-Bawerk then turns to interest to consider both its nature and the laws which determine and govern it. We can appreciate his work more readily by referring to Chapter 7 where

---

[9] *Positive Theory of Capital*, Libertarian Press, South Holland, Ill., ch. 2, Book 1, p. 11.

[10] *Ibid*., p. 95.

the idea of interest was introduced within a Fisherine time concept. The underlying principle there was that no "rational" individual would forego current liquidity for exactly the same amount of future liquidity. This is not good enough for Böhm-Bawerk. He asks the question *why* do people want more future liquidity than current liquidity? In seeking the answer he arrives at his first two Causes (or Grounds) of interest which lie within the bounds of the human psyche.

The first of these Causes is a basic difference between supply/demand conditions for the present vs. the future. (Actually, in the first two Causes it is only demand conditions which change between the present and future—supply is assumed constant.) Present demand for goods and services can only be satisfied by means of economic activity which involves the "pain" or suffering of work at the present time, and by virtue of the fact that it is "now" pain, it is greater than "future" pain. This is a difficult idea to accept at first sight and Böhm-Bawerk is quick to illustrate his argument. Consider first a younger employee at the beginning of his career and who looks forward to future advancement. His demand for goods is greater now than it will be, hence, his psychological "pain" of work is greater, and, it follows, the "now" goods are more valuable than the future goods.

Strange as it might seem, the older worker in mid-career and at the height of his earning power also has a greater demand for now goods than future goods when he will be likely pensioned off in retirement. The reason for this is that he is busy amassing material goods which will last into his retired future (for instance, paying off the house mortgage). Finally the retired pensioner without much of a future left (it goes without saying) will also have a demand for purely "now" goods. In other words, the whole population will have a preference for present goods so that the utility of present income is greater than the utility of future income.

This leads directly to Böhm-Bawerk's second Ground (or Cause) for interest — "we systematically undervalue our future wants and also the means which serve to satisfy them."[11] This is *not* the same as the first Cause though it may indeed

be related to it. That is, while the first Cause was concerned with the actual demand for goods, which is always greater in the present than in the future, the second is a psychological tendency to underestimate what we will need in the future. To a certain degree it is a human weakness; thus, a laborer may squander his weekly paycheque in drinking only to impose hardship and hunger on himself and his family the rest of the week. This may appear to be an extreme example, but it is not difficult to identify other better examples by simple introspection. We are all aware of the tendency to overspend from present income; in fact, the entire principle of consumer credit is based upon the undervaluation of future wants and, consequently, overvaluation of our future income. Böhm-Bawerk even includes life expectancy in his analysis preferring, as he did, a small gift now to something worth $100,000 when he reaches the age of 100. (Actually he died in 1914 at age 63.)

For this third Cause of interest, Böhm-Bawerk turns to another portion of the market; actually it is concerned more with saving and the fruits thereof. Interest arises from the fact that present goods have a technical superiority over future goods. This is a difficult point to grasp and it derives from the fact that productive factors are more fruitfully applied in the more lengthy, roundabout methods of production. By using saved present goods to supply productive factors (actually nothing more than labour) with their current needs during their employment in the production of capital goods, these present goods become superior for the reason that they make possible future consumer goods which are more plentiful and cheaper. Since the present goods so utilized are derived from saving, the saver is entitled to a reward—interest. Of course, this raises the point why not continuously extend the productive process to infinity? To this question Böhm-Bawerk replied by resorting to the first two psychological Causes of interest — the preference for present goods over future goods which overcomes very quickly the technical superiority which would result *by itself* in huge and ever growing savings. There is a limit, in other words (aside from actual income earned) which checks the capacity of people to save.

We may imagine how the very careful and precise scientific analysis of Böhm-Bawerk must have

---

[11]*Ibid.*, p. 268.

excited considerable thought and discussion on the subject of capital and interest. Certainly the greatest of the Austrian School, he carried the theory of capital much further than either the British or French writers up to his time. But, most important, capital and interest, instead of occupying a subordinate position in economic thinking, as they had with English writers, in the hands of Böhm-Bawerk became not only an integral part of economics, but also assumed a pivotal position in the economic scheme of things. Certainly the futility of the Exchange Bank of Proudhon is much more obvious with the aid of Böhm-Bawerk's penetrating analysis. Likewise we can readily see how inadequate Adam Smith's treatment of capital was.

To show how capital and interest are integrated into the production process, Böhm-Bawerk noted the relationship between the lengthening of production and output. In this way capital becomes a factor of production in a true sense though not an *original* factor of production. He began his analysis with an assumption of a fixed amount of capital (say $50,000) and a fixed annual wage rate ($1,500) in money terms. This capital can be utilized by employing many workers for one year ($50,000/$1,500), less workers for two years ($50,000/$3,000), etc., with the product per worker increasing with the length of the production period. The annual gain (or profit) per worker increases, of course, but it increases at a decreasing rate; therefore, total gain will be maximized when the marginal wage cost ($1,500) equals the marginal product. At that point the gain from capital is maximized and the interest rate is determined. As Böhm-Bawerk expressed it, "the rate of interest. . .is limited and determined by the productivity of the last prolongation of the production period which is still economically permissible."[12] By the terms "limited" and "determined" Böhm-Bawerk meant both a maximum limit to the rate of interest obtainable by a given unit of prolongation and a minimum as set by the next less fruitful prolongation. Here it should be noted that an increase in the wages of workers forces the entrepreneur into a longer period of production, a demonstration of the "Ricardo effect" discussed by Hayek in *Profits, Interest and Investment* and mentioned in Chapter 1.

Without doubt Böhm-Bawerk stands out as the

original thinker who developed capital theory, and certainly very many of the ideas of the Austrian School can be attributed to him. But even as careful and close a scientific thinker as he was there was still much to be done in capital and interest theory. It was Knut Wicksell, the great Swedish economist, who refined capital theory even further, giving it the keen "cutting edge" of a useful tool of analysis. It is always true that no single lifetime is sufficient to produce a theory in finished form; each of the contributors to economic theory draws upon his predecessor.

2. K. Wicksell

While Böhm-Bawerk laid stress on the lengthening of the productive process, thus implying a time relationship, Wicksell developed the concept of time (or waiting) as a producing agent which generated a surplus (interest). His methodology was to use an example of wine which increases in value with time, i.e., time itself becomes a productive factor. Suppose the market value of 4-year-old wine happens to be 100 shillings, 3-year-old wine 90 shillings, and 5 and 6-year-old wine 110 and 120 shillings respectively. Further, suppose that only a fixed amount of capital is available in the community for storing wine which is just sufficient for 4 years. It follows that the rate of interest must be between a maximum 10/90 or 11.1%, and a minimum 10/100 or 10%. Why? Because all the capital must be used and an increment of capital from 3-year to 4-year wine will bring a reward of an additional 10 shillings from 90 to 100, or 11.1%. Further, *if* there were just a little more capital than is just sufficient for 4-year wine, it could bring another 10 shillings, from 100 to 110, or 10%. It follows that $10\frac{1}{2}$% is quite close enough as an approximation to the rate of interest. We can now easily compute the value of new wine which is really the value of wages and rent in viniculture. The formula, just like the present value of bonds, is

$$V_o = \frac{100}{(1.105)^4} = 67 \text{ shillings.}$$

Furthermore, the value of the "wine capital," assuming equal amounts in the process of maturation is

$$K = 67(1 + 1.105 + 1.105^2 + 1.105^3)$$
$$= 314 \text{ shillings.}$$

Now the thrust of Wicksell's argument is as follows: Suppose the savings of the viniculture com-

[12]*Ibid.*, p. 361.

munity should increase so that 5 years maturation could take place. The value of 6-year-old wine is 120 shillings, or, in percentage terms, an increase of 10/110 or 9.1%. This, therefore, is the interest minimum. The maximum is, of course, 10/100 of 10%. Selecting $9\frac{1}{2}$% as the likely value of interest, we can derive the value of wine at year zero (which is the value of wages and rent) as follows:

$$V_o = \frac{100}{(1.095)^5} = 69.88 \text{ shillings.}[13]$$

There are, therefore, *two* phenomena which have resulted—the rate of interest has declined because of the increase in capital, and, most important, the value of wages and rent have increased from 67 shillings to 69.88 shillings.

The raising of the wage rate is known as the "Wicksell Effect" and is an explanation via simple arithmetic of what has been observed consistently in economics. An increase in available capital not only lowers interest but raises wages which in turn tend to "swallow up" some of the savings. The argument here is important from another point of view. Both Böhm-Bawerk and von Thünen before him had asserted that the rate of interest was determined by the marginal productivity of capital—much as any other factor of production. Theoretically, then, the rate of interest could fall to zero if wages and other rewards of factors are held constant and enough capital happened to be at hand. But this cannot be true because wages are not (and cannot be) held constant. The true marginal product of capital is always lower than the rate of interest which is really a *social* marginal product, i.e., a kind of macroeconomic concept.

The rationale behind the Wicksell Effect can be further explored by considering the nature of both capital and labour. Since the analysis really is concerned with market values (as in the case of bonds) we know that increments of capital actually add to an existing pool of capital. This pool exists because it is really stored up labour. Labour, on the other hand, vanishes the moment it is performed. It can, of course, become part of capital and thereby "preserve" itself in which case it ceases to be labour.

It is the fact that capital is stored that causes the

rate of interest to fall with additional increments. The wage rate, however, will not fall unless the number of workers happens to increase. Quite the contrary, since capital is always increasing and workers may not, labour enjoys an "automatic monopoly." This is why in order to use this scarce factor a portion of capital must be used to pay the additional wages that are demanded. A kind of wage absorption of savings is taking place.

This tendency to absorb savings in this way can be counteracted to some degree by the imposition of forced savings through price increases, which, in turn, lower real wages. Any expansion of credit, as we already know, must take place by lowering the rate of interest below what it would ordinarily have been. Manufactured deposits, then, become "artificial savings" and encourage further investment. The process of wage absorption along with the increased capital investment takes place, and it may require several rounds of additional deposit manufacture before prices begin to rise. Eventually the forced savings sequence *will* take place, especially for those incomes which do not rise so fast as prices. Prices of consumer goods will rise because the demand for factors of production in the capital goods industries is continuously increasing with the expansion of credit, thereby depleting the supply of factors for producing consumer goods. A shortage of consumer goods, therefore, is inevitable, and the process of additional liquidity flowing into the hands of workers must mean a lowering of resistance to price increases. Thus, the "forced saving" process finally arrives but it may be longer in coming than one might wish, in the first place, and it strikes incomes other than workers who have been absorbing the capital in the second.

As an outgrowth of his capital theory, the rate of interest which measures the marginal social productivity of capital is clear and precise. Suppose we call this the "natural" rate of interest. It is natural because it is determined by the amount of capital, or savings, on the one hand and the desire of entrepreneurs to maximize their profits on the other. This is the reason for investing in wine or any other type of roundabout production in the first place.

The "natural" rate of interest to Wicksell was the marginal productivity of capital in a moneyless

[13]K. Wicksell, *Lectures on Political Economy, Vol. I,* Routledge and Kegan Paul Ltd., London, 1949, p. 176.

society, a concept inherited directly from Böhm-Bawerk.

Now, at the same time, Wicksell was deeply concerned with banks and the theory of money and the price level. It was necessary, therefore, for him to reconcile what to him were *two* different interest rates, the money rate and the natural rate, and in the process of reconciliation, he developed the dynamic analysis for which he is so well-known. In the final analysis, of course, the money rate and the natural rate are really two different aspects of the same phenomenon, but this Wicksell did not recognize until, perhaps, the latter stages of his career.[14]

> Besides the somewhat too vague and abstract concept of natural rate of interest I have defined the more concrete concept normal rate of interest, i.e., the rate at which the demand for new capital is exactly covered by simultaneous savings.[15]

Following Wicksell, if we have two different interest rates, it is possible for them not to be the same even though they might tend to be equal in the long run. It was the possibility of this divergence of the two rates which led to his dynamic analysis of the business cycle and brought the theory of money from a purely mechanistic Quantity Theory into the heart of the process of economic decision-making. In this there was an undoubted influence on J.M. Keynes whose *Treatise on Money* was yet to be written. In brief, and we need go no further than this, there are "capitalists," so-called, who own bank deposits upon which they earn interest equal to the money rate of interest. Banks, then, loan these funds to entrepreneurs who use the proceeds of the loans to pay their workers and their raw material expenses. The output is sold for an amount equal to the original loan value *plus* an amount equal to the natural rate of interest which, in equilibrium, equals the money

rate of interest. This permits the loan to be repaid plus interest and since the natural rate equals the money rate there is an equilibrium flow. Capitalists, those who own the bank deposits, are the savers who spend from their interest earnings just as everyone else so that there is no "leakage" of funds. In Diagram 10-1, this circular flow can be readily seen. Banks loan to entrepreneurs 100 at 5% interest (money rate). Entrepreneurs pay out this 100 to productive factors who are also "capitalists." Since the natural rate of interest equals the money rate of interest, entrepreneurs receive 105 for their output which exactly equals the banks' loan plus the deposit interest.

Now suppose that, for reasons of productivity increases, the natural rates should exceed the money rate. Entrepreneurs would earn excess profit and proceed to expand their output with the objective of profit maximization. Assuming full employment (this is Wicksell's basic assumption) entrepreneurs would borrow more money from the banks to "pirate" workers from each other. This would raise wages, and, ultimately, prices, with the prospect of further increases in wages and prices as long as banks are willing to supply additional funds at a money rate of interest lower than the natural rate. Ultimately, banks must exhaust their money expansion power, depending upon the reserve ratio, drain of cash, gold, etc., in which case they will raise the money rate of interest to a higher level.

Diagram 10-1

WICKSELL'S CIRCULAR FLOW

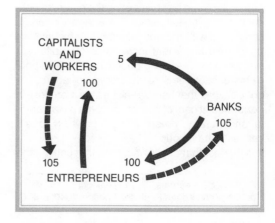

---

[14] It was undoubtedly the experience of World War I which must have convinced Wicksell that prices could rise or fall even if savings and investment were equal; hence, there is really no significance in the difference between the two rates.

[15] Quoted by B. Ohlin in the Prefare to K. Wicksell, *Interest and Prices*, Macmillan and Co. Ltd., 1936, p. xiii.

If banks should raise their money rate above the natural rate, it follows that there must be a net reduction in total money being lent because entrepreneurs will find their profits shrinking due to the additional repayment of loan interest to the bank which is in excess of what they earn. Entrepreneurs must lower wages and prices since consumers will no longer be able to purchase their output at higher prices, and must ultimately, result in reduced employment. This process could also continue until banks somehow are willing to accept lower loan rates, and capitalists, in their turn, agree to accept a lower rate. When this takes place, a "business cycle" is complete.

There are, of course, deficiencies in Wicksell's model, the most important of which is at the very beginning. Why should entrepreneurs not sell their greater product, due to increased productivity, at a *lower* price? This would seem to be a logical outcome of perfect competition in which case they would have to be content with the same level of profits; in this way equilibrium would not be disturbed and the cumulative process could never begin at all. Wicksell later attempted an answer to this criticism.

> Even if it were desired to associate the increase in the quantity of goods with a tendency for a fall in prices, the fall that could on such grounds be expected would be a very small one. More important, it would, so far as I can see, occur only *once and for all*, and it would thus be put completely in the shade by the cumulative effect on prices that is to be ascribed to a difference between the two rates of interest.[16]

It is doubtful, however, that the "answer" is perfectly satisfactory.

One of the great advantages of the hindsight of some fifty-odd years is the capacity to look with a critical eye at the giants of Economics who lived and wrote during the great period of high theory. There is a secondary advantage in this in that there is a heightened appreciation of the difficulties and problems with which they wrestled in those years. After all, these were the formative years of modern Economics as a science.

---

[16]K. Wicksell, *Interest and Prices*, Macmillan and Co. Ltd., London, 1936, p. 142.

Certainly Wicksell's contribution in helping to shape Economics was very great. It was he who first began the analysis of economic dynamics, i.e., the processes of change and how these processes come about, yet the modern reader of his works cannot avoid being struck by the lack of firmness in his ideas and principles. Quite simply, he could not make up his mind.

In retrospect, hindsight bestows a tremendous advantage. We recognize that Wicksell's tentative conclusions marked a crossroads in the stream of economic thought. We can see this because of two almost irreconcilable positions in his thinking which later became the basis for two quite divergent points of view. The first is the capital theory which Wicksell had inherited from Böhm-Bawerk and the second is the concepts of the natural, money, and neutral rates of interest, which, though in embryo stage, were to be developed more completely in the work of J.M. Keynes.

3. Keynes—Treatise on Money

We can see this not only in the ideas and principles which received concrete expression in the *Treatise on Money* but also in the specific references to Wicksell which Keynes made throughout his work. Prior to the publication of the *Treatise*, Keynes would have been considered not only a monetary theorist but a Quantity Theorist inheriting much from Marshall and the Cambridge version of the Quantity Theory. His *Tract on Monetary Reform* was concerned largely with a revision of this Cambridge version; it was, however, purely a revision. By the time of the publication of the *Treatise*, a definite change became apparent in his thinking. What would appear to have taken place was not an abandonment of the Quantity Theory but an integration of it into a more general format along the lines suggested by Wicksell.

The format which he developed consisted of four Fundamental Equations which were really the beginnings of what was later to develop into National Income analysis. The equations were, admittedly, crude in the sense that there was considerable development yet to come; however, the idea was clearly there and once begun there was no stopping its future growth and development. There was no doubt, however, that it was

Wicksell's original concept which was at the heart of the matter.

If we refer once more to Diagram 10-1, it is obvious to modern students of Economics that this is a kind of National Income Income/Expenditure approach. As in all such analyses of a circular type, this suggests an identity, i.e., "something is equal to something else" not because the two somethings are related functionally but because they *are* the same. The identity in this case would appear to be a statement of what is apparent, but if it is obvious, why bother to state it at all? The reason is that it was apparent only to Keynes at first and it required a fairly rigorous exposition to make it similarly apparent to the rest of us.

The best way to look at the equations is to reverse their order, i.e., to begin with the pure identities first. We have, therefore, the price level of consumer goods, P, equal to the wages per unit of output, W_1, plus profits, Q, divided by the output of consumer goods, R.[17]

$$(1) \qquad P = W_1 + \frac{Q}{R}$$

This is, to be sure, an identity, a mere truism as Keynes himself put it. The second equation is also an identity. It states the price level of output as a whole, Π, equals wages per unit of output plus total profits divided by total output.

$$(2) \qquad \Pi = W_1 + \frac{Q}{O}$$

Note carefully that Keynes assumed that W_1 is the same in both (1) and (2).

Continuing the backward analysis of the Fundamental Equations, we consider the next step which is not really an identity at all. This is the relation of profits to both investment and savings. We recall the Wicksell circular analysis which states that investment will proceed when the natural rate of interest exceeds the money rate of interest. This is the same thing as saying that the

marginal product of capital exceeds the cost of borrowing funds from the banks and since the marginal product of capital is a "gross" profit concept which derives from the last unit of time prolongation and the cost of bank loans is the rate of interest on savings, additional investment must proceed from new money. Clearly this new money must go someplace in a circular flow, and if wage costs are constant, it must flow into profits.

A similar situation applies to savings. Here the portion of incomes which are not spent on consumption goods are used to finance a good part (the largest part) of the loans to entrepreneurs and if savings are just sufficient to finance all these loans, there will be no additional excess marginal product of capital in the first place. Only when consumption is high, i.e., savings are insufficient to finance loan investments, does the greater marginal product of capital arise. This is why it is possible to substitute in equations (1) and (2) the difference between savings and investment *(S and I)* for profits to derive equations (3) and (4). Thus,

$$(3) \qquad P = W_1 + \frac{I'-S}{R}$$

I' is defined as the cost of production of new investment goods.

The last version, equation (4), is somewhat more complicated. Keynes' introduction of the value of investment, I, as opposed to the cost of production of investment goods, I', is really what "ties" together the circular process and relates saving and investment. The value of investment depends upon how the public wishes to hold its savings, i.e., suppose the public decides to purchase securities—it is, as Keynes used the term, "bullish." Banks will find themselves short of savings deposits, the value of securities would rise (interest rates would likely fall) and the value of new investment would also rise. In this case the banking system must be prepared to expand the money supply to accommodate entrepreneurs' loan demands. On the other hand, suppose the public is "bearish," i.e., it prefers bank deposits to securities. In this case the value of securities would fall, and the value of new investment would likewise fall. But why should the public prefer deposits? This, according to Keynes, is a decision which the public makes in response to the relative attractiveness of savings deposits, i.e.,

---

[17]The Fundamental Equations are discussed on pages 135-138 of Vol. I, *A Treatise on Money*, Macmillan & Co., London, 1958. Keynes defines his W_1 as $W_1 = \frac{1}{e}W$ with e equal to "efficiency-earnings" and W_1 the rate of earnings per unit of human effort. This refinement is unnecessary for our purpose, but we keep the odd nomenclature W_1 for consistency's sake.

Note the absence of any other factor income than the wages of labour. Profits are simply residuals. This may seem strange to us in a more sophisticated era, but, of course, this was only the beginning.

because interest rates are high.

The result, then, of these equations is to relate the general price level to both the wage costs per unit of output and the value of new investment in relation to savings as follows:

$$(4)\ \Pi = W_1 + \frac{I-S}{O}$$

This is an important idea. It means that the general price level, and the term is subject to the same difficulties of definition as Fisher's general price level in his Equation of Exchange, is determined by wages per unit of output along with the value of investment less the value of savings relative to total output. Of course, since the volume of savings results from decisions of income earners which are quite independent of the value of investment, the price level depends upon *all* the variables in the equation which actually interact with each other.

It was, perhaps, unfortunate that Keynes abandoned this particular approach when he wrote the *General Theory*, concentrating as he did on the problems of the Great Depression and underemployment equilibrium. Certainly equation (4) is rudimentary, but it holds considerable promise for further development.

Everyone would agree that the equation as it stands is a clear demonstration of Keynes' well-known aversion to mathematics. There is an ambiguity between equations (3) and (4) which was never really clarified. We can see this in the fact that both these equations use W_1 but equation (3) uses I' and equation (4) uses I. At the same time, prices of total output Π must include P, prices of consumer goods (determined by I' instead of I) and prices of investment goods. Note also that he did not specifically define any relationship between prices of new investment goods and the prices of consumer goods, preferring instead the loose additive version of equation (4) to arrive at a general price level. Is it conceivable, for example, that the price level, or value, of investment goods could rise without affecting in some way the prices of consumer goods? If the answer to this question is negative then equation (3) must include I in *some* form.

Keeping in mind, then, the rudimentary form in which the equations stand, it is worthwhile quoting a passage from the *Treatise* in the hope of clarifying some of the waters which may appear slightly muddy from the mathematics.

Wicksell conceives of the existence of a "natural rate of interest" which he defines as being the rate which is "neutral" in its effect on the prices of goods, tending neither to raise nor to lower them, and adds that this must be the same rate as would obtain if in a non-monetary economy all lending was in the form of actual materials. It follows that if the actual rate of interest is lower than this prices will have a rising tendency, and conversely if the actual rate is higher. It follows, further that so long as the money-rate of interest is kept below the natural-rate of interest, prices will continue to rise—and without limit. It is not necessary for this result, namely the cumulative rise of prices, that the money-rate should fall short of the natural-rate by an ever-increasing difference; it is enough that it should be and remain, below it.

Whilst Wicksell's expressions cannot be justified as they stand and must seem unconvincing (as they have to Professor Cassel) without further development, they can be interpreted in close accordance with the Fundamental Equation of this Treatise. For if we define Wicksell's natural-rate of interest as the rate at which Saving and the value of Investment are in equilibrium (measured in accordance with the definitions of Chapter 10 above), then it is true that, so long as the money-rate of interest is held at such a level that the value of Investment exceeds Saving, there will be a rise in the price-level of output as a whole above its cost of production, which in turn will stimulate entrepreneurs to bid up the rates of earnings above their previous level and this upward tendency will continue indefinitely so long as the supply of money continues to be such as to enable the money-rate to be held below the natural-rate as defined.[18]

This rather lengthy quoted passage expresses more completely what Keynes had in mind than his mathematical equations. We note in the passage that the supply of money must continue to expand as long as the money rate is below the natural rate (or investment exceeds savings). This is the central point of his argument — an expansion of the money supply will increase prices not necessarily in the mechanistic Quantity

---

[18]*Ibid*., pp. 197-8.

Theory of Money format but through its influence on investment, and investment, in turn, depends upon the rate of profit. But there is also something else involved—the bullishness or bearishness of the public. Money, that is, may flow into financial circulation leaving the goods "circulation" unaffected; indeed, an outflow of funds from financial circulation (bearishness) may increase prices and profits as well.

But *still*, despite his careful development of the idea of the supply of money affecting prices through investment, Keynes was not prepared yet to completely abandon the mechanistic Quantity Theory. He noted that even under condition of equilibrium when $I = I' = S$ we can *still* have rising prices. He concluded his Chapter 10 by developing his Fundamental Equations purely on the basis of money and velocity deliberately to show a "family relationship to Professor Irving Fisher's familiar equation."[19]

4. Hayek

The second stream of economic thought which developed from Wicksell's writings was really a continuation of the Austrian School of Böhm-Bawerk to emerge as a fully developed theory of capital under the careful and precise analysis of F. von Hayek. Just as with Keynes, it is not possible to do justice to the great work and contributions he has made to "high theory" in a single chapter. All that one may hope is that the violence done to his work by the process of condensing and distilling is minimized. The paragraphs which follow are fundamentally a description of Professor Hayek's simple "point input-point output" case which is discussed in Chapter 14 of his *Pure Theory of Capital* and which is only the beginning of his exhaustive treatment of capital theory.

Both Böhm-Bawerk and Wicksell considered the rate of interest to be determined by the marginal product of time prolongation of the production process. But this does not quite fit the facts in the sense that interest on savings accounts, for instance, may be a long way from entrepreneural decision-making, yet somehow there is a direct relationship with the marginal product of capital. Our first task, therefore, following Hayek, is to establish this relationship. Of necessity the analysis assumes a background of a few mathe-

matical fundamentals; however, by careful examination of the diagrams the basic prinicples should be clear with only the minimum mathematical knowledge.

Money as a bank savings account grows at a rate of interest compounded. This may be annual, semi-annual, or even monthly depending on the bank or financial intermediary. Most of us are sufficiently familiar with the compounding process, which means earning interest on interest, that we may begin the analysis with an imaginary bank which offers interest compounded not monthly, not weekly, but continuously. This is not so unusual as it might appear because compounding in this way actually is a remarkably close approximation to monthly compounding—so close that the gain in analytical convenience relative to the sacrifice of realism is worth it. We can do this by using the number e raised to a certain power. The power is determined by the rate of interest multiplied by the time the deposit is left in the bank. Thus the value of a deposit left in a bank for 20 years at 6% per year is as follows:[20]

$$V = De^{.06(20)} \text{ or } V = D(e)^{rt}$$

We can easily show this in Diagram 10-2. A savings deposit, D, is entered at time 0 which will increase in value with the passage of time in accordance with the compound interest function e^{rt}. We assume, for simplicity, that all savings are deposited with banks in this way and earn the same interest.

The concept of increments of production due to time prolongation alone is a little more awkward to grasp; after all, labour and raw material are the true elemental productive factors. What this means is simply that these factors are applied at a constant rate to a certain piece of capital equipment, and as time passes a flow of output results.

The situation can be best illustrated in terms of an oil well because the application of productive factors is separate in time from the actual output. Imagine an oil well which is the result of a lengthy process of exploration and development, with everything in place ready to begin production. Imagine further that the moment has arrived to turn a valve which will set the stream of oil

---

[19]*Ibid*., p. 150.

[20]For a demonstration of the close approximation of the continuous compounding function to monthly compounding, a deposit in the bank for 20 years at 6% compounded monthly is
$D(1.005)^{240} = 3.31D$, or $D(e)^{.06(20)} = 3.32D$

Diagram 10-2

INTEREST RATE DETERMINATION

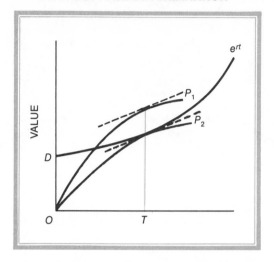

erty of the number e is useful in describing this function which would appear mathematically as something like the following:

$$V = It(e)^{-s(t)}$$

The value of output for a specific capital investment is equal to the value of the input, I, multiplied by time, t, "discounted" by means of e raised to an $s(t)$ power. The coefficient, s, simply determines the rate at which time influences the discounting. It is the production equivalent of the rate of interest in the compound interest growth function.

As will be recognized from Diagram 10-2, profits will be maximized when the slope of production function, P, just equals the slope of the compound interest function. In other words the marginal rate of prolongation of production ($s(t)$) just equals the *compounded* rate of interest ($r(t)$) for the deposit, D. This occurs at a time T as indicated by the dashed parallel lines. It is also apparent that excess profits are being earned so that additional investments should take place in the industry until the P curve shifts downward through the force of competition to assume the position P_2. This would represent the equilibrium point where the proceeds of the investment project are just sufficient to repay the borrowed bank deposit, D, plus accrued interest. The rate of interest is determined by this relation between the demand for and supply of borrowed funds.

A more interesting and realistic example involves a scarcity of funds as opposed to a shortage of investment outlets which is implied in Diagram 10-2. In this case it is savings which are scarce, and, as a consequence, changes in demand for deposits are rather quickly reflected in the rate of interest. Diagram 10-3 shows three different interest rates on the compound interest curves. At a point in time, T_1, the curve R_1 is tangent to the output curve P_1. At that particular interest rate which generates R_1 investment projects (oil wells, factories, etc.) generate a value, V, of output which is in equilibrium with the rate of interest. This equilibrium exists when the marginal rate of prolongation of P_1 just equals the rate of interest compounded (the slope of R_1) with no excess profits.

Suppose, because of a heavy demand for capital vis-à-vis a scarce supply, the rate of interest rises to a level to produce a compound interest curve R_2. The investment project P_1 is now no longer feasible. It must be abandoned in favour of pro-

flowing. As the valve is turned, the oil flows rapidly at first with the value of production rising steeply in the manner similar to P_1 (Diagram 10-2). As time passes, the value of production (cumulative) increases but with steadily decreasing increments because of the declining pressure within the pool of oil itself. It is simply a matter of time until the pressure exhausts itself, or, to express it differently, time is the only remaining productive "factor," the other genuine factors having already been used in exploration and development of the well. The longer the well is in production the more is produced, but the marginal product due to a given unit of time (or "prolongation") is declining.

The same analysis can be applied to any piece of capital equipment, e.g., a factory; in this case, however, the other productive factors are applied *simultaneously* with time. In the process of production the machinery wears out faster or more slowly depending on whether the factory is run "flat out" or more slowly just as an oil well can run with its valve wide open or partially open.

We can describe the shape of the P curve in Diagram 10-2 as an exponential function which changes its slope continuously with time, in this case, meaning "factor time" or the amount of time in which a specific unit of a factor of production is locked into a waiting period. Once again the prop-

Diagram 10-3

INTEREST RATE CHANGES AND EFFECTS

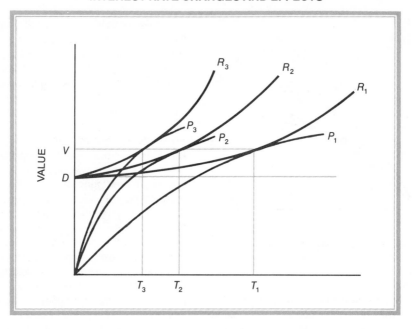

ject P_2 which matures much more quickly than project P_1. This is apparent from the point of tangency to the curve R_2 at T_2. Finally, a still higher rate, R_3, results in project type P_3 which reaches its maturity-equilibrium point at time T_3.

We have now reached a stage in our analysis of the highest importance. All three equilibrium points result in the same value of production. The longer, more roundabout process of production P_1 will certainly produce a greater quantity of output at a lower price simply because at a specific low price there is no *other* method of generating that output value. In order to produce this output, market interest rates, R_1, must be sufficiently low so that entrepreneurs may be able to borrow the sum, D, at a low rate. Failing this, they will seek the same amount of funds at higher rate, R_2. But this means a less roundabout, or more direct, method of production so that the time for the production process will become T_2, and, most important, higher prices for a smaller amount of output will result.

In general, the shorter the period of production the greater the degree of "labour intensity." Certainly, the shorter the production the less capital

intensive is the productive process. To express the concept in terms of a factory producing certain consumer goods, the entrepreneur will refrain from selecting a specific machine which would increase output, but the increase will not bring sufficient returns to cover the cost of the machine. Hand labour with a higher market price for the product is preferred. Even though less productive, hand labour is economically more efficient.

It is now possible to see more clearly the results of changes in interest rates on the production planning of entrepreneurs. Lower interest rates will encourage more lengthy, roundabout, capital-intensive techniques which are generally labour saving. Higher interest rates, on the other hand, will encourage more direct production of consumer goods using more labour intensive production techniques. This is in accord with Professor Hayek's "Ricardo Effect" discussed briefly in Chapter 1.

Higher prices of directly produced consumer goods, on the other hand, *encourage* direct output by lowering the real cost of labour, the more intensively used factor. The P curves rise more steeply with the increasing value of total output, and in this way, production is directed toward the output of directly produced consumer goods. On the other hand, lower prices of directly produced consumer goods, relative to more "roundabout" goods, encourage the longer productive techniques.

We can see now how the entire structure of demand for capital develops within the pricing structure of the economy itself, and how this, in turn, affects interest rates. The beginning of the process is the actual community's savings which consumers elect to perform. By saving they are reducing the pressure of demand for consumer goods, and this, in turn, lowers the prices of these consumer goods. The additional saving also lowers the interest rate so that entrepreneurs recognize both the lower price of labour intensive consumer goods as well as the lower cost of capital. This encourages cost saving productive techniques by more roundabout methods of production which means in turn that the demand for investment goods rises adding a price stimulus to the additional production of these goods. Labour that is displaced by lower consumer goods production is therefore re-employed in the investment goods industries.

As a result, there are two necessary qualifications for the free market system to operate successfully. The first is flexible relative prices. Relative prices of consumer goods must be capable of downward as well as upward adjustment in the same way as prices of investment goods. This is essential to the efficiency of the market's operation as an indicator of the correct structure of production. The second is mobility of labour. Workers must be prepared to move from one industry to another, seeking, we must add, higher real wages with each move, for only in that way can labour as a factor of production be applied with its maximum efficiency. Certainly, immobility of labour combined with the threat of strikes as pressure for higher wages reduces efficiency.

A macroeconomic concept of a general level of prices obscures the important function of individual market prices in directing the factors of production into their most efficient use. Suppose, for example, that the prices of "roundabout" produced consumer goods happen to be relatively high because of a great demand for these types of goods — great, that is, relative to demand for goods produced directly by productive factors.

Suppose further that the rate of interest is kept artifically low by means of a central bank policy of easy money. The incentives, therefore, exist for "laying in" further roundabout techniques of production, but these happen to be generally labour saving. The consequence is structural unemployment in the sense that the productive system itself is no longer capable of providing enough jobs.

At the same time that unemployment results from structural maladjustments, another phenomenon is taking place. We recall that the assumption was made at the outset that prices of roundabout consumer goods were high in relation to directly produced consumer goods. Such goods are often consumer durables, automobiles, appliances and the like which are heavy users of raw material and resources. But, being roundabout, they require an accumulation of capital which can be provided in either of two ways — saving on the part of the public or an expansion of deposits through an easy money policy. The latter is really a kind of "false" savings since no one, at the moment of investment, is undergoing the "pain" of waiting. An excessive consumption of goods, therefore, for which we have not saved and to which we are not entitled, is taking place.

Ultimately a *forced* savings will be imposed upon a sector of the public whose incomes have not risen so fast as prices, and prices *must* rise as a result of the great demand created by the desire for excessive consumption. But, unfortunately, we are not yet finished. The very rise in prices of roundabout goods encourages further "laying in" of investment for additional production. This again puts pressure on scarce capital and tends to force up interest rates unless a central bank easy money policy continues. We, therefore, move into a second round of inflationary demand.

But the forced savings imposed on incomes which fail to keep pace with each successive round of inflation is by no means the only source of finance for capital investment. Those members of the public who have accumulated past savings discover that the real value of their savings is considerably less in terms of purchasing power for the reason that interest rates are simply too low to keep pace with the inflation rate. This is especially true when the tax system is such that interest net of *tax* is substantially lower than rates of inflation. In this way, inflation combined with taxes effectively imposes a confiscatory tax on savings as well as upon those incomes which are relatively fixed. It is from these two sources that the *real* finance of investment is derived. We shall have occasion to consider the consequences and results which flow from Austrian capital theory again in the final section of this chapter. At the moment the important Hayekian principle to keep in mind is that the structure of investment is influenced by interest rates (as opposed to a single "rate"). This is the central idea of the modern Austrian School.

In terms of our modern capital market, corporate business enterprise may be forced to tailor its capital investment in accordance not only with its own requirements but also with the particular financing instruments within the market itself. The reason for this is really a combination of both cost and risk. Equity financing does not require repayment of capital and so long as real capital expansion means a corresponding increase in earning capacity, the sale of additional shares would seem, other things being equal, to be the ideal form of financing. But other things are not equal and equity markets may not prove capable of providing sufficient funds for the purpose. In this case debt financing with some kind of option for conversion into stocks might prove sufficiently attractive to investors.

Thus, while we ordinarily think of corporate debt as appropriate for financing projects with a promise of a cash flow sufficient to service the debt, including repayment of principle, this may be the *only* method of raising capital. To corporate managers this means assuming a higher risk and therefore is the equivalent of a higher cost of capital, or, in terms of our analysis, higher interest rates. Such decisions of corporate management as to how capital will be structured relative to the obligations incurred in the process of acquiring the finance are precisely what is involved in the simple "point-input, point-output" case discussed above.

5. Keynes, The General (?) Theory

The Austrian theory discussed above reached its climax in the *Pure Theory of Capital* of Professor Hayek which was first published in 1941. The basic ideas incorporated and developed therein, were, however, well-known long before. It is unfortunate that they never became integrated into English economic theory, partially, perhaps, because of the language problem (although the Wil-

liam Smart translations of Böhm-Bawerk's major works were available long ago in 1890 and 1891) and partly, one presumes, because they were not clearly understood. Alfred Marshall in a footnote in his *Principles* (referred to by Keynes in the *General Theory*) criticized Böhm-Bawerk for laying too great stress on the higher productivity of lengthy periods of production noting that roundaboutness does not nessarily guarantee increased productivity. Keynes also observed " . . . Some, probably most, lengthy processes would be physically very inefficient for there are such things as spoiling or wasting with time."[21]

There is almost a naïveté in a criticism of this kind which can be answered in two ways: firstly, and obviously, a specific, lengthy, roundabout technique of production would not be undertaken unless it were more profitable than an alternative less roundabout method, i.e., all production techniques must be feasible in the sense of being more profitable before being undertaken; otherwise, they would be scrapped in the planning stage. The second is that the investment process involves not merely "time" alone but time *weighted* by the amount of a factor input. Thus, of two production techniques, one may involve a short waiting period (or actual passage of time) and heavy labour input, and another a long waiting period and a light labour input. Which of the two is likely to be the more roundabout? The former because so much more of the factor is involved in the shorter waiting process. "Time" in this sense is not mere passage of clock time but a weighted value.[22]

In Chapter 16 of the *General Theory*, "Sundry Observations on the Nature of Capital," Keynes made quite clear his own position on the nature of the returns of capital.

> It is much preferable to speak of capital as having a yield over the course of its life in excess of its original cost, than as being *productive*. For the only reason why an asset offers a prospect of yielding during its life services having an aggregate value greater than its initial supply price is be-

---

[21]J.M. Keynes, *General Theory of Employment, Interest and Money,* Macmillan, London, 1949, p. 214 by permission of the International Economic Association and Macmillan, London and Basingstoke.

[22]For a complete discussion of this point see Chapter 11, Hayek, *op. cit.*

cause it is scarce; and it is kept scarce because of the competition of the rate of interest on money.[23]

This is strange indeed. Capital earns a surplus not because it is productive but because it is scarce—a kind of payment as economic rent. But even rent, as J.B. Clark had explained in 1899, is earned because of the excess of production of earlier doses of capital over the marginal dose. It has its foundation, in other words, in productivity.

To the impartial observer it must seem incredible that Keynes would have rejected in one short chapter the careful scientific work of his many predecessors and colleagues of the Austrian School, especially on the basis of such apparently flimsy logic. Why, then, did he do it? By severing the relationship between capital and productivity he likewise severed the connection between the rate of interest and productivity, and this it was necessary for him to do before his structure of aggregate demand could be erected.[24]

Keynes and the Austrian School were not always so far apart however. In the *Treatise*, prices of consumer goods were seen as determined by both wages and the decisions of the public to save. (See the fundamental equation (3) above.) In that equation an increase in the desire to save, unless counteracted by a corresponding increase in investment, would result in lower prices of consumer goods. In the *General Theory*, on the other hand, prices are seen to be determined individually by supply and demand in the marketplace; there is, however, a general price level which depends upon the relationship between aggregate effective demand and aggregate sup-

ply. Aggregate demand is made aggregate *effective* demand with the inclusion of money.

The impact of any change in the money supply on the general price level depends upon a fairly complex set of demand and supply elasticities which determine the elasticity of aggregate supply and which may be summarized as the consequence of the level of unemployment within the economy. The emphasis on the general level of prices seems to place Keynes once more in the Quantity Theory of Money camp, although in a much more sophisticated version. As such, his "general price level" is exposed to the same criticism as Fisher's price level, i.e., does it really exist, and if so, has it any economic meaning other than a statistical index number? The importance of a relative price structure determined in the marketplace to serve as an indicator of the direction toward which productive factors should go has disappeared.

Another break which Keynes made was with his own work in the area of interest rates. In this regard it may be best to include a direct, though somewhat lengthy, quotation from the *General Theory* itself.

> In my *Treatise on Money* I defined what purported to be a unique rate of interest, which I called the *natural* rate of interest— namely, the rate of interest which, in the terminology of my *Treatise*, preserved equality between the rate of saving (as there defined) and the rate of investment. I believed this to be a development and clarification of Wicksell's "natural rate of interest," which was, according to him the rate which would preserve the stability of some, not quite clearly specified, price-level.
>
> I had, however, overlooked the fact that in any given society there is, on this definition, a *different* natural rate of interest for each hypothetical level of employment. And, similarly, for every rate of interest there is a level of employment for which that rate is the "natural" rate, in the sense that the system will be in equilibrium with that rate of interest and that level of employment. Thus it was a mistake to speak of *the* natural rate of interest or to suggest that the above definition would yield a unique value for the rate of interest irrespective of the level of employment. I had not then understood that, in certain conditions, the system could be in equilibrium with less than full employment.

---

[23]Keynes, *Ibid.*, p. 213.

[24]In the words of Professor Hayek, a close friend of Keynes, "though a genius, his (Keynes') ignorance of anything but Marshallian economics was incredible." This explains the very serious shortcoming of Keynes' otherwise brilliant work, capital theory.

Keynes' view of the rate of interest, however, did not originate with the writing of the *General Theory*. Hayek observed that his first clash with Keynes occurred in 1928 on the very issue of interest. It was because of Hayek's refusal to yield ground on this issue, so he believes, that he won the respect of Keynes. The clash, incidentally, would have occurred during the preparation of the *Treatise on Money* when Keynes was involved with Wicksellian interest.

I am now no longer of the opinion that the concept of a "natural" rate of interest, which previously seemed to me a most promising idea, has anything very useful or significant to contribute to our analysis. It is merely the rate of interest which will preserve the *status quo*; and, in general, we have no predominant interest in the *status quo* as such.[25]

In the first (and equally lengthy) quotation from the *Treatise* noted above, Keynes made it clear that if the rate of interest is held below the natural rate, prices will rise. (Unemployment was ignored.) In this quotation from the *General Theory* he rejects the natural rate of interest which equates savings and investment because this could occur at levels of employment which are less than full. It was aggregate demand that really mattered, not the rate of interest as such, and the deficiency of aggregate demand was responsible for the level of unemployment which existed. Increased aggregate demand and unemployment would disappear. But this could not be done simply by lowering the money rate of interest below the natural rate since, in Keynes' "new" view, there was a different natural rate for every level of employment. All that could be accomplished, therefore, by lowering the money rate of interest would be an increase in prices but no increase in employment.

The reason for the failure of effective demand to Keynes was the failure of investment which, in turn, was the consequence of a collapse in the marginal efficiency of capital. This Keynes defined as "being equal to that rate of discount which would make the present value of the series of annuities given by the returns *expected* from the capital-asset during its life just equal to its supply price (or cost of production)."[26] Further, this capital asset must be a marginal asset in the sense that its rate of discount (actually a rate of return to the entrepreneur) is the least profitable. The amount of investment will be determined when this rate of return to the marginal unit of capital just equals the rate of interest. Armed with this concept Keynes was clearly in a position to show why investment could decline through general pessimism, etc., for the reason that the marginal efficiency of capital is an expectational phenomenon, and when it falls short of the cost of borrowed money (the rate of interest), entrepreneurs will cut back investment to reduce aggregate demand via the familiar multiplier mechanism.

The last "link" in Keynes' chain of causation in the system was the rate of interest itself which was the original source of contention between Hayek and Keynes. Interest, quite different from the interest of the *Treatise*, was purely the consequence of demand for money, a present phenomenon which is determined purely by liquidity preference. "The rate of interest is not the 'price' which brings into equilibrium the demand for resources to invest with the readiness to abstain from present consumption. It is the 'price' which equilibrates the desire to hold wealth in the form of cash with the available quantity of cash..."[27]

The break with the Austrian theory of capital is, then, complete and almost irreconcilable. Clearly the conclusion to be developed from the Keynesian system, despite his own words of caution on page 173 of the *General Theory*, is to lower the rate of interest to encourage investment, and, in turn, stimulate employment.[28] But this solution is at best a short-term measure because a lower rate of interest will, according to Hayek, alter the structure of capital by encouraging roundaboutness. Eventually the stimulation of investment in this way must involve a collision between the necessity for increased aggregate demand to create more employment and the structure of capital investment which *discourages* additional employment through a limitation on the technique of directly produced consumer goods which is labour intensive. We are on a perpetual treadmill —a "tiger by the tail"— just one step ahead of unemployment.

B. Long-run vs. Short-term

It is possible to attempt a reconciliation between

---

[25]Keynes, *op. cit.*, pp. 242-3.
[26]Keynes, *op. cit.*, p. 135.

[27]Keynes, *General Theory*, p. 167.
[28]This is the famous caution that if we seek to stimulate economic activity by increasing the money supply and lowering the rate of interest, "there's many a slip 'twixt the cup and the lip."

Hayek and the *General Theory*, which was not really "general" at all but highly specific, on the basis of a long vs. short-term analysis. The Marginal Efficiency of Capital is expectational involving what can be foreseen for the future, and investment plans will be made and carried out in accordance with these expectations. We can, however, envision a process of abandonment of the less efficient production techniques (including those already in place) as expectations are revised, ultimately to arrive at a fairly reasonable estimate of the true marginal product of time prolongation (the slope of the *P* function in Diagrams 10-2 and 10-3). By the time, then, that investment plans have assumed a permanent form, something approaching equilibrium vis-à-vis the rate of interest (or set of rates) appropriate to the investment may be achieved. Since Keynes was concerned only with the short-term in his *"General"* Theory, we can accept this interpretation of the Marginal Efficiency of Capital as being under a constant state of revision.

Let us suppose, then, that an easy money policy is followed by the Bank of Canada which can lower interest rates for short-term loans and securities. Long-term rates may, and will likely be, unaffected. It is quite possible for entrepreneurs to borrow short and refinance on a continuing basis within the planning horizons of their marginal efficiencies of capital so long as the cost of borrowing, the short interest rate, is below their expected rate of return.

In the long-run, the structure of investment must adjust itself to such a series of short-term, easy money policies if they are consistently followed. A highly capital intensive form of capital investment must therefore result. At the same time the additional funds made available to the public via the easy money policies of the central bank will provide the necessary purchasing power to finance a living standard to which the public aspires but for which it has not actually saved. As a nation we want the consumer products at the end of a roundabout production technique but we are unwilling to undergo the pain of saving to provide, in real terms, for the capital investment which has been laid down.

There still, however, remains a matter which is more difficult to reconcile and that is the Keynesian interpretation of Aggregate Demand, especially in the form that it is currently used in econometric models. In the famous Keynesian identity,[29]

$$Y = C + S$$
$$Y = C + I$$
$$I = S$$

investment always equals saving. There is nothing at all unique about such a statement because it is purely a tautology. But it was precisely this "static" analysis of Keynes which came under attack by the Stockholm School shortly after the publication of the *General Theory*. Keynes had not sufficiently developed the idea that it is what people *wish* to save that really matters as well as what business *wishes* to invest. When seen in this light, such matters as the excess of savings (the paradox of thrift) or the finance of investment from "new money," are really quite meaningless. Of course savings will always match that investment which is financed by additional bank loans for the reason that the public will have extra income on hand. Should the public attempt to spend its additional income on goods which are not yet available, rising prices will transfer the burden of savings to fixed incomes as "forced savings."[30]

There is also something else in the concept of aggregate demand, $C + I$, which does not hold true in a dynamic sense; the components of aggregate demand are not additive except in the purely *ex post* (using the Stockholm School terminology) context. Let us consider the consumption component, C. We know that it is the structure of consumption, whether directly produced goods, roundabout goods, etc., which determines the structure of investment. This is done via the price mechanism. It follows that in anything but a purely static sense, I, investment, is functionally related to consumption itself. In a word, I and C cannot be simply added together to arrive at a level of aggregate demand.

Furthermore, a decision to save is a decision not to consume. But, not to consume what? The particular item which is not consumed is in surplus and its market price will fall. This will direct investment away from that particular item into

---

[29]Keynes, *op. cit.*, p. 63.
[30]B. Ohlin, "Some Notes on the Stockholm Theory of Savings and Investment," *Economic Journal*, Vol. XLVII, 1937. Reprinted in *Readings in Business Cycle Theory*, Allen and Unwin, London, 1950, p. 87.

other areas in which consumers have stronger preferences so that both components, C and S, influence the structure of investment, and this, in turn, determines its size. For example, Canadians have a strong preference for consumer durables which are financed largely by consumer credit—automobiles, television, appliances, etc. The output of these goods (those which are produced domestically) require large expenditures for capital equipment in the roundabout technique of production. The use of consumer credit, which is really contractual saving after the purchase, means that some other consumer goods will not be purchased during the post-purchase savings period. In this way the structure of consumption will not only determine the level of savings but also the type of investment as well.

What we might refer to as "genuine" savings, i.e., savings for the purpose of acquiring additional future liquidity also reduces consumption, and, in addition, makes available more funds for investment. In this way, the market rate of interest is less than it would otherwise be; savings to repay consumer debt, on the other hand, have no effect on interest rates unless there is a net increase in consumer credit through time. In this case, it would add to the pressure of demand for funds from the capital market and increase market rates of interest.

Since all the components of aggregate demand mutually interact it is not possible to express them all with just positive signs alone. Any change in one component will have its reaction on another in the complete adjustment process. Aggregation by addition is only possible after the adjustment process is complete and this may require more or less time depending upon the speed of entrepreneural decision-making, consumers' reaction to changes in income, etc. In sum, the whole concept of aggregate demand which has been expressed as additive in macroeconomics even when it includes very many components and subcomponents is only a rough approximation of reality in the shortest-term only, and is certainly not appropriate for forecasting beyond anything but one or two years hence, depending of course upon the speed of adjustment of each of the variables to each other.

To this point we have been concerned with the effect of interest rate changes on entrepreneural demand for investment. We now consider the other side of the coin to examine the impact of price and interest changes on those who must provide the wherewithal for investment. In the Economic literature, this analysis has been known by various names, but, for consistency, we will use the simple title, Wealth Effect.

The years of the Great Depression were characterized by considerable debate amongst academic economists—a debate that never reached a conclusion. It was, in fact, not until after Keynes' death in April, 1946 that academic economists began to genuinely swing toward the view that there might just be a genuine Keynesian Revolution in economic thinking after all. It was shortly thereafter that the term "macroeconomics" came into general use and the concept of national income and its components as an analytical and regulatory device became popular.[31] In particular, the idea that national income aggregates could be manipulated and adjusted with the objective of ensuring full employment and the maximum of economic welfare became current with the publication of the famous "Beveridge Report."[32] It was then, too, that Keynes became a "saint." However, all the academic economists were still not convinced and one of the last "holdouts" was A. C. Pigou, professor emeritus at the University of Cambridge. His concern was the Keynesian assumption of a downward rigidity of money wages and its implications, and it is really his argument which concerns us in this section.[33]

As a first approximation, we can begin with the Pigou version of the Quantity Theory of Money which was discussed in Chapter 1. In that presentation it was shown that the demand for money was a rectangular hyperbola which related the inverse of the price level of goods to the amount of money. See Diagram 10-4.

Now, the nature of the great debate between Keynes and his followers and Pigou and the clas-

---

[31]Kenneth Boulding used and defined the term "macroeconomics" in *Economic Analysis*, published by H. Hamilton, London, 1948.

[32]Sir William Beveridge, *Full Employment in a Free Society*, Allen and Unwin Ltd., 1944. It was in this report that the extension and concern of the State in the purpose of control of the economy was argued.

[33]The argument here is principally that presented by Don Patinkin, "Price Flexibility and Full Employment," *American Economic Review*, Vol. 38, (1948), pp. 543-64. Reprinted in *Readings in Monetary Theory*, Allen and Unwin Ltd., London, 1952, p. 252.

Diagram 10-4

DEMAND FOR MONEY

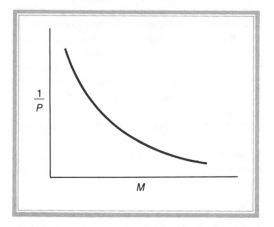

sical economists turned round a single issue: Is it possible for full employment to be restored by means of flexible prices and wages? To the Keynesian the answer was negative, for, as discussed above, equilibrium at less than full employment was quite possible, depending upon the level of aggregate demand. Pigou and G. Haberler in his *Prosperity and Depression* argued to the contrary, that savings was a function of interest rates, income, and real money balances as follows:

$$S = s\left(r, Y, \frac{M}{P}\right)$$

When prices fall the propensity to save is satisfied so that demand for consumer goods would rise again and thereby increase employment.

The Keynesian argument, on the other hand, was that savings are insensitive to the rate of interest in the first place and that they depend entirely upon the level of real income in the second.

$$S = f(Y)$$

If this is true, there is no automatic mechanism by which full employment could be achieved. In the Pigou version, however, full employment could be reached by satisfying the desire to save by means of a falling price level and a consequent higher real value of money balances.

It is unfortunate that Pigou, once he had established his argument regarding flexible wages and prices, decided to destroy it in his concluding paragraphs. Having asserted that falling wages, prices, and interest rates will be checked by the "stock of property," which in terms of consumption goods grows larger until full employment equilibrium is once more established, he proceeded to note that no government would ever permit such a catastrophic fall in prices and wages so that his automatic mechanism designed to ensure full employment could never be utilized on the "chequer board of actual life."[34]

However, in his classic paper Patinkin developed what he termed the "Pigou Effect" by considering that in our society there are both creditors and debtors and when the money supply, as it does, consists of loans and corresponding deposits (or cash in circulation against these loans as in Great Britain), any price decline places an enormous burden on the debtor who must repay in more expensive currency, but for the creditor, the corresponding gain is considerable. Thus, the Pigou effect would largely cancel because at the same time that those who gain, the creditors, spend more as their savings propensities are satisfied, the losers, the debtors, would be forced to increase their savings considerably by spending less so as to pay back their costly debt. This would be true *except* in the case of government debt, because money balances which consist of fiat currency (interest-free government debt) bonds, etc., would genuinely increase in real value with falling prices since there is no corresponding debt in the private sector. This would result in a genuine Pigou Effect.

Under any circumstances, wages did prove in the end to be "sticky" downwards so that it was not possible to lower money wages; hence, the controversy was finally laid to rest. Keynes' original prescription was that a flexible wage policy could be better achieved by what amounted to the same thing, a flexible money policy.[35] Post-Keynesian economists generally adhered to this idea, and, indeed, events did seem to bear out their hypothesis. With the onset of the post-war inflation, however, it became clear that prices and wages were not symmetric, i.e., though they were

[34]A. C. Pigou, "Economic Progress in a Stable Environment," *Economica*, New Series, 14 (1947), 180-88. Reprinted in AEA Series, *Readings In Monetary Theory*, Allen and Unwin Ltd., London, 1952, p. 241.
[35]Keynes, *op. cit.*, p. 266.

likely inflexible downward both were flexible upward.

II. THE WEALTH EFFECT

A. Real Balances

Certainly the position of the classical economists left much to be desired. In the Quantity Theory of Money, which was really the theoretical underpinning of their analysis, there was no functional relationship between money and the price level. Neither Fisher's velocity nor Pigou's k adequately served this purpose because there was always an implicit assumption that no rational individual demanded money for its own sake. Demand for money was only to get rid of it by spending, and, therefore, money was neutral in the sense that it had no impact upon real income at all, only the nominal value of prices and incomes. Professor Patinken later, in *Money, Interest, and Prices*, criticized this position of the classical economists, particularly their assumption that money is neutral. They had assumed that as the price level of goods and services rose, the demand for money would increase by the same proportionate amount. In elasticity terms, $E = -1$, or unit elasticity of money demand as shown in Diagram 10-4. Always the assumption which underlies this position is that no one wants money for the sake of having money (except misers).

But this is not the case. As has been argued consistently in the chapters preceding, money does indeed serve a useful purpose and this useful purpose is the need for holding current liquidity in the form of real balances. Suppose we have the demand for money curves as shown in Diagram 10-5. Now the demand for money assumes a shape different from that of Pigou's rectangular hyperbola since price increases of goods do not generate equi-proportionate increases in demand. In A of Diagram 10-5, an increase in prices results in a less than proportionate increase in demand for money; whereas in B the opposite is true. The reasoning underlying these two different demands for money curves is that in A, it may be possible to "economize" in the use of current liquidity, hence, less money will be required as real balances. In B, the

opposite may be true; more current liquidity is required because of a price change so that demand for money as real balances may rise proportionately more than prices.

Considering real balances in this way makes it possible to attach, for the first time, a concrete meaning to the "general price level," which, until now, really made little sense. Now, money is a commodity which may be inferior (Section B) or superior (Section A), and if it is a superior good, a fall in prices of commodities will mean less of a demand for commodities and more of a demand for money, hence, downward price stability is not possible. Conversely, rising prices can mean instability upward if money is an inferior good (Section B).

We can see this in our own analysis of offer curves in Chapter 2 above. When consumers' demand for current liquidity is inelastic, so that as prices of commodities rise the buyers' demand for money rises by less than the sellers' demand for money, buyers' offer curves (the complement of demand for current liquidity) will be elastic and price instability will be the result. In Patinkin's terms, money is an inferior good. Conversely, if money is a superior good, offers of current liquidity will be less when prices fall, hence, prices become unstable downward.

Whether or not money is superior or inferior, real balances *are* affected by price change. Current liquidity will rise or fall in response to price changes as the public adjusts its liquidity structure. We can see this more readily by reference once more to the liquidity structure equation discussed in Chapter 8. Suppose we consider liquidity in real terms, i.e., liquidity divided by the price level.

$$(1)\quad \frac{L_1}{P} + L_2 = \frac{L_c}{P} + \frac{L_{f0}}{(1 + r_0)^t} + \frac{L_{f1}}{(1 + r_1)^t} \cdots \frac{L_{fn}}{(1 + r_n)^t}$$

For the moment the assumption is made that a rise in the price level only affects current liquidity leaving future liquidity unaffected. This is why liquidity, L, is divided between L_1 and L_2; the portion of total liquidity affected by the price increase is L_1 whereas discounted future liquidity, L_2, is just the same as before.

A once-for-all price increase will have no effect on the stock of future liquidity for the reason that the stock of current liquidity must be increased to the point where the marginal "pain" of current liquid-

Diagram 10-5

REAL BALANCES

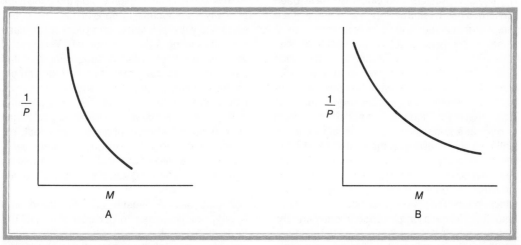

 A

B

ity foregone just equals the interest reward of the most liquid of the future liquidities. (This would be r_0.) This stock adjustment will require only a one period additional saving from current income, or a slight reduction of consumption from many periods of income, so that in the long-run the stocks of future liquidity will be unaffected. The stock of real balances of current liquidity will also be just the same as before.

This conclusion would not be reached if a continuous price increase takes place. In order to maintain the stock of current liquidity constant in real terms (constant real balances of money) and if income is not rising so fast as prices, a readjustment of future liquidity must take place. This readjustment will consist of a transfer from areas of future liquidity into current liquidity so that L_2 will now be affected as well. The question now is will current liquidity be a "superior" or an "inferior" good? In most cases it is likely that L_c will be superior because a transfer from future liquidity will result in a shortage of funds in the areas so affected with the result that interest rates will rise. This transfer will, generally, be accompanied by rising rates throughout the entire spectrum of future liquidity because of the highly competitive nature of the demands made upon a limited supply. The consequence will be to encourage the public to "stretch" current liquidity as far as possible for the reason that the opportunity cost of interest foregone will be higher. Offer curves, therefore, will become less elastic.

Lastly, suppose that annual price increases are anticipated at a certain rate, p, per year. This means that real future liquidity will be affected by price changes as well as the interest rates. We can see this by subtracting the rate of price increase from each of the rates, r, as follows:

$$(2)\ \frac{L_1}{p} + \frac{L_2}{p} = \frac{L_c}{p} + \frac{L_{f_0}}{(1 + r_0 - p)^t}$$
$$+ \frac{L_{f_1}}{(1 + r_1 - p)^t} \cdots \frac{L_{f_n}}{(1 + r_n - p)^t}$$

The problem is now considerably more complicated because the real values of future liquidity are declining rather substantially. We can readily see the consequence of both actual and anticipated inflation for the fixed income earner who must (if he can) maintain his real current liquidity at a constant level but does not have the means of increasing his total liquidity, $L_1 + L_2$. Real interest rewards are declining at the same time that real total liquidity declines. Assuming that real balances of current liquidity are maintained intact (L_c/p is constant), a substantial drain from future liquidity must take place. There are, thus, three sources of liquidity transfers: (1) a declining value of real income making it difficult to maintain a constant value of total liquidity, (2) a drain from future liquidity into current liquidity, and (3) declining real rates of return. These latter rates can easily become negative so that $1 + r - p$ could become less than unity. This is particularly true if the rate of tax is also included, so that real rates of return net of tax are even less.

B. Supply of Wealth

The liquidity structure with which we have been concerned has been developed with the tacit assumption that a source of funds is already in existence. A complete analysis of wealth effects, however, cannot assume either that the funds themselves or their distribution can be taken for granted. In recent years, there has been a resurgence of interest amongst monetary economists in the Wealth (or Pigou) Effect not so much from its original anti-deflation emphasis but as a potential for the analysis of the problems of inflation.[36] Generally, the thrust of this research has been directed toward the impact of a growing quantity of money and rising prices and their effect on the distribution of wealth.

Actually, to follow a long tradition, money and the money supply is not real wealth at all but claims to wealth. As these claims are redistributed in value terms, certain sectors of the population gain control over more wealth while others lose. It has become customary, however, to refer to money in this context as wealth itself, hence, the "wealth effect," though it should be understood that claims and real wealth are quite different.

As has been shown in previous chapters, our chartered banks combine two distinct functions in one institution — deposit manufacturing and intermediation. This latter function the banks have in common with other financial intermediaries; however, in the analysis which follows our chief concern is the deposit manufacturing function.

Deposits which are "newly manufactured" by banks are really no different than "old" deposits, hence, are quite indistinguishable, since *all* deposits were manufactured at some time or other. Should we wish to statistically identify the process of manufacture through time, we could, presumably, use the annual increase in the total of deposits of chartered banks as deposits newly manufactured during the year. Beyond this we cannot distinguish new from old deposits; therefore, for the sake of the analysis we shall refer to all deposits in equation (3) simply as D.

---

[36]Pesek and Saving, *Money, Wealth, and Economic Theory*, Macmillan and Co., New York, 1967. This book is among the last of a series of published materials including work by Metseler, Patinkin, A. L. Marty, Archibald and Lipsey, and others. The analysis here draws upon the Pesek and Saving book.

Another type of money is, of course, cash and deposits at the Bank of Canada. Some of this cash which is in circulation will be the equivalent of newly manufactured deposits, i.e., the public prefers to withdraw some loan proceeds in cash instead of using a demand deposit. This type of cash we will refer to as C_P suggesting that it is cash which has been manufactured (or printed) as the counterpart of loans to the private sector. Not all cash, however, is of this type. Some is purely "fiat" currency which comes into existence as the cash counterpart of government debt, but again is indistinguishable from any other cash. Again, for the sake of our analysis, we will use an artificial distinction, C_g to refer to cash created against this government debt.

For purposes of wealth holding, there are, broadly, three sectors in our economy: (1) The Federal Government, (2) The Private Sector, which is further subdivided between creditors and debtors, and (3) Banks. We shall examine each of these in turn. Of the three sectors, the federal government is unique in the sense that it can borrow money by increasing the national debt cost free (aside from negligible cost of paper, etc.). The debt when it falls due is simply rolled over in a perpetual reborrowing process with only the interest to be paid by taxation proceeds. The money counterpart of this debt is deposits within the banking system including the Bank of Canada and some cash, C_g. This money has been referred to in the literature as "outside" money.

The second sector, the private sector, consists of two parts, creditors and debtors. Creditors are those individuals who possess an excess of liquidity and are willing to transfer this surplus to debtors who have insufficient liquidity. In acquiring this extra liquidity, the debtors have obligated themselves to repayment of their debt plus interest which will consist of current liquidity in the form of any one of the different money "types." Creditors, incidentally, are those of the population who have elected to store their liquidity in any of the several forms of bank deposits and other forms of future liquidity indicated within the liquidity equation. Private debtors, then, are those of the public who are in debt to creditors through the medium of the banks.

The third sector is the banks themselves. They are a separate sector from the other two for the reason that their deposit manufacturing function entitles them to a reward of interest at zero marginal cost. That portion of the deposits at the banks which requires no deposit interest payment, demand deposits, are "free" since there are no corresponding creditors in the private sector who forego current liquidity; therefore, the interest which is paid to the banks from loans accrues as income to the banks. In a sense, banks are money manufacturing institutions which earn an economic rent on the basis of their legal monopoly. These deposits manufactured by banks are often referred to as "inside" money.

A moment's careful thought is sufficient to show that no other forms of primary wealth (or rather *claims* to wealth) exist in our society. We have identified all primary money claims and classified them in accordance with our objectives. Note that deposits at financial intermediaries are excluded —they are not primary claims and will be "captured" in another form. What we have, then, are all the wealth sources *in money form* which will be apportioned amongst all the various forms of liquidity in the liquidity side of the equation. All these primary wealth forms can be summed as the first four terms in the equation:

$$(3) \quad \frac{C_p}{P} + \frac{C_g}{P} + \frac{D_p}{P} + \frac{D_g}{P} - \frac{Q}{P} + \frac{y_h}{r} + \frac{y_n}{r} = \frac{L}{P}$$

with

C_p = cash against private debt
C_g = cash against government debt
D_p = deposits against private debt
D_g = deposits against government debt
Q = private debt
y_h = expected real income of individuals
y_n = expected non-human real income
P = general price level
r = a suitable discount rate

The first four terms represent the forms of primary money, as distinct from deposits with financial intermediaries, etc., which are distinguished by sectoral origin. They are expressed in real terms, i.e., divided by the general price level, P. Both C_g and D_g are "outside" money whereas C_p and D_p are "inside" money. The debt term Q/P applies only to inside money and is the private sector's debt repayment responsibility. The government has no such responsibility.

Provincial and municipal governments, while technically part of the government sector, do not have the money creation capacity, and are, therefore, not specifically included in the equation. They are subsumed under the "private" sector, though, to be sure, a more detailed breakdown of

the wealth equation would include these governments as "hybrids," neither government nor private. This is a matter of detail only which is not necessary for our analysis.

The term for real debt, Q/P, carries a negative sign. This is the debt counterpart of the inside money created by banks and constitutes the largest part of the assets side of the banks' balance sheets. Once again, one might wish a more detailed analytical breakdown of private debt, for example, between corporate borrowing and borrowing by private individuals with the objective of defining which type of borrowing might be more "negative" than another. However, just as governments other than federal are specifically excluded as an unnecessary complication, distinction between types of debt are omitted for the same reason.

The same reasoning does not apply to the next two members of the wealth equation. These are *not* an unnecessary complication but are an essential part of total wealth. The term, y_h, refers to a stream of expected real income earned by all individuals in the future. It is discounted by a certain rate of "interest," r, because we want to know its present value before including it in the wealth equation. Notice that as expected income there is no monetary counterpart as yet as in the case of present wealth; there are no primary deposits in existence which can represent future income as wealth. This does not exclude future income from the wealth equation, however.

The same is true for a future flow of real income from non-human wealth. It is this member of the equation which captures all the wealth which has been created by means of intermediation by banks, financial intermediaries, capital markets, etc., and which like human wealth cannot yet be represented by primary deposits. As before, this flow of expected real income must be discounted to arrive at its present value. All the variables in equation (3), therefore, should represent total real wealth in our society at the present time. It is this real wealth which must be disposed of in some form or another in terms of liquidity, and we do this by setting equation (3) equal to the liquidity equation (2) to arrive at an identity similar to the income identities of Keynesian analysis.

$$(4) \quad \frac{C_p}{P} + \frac{C_g}{P} + \frac{D_p}{P} + \frac{D_g}{P} - \frac{Q}{P} + \frac{y_h}{r} + \frac{y_n}{r}$$

$$= \frac{L_c}{P} + \frac{L_{f_0}}{(1+r_0-p)^t} + \frac{L_{f_1}}{(1+r_1-p)^t} + \cdots \frac{L_{f_n}}{(1+r_n-p)^t}$$

C. Inflation and Distribution

It is now possible to gain some insight into wealth effects and how the distribution of real income takes place amongst all three sectors of the economy, especially during periods of inflation. Suppose we have an expansion of the outside money supply due to borrowing by the federal government from the banking system, some of which, as is true in Canada, will likely consist of government securities sold to the Bank of Canada. There will be, at first, a transfer of real wealth from the private to the public sector as this outside money is used to purchase the goods and services required by the government. In addition, there will be an increase in both C_g and D_g in the wealth side of equation (4). This will, of course, be reflected in the liquidity side, probably as an initial increase in current liquidity. This would not be true if the finance of additional federal debt were by Canada Savings Bonds, or any other bonds sold to the public. The increase in outside money would be accompanied by an initial increase in future liquidity. However, regardless of which of the forms of liquidity are increased, current or future, the wealth counterpart is outside money which carries with it no corresponding negative debt.

To the extent that the Bank of Canada purchased government securities to finance federal borrowing, chartered banks have an increase in reserves and are now in a position to expand inside money. But this they cannot do unless the private debtors of the private sector wish to acquire additional liquidity in exchange for future liquidity foregone. In Keynesian terms we could say that the marginal efficiency of capital must be sufficiently high, or in Hayekian analysis, the marginal product of investment must be above the rate of interest. If the private debtors do not wish additional liquidity at that price, or, to express the same thing in a different way, the cost of liquidity to them is less than the market rate of interest on government securities, banks will prefer not to expand inside money. They will, instead, purchase existing government securities on the market. These securities will be sold to finance additional inside money when debtors are willing to pay the market price.

The result of this transaction is to increase the real wealth owned by the government sector, and, in all likelihood, increase current liquidity of the public. The distinction between "outside" and "inside" money now becomes important because an expansion of inside money is very definitely limited by the debt obligation, Q/P. Because of the discipline of the debt constraint, additional current liquidity generated by inside money is more likely to be accompanied by an increase in real wealth unless an excessive prolongation of output takes place. Outside money expansion, however, unless used for some productive investment by the government, will *not* result in an increase in total real wealth, while an increase in inside money will increase real wealth some day in the future.

Prices rise because the public has now acquired either excessive current liquidity or future liquidity which can be readily transferred into current liquidity when required and resistance to sellers' demand for money is weakened. This now ushers in a "price-induced" wealth effect. This gives the debtor section of the private sector a great advantage because the real value of debt is reduced. At the same time all the positive members of the wealth side become less in real terms. Total wealth is constant but a massive redistribution of wealth is taking place. This occurs because owners of deposits are transferring their claims to real wealth to the debtors.

Meantime, as a result of a rise in the general price level, real income, both y_h and y_n, have declined. It is likely that those income earners who suffer this loss, particularly y_h, will attempt to restore their real income to at least its former level. This they can do because the entrepreneural debtors of the private sector have experienced a windfall wealth transfer and are in a position to pay higher wages. Like outside money, the amount of claims to real wealth has now increased by an amount equal to the discounted value of the future higher stream of income.

It is, of course, possible that non-human real income could also rise if an increased flow of dividend and interest payments should occur. But there is no automatic guarantee that such will take place, particularly because of the inherent competing nature of the two forms of income, human and non-human. Corporate businesses can accommodate the demands of one form of income from their windfall gains but hardly both. This is why common stocks are no longer a successful hedge against inflation.

The only sector in the economy that is untouched by rising prices is the banks. They enjoy windfall gains of real wealth from the fact that additional inside money is manufactured at zero cost to them at the same time that they earn a reward supported, as it were, by the market rate of interest on government securities. Their excess earnings are, presumably, distributed as salaries and dividends to shareholders.

There is another side to the wealth effect which remains yet to be considered — the interest-induced wealth effect. We have already had occasion to examine the impact of interest rate changes on the equity markets in particular and have seen that rising interest rates can and likely do have an impact on stock prices. For many individuals the collapse of equity values constitutes a real and genuine loss for the reason that they may be forced to sell their shares or their bonds in the market. In terms of additions to stocks of liquidity, increasing rates of return in general will mean better yields in some areas than in others, for it is not true that *all* rates of return march together in lock step. Some do, especially those of financial intermediaries, but it is possible to find still better rates of return especially if one is willing to accept a slightly greater risk.

But, why *should* interest rates rise in the first place? As we have seen earlier in this chapter, shortages of funds relative to demand ensure rising rates which, if permitted to feed back into the demand mechanism, would reduce the demand for funds by making roundabout methods of production less profitable. More direct methods would be preferred. Even though these more direct methods might be less productive in the long run than roundabout methods, they would absorb more employment since they tend to be more labour intensive. This is most important because it increases economic efficiency overall. Thus, an interest induced wealth effect is not *of itself* harmful if scarce resources are channeled to their most productive uses. The system of relative market prices left to itself would ensure this distribution, but a general increase in the price level does not. Furthermore, rising rates which derive from speculative ventures based upon the prospect of higher prices completely distort the market mechanism. It is, in fact, a combination of both the interest induced and an "expected-price-increase-induced wealth effect"

which has the greatest impact.

In equation (4), the expected rate of price increase has been assumed to be zero to this point. We move into the final stages of the inflationary process when expectations of rising prices begin to become general. This means that it is no longer possible to expect future liquidity to maintain its real present value, let alone increase. Just to emphasize this point, we might consider a simple example which will show not only the nature of the impact of expected inflation but its strength as well.

Suppose there is an individual who expects to retire in 10 years time with an annuity of $8.00 per year in perpetuity (he expects to live forever, or plans it that way just to be on the safe side). At a rate of interest of 8% he must provide $46.32 as an investment because that is the value of $100 (8/.08) in ten years.

$$\frac{8}{.08(1.08)^{10}} = \$46.32$$

Suppose, now, that he anticipates an 8% rate of inflation and wishes to provide $8 per year of current purchasing power in 10 years time. He must provide now exactly $100 which will be worth in money terms $215.89 in ten years.

$$100(1.08)^{10} = \$215.89$$

But *still* this is not all. In order to provide for $8 per year of current purchasing power after the initial decade, the annual annuity payments must also grow at 8% per year, and this means that the capital value of the annuity must also grow sufficiently to provide this 8% increase in money terms. This would mean an approximate 16% annual growth rate in the value of the capital after the lapse of 10 years, a rate which seems almost impossible. This is the process of discounting inflation which market rates tend to do if left to themselves. Such phenomenal rates as 15.79% for British government securities and 16.59% for debentures were reached in Britain in October, 1976, at the peak of the recent British inflation.

At the same time that interest rates are pushed upward by inflation rates, capital values in the market shrink rapidly. Suppose in the above example it became necessary to sell the asset which was to provide $8 per year in perpetuity and the market rate increased from 8% to 10% meantime. The result would be a loss of $20, $8/.10 = $80 instead of $100 which, when discounted at 10% for 10 years would be

$$\frac{20}{(1.10)^{10}} = \$7.71 \ .$$

Still, the process is not finished, for there yet remains taxes to be paid from interest and dividend income. All we have to do is imagine the plight of the poor Canadian who hopes to establish an annuity of $8 per year of current purchasing power *net of tax* to understand the enormous redistributory effects of a price-interest-tax-induced wealth effect. It is savers who are methodically and consistently stripped of their wealth by an inflationary process which likely began with an original expansion of outside money. In the last analysis, it is the saver who bears, unprotected, the full burden of inflation.

CONCLUSION

Within the limits of a single chapter it is not possible to do justice to the great contributions to our knowledge made by the great economists and which have now been part of our heritage for so many years. The best anyone can hope is to be selective, to limit his scope to include only that which is relevant and hope that not too much violence is done. This has been the modest objective of this discussion; any reader who expects to be satisfied with this chapter as a digest of Keynes, Wicksell and Hayek must be disappointed.

There is, however, a stream which runs through the theory of capital and interest from the Austrians, through Wicksell, to split into two distinct divisions. The split was due largely to the circumstances of the time, viz., the greatest depression in modern times. Because of this there was a concentration of attention upon the very pressing problems of unemployment and it is to be expected that different economists with different backgrounds should propose varying theories and remedies. The "split" with which we are concerned here, upon reflection, does appear to be the result of two different points of view—the long vs. the short-run. However, a categorization of this nature does run the risk of distortion of the truth. One doubts, for instance, that Keynes would entirely agree that his *General Theory* was a purely short-term analysis, yet his entire approach does appear to be a concentration on the problems of unemployment.

It has become fashionable in recent years, in the process of developing a system of macro-economics, to attribute to Keynes a "generality" which is unwarranted. He has, in effect, become a patron saint of a complete system of macroeconomics. The trouble with this type of "reverence" is that his name can be invoked as a justification for an economic policy which has as many variants as there are ideological proponents. It leads to the illusion that the components of aggregate demand are subject to manipulation and control in such a way that our economic problems, be they unemployment or inflation, a standard of living which somehow fails to grow, a deficit in the balance of payments, etc., can be readily solved, and the fact that they are not is due entirely to some perversity on the part of governments. It is this illusion that politicians seem to have seized upon when they accuse the government of failing in its responsibility when the unemployment percentage rises or the consumer price index moves up by a few tenths of a point. Since the government has the power to tax, to spend, and, in the final analysis, to control the Bank of Canada, it is believed that it is directly responsible for the economic well-being of the nation.

Nothing could be further from reality. It is neither possible nor desirable that governments have such all-embracing powers. It is not possible because the individual components of aggregate demand cannot be changed or even adjusted without affecting every *other* component; hence, what may appear to be a preferred outcome of a specific policy may prove in the end to be quite damaging because of the unexpected and unforeseen effects upon the other components. Furthermore, it is not desirable that governments have such powers because, given the state of our economic knowledge, we cannot be certain that economic welfare is truly being served by any specific policy. We can say, for instance, that unemployment is undesirable, but putting people to work by government "make work" projects does not remove the *cause* of unemployment. Quite the contrary, by creating jobs, the one mechanism that could correct the difficulty, surplus labour in the job market, is removed. Political interests which reflect certain groups within our society cannot be relied upon to produce the most efficient economic policy.

In the last analysis, this appears to be the principal difference between the short and the long-term approach in economics. So long as we adhere to the principles of a free market, free enterprise economic system, we cannot serve a long-term objective with short-run policies. In terms of pure time, the long-run is simply an extension of a series of short-runs. When the two are in fundamental conflict, a reconciliation is necessary.

But this appears to be far removed from our original narrow topic of Canadian money and assets. Our subject is not concerned with the theory of value, employment, labour markets, etc., yet of necessity the study of money and its relationships within our economy must include some aspects of these related topics if for no other reason than that we all share a common currency unit. This is why the theory of business cycles became in so many cases a monetary theory. Friedman's money cycle and its relationship with the business cycle is an excellent example of this.[37]

Lastly, of the two protagonists, Keynes and Hayek, which is likely to be correct? At the present time, the evidence would suggest that Hayek and the Austrian School have been neglected for far too long. Events of the recent past in Canada, the U.S. and Great Britain seem to point to the end of the "Keynesian era" in economics. However, it should be made very clear that Keynes himself, were he alive today, would be appalled at the manner in which his own work has been used to justify economic policies and ideas. He had conceived his theories as important for the 1930s, not for the post-war world in which we live now.[38] It is rather the pupils of Keynes as well as his followers who have turned our world into the dangerous and unjust combination of inflation and unemployment of which we are all so painfully aware.

---

[37]In what is probably one of the largest and most exacting econometric studies of all time, Milton Friedman and Anna Schwartz have demonstrated the relationship between changes in growth rates of the money supply and the business cycle itself. This study covered a period of some 90 years of U.S. history. *Monetary History of the United States, 1867-1960*, Princeton University Press.

[38]Keynes himself was very adaptable and prone to change in his views. His untimely death was responsible for the fixed Keynesianism we know today. In a conversation with Professor Hayek, he pointed out that should his theories ever become "dangerous" he would "turn round public opinion at once." Six weeks later he was dead and couldn't do it.—An interview with Professor Hayek in Freiburg, Germany, May, 1978.

ADDITIONAL READINGS

Böhm-Bawerk, Eugen von, *Capital and Interest*, Libertarian Press, South Holland, Illinois, 1959. Particularly, Vol. II, *Positive Theory of Capital*.

Harrod, R. F., *Money*, Macmillan, London, 1969, ch. 7.

Hayek, F. A., *The Pure Theory of Capital*, Routledge & Kegal Paul, London, 1950. A rigorous treatment of capital theory.

_____, *Monetary Theory and the Trade Cycle*, Jonathon Cape, London, 1933.

_____, *Profits, Interest, and Investment*, A. M. Kelley, New York, 1969.

_____, *A Tiger by the Tail*, Institute of Economic Affairs, Great Britain, 1972. Highly recommended for a background knowledge of the Hayekian position vis-à-vis Keynesian economics.

Hicks, J. R., *Critical Essays in Monetary Theory*, Oxford, 1967, chs. 11 and 12.

Keynes, J. M., *A Treatise on Money*, Macmillan, London, 1960. Particularly, Vol. II, *The Applied Theory of Money*.

_____, *A Tract on Monetary Reform*, Macmillan, 1923, ch. 5 expresses an early Keynesian view of money.

_____, *The General Theory of Employment, Interest and Money*, Macmillan, London, 1949, Book IV is particularly relevant.

Leijonhuford, Axel, *On Keynesian Economics and the Economics of Keynes*, Oxford University Press, Toronto, 1968, pp. 187-231. One of the best treatments of capital theory.

Schumpeter, Joseph A., *Capitalism, Socialism and Democracy*, Allen & Unwin, Ltd., London. Highly recommended for thoughtful readers, particularly Chapter 10.

Uhr, Carl G., *Economic Doctrines of Knut Wicksell*, University of California Press, Berkeley, 1960. Discusses Wicksell's life and economic theories.

Wicksell, Knut, *Interest and Prices*, Macmillan, London, 1936, chs. 8 and 9.

_____, *Lectures on Political Economy*, Routledge & Kegan Paul, London, Vol. I, Part II is a particularly good discussion of capital theory.

APPENDIX

1. A Macroeconomic Relationship

Anyone who has considered seriously the capital market and its operation will certainly testify to its complicated structure with many interrelationships, each part affecting another. At the same time, the details of these relationships are not known. There has not been a sufficient consistency amongst the behaviour patterns of variables to identify cause and effect. Nevertheless this entire complex structure of the capital market and its relationship to the public can be (and has been) collapsed into a single function which relates the rate of interest and the Gross National Product. Initially the work of Sir John Hicks, this functional relationship is now widely accepted and used in many textbooks on macroeconomics. Briefly, it identifies a locus of points on which liquidity preference is satisfied, given both a certain level of interest and the GNP in real terms and a money supply. It is because of this latter that the function is designated as L,M (See Diagram A10-1).

It is easy enough to see why the function is positively sloped. As the GNP increases, the demand for current liquidity increases, and this means that the "pain" of current liquidity foregone increases as well. Since, in equilibrium, this pain equals the rate of interest, interest rises accordingly. But what is not so easy to recognize is that implicit in the function is the fact that the very process of arriving at equilibrium in the capital market *has already taken place*. The capital market is a complex business at best and equilibrium is just as elusive there as in other markets. If we keep in mind that equilibrium means the absence of any incentive on the part of the public to shift assets from one part of the market to another, we can readily see how difficult it is to imagine such an equilibrium in the real world, let alone achieve

Diagram A10-1

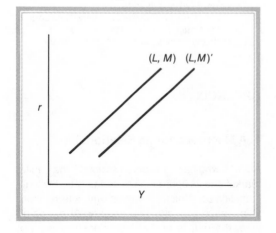

it. And, of course, the same practical problem of identifying a single rate of interest appropriate for the vertical axis exists as in our own analysis.

Another aspect of the diagram which deserves careful attention is the shift of the (L,M) function to $(L,M)'$, the consequence of an increase in the money supply, M. It is not really an increase in the money supply per se which is the main factor but an increase in liquidity. While any increase in the money supply constitutes *some* addition to total liquidity, (hence, to this extent the analysis is valid) there is an important distinction to be made in the amount of liquidity which a given increment of money supply, ΔM, will produce. Since we are dealing largely with liquidity preference, it is important that this distinction be made clear. Money, as we have seen, consists of both debts of the chartered banks (for our purposes we consider only deposits of the chartered banks as "money") owed to the public on the one hand and debts *of* the public and the various levels of government to the banks on the other. It follows that any increase in the money supply must constitute an increase in debts of either the public or the government. Now the result of such an increase in private debt to the banks must be a decrease in the liquidity of the borrower. For instance, a corporation which has incurred a higher debt to equity ratio than before as a result of its increased borrowing is now *less* liquid since a greater portion of its future earnings are obligated to the creditor. Similarly, individuals who have utilized their available consumer credit more extensively are also less liquid than before. So it is that the *availability* of credit enhances the liquidity of both business enterprises and consumers while the utilization of this credit does just the opposite, it reduces liquidity. Since most of our money supply consists of deposits of the banking system, they have been referred to as "inside money" as opposed to fiat money, gold, etc., which would be "outside money." Thus the addition to liquidity of an increase in inside money is to some degree cancelled by the reduction of liquidity of debtors. While this is certainly true, it does not follow that the net effect is zero, for the reason that an increment of debt of General Motors Corporation, when converted by the banking system into deposits which, in turn, are eventually owned by private individuals, need not mean that the reduction in liquidity of General Motors exactly equals the total of the gains in liquidity of individuals. Nevertheless, we can be certain that *some* reduction in the increment of liquidity occurs when inside money is created as the counterpart of private debt. We cannot, however, be so certain that any reduction in the increment of liquidity at all occurs as the consequence of an increase in government debt which is really a form of outside money. In fact, the federal government's borrowing capacity seems to be virtually infinite and provincial and local governments only less so. (The New York City case would appear to prove the existence of a ceiling to debts of local governments.) There is no debt/equity ratio to consider in the cases of public debt, only the willingness of the market to accept the debt instruments. The consequence is that an undiluted addition to liquidity takes place due to an increment of public debt, and this is not true of private borrowing.

For these reasons, a rightward shift in the *LM* function, which, by the definition of the function results from an increase in the money supply, need not *necessarily* result in an equal shift to a new schedule of liquidity preference. It is most likely to do so when the money supply is expanded through an increased holding of government debt instruments by the banking system with federal debt having the greatest impact.

In sum, then, we can identify two major shortcomings of the *LM* function. The first is the assumption of equilibrium in the capital market which automatically obscures the most important part of our study and which is the subject of much of the chapters preceding, i.e., the process of adjustment through which the capital market goes in striving toward equilibrium. Here is where the real action is! The second is the emphasis upon an expansion of the money supply which is assumed to result in a corresponding shift in the liquidity preference function, *LM*. This latter assumption stems, in all likelihood, from the inability of economists to quantify liquidity and to prefer an objectively defined measure of the money supply which can be readily inserted into econometric models.

Hicks' 1937 "paradigm" also includes the well-known investment/savings equilibrium conditions which determine, in turn, the equilibrium level of national income. Here, the locus of points of equality relate the rate of interest to the national income in such a way that the function is negatively sloped. This is the familiar marginal efficiency of investment function which relates net investment as a flow during a time period to the rate of interest. Lower interest rates, especially lower long-term rates, tend to encourage longer term, capital-intensive production techniques for the reason that the present value of an income from long-term investment is much higher when discounted by a low interest rate rather than a high rate.[1]

It is because of this encouragement of investment through lower interest rates that it is possible to influence the level of economic activity by means of interest rate control. This, of course, is aside from the question: *Ought* such control be attempted? Through the familiar multiplier mechanism, the value of the national income is increased until savings and investment are equal. This generates our second curve relating interest and national income (or GNP) by means of the points of equilibrium between investment and savings (Diagram A10-2).

It is also this relationship between the GNP and the interest rate which supplies the missing ingredient, i.e., the process of investment which constitutes the demand for the funds which pass

[1]Probably the acid test of any hypothesis involves empirical evidence, i.e., *does* investment actually respond to changes in interest rates? Many attempts, using mostly U.S. data, to determine an elasticity of response of investment to rate changes have been made. Earlier studies involving both survey techniques and regression analysis yielded no relationship at all between investment and interest. Surveys, in particular, were disappointing in that interest rates appeared to have no impact whatsoever on investment decisions. Later empirical investigations, employing more sophisticated econometric techniques, have reversed these earlier conclusions. Elasticities of response of investment have been found which vary between $-.15$ for short rates to $-.5$ or $-.6$ for long rates and even as high as -1.0 to -1.4. For a review of results of these studies see Thomas Mayer, *Monetary Policy in the United States*, Random House, New York, pp. 118-123. Obviously the difficulties encountered in such empirical investigations are many. Such problems as: Does investment *cause* higher rates because of greater demand for borrowed money? Do investment and interest rates move inversely during a stage of the business cycle because of a third and more significant cause affecting both investment and interest? Does one measure the demand curve (negatively sloped) for borrowed money given the interest rate, or the supply of credit (positively sloped) given the interest rate? It is such formidable questions as these which force one to rely on the rational hypothesis for his conclusions.

Diagram A10-2

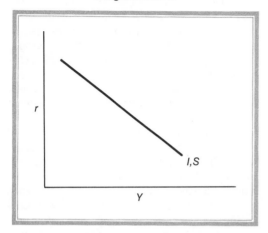

through the capital market. This is a negative relation which indicates that the lower the cost of funds the greater is investment, and, consequently, the greater is the equilibrium value of the GNP. This latter follows from a purely mechanical interpretation of the multiplier mechanism.

We note, however, that the I,S function consists of points of *equilibrium* between savings and investment; in other words, all the components of aggregate demand and supply, consumption, government expenditure, and investment demand equal the production of consumer goods, taxation, and savings. Since all of these are the results of quite separate decisions in diverse areas, it is obvious that we are not likely to encounter such equilibria in the real world.

Following the standard macroeconomic procedure, we can superimpose the L,M function on the I,S function (Diagram A10-3) to combine both the capital market equilibrium with the equilibria of the goods market. This gives us a kind of "Marshallian" relationship with an Equilibrium Point which is the intersection of two equilibria. Suppose we take an arbitrary interest rate, r_1 (remembering that r_1 is really some weighted average of all capital market yields in equilibrium). At that particular rate, the GNP, Y_1, would satisfy capital market equilibrium, i.e., savers would be adequately recompensed in the sense that they are satisfied with the rewards for exchanging current liquidity for some form of future liquidity. This level of Y_1, however, is less than Y_2 which would be the GNP which satisfies equilib-

rium in the product market at the same rate of interest, r_1. Business enterprise, therefore, will seek to borrow money and generally expand their productive capacity for the reason that the marginal efficiency of investment is high enough to warrant such an expansion. The GNP will, therefore, rise to approach Y_2, but as it does so, a shortage of funds for investment purposes will appear in the capital market. This will result in a disequilibrium in the capital market and consequent higher interest rates. If savers respond with a transfer of additional savings from current liquidity to future liquidity, equilibrium could be restored at a new and higher level of interest rates indicated by the intersection of the I,S and L,M functions. But note carefully once more that this intersection is *the equilibrium of two equilibria*.

The real dilemma arises when this "equilibrium of equilibria" is incompatible with the prevailing policy of the government. Thus, suppose a level of GNP equal to Y_2 is the "target level" for the reason that full employment is achieved there. To reach this level means that the interest rate (capital market yields) must always be below what the public wishes it to be. This rate happens to be r_2. We can achieve Y_2, of course, by forcing an interest rate of r_1 and this can be done by means of a money supply expansion which shifts the LM function to LM'. The chartered banks, in effect, provide the additional capital funds which the capital market itself lacks at the lower rate.

The IS/LM functions have been used as theoretical "underpinnings" for very many econometric studies which attempt to identify the mechanism through which changes in money supply, government deficits, etc., impact upon the price level and real income.[2] Such a formulation has the great advantage of simplicity, and, therefore, lends itself well as a framework for econometric analysis. However, assuming that the criticisms mentioned above are valid, what value can we attribute to the conclusions of quantitative anal-

[2]Professor Laidler has, probably more than any other economist not only worked extensively in this field but has also carefully studied the work of others. The results of his efforts are neatly brought together in *Demand for Money, Theories and Evidence*, International Textbook Co., Scranton, Pa., 1969, and in "Money and Money Income: An Essay on the 'Transmission Mechanism'," *Journal of Monetary Economics*, Vol. 4, p. 151.

Diagram A10-3

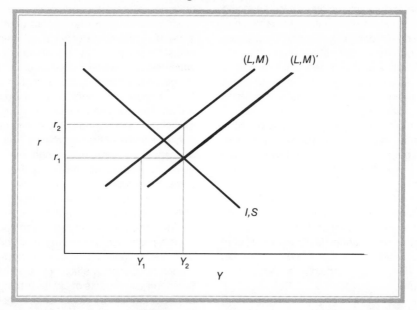

ysis based upon a massive oversimplification of a highly complex set of equilibria? The answer is very little, and Professor Laidler, probably the best authority on the subject, concludes that aside from the fact that " ... there is an overwhelming body of evidence in favour of the proposition that the demand for money is stably and negatively related to the rate of interest,"[3] very little of the transmission mechanism between money and prices has been uncovered, particularly because so much of the mechanism itself depends upon how a monetary policy is carried out. The private sector itself, businessmen, the public, etc., guage their actions in accordance with the very policy measures which are being implemented; hence, "If the structure of the economy through which policy effects are transmitted does vary with the goals of policy and the means adopted to achieve them, then the notion of a unique "transmission mechanism" for monetary policy is a chimera. It is small wonder that we have had so little success in tracking it down."[4] Very much aware of the shortcomings within the LM/IS analysis, Brunner and Meltzer have devel-

oped a different set of functions which are similar to the LM/IS curves but are defined differently.[5] These writers develop an Asset Market (AM) function which relates a set of interest rates, r, to the national income. At the same time an Output Market (OM) function, similar in shape to the IS function of Hicks, relates output and national income negatively. See Diagram A10-4.

Diagram A10-4

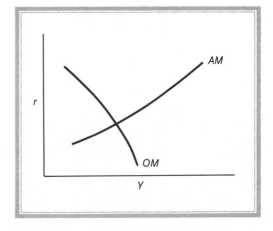

[3] *Demand for Money*, Ibid., p. 97.
[4] "Money and Money Income," op. cit., p. 184.

[5] K. Brunner and A. Meltzer, "Money, Debt, and Economic Activity," *Journal of Political Economy,* p. 951.

Since the *OM* function includes demand from both private and public sectors, deficit financing shifts the curve to the right, but, at the same time, since additional money is generated (how much depends upon the method of financing the deficit), the *AM* curve is also shifted. There is, therefore, an interaction between the two functions such that an equilibrium level of the interest rate and the national income is achieved. Interestingly, if an increase in output demand is financed by substantial expansion of the money supply, the convergence of the system toward equilibrium is faster than when the money supply expands less.

Most important, however, is the fact that the "heroic equilibrium" of two sets of equilibria inherent in the Hicks paradigm is not necessary. Equilibrium in the Brunner/Meltzer model consists of the asset market and the output market in joint relationship, certainly a substantial improvement.

2. Long-term Considerations

There is a second aspect of investment and the national income which should be considered as well. This may be considered the "long-term transmission mechanism." The marginal product of capital is, of course, the product due to the last unit of capital invested which really means a unit of "roundaboutness" (or time). Further, as we have already seen, capital like any other productive factor is subject to the law of diminishing marginal productivity. Diminishing productivity in this sense implies that if labour were the fixed and capital the variable factor of production, output due to the last unit of capital input would ultimately decline. Since it is not possible for businessmen to vary inputs of capital in this way, the rational businessman will seek that particular project which yields the highest return in terms of productivity. Having identified the project, he will then locate the necessary financing either from his own resources or from the capital market. Thus, having put the capital into place as a productive factor, capital ceases automatically to be a variable factor of production in the short-term—only labour can serve this function.

Nevertheless, we must consider the marginal product of capital to be the output due to the last unit of capital employed, even though it is a fixed production factor. This "unit" of capital may be quite large, say, the equipment necessary to produce oil from the tar sands, or, at the other extreme, quite small when a businessman decides to purchase an additional delivery van which will also yield a particular marginal product. In both cases there is nothing "marginal" as far as the individuals or groups undertaking the project are concerned. The principle of marginality only exists from the standpoint of the pool of capital available to the entire community. This is why the concept of the marginal product of capital takes on a much greater economic significance when a decision is made as to the particular form capital must take. It is a problem in economic efficiency, and, consequently, involves not just the individual businessman but society as a whole. Capital is a scarce productive factor and must be allocated amongst a variety of uses. At the same time, criteria of economic efficiency is achieved when the marginal products of capital amongst all uses are equated just as would be the case for other factors of production. We can readily see why this is true by imagining the marginal product of capital in one industry to be less than the marginal product of capital in another. Total output would be increased by a reduction of capital investment in the former industry and a corresponding increase in investment in the latter; this is the consequence of the principle of diminishing marginal productivity.

We can carry this efficiency criteria a step further by considering the marginal cost of the products of productive factors. An inefficient allocation of capital means that the relative costs of these products will be different from the optimum. We can define the optimum as the equating of the ratios of marginal costs of products with the ratios of their market prices, i.e.,

$$(1) \quad \frac{MC_1}{MC_2} = \frac{P_1}{P_2}, \text{ or}$$

$$\frac{MC_1}{P_1} = \frac{MC_2}{P_2} = \frac{MC_3}{P_3} = \frac{MC_n}{P_n}$$

This equation states that maximum efficiency exists when the ratio of prices of products equals the ratio of their marginal costs. Or, to put it another way, the marginal rate of substitution of products for buyers (P_1/P_2) equals the marginal rate of substitution of products for producers (MC_1/MC_2). From this it follows that the most efficient combination of productive factors will result in the least marginal cost which, under perfect competition, leads to the most efficient allocation of resources in such a way that the ratios of marginal products of all factors to their respective costs will be equal. Thus,

(2) $\dfrac{MP_1}{MP_2} = \dfrac{C_1}{C_2}$, or $\dfrac{MP_1}{C_1} = \dfrac{MP_2}{C_2} = \dots \dfrac{MP_n}{C_n}$

For capital, the cost, C, would be expressed in terms of an interest rate on borrowed funds, and the marginal product of capital would be similarly expressed as a rate of return.

A parallel concept which is even more important for our purposes is the marginal efficiency of capital. This is a rate of return over cost, as Fisher expressed it, and is not the same as the marginal product. Keynes' definition of the marginal efficiency of capital is as follows: "...as being equal to that rate of discount which would make the present value of the series of annuities given by the returns expected from the capital-asset during its life just equal to its supply price."[6] Of course, the key words are "expectations" and "supply price," for expectations look to the future and the supply price (the cost in terms of productive factors of a capital asset) is a current concept.

It is the marginal efficiency of capital which provides the link between the capital market and the process of investment. It is, in fact, the relationship between the marginal efficiency of capital and the cost of borrowed money (the investment rate of interest as opposed to the savings rate) which determines the profitability of investment, and, in turn, acts as the stimulus encouraging the flow of capital into the process of production.

Suppose, to use an example, that the marginal efficiency of capital is 20%. This is the expected rate of return (a profit concept) and the rate of interest on borrowed funds is 10%. It follows that the particular project to which this 20% applies (a marginal project to society but not to the businessman) would be undertaken in response to the profit motive. Having secured the amount of capital required for the project, the rational businessman will then seek to maximize his return per unit of capital by setting the ratios of the marginal products of his factors to their costs equal to each other, including, of course, capital. Thus, instead of an expected rate of return over

cost of 20%, the actual rate may be more or less depending upon the entrepreneur's skill. Marginal productivity, therefore, determines the level of the marginal efficiency of capital only insofar as the businessman *expects* to achieve a certain degree of efficiency.

Equally important is the fact that marginal productivity determines the *amount* of capital required. A declining marginal product of capital could, in general, be the result of either inefficiency in allocation of capital resources or a decline in the capacity of new capital resources to produce to the same extent as formerly. This could be the result of an exhaustion of the most favourable opportunities for investment so that the less favourable, or least productive, investments are all that are left. In either case, the result must be a need for more capital to invest to attain a given increment of output.

If the marginal productivity of capital is, in fact, declining in the manner suggested, either the marginal efficiency of capital (the expected rate of return over cost) must increase or the investment rate of interest must decrease so as to make possible the necessary capital flows into the industry. This is a conclusion of some significance.

Equations (1) and (2) suggest the bare outlines of economic efficiency conditions for production in any society. Insofar as conditions of perfect competition hold, these equilibrium conditions will be more nearly achieved than under less than perfect competition. But the significant feature of these conditions, for our purposes, lies in the distinction between goods produced by means of more capital intensive techniques than those of less capital intensity. Capital goods derive their value from the promised consumer goods embodied within them. Thus, should society prefer those particular consumer goods as opposed to goods produced with more labour intensive techniques, the prices of these goods should rise relative to those produced with more labour intensive techniques. Likewise, the value of the capital resources required to produce these consumer goods will also rise as entrepreneurs seek to maximize the profits via the more capital intensive techniques. Productive factors and resources must be enticed away from the alternative, more direct production of consumer goods, unless there are idle resources available,

[6]Keynes, *The General Theory*, p. 135.

with the result that their costs rise.

It is this cost, in terms of consumer goods not produced directly, which constitutes the real cost to society of capital intensive production, for production factors and resources devoted to the production of capital equipment are not available for the production of consumer goods. This is the opportunity cost, and when consumers indicate their preferences for capital intensive production via the free market, profits in that particular type of production increase.

The method of financing such machinery and equipment is, of course, the capital market. This must be true whether or not internal funds are used because the cost of funds must be calculated as if they were either borrowed or acquired through equity financing for the reason that they could be otherwise employed via the capital market itself. This is, again, opportunity cost.

As productive factors rise in cost, because of the necessity to attract additional quantities into capital intensive industry, it becomes necessary to increase the flow of funds to defray this higher cost. This, in turn, puts more pressure on the capital market which will force up the structure of interest rates. Additional funds should be attracted by these higher rates; in fact, if it is society's collective wish to continue producing by means of capital intensive techniques, these funds must be forthcoming in sufficient quantities to provide a rate of interest low enough to maintain a relatively high spread between the marginal efficiency of capital and the rate of interest. Now, the unfortunate feature about all this is that once capital intensive industries are developed, society becomes locked into that particular productive process. That is, the equilibrium conditions as stated in equation (2) (assuming that some of the ratios MP/C represent more capital intensive industries than others) can only hold true if adjustments by *withdrawals* of factors can take place. Of course, this is absurd in the short run since the only withdrawal possible for capital equipment is a wearing out process without replacement. In the real world, therefore, an equilibrium of the type expressed in equation (2) can only be of short duration at best. What this means is that the cost of capital may increase (the C in equation (2)) but there is no feasible method of immediately reducing the amount of capital invested so as to increase the marginal product to restore equilibrium. In a word, society might change its collective mind and decide not to increase the flow of funds to the capital market with the result that the interest rate (or cost of capital) would rise, and, at the same time, it is not possible to raise the marginal product of capital to maintain equilibrium.

It is also because of this "locked in" effect that when the marginal productivity of capital falls for any reason, instead of reducing the amount of capital employed so as to raise the marginal product (a rational approach) as a nation, we tend to compensate by encouraging an increase in the amount of foreign capital so as to achieve a higher level of production. This adds further to the pressure on a limited capital market, forcing the interest rate higher unless, and this is a crucial point, the banking system supplements the inadequate capital funding with its own increased supply of money.

The reason for this is not difficult to grasp, but it is sufficiently important to be worth developing further. Consider equation (2) once more which states equilibrium conditions as follows:

$$\frac{MP_1}{C_1} = \frac{MP_2}{C_2} = \cdots \frac{MP_n}{C_n}$$

Suppose that the marginal product of existing capital (for instance MP_2) should decline for the reason that the most profitable opportunities for investment have already been used up. Thus, not only is the marginal product of capital falling because of an increase in its quantity within a specific project but also between projects. Investment funds seek the most profitable outlets first and these are, generally for Canada, those in southern regions as opposed to the less hospitable north. In terms of economic efficiency, there are two equally rational alternatives open to a businessman: (1) reduce his existing capital investment by pounding his machinery into dust, and, at the same time, wiping out his debt to the satisfaction of his creditors, not by payment but by some more mysterious means, or (2) increase his capital investment by incurring more debt. By increasing investment in this way, employment and output may be encouraged, but this can only be done if either the marginal efficiency of capital is increased (by means of higher prices) or the interest rate is lowered. This is the dilemma facing a society with "locked in" capital equipment.

This "dilemma" highlights a fundamental conflict between a microeconomic principle and a macroeconomic objective. The first alternative above could be accomplished in the long-term by a wearing out process for machinery and equipment and a gradual liquidation of debt. Our macroeconomic policy, however, dictates otherwise. Because of a tendency for the *MP* of capital to fall, our total output is likely to be below our economic capacity, however defined. We therefore encourage an increase in investment by means of an expansion of the money supply by the chartered banks, which, in turn, lowers the interest rate in general. Lower rates tend to "force" equation (2) into an equilibrium at an efficiency level which may be quite different from that which society itself desires.

PART 3

International Money

Some of the most interesting facets of money are to be found in the areas of finance which arise outside Canada or Canadian jurisdiction. They are more interesting than purely domestic finance in that they are much more complex, in the first place, and in the second, they extend more widely throughout the international economy. It is through the international financial mechanism that our domestic monetary system is linked to those systems in the western world. In fact, it is no exaggeration to argue that we are not independent in a financial sense and our dependence upon other monetary and banking systems is becoming even closer as the years roll by.

Canadian sovereignty ends, as far as the Canadian dollar is concerned, with the borders of Canada, but since our international trade is so important to our economic well-being, the relationship between our dollar and other currencies is likewise very important. This raises a whole host of problems involving exchange rates, balance of payments, flows of capital, etc., all of which occupy prominent positions in the news headlines of the day. In working with problems such as these Canada is only one member of a group of nations which must find cooperative solutions.

Still, the most interesting developments in international finance have little to do with the Canadian dollar itself. In fact, our currency is a relatively minor one compared to the U.S. dollar, Sterling, and the great West European currencies which occupy the centre of attention. It is these currencies and the events which have shaped their values which occupy our attention in Part III. Chapter 11, of necessity, involves definitional concepts designed to clear up a great deal of confusion which arises from not knowing what things really are. Chapter 12 explores further the foreign exchange markets as well as the flows of international capital which are so important to Canada and other countries. Chapter 13 considers Euro-currencies, the newest of the phenomena in international finance. Chapter 14 examines international money within its international context very much as domestic currencies are related to domestic economic affairs.

As is true in Parts I and II, the discussion and analysis in the following chapters are not final and conclusive; quite the contrary, events are continuously shaping the nature of institutions so that what is true today may not be true next year. Nowhere is the speed of change so rapid as in international finance. In fact, in the last analysis, this is why the subject of international money is both exciting and challenging.

CHAPTER 11

Foreign Exchange Markets

INTRODUCTION

It was not so long ago, at least in an historical context, that the question of what determines the value of foreign currencies in relation to a domestic currency could be answered simply as "gold." The reason for this was that the value of one currency against another was determined by the price of gold and could only fluctuate within a range determined by the cost of shipping gold. These gold shipping "points" determined the upper and lower limits of a currency's fluctuation since any loss on a transaction involving foreign exchange could not be greater than the cost of sending gold instead. But like so many of our institutions which arise from the human psyche, gold and its functions have undergone enormous changes. Today, gold attracts considerable attention because changes in its price and the amounts purchased thereof are symptomatic of underlying causes.

For us, in the modern world, a study of foreign exchange can begin with an experience common to us all, that of exchanging Canadian dollars for foreign currency (likely U.S. dollars) at a local branch bank. This could be either in the form of cash or traveller's cheques, whichever happens to serve our purpose. In the process of exchange, a certain ratio is expressed as, say, $C1 = $U.S.85 or £1 = $C2.00, etc. How this ratio was determined is the subject of the next section. For the moment we should note that banks do have on hand foreign exchange either in the form of cash or deposits.

Just as in the case of domestic currency, the amount of foreign cash on hand is very small. Furthermore, since this cash results from tourist traffic, it may accumulate at points of entry into Canada from the U.S., and, should an excess of cash result, it would be returned, ultimately, to the U.S. bank on the other side of the border where it would be credited to the Canadian bank's ac-

count. Generally even this would hardly be necessary because points of entry are also points of exit, and tourists will wish to exchange Canadian cash for U.S. currency. Traveller's cheques are also issued by Canadian banks on behalf of the agency (American Express, etc.) which has an account at that bank. These may be used for payment abroad or exchanged for cash when the tourist arrives at his destination, but it is the agency's bank accounts, not those of the bank, which are the ultimate source of foreign funds.

I. FOREIGN ASSETS AND LIABILITIES

By far, the bulk of the foreign currency holdings of banks is in the form of deposits. We can see these in Table 11-1, Foreign Currency Assets and Liabilities. On the assets side are deposits with banks, i.e., deposits in foreign exchange which are liabilities of foreign banks to Canadian banks. On the liabilities side are deposits of banks, i.e., deposits of foreign banks with Canadian banks, hence, are liabilities *of* Canadian banks. It is apparent that total liabilities in foreign currencies have grown considerably over the years from $6.3 billion in 1967 to, roughly, $48.7 billion only ten years later. This, of course, reflects the enormous growth in activity in the foreign banking field which chartered banks have experienced over the past decade.

A. Origins of Foreign Payments

At this point, we should be clear as to how these assets and liabilities originate. In the transfer of ownership of funds, so as to make possible a flow of payments among their customers, the banks are by far the most important agents. Their customers may be domestic, as when a Canadian makes a payment to another Canadian, or foreign, i.e., a Canadian makes a payment to a

Table 11-1
CHARTERED BANKS: TOTAL FOREIGN CURRENCY ASSETS AND LIABILITIES
Millions of Canadian dollars

End of period	Assets						Liabilities			
	Call loans	Other loans	Securi-ties	Deposits with banks	Other assets	Total	Deposits of banks	Other deposits	Total	Net foreign assets
	B1801	B1802	B1803	B1804	B1805	B1800	B1807	B1808	B1806	B1809
1967	744	2,658	788	2,326	−46	6,470	1,529	4,780	6,309	162
1968	712	2,943	814	3,263	75	7,806	2,134	5,243	7,378	429
1969	676	3,853	860	6,381	−138	11,632	3,240	8,390	11,630	2
1970	623	4,671	733	7,526	138	13,691	4,915	8,618	13,533	158
1971	715	5,315	516	7,669	254	14,469	6,419	7,743	14,162	307
1972	973	5,510	613	9,524	−48	16,572	8,411	8,607	17,018	−446
1973	537	7,082	546	14,759	375	23,298	13,323	11,255	24,577	−1,279
1974	526	11,692	726	14,885	705	28,534	15,197	14,156	29,353	−818
1975	427	14,430	603	15,468	281	31,209	16,268	15,193	31,461	−253
1976	454	16,508	618	19,330	703	37,614	20,751	17,552	38,303	689
1977	883	21,828	2,164	21,774	1,009	47,658	27,353	21,311	48,664	1,006
1975 A	286	13,914	580	14,750	614	30,144	15,599	14,604	30,203	−58
S	383	14,117	571	14,486	665	30,222	15,898	14,574	30,472	−249
O	408	14,070	588	15,299	491	30,856	16,575	14,260	30,835	22
N	390	14,077	590	15,078	426	30,561	15,737	14,818	30,555	6
D	427	14,430	603	15,468	281	31,209	16,268	15,193	31,461	−253
1976 J	278	14,199	595	15,998	361	31,431	16,595	15,077	31,673	−241
F	337	14,143	572	16,349	201	31,602	16,428	15,464	31,892	−289
M	460	14,253	571	16,266	416	31,966	16,617	16,431	33,048	−1,082
A	429	14,454	575	17,158	513	33,129	17,106	16,815	33,921	−792
M	258	14,826	569	17,456	374	33,484	17,223	16,704	33,926	−442
J	508	15,048	576	17,032	525	33,689	18,036	16,375	34,411	−722
J	452	15,042	579	18,061	449	34,583	17,836	17,611	35,446	−863
A	483	15,234	596	17,533	472	34,318	17,727	17,650	35,378	−1,060
S	466	15,325	599	18,192	272	34,855	17,879	17,784	35,663	−808
O	598	15,397	595	18,256	571	35,417	18,479	17,655	36,135	−718
N	391	16,854	606	19,190	577	37,618	19,506	18,935	38,442	−824
D	454	16,508	618	19,330	703	37,614	20,751	17,552	38,303	−689
1977 J	400	16,767	614	18,858	631	37,270	20,158	17,712	37,870	−599
F	439	17,495	661	19,600	572	38,767	20,785	18,440	39,225	−458
M	611	18,146	693	20,110	928	40,488	21,946	19,160	41,107	−619
A	503	18,092	738	20,473	846	40,653	22,324	19,004	41,328	−675
M	562	18,660	1,134	19,800	927	41,082	22,488	19,384	41,871	−789
J	595	18,995	1,137	19,786	657	41,170	22,620	19,573	42,193	−1,023
J	519	19,588	1,492	19,936	855	42,389	22,953	20,444	43,397	−1,009
A	668	20,010	1,586	19,673	763	42,699	22,865	21,562	44,428	−1,728
S	701	20,457	1,698	20,184	1,091	44,132	24,206	21,277	45,483	−1,351
O	909	21,570	1,748	21,742	951	46,919	25,647	22,854	48,501	−1,582
N	762	21,759	1,962	20,842	779	46,105	25,078	22,403	47,482	−1,377
D	883	21,828	2,164	21,774	1,009	47,658	27,353	21,311	48,664	−1,006
1978 J	754	22,295	2,132	22,412	864	48,456	27,169	22,584	49,753	−1,297
F	856	22,621	2,159	23,114	976	49,726	27,395	24,016	51,411	−1,685
M	956	24,211	2,520	24,245	996	52,928	29,390	25,124	54,514	−1,587
A	809	24,927	2,651	24,819	793	54,000	29,570	26,228	55,798	−1,797
M	914	24,311	2,632	25,424	921	54,202	30,088	25,982	56,070	−1,867
J	1,058	25,239	2,923	24,328	1,364	54,912	30,830	26,167	56,997	−2,085
J	890	25,290	3,055	25,013	1,156	55,404	30,717	27,146	57,863	−2,460
A	1,012	26,176	3,085	25,963	1,631	57,867	30,883	29,276	60,159	−2,292

foreigner, or vice versa. In the former case, the clearing house mechanism is used while in the latter, a transfer of funds from one currency into another is necessary.

In the area of foreign business, virtually every transaction involves some form of credit. This could be a letter of credit which authorizes an exporter in some other country to draw foreign funds from either a Canadian branch bank abroad or a correspondent bank. The exporter, in his turn, draws a draft against the Canadian branch (or correspondent) then turns it over to his own bank for completion of payment. However, most international payments are made more simply than this. For example, a U.S. exporter acquires his own credit from his own bank to await payment from a Canadian importer. The importer simply purchases a U.S. dollar deposit in Canada, probably with the proceeds of a loan from his bank, then instructs his branch to have its correspondent credit the U.S. exporter's account with these U.S. dollars. This is simply a "telegraphic transfer" or an "open account" system which the banks carry out wherever appropriate banking facilities exist. The important thing here is that they have sufficient foreign funds in their accounts in banks in other countries to honour the transactions.

Consider, for example, how debtors and creditors, each in two different countries such as Canada and the U.S., would discharge debts via the banking system. This assumes that there is sufficient business activity (true in this case) to make it profitable for the banks to enter the field in the first place. Suppose a Canadian debtor is required to pay his creditor, presumably for payment of imported goods, a stipulated sum in U.S. dollars.

This could be accomplished by debiting the debtor's account (M in T table 11-1) and crediting the correspondent bank's account by the same amount (as indicated by the downward-pointing arrow). And this is what correspondent banking really means—banks hold accounts in favour of their correspondents for the purpose of discharging these payments.

The U.S. bank now has acquired an additional foreign exchange asset (a deposit with a Canadian correspondent). It is now in a position to increase the exporter's (X) account by the same amount (the upward-pointing arrow), and in this way a foreign exchange transaction has taken place (see T table 11-2).

It is now possible to see why it is so important that our Canadian banks have sufficient balances in their correspondent banks' accounts. Furthermore, since these are in foreign currency ($U.S. in this case) they must always be replenished should they become excessively low. If, for example, the Canadian bank only had 100 in its U.S. account, the U.S. exporter would have absorbed the entire amount in receiving his payment and the Canadian bank would be unable to finance any more imports.

The direct transfer method, as outlined above, is the most common method of making payments in foreign currency. Of course, the transaction can be made in the reverse order, i.e., a cheque, bank draft, etc., is drawn on M's account, sent to X for payment who then presents it to his bank for crediting to his own account. The U.S. bank then asks for its Canadian dollar account to be increased by presenting the cheque for payment which the Canadian bank does by decreasing M's account.

This is an enormous convenience and improvement in the process of discharging obligations, and certainly facilitates the movement of trade between countries. In former times, bills of exchange would be drawn up against an importer and turned over to a bank by the exporter for payment in his own currency. This was an awkward mechanism at best and is now almost completely displaced by the modern "open account" system. The only foreign bills of exchange business which remains is that of those countries without adequate facilities for the telegraphic transfer and whose foreign business is not sufficiently large to warrant the installation of the necessary capital equipment. Now, debts are discharged as easily outside the country as within, and banks find themselves in the happy

T table 11-1

A CANADIAN BANK

Assets		Liabilities	
$U.S. Deposits with banks	100	M	100 ↓
		Deposits of banks	100 ($C)

T table 11-2
A U.S. BANK

Assets		Liabilities	
$C deposit with banks	100	*X*	100 ($U.S.)
		Deposits of banks	100 ↑

position of earning more profits as long as the payments flows are great enough in volume. The only significant requirement for the banks is that they maintain deposit in their own currencies in favour of their correspondents. At the same time, trade and commerce are not the only means by which banks may secure foreign deposits. Additional methods will become apparent in subsequent sections and chapters, and these, combined with the requirements of trade, constitute the origin of the "deposits with banks" and "deposits of banks" as shown in Table 11-1. But just to give an idea of how extensive the foreign services of Canadian banks are, J. A. Galbraith suggests that "...perhaps well over a thousand different foreign banks all over the world serve as correspondents for Canadian banks...."[1]

It is now time to introduce the economics of payments flows into the banking structure. Suppose, as an example, the flow of payments from Canada to the U.S. should exceed that from the U.S. to Canada. We recall that a correspondent bank in the U.S. deducts the Canadian bank's account by the amount of the payments when payments are made by Canadians to Americans and adds to the Canadian bank's account when payments are made by Americans to Canadians. It follows that under the hypothesis of a new outflow of payments to the U.S., Canadian banks' foreign assets will decline. The "deposits with banks" will fall at the same time that "deposits of banks" will rise. Ultimately, a negative net asset may appear if the payments outflow is sufficiently great. Of course, the contrary situation, i.e., a net inflow of payments will result in a build-up of foreign assets.

One may readily imagine the situation which exists in a major trading area such as Vancouver, Toronto, or Montreal. Branch offices of the chartered banks will "marry-off" outpayments and inpayments all day long, but at the end of the day a net inflow or outflow will be inevitable. If, say, a surplus of inpayments exists, this will likely be offset by other branches of the same bank, but if

a surplus *still* exists, an increase in the entry, "deposits with banks" will occur.[2]

Once the banks have accrued a surplus of deposits with banks in this way they are free to use them in any way they see fit. Indeed these uses are many and varied and can be very much more diverse than domestic currencies.[3] But for our purposes at the moment it is important to recognize that foreign currency deposits are acquired, as opposed to "manufactured," by the domestic banking system. They are not subject to a required reserve ratio as are domestic deposits; hence, there is no cost of deposit manufacture as there is for domestic deposits. There is a cost of acquisition, of course, which arises when a Canadian bank wishes to acquire more foreign exchange deposits than it currently has on hand, and this cost arises from either (1) a purchase cost on the foreign exchange market, or (2) an interest cost which results from competitive bidding for foreign exchange deposits.

B. The Market For Foreign Exchange

In economics we have very many markets; in fact economics *is* the study of markets. The foreign exchange market is, however, unique in the sense that there is no other market quite like it. It is unique in its size, embracing, as it does, the entire world; it is unique in its structure of supply and demand because the forces of supply and demand are remote from the market itself; and, finally, it is unique in that only one item, the U.S. dollar, is being bought and sold. All this means that to understand the foreign exchange market a reorientation of our thinking is required.

We might begin by laying out the basic problem. It is the responsibility of Canadian banks, and *all* banks which participate in foreign exchange payments, to maintain a volume of foreign exchange

---

[1] J.A. Galbraith, *Canadian Banking*, The Ryerson Press, Toronto, 1970, p. 33.

[2] See the *Report of the Royal Commission on Banking and Finance*, 1964, pp. 292-293 for a discussion of this payments mechanism.

[3] Galbraith, *op. cit.;* his Chapter 36 is an excellent introduction to these possibilities.

deposits. This they must always do; and should they happen to run short, they must replenish them as soon as possible. Consider the situation. A German automotive manufacturer has completed a sale of automobiles to his representative dealers in Canada for, say, $C 1,689,432.84 and he wishes payment in DM on July 14, 1979. This is an odd sounding sum on a strange date in the future which the banks must be prepared to accommodate by having sufficient DM deposits in their accounts on that specific date. How is this possible?

Before answering this question directly, we should consider the physical structure of the market. All banks, Canadian banks included, have not only branches in the various financial capitals of the world but each branch is equipped with modern telex communication systems so that, by simply pressing buttons, rates of exchange, volumes of currencies traded, etc., can be instantly made available. The trading centres in Singapore, Frankfurt, Paris, New York, Toronto, etc., are just as close to each other as modern technology can make possible.

Now the difficult point to grasp is this. While we wish to provide a German exporter with DM deposits on a specific date in the future, we actually have *no* market which can provide a market price (or exchange rate) between these two currencies. The only market in the true sense of the word which exists is the market between the U.S. dollar and the deutsche mark, and the U.S. dollar and the Canadian dollar. It is the U.S. dollar which is the true *numeraire* for all foreign exchange markets so that both the DM and the $C are quoted against the $U.S., and, therefore, quoted against each other.

Once more, we ask the question, why? Why should foreign exchange markets treat, as it were, the Canadian dollar as a second-class citizen? The answer here, though not apparent at first sight, really underlies the whole structure of a foreign exchange market and distinguishes this market from all others. The fact that a flow of trade between Germany and Canada exists does not mean that a market in these respective currencies exists. There is very much more to a market than this. Markets consist of specific commodities which are bought and sold at a price, and remember that the specific commodity in our case is $C 1,689,432.84 to be sold for deutsche marks on July 14, 1979. What are the chances of

finding a buyer for that exact same sum on that exact date willing to pay in DM? The problem, then, is to *create* a market which would otherwise not exist in a currency for which any amount at any time, or date, can be traded.

This can be done by trading huge volumes of U.S. dollars against all the major currencies (including the Canadian dollar) *all* the time. These are purely interbank transactions and actually amount to some 90% of the total of market transactions. The balance, about 10%, will be the actual commercial transaction such as the one suggested above. Since the DM/$U.S. quotation exists for July 14, 1979 (which is actually a forward exchange transaction) and the $C/$U.S. quotation exists for that same date, it follows that the DM/$C rate exists for the precise amount.

We can readily grasp the significance of "making a market" in foreign exchange and the importance of using a single currency as numeraire, by imagining how much in terms of volume of trading would be required in order to make a market in *all* currencies against each other. The situation would be exactly the same as barter trade within a society, simply impossible to conduct. But, to ask one more question, why the $U.S. as a numeraire? The answer here is purely custom or habit. Any other single currency *could* be used, and, indeed, *would* be if customers wanted it that way. To be sure the day may well come when a single composite European currency (the "Europa") may supplant the U.S. dollar in this role of numeraire; until that time it is likely that the U.S. dollar will remain as the single commodity against which the "price" in terms of other currencies is quoted.

Changes in market prices between the $C and the DM also occur via the $U.S. and the $U.S./DM markets. For example, if a large payment must be made from Canada to Germany to service a loan, the Canadian demand for $U.S. will rise, exhausting $U.S. deposits in Canadian banks. This must be replenished at a price which will likely be higher than before the payment was made. Furthermore, the $U.S. demand for DM will (temporarily) rise making that currency relatively scarce and more difficult to replenish with a corresponding increase in its price. The result is that the $C/DM ratio will rise as the value of the Canadian dollar declines vis-à-vis the deutsche mark. Of course there is the remote possibility that using the $U.S. in this way would cause an unwarranted depreciation of the $U.S. also; however, as far as the $U.S. is concerned such payments as these are random so that payments to Germany from Canada would be cancelled by payments flowing from Germany to other countries.

As pointed out above, the market for foreign exchange is world-wide. The London market, with some 300 banks authorized to deal in foreign exchange, is the largest single centre in the world and certainly the most important. At the same time it is the most "perfect" in the sense that the Bank of England,which administers the British Exchange Control Act, maintains a tight control over the entire operation. The London market is set up with approved brokers as middlemen and all banks are required to buy and sell large amounts of currency through these brokers. This avoids any possibility of collusion and ensures that a customer is getting the best buying and selling price possible.

A typical day in this world-wide market would begin in Singapore after the Canadian markets have closed for the previous day. The Singapore centre will quote various prices for the Canadian dollar, with, perhaps, a trend up or down discernible. By the time the Singapore market is closing the London market is opening, with a possible slight overlap in time, so that the London banks will begin trading in Canadian dollars according to the commercial trends in London, taking over, as it were, from the Singapore markets, perhaps continuing or even reversing the Singapore trends. As the time for opening in Canada approaches, London banks will begin anticipating the value in Canada; for example, if there is a rising trend being suggested by the events of the day, London banks will likely buy more Canadian dollars than they otherwise would.

Before noon, London time, the North American banks will begin calling London banks for their Canadian dollar prices. About noon, the Toronto/Montreal markets will begin their trading and what happens in these markets will "swamp" the other world markets; in fact the rest of the day will be spent largely in arbitrage, i.e., buying in one market and selling in another where the price is higher. The rest of the trading day in London, then, will be dominated by what happens in Canada itself, because the Canadian dollar, not being one of the world's major currencies, is strongest within Canada. No one really wants the Canadian dollar as a trading currency in the same way as the DM, the Japanese yen, or the U.S. dollar.

In Canada the foreign exchange market, or "interbank market" as it is referred to, is different. It consists of salaried brokers in Toronto and Montreal who are paid by the Canadian Bankers Association for the purpose of bringing buyers and sellers of foreign exchange together on a strictly impersonal basis. The prices at which deals are arranged are made known to all market participants—including the Bank of Canada which also participates in the interbank market—without the names of the transactors being divulged. This maintains the perfection of the market in much the same way as the London brokers do, but instead of private companies acting as middleman, the CBA supplies the same service.

The interbank market was instituted in 1950 following the relaxation of wartime exchange controls. Prior to World War II, individual dealers were active in the market on a commission basis much as is common in European countries today. What we have now is a *de facto* market oligopoly which is maintained by performing the service of exchange at such a low cost that no other firm or dealer can possibly compete. There is just not enough profit in the business for any competing brokerage firm to survive.

The buyers and sellers, or market participants, are actually restricted to the wholesale offices of the chartered banks. These banks will likely find a surplus or deficit in their foreign exchange deposits and will wish to dispose of the surplus or purchase additional deposits at the most favourable terms. A price is agreed upon, and at that moment, the price of the foreign exchange in terms of the Canadian dollar becomes the exchange rate. It is widely disseminated throughout Canada and becomes the basis for all transactions involving foreign exchange.

It should be clear at this point that the "foreign exchange" in the interbank market is really the U.S. dollar. This is the consequence of the predominance of trade on the one hand, and the fact that our foreign trade is denominated in U.S. dollars on the other. It is because of the latter that the burden of transferring Canadian dollars into U.S. dollars rests upon the Canadian trader. It is also the reason that the exchange rate of the Canadian dollar is largely determined in Canada rather than elsewhere, for it is the Canadian dollar which is most actively traded in our own local market. Nevertheless, the great international markets are not completely excluded from the Canadian market, for at any time the foreign exchange offices of the chartered banks may contact their counterparts anywhere in the world for a quotation of any currency. If the price quoted for $U.S. in London happens to be better than in the interbank market, they are perfectly free to purchase in that market. Similarly, London banks may purchase $U.S. through their Canadian counterparts from the interbank market, thereby maintaining a two-way link between the Toronto/Montreal market and the rest of the world.

C. The Interbank Market

In Diagram 11-1 there are two parts: A, the demand for Canadian dollars in foreign exchange markets abroad and B, the demand for the $U.S. within the Canadian market (the interbank market). Part A uses the U.S. dollar to measure the "price" of the Canadian dollar and part B inverts this with the $U.S. as the commodity and the $C as the "price." The switch, of course, is to reflect the change in the point of view.

To inject a little realism in the analysis, suppose that an upward trend in the value of the $C appears in Singapore and events portend that this same uptrend is likely to continue in Canada. The reason for this can only be an expected shift in demand for $C to D' which may or may not materialize; at any rate, banks anticipate such a shift in demand which must, ultimately, be concentrated in the North American market. London banks, accordingly, increase their purchases of $C to remove from the market (or increase their holdings of) the supply, $S_3 - S_2$ to raise the price to $.90 U.S. They do this with the expectation of some profit after the shift in demand to D, when all their holdings, purchased at between $.85 and $.90, may be sold at a profit at $.90. Suppose the demand increase fails to materialize. By the end of the trading day there will be a surplus holding of $C deposits which banks will attempt to dispose of on the market. This will shift the market supply back to S_3 (or even further to the right) with the result that the price of the $C declines to or below its original level. A price fluctuation has occurred on the market.

Meanwhile, in the interbank market in Canada, the approach to foreign exchange demand and supply is different. The "commodity" to be traded is the $U.S. dollar and the price is indicated in $C. The two markets, London and Toronto/Montreal, are connected because the supply of $U.S. is a

Diagram 11-1

SHORT-TERM DEMAND FOR FOREIGN EXCHANGE

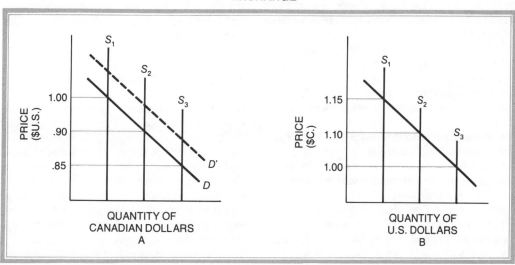

demand for $C, and had the expectations of London banks materialized, there would have been an increase in the market supply of $U.S. Our "market supply" now is the surplus $U.S. deposits which Canadian banks find they do not require in the foreseeable future. And, of course, "surplus to requirements" suggests that a demand function exists, and, given the price, there is an excess of supply.

The demand for U.S. dollars means the deposits necessary to satisfy the needs of trade and commerce between the U.S. and Canada (which is considerable) and any further payments which bank customers may wish to make to Americans for whatever reason. In addition, banks themselves may use their own U.S. dollar deposits for investments if the U.S. interest rate happens to be above the Canadian rate. Once all these needs are satisfied, any bank can offer the surplus for sale on the interbank market. The Canadian demand for U.S. dollars is, thus, quite different from the demand in London for Canadian dollars (aside from the obvious switch in "commodity"). It is different in the sense that it is more stable, originating, as it does, through the needs of trade instead of for the purpose of creating a market. The market, in other words, does not need "creating"—it already exists.

In both cases, London and Canada, demand curves are negatively sloped, but for different reasons. In London, the objective of the banks in purchasing $C is purely to make a market, in which case the lower the price, the more will likely be purchased by the banks' customers. At the same time the slope of the demand curve for the $C will likely be steep (a lower value of elasticity) relative to the demand curve for a currency such as the DM. It will, in other words, require a wider fluctuation in the price of the $C to stimulate interest amongst buyers and sellers than for the DM. The Canadian dollar is *not* a major world currency.

The demand curve for the $U.S. in Canada is also negatively sloped because it is the customers of the chartered banks who will ultimately determine demand. It is through the high price for the $U.S. that the scarce dollars are "rationed" amongst would-be buyers.

Suppose the supply of U.S. dollars on the interbank market should shift to S_1 (Diagram 11-1, B). The cost of the U.S. dollar rises from $C1 =

$U.S.1 to $C1.15 = $U.S.1, and this means that a $U.S.1000 item now costs $C1150, and since the major portion of our trade is with the U.S. the bulk of our imported goods is now more expensive than before. A rationing by price is taking place because the supply, S_1, of U.S. dollars is relatively scarce. Some would-be buyers of U.S. dollars are therefore forced out of the market, and since most of the ultimate "buyers" are actually commercial importers, they are sensitive to the higher cost of foreign exchange deposits and will purchase less.

Similarly, lower costs of U.S. dollars, say $C1.00 or $C.95 mean that imported items become cheaper. Importers will be inclined to purchase more from the U.S. and banks will find foreign exchange deposits more profitable. (The use, to which these foreign exchange deposits can be put by the banks other than meeting "traders' requirements", is discussed in Chapter 13, Eurocurrencies). We have, therefore, a negatively sloped demand curve for foreign exchange just as for any other commodity.

It is important to keep in mind exactly what is being sold (exchanged) for Canadian dollar deposits. These are U.S. dollar deposits manufactured by U.S. banks, of course, which have, through the normal course of business activity, become the property of Canadian banks. As "deposits with banks" they can be sold, loaned, or otherwise disposed of in accordance with the wishes of their owners, Canadian banks. This means that the ownership of these deposits may change, and since they are deposits in U.S. banks, the book entries in these banks may likewise be changed.

D. The Bank of Canada

In the market structure as presented in Diagram 11-1, there are three short-term supply curves for foreign exchange, S_1, S_2, and S_3. They represent the amount of U.S. dollars which are available in the market on a daily basis. These supplies are the result of a *demand* on the part of Americans for Canadian dollars for imports, for Canadian capital investment, or whatever, and flow continuously through the market. If the balance of trade and payments is unfavourable to Canada, banks will find that their U.S. dollar deposits are running down and will seek to replenish them in the foreign exchange markets. This would mean a general shortage of U.S. dollars in the market on any particular day, and since Canadian banks would actively seek and offer high prices for U.S. dollar deposits to supplement their own inadequate supplies, the cost would rise to higher levels. To prevent this the Bank of Canada might move in to augment the meagre market supply by selling from the Exchange Fund Account at a price, say $C1.15 = $U.S.1.00. (See Diagram 11-2.) This has the effect of stabilizing the price upward by keeping the market supply at S_1 or above.

In the same way, if the balance of payments is in Canada's favour and a surplus of U.S. dollar deposits exists among Canadian banks, they would wish to sell the surplus in the market. But since buyers would be generally hard to find, the price would fall to a very low level, and to prevent this, the Bank of Canada purchases for the Exchange Fund Account any U.S. dollar deposits in excess of S_3. This effectively prevents the price from falling below $C.95.

It should be pointed out that the Bank of Canada, in operating in the interbank market in this way, is acting on behalf of the Ministry of Finance which is the "owner" of the Exchange Fund Account. (Actually it is the people of Canada who are the ultimate owners.) By making purchases of foreign exchange it is using Canadian dollars which have accrued as proceeds of taxes or of bond sales to the public. These dollars then become the property of the chartered banks which sold the U.S. dollars and can readily be used to replenish their Bank of Canada deposits, i.e., cash reserves.

The Bank of Canada can enter the market at any point to stabilize the value of the Canadian dollar at a particular level. It can also intervene in the market with the objective of maintaining an "orderly market," i.e., to avoid abrupt swings in the exchange rate. This would involve selling or buying limited amounts of foreign exchange at various price levels. There is considerable evidence that this has been the more usual case. Since May, 1970, the Canadian dollar has been "floating" in the sense that the price of the U.S. dollar is supposed to be determined purely by the intersection of the demand curve and the short-term supply curve (stock equilibrium) without interference by the central banks. Despite this it is

Diagram 11-2

BANK OF CANADA OPERATIONS IN THE INTERBANK MARKET

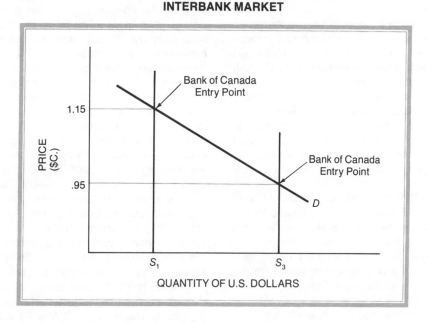

obvious that the Bank of Canada has "steadied" the market so as to influence the exchange rate. We know this because the amount of U.S. dollars in the Exchange Fund Account fluctuates rather considerably.

At the same time that the Bank of Canada intervenes in the interbank market, we know that other central banks, the Bank of England, for example, has intervened in the London market with the objective of steadying the Canadian dollar. This the Bank of England would do upon the request of the Bank of Canada. On the other hand, a much more likely occurrence would be foreign central banks assisting the U.S. by propping up the U.S. dollar, i.e., selling foreign currencies which buying banks might wish to purchase with U.S. dollars.

II. FLOW EQUILIBRIUM IN THE FOREIGN EXCHANGE MARKET

To this point the analysis has been concerned with stocks of foreign exchange which appear on foreign exchange markets on a daily basis as a consequence of Canadian banks acquiring a surplus of foreign deposits — a surplus relative to their requirements at a particular time. This is why vertical supply curves were applied to market demand to determine an equilibrium price or exchange rate. Like the equity markets, the price, or exchange rate, is the result of stock equilibrium.

In the case of flow equilibrium, we are concerned with the changes in the exchange rate through time. In this case the demand curve for foreign exchange will be negatively sloped just as before, i.e., the lower the price the more will be demanded, but we can expect a greater elasticity because there is sufficient time for increases in the amount of foreign exchange demanded to work themselves out. As the price falls and as old contracts expire, etc., new ones will be written so that importers have adequate time for adjustments.

In flow equilibrium also the significance of commodity trade as a component of demand for foreign exchange will be greater than in stock equilibrium. In the latter, banks themselves will have a significant impact on the price as they adjust the levels of their foreign exchange deposits on a day to day basis. These adjustments tend to behave in a manner similar to variations around a long-term trend. Also, in stock equilib-

rium it is the foreign exchange offices of banks which are purchasing at lower cost in anticipation of their customers' increased demand. In flow equilibrium, on the other hand, it is the increased demand *itself* which is working its way through the banking system, and, ultimately, to the market. This increased demand is the consequence of the lower cost of imports due to the cheaper price of the U.S. dollar.

The flow supply function is more complex since it involves an analysis of demand for Canadian exports. In this case we must examine the situation from the U.S. point of view. Suppose the stock equilibrium rate is $C1.05 = $U.S.1. This is a cheap price for an American importer, for now an item costing $C1000 requires only $U.S.952.38. On the other hand, should stock equilibrium produce a rate of $C.95 = $U.S.1, a $C1000 item would cost $U.S.1052.63, substantially more expensive.

We can draw up a demand curve for Canadian exports (which generates the supply of U.S. dollars) that is negatively sloped. On the vertical axis, however, are the *reciprocals* of the Canadian price of the U.S. dollar multiplied by the price in Canadian dollars of the items in question. (See Diagram 11-3.) There are two demand curves drawn, D_1 which is inelastic and D_2 which is elastic. As to which of the two curves applies to Canadian exports in general, we do not know. In the past it has appeared from observation that the curve D_1 has applied. This would be characteristic of such exports as oil and gas, raw material, etc., which are essential to the U.S. economy. However, more recent experience suggests that D_2, the elastic curve may be more appropriate. This seems to be true during recent U.S. recessions which have resulted in a reduction in demand for Canadian exports. While this is, strictly speaking, a combination of both high *income* elasticity and price elasticity of demand, the result is a heightened sensitivity to Canadian price changes during recessionary periods. Our manufactured goods, particularly automobiles, seem to be overpriced and if either (1) the price, P, were to fall, or (2) the Canadian dollar were to depreciate, our exports could increase substantially.

If we note carefully the size of the rectangles subtended by D_1, the inelastic curve, it is apparent that they increase in size as the exchange rate appreciates from $C1.05 = $U.S.1 to $C.95 = $U.S.1. The opposite is true for the elastic

Diagram 11-3

U.S. DEMAND FOR CANADIAN EXPORTS

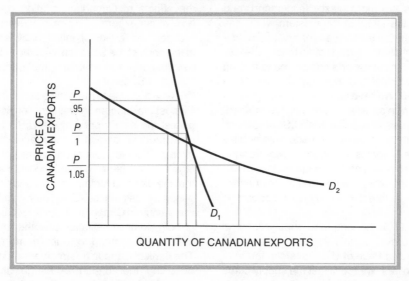

demand curve, D_2—the rectangles decrease in size. Since each rectangle represents the price in U.S. dollars multiplied by the quantity of our exports, it follows that total value of our exports will represent the inflow of U.S. dollars into the banks. In this way the amount of U.S. dollars coming into the interbank market (the excess above that which banks wish to hold) will depend both upon the exchange rate and the elasticity of demand. The supply curves of U.S. dollars will appear as shown in Diagram 11-4. For the inelastic demand curve for Canadian exports, D_1, the supply curve, S_1, bends backward—just about the only negatively sloped supply curve in Economics. For the elastic demand curve, D_2, the supply curve, S_2 is normal, positively sloped. The question as to which curve is more appropriate for Canada is considered in the next section.

A. A Theoretical Analysis

The problem of a backward-bending supply curve of foreign exchange is not confined to Canada alone — after all, we are just one of very many primary producers in the world. A clear example of such a curve is that of the OPEC countries whose recent increases in the price of oil have brought enormous amounts of foreign exchange to them. As in Diagram 11-3 above, the curve D_1

applies in this case and it matters little whether the price, P, rises or the exchange rate appreciates; the effect is precisely the same; the importing country will pay much more. Both curves D_1 in Diagram 11-3 and S_1 in Diagram 11-4 apply. The same would be true of that portion of our exports to the U.S. which consists of energy sources, minerals, etc., which are essential to the U.S. economy.

Diagram 11-4

SUPPLY OF U.S. DOLLARS IN THE CANADIAN MARKET

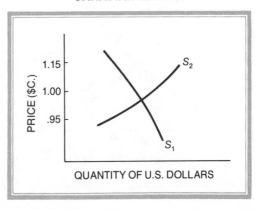

However, the events of the more recent past suggest that we now have a positively sloped supply curve of foreign exchange. This means that our total exports are more elastic in demand, and stems from the fact that the western world has been plagued by both recessionary unemployment and inflation. In geometric terms, the demand curve for our exports has shifted to the left and changed its shape to something like D_2 in Diagram 11-3. We have lately become more of an industrial nation as far as exports are concerned, largely because of the Canada/U.S. auto pact, and substitutes for Canadian-made automobiles are available. There is, therefore, a two-pronged problem—recession and consequent loss of demand in the importing country and rising prices in Canada which threaten to "choke off" demand still further.

In Diagram 11-5, the long-term supply/demand curves are drawn against the axes Quantity of U.S. dollars and Price of U.S. dollars in terms of Canadian dollars. We recall that the supply curve is drawn by identifying the locus of points which indicates the area of a rectangle subtended by the demand curve in Diagram 11-3. However, there are two variables expressed as a ratio in Diagram 11-3 — price divided by the $U.S./$C exchange ratio. Any increase in the Canadian price of exports, therefore, reduces the area of the rectangle.

Diagram 11-5

LONG-TERM MARKET SUPPLY AND DEMAND

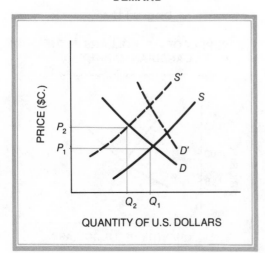

QUANTITY OF U.S. DOLLARS

In Diagram 11-5 we cannot show this Canadian price increase in the supply function itself. We must shift the supply function to the *left* to show the effects of Canadian inflation on the price level of our exports. We can, however, effectively "cancel" the effect of inflation by an increase in the price of the $C in terms of the U.S. dollar (a devaluation) and maintain the same quantity (Q_1) of U.S. dollars.

If it were possible to maintain a constant Personal Disposable Income in the face of rising export prices, the higher price of the U.S. dollar would have reduced demand to the level of Q_2. However, our Canadian inflation means not only rising export prices but also rising incomes after tax so that the demand for imports shifts to the right and becomes less elastic (D'). The result, therefore, is a devalued Canadian dollar as a consequence of both domestic inflation and the recessionary collapse of demand for our exports to the U.S. The Bank of Canada has intervened in the market by using the foreign exchange proceeds of several loans negotiated in the U.S. as well as by drawing down the Exchange Fund Account for selling to buyers in the market. The effect has been to stabilize the Canadian dollar at about $C1 = $U.S.0.85 ($U.S.1 = $C1.18).

It is interesting that recent statistics of merchandise exports have shown increases in our export volume, some 31.2% greater in 1977 than in 1971. Imports, on the other hand, have grown in volume by 53.2% during the same period. This suggests both that the Canadian inflation rate has been high enough to maintain growing imports at the inevitable higher costs and that the lower value of the Canadian dollar has indeed succeeded in making our exports more competitive in world markets. However, it is not merchandise trade which is the difficulty, but Services.

Of the various components of our balance of payments, it is the Service Transactions which have been showing the clearest trends, and at the same time, generate by far the greatest of our annual deficits in the balance of payments. A breakdown of these Service Transactions shows the following classifications, (Table 11-2).

It is the two largest components, Interest and Dividends, and Other, which are of principal concern. The "other," incidentally, as a little search in Statistics Canada material reveals, includes government transactions, business transactions,

Table 11-2
COMPONENTS OF
SERVICE TRANSACTION DEFICIT[1]
1975

Category	%
Travel	15.4
Interest and Dividends	41.6
Freight and Shipping	7.8
Other	25.4

[1]Exclusive of withholding tax.
Source: Bank of Canada Review, March, 1977, Table 70.

(commissions, etc.) and a host of other payments which arise during the course of normal business activity involving non-Canadian business firms. Foreign payments made by Polysar as well as those involving the sale of CANDU reactors are comfortably tucked away in this "other" category.

It is actually not so much the size of the deficit in services but the growth trend over the years which sets the Canadian dollar on an inevitable collision course. Since 1956, there have been three distinct patterns in this trend — a 6.2% growth rate from 1956 to 1963, a 10.8% rate from 1963 to 1972, and, finally, a 21.9% rate for 1972 to 1976. We can gain an insight into the magnitude of the "collision course" by simply projecting the deficit to the year 1980 on the basis of the three growth rates using the year 1976 as a base. The following is the result:

By 1980, assuming the current rate of growth, our service deficit will have reached $14 billion; however, at the lowest 1956-63 growth rate, the deficit would be $7.7 billion, an amount already surpassed by the latest Statistics Canada reports for 1978. An arbitrary selection of a figure of $11 billion, halfway between the two extremes, likely gives a reasonable approximation of our 1980 Service Transactions deficit.

Obviously, there is not the slightest possibility of exporting sufficient merchandise to finance a deficit of such a magnitude; this means that a devaluation of the Canadian dollar is inevitable, the only question being when. As we shall see in the next chapter, it is possible to sustain balance of payments deficits for considerable periods by means of capital imports.

B. A Backward Bending Supply Curve of Foreign Exchange

The situation described above would not have occurred if the demand for our exports were inelastic. Demand for Canadian exports could, conceivably, collapse because of a recession in U.S. industry which requires our raw material, but failing this, the situation would be improved by a *lowering* of the price of the U.S. dollar (an appreciation of the Canadian dollar). This would bring in more U.S. dollars into the market and thereby correct the disequilibrium.

Table 11-3
BALANCE OF PAYMENTS ON SERVICE TRANSACTIONS
(Deficit in $millions)

	I	II	III[1]	Actual Values
1976	6,002	6,002	5,907.6	5,651
1977	6,389	6,690.9	7,354	7,432
1978	6,800.8	7,457.7	9,154.5	8,727
1979	7,238.7	8,312.4	11,395.8	—
1980	7,704.8	9,265.0	14,185.8	—

[1]Projections from 1976 for trends I and II are based on the following trends fitted to the data for the years indicated, using the 6 billion deficit for 1976 as a base. For trend III the base year 1972 was retained.

I. 1956-1963, $\ln y = .064t + 8.7$
II. 1963-1972, $\ln y = .1085t + 8.7$
III. 1972-1976, $\ln y = .219t + 7.589$

Source: Bank of Canada Review, November, 1978, Table 68.

In May, 1970, Canada officially freed the Canadian dollar from the rigid limits of the IMF parity and began the period of "floating." Prior to that time, the Canadian dollar had fluctuated only 1% above or below the official parity rate of $C1.08108 = $U.S.1 in accordance with the IMF regulations. Of course, this involved considerable intervention by the Bank of Canada in the market and required a fairly continuous purchasing of U.S. dollars for the Exchange Fund Account so as to avoid an appreciation of the Canadian dollar. From January to May, 1970, U.S. dollars in the EFA rose from 1,827.6 millions to 2,526.3 millions, almost a $700 million increase.[4] Remembering that these purchases are made with the proceeds of taxation or by borrowing from the Canadian public, we can readily see how the maintenance of such an exchange rate could present an awkward problem. Sometimes it is not correct, as far as domestic economic policy is concerned, to borrow such large sums either from the banking system or through the bond market.

This means that the value of the Canadian dollar was simply too low given the economic circumstances of the time. By the end of May, 1970, the last month in which the Canadian dollar was pegged, the monthly average of noon rates was 1.0728 for one U.S. dollar. By the end of September it had slid to 1.0159, a drop of some 6.6%. At the same time, the Bank of Canada purchased U.S. dollars for the Exchange Fund Account to an amount of 378.6 million. This *suggests* (it does not prove) that the flow of U.S. dollars into the market exceeded the demand without a narrowing of the difference until the equilibrium level was reached, i.e., a backward bending supply curve. Such a situation would appear as shown in Diagram 11–6. Under the pegged rate system the Bank of Canada was purchasing U.S. dollars to the amount of $Q_2 - Q_1$ so as to remove the surplus from the market, and, in effect, shift the supply curve to the left so as to intersect demand at 1.08. When this support was removed in May, 1970, the supply curve resumed its normal position and the Canadian dollar appreciated until the equilibrium price of the U.S. dollar was reached at about $C1.01 = $U.S.1.

---

[4] *Bank of Canada Review*, December, 1971, Table 61.

Diagram 11-6

MARKET EQUILIBRIUM FOR FOREIGN EXCHANGE, 1970

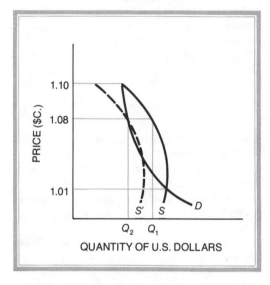

QUANTITY OF U.S. DOLLARS

One tends to accept this hypothetical supply curve as characteristic of Canada at the time for the reason that it is the simplest, most rational explanation of economic events. It might be asked, however, since there were clearly two points of equilibrium, why, once the Canadian dollar was freed, did it not depreciate further to 1.10? While such an equilibrium point is theoretically possible, it is not *practical* because in the free market, a surplus is disposed of by lowering the price, not raising it.

On further inspection, however, we can see that the backward bending supply curve does not exist for long. It turns so as to intersect demand and in so doing it acquires a positive slope and this is how we find it under the conditions described in the previous section.

CONCLUSION

It might appear disturbing at first that probably in no other aspect of Canadian-U.S. relations is there a closer tie than in the area of foreign exchange rates. But, having accepted this fact, why should it be true that whenever the U.S. dollar depreciates against the Japanese yen, or European currencies, the Canadian dollar also depreciates against these currencies? Are we not the innocent victims of a "raw deal?" After all, we are two separate independent countries which happen to share the name "dollar." (Of course, having the same name for our currency has nothing whatever to do with the problem. Foreign exchange markets and dealers are not confused into thinking that these two currencies will move together in the markets for this reason.)

Our devaluation against other currencies is based on a much stronger rationale than this. There is the first characteristic of foreign exchange markets discussed earlier in this chapter and that is the essentiality of a numeraire. One currency, or even a group of currencies, must be a standard against which all others may be measured. This is precisely the same situation that would be found in a domestic economy which has to use money as its measuring rod of value. For example, in a barter situation, apples and oranges may be compared in some ratio of nutrients, but in a market where the forces of demand and supply are at work, it is impossible to compare value ratios without money. The same is true for currency markets. But why not use some other device than the U.S. dollar, a Special Drawing Right, a "basket" of currencies, etc.? The answer to this is purely because the public wants it that way. The markets are consumer oriented and will change if and when the public wishes.

There is one exception to this general rule. The Swiss franc and the German mark actually do have a single market between them without using the U.S. dollar as a numeraire. This is the result of a historically close relationship peculiar to these countries alone. All other currencies must pass through the U.S. dollar. In the table included in the appendix to this chapter, this general rule was tested to see if, by any chance, there was some possible deviation, i.e., did some banks attempt to relate the Canadian dollar directly to Sterling after the fashion of the "Swiss mark?" The monthly values of the ratio of the Canadian dollar to the U.S. dollar were correlated with monthly values of the ratio of *two* ratios — $C against sterling divided by the $U.S. against sterling. If there were any possibility of evaluating the Canadian dollar directly with sterling, the values of the second "ratio of ratios" would move differently from those of the first ratio. Such is not the case. The correlation was almost perfect, $r = .9154$.

If one were to seek for a reason for the "raw deal" for Canada, he would have to look at the closeness of the trade and payments position between Canada and the U.S. The situation is precisely the same as the stock exchange relationship between Canada and the U.S. discussed in Chapter 8 above. The volumes of currencies traded and the elasticities of demand and supply are so great relative to other smaller markets that it is impossible (unless the markets are segregated) for the prices of smaller markets to deviate by any but the smallest degree from the price set in the larger. When, and if, the day arrives that Canada's trade becomes world oriented instead of U.S. oriented, our currency will find its own true value against other world currencies just as any other currency in the world. It is not the fact that the U.S. dollar is the numeraire but the trade and payments orientation which matters.

It follows that the value of the yen, for instance, in terms of Canadian dollars has no economic significance. It is the cost of the U.S. dollars with which one purchases yen that is important. This is why the only significant foreign exchange for Canada is the U.S. dollar, and also why the interbank market, which determines the Canada/U.S. rate of exchange, is so important. We are at one and the same time arriving at our exchange rate against all other currencies as well as the U.S. dollar.

In this chapter, rather careful and detailed attention has been devoted to the market mechanism itself so as to dispel confusion and clear up any erroneous concepts regarding the nature of the exchange rate. It can hardly be overemphasized that in the Canadian interbank market the analysis applies only to that portion of foreign exchange deposits which are considered surplus to the banks' requirements. These are "marginal deposits" in the sense that their value to the banks is less than the Canadian dollar deposits which they could acquire in exchange. Sometimes these U.S. dollar deposits may be very valuable especially during periods of tight money when chartered bank reserves at the central bank are scarce. Foreign deposits can be sold to the Bank of Canada, and in that way the chartered banks' deposits at the central bank will rise; hence, reserves will be eased. At other times, foreign exchange deposits loaned in Eurodollar markets may earn higher interest than Canadian dollar deposits; we will see how this is done in a later chapter. So it is entirely the responsibility of the banks how much foreign deposits enter the market to determine the exchange rate.

It follows that although the balance of trade may be in Canada's favour, it does not automatically ensure an appreciated exchange rate. Canadian banks may prefer to hold their surplus foreign deposits rather than sell them on the market. On the other hand, when the balance of trade is against Canada, banks will be short of deposits and will be more prompt to enter the market to buy. This depreciates our dollar as the cost of the U.S. dollar rises. But there are ways of counteracting trade deficits by means of capital flows and this follows in the next chapter.

ADDITIONAL READINGS

Caves, R.E. & R.W. Jones, *World Trade and Payments*, Little, Brown & Co., 1977, ch. 17.

Friedman, Milton, "Exchange Rates, How Flexible Should They Be?". Paper presented to Joint Economic Committee, 88th Congress, reprinted in *Current Issues of Economic Policy*, Reynolds, Green, Lews (eds.), Irwin-Dorsey Ltd., 1973, p. 465.

Harrod, R.F., *International Economics*, University of Chicago Press, 1958, ch. 5.

Krause, L.B., "Fixed, Flexible, and Gliding Exchange Rates," *Journal of Money, Credit and Banking*, May, 1971, p. 321, reprinted in *Readings in Money, National Income and Stabilization Policy*, Smith, Teigen (eds.), Irwin, Homewood, Ill., 1974, p. 480.

Officer, L.H. & T.D. Willett, *The International Monetary System*, Prentice-Hall, Englewood Cliffs, 1969. A very good selection of readings on the subject title. Friedman's "Free Market Determination of Exchange Rates" is appropriate.

Robinson, J., "The Foreign Exchanges," from *Essays in Employment*, Blackwell, Oxford, 1947, reprinted in *Readings in the Theory of International Trade*, Ellis, Metzler (eds.), Allen & Unwin, Ltd., London, 1950, p. 83. Excellent analysis by a great economist.

Triffin, Robert, *Our International Monetary System: Yesterday, Today, and Tomorrow*, Random House, New York, 1968. Highly recommended for history and background.

APPENDIX

The fact that the Canadian and U.S. dollars are closely related, insofar as other currencies are concerned, is quite easily shown by statistical

Table A11-1
FOREIGN EXCHANGE RELATIONSHIPS

		$C/$U.S.	$C/£ $U.S./£
1976	S	0.971	1.01
	O	0.972	1.00
	N	1.036	0.98
	D	1.009	1.00
1977	J	1.018	1.01
	F	1.046	1.03
	M	1.054	1.05
	A	1.046	1.05
	M	1.052	1.05
	J	1.059	1.06
	J	1.070	1.05
	A	1.075	1.07
	S	1.075	1.07
	O	1.106	1.06
	N	1.108	1.11
	D	1.094	1.06
1978	J	1.107	1.09
	F	1.115	1.12
	M	1.134	1.15
	A	1.130	1.16
	M	1.122	1.11
	J	1.123	1.11
	J	1.135	1.10
	A	1.150	1.14
	S	1.184	1.17

$r^2 = .8379$
$r = .9154$

Source: $C/$U.S. and $C/£ *Bank of Canada Review*, October, 1978, Table 65. $U.S./£ *Bank of England Quarterly Bulletin*, September, 1978, Table 28.

observation. In the table a time series of 25 monthly prices was selected during a period of general decline in the foreign exchange value of the Canadian dollar.

In the first column the U.S. dollar in terms of the Canadian dollar is tabulated. The price movement is shown as ranging from $.97 Canadian for one U.S. dollar to $1.18 Canadian per U.S. dollar—a devaluation of some 22%. The second column, slightly more complex, is the more interesting. It is the "ratio of ratios" and it measures the Canadian dollar devaluation against the pound sterling relative to the devaluation of the U.S. dollar against the pound. Thus, if the exchange rates of the two dollar currencies were exactly the same, the values in the second column would all be unchanging at 1.0. But this is not the case; in fact, a devaluation of the Canadian dollar against the U.S. dollar of 22% produces a 42% devaluation against the pound because the U.S. dollar has suffered a 20% devaluation against the pound during the same period. This is why the values in the two columns are so close and the correlation is so high. The fact that the two columns are not identical is due to the variation in sources and times of data collection as between the Bank of Canada and the Bank of England.

CHAPTER 12

Forward Exchange and Capital Markets

INTRODUCTION

The foreign exchange market discussed in the chapter preceding is certainly one of the greater achievements of the world banking system, not only in terms of technical "hardware" and communications equipment but also from the standpoint of market expertise. The capacity to create a market with the objective of offering the customer the best possible spot price for foreign currency at any time *and* transmit payments in that currency is a great technical achievement.[1] But the banks do more than this. They offer, in addition, payments on specific dates in the future for specific amounts, again at the best possible price. It is this aspect of the banks' services which is most often taken for granted but which, in importance, greatly outweighs the spot market.

Consider, for a moment, what it means to a contractor who has a project in Saudi Arabia involving millions in capital and for which he expects to pay out considerable sums for many years in the future. It is vital for him to fix his exchange rates so that contract costs can be met without the uncertainty of fluctuating exchange. This is particularly important in these days of "floating" exchange rates.

Under the former IMF regime, parities existed for the express purpose of avoiding fluctuating exchanges which had proved disastrous for foreign investors. It was just not possible for capital to go abroad under conditions of uncertainty, and now that the Bretton Woods system has collapsed, it is

just as imperative that we have another system to replace it. This the banks have done with an extraordinary efficiency which even excels the old fixed parity system. We now have the advantage of fluctuating exchanges without the disadvantage of not knowing what the exchange rate will be in the future.

I. FORWARD EXCHANGE

In principle the idea of forward exchange is simple enough. It is just a contract to buy or sell foreign exchange at a stipulated rate, but for delivery in the future. This is a service all modern banks are quite prepared to provide.

The underlying reason for the existence of forward exchange is commercial. Importers who wish to contract for a shipment of goods may prefer to fix the foreign exchange rate at which the purchase will be made. If the payment is to be made upon receipt of the requisite set of documents, the trader can purchase forward exchange at the current prevailing rate. This avoids the risk involved in a fluctuating exchange "spot" rate and can be especially useful if the trader is nervous regarding a possible depreciation of the currency in the near future.

There is another advantage to the importer which follows automatically from the negotiation of a forward contract. No payment is required until the time of the contract has elapsed, hence, by definition, credit is involved and only those with the best credit ratings may request a forward contract. This frees the trader's capital for other uses.

The exporter too has as good a reason for using the forward exchange service as the importer. We recall that Canadian international trade is in U.S. dollars. The exporter will wish to sell the U.S. dollars he will receive in payment for his goods.

---

[1] "Spot" is defined as two days (48 hours) in London. In Canada it is the day following the negotiation; however transactions for two or three days in the future are also spot rate. Beyond this the forward rate applies. *Royal Commission on Money and Credit*, 1964, p. 292, footnote 2.

But what if the Canadian dollar appreciates in the interim? He could lose in the process, and to avoid this possible loss he sells U.S. dollars forward at a specified rate. Again, the banks provide this service just as readily as selling Canadian dollars forward.

It is because of the instability of spot foreign exchange rates that forward exchange exists in the first place. That is, if the spot rate were fixed absolutely, the forward exchange system would vanish but so long as even a small degree of flexibility exists, forward rates are useful. Even under the former IMF regime with only a one percent variation on either side of parity, the forward system operated effectively.[2] This is the result of the enormous volume of payments which can result in substantial losses with only minute changes in the spot rates. One can readily appreciate why only a relatively few currencies have forward markets. Only those of the great trading nations which have the sophisticated banking systems are capable of handling the complexities of the market as well as the huge volume of trade.

In supplying their customers with the necessary foreign exchange forward, the banks will match their contracts as nearly as possible so that when the time for delivery arrives, the customer who supplies one currency is actually satisfying the requirements of the customer who supplies the other. The banks are merely a market medium through which the currency flows when the time arrives. Of course, such a perfect matching would be a happy coincidence which just does not happen, so there is always a residual of forward contracts in either currency to be accounted for. It is this residual, just as in the spot case, which finds its way to the market.

Let us consider the task facing a typical bank, say in London, which undertakes the responsibility of satisfying its customers with a forward exchange contract for one year. To take an example, suppose a customer wishes to purchase 2 million Swiss francs for delivery in one year for $U.S. 1 million (assume an exchange rate of 2/1). The customer, of course, need not produce his $U.S. 1 million until the delivery date. How does the

bank accomplish this? If it could locate a forward contract which would *sell* SF 2 million for $U.S. 1 million on the precise date, no difficulty need arise. But suppose it does not. The bank will then set about creating its own forward contract purchase to match the sale in the following manner: Firstly, the bank purchases 2 million Swiss francs on the spot market. This creates no difficulty because it can make the purchase with sterling deposits which will return, as we shall see presently, to their origin, i.e., they will never be disturbed. With the SF 2 million it enters the swap market where it arranges a spot sale of SF along with a forward purchase of SF with U.S. dollars. Such swaps are advantageous in that they involve the least possible cost to the banks when conducted simultaneously, and since the spot sale was arranged in sterling, the sterling deposits are right back at the beginning! The original spot purchase is cancelled by the spot sale of the same currency (the Swiss franc) and what is left over is the forward purchase of SF 2 million to meet the forward sale of $U.S. 1 million. (See Diagram 12-1.) Note carefully that a total of four transactions (count the arrows) are involved, three supporting transactions and one original. Now, to complicate matters, suppose the customer was a Canadian who wished to purchase SF 2 million one year forward with Canadian dollars. A transaction of this kind must, of course, pass through the numeraire, the U.S. dollar first. How many transactions would be involved to support the single original transaction?

1. A spot purchase of Swiss francs (one transaction).
2. A spot sale of SF and a simultaneous purchase forward with $U.S. in the swap market (two transactions).
3. A spot purchase of $U.S. (one transaction).
4. A spot sale of U.S. dollars and forward purchase with Canadian dollars in the swap market (two transactions), and, finally,
5. A forward sale of Canadian dollars to acquire the necessary $U.S. forward to pay for the Swiss francs forward purchase in step 2 (one transaction).

A simple count will reveal a total of seven supporting transactions. Note carefully that the whole operation has been conducted with sterling deposits (or any other currency for that matter) which are really not important at all. Also, the

[2]In actual practice, central banks intervened at about a ¾% variation on either side of parity. Still, a total of 1½% flexibility was sufficient to establish forward markets.

Diagram 12-1

A FORWARD CONTRACT

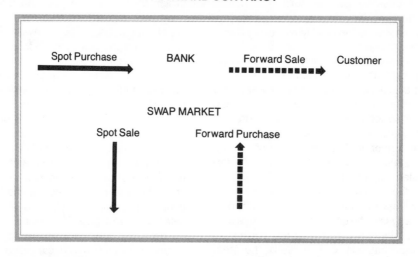

bank is completely covered throughout with no risk of exchange depreciation.

Canadian banks dealing in U.S. dollars do not have such a complicated procedure as this, but they do indeed make use of the swap market. They will, if possible, match their forward commitments, and when this is not possible, they will cover their surplus (or deficit) forward commitments with spot purchases (or sales). They do so for the reason that to locate the compensating purchases of forward exchange, so as to balance out their commitments, is more time-consuming than spot purchases. But time is of the essence, because to delay could mean an increase in the price of U.S. dollars both spot and forward, the two markets generally moving together. Having insured against this risk by immediate spot purchases, the banks can then sort out their forward contracts so as to match purchases and sales. There are, thus, two equilibria which the banks seek — the overall equilibrium of foreign exchange commitments and the forward contract equilibrium.

The forward contract equilibrium can be achieved by means of a swap. This is a transaction involving a simultaneous sale and purchase (or purchase and sale). In the case of having purchased U.S. dollars spot to cover its excess forward commitments, the bank can now proceed to swap, i.e., sell these dollars spot and simultaneously purchase U.S. dollars forward so as to meet the

required forward sales. The "insurance" is now complete with both the risk of a depreciating exchange rate covered and the danger that the differential between the spot and forward rates may increase, forcing the bank to pay more, covered as well. If we ask the question why does the bank not retain its spot U.S. dollars in the first place, the answer is that it can, but in so doing it may forego a profitable short-term investment in Canadian dollars. In fact, the only occasion in which a bank would not swap would be when short-term investment in U.S. dollars is more profitable. Bank funds must be continuously employed; otherwise profits will not be maximized.

A. Short-Term Capital Movements

International payments involving foreign exchange originate in ways other than purely commercial. For Canada, capital flows are very important, involving, as they do, the flow of U.S. dollars into the banks. The reason that we have such capital inflows lies in the fundamental fact that the marginal return to capital is lower in the U.S. than in Canada. Thus, when Americans have an excess of funds to place in capital markets on a short-term basis, they can put them to the most profitable use, be it in Canada, Europe, or the U.S. Since they are interested in security, as well as yield, they will choose those countries with developed capital markets which are particularly adapted to short-term investments.

It is interesting that it was neither the government nor the Bank of Canada which initially started the original short-term capital market. By the time the Bank of Canada had arranged Purchase and Resale Agreements so that federal Treasury Bills could be purchased by dealers, sales finance companies were already active in selling "commercial paper" with 90 days maturity. This practice began in 1951 and has continued for the reason that it is a cheaper method of obtaining funds than by chartered banks borrowing.[3] Other companies which require large sums of finance, such as grain dealers, wholesale marketing companies, etc., have also found it to their advantage to use this market. There are even some municipal and provincial governments selling Treasury Bills as well. By the end of 1977, short-term paper outstanding in this market amounted to a total of $9.5 billion, about one-third ($3.3 billion) of which was sales finance and consumer loan paper. Another 48% ($4.6 billion) consisted of "other" commercial paper sold by all other business firms. Bankers' acceptances amounted to $1.2 billion and Treasury Bills of local and provincial governments were $447 million.[4] Considering that the Treasury Bills of the federal government outstanding at the end of December, 1977, came to $10.3 billion, the "private sector" short-term money market is surprisingly large.

Statistics Canada is able to identify to some extent the flow of short-term capital from foreign sources and the particular market, federal or "private," and the particular market instrument which it uses. Since such investment comes from outside the country, it is included in the balance of payments capital account along with other forms of capital movements such as bank deposits, etc. As frequently occurs in such cases there is a large "errors and omissions" entry to reconcile the discrepancies in the statistics so that we cannot be certain of their accuracy. Neither is such capital a one-way proposition, for Canadian capital flows out of Canada as well so as to take advantage of the interest yields, security, etc.,

available in foreign markets. However, from the balance of payments accounts we can get some idea of the net flow of this capital.

Table 12-1
NET SHORT-TERM CAPITAL MOVEMENTS ($ MILLIONS)

1970	1972	1974	1976	1977
-196	472	1,310	93	902

Source: Bank of Canada Review, October, 1978, Table 68.

As is suggested in Table 12-1 swings in short-term capital flowing in and out of Canada are rather violent and wide. The reason for this will be apparent shortly.

We can more easily clarify how and why such capital movements occur in the first place with the aid of an example. Suppose a U.S. corporation has a temporary surplus of funds which it wishes to invest at the maximum profit. It can purchase U.S. credit instruments on the short-term market, or, if the Canadian market looks attractive, Canadian instruments. But, and this is the main point, if it elects the Canadian market, it encounters a difficulty in the form of the exchange rate, for it has no guarantee that the rate, say, 90 days hence will be the same as the present.

This difficulty can be overcome with the aid of the forward market. Forward exchange is always quoted both in Canada and abroad as a certain amount (generally in hundredths of a Canadian cent) above (+) or below (−) the spot rate. This means, simply, that the cost of a forward contract is included in the actual exchange rate itself and this cost varies quite on its own just as the spot rate varies depending on the forces of supply and demand in the interbank market.

Any corporation, therefore, can purchase the necessary Canadian dollars spot and simultaneously sell these dollars forward and have the rate for the entire investment transaction fixed so long as it is prepared to pay the spot rate plus (or minus) the forward spread, and this the corporation considers in its initial decision to invest in Canada in the first place. It subtracts, that is, the forward spread from the Canadian interest and then compares this with the U.S. rate. We can state this as a "hedging equation" more precisely. For convenience, we assume Treasury Bills are

---

[3]Submission of the Industrial Acceptance Corporation to the *Royal Commission on Banking* and Finance, 1964, p. 122.
[4]*Bank of Canada Review*, October, 1978, Table 35.

the credit instruments with 90-day forward rates.

$$R_C - \frac{F. \text{ Spread (4)}}{\text{Spot Rate}} - R_{US} = \overset{+}{\underset{-}{0}}.^5$$

With R_C = Treasury Bill rate in Canada.

With R_{US} = Treasury Bill rate in U.S.

Notice that each of the members in the equation is expressed in annual rates, purely a convention, for comparison purposes with longer-term rates. This is why the percentage spread between 90-day forward and spot rates is multiplied by four. At the end of the equation a plus sign indicates that Canada is more profitable than the U.S. for short-term investment, a negative sign means the U.S. is more profitable than Canada, and a zero is neutral.

To illustrate, suppose that an interest rate in Canadian Treasury Bills of 10% *per annum* is being earned. If a positive forward spread of 1% (annual rate) exists, a portion of the 10% would be lost because a U.S. corporation purchases Canadian dollars spot at a specific rate and must sell them at a higher rate, hence, completing the exchange transaction with less U.S. dollars than it started with.[6] The "covered rate" (9%) would be compared with the comparable interest rate in the U.S. If the difference between this 9% and the U.S. rate is positive, it is worthwhile investing in Canada.

Suppose, now, the forward spread were negative which, indeed, it can easily be. In the "hedging formula" above, this enhances the Canadian interest rate and could actually compensate for a rate *lower* in Canada than in the U.S. Short-term capital could easily flow to Canada under these circumstances.

Now what about a Canadian corporation with an excess of dollars to invest in *either* the U.S. or Canada? The same formula applies in this case as well. Consider again a numerical example. As before, Treasury Bill rates are 10% in Canada and 8% in the U.S. and a 1% spread (annual rate) exists. The Canadian can purchase U.S. dollars at the rate of $C1 = $U.S.1 and sell them at a forward rate of $C1.01 = $U.S.1. In this way he

gains an extra Canadian cent in the exchange transaction. Despite this it still is not worthwhile to invest in the U.S. because he earns 8% + 1% = 9% which is below the Canadian rate. Thus, the equation is true for both U.S. and Canadian capital.

For those who do not wish to bother with all the arithmetic to decide in which country one should invest his short-term capital, "hedged" rates are available from private dealers. One of these is Greenshields whose excellent "Canadian Money Market Review" supplies such information. From this, Table 12-2 is extracted.

One year before the publication of the Review (July 23, 1974) it was substantially more profitable to purchase Canadian Treasury Bills than U.S. Bills. This was true for both Canadians and Americans and was the result of both a higher interest rate in Canada than in the U.S. and a rather large *negative* forward spread. For both Canadians and Americans almost a 3% difference between their two alternatives existed in favour of Canada. It is hardly surprising, therefore, that in 1974 (see Table 12-1 above) a subtantial amount of short-term capital came to Canada.

In addition the Bank of Canada includes in its monthly Review both the forward premium (+) or discount (−) calculated on the basis of an annual interest rate and the "covered differential" (the solution of the hedging equation) in its table on Canadian and international interest rates (Table 20). It is interesting that over the past four years these monthly differentials have averaged .36% for commercial paper and .43% for Treasury Bills. This suggests that the commercial paper is more attractive than federal Treasury Bills since it requires less differential for capital to flow into Canada for commercial paper than for Treasury Bills. In terms of standard deviation, the commercial paper also has a narrower spread, i.e., .047% instead of the Treasury Bill, .083%.

We can now recognize the reason for the wide fluctuations in net short-term foreign capital flows. It is the interest rate difference between the U.S. and Canada combined with the forward spread. When the covered differential is positive, it is in Canada's favour, when negative, it is in favour of the U.S. Most of the time in the recent past (44 of the past 49 months for commercial paper and 37 of the past 49 months for Treasury Bills) the differential is positive so that net inflows

---

[5]Sometimes the formula is written $(R_C - R_{US}) - F.$ Spread $= \overset{+}{\underset{-}{0}}$. The expression in the parenthesis is the interest rate differential between Canada and the U.S.

[6]If $C1=$U.S.1, spot, and a one cent forward spread exists, a U.S. investor will have $1.00 − .01 = .99$ after the transaction. A negative forward spread would yield $1.01 for each U.S. dollar invested in Canada.

Table 12-2
COMPARABLE SHORT-TERM RATES*

	Today	Week Ago	Month Ago	Year Ago
Government of Canada Treasury Bills	7.25	7.15	6.90	8.85
U.S. Terms fully hedged	6.79	6.47	6.04	10.33
U.S. Treasury Bills	6.24	6.05	5.66	7.60
Canadian Terms fully hedged	6.58	6.61	6.40	5.90

*All rates are percentages for 91-day Treasury Bills (annual rates). *Source: Canadian Money Market Review*, July 23, 1975.

---

of short-term capital have been more generally true than not. All this suggests that if the government and the Bank of Canada so wish, they can readily attract short-term capital into Canada simply by pushing up the Treasury Bill rate in the manner outlined in Chapter 6.

B. Capital and the Exchange Rate

Canada is in a situation similar to that of Great Britain in that adjustments in the interest rates affect the inflow of foreign capital rather considerably. Of course the reasons are very different; i.e., Canada requires long-term capital for investment within the country; whereas Great Britain is an international capital market so well established that large sums of foreign capital can always find temporary accommodation in London. In our case, savings from the U.S. in particular are often directly invested by corporations or used to purchase Canadian stocks and bonds. The importance of such capital cannot be overemphasized; in fact, both within our national economy and in the foreign exchange market the effects of capital flows are very strong.

The reason for this lies in the fact that capital inflows provide an additional increment to the foreign exchange deposits of the banks which keep the exchange rate at an appreciated level. We recall that the interbank market itself is incremental to the amounts of foreign exchange assets of the banks so that capital flows increase these increments of foreign exchange, and have, therefore, a correspondingly greater impact in the interbank market. This is why substantial shifts in the market supply curves will take place as these capital inputs appear. (See Diagram 12-2.) The impact of capital flows on the market price is greater in the case of the backward bending supply curve, the amount of the impact depending

upon the slope of the supply curve relative to the demand curve.

Broadly, this was the problem during the free-floating exchange rate years prior to 1963. With the huge influx of direct investment, the supply of foreign exchange shifted to S' whether backward sloping or not. Such appreciated exchange rates encouraged imports but discouraged exports, and with unemployment at high levels in the early 1960s, either capital inflows had to be discouraged, so as to lower the exchange rate, or a fixed rate of exchange at a depreciated level had to be assigned with the Bank of Canada absorbing the surplus. The government chose the latter course and direct investment continued to flow into Canada.

There was actually very little the government could do under the circumstances. Continued appreciation of the Canadian dollar would likely have hurt export markets and to reduce foreign investment would also have cut back employment in the investment industries. In electing to build up the Exchange Fund Account by pegging the dollar at a low level, the government was simply avoiding a two-pronged dilemma. Certainly there was nothing that could have been done by way of monetary policy to influence investment which at the time was largely direct investment.[7] Such investment is motivated by profits which, because of a host of technical reasons peculiar to the various industries (proximity to raw material, the labour force, etc.), were, in the past, higher in Canada. It is this same direct investment, incidentally, which has been leaving Canada for the opposite reasons — high costs, lack of profits, etc.—during the recent inflationary years of the 1970s.

---

[7]In the years 1960 to 1963 direct investment varied between 60 and 73% of total long-term investment in Canada.

Diagram 12-2

FLOW EQUILIBRIUM WITH CAPITAL INPUT

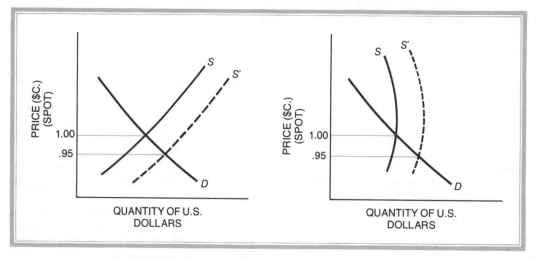

In the case of portfolio investment, particularly bonds, a tight monetary policy, which limits the availability of Canadian bank financing and raises interest rates, encourages Canadian borrowers to seek accommodation in the U.S., assuming that conditions are easier there. Equity investment, on the other hand, flows to Canada from foreign countries in response to differentials in dividends, growth prospects, etc., and to the extent that interest rates affect the market prospects for equities, will be subject to some influence from monetary policy.

Short-term capital, on the other hand, is strongly influenced by monetary policy which affects the short-term interest rate. The forward differential is also instrumental in attracting or discouraging such investment. All this means that Canada can significantly influence the exchange rate of the Canadian dollar by policies which affect the rate of interest.

But oftentimes economic policies may be conflicting as, for example, government deficit financing which stimulates employment but which raises interest rates through government bond sales on the capital market. This increased interest rate can widen the differential between the U.S. and Canadian rates, attract more capital, appreciate our exchange rate and *discourage* employment in the export industries. It is because of such complex and difficult policy mixes as this

that it is often easier and more effective to simply follow the monetary policies of our giant neighbour to the south.

A fixed exchange rate with Bank of Canada intervention within strict limits in the interbank market avoids this exchange rate problem so long as we are content to accumulate reserves in the Exchange Fund Account. But this again has its difficulties, for the Exchange Fund Account is financed almost entirely by "Advances from The Receiver General of Canada." This means that either taxes or proceeds of bond sales must be used to purchase the foreign exchange in the interbank market. It is interesting also that none of the funds so accrued, with the exception of gold and SDR's, is "idle." They are reinvested in the U.S. itself, largely in the form of Treasury Bills and Treasury Notes; in other words, they are recycled through the U.S. where they came from in the first place! The only difference is that we, the Canadian public, have become the lenders instead of, say, large U.S. corporations, banks, etc. Considering the fact that we "earned" these funds in part by surrendering title to our own resources, industries, etc., through inflows of capital, any long-term benefits to Canada derived in this way may be questioned.

There is one other aspect of capital investment which is even more disturbing. Capital inflows, whether direct or portfolio, are automatically self-reversing, i.e., they generate reverse flows of payments in the form of interest and dividends and repatriated profits. The time lag between the inflow of capital and the outflow of profits may be long enough, but in the last analysis it is there. We can see part of this outflow and its growth during the 1970s in Table 12-3.

Since the year 1957, the growth rate of these payments has been 9.1% per year, a rather substantial amount. This means that the demand for U.S. dollars with which to make these payments is continuously growing as well. This demand would likely be transmitted to the interbank market as a shift in the demand curve (see Diagram 12-2) to the right, raising the price of the U.S. dollar (depreciating the Canadian dollar). But, as we know, the rather typical Canadian solution to a depreciating exchange rate is to encourage provinces and municipalities to borrow in the capital markets of the U.S. to relieve the pressure on the exchange rate. This can be done by monetary policies which maintain a high differential between interest rates in Canada and the U.S., and in so doing, the result is a shift of the supply curve to the right at S'. But this automatically ensures a further increase of demand for foreign exchange for the future payment of dividends and interest, etc.—an excellent example of short-run solutions to create long-run problems. This has the effect of increasing the *potential* future demand for foreign exchange when such investments are either liquidated or the profits therefrom are repatriated instead of being reinvested.

C. Swaps

Another method by which short-term capital can be invested abroad is through the banking system itself—the swapped deposits. These involve a commitment on the part of the bank to a depositor to convert his deposit into a foreign deposit with a specific rate of interest. When the period of the commitment has expired, the bank agrees to convert the foreign deposit into a Canadian dollar deposit once more. The "swap" arises because a simultaneous sale of U.S. dollars forward accompanies the purchase spot of U.S. dollars.

The process of swapping in this way gives rise to a new foreign currency deposit on the liabilities side of the bank's balance sheet. It is balanced by a foreign currency asset indicating the use to which the funds are put. Of course the interest rate on these deposits is often higher than domestic deposits, especially if the forward spread happens to be positive. In this way more Canadian dollars are acquired through the forward transaction than are sold through the spot.

A very interesting development is the use of foreign exchange deposits to increase reserves during a period of monetary stringency imposed by the Bank of Canada. This can be done in the following manner: Cash reserves are required to be held against Canadian dollar deposits only, so when reserves are scarce, banks can temporarily *reduce* their Canadian dollar deposits by satisfying the customer with a foreign exchange deposit instead. In so doing foreign exchange liabilities are increased.

Ordinarily, the banks would purchase a foreign exchange asset with the Canadian dollar deposit so acquired, and thereby balance their liabilities. But in this case, they may redeposit the Canadian dollars with the central bank to satisfy their liquidity requirements. This process of swapping to increase reserves could go on indefinitely and would be checked by a decline in the forward spread to a negative level making such activity unprofitable. It would be characterized by negative foreign assets because foreign liabilities increase without corresponding increases in foreign assets. Another possible, though improbable, check would be a "run" on the foreign liabilities of the banks sparked by a loss of confidence in the foreign banking activities of all of the banks in the western world. In such a case, (see Chart

---

Table 12-3
ANNUAL PAYMENTS OF INTEREST AND DIVIDENDS
(millions of dollars)

						Projected	
1970	**1972**	**1974**	**1976**	**1977**	**1978**	**1979**	**1980**
1550	1713	2435	3297	4300	3838	4204	4605

Source: Bank of Canada Review, October, 1978, Table 70. Projections based on a growth trend fitted for the years 1957-1977.

Chart 12-1

NET FOREIGN ASSETS OF CHARTERED BANKS

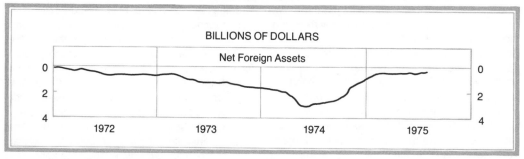

BILLIONS OF DOLLARS

Source: Bank of Canada, Weekly Financial Statistics, August 7, 1975, p. 6.

12-1) Canadian banks would be hard put to it to locate an additional $2 billion or so of foreign liquid assets.

During 1973 and 1974, monetary policy was mildly restrictive, or to put it in the words of the Governor of the Bank of Canada:

> During 1973, the Bank of Canada so managed the cash reserves of the chartered banks that the bank's total assets were not permitted to rise in line with the rapid growth of their loans and mortgages.[8]

and again,

> During 1974 until late in the summer the Bank of Canada maintained a cash management policy that was designed on balance to offer resistance to strong credit demands and to moderate the rate of monetary growth.[9]

In a manner akin to the British clearing banks, our chartered banks appear to have discovered the potential for avoiding tight money policies in foreign deposits. It is not inconceivable that in the future, the Bank of Canada may be forced to find a method of closing this "loophole" in the interests of conducting a successful monetary policy.

[8]Bank of Canada Annual Report for 1973, p. 31.
[9]Bank of Canada Annual Report for 1974, p. 31.

The decennial revision of the Bank Act is the appropriate time to consider this.

II. SPECULATION

In the process of balancing their forward exchange commitments, banks will only enter into agreements with firms with established lines of credit. This is important for them because, should there be a default of payment, the banks must carry out their end of the agreement even though losses result. For instance, a forward sale of U.S. dollars, even though covered initially by spot purchases, will be matched by a forward sale of Canadian dollars. Once the matching sale has taken place, the bank is free to sell or otherwise dispose of its spot cover. If the firm fails, for any reason whatever, to deliver the U.S. dollars as per its contract, the bank still is obligated for the delivery under the original contract of U.S. dollars. This is why only firms with established lines of credit will find forward accommodation at the banks.

This does not mean, however, that speculation would not take place, since any corporate treasurer who is responsible for large amounts of funds can take advantage of an open position on the market. In so doing he is not, as politicians sometimes like to imply, performing an act designed to force down the exchange value of a currency. There is nothing reprehensible about speculation; rather, it is the deterioration of the economic conditions of a country that makes speculation possible.

If we define speculation as any "open" position, i.e., uncovered or unhedged, then the majority of firms, according to the Royal Commission of Banking and Finance in 1964, were speculators[10] However, it is unlikely that this would be true today. When the Porter Commission was preparing its report, the Canadian dollar was pegged under the IMF parity system so that the spot variation was never much more than 3/4% on either side of parity. Unless very large sums of money were involved, forward contracts to fix the exchange rate were unlikely to be worth the extra expense. There was no incentive to use forward markets at that time.

More to the point, foreign exchange speculation should be defined as an open position with an *objective*, i.e., the speculator is sufficiently certain of what the future will bring forth that he is willing to gamble with what he believes are odds in his favour. By the open position he is laying his money "on the line." Sometimes the speculator's degree of certainty becomes almost 100%, and it was this which led *The Economist* to remark, regarding the devaluation of the U.S. dollar in February, 1973:

> By last week every blind beggar could see that the purchase of a D-mark at the old Smithsonian ceiling price of 31³/₄ American cents would bring in something that could not conceivably be worth less than 31³/₄ American cents this week and that would most probably be worth more.[11]

A speculative, or open position, can be shown most easily in diagrammatic form. Let time be represented on the horizontal axis and the cost of the U.S. dollar on the vertical. There are only two points in time that are relevant—the present, and the time of the forward contract, e.g., 90 days hence. Spot prices are indicated as solid lines and forward exchange prices as dashed. A first example of speculation would be very simply an open position much as a trader might assume. A

---

[10]Of the membership of the Canadian Manufacturers Association, 77% reported that they never used the forward market. *Report of the Royal Commission of Banking and Finance*, 1964, p. 298.
[11]*The Economist*, February 17, 1973, p. 13.

Diagram 12-3

OPEN FUTURE SPOT

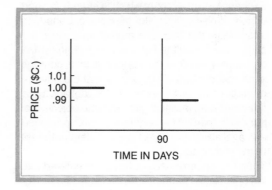

delivery of goods is expected in 90 days and he hopes to profit from an expected appreciation of the Canadian dollar from $C1 = $U.S.1 to $C.99 = $U.S.1. (See Diagram 12–3.) The purchase of U.S. dollars is made 90 days into the future when the expected spot price is .99. The importer has gained a 1% windfall from guessing correctly and postponing his purchase rather than "closing" with a forward contract. This is, of course, an expectation of an appreciation of the Canadian dollar.

A second form of speculation would be an expected depreciation of the dollar to take the form of an outright purchase of U.S. dollars spot to be sold back to the banks in 90 days after the Canadian dollar depreciates. This is shown in Diagram 12–4.

Diagram 12-4

SPOT SPECULATION

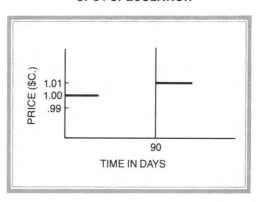

Such speculation as this, if sufficiently general, increases the demand for U.S. dollars in the market. In so doing it removes U.S. dollars from the Exchange Fund Account which, if already in short supply, makes it difficult for the Bank of Canada to intervene in the interbank market. In a word, the speculator himself is helping to bring about the devaluation which he hopes for. It is to discourage such speculative activity as this that the government borrows large sums of U.S. dollars, uses IMF borrowing facilities, etc., with the objective of *not* using them. The very fact of their presence and availability if required is a sufficient deterrent to the speculator.

Thus far, forward markets have not entered into the speculative pattern. However, it will be recognized at once that purely spot speculation can be costly since it involves a considerable outlay of cash. The speculator can avoid this if he can contract forward since no cash is involved until the actual date of transfer. In this case, he purchases U.S. dollars forward in the expectation that the price will rise. (See Diagram 12-5.) A rise in the future spot price of the U.S. dollar from $.99 to $1.00 means a profit with no cash outlay since the speculator closes his forward contract with a simultaneous purchase and sale.

The banks would be caught in the middle of this situation. Their first action would be to cover the speculative forward contracts with spot purchases of U.S. dollars. Having done so, they would then, if they could, line up their forward purchases, but this may be difficult if expectations for a depreciation are general. To the extent

Diagram 12-5

FORWARD SPECULATION

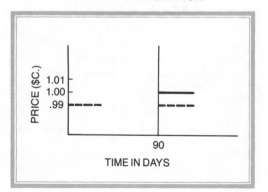

that they *would* be unable to match their forward contracts, they would rely on the Exchange Fund Account for additional forward sales.

Eventually, as the forward contracts are wound down, the "unmatched" forward sales would draw from the original spot purchases which would constitute a net drain from the Exchange Fund Account. Assuming that devaluation is not forthcoming, i.e., the speculators are disappointed, all the Bank of Canada need do is to push up Treasury Bill rates to increase the differential in the "hedging equation." This would counteract the forward spread and would encourage an inflow of short-term capital to finance the outflow due to maturing forward contracts. In this case the original spot purchase by the banks may be returned to the Exchange Fund Account so that no loss of U.S. dollars need occur.

Forward speculation, then, can be extremely damaging to the exchange value of any currency, including the Canadian dollar. Suppose that Canada, with a relatively "weak" currency, shows poor balance of payments figures, or, even more speculative, inflationary tendencies which would probably worsen the balance of payments in the future. This is precisely where forward speculation enters in, because it is likely that the future spot price of the Canadian dollar will decline. A forward sale to be covered with a future spot purchase after the currency has gone down in value will reap a tidy profit.

Banks who offer to purchase the forward contracts will, if speculation is general, find it difficult to match them with forward sales, and, therefore, will be obligated to cover spot. They must, as a consequence, buy the $ U.S. spot and this will drain the Exchange Fund Account to force a "premature" devaluation. This is why the forward markets are so important as barometers of the weakness, or strength, of a currency. Should forward rates decline in the markets, we can be certain that our currency is facing rough weather ahead unless the Canadian government shows its determination to hold the exchange rate firm.[12] Undoubtedly the most interesting examples of speculation have been not in Canada at all but in

---

[12]The government insists on the fiction that the Canadian dollar is "floating" free with its value determined by the forces of supply and demand. The Bank of Canada intervenes only to smooth out fluctuations. Forward market speculators know better, however.

Europe, Japan and the U.S. In fact, one can say that it was speculation which administered the final blow to the old IMF fixed rate system of currencies, for it is the speculator who wagers on the capacity of the central bank to hold the value of foreign exchange within specified limits. After all, to supply the foreign exchange markets with the amounts of foreign exchange that may be required is to have almost an unlimited supply in the various official accounts. When the speculator realizes that the central bank in question is weakening, he purchases the foreign exchange (adding further to the difficulties of the central bank) with the expectation of selling it back to the same central bank (ultimately) at an appreciated rate and at a tidy profit.

The Economist estimated that during the dollar devaluation crisis of February, 1973, $6 billion of currency was "rushed into marks at the Bundesbank's inanely fixed price, ($U.S.3175 = 1DM), so that 10% devaluation of the dollar will cost the German people up to $600 million from a week's dealings."[13] What was happening at that time was a great wave of short-term capital washing out of the ailing U.S. dollar into the stronger D marks. After devaluation the Bundesbank found itself in the unhappy position of supporting a devalued price of $U.S.3525 = 1DM, offering to speculators a cool 10% profit. In this case it mattered little whether the purchase of DM's was spot or forward, the profit was great enough in a very short time.

Speculators, however, were not the "international money speculators" about whom former President Nixon spoke so disparagingly in August, 1971. Quite the contrary, they were giant multinational corporations with specialized offices that perform the important service of managing the corporation finances both to avoid losses and to maximize profits. It was simply sound business management. Freely floating rates, of course, would avoid such massive floods of capital since the market would correct any excess of demand for a currency by automatically increasing the price. Thus, had the D mark floated in the above case, its price in terms of the U.S. dollar would have risen as soon as capital flowed into the country, thereby choking off any possible speculative profits.

In the days of the Bretton Woods system of fixed rates, speculative action against the Canadian dollar was not at all significant. As the Royal Commission on Banking and Finance put it, "Our enquiries suggest that such speculation is much less important than that carried on by firms and individuals whose regular business brings them into the exchange market."[14] However, what was true a decade ago is certainly not true today.

When the IMF system (or "Bretton Woods" system as it is sometimes referred to) collapsed in 1971 to be replaced by the Smithsonian Agreement with a fluctuation of $2^{1}/_{4}$% on either side of parity instead of the IMF 1%, forward exchange became much more important. With the further breakdown of the Smithsonian Agreement, all currencies began to "float" on the free market though the floating process was a "dirty" one in the sense that central banks (including the Bank of Canada) intervened.[15] So long as central banks do intervene, speculators have an added incentive to enter the market to wager against the central bank. But even if the market is absolutely free, speculation in forward contracts would still take place in the same way as commodity futures speculation, discussed in Chapter 9 above.

Who are these speculators? Originally, they were banks (the Gnomes of Zurich) particularly the great Swiss private banks, multinational corporations, traders, etc., who simply protect the value of their liquid capital or their clients' capital. Now, however, speculators may be anyone because in 1972 the Chicago Mercantile Exchange opened its International Money Market to deal in futures contracts of the great currencies of the world. These currencies are German marks, Swiss francs, British pounds, Mexican pesos, Canadian dollars, French francs, Dutch guilders, and the Japanese yen. Naturally the U.S. dollar is implicitly included in the list because it is the numeraire (N.B., The IMM refers to its market as "futures" as opposed to the forward market in which banks, brokers, and multinational companies participate and in which public speculation is specifically discouraged.) Anyone, therefore, who wishes, may speculate or hedge, if he is a

---

[13]*The Economist,* February, 17, 1973, p. 13.

[14]*Op. cit.,* p. 298.
[15]There was an exception to this, which should be mentioned, and that was the currencies of those countries which made up the EEC and which agreed to fix their currencies against each other to form a "snake."

Table 12–4
NET OUTSTANDING FORWARD CONTRACTS IN U.S. DOLLARS.
Millions of U.S. dollars
As at month-end

Mths/	1962	1963	1964	1965	1966	1967	1968	1969	1970	1971	1972	1973	1974	1975	1976	1977
J	-11.4	-2.2	63.4	8.3	28.9	1.0	-296.5	51.0	-1.4	2.3	-0.3	-8.3	9.5	-14.3	-7.4	21.5
F	-1.1	—	38.5	10.0	9.2	-3.5	-524.3	42.4	-0.3	-4.9	9.9	-11.6	27.2	-22.8	-11.2	43.6
M	-4.6	-1.4	104.5	43.6	11.0	-7.5	-705.0	41.7	3.3	-3.8	-4.9	-13.2	-0.3	9.0	-2.9	29.3
A	-51.4	48.5	40.4	3.0	12.9	-3.5	-553.0	-0.5	15.0	-5.5	-6.1	-4.5	15.7	-42.5	10.2	27.1
M	-78.4	30.5	32.6	—	22.0	-2.2	-432.8	-2.9	360.2	-7.3	20.1	1.4	-0.2	27.3	-12.7	0.2
J	-605.4	18.0	-1.0	—	7.0	-2.0	-201.7	-0.3	187.4	1.6	-38.1	-0.6	-18.0	-11.1	-152.6	37.8
J	-563.7	0.6	0.5	-5.2	-4.8	-5.9	-33.5	36.0	146.7	5.9	-11.1	-7.1	-0.8	-1.3	-45.9	44.1
A	-464.5	-4.0	0.1	95.5	-20.0	-11.7	31.6	-2.0	91.9	-20.8	-2.2	-5.0	-16.6	-1.3	102.7	-5.8
S	-361.8	104.6	23.0	72.3	-24.7	9.1	27.0	-3.4	51.1	0.2	-3.5	-13.5	0.3	5.0	8.2	-15.1
O	-71.3	78.3	28.0	41.9	-17.6	37.8	134.5	19.1	54.5	-13.4	-49.0	-38.3	-	42.8	-19.0	7.6
N	-100.0	56.8	11.3	-5.7	-7.7	29.7	117.0	1.2	14.1	-2.0	-100.5	5.0	-0.8	-16.2	-133.6	-7.1
D	-0.8	54.0	9.3	-14.6	-5.5	16.7	25.2	7.5	-6.4	-4.0	-2.5	-	-8.3	-4.9	30.7	-5.4

Source: Bank of Canada Review, June, 1978.

trader, simply by contacting participating brokers. A small security fee will be required because no actual currency delivery need take place. In this sense the situation is exactly the same as commodity futures whereby speculators sell before the contract matures.

Since no delivery actually occurs, a great "balloon" of futures trading volume (and value) surrounds a small core of actual delivered currency. As such it poses no threat *per se* to a specific currency other than being a signal as to what markets are actually thinking. The forward market, therefore, will likely use the futures market as an important indicator, and, as we have seen, it is the forward market which can, and does, put pressure on a currency's spot value.

Canada's experience with speculation in the past has not been spectacular; after all, in the list of currencies traded in Chicago, it is not difficult to identify which are of least importance in trade. There have, nevertheless, been periods of speculation in Canadian dollars in the past. In Table 12-4, published by the Bank of Canada, these periods are identified in the form of net outstanding forward contracts of the Exchange Fund Account. Negative signs identify future losses of U.S. dollars when the forward contracts are eventually unwound. These identify expectations of declining values of the Canadian dollar because speculators expect to sell U.S. dollars spot at a profit having purchased them at a cheaper forward rate. Similarly, Canadian traders prefer to have the cheaper U.S. dollar forward contracts as

long as possible into the future after the dollar has become more expensive spot.

This is why, in 1962, a large amount of negative forward contracts was recorded. With an expectation of a possible further exchange depreciation (the Canadian dollar was re-pegged at $U.S. .925 in May, 1962), business enterprises purchased forward large amounts of U.S. dollars while they were still cheap so as to satisfy, as much as possible, their foreign exchange requirements at the lowest price. The drain of U.S. dollars from the Exchange Fund Account in terms of forward contracts is recorded as negative. It should be pointed out, however, that the figures recorded in 1962 in Table 12–4 were swollen by $350 million from June to October, 1962. This was the amount of spot borrowing for the purpose of protecting the value of the Canadian dollar from the Federal Reserve Bank of New York and the Bank of England and was recorded as forward obligations. This was reduced to $175 million in October, $100 million in November, and zero in December, 1962.

The second occasion when negative forward contracts appeared in large amounts was in 1968. This was a "mini-crisis" which was hardly warranted but was the consequence of the gold/dollar crisis in Europe. A loss of confidence in the U.S. dollar was spreading rapidly so that dollar claims were being exchanged for gold at the official price of $35/ounce. Successive waves of gold buying were engulfing the gold market so that it ultimately became no longer possible for the U.S. to maintain the official price. A "two-tier" price system was resorted to with the official price of gold to be sold to central banks at $35/ounce and a free market price which would find its own level. Surprisingly, this had an effect on the Canadian dollar because it was generally expected that the U.S. would change to a policy of restriction of capital outflow. This would lead once more to a devaluation of the Canadian dollar if such a policy materialized because of our heavy dependence upon U.S. capital as a source for keeping our Exchange Fund Account solvent, and for this reason, heavy forward purchases of U.S. dollars once again appeared. In addition, another $250 million was recorded as a forward purchase of U.S. dollars through a "reciprocal currency facility" between the Banks of Canada and the Federal Reserve System. This was reduced to $125 million in June, 1968, and zero in July.

A third occasion appeared in May and June, 1970 when the Canadian dollar was free to float once more. Now the speculation is in the other direction, i.e., an *appreciation* of the Canadian dollar was expected. In other words, the *expensive* U.S. dollar was being sold forward at a higher Canadian dollar price to be purchased at a cheap price spot after the Canadian dollar had appreciated. So long as this continued expectation of appreciation existed, net forward contracts were positive, indicating inflows of forward U.S. dollar contracts into the Exchange Fund Account.

III. THE COLLAPSE OF THE DOLLAR

There is rarely an event in our history which could have been more easily forecast than the decline of the foreign exchange value of our Canadian dollar. There was no doubt of its inevitability; the only question was when.

It is unfortunate for Canadians that the drop in value vis-à-vis the U.S. dollar coincided with the decline of the U.S. dollar because this has resulted in an accelerated collapse of our dollar against the European and Japanese currencies. But there is something apocalyptic in this because for a long time Canadians have enjoyed a relationship with the United States which has been such that so long as the U.S. dollar enjoyed the prestige of, first, a "hard" currency, second, the numeraire of other world currencies, and third, a world reserve currency, our dollar too

could enjoy the equivalent prestige simply by maintaining a close trading relationship with the U.S. Thus, a devaluation of any European currency against the U.S. dollar was an equivalent *appreciation* of the Canadian dollar against the depreciated European currency without any effort or "pain" as far as Canada was concerned. With no increased effort to export our goods to these countries, we could acquire inexpensive imports from Europe and Japan: automobiles, durable goods, etc.

It is more difficult to export to Europe, and, especially, Japan compared to the United States where proximity, absence of language barriers, similar customs and laws, and even joint ownership of producing facilities ensure an easy flow of exports to the U.S. In this easy, "painless" manner we could enjoy the best that other countries had to offer to us, including a thriving tourist industry as Canadians travelled more extensively abroad. This is why the collapse of the Canadian dollar is all the more dramatic — we are at last paying for a standard of living to which we were never really entitled by our own efforts alone.

We can see this in the extent to which the Canadian dollar has declined in value over the past two years. See Table 12-5.

These percentages, confined as they are to only a 2-year period, do overlook longer-term devaluation which would really reflect the appreciation (or revaluation) of the DM and the Swiss franc. Since 1967 our dollar has declined by 127% against the German mark and 205% against the Swiss franc.

Old habits die hard. Canadians find it difficult to

Table 12-5
DEVALUATION OF THE CANADIAN DOLLAR AGAINST WORLD CURRENCIES
September, 1976 to October 4, 1978

Currency	%
British pound	39
French franc	38
German mark	57
Japanese yen	58.3
Swiss franc	93
U.S. dollar	21.6

Source: Bank of Canada Review, October, 1978, Table 65.

readjust to new conditions such as cutting back on expensive foreign travel, substitution of domestic products for imports, etc., especially since whole industries such as travel bureaus, import companies and the like have grown up with the specific objective of encouraging the consumption of imported goods and services. Furthermore, the exporting industries in those countries will likewise do all they can to maintain their export markets. This they would do by cutting costs in their own producing facilities to counter the depreciation of the Canadian dollar.

What, then, has gone wrong? There are a number of factors within the Canadian economy itself which are responsible. The first of these, an excessive reliance on the U.S. for export markets, has already been mentioned, and this leads directly to the second factor. Since our commercial relationship with the U.S. is so close, we must maintain our competitive position with that country, and that, briefly, is the difficulty as Table 12-6 indicates.

Our rate of inflation during the 1970s has been greater than that of the U.S., but even more significant is the change in hourly earnings in manufacturing. When these are compared to the comparable increases in industrial production in both countries, it follows that wage costs per unit of output *must* increase in Canada relative to that of the U.S. This is made very clear in Chart 12-2 where it can be seen that during the years 1971-76, unit labour costs rose by 11% per year in Canada compared to 7% in the U.S. Further, the impact of Canadian devaluation on relative costs in terms of U.S. currency is highlighted in the righthand chart in which Canadian costs actually "declined" in 1977.

The result of this can only be rising export prices. Assuming that U.S. demand for our exports has been elastic, and the statistics would suggest that

it may well be, this must result in a shift leftward in the supply curve of foreign exchange (see Chapter 11, Diagram 11-3).[16]

Still, however, the "collision" course of the Canadian dollar was set not so much by rising costs of exports as the annual growth of interest and dividend payments and tourism. The services sector in general, which includes both these items, was growing at a rate (see discussion in Chapter 11) which was impossible to sustain.

The rather typical Canadian solution for the problem for many years has been to encourage an inflow of foreign capital, thereby shifting the supply curve for foreign exchange rightward. Theoretically such capital investment should enhance the nation's productivity so that output in general and export volume in particular should rise sufficiently to defray the cost of the additional interest and dividends burden. Such, however, has not been the case in actual experience especially during the 1970s when growth rates of real GNP have been substantially below those of the 1960s.

Unfortunately, however, foreign investment has not been the answer lately, due to an unfavourable investment climate. This is again made clear in Table 12-6 and Chart 12-2. Unit labour costs in the U.S., which rose as rapidly in 1971-76 as those in Canada *discouraged* direct investment and encouraged its outflow instead. This, combined with the Quebec PQ election with its uncertainties for the future of the country, was sufficient to significantly reduce capital inflows. (Net capital movements into Canada fell from $8 billion in 1976 to $5.5 billion in 1977. It is likely that this drop is understated because of the very large, $1.4 billion, *negative* "errors and omissions" for that year.)

Perhaps the most surprising development during the period of the decline in the market value of the Canadian dollar has been the capacity of the forward market to insulate Canadian short-term interest rates from those of the U.S. This is, after all, the first time since the "floating" of the Canadian dollar in 1970 that the mechanism has been truly tested. The point at issue was a question of

Table 12-6

U.S./CANADA COMPARISONS,
% CHANGE, 1971-77

	U.S.	Canada
Consumer Prices	49.9	60.8
Hourly Earnings (mfg.)	57.7	94.6
Industrial Production	25.2	22.0

Source: International Financial Statistics, International Monetary Fund.

[16]We can infer (we cannot prove) from statistics that export demand is elastic from the decline in export volume from 1973 through 1976 coinciding with the period of rising costs in Canada. Import volume declined slightly in only one year, 1975.

Chart 12-2

UNIT LABOUR COSTS[1]
**(Average annual percentage changes based
on fourth quarters)**

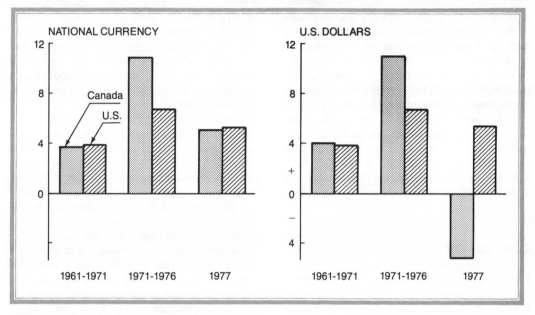

1. Wages, salaries and supplementary labour income (for Canada excluding retroactive payments) per unit of real GNE. *Source:* Bank of Canada Annual Report of the Governor, 1977, p. 13.

the capacity of Canada to have an independent monetary policy with higher interest rates. In the past, Canadian rates have maintained a fairly static positive differential with U.S. rates. Any variation in this differential would result in a "rush" of U.S. funds which would lower Canadian short-term rates or a flight of funds which would raise short-term rates to a level appropriate to the differential. This would take place leaving the forward spread intact.

During the 1976 period of a relatively high rate of inflation, the Bank of Canada, by means of an increase in the Bank rate up to 9.50%, pushed up Treasury Bill rates with the objective of reducing inflationary pressures. The result was a forward spread, at annual rates, of an average of 3.89% during the entire year and a high of 4.54% in March. Forward spreads as high as these meant that the interest rate differential in the "hedging equation" was being effectively cancelled so that only a small covered differential existed on the right of the equal sign. When this equilibrium ex-

ists (the covered differential approaching zero), it means that the world looks upon Canada as a stable country in the short-term without any economic or political dislocations which would encourage flights of capital. Similarly, the Canadian dollar, though floating within a much broader range than the fixed rates of the Bretton Woods System, was not expected to either increase or decrease in value in terms of foreign exchange. At the same time the Canadian economy could hardly become a refuge for the world's short-term capital.

When conditions of equilibrium apply in this way, the hedging equation actually becomes a tautology so that the forward spread *is* the short-term interest rate differential. At this time pure arbitrage on the part of banks will equate the interest differential with the forward spread. Many banks, incidentally, use computers for this purpose to calculate instantly what interest rates *ought* to be given a specific forward spread, etc. This is why in Table 12-4 the last period of devaluation of the

Canadian dollar, 1976 and 1977, was not accompanied by substantial negative forward contracts which were characteristic of the two previous periods of threatened devaluation.

The last question which must remain unanswered at this point is, Will our now devalued dollar make possible some improvements in our balance of payments so that we can expect no *further* devaluation? Certainly there has been considerable improvement in our merchandise exports, and reduced import volumes do appear to be showing the results of their higher cost. This is by no means enough, however, to reduce the huge deficit in the services sector. In 1977 our merchandise trade earned a surplus of $2.9 billion, but services incurred a deficit of $7.4 billion. We cannot say yet, therefore, what the answer will be for there is still a long way to go.

CONCLUSION

It is no exaggeration to argue that capital movements are the dominant feature of Canada's balance of payments and foreign exchange equilibrium; indeed, there is likely no other developed country in the western world that can demonstrate such a dependence on capital imports.

In the past, Canada's balance of payments current account has been negative. This was due not so much to merchandise deficits in trade but to the heavy deficit in the services and transfers area which includes interest and dividend payments. It is these services which have proved to be intractable in the sense that the deficit in this area has increased faster than our surplus in merchandise trade. The consequence has been the decline in the foreign exchange value of the Canadian dollar.

Should it become impossible for Canada to contain inflationary cost increases and our exports suffer from being no longer competitive, we would find ourselves once more in the position of a further declining exchange rate. Capital inflow could sustain a free market exchange rate higher than this in which case our imports would cost less and our standard of living would be correspondingly higher. But this would be at best a short-term, short-sighted solution since we would inevitably increase our dividend and interest obligations for the future. Perhaps a more sensible long-term policy would be not to encourage *any* foreign capital investment but only productive capital to establish new industries which would result in an increase in both our exports and import substitution production. Such a policy might be implemented by FIRA. Failing this, the result of continued reliance on foreign investment purely to maintain a higher exchange rate of our dollar must involve us in a kind of fruitless economic *la ronde*.

Here one should keep in mind that it is not short-term capital which causes the difficulty. Such capital "washes" back and forth across the border in response to a combination of short-term interest rates and forward spreads. It is both direct and portfolio investment which sustains a high level of our exchange rate and which flows to Canada because of the profit incentive.

A fact which emerges from the study of the Canadian dollar and the foreign exchange markets is the virtual complete integration of the two dollars, U.S and Canadian, in matters of foreign exchange and finance. To a certain degree there has indeed been an assertion of a measure of independence during the mid-1970s (1975-77). At that time, tighter monetary policies in Canada in the interest of combatting inflation had coincided with easier policies in the U.S. with the result that short-term rates in both countries diverged considerably. This was made possible through equilibrium in the "hedging equation," an achievement which had never really occurred before. However, one does not have to be cynical to observe that our domestic monetary policies must follow closely those of the U.S. to be effective; otherwise it is too easy to use the American capital market to circumvent tight Bank of Canada policies. In matters of foreign exchange, there really is only one currency, the U.S. dollar, which is of concern to Canada. Our currency relates to other currencies via the U.S. dollar not just as a numeraire but as a trading currency. Perhaps one day in the future this may change, especially if our trading relations with the European Common Market become sufficiently great to warrant separate supply demand relationships between European currencies and the Canadian dollar which are equally as strong as those between the U.S. and Canada.

ADDITIONAL READINGS

Caves, R.E. & R.W. Jones, *World Trade and Payments*, Little, Brown & Co., 1977, ch. 19.

Grubel, Herbert G., *Forward Exchange, Speculation, and the International Flow of Capital*, Stanford University Press, 1966. An in-depth study recommended as follow-up reading.

Levin, Jay H., *Forward Exchange and Internal External Equilibrium*, Michigan International Business Studies, #12, 1970. Somewhat technical and broader in scope.

CHAPTER 13

Eurocurrencies

INTRODUCTION

It is no exaggeration to say that the most interesting as well as the most significant development in banking in this century is the Eurocurrency. Indeed, it is Eurocurrencies which make banking truly international in the sense that banks are no longer confined to their own national boundaries for assets or liabilities for any reason other than choice. This is why the development of Eurocurrencies constitutes a true watershed in the history of banking, for no longer is it possible to consider a national banking system in isolation; it is rather a single system set within a context of international banking. Any monetary or banking policy, for instance, initiated within a country for purposes of economic stabilization directly affects the banking systems of other countries, and this is the consequence of the close interrelationships of national banking systems by way of the international markets for Eurocurrencies. In a real sense we now have a world banking system.

I. THE EUROCURRENCY CENTRE

The growth of Eurocurrencies is itself fascinating enough in that the banking technique involved is different from more normal domestic banking practice. In Chapter 6, British banking was discussed with particular emphasis upon the contribution of foreign deposits; indeed, London was, and is today, a world banking centre. The foreign deposits upon which British banks rely, when converted into sterling via the Exchange Equalization Account, become ordinary sterling deposits available for lending in Great Britain or wherever sterling is required. This ability to attract foreign currency deposits has been a great asset, especially in recent times when some of the huge oil revenues of OPEC countries have been deposited with British banks.

It may be worthwhile explaining, as an aside, that the British Exchange Equalization Account is really the counterpart of our own Exchange Fund Account. The British version was established in 1932 by the Finance Act and provides for the stabilization of the foreign exchange value of the pound sterling. In its operation, it is financed by public revenues through the sale of "tap" Treasury Bills (Bills sold directly to the Account instead of via the market mechanism) in such a way that there is no effect on the domestic money supply. Canada's Exchange Fund Account operates in the same way in that government deposits with chartered banks are drawn down when foreign exchange is purchased by the Bank of Canada for the Account. This effectively by-passes the reserves of the banking system because only the government deposits change as chartered banks sell (or buy) excess foreign deposits to the Bank of Canada. In effect, transactions for the Account are really not Bank of Canada transactions at all but government transactions.

Now suppose incoming foreign deposits are not used to purchase sterling from the Exchange Equalization Account at all but are "on-lent" as foreign currency. This is quite a different situation because in this case, loans are made to customers who would ordinarily have borrowed from banks within the countries in which the currency originated in the first place. Why go to London to borrow, say, U.S. dollars instead of going directly to New York? The answer to this question will become apparent in the sections which follow, for it is this answer which underlies the entire structure of the Eurocurrency market.

The practice of on-lending foreign deposits, while new in the sense that it became a major development of the 1960s, actually had its beginnings in the 1920s to end in the financial crises associated with the world depression of the 1930s.[1] With the outbreak of World War II in 1939 and the strict exchange control which ensued, any further development of such banking practice became impossible. We can see more easily why this is true, and, at the same time, recognize the important contribution of exchange restriction to the Euro-

---

[1]"U.K. Banks' External Liabilities and Claims in Foreign Currencies," *Bank of England Quarterly Bulletin*, June, 1964, p. 101.

currency market if we first digress briefly to consider how restriction was practised during the years immediately following the reopening of the London foreign exchange market in 1951.

In Chapter 11, a typical foreign exchange market was represented as the interplay of supply and demand. It really makes no difference to the analysis whether the market is Canadian, British, or Continental — the same principles apply to any market anywhere. The central bank, in that case, intervened in the market to augment the supply of foreign exchange or purchase any surplus so as to stabilize the value of the domestic currency vis-à-vis the foreign currency. The same, of course, is true for the London foreign exchange market but with the Bank of England as the specific central bank. But suppose the Bank of England has been running down its supply of foreign exchange in the Exchange Equalization Account to dangerously low levels in an attempt to prevent the depreciation of the pound sterling? In that case, if it wishes to maintain the high value of the pound it must take other action, and this it can do by shifting the *demand* curve for foreign exchange to the left since it is no longer able to supply the necessary foreign exchange at the central bank selling point. (See Diagram 13-1.) The British government can accomplish this by restricting the supply of domestic currency (demand for foreign exchange) which comes onto the market. For example, amounts of foreign exchange which British tourists may have for travel purposes would be restricted, remittances abroad would be curtailed, and only certain strategic imports would be permitted. In the British case, post-war restriction applied only to currencies of countries outside the sterling area, i.e., those countries which use the Bank of England as their "central bank" as far as foreign exchange is concerned.[2] Of course, such restriction requires the force of law—the Exchange Control Act of 1947.

---

[2]The sterling area had its origins with the suspension of gold payments by Britain during the Great Depression in 1931. Countries using sterling as an international reserve currency found it necessary to link their currencies either to gold or sterling. If they chose sterling, they became members of the sterling area. Currently the members are the Commonwealth countries except Canada, the dependent territories of the U.K., and Bahrain, Iceland, Eire, Jordan, Kuwait, Qatar, South Africa, Southern Yemen, the United Arab Emirates.

Diagram 13-1

EXCHANGE RESTRICTION

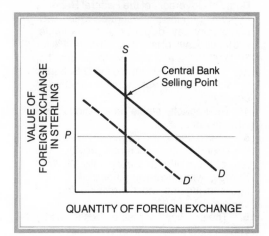

The objective of such restriction, i.e., maintenance of a relatively high value of the pound, is to avoid an increase in costs of essential imports to the British public. It serves little purpose to permit these imports to be more expensive than they need be, especially during emergency periods, for the increased costs would only contribute to unnecessarily higher costs of living. Unfortunately, however, the "emergency periods" have tended to be extended well beyond the immediate emergency and the practice of restriction has been used as a substitute for the devaluation of the pound which was really necessary to correct fundamental disequilibria in the balance of payments.

A totally unexpected outcome of this policy of exchange restriction was the Eurocurrency "era." We can identify the year 1958 as the beginning because in that year a number of factors contributed to the formation of a Eurodollar market; these have been identified as follows:

1. The greater freedom which banks were allowed in the conduct of their foreign exchange operations as a result of external convertibility in Western Europe at the end of 1958—in effect, arbitrage operations;
2. Other exchange control relaxations in West European countries, which have given commercial banks and business

firms more freedom to conduct foreign capital operations;

3. Regulation Q (the limitation by the Board of Governors of the Federal Reserve System upon the interest rates which U.S. banks may pay for deposits, for example, 0% for deposits of less than 30 days, 1% for 30 to 90 days, and 90 days to six months, $2\frac{1}{2}$%) effectively eliminated the U.S. banks from competing for foreign exchange deposits;

4. Reasonably stable international exchange rates;

5. The balance of payments deficit of the United States which has provided the rest of the world, and especially Western Europe, with increasing holdings of dollars seeking the most profitable form of investment;

6. The practice adopted on occasions by certain central banks of offering their commercial banks special inducements to hold dollars in order to reduce internal liquidity; and, to a lesser extent;

7. The tendency of East European countries to hold dollars through West European intermediaries.[3]

At the same time that these conditions were generally prevailing throughout western Europe, the British government imposed *additional* exchange restrictions which took the form of, first, a ban on the lending of sterling to finance foreign trade outside the sterling area, and, second, the prohibition of further increases in overseas sterling credits. This was, in effect, a substantial cutback in the British banks' highly profitable foreign business, and, in order to restore some of these lost profits, the banks resorted to the practice of directly on-lending their U.S. dollar balances. This they could do since the U.K. liquid asset reserve requirements did not apply to foreign balances, and, at the same time, the customers were already waiting to be supplied with their necessary credit.

The combination of demand in the form of customers who had formerly relied upon sterling trade credits and the supply of U.S. dollars which were available because of the deficit in the U.S. balance of payments meant that the necessary ingredients for a true market for U.S. dollar bal-

ances existed. It only remained for the technical expertise of the British banks to act as the medium through which demand and supply could be brought together.

We must keep in mind that what was actually happening was an expansion of an entry known as "External liabilities and claims in foreign currencies," in other words, foreign currency deposits. These liabilities and claims (or assets to the British banks) were, and are, no different from any other external asset acquired for more "normal" purposes of foreign business transactions. When the circumstances became propitious, as outlined above, substantial increases in foreign assets were experienced by British banks with the consequence that corresponding increases in foreign liabilities could occur to "balance" these assets. Seeking to maximize profits, they simply behaved rationally by on-lending their surplus dollar deposits, and so the "Eurodollar" was born.

By the time the ban on the sterling financing of trade credits was lifted in 1959, the Eurodollar market was firmly established as an integral part of the banks' activities, and it was no longer possible to stop it.

One factor, however, which was of great importance in the growth of the Eurodollar market should be discussed further — number 3 above, Regulation Q. Somewhat like the practice of exchange restriction, this regulation is an outmoded hangover from the past with very little by way of economic justification remaining. It dates back to 1933 and gives the Federal Reserve Board the power to set interest rates on time (savings) deposits. Even at that time there was very little rationale for it though it was believed that banks were excessively competitive during their earlier years and tended to invest in high yield (and high risk) assets. This was supposed to have been a cause of bank failures during the early years of the Great Depression.

At any rate the logic which may have existed then certainly no longer applies. It is comparable to the 6% ceiling on chartered bank loan rates which was in effect from 1944 to the Bank Act of 1967. (Prior to 1944, the ceiling was 7% which had been in effect since 1867.) It would appear that interest rate ceilings of this kind (either loans or deposits) may have some foundation in the deposit manufacturing mechanism of commercial banks which was supposed to have given them an excessive

---

[3] *Bank of England Quarterly Bulletin, op. cit.,* p. 102.

advantage over their competitors. Whatever the rationale, when U.S. market rates are higher than "Q rates," savings deposits of all kinds are channeled, not through commercial banks, but through competing financial intermediaries alone. Competition is severely restricted in this way. But, and this is the main point, foreign banks, particularly foreign branches of U.S. banks, are not and cannot be subject to Regulation Q. As we shall see presently, this was a major stimulus to the growth of the Eurodollar market.

II. EUROCURRENCIES AND THEIR ORIGINS

A. Banks as Intermediaries

There is a fundamental difference between lending domestic currencies and foreign currencies. In the former case, banks make loans by creating claims against themselves, and as we have seen, these claims are additional deposits which increase the domestic money supply. In the case of foreign exchange deposits banks are not creating new claims but are simply transferring the ownership of an existing claim against a foreign bank. This foreign bank could be U.S. (Eurodollars), a German bank (Euromarks), a French or Swiss bank (Eurofrancs), a Japanese bank (Euroyen), etc.

The difference between the two types of lending is crucial. With foreign exchange, a deposit is acquired either through the normal financing of international trade or by actively bidding for foreign exchange deposits. If the deposit is acquired by means of trade, an excess of foreign assets over liabilities will develop if the balance of payments of the country of the bank in question happens to be in surplus. Such foreign balances in U.S. dollars were typical during the decade of the 1950s when the U.S. balance of payments was in deficit, and these balances accrued in many countries, including British banks. These banks, having already had many years of experience with foreign exchange deposits, had no difficulty in attracting and disposing of these deposits.

The enormous expansion of external liabilities and claims during the decade of the 1960s re-flects the growing importance of London as a Eurocurrency centre. While it is not possible to distinguish Eurocurrencies from any other foreign deposit, we may be certain that practically all of the huge increase in "external liabilities and claims" in British bank balance sheets is due to the growing activities in the Eurodollar market.

B. "Creation" of Eurodollars

Since 1. by far the largest proportion of Eurocurrencies consist of U.S. dollars, 2. the Eurodollar was the first of these currencies, and 3. the Canadian banks' activity in the Eurocurrency market is entirely in U.S. dollars, the more feasible approach would be to concentrate, for purposes of analysis, on that currency alone. This is not to suggest, however, that other Eurocurrencies are unimportant, but rather that the analysis of these currencies would be the same as the Eurodollars.

We recall in Chapter 11 that a surplus of foreign currency deposits arises from the existence of an excess of inpayments over outpayments. These deposits are carried on the books of U.S. banks as liabilities, and, at the same time, are *assets* to the banks of Canada. Since they are the property of the chartered banks, these banks are free to do with them as they see fit, e.g., they could be invested in U.S. money markets, loaned directly to U.S. businessmen, or, and this is the main point, loaned abroad as Eurodollars. In many cases, they will be loaned to an intermediate bank, say in London, which will in turn re-loan the $ U.S. asset to an ultimate borrower. A good deal of intermediation of this type is taking place, so that in order to estimate the true size of the Euromarket, (i.e. all Eurocurrencies) a "netting out" process should be gone through in order to avoid double counting: this is, however, not possible since accurate international accounting of these loans does not exist, but informed estimates give the total "gross" size as $657 billion with a "net" size of $405 billion.[4]

To see precisely how a Eurodollar arises, we might consider a simple T table once more.

---

[4]47th Annual Report of the Bank for International Settlements, 1977, p. 86.

Canadian Bank

Assets	Liabilities
1. Deposits ($US)	
2. $US Loans or deposits with banks	2. Deposits ($US)

A bank in Canada can acquire assets in foreign exchange as the consequence of foreign trade or it can also acquire a liability in foreign exchange quite apart from its normal commercial business. This would be the result of bidding for $US deposits, i.e., encouraging holders of $US claims against U.S. banks to deposit with a branch of a Canadian bank in the U.S. In such a case, a book entry in the Canadian branch is made on the liabilities side. In the home office, this liability is recorded as a foreign currency liability booked outside Canada, and is, in effect, a short-term loan from the branch bank.

In this case (Deposit #2 in the T table) the U.S. dollar deposit will be accompanied by a corresponding entry on the assets side in U.S. dollars (Asset #2 in the T table). This follows from the fact that the deposit liability is a cost to the bank to be matched with an asset which yields a revenue. The asset reflects the use to which the deposit is put, e.g., a loan to another bank (a deposit with a bank) or a loan directly to a final borrower. What is significant here is that these loans, unlike loans in domestic currency, are not claims manufactured by the chartered banks against themselves or against U.S. banks.

C. A Multiplier?

When a domestic deposit is acquired by a specific bank, it is accompanied by a corresponding asset as a result of which the deposits are cleared via the clearing house. This becomes the liquidity base necessary for the support of further deposit liabilities. This is not true in foreign exchange banking. U.S. dollar deposits acquired as assets are not necessarily accompanied by a corresponding liability. This may, at first sight, appear to be an advantage, but when we recall that the original deposit is actually the "raw material" for the manufacture of another deposit, it becomes a *dis*advantage. Suppose, as an

example, a chartered bank in Canada did loan $U.S. by "on-loaning" so that claims against itself — i.e., promises to pay $U.S. are now the property of a borrower. The borrower, disbursing these, would circulate these promises to pay outside the U.S. as well as inside the U.S. Suppose further that a second bank in some other country followed the same practice and received the same promises to pay as the first bank. Receiving these promises in $U.S., it would request payment from the original Canadian bank which would be forced to transfer ownership of the first deposits without altering the assets side of its balance sheet, i.e., loans in U.S. dollars would still be outstanding until ultimately repaid. The process could theoretically continue *ad infinitum* since there is no reserve requirement in this case, and an enormous expansion of loan assets against a single (though highly active), U.S. dollar deposit.

It only requires a little imagination to visualize what could happen next. Any recipient of the "created" U.S. dollar deposit could request a cash withdrawal, or its equivalent in the form of a bank draft requesting a transfer to an account in a U.S. bank, gold, etc., and no cash "reserves" in the U.S. would exist except for the original lending bank. Since loan assets cannot be collected immediately, i.e., the loans may not have become due for repayment, a complete collapse of the bank's foreign business could result. This is why each U.S. dollar claim must be "genuine" in the sense that it represents a true claim against a U.S. bank.

Actually, in the process of lending U.S. dollars, Canadian banks, as well as other banks in other countries, are nothing more than intermediaries, or conduits, through which U.S. dollars pass *en route* to their destination, the Eurodollar market. One might think of these foreign deposits as interbank deposits; indeed, a highly developed interbank market has grown up in London in which such deposits are traded at specified interest rates.

But this still does not preclude the possibility of redepositing the *spent* proceeds of a Eurocurrency loan in a bank in the form of a foreign exchange deposit in which case the same original deposit would reappear once more, in effect, to be recycled and thereby counted twice. Such double counting would not be the same as that which results from the relending of deposits from one bank to another. It is rather the consequence of redepositing and reloaning in the Eurobanks themselves to build up assets in Eurocurrencies which is really the consequence of what would be, in the case of a domestic banking system, an increased velocity of circulation.

During the early 1970s this process of "round tripping" was, rather surprisingly, prevalent amongst central banks other than the Group of Ten which were specifically requested not to engage in the practice. As these banks acquired more U.S. dollars in their official accounts, instead of investing them in U.S. Treasury Bills, etc., as would ordinarily be the case, they preferred the higher yielding Eurodollar market. The result was a recycling of the U.S. dollars within the same market.

Ultimate borrowers of Eurocurrencies are a whole range of institutions, financial and commercial, which have bills to pay and obligations to meet. For example, an importer of goods denominated in U.S. dollars may wish to borrow Eurodollars to meet his commitments on time. The exporter (the recipient of the proceeds of the loan) will likely use the dollars so acquired to defray his own domestic manufacturing costs, etc., and such payments necessitate a conversion into domestic currency rather than a redeposit as a U.S. dollar account in a Eurobank. On the other hand, if the exporter does not require his cash immediately he could very well redeposit with a Eurobank for the reason that the rate of interest is likely to be higher than corresponding rates in his own domestic banks. Such redepositing would result in a Eurodollar bank multiplier, which, though not large, is nonetheless real.

It is, therefore, quite possible that a portion (about one-half) of the $650 billion worth of Eurodollars is the result of a multiplier effect which can be calculated by relating total non-U.S. resident holdings of short-term dollar assets to actual Eurodollars (specifically total U.S. short-term liabilities to non-residents). In 1969, such a calculation resulted in a value of the multiplier as 1.9213.[5] By 1978 it is likely that a value of something in excess of 2.0 may be expected.

D. Eurocustomers

For obvious reasons of confidentiality, it is difficult to identify Eurobank customers, i.e., governments, private industry, etc., as well as the uses to which loans are put. The Bank of England does attempt, however, to analyze the employment of these funds, particularly those which U.K. banks lend. Thus, some loans can be identified which were used for speculation during the period of the revaluation of the deutsche mark in 1969. In this case, a purchase of deutsche marks financed by a Eurodollar loan, when expectations of revaluation were general, could mean a tidy profit after revaluation since cheap deutsche marks were purchased with dollars and more expensive DM's were sold. Another use for Eurocurrencies was found by the Japanese banks which used the Eurodollar market to finance domestic lending to industry by borrowing dollars and exchanging them for yen.

But, perhaps the most interesting employment of all was the use of the Eurodollar market by U.S. banks to borrow *their own* dollars for the purpose of avoiding the Federal Reserve tight money policy, specifically Regulation Q, during the latter 1960s. This was, in fact, a principle reason for the expansion of the market during that initial period. U.S. bank branches borrowed short term on the Eurodollar market and re-lent these funds to their parent banks in the U.S. In so doing, part of their deposits (Eurodollars are actually deposits *already* on the books of U.S. banks in favour of foreign banks) were excluded from the domestic reserve requirement. Prior to October, 1969, foreign borrowings were free from reserves, and, therefore, a portion of their deposits outstanding could be deducted before calculating their legal reserves. In this way Eurodollar borrowing became a convenient way of avoiding credit stringencies. This loophole was closed in October, 1969, by the imposition of a 10% reserve requirement on borrowings by banks from their overseas branches "in excess of the average level of borrowing outstanding in May, 1969."[6] However, there is no doubt that prior to closing this loophole the huge amounts of U.S. branch

---

[5]Boyden E. Lee, "The Eurodollar Multiplier," an unpublished paper prepared for the Bank of Canada.

[6]"The Eurocurrency Business of Banks in London," *Bank of England Quarterly Bulletin*, March, 1970, p. 35.

bank borrowing was responsible for the rising rate of interest on Eurodollar loans.

Since the beginning of the 1970s the Eurocurrency market has been a major source of loans to less-developed countries. This may appear strange, at first sight, for the reason that Eurocurrency loans have been relatively short-term with high interest rates.[7] The ability to repay such loans on the part of less developed countries would seem to be questionable; indeed, it is for this reason that foreign aid made available by the wealthier countries, such as Canada, is generally preferred. This takes the form of grants and long-term, low-interest loans. There were, however, a significant number of "less-developed" countries, including Spain, Brazil, Greece, Algeria, Indonesia, etc., which were sufficiently credit-worthy to find accommodation in the Euromarket. This was made possible because of rising prices of commodities produced by these countries and which Eurobanks found sufficiently attractive as investments. Unfortunately, with the exception of oil producing countries, the commodity price boom did not continue and the heavy burden imposed by the growing cost of oil imports made further financing from the Euromarket not feasible; in fact, it has been becoming increasingly difficult to collect repayments from past loans as they fall due. The problem faced by all of these less developed countries is a long-term one of financing balance of payments deficits which are the consequence of importing capital equipment and such other commodities necessary for economic growth, both directly and to supplement domestic production. Foreign assistance and aid from the OPEC countries are just not sufficient; hence, more financing is required and the burden has fallen on the Euromarkets themselves. It has been estimated that about $150 billion will be required from Eurosources by 1980.[8] This is why another instrument of lending by way of Euromarkets is so important—the Eurobond.

E. The Eurobond

The principle underlying the Eurobond is the same as that for Eurocurrency deposits—bonds are denominated in a currency and offered to nonresidents of the currency area. This means that Europeans (hence the origin of the prefix, "Euro") may purchase U.S. dollar bonds which American residents will likely not purchase. The U.S. resident *could* purchase the Eurobond if he so wished, but the purpose of the Eurobond is not to acquire U.S. dollars for investment in the U.S.; these Eurodollars will be sold to non-resident investors who happen to own U.S. dollar deposits. The proceeds of the sale of these bonds will be exchanged for other currencies which will, in turn, finance capital expenditure in these other currencies.

If we follow the "movement" of the original dollar deposit for a moment, it is clear that the ownership will transfer from the original deposit holder to finally become part of the official reserves of another country or countries, likely changing ownership several times in the process. Suppose, for example, an international film star who has no particular residence but lives in hotels throughout the world has accumulated some U.S. dollar balances. To avoid payment of tax, he decides to entrust this sum to a Swiss bank which manages such foreign accounts in great amounts.[9] The Swiss bank purchases a Eurodollar bond (or bonds) which is a debt of some well-known private multi-national enterprise, an international organization, or a government enterprise. The proceeds of the sale accrues to the concern which then exchanges the U.S. dollars for any currency it happens to require in payment for imports of capital equipment, local construction costs, or whatever. The original U.S. dollar account then has simply changed ownership in precisely the same fashion as a financial intermediary acquires ownership of a commercial bank account in exchange for a promise to pay. Of course, the film star must have his U.S. dollar account restored eventually when the bond matures in which case the ownership of the account

---

[7]The majority of Eurocurrency loans to less developed countries (75-80%) are for periods of less than 10 years. Pierre Latour, "Euromarkets Wait for LDC's Credits to be Repaid," *Euromoney*, October, 1975, p. 7.
[8]David I. Levine, "Developing Countries and the $150 Billion Euromarket Financing Requirement," *Euromoney*, December, 1975, p. 14.

[9]Julius Bär, a small Swiss private bank, has only about $210 million in assets and liabilities, but about *$2 billion* in foreign accounts.

must retrace its steps. All that has really happened is the film star has voluntarily surrendered claim to his own U.S. dollar balance to someone else who requires it.

The fundamental difference between Eurocurrency and the Eurobond, therefore, is time. Both derive from the same original source, U.S. dollar accounts, which are transferred abroad to non-residents because of a U.S. balance of payments deficit.

But a deficit is not *essential* to Eurobonds. During the mid-sixties, the DM was considered to be an appreciating currency so that foreign capital was moving into the country in great amounts away from the U.S. dollar. To restrict this inflow the government imposed a 25% coupon tax; of course, this had no effect on domestic investors. The Germans, therefore, began the process of switching their deposits outside the country to take advantage of higher interest rates in Euromark bonds which were already well-established in foreign banking circles. To illustrate, German banks have already opened branches in Luxembourg for the purpose of handling DM bonds *outside* Germany, i.e., Euromark bonds. German residents can transfer their DM accounts to these bank branches to take advantage of higher interest rates offered by Euromark bonds — higher, that is, than domestic bonds. There is no balance of payments deficit in Germany, quite the contrary, yet Germans may now arbitrage between their own bonds and Euromark bonds. So it is that non-resident owned currencies can be artificially created, as it were, without any relationship to the balance of payments. In a real sense, our national currencies are becoming international.

All this is made possible by the existence of bank branches abroad, in particular, foreign bank branches. They must be foreign to be non-residents and thereby participate in the Eurocurrency market. Canadian banks, for instance, will have branches in financial capitals of the world offering loans to companies in competition with local banks. To the casual observer it would seem that there exists a massive "overbanking" situation in London, Frankfurt, Zurich, Brussels, etc., with banks on every corner, and he would ask the question: How is it possible for a relatively small European country to generate sufficient savings to warrant so many banks? The answer is that the host country does *not* generate the savings at all – only a small portion thereof. The banks themselves bid for Eurocurrency deposits, switch these into the currency they wish, and offer that particular currency as a loan to a borrower. Indeed, they are not really interested in the small local "retail" deposits at all.

The latest "spur" to international banking of this type is the offshore bank branches, particularly those which are located advantageously for the collection of oil revenues. These are set up under the authority of the host government but are not permitted to participate in banking within the host country itself. The overseas banking unit (OBU) will gather in foreign exchange deposits to reloan them through the interbank market in the European financial centres or to final borrowers. In this way the petro-dollars are recycled through the world's financial system. We find these offshore banks in odd corners of the world such as in the Bahamas, Barbados, Cayman Islands, Hong Kong, etc. One of the latest is Bahrain, an island in the Persian Gulf.[10] Here the location is obviously important, and while the ultimate source of funds for the off-shore banks located here is oil money, "interbank funds" are the nominal source for balance sheet purposes. At the same time, from the assets side, the funds are invested in the "interbank" markets indicating the recycling process which is continuously in progress.

to keep watch on the latest developments in these areas, but it is obviously a difficult task. At the end of December, 1977, it reported that the U.S. offshore banks collected slightly over $70 billion, whereas loans from these centres amounted to $97.8 billion. (N.B., Assets and liabilities do not match in foreign currency banking.)[11]

From the removal of the Canadian withholding tax on interest payments until the collapse of the value of the Canadian dollar, there was a surprisingly active market in Euro-Canadian bonds. It is surprising because the Canadian dollar is not a major world currency and the tendency has been to seek only "hard" currencies for Euro-lending for the obvious reason that any variation in a

---

[10]Reported in *Banker*, January, 1977, "Survey of Euro-Markets—Bahrain's Banking Boom," p. 69.
[11]Bank for International Settlements, *op. cit.*, p. 92.

currency's value can mean a loss in value of investment. Undoubtedly it was the close relationship with the U.S. dollar which was primarily responsible for the "promotion" of the Canadian dollar in international finance.

At the same time there is a tendency for Eurobond markets to broaden their currency base whenever possible — the greater the number of "safe" currencies the less is the risk. The result is Euroyen, Eurofrancs, Euromarks, Eurosterling, and Euro-Canadian. However, as would be expected, the recent devaluation and the political events in Quebec have resulted in a substantially reduced market for Euro-Canadian bonds. In Eurocurrency investment, it is the future of a currency which matters.

Fundamentally it is the absence of optimism within the short-term outlook for stability of the Canadian dollar which is responsible for the absence of demand for Euro-Canadian bonds. As a primary producer dependent upon export markets for minerals, lumber, and agricultural products, Canada has suffered considerably from world-wide recession and the shrinking of demand for such products. Devaluation does help to some degree but such products are generally price inelastic in demand so that within the near future there is little likelihood of an export expansion sufficient to return the Canadian dollar to stability.

According to *Euromoney*, it is the services sector in the Canadian balance of payments which is the difficulty. Debt servicing combined with the excessive demand for foreign services (tourism and the like) ensure the rather poor short-term outlook for Canada's dollar. "There are those that say that Canada's longer-term prospects, given its range of natural resources are good. There are others who are not prepared to wait that long."[12]

F. Eurocredits or Medium-Term Euroloans

Broadening the Euromarkets to include the Canadian dollar may be important from our point of view, but of much greater significance has been the invention of the Eurocredit. This interesting banking device is the latest in a long series of adjustments and adaptations of Euromarkets to the changing requirements of world finance.

---

[12]Peter Field, Assistant Editor of *Euromoney*, June, 1978, p. 43.

Initially, the Eurodollar loan consisted of short-term credit designed for the purpose of meeting a temporary demand for funds in foreign currencies. As the market expanded and the use to which these funds were put grew in variety, it was inevitable that the length of time of the credit facility would grow. It would have been inconceivable, for example, in the early years of Euromarkets that less-developed countries could have borrowed in these markets to finance balance of payments deficits, yet this is precisely what has been happening. It is occurring because of the application of a well-known bank lending technique to international finance — the revolving credit.

The principle of the revolving loan is simple enough; it is a device by means of which a short-term liability is converted into a longer-term loan. It operates on the principle that a short-term loan can be renegotiated at higher (or lower) interest rates for an ensuing short-term period simply by paying the interest as it accrues from the date of renegotiation. In this way it is effectively converted into a longer-term loan.

In Euromarket financing, the Eurocredit is precisely the same. A banking consortium arranges for a medium (or long) term loan initially at a rate of interest fractionally above the British interbank offering rate (LIBOR). This loan is financed by short-term liabilities in foreign exchange, and since the loan is "revolving" at short-term intervals, the interest rate is periodically adjusted to that which is required to secure the necessary deposits. The original depositor is repaid by a new deposit until the term of the Eurocredit has expired.

Since billions of dollars in loans are involved, it is easy to understand and appreciate the Eurocredit as by no means a small achievement of the Euromarket. It involves a matching of short-term liabilities with long-term assets with sufficient accuracy to maintain bank liquidity. When one considers the uncertain world of international finance and the possibility of political decisions which might affect the movement of currencies or their convertibility, one can appreciate the enormous risk involved. Indeed, the logic could run the other way; i.e., considering the importance of convertibility and the free flow of currencies to the Euromarket as a whole, the very existence of Eurocredits and Euromarkets is an insurance against political actions which might affect them in an adverse manner. The loss of the enormous benefits of Euromarkets is greater than the gain from any move toward non-convertibility.

With the development of the principle of Euro-credits, now pretty well established within the Eurocurrency lending system itself, we have a complete international money and banking system complementary to the many different domestic systems of Europe and North America. Short, medium, and long-term loans are now available to borrowers with approved credit standing in various types of currencies, all with the prefix, Euro, in addition to ordinary domestic credit. Thus, should domestic credit be *not* available for any reason, a borrower may turn to the Euromarkets because Euromoney has assumed a life of its own quite independent of the individual currencies of any country. A tight money policy, for instance, in any country (except possibly the United States) can be readily circumvented by Euro-borrowing.

The success of the Eurosystem appears to rest upon two foundations, the banks themselves which establish bank branches at strategic centres and a highly efficient market system which operates along with the British domestic whole-sale deposit market. This latter is an institution quite foreign to North Americans. It consists of brokers who receive deposits "wholesale" from large corporations and financial institutions and place them with banks which offer the highest rate. Their function is as middlemen who maintain a contact with banks and depositors. The London Interbank Offering Rate (LIBOR) is the rate for wholesale deposits which forms the base for further rates quoted as a certain number of percentage points above this rate. Eurocurrency loans to customers which are made on a roll-over basis also use LIBOR.

It can be easily recognized that the existence of an efficient market is absolutely vital to the success of a Eurocurrency system. Those who have a demand for funds must be brought into contact with those who have a surplus of funds; it is as simple as that. And, since we are dealing with world-wide demand and supply, the development of an efficient market system is itself a remarkable achievement. Certainly, the Eurocurrency system has a life of its own. It no longer matters whether one nation, say the U.S., manages to correct its deficit on the balance of payments, the system will grow to find alternate currencies if the U.S. dollar is no longer available. It will grow because there is a need for it.

III. CANADIAN BANKS AND EUROCURRENCIES

A. Canadian Participation in Euromarkets

Since banks are lending to customers in Euromarkets (be they other banks or final borrowers) in foreign currencies only, it follows that there will be no effect upon the domestic currency itself. The money supply, however defined, so long as it is in domestic currency alone, is unaffected by events in the Eurodollar market. However, the broadest classification of "money," M_3, does include foreign currency deposits booked in the specific country on the assumption that such deposits can be readily transferred into local currency when required. M_3, then, includes all "money" in terms of domestic deposits of all kinds (exclusive of government deposits) plus currency in circulation *plus* potential domestic money. These definitions have tended to become standardized amongst countries so that international comparisons may be readily made—Canada is no exception.

What we cannot do at the present time is derive from Canadian statistics alone the amount, in money terms, of Eurocurrency participation on the part of Canadian banks. We can be certain, however, that the large chartered banks do have branches in foreign financial centres and are extremely active. These branches always conform to the laws and regulations of the country in which they reside, and, sometimes, the laws are more stringent regarding foreign branches than for local banks. The personnel that staff the branches are highly qualified and knowledgeable, with experience appropriate to their particular level within the bank. Of course, being in an atmosphere of intense bank competition, the personnel of Canadian banks tend to forget the fact that their employers themselves are competing with each other and often meet informally and exchange ideas and information—certainly more so than within Canada.

We can gain some measure of the activity of chartered bank branches by using two tables from the

Table 13-1
FOREIGN ASSETS AND LIABILITIES ACQUIRED ABROAD
(Millions of Canadian Dollars)

	Assets		Liabilities		BIS	
	1	2	3	4	5	6
	Total	Banks	Total	Banks	Assets	Liabilities
					(billions of U.S. dollars)	
1970	4,799	450	4,776	1,540	—	—
1971	6,308	1,466	6,158	2,419	—	—
1972	7,360	2,269	7,311	2,759	—	—
1973	10,182	4,047	10,061	4,901	—	—
1974	12,764	3,264	12,668	7,700	—	—
1975	14,622	4,086	14,526	9,019	9.9	7.1
1976	17,202	5,313	17,158	11,397	12.6	9.4
1977	22,201	6,080	23,207	14,724	12.5	11.6

Source: Bank of Canada Review, October, 1978. Table 15 less Table 16.

Bank of Canada Review. The first table (Table 15 in the Review) gives total foreign currency assets and liabilities while the second (Table 16 in the Review) gives total foreign currency assets and liabilities booked in Canada. The difference between the two should be an approximate measure of the deposits in foreign currencies secured by foreign branches from foreign sources.[13]

It is not possible to identify the Eurocurrency portion of foreign claims booked abroad. The sub-classification "banks" in both Tables 15 and 16 of the Review *suggests* that on-lending of foreign currencies via the interbank market (or Eurocurrencies) is taking place when foreign assets are so acquired (col. 2). Foreign currency lending to "principals" (final borrowers) takes place when the total (col. 1) exceeds lending to banks (col. 2) which it does by a considerable amount.

Foreign currency liabilities (deposits of banks) are acquired by bidding in the Eurocurrency markets and from available sources in the local deposit market. The Eurocurrency market would be interbank borrowing (col. 4) whereas deposits acquired from sources other than banks would be the difference between columns 3 and 4. By simple comparison of the first four columns, it is

apparent that Canadian branches acquire very much of their funds (63%) from the Eurocurrency markets. On the other hand, lending to the Eurocurrency markets (col. 2) is relatively small (27% for 1977). These ratios are, roughly, confirmed by personal interviews with some Canadian branches in Europe.

The great mystery lies in the complete discrepancy between the Bank of Canada statistics and those of the Bank for International Settlements (cols. 5 and 6). The BIS gives "External positions in Domestic and Foreign Currencies" of banks in the "Group of Ten" (in which Canada is included) and specific data for Canada. The Canadian position in U.S. dollars is impossible to reconcile with the Bank of Canada figures; indeed, differences are such as to cast doubt on the accuracy of the BIS data.

On the whole, the expansion of Canadian participation in Eurocurrency activity is very much in line with the general expansion of the entire market. Assuming a reasonable accuracy of BIS statistics for the entire market is reasonable, total net assets of reporting banks have grown considerably since 1970 from $61 billion to $405 billion by the end of 1977, a growth of 131% per year.[14]

---

[13]It is, of course, possible that foreign currency deposits could be booked through non-Canadian branches such as foreign correspondent banks, but such deposits are likely to be small.

[14]Statistics taken from Crocket and Knight, "International Bank Lending in Perspective," *Finance and Development*, Vol. 15, No. 4, December, 1978, IMF and World Bank, Washington, D.C., p. 45. The ultimate source of these figures is, of course, the Bank for International Settlements.

B. Relation Between Canadian Dollars and the Eurocurrency Market

Canadian chartered banks enter the Euro-currency market and the business of lending in foreign currencies purely for the profit motive. As we have seen, some 47% of the foreign currency deposits arise from "collection" in foreign countries. The balance, 53%, derives from foreign currency deposits which are booked in Canada. Now, even though booked in Canada, such deposits arise from residents of foreign countries—U.S., Great Britain, OECD countries, etc. — and will likely develop through normal trade and payments relationships, most of which are commercial.

There is, however, a residual of these deposits which consists of foreign currency liabilities of banks booked in Canada and owed to the residents of Canada. It is these which are included in M_3, the broadest of the categories of the money supply. In Table 13-2 below, these foreign currency deposits are shown for the past seven years.

There are three clearly defined periods of growth of these deposits; the first, 1972-1974, was characterized by considerable growth from $1.5 billion to $5.0 billion. During the period (see Chart 13-1), the Eurodollar interest rate rose rather sharply pacing the swapped deposit rate and the Canadian certificate of deposite rate.[15] At times, the Eurodollar rate was as much as 2 percentage

points above the swapped deposit rate so that the incentive, in terms of profits, was to encourage the transfer into foreign currency deposits both swapped and uncovered. From 1974 through 1977 foreign deposits rose very little until the end of 1977 when they reached $8.3 billion in October to close the year at $7.4 billion. Throughout this second period, interest rates on Eurodollars stood well *below* the *CD* rate. The third period of growth, 1978 to the present time, is also characterized by rising Eurodollar rates which "pull" the other rates upward (see Chart 13-1).

The statistical evidence is clear enough to justify the conclusion that higher rates in Eurodollars attract Canadian dollar deposits into the foreign currency sector on a short-term basis. The presumption is (we have no statistical proof of this) that Eurodollar loans are being partially financed by such transfers. We can see how this can take place as well as the implications which derive therefrom with a theoretical analysis.

In Chapter 3, Diagram 3-1, the cost/revenue functions of chartered banks were described as a linear total revenue function and a total cost function that turned upward at higher levels of deposit manufacture. Profit maximization would result from the equating of marginal revenue with marginal cost. Such a relationship would appear as shown in Diagram 13-2.[16] which shows the relationship between Canadian dollar deposits manufactured by the chartered banks and foreign currency deposits acquired from residents of

---

Table 13-2
FOREIGN DEPOSITS IN THE M_3 AGGREGATE
(MILLIONS OF DOLLARS)

End of Period		Swapped	Other	Total
	1972	270	1,206	1,476
	1973	880	2,022	2,902
	1974	1,787	3,250	5,037
	1975	848	3,528	4,375
	1976	1,281	5,403	6,684
	1977	1,545	5,845	7,390
Oct.	1978	1,599	8,666	10,265

Source: Bank of Canada Review, Table 14, *or* Table 6.

---

[15]Certificates of deposit are fixed term deposits which are sold on the money market to corporations with temporary surplus funds generally in blocks of $100,000. In effect, they are competitive with Treasury Bills and commercial paper.

[16]The *MR* function is, as normally described, *MR* = (*dTR/dD*) which is a constant because the *TR* function has a constant slope. The *MC* function, on the other hand, *dTC/dD*, is equal to zero until the *TC* function increases at an increasing rate.

Chart 13-1
INTEREST RATES
SHORT-TERM (90-DAY) RATES
MONTHLY

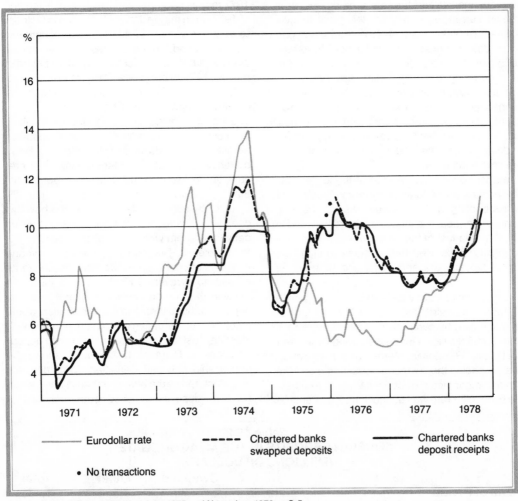

Source: Bank of Canada Review, July, 1975 and November, 1978, p. S-5.

Canada. On the left, the marginal cost function is shown as sharply rising from the origin; this is in contrast to domestic deposits which have an *MC* function rising from the zero axis at the point where competitive bidding for domestic deposits takes place. In both cases the *MC* functions increase steeply for the reason that in order to acquire additional deposits, higher interest must be paid on *all* deposits (not just the marginal incre-

ments), and for foreign currency deposits, competitive bidding begins at the zero point.

Firstly, suppose the banking system exists in isolation so that no foreign deposits are available. The level of domestic deposits (D_d) would equate marginal cost and marginal revenue and be the equivalent of the maximum spread between the *TR* and the *TC* functions in Diagram 3-1 of Chapter 3. Now interject an international market for

Diagram 13-2

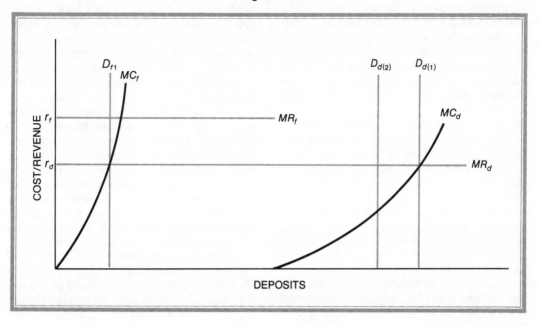

foreign currency deposits with an interest reward higher than domestic rates at MR_f. It is clear that disequilibrium exists at a level of D_{d1} domestic deposits and zero foreign currency deposits from residents. It would be to the banks' advantage in terms of profit maximization to reduce their domestic deposits to $D_{d(2)}$ and increase foreign currency deposits to $D_{f(1)}$, for at these levels of deposits, the differences between marginal revenue and marginal costs for foreign deposits equal the differences between marginal revenue and marginal costs for domestic deposits. (The technique of reducing domestic deposits in favour of foreign currency deposits in this case is shown in the T table on page 318.) Of course, profits may be further increased until deposit expansion in both foreign currency and domestic deposits results in equating both marginal costs with their respective marginal revenues.

The incentive to switch into foreign currency deposits for deposit owners will be greater, and bank profits will increase faster, the greater is the spread between r_f and r_d. This higher rate on foreign currency deposits stems from the higher revenue on foreign currency loans than on domestic loans. Further, these foreign currency deposits will take the form of either swapped or non-swapped deposits depending upon whether the bank covers with a forward contract. In either case, the banks will set deposit rates for them and accept all offers which come forth.

The process of shifting from Canadian deposits into foreign currency deposits will continue so long as the differentials between the marginal revenues and marginal costs of both deposits are unequal. But we note that a shift from Canadian deposits into foreign currency deposits will result in a reserve ratio higher than the legal requirement, for foreign currency deposits require no reserve ratio. This would make possible a *further* manufacture of Canadian dollar deposits because of a rightward shift in the marginal cost function. So the process of shifting into foreign currency deposits would begin anew with Canadian dollar deposit manufacture continuing until equilibrium is reached at the levels of both types of deposits at D. This equilibrium would be where the Marginal Costs of both deposit types equal their respective Marginal Revenues.

Now suppose that a tight monetary policy is being followed which entails a shrinkage of reserves. The banks would be encouraged to switch into foreign exchange deposits so as to maintain their legal reserve ratios as well as to maximize profits. This process of switching would take place until the Marginal Revenue (interest rate) on Canadian dollar loans would rise to equal that of the foreign currency, or Eurodollar, loans (MR_f) in Diagram 13-2. Thus, through a tight money policy, the Canadian loan rate will follow closely the Eurodollar rate.

About 20% of the chartered banks' foreign exchange liabilities are derived from Canadian residents — the balance being acquired from non-residents. Some of these will likely be earned by Canadian business enterprise as a result of commercial activity in foreign countries and may be held as foreign exchange deposits for both convenience and higher deposit rates. Still others will derive in the manner discussed above, a process of switching into foreign exchange deposits either as swapped or non-swapped deposits.

For the balance of foreign currency deposits, those which are acquired from non-residents, the equilibrium as shown in Diagram 13-2 is absent. There is no domestic constraint on any increase in foreign currency deposits from non-resident sources. In fact, Canadian chartered banks are free to compete for foreign deposits in any country in which branch banks or similar facilities are permitted to exist. The difference between resident and non-resident deposits lies in the nature of marginal cost and marginal revenue which will result from the competition for deposits within the country of origin. Again, in this case, the marginal cost function will rise steeply and profit maximization will occur at the point of equalization between marginal costs and marginal revenue for foreign deposits without having any relationship to domestic Canadian dollar deposits. This is the consequence of the intermediation function of the chartered banks in foreign currencies.

It is now quite easy to recognize the nature of the link between chartered bank interest rates and Eurodollar rates. Since the Eurocurrency market is large relative to the Canadian banks' contribution, Euromarket rates will be unaffected by any changes in the Canadian flows of deposits. Our banks are price-takers in this case. Similarly, the deposit rate on non-resident foreign currency deposits will be the result of a complex of monetary and financial forces within the host country and the Canadian branch will be in a position of perfect competition—again a price-taker. In fact, the Canadian branch's share of foreign deposits in the host country will likely be a fairly constant proportion of the total destined for the Euro-markets.

But this is not true of resident foreign exchange deposits. The flow of deposits from Canadian dollars will be elastic relative to changes in deposit rates. This appears to be verified by the considerable transfers which have been reported in recent years from Canadian dollars into U.S. dollars. This high elasticity of response suggests that the domestic interest rates will be forced to compete with the Eurodollar rate; the 90-day certificate of deposit, in particular, will adjust in response to changes in the Eurocurrency markets so that in Diagram 13-2, MR_d will shift upward as deposit switching takes place. We should note, however, that it is the Eurodollar rate which is dominant — a dog/tail relationship — and leads the domestic rates in Canada.

We cannot, however, draw the same conclusion regarding the interest rates on U.S. short-term deposits. Here the dog/tail relationship is not obvious, for Euromarket rates, because of the large amount of U.S. dollars in the Euromarkets, may themselves be determined by the U.S. structure of interest rates. Cause and effect in this case are by no means so clear.

Interest rates on swapped deposits will be similarly related to Euro-rates for the reason that Canadian dollars "swapped" into U.S. dollars with forward exchange cover will also be a means of profit maximization. Whether or not U.S. rates lead or follow Euro-rates, swapped deposits rates will reflect the elasticity of supply of foreign currency deposits. Again the dog/tail relationship applies since the amount of swapped deposits is large relative to Canadian deposits but small relative to U.S. deposits. Clearly this effect will be stronger the greater the degree of competition between particular types of Canadian dollar deposits and the foreign exchange deposit. Thus, similarity in time, whether short or long-term, degree of liquidity, etc., will increase the competition.

C. Net Foreign Assets

Assets and liabilities in foreign currency need not be equal for reasons already examined in Chapter 11. Only in cases in which a deposit is acquired through competitive bidding or through the swapped deposit will corresponding assets be acquired for the reason that the deposit is a cost which would not be incurred without a prospect of revenue from assets. This is the Eurocurrency case with market demand for the assets already in existence which can be satisfied by Canadian banks' incurring additional liabilities.

But it does not follow that banks need *always* balance foreign assets and liabilities even in this instance. Prudence, of course, would dictate a reasonable balance since assets are the "cover" for the liabilities. Indeed, regulations are often imposed by the central authority. The British banks have specific limits to the amount of net foreign assets which they may have at the end of each business day. In this case, the limits are defined in terms of an *open* position (total foreign currency assets against total liabilities of foreign currency) and a *spot against forward* limit (net spot assets against net forward liabilities). The enforcement of these exchange controls is the responsibility of the Bank of England.

In our case, the Bank Act, (18), Section 72, sub-section 7, stipulates that banks must "maintain adequate and appropriate assets against liabilities payable in foreign currencies."[17] What is "adequate and appropriate" is, presumably, the responsibility of the Inspector General of Banks. But it should be observed that an excess of foreign assets in one currency (a long position) can be balanced by an excess of foreign liabilities in another currency (a short position). Such a situation could well arise if profit maximization dictates a long position in say, U.S. dollars for investment in the Euromarket. The funds needed could be acquired by means of a short position in another currency, thereby increasing the risk factor in that other currency.

On the other hand, since most of the chartered banks' foreign currency assets and liabilities are in U.S. dollars, a long position in U.S. dollars with a specific country of residence, such as the United Kingdom, can be balanced with a short position with other OECD countries. In such a case, it is likely that loans to the Eurodollar market via U.S. banks are being financed by borrowings from other OECD countries. The *total*

---

[17]C. Freedman, *The Foreign Currency Business of the Canadian Banks*, Bank of Canada Staff Research Studies, #10, 1974, p. 120.

net foreign asset position on the other hand may be long or short (positive or negative) depending upon the banks' capacity to balance risk against profit.

One rather interesting aspect of this is the heavy short position in foreign currency deposits with Canadian residents in 1974–75. In this case there is no risk involved; in fact, it is merely a means by which chartered banks may reduce their reserve requirement during tight money. To show how this operates, we can use a simple T table page 318. The banks can reduce their Canadian dollar deposits during times of tight money by the simple expedient of selling foreign currency assets to the Canadian public. In so doing, the Canadian dollar deposits are reduced by the amount of the assets sold. It has been the practice in the past to sell these foreign securities with a forward contract to repurchase, but this need not necessarily follow. Under either circumstance, the reserve position of the banks is improved by means of a short foreign exchange position and a corresponding reduction in Canadian dollar deposits.

IV. CONCLUSION—EUROCURRENCIES AND THE FUTURE

From the barest outlines of the Euromarket presented in the preceding pages, as well as the relationship between the Canadian banking system and Eurocurrencies, a few conclusions can be reached which will serve as a bridge to the many complex issues raised in the next chapter.

1. Of all the separate monetary and financial systems in existence, the Eurocurrency system is certainly the most complex. This is not just because it is international in scope, that is significant enough, but because it is superimposed upon individual domestic systems to become a *part* of each domestic system. Or, conversely, the domestic systems have become part of the Eurocurrency system. Even the central banks have found the Eurobanks to be excellent repositories for surplus funds in foreign exchange. In a real sense we are only a small part of a world financial system.

At the same time, the Euromarkets extend credit in many different currencies to many different nationals, and lately, to governments themselves. Apart from the sheer technical expertise involved in making multi-currency loans, there is always

Assets	1	Liabilities	
Cash	500	Canadian Deps.	8000
Loans and Securities	7500	Foreign Currency Deps.	800
Foreign Currency Assets	800	Total	8800
Total	8800		

Assets	2	Liabilities	
Cash	500	Canadian Deps.	7950
Loans and Securities	7500	Foreign Currency Deps.	800
Foreign Currency Assets	750	Total	8750
Total	8750		

Source: Illustration 25 "Net Foreign Assets of the Chartered Banks and the Money Supply," *How the Canadian Money Supply is Affected by Various Banking and Financial Transactions and Developments*, The Royal Bank of Canada Economic Research Department, 1973, p. 55.

the question in which currency a loan will be negotiated. Obviously a perfect arrangement for borrowers is to take delivery of a loan in a hard currency and repay in a soft currency. Exchange rates for hard currencies tend to be overvalued, whereas soft currencies are often undervalued. Banks, on the other hand, prefer loans in soft and repayment in hard, and to reach a compromise is not easy; in fact, Eurobonds denominated in Special Drawing Rights have recently been issued during a period of weakness on the part of the U.S. dollar. The resurgence of the U.S. dollar seems to have resulted in shelving, at least temporarily, the SDR as a unit of account for Eurobonds.

Aside from these problems there remains the whole range of questions as to the use to which the Euroloans are put. Ordinary short-term commercial loans in specific currencies are simple enough, but loans for economic development purposes involve considerable risk to the lenders. Additionally, there are loans used for speculative purposes, i.e., a short-term Eurodollar loan used for the purchase of francs at F 5 = $1 U.S. to be sold later at F 4 = $1 U.S. means a 20% return (less interest on the loan). Or, conversely, a Eurofranc loan to purchase dollars at F 4 = $1 U.S. can result in a 25% return after devaluation to F 5 = $1 U.S. It is clear also that the actual purchase of francs in anticipation of revaluation adds to the demand for the franc and forces its value upward. Conversely, adding to the supply of francs on the market tends to lower its value and helps to make devaluation a certainty. In such cases, the very existence of Eurocurrency markets tends to destabilize market values of currencies.

2. Then there exists what is known as the "dollar overhang," i.e., an excess of U.S. dollars which gluts the Eurocurrency market. This is, generally, the consequence of continued U.S. deficits in the balance of payments, and, like a Damocles sword, threatens the external value of the U.S. dollar. However, in the short-term, there appears to be a more immediate problem of the declining value of the U.S. dollar vis-à-vis the strong continental currencies. This is particularly difficult for Canadians because of the "double jeopardy" position of our dollar against the U.S. dollar, and, in turn, against the European currencies. The matter of the overhang will be considered again in the next chapter.

As part of this overhang of U.S. dollars, there is some evidence of a Eurodollar multiplier, i.e., an expansion of non-resident short-term dollar assets on a cash base of U.S. short-term liabilities to non-residents. The Euromultiplier, in this sense, is analogous to the domestic money multiplier relating total deposits to a base of high-powered money. It is the direct consequence of recycling Eurodollars through Eurobanks, central bank deposits in Eurobanks, and an increasing tendency on the part of commercial enterprises to use Eurobank facilities.

3. This leads to the third point of this conclusion which is perhaps the most intriguing of all. The Eurocurrency system acts as a super-national financial structure of which most western countries (including Canada) are a part. Smaller countries will be dominated by the system, making independent monetary and financial policies difficult if not impossible. But even more significant is the fact that the U.S. dollar, being the major Euro-

currency, is subject to the monetary policy of the Federal Reserve Board in Washington as well as the decisions on the part of the U.S. Congress and Executive. In a word, stringency or glut in the Eurocurrency markets can theoretically be dictated by Washington, an awesome thought these days.

ADDITIONAL READINGS

Clendenning, E. W., *The Euro-dollar Market,* Oxford University Press, 1970.

Einzig, Paul, *The Euro-bond Market*, Macmillan, London, 1969.

Euromoney, Euromoney Publications Ltd., 20 Tudor Street, London. A sophisticated journal highly recommended for those interested in keeping up to date in a rapidly changing area.

Herring, R. J. & R. C. Marston, "The Forward Market and Interest Rates in the Eurocurrency and National Money Markets," *Eurocurrencies and the International Monetary System*, Stern, Makin and Logue (eds.), American Enterprise Institute for Public Policy Research, Wash, D.C., 1976. Other papers in this same volume are recommended.

CHAPTER 14

Money in an International Environment

Introduction

Some of the most interesting and controversial developments in all economics have taken place in an area which is outside national boundaries and jurisdictions, and, therefore, is subject to no national law or discipline. Yet it is an extraordinary fact that international money does have a rationale of its own. It follows some logical principles in its course so that it is possible to expect developments in the future as events work themselves through to their logical conclusion.

But, what is perhaps most interesting of all is that some of mankind's best minds have attempted to shape an international order in accordance with their own views. Yet international banking has developed quite separately from what these men might have preferred. This is the impression one gets from a study of money in an international environment, and it is the theory and logic behind these developments that are the subject of this chapter.

So it is that the world's monetary system which we have today has been shaped by two major influences, the first being the course of events themselves and the second, the Bretton Woods Conference which led to the establishment of the International Monetary Fund. What we know today as the "Bretton Woods System" was the outgrowth of that Conference and the experience of the men who participated in it. It has now been completely replaced by a payments mechanism which is not yet clear except in general principles; in fact, it is still in the process of evolutionary change.

This chapter explores in some detail the attempts which have been made in the past to create a payments mechanism which can satisfactorily discharge obligations between nations. These "creations" are not futile, but while they attempt to address with more or less success the problems and difficulties in international payments which exist at the time of their creation, they quickly become outpaced by changing circumstances. The result is that our international payments system which we have today is a combination of both man-made creations and institutions which have developed in response to needs as they arose.

I. THE BRETTON WOODS SYSTEM

A. A Quantity Theory of International Money

A theoretical beginning has the advantage of focusing on the essentials. For this purpose the Quantity Theory of Money in its application to international trade is particularly useful. We can, in fact, apply the Quantity Theory to international trade with even more confidence than in domestic trade because of the fact that international money, be it gold, SDR's, bilateral accounting, or whatever, is an essential prerequisite for the exchange of goods and services between countries. To put it simply, in domestic exchange we are never quite sure which comes first, the economic activity and exchange which call forth an addition to the money supply in the form of bank deposits, or the availability of additional bank deposits which enables an expansion of economic activity to take place. It is truly a chicken/egg situation.

This dilemma does not exist in international trade. International money in some form is essential for the evaluation of exports and imports *before* trade takes place. This is true even for so-called "barter" agreements which require an evaluation of the items which are traded in terms of an agreed standard, generally U.S. dollars. This fact lends a greater degree of credibility to a Quantity

Theory analysis in international finance than when it is applied in its simplest forms to domestic trade. Also, because of the forward exchange requirements, a kind of multiplier effect exists which results from an expansion of payments of many kinds to support a given increment of international trade. Before any movement of goods can take place, bank credit must be advanced to importers and exporters in an amount considerably in excess of the actual value of the trade. The nature of this credit and how it arises was discussed earlier in Chapter 11. As was pointed out, some seven separate transactions are required to enable a single monetary transfer between Canada and a country other than the U.S.

For our analysis, we shall consider a form of abstract international money somewhat similar to a basket of currencies like the IMF Special Drawing Right, consisting of dollars, sterling, and all other currencies, in a kind of "amalgam" of national currencies each of which is weighted by the value of the foreign trade respresented by the currency.[1] Such an amalgam would be designated as M.

Since no international consensus exists as to the nature of M, other than gold itself, we will make the assumption that a certain ratio $1/g$ of gold to the amalgam, M, exists. The expression $1/g$, could be the official price of gold (formerly \$U.S.35/oz.) if just one of the currencies, albeit the most important one, of the amalgam is used for comparison purposes. In our case,

(1) $G = (M/g)$, with G as the gold portion of the amalgam and $1/g$, the reciprocal of the price of gold in terms of the balance of the currencies which make up the amalgam. Using the Quantity Theory in international trade analysis, we can express

(2) $MV = Tm$, which states that the amalgam M multiplied by its velocity of circulation during a time period must be the same as the value of trade, Tm being expressed in terms of the amalgam. If we divide both sides of the identity (2) by g, we have

(3) $(MV/g) = (Tm/g)$ and substitute gold, G, for M/g we have further,

(4) $GV = (Tm/g)$, which is the value of trade in

terms of gold and which was at one time the only truly acceptable means of payment for international obligations. The Quantity Theory in this form is useful because it focuses on the basic essentials which for the moment are gold, the price of gold, its velocity of circulation, and the value of trade. Thus, the question of accommodating a limited supply of gold to the requirements of trade can be addressed in either of two ways, increasing the velocity or increasing the price of gold. More importantly, it provides a framework for the analysis of the events of the past.

The unfortunate feature of the gold standard in its earlier forms was that nations preferred to hoard gold as a security against those years when exports were insufficient to equal the value of imports. In addition, the United States followed a policy during the years after World War I of amassing most of the world's existing gold supply both as payment for war debts and surpluses in its balance of trade. This gold hoard remained virtually intact until the last decade of the 1960s when U.S. deficits in the balance of payments led to an outflow of gold to the rest of the world.

In general, the objective in accumulating stocks of gold, or M, is simple enough when the world's currencies are fixed in terms of each other. There are periods during, say, the expansionary phase of the business cycle when domestic prices and incomes are rising faster than those of other countries. A reserve of gold would permit a continued import of goods and services during which time either the cycle would resume a more normal trend or domestic economic policies would have an opportunity for corrective action. Such imports could continue without the compensatory action of a devaluation of the exchange rate which would ordinarily act to reduce imports.

This, of course, poses the real dilemma. Hoards of gold amassed within the country for reserve purposes have a zero velocity of circulation during the period within which they are held. This reduces average velocity of circulation of all the world's monetary gold (V in equation 4). Unless this is accompanied by an increase in the world's stock of gold or an increase in its price, the value of trade, Tm, must decline. More realistically, stresses and strains within the international payments system will result as the world adjusts to new equilibrium values of trade which are less than what they could be. (See Table 14-1.)

We can see these stresses from the fact that the

---

[1]This is not far from reality. Since the Smithsonian Agreement, currency values in terms of each other have been determined by just such a weighting system.

Table 14-1
VALUE OF FOREIGN TRADE (EXPORTS PLUS IMPORTS)
(MILLIONS OF U.S. DOLLARS)

1948	1950	1955	1960	1965	1970	1974	1977
110,094	114,049	171,952	232,724	340,906	574,695	1,556,900	2,077,700

Source: *International Financial Statistics,* International Monetary Fund, Tables, "Exports" and "Imports."

actual value of foreign trade, *Tm*, has *not* declined at all; quite the contrary, a considerable expansion in the value of exports and imports has taken place over the years since World War II.

At the same time that the value of trade has been growing, the supply of monetary gold has increased very little through the years. We cannot be certain of the actual increase in the quantity of monetary gold over the past, but according to the International Monetary Fund, the amount of monetary gold in the world was $U.S. 24.8 billion before World War II while in 1977 it was SDR's 35.5 billion. (Actually, the shift from $U.S. to SDR's gives a better measure of quantity than U.S. dollars because of the increased price of gold in terms of dollars.)

While the world's supply of gold was practically static, the growth of gold hoards resulted in a decline in velocity of circulation so that either the development of substitutes for gold as means of payments or an increase in the price of gold (or a combination of both) was essential. This is what the Quantity Theory states and why it is useful.

The dilemma thus posed has been the subject of considerable discussion for many years. Keynes, in his *Tract on Monetary Reform*, advocated the freeing of the domestic currency from gold but would have retained the use of gold for international payments only. This would increase the supply of gold available for international exchange. Much later in his International Clearing Union submission to the Bretton Woods Conference in 1943, a new unit of international currency was proposed which was not freely convertible into gold but *purchasable* by gold—a kind of one-way convertibility.

B. The Keynes Plan

In this famous proposal of the British Treasury, published and circulated in 1943, a new currency was to be developed which would have "general acceptability between nations," and would be

subject neither to the technical supply restrictions of gold mining nor the gold hoarding policies of nations (e.g., the United States or France). The currency would be elastic, subject to expansion or contraction depending upon the needs of trade, and would, at the same time, be administered by an international bank—the International Clearing Union—similar in operation and name to the London clearing banks. The international bank would, precisely as a national bank in its domestic business, make available to debtor nations (those which have deficits in their balance of payments) lines of credit denominated in terms of the new currency instead of gold.

It was not anticipated that the ICU would advance *unlimited* lines of credit (or overdrafts in the British case) to debtor countries any more than a national bank would in relation to its more improvident customers. In all cases, debtor countries would be expected to take necessary measures to correct their deficits, but the borrowing facility would give them time, an essential ingredient for economic policy. It followed that any chronic debtor would require some other borrowing facility in addition to the ICU which could only provide short-term credit to temporary debtor nations. Most important in the scheme, however, was the revolutionary concept that chronic creditor nations (such as the U.S. at that time) were subject to "international disapproval" just as chronic debtors. The reason for this is quite simply that for every debtor nation in the world there must be a corresponding creditor nation — every deficit in the balance of payments must be accompanied by a surplus, somewhere. Thus, to run up a high credit balance in the union was indicative of poor international citizenship as was excessive borrowing; hence, penalty interest charges were to be levied on excess credit balances — a novel departure from ordinary national banking.

At the outset, the members of the clearing union would be assigned a quota of reserve currency (a *bancor*) which would be based upon an objective measure such as a member country's volume of trade.[2] These quotas were to have been revised periodically as the need arose ("need" being defined as volume of trade). In this way the Union addressed the twin prongs of the dilemma, inadequate velocity of circulation created by hoarding and an inadequate supply of international money relative to the volume of trade which was expected to grow in post-war years.

But the clearing union embraced much more than its immediate objective of creating a new international money with a higher velocity of circulation. In Section IX of the proposal there are numerous "might" clauses relating to what the Union could become in the future. These included a future economic government with the power of overseeing post-war reconstruction, policing authority via the freezing of a recalcitrant state's bancor account, the finance of buffer stocks of primary commodities, such as "ever-normal granaries," and, finally, a link with an international investment board for longer-term lending which was beyond the capacity of the Union. In the case of the buffer stocks, it was envisioned that they could eventually become an instrument for control of the trade cycle through price stabilization — a grandiose idea worthy enough of the genius of Keynes.

C. The International Monetary Fund

At the same time that the British Treasury was preparing its proposal for the International Clearing Union, the U.S. Treasury under the supervision of Dr. Harry D. White, the chief assistant to Treasury Secretary Henry Morgenthau, was preparing its own plan for publication in April, 1943. It was entitled *Preliminary Draft Outline of a Proposal for a United and Associated Stabilization Fund*. Broadly, the plan was based upon the successful United States Exchange Stabilization Fund which had supported the exchange rates of sterling and the French franc in the New York market before World War II. In that case, the

U.S. dollars were purchased from the Fund and sold back to the Fund when they were no longer required at rates agreed upon in the so-called Tri-Partite Agreement. It was a novel idea in that, for the first time during those depression years, the responsibility for the maintenance of stability of the exchange rate of the debtor country's currency became the responsibility of the *creditor* country, in this case, the United States, because the U.S. had to make its own currency available for sale to the debtor country when it was required.

When broadened into a truly international fund, it would mean that member nations could purchase necessary foreign exchange with their own currencies, a rather different concept from the clearing union which was so devised as to *create a new currency* and operate exactly as a domestic bank, including overdraft facilities. In the American case, the amount of foreign exchange so purchased was not to be unlimited and would require a certain amount of gold as security. It was, in fact, the White Plan, which, after considerable negotiation between Lord Keynes and Mr. White, was to emerge with some slight modification in the Articles of Agreement of the International Monetary Fund at Bretton Woods.

In April, 1944, the famous Joint Statement, the result of discussions between Keynes and White in September and October, 1943, was released. This was followed by a speech delivered by Lord Keynes to the House of Lords in May in which he was forced to concede that his clearing union would not be accepted. While he was full of praise for the efforts of the Americans, he could hardly conceal his own disappointment. "Perhaps we are laying," he said, "the first brick, though it may be a colourless one, in a great edifice."[3] Of course, subsequent events have proven that far from being the great edifice that Keynes hoped, the International Monetary Fund which emerged has proven to be, in reality, the somewhat colourless brick which was first laid.

In his speech to the Lords, he outlined five benefits to be gained from the Fund which would be of great advantage to Great Britain: (1) A breathing space for retaining non-convertibility of sterling until economic conditions improved, (2) inter-convertibility of all currencies

---

[2]Keynes himself deplored the new name. In presenting the plan to the House of Lords, he made amused reference to the fact that Ms. Churchill and Roosevelt could have done better at selecting a title for the new international unit of currency than all the civil servants who worked with him on the plan. *The New Economics*, Seymour Harris, ed., ch. 26, "The International Clearing Union," p. 361. Published by Dennis Dobson Ltd., London, 1949.

[3]Keynes, "The International Monetary Fund," *op. cit.*, p. 379.

after an initial adjustment period, (3) a substantial addition to the world's monetary reserves in the form of quotas (considerably less, however, than the Union had conceived), (4) the drain of gold from debtor nations to the U.S. and future creditor nations would cease, and (5) a forum for regular discussion of exchange rates and other matters would exist.[4]

> Therefore, for these manifold and substantial benefits I commend the monetary proposals to your Lordships. Nevertheless, before you will give them your confidence, you will wish to consider whether, in return, we are surrendering anything which is vital for the ordering of our domestic affairs in the manner we intend for the future. My Lords, the experience of the years before the war has led most of us, though some of us late in the day to certain firm conclusions. Three, in particular are highly relevant to this discussion. We are determined that, in future, the external value of sterling shall conform to its internal value as set by our own domestic policies, and not the other way round. Secondly, we intend to retain control of our domestic rate of interest, so that we can keep it as low as suits our own purposes, without interference from the ebb and flow of international capital movement or flights of hot money. Thirdly, whilst we intend to prevent inflation at home, we will not accept deflation at the dictate of influences from outside. In other words, we abjure the instruments of bank rate and credit contraction operating through the increase of unemployment as a means of forcing our domestic economy into line with external factors.[5]

It is obvious from the cited passage that even Keynes himself was not endowed with the gift of prophecy, for, despite his "determination," subsequent developments were to show that all three of his "firm conclusions" could not be realized.

It would be helpful to return to a theoretical analysis of the problem and the proposed solutions in diagrammatic form. First, equation (4), will be restated as follows:

$$(5) \qquad V = \frac{Tm}{gG}$$

[4] *Ibid.*, pp. 370-374.
[5] *Ibid.*, p. 374.

Velocity of circulation is equal to the value of trade as measured in terms of the amalgam M, divided by the quantity of gold multiplied by its price level. Now let the term G represent an acceptable international currency, gold, bancors, IMF credits and drawing rights, etc. In Diagram 14-1, Tm, volume of trade in terms of M is measured on the horizontal axis. The vertical axis is the amount of international currency multiplied by its price level in terms of M. It follows that the velocity of circulation of international currency is the cotangent of the angle θ, (Tm/gG), i.e. the greater the velocity of circulation the less the angle θ.

The merit of the ICU in addressing the basic problem lay in the fact that both the quantity of international currency and its velocity would be increased. The latter would arise from the fact that the international reserves of members would be deposited with the Union which in turn would lend them to countries with deficits in their balance of payments. This would have eliminated the problem of gold hoards which always have zero velocity of circulation, and, therefore, reduce total velocity. By lending out the "hoards" total velocity would be maintained at its former level. Thus, an increase in the quantity of international money would be shown by a new and higher level (2 in Diagram 14-1) of existing reserves, while at the same time the greater velocity of circulation due to lending would sustain a volume of trade Tm_3. Or, in terms of our Quantity Theory analysis, an increasing velocity of circulation would be maintained for accepted international money.

The U.S. plan, on the other hand, could do no more than increase the volume of international currency by means of its quota system. But this was a once for all affair, and any further increase in the supply of international currency would involve an increase in quotas, a more difficult feat since it involved a general agreement of the membership. But even when quotas were increased, there was still no method of avoiding a reduction in velocity of circulation. Nations in deficit would *purchase* (they would not borrow) from the fund of quotas so that the actual amount of quotas was always the same—only the composition in terms of national currencies was different. In a word, all that could be expected in terms of financing the volume would be Tm_2.

However, in retrospect, it must be admitted that the U.S. plan, which later became the Interna-

Diagram 14-1

KEYNES VS. WHITE PLANS

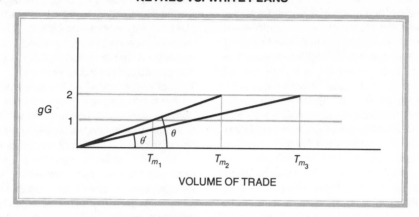

VOLUME OF TRADE

tional Monetary Fund, was the more logical of the two. It was more logical in the sense that it was an extension of the *existing* system of international payments insofar as the U.S., Great Britain and France were concerned. Outside the Tri-Partite Monetary Agreement, there had existed a disorderly system of fluctuating exchange rates, an excessive reliance on bilateral trade agreements, and a massive international disequilibrium in flows of trade and payments. All this was the result of the Great Depression, and since the delegates to the Bretton Woods conference were, generally, well-established in the field of finance (bankers, etc.), their memories were long.

The difficulties which the delegates had experienced were that during periods of unemployment, nations discovered that they could encourage exports and discourage imports through a process of devaluation of their currency relative to that of their neighbours. In so doing, the employment of exporting industries could be stimulated and at the same time employment within domestic producing industries could be encouraged through a reduction of competing imports. This meant that employment could be increased in times of heavy unemployment at the expense of the trading partners. Of course, since other countries could do the same thing, and did, the consequence was that, relatively speaking, exchange rates were just about the same as before devaluation. In the end it is doubtful that much was achieved in terms of employment stim-

ulation, but no end of confusion resulted for bankers and others concerned with exchange rates.

D. The Gold Exchange Standard—A Digression

There is another aspect to the international payments system which existed at the time of the 1920s and 30s and which contributed to the prestige of the White Plan as opposed to the Keynes Plan. This was an already well-developed Gold Exchange Standard of which the White Plan was also a logical extension. While it is neither appropriate nor necessary to develop a detailed discussion of this system, a few of its important aspects will assist in understanding the structure of the international payments system as outlined at Bretton Woods.

During the years following World War I most nations made sincere attempts to restore the international gold standard which had existed prior to the War. The domestic gold standard was, of course, impossible to restore as Keynes and others recognized.[6] Internationally, however, it was a different matter, for the utilization of monetary gold, hitherto required for domestic circulation, became available for international use — a substantial increase in the supply of international

---

[6]J. M. Keynes, *The Tract on Monetary Reform*, Macmillan, London, 1923.

currency. Still, despite this advantage, it became an impossibility to overcome the fundamental difficulty that creditor countries, the United States in particular, absorbed much of the world's gold in payments for war munitions, etc. In addition, the central banks of Europe learned how to absorb hoards of gold within their vaults to be used as a base for credit expansion, a further method of economizing in the use of gold.[7] Generally rising prices, of course, absorbed this extra credit money making a restoration of the pre-war domestic gold standard impossible and the international standard extremely difficult.

Nevertheless, most countries climbed back onto the international gold standard so that by 1929, only China, Spain, and Mexico were still not included in the list of gold standard countries. The question of *how* most countries could be on a "gold standard" when only a few countries had practically all the gold was resolved at the Brussels Conference in 1920 and the Genoa Conference in 1922. At the latter conference the idea that central banks could hold reserves of both gold and/or foreign exchange was pretty much accepted by the delegates. It followed directly from this that the currency with which gold could be purchased at a fixed price (the U.S. dollar) was the equivalent of gold. In a word, the U.S. dollar as a reserve was the equivalent of gold and became the basis for the Gold Exchange Standard (actually loosely referred to as the "gold standard").

But the "gold standard" thus developed was short-lived. It collapsed with the onset of the Great Depression not so much *because* of the Depression but because of a cumulative series of stresses placed upon the system. There was, according to Keynes in his *Tract on Monetary Reform*, a confusion in the minds of the public between "deflation" and "devaluation."[8] Central banks and governments believed that the process of establishing a gold standard meant restoring the value of gold as a commodity to its

pre-World War I level, and this could only mean deflation. The incredible fact, according to Keynes, was that the principal delegates to the Genoa Convention to whom the situation applied, the representatives from Italy, France, and Belgium, asserted that they would *not* devaluate (entailing a loss of national pride) but deflate so that pre-war prices would prevail!

This, of course, doomed the new gold standard (or more correctly the gold exchange standard) from the start simply because of the impossibility of its implementation. As Keynes noted, the burden of taxes, dislocation of business, unemployment, etc., were insupportable and it only remained for the Great Depression to end the system forever. Under any circumstances attempts to deflate must of necessity be self-defeating in the end since they involve the accumulation of a quantity of gold or U.S. dollars in reserves without a domestic expansion of credit. In other words, hoards of gold were for sale at a fixed price in terms of a foreign currency when the foreign exchange markets could not accommodate the currency at a certain "parity." But every country cannot accumulate hoards in this way and the result must be a "scramble" for scarce gold or foreign exchange by contracting bank credit until the country collapses in severe depression.

By 1936 the gold standard, or rather the gold exchange standard, was generally abandoned by almost all countries. France was the last of the leading western countries to give up amidst a system of fluctuating and depreciating currencies which had already become universal. The German Reich under Hitler's brilliant Hjalmar Schacht had developed a system of different rates of exchange for different commodities and for different countries. Ultimately a total of 237 separate rates for the mark existed, a symptom of the degree of degeneration of foreign exchange markets which had already occurred.[9] It was, in fact, this chaos in exchange rate determination which led to the formation of the Tri-Partite Agreement in 1936, after France's abandonment of the gold standard, among the United States, Great Britain, and France. Ultimately, by the outbreak of

---

[7]G. Crowther, *Outline of Money*, Thomas Nelson and Sons Ltd., London, 1949, p. 310.

[8]Keynes used an extraordinary definition of "devaluation" which could only have meaning within the context of the period, viz., "The alternative policy of stabilising the value of the currency somewhere near its present value, without regard to its pre-war value, is called *Devaluation*." Keynes, *op. cit.*, p. 142.

---

[9]William L. Shirer, *The Rise and Fall of the Third Reich* Mr. Shirer indicates that "some economists" estimated that the number of rates of exchange for the mark was as high as that. This could be an exaggeration.

World War II in 1939, many other countries had joined as well.

Considering this background, then, it is not difficult to understand why the delegates to the Bretton Woods Conference would swing back to the gold exchange standard (or the U.S. dollar standard) preferring the monetary stability as they had seen it to the alternative of chaos preceding World War II. Accordingly, Article IV, Section 1(a) of the Articles of Agreement states:

> The par value of the currency of each member shall be expressed in terms of gold as a common denominator or in terms of the United States dollar of the weight and fineness in effect on July 1, 1944.[10]

Thus, despite the fact that the original White Plan had provided for "unitas" equal in value to 137$\frac{1}{7}$ grains of fine gold, the Articles of Agreement restored, in effect, the gold exchange standard at the same time elevating the U.S. dollar to the status of an international reserve currency. This was what it had been before, amongst the participating countries in the Tri-Partite Agreement, but this time it received the official sanction of the Bretton Woods delegates.

Through this device, the restoration of the gold exchange standard, the strain on a given supply of gold for payments purposes was enormously relieved. The future growth in international trade could be accommodated by the simple expedient of acquiring and using U.S. dollars as a means of payment so long as all countries were willing to accept dollars for their exports.

One is hardly being cynical in arguing that this position of being the source of the free world's international money carried both enormous prestige and economic advantage. The advantage lay in the fact that the United States need not (indeed must not) balance its international payments. It meant that imports and payments abroad would exceed exports for the reason that there is no other way for U.S. dollars to move into the stream of international payments.

If we consider a country, France, for example, which preferred not to accept U.S. dollars in payment for its exports to the United States but did so

because it had no choice, its exports would be tantamount to an interest-free loan to the U.S. without definite term. The United States, since it could not and must not balance its payments, was acquiring additional wealth in the form of imports without a corresponding loss of wealth in the form of exports. Further, the loans and grants made to various countries in U.S. dollars meant that allies and friends could be "purchased" without sacrifice since these dollars could be used for payments for imports from a third source. In this way a dollar "empire" was created with influence and power equal to the Victorian empire.

Whether for these reasons or others, the International Monetary Fund certainly laid the ground work for the extension of the pre-war gold exchange standard into the future. Had either the Keynes or White Plans been accepted in entirety, *bancors* or *unitas* would likely have replaced the U.S. dollar and many years of confusion in international finance could have been avoided. In the end, of course, the Special Drawing Right superceded the U.S. dollar, but the road to that end was rocky and progress was much too slow.

E. Other Proposals: France and Canada

The British and American proposals were not the only ones submitted to the Bretton Woods Conference for consideration. The French delegates too had their own vision of a future world of international finance. This, again, was fundamentally an extension of the past into the future, and this, to them, was the Tri-Partite Agreement of 1936 on the one hand and the Franco-British Agreement of 1939 on the other. In both cases the creditor country (or countries) had agreed to support the debtor country's currency in terms of its foreign exchange value by continuous purchasing in the foreign exchange markets. In the latter case, there was no limit to the amount purchased because of the emergency of war.

To this point, there was nothing of substantive nature about the French proposal to distinguish it from the White Plan; however, from there on the proposals diverged. After an initial adjustment and reconstruction period, the French believed that all credits earned in the process of trade should be redeemable in gold. In other words, the final settlement of international payments should take place in gold after the credits and debits had been cancelled.

---

[10]*The International Monetary Fund*, 1945-65, Vol. III Documents, IMF, Washington, D.C., 1969, p. 189.

Considering the difficulties which nations would encounter if they attempted to agree upon the adoption of a new international currency, is it not providential that they have at hand such a currency, consecrated by a mystic thousands of years old, in the form of yellow metal? Gold is the international currency of the future.[11]

This "faith" in gold, as we shall see later, has been characteristic of the French position even to the present day.

Canada's contribution to the IMF as an international organization actually began during the preliminary discussions preceding Bretton Woods with a submission of its own—"A Tentative Draft Proposal of Canadian Experts for an International Exchange Union" (July 12, 1943). The "experts" were officials of the Canadian government, in particular the Ministry of Finance, and the proposal followed from an examination of both the Keynes and White Plans. In the discussions which ensued, there is no evidence that it was ever seriously considered as an alternative to either of the major submissions, and, like the French Plan, was politely accepted and filed away for future reference.

The Canadian Plan was fundamentally different from the French in that, while attempting to steer a course between Keynes and White, it veered toward the Americans. While the Canadians did conceive of a new unit of currency, referred to simply as the "Unit," like the White Plan, quotas to an amount of $8,000 million were to be assigned —15% payable in gold or gold equivalent and the balance in national currency. While there is no evidence that the drafters had conceived of increasing the amount of Units so as to provide for an elastic international currency, they were aware of the difficulties attendant upon a "penury in the foreign means of payment." Beyond this it is difficult to identify anything very original in the Canadian Plan with the possible exception that the Canadians did recognize the importance of extending credit to the "International Union," foreshadowing the General Arrangements to Borrow almost 20 years later.

F. International Liquidity

At the same time that the western countries (the Soviet Union refused to ratify the Articles of Agreement and was therefore excluded from membership) agreed on the basic structure of the International Monetary Fund, they effectively ensured its weakness as an international organization. The first, and foremost, of the built-in weaknesses lay in the fact that drawing rights for debtor countries were conditional, not free as Keynes himself had wished. Article V, Section 3(iii) severely limits a member state's capacity to purchase currencies of other countries. With both time constraints as well as an upper limit of 200% of the member state's quota.

Sir Roy Harrod argued that these limitations were the result of insistence on the part of the Americans. "It is easy to see why the American view in favour of making drawings conditional should have gained ascendancy at the beginning. Most of the currencies of the members were still inconvertible, and since they were thus not discharging their full duties as members of the Fund, it was quite reasonable to restrict their privileges."[12] He notes further that the world was passing through " ... a highly abnormal period with the vast structural adjustments required as an aftermath of the war not yet achieved and with an acute dollar shortage prevailing."[13] A rather curious contradiction in the Articles of Agreement results from just this situation. Article VII deals with the problem of scarce currencies with specific measures to be taken in the event that scarcity exists. Section 3 of this article requires the Fund to "apportion" these scarce currencies among members with due regard for their relative needs. On the other hand, Article VIII, Sections 2, 3, and 4, "General Obligations of Members," discourages anything *but* free convertibility of currencies and specifically forbids (Section 3) discriminatory currency arrangements! Thus, if the latter article is strictly adhered to, scarce currencies are an impossibility and Article VII is superfluous, because it is a simple matter to convert into any currency first and the "scarce" currency second on the assumption that the country which

---

[11]*Ibid.*, p. 101.

[12]R. Harrod, *Reforming the World's Money,* St. Martin's Press, New York, 1965, p. 121.
[13]*Ibid.*, p. 122.

Table 14-2
INTERNATIONAL RESERVES
(MILLIONS)

IMF Portion	1967 $U.S.	1970	1973	1976	1977
			SDR's		
Special Drawing Rights	—	3,124	8,807	8,656	8,133
Reserve Position in the Fund	5,748	7,697	6,168	17,736	18,089
Gold	39,500	36,996	35,608	35,346	35,536
Foreign Exchange	29,040	45,435	101,679	160,615	200,666
Total	74,288	93,252	152,262	222,353	262,424

Source: International Financial Statistics IMF, Washington, D.C.

issues the first currency happens to have some of the "scarce" currency in its reserves.

Secondly, the fact that the U.S. dollar became the underpinning for the entire structure meant that once the dollar weakened, so would the Fund. Of course, since the strength or weakness of the U.S. dollar depended entirely upon the policies of the United States, the Fund in turn was dependent upon the behaviour of one country, hardly a stable or secure foundation.

And thirdly, the eternal problem of international liquidity remained, and the success of the IMF depended in turn upon its success in addressing this important problem. Unfortunately, increases in quotas, standby arrangements, and the General Arrangements to Borrow all required lengthy discussion at annual general meetings. The consequence has sometimes been delayed response to what actually is an emergency situation. This was especially true of the Special Drawing Rights proposal which was a solution to a problem of international liquidity recognized as early as 1963. In 1967, four years later, the Directors submitted a plan for these SDR's to the Governors at the annual meeting, but the proposals for the amendment to the Articles were not submitted until 1968. Ultimately, the Special Drawing Rights were included in member states' reserves on January 1, 1970, over six years after the initial concern over a shortage of liquidity.

Table 14-2 above indicates the almost painful slowness with which the "official" IMF portion of reserves has grown over the recent past.

The IMF contribution to the world's reserves (SDR's plus the reserve position in the Fund) was only 7.7% of total reserves in 1967 and 9.9% in 1977, including the new SDR's. The foreign exchange portion, on the other hand, has grown very rapidly over the past ten years.

It was the rapid growth of the foreign exchange portion of reserves (largely U.S. dollars) which led the staff of the IMF to the conclusion as long ago as 1958 that no problem of international liquidity existed. Nations, it was argued, had sufficient reserves to give the fiscal and monetary measures designed to correct their balance of payments deficits time to take effect. This improvement in liquidity stemmed largely from the fact that the proportion of the world's monetary gold held by the United States had been declining from a high of 74% in 1949 to 62% in 1957. Of the total gold and foreign exchange reserves, the United States held 56% in 1949 and 43% in 1957.[14] The decline in these percentages over the years was seen as a favourable sign indicating an improvement in the current and projected liquidity of the world. Of course, the huge U.S. balance of payments deficits of the 1960s which accompanied the Vietnam War were yet to come, and it was these which pumped out U.S. dollars into the stream of international liquidity on a scale undreamed of during the latter 1950s.

The effect of the inclusion of foreign exchange on the world's liquidity can be readily seen in Diagram 14–2. The vertical, jG, is the amount available for trade and for reserves. The coefficient j is the price of the reserve currency, G, which consists of a weighted average of the prices of the component reserve currencies (specifically gold and U.S. dollars).[15] As before, the cotangents of the angles θ and θ' measure the velocity of circu-

---

[14] *IMF, op. cit.*, Vol. III, Documents, p. 406.
[15] The weighted average would be $j = h(H/M) + k(K/M - K)$ with H, the amount of gold, and h, its price in terms of M. K is the amount of U.S. dollars and k the exchange rate as measured against all other currencies, $M - K$.

Diagram 14-2

GOLD PLUS FOREIGN EXCHANGE

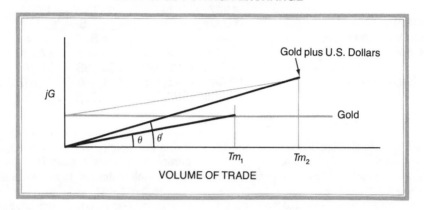

VOLUME OF TRADE

lation, with respect to the volume of trade, Tm. Instead of a static level of monetary gold, indicated by the gold horizontal, the total of gold plus U.S. dollars now has a positive slope, i.e., the amount of U.S. dollars plus gold is functionally related to the volume of trade. As the volume of trade, as measured by T_m, increases, the amount of U.S. dollars to finance this trade increases to the extent that the U.S. participates. Furthermore, the deficit in the U.S. balance of payments must be sufficient (no more and no less) to satisfy both the increased volume of trade and the foreign exchange reserve requirement of each of the countries which participate in trade. This reserve requirement is indicated by the cotangent of the angle θ, since the greater the exchange reserve of each country is, the less is total velocity of circulation.

Diagram 14-2 can be easily extended to include other forms of liquidity, particularly the "reserve position in the Fund" and Special Drawing Rights. We would simply superimpose these on the "Gold plus U.S. dollars" expansion path. This total expansion path has a somewhat greater slope than before for the reason that these additional forms of liquidity have been increasing along with the volume of trade. Of course, Special Drawing Rights are not functionally related to trade in the same way as U.S. dollars or the reserve position in the Fund since their increase depends upon independent decisions of the Fund. However, these decisions have been taken in response to a need for additional liquidity so to include SDR's

as functionally related to trade does not violate logic too greatly.

In Diagram 14-3 jG is, as before, the amount of liquidity available for trade as well as for holding as reserves of foreign exchange by all countries. The coefficient j now includes the "price" of both SDR's and the reserve position in the fund which is also now measured in SDR's.[16] Also as before, the cotangent of the angle indicates the velocity of circulation of all liquidity, hence, measures the strength of the desire for nations to hold reserves. Should this desire for reserves decrease, so that less would be required, the angle θ would decrease as the velocity of circulation increased and more trade could be financed.

1. Canada and the IMF

Of much greater significance to the IMF than the Exchange Union submitted to the Bretton Woods Conference were the *negative* contributions of Canada, for it is here that the Canadian government has been much more active, specifically in

---

[16]The weighted average would consist of the following:

$$J = \frac{h\dfrac{H}{M} + k\dfrac{K}{M-K} + 1\dfrac{L}{M} + n\dfrac{N}{M}}{\dfrac{H}{M} + \dfrac{K}{M-K} + l\dfrac{L}{M} + \dfrac{N}{M}}$$

where h = price of gold, k = exchange rate of U.S. dollars against all other currencies $M - K$, 1 = the price of Fund reserves in terms of SDR's and N = the price of SDR's in terms of all currencies.

Diagram 14-3

INTERNATIONAL LIQUIDITY
(Gold Plus Dollars Plus SDR's)

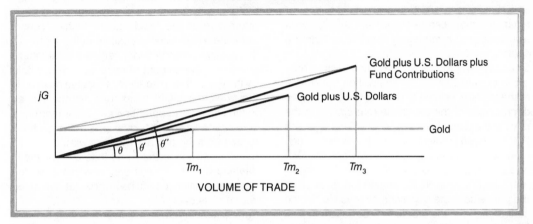

Gold plus U.S. Dollars plus Fund Contributions

Gold plus U.S. Dollars

Gold

jG

θ θ' θ''

Tm_1 Tm_2 Tm_3

VOLUME OF TRADE

violating Article IV both in letter (Section 3) and in intent. In a word, Canada was among the first countries to introduce the floating exchange rate. In September, 1950, Mr. Rasminsky, Canada's representative on the Board of Governors, had the unwelcome responsibility of explaining the Canadian decision to suspend the par value of the Canadian dollar and permit a fluctuating rate of exchange.[17] The reason for the change in policy on the part of the Canadian government was the heavy inflow of U.S. capital which was depressing interest rates and making control of the supply of money and credit difficult. Open market operations on a scale necessary to cancel the impact of additional foreign exchange inflows on the reserves of the banks were just not feasible for the simple reason that there was insufficient government debt for the Bank of Canada to sell on the open market. And, since quantitative restrictions on U.S. capital were difficult to implement (there was no Foreign Investment Review Act then) the Canadian Government decided that a floating rate was the only practicable solution.

The logic of this stand is not easy to grasp. It does, in fact, imply an elasticity of response of capital flows to exchange rate adjustments, a proposition which is only tenable for short-term

---

[17]For this and much of the chronical of events which follows, the excellent work of Margaret G. de Vries is extremely helpful. See ch. 7, "Fluctuating Exchange Rates," Vol. II, *Analysis*, IMF Documents, p. 152.

capital. Long-term capital inflows, as recorded in the balance of payments capital account, actually continued to increase during the decade of the 1950s, rising by 227% from 1952 ($455 million) to 1956 ($1,490 million). What actually happened was that the Bank of Canada was relieved of the necessity for buying huge amounts of U.S. dollars for the Exchange Fund Account. The permitting of an appreciation of the Canadian dollar (the original par value of 100 U.S. cents for one Canadian dollar) encouraged more imports from the U.S. and reduced the balance of payments surplus to more meaningful proportions. Short-term capital flows, in response to interest rate differentials and forward exchange spreads, were mostly negative during this period which also helped to reduce the balance of payments surplus, suggesting that for the period of the 1950s, at least, such capital was more responsive (elastic) to changes in the exchange rate than to interest rate changes, a curious development. Events notwithstanding, Mr. Rasminsky defended Canada's position on the basis that capital inflows had indeed been reduced.

The significance, of course, of Canada's decision to float was not lost on the Executive Directors, and Mr. Stamp of the U.K. considered that there was a general principle at stake and that danger to the Fund's operations existed if floating rates became general. Other Directors, Mr. Melville of Australia and M. Largentaye of France, were equally critical. But the situation was already being remedied by Canada's balance of payments deficit on current account which reached almost 1½ billion dollars in both 1957 and 1959. The deficit with the United States alone was $1,579 million in 1957. In 1961 the Minister of Finance announced in Parliament that Canada would move to a *managed* float rather than the current free float.

One may sympathize with Mr. Rasminsky's having to explain Canada's new position because a managed float implied a return to the competitive depreciation of the exchange rate similar to the days of the Great Depression, precisely what the IMF had been created to avoid. There did, in fact, emerge a sharp disagreement between the IMF and Canada, and the staff of the IMF in a report on Canada's position recommended a return to the par value system as soon as feasible. To the staff at the IMF, the problem of Canada's capital inflows was not the result of the exchange rate but the government's policy toward interest rates and credit in general.

It was on the basis of this staff report that the Board of Directors attempted to exert pressure on Canada under Article VII, General Obligations of Members, in the form of consultations in February, 1962. At the same time, mounting unemployment in Canada and massive imports combined with the encouragement of the Board of Directors convinced the Canadian government that it was time to establish a new par value at $C1 = $U.S. .925 or, conversely, $C1.08 = $U.S. 1.00. Canada was "welcomed" back to the par value system.

Of course, Canada was not alone in its fluctuating rate. Other countries — Lebanon, Peru, Syria, and Thailand — were also floating. However, Canada's position as a relatively wealthy country to be included among the Group of Ten under the General Arrangements to Borrow could only serve to weaken the prestige of the IMF if the Canadian dollar continued to float, a fact of which the Directors were certainly aware. Ultimately, however, the Directors did accept the principle that temporarily a free-floating rate could be a useful device for establishing par values, but they were not at all prepared to abandon the par value system itself. It is this which remained as the ultimate objective to the last.

2. The Mechanism of the Fund

In its actual day-to-day operation, the IMF does not "loan" any currencies at all. Each member country is required to pay its quota in the form of 25% in gold and 75% in its own currency in accordance with the exchange rate as determined by the par value of its currency.[18] It is the 25%, referred to as the "gold tranche," which constitutes the initial reserve position in the Fund, for the reserve position is defined as the member's quota less the amount of national currency held by the Fund. It is, in addition, a reserve position in the *true* sense of the word, for a member has an automatic right to purchase any other member's currency to an amount equal to its gold tranche. It follows from this that any member will increase its reserve position in the Fund if its currency is in demand by other members, in which case the reserve position could be 100% (at the maximum) of its quota.

Purchases of members' currencies with a single member's currency to an amount equal to 25% of its quota (in addition to the gold tranche), may be made with justification under Article VII, the scarce currencies article. Such rights of purchase are, however, not included under the reserve position in the Fund because they are not automatic. An additional purchase of up to 100% of a member's quota may be made with detailed justification, hence, it follows that the use of the Fund's "credit" actually begins at the point where the 25% gold tranche is exhausted. In other words, when the IMF holdings of a member country's currency exceeds its quota, credit is being extended; in this way it is possible to compute a country's use of IMF credit by simply subtracting its quota from the IMF holdings of the country's currency. Similarly, a country's reserve position in the Fund may be calculated as the difference between a member country's quota and the actual holdings of that country's currency. Fortunately, such purchasing (actually borrowings because all currencies must be repurchased from the Fund within three to five years) can be arranged in advance with standby agreements. Nevertheless, the Fund's resources have been strained in the past and in 1962 they were augmented by the General Arrangements to Borrow, a standby credit offered to the IMF by ten industrial nations, including Canada. In 1974, Mr.

---

[18]Since May, 1973, the exchange rate of a currency has been determined by the month-end market closing rate.

J. Witteveen, the Fund's managing director, was able to arrange an oil facility amounting to $3.4 billion (U.S. dollars) of which Canada's share has been $300 million. This was designed to assist member countries which are in a balance of payments deficit position due to the rising import costs of oil.

The operation of the General Account of the International Monetary Fund can be seen from Table 14-3 extracted from the *Bank of Canada Review*. It is divided into three parts, (1) Canada's position in the Special Drawing Account, (2) Canada's position in the General Account, and (3) the transactions in the General Account.

(1) The Special Drawing Account is a net addition to Canada's foreign exchange reserves, granted purely by agreement and allocated according to the relative size of each country's quota. SDR's are a creation, literally additional reserves of liquidity without any "backing" of gold or national currencies to ensure confidence, etc. As can be seen from the Table, Canada has increased its holdings of SDR's beyond the original allocation for the reason that other countries have used some of their own allocations for the purchase of Canadian dollars.

(2) Canada's position in the General Account (as opposed to the Special Drawing Account) begins with the current quota of 1.357 billions of SDR's. The SDR, incidentally, is the "new" international currency unit reminiscent of the bancor or unitas which is now made necessary by the demise of the gold exchange standard. As such, it cannot be used by any country directly for the purchase of imports but must be exchanged for national currencies first. The national currency is then used for supplementing a member state's reserves.

Originally, when the SDR was created from thin air in January, 1970, it was given the exchange rate of 1 U.S. dollar equal to 1 SDR. It followed that the SDR had the same gold equivalent as the U.S. dollar and was tantamount to an increase in the *volume* of U.S. dollars in the IMF. Since then, two devaluations of the dollar, in December, 1971 and February, 1973, have taken place. These "devaluations" are actually increases in the price of gold in terms of U.S. dollars and thus mean that the SDR was valued at $1.20635 in February, 1973, an increase of 11.1% from the December, 1971, value of $1.08571. As of July 1, 1974, the SDR has assumed a floating value in accordance

with the value of 16 currencies against the U.S. dollar. In effect, the SDR has become simply an index number consisting of weighted averages of exchange rates. The methodology is simple enough. It consists of assigning a base date of June 28, 1974 when the value of the SDR was still $1.20635. The exchange rates of 15 currencies relative to the U.S. dollar were used as weights so that as the values of any of the *sixteen* currencies (including the U.S. dollar) move, so does the SDR value move in accordance with each currency's weight. The currencies which make up the SDR and their units within it are as follows:

Currency	Unit
U.S. $	40 cents
S. African rand	.8 cents
Austrian schilling	22 groschen
Peseta	1.1 peseta
Nor. krone	9.9 oere
Dan. krone	11 oere
Australian $	1.2 cents
Swed. krona	13 oere
D-mark	38 pfennigs
Sterling	4½ pence
Fr. franc	44 centimes
Japanese yen	26 yen
Canadian $	7.1 cents
Italian lira	47 lira
Dutch guilder	14 cents
Belg. franc	1.6 francs

Source: *The Economist*, July 6, 1974, p. 96.

By "floating" its SDR in this way, the IMF has succeeded in restoring the confidence in its currency unit that was lost after the last dollar devaluation; in fact, the SDR is increasingly being used as an accepted standard for evaluating the world's purchasing power.[19]

By subtracting the IMF holdings of Canadian dollars (denominated in SDR's) from the quota and adding the Notes Held Outstanding under the General Arrangements to Borrow and the new

[19]Three public bond issues took place in June and July, 1975, Alusuisse (SDR 50 million), Sveriges Investeringsbank (SDR 30 million) and Electricite de France (SDR 50 million). A. Middernacht, "The Future of SDR Deposits," *Euromoney*, November, 1975, p. 70.

Table 14–3
CANADA'S POSITION IN THE IMF
(MILLIONS OF SDRs)

Years and months	Canada's position in the Special Drawing Account			Canada's position in the General Account					
	Cumulative allocation of SDRs	Balance on transactions in SDRs	Total holdings of SDRs	Canada's quota	IMF holdings of Canadian dollars		Notes held under outstanding IMF borrowings	Use of IMF credit	Reserve position in the IMF
					Amount	Percentage of quota			
1967				740.0	341.6	46	35.0		433.4
1968				740.0	533.8	72			206.2
1969				740.0	357.4	48	95.5		478.1
1970	124.3	57.8	182.1	1,100.0	550.4	50	120.0		669.6
1971	242.0	129.9	371.9	1,100.0	767.4	70			332.6
1972	358.6	106.7	465.3	1,100.0	784.1	71			315.9
1973	358.6	108.7	467.3	1,100.0	819.6	75			280.4
1974	358.6	110.5	469.1	1,100.0	808.1	73	140.7		432.6
1975	358.6	115.8	474.4	1,100.0	793.4	72	246.9		553.5
1976	358.6	121.5	480.1	1,100.0	534.0	49	246.9		812.9
1977	358.6	57.4	416.0	1,100.0	604.0	55	205.4		701.4
1975 O	358.6	115.8	474.4	1,100.0	785.2	71	246.9		561.7
N	358.6	115.8	474.4	1,100.0	793.4	72	246.9		553.5
D	358.6	115.8	474.4	1,100.0	793.4	72	246.9		553.5
1976 J	358.6	115.8	474.4	1,100.0	787.5	72	246.9		559.4
F	358.6	115.8	474.4	1,100.0	788.4	72	246.9		558.5
M	358.6	115.8	474.4	1,100.0	783.8	71	246.9		563.2
A	358.6	120.3	478.9	1,100.0	780.9	71	246.9		566.1
M	358.6	121.5	480.1	1,100.0	722.5	66	246.9		624.4
J	358.6	121.5	480.1	1,100.0	714.9	65	246.9		632.1
J	358.6	121.5	480.1	1,100.0	659.0	60	246.9		688.0
A	358.6	121.5	480.1	1,100.0	607.9	55	246.9		739.0
S	358.6	121.5	480.1	1,100.0	591.6	54	246.9		755.3
O	358.6	121.5	480.1	1,100.0	578.9	53	246.9		768.1
N	358.6	121.5	480.1	1,100.0	531.9	48	246.9		815.1
D	358.6	121.5	480.1	1,100.0	534.0	49	246.9		812.9
1977 J	358.6	119.5	478.1	1,100.0	541.9	49	266.5		824.6
F	358.6	119.5	478.1	1,100.0	556.5	51	266.5		810.0
M	358.6	115.2	473.8	1,100.0	556.5	51	266.5		810.0
A	358.6	119.8	478.4	1,100.0	546.5	50	266.5		820.0
M	358.6	109.0	467.6	1,100.0	532.7	48	276.7		844.0
J	358.6	85.5	444.1	1,100.0	553.7	50	276.7		823.0
J	358.6	83.5	442.1	1,100.0	576.9	52	257.5		780.7
A	358.6	62.6	421.2	1,100.0	577.4	52	243.8		766.4
S	358.6	62.6	421.2	1,100.0	581.4	53	243.8		762.4
O	358.6	62.6	421.2	1,100.0	581.4	53	243.8		762.4
N	358.6	61.0	419.6	1,100.0	591.9	54	243.8		751.9
D	358.6	57.4	416.0	1,100.0	604.0	55	205.4		701.4
1978 J	358.6	51.2	409.8	1,100.0	611.0	56	205.1		694.1
F	358.6	50.4	409.0	1,100.0	619.5	56	203.3		683.8
M	358.6	49.7	408.3	1,100.0	633.4	58	199.7		666.3
A	358.6	38.7	397.3	1,100.0	794.9	72	198.9		503.9
M	358.6	45.3	403.9	1,357.0	1,051.9	78	194.4		499.5
J	358.6	45.3	403.9	1,357.0	1,047.9	77	182.8		491.9
J	358.6	44.3	402.9	1,357.0	1,053.7	78	178.1		481.5
A	358.6	44.3	402.9	1,357.0	1,053.6	78	171.7		477.1
S	358.6	42.5	401.1	1,357.0	1,053.6	78	167.4		470.7
O	358.6	40.0	398.6	1,357.0	1,050.3	77	147.6		454.3

Transactions in the General Account

	Canadian transactions with the IMF				Canadian dollar transactions of other countries with the IMF (net)	Canadian transactions with other countries in notes issued by the IMF	Total
	Drawings (-)	Repurchases	Purchases (-) of gold and SDRs from the IMF	Other trans- actions net			
1967					−15.1		−15.1
1968	−426.0	64.8		2.8	131.2		−227.2
1969			−8.6	0.2	250.3	30.0	271.9
1970			−45.2	91.0	145.7		191.5
1971			−66.3		−270.7		−337.0
1972					−16.6		−16.6
1973					−35.5		−35.5
1974					11.5		11.5
1975					14.7		14.7
1976					259.4		259.4
1977			−16.4	−21.8	−31.5		−70.0
1975 O					−0.6		−0.6
N					−8.2		−8.2
D							
1976 J					5.9		5.9
F					−0.9		−0.9
M					4.7		4.7
A					2.9		2.9
M					58.4		58.4
J					7.7		7.7
J					55.9		55.9
A					51.0		51.0
S					16.3		16.3
O					12.8		12.8
N					47.0		47.0
D					−2.2		−2.2
1977 J			−8.2	−3.6	4.0		−7.9
F				−13.8	−0.8		−14.6
M					10.0		10.0
A							
M				8.7	5.1		13.8
J				−9.2	−11.8		−21.0
J					−23.1		−23.1
A					−0.5		−0.5
S					−4.0		−4.0
O							
N					−10.5		−10.5
D			−8.2	−3.9			−12.1
1978 J					−7.0		−7.0
F					−8.5		−8.5
M					−13.9		−13.9
A					−161.6		−161.6
M							
J					4.0		4.0
J					−5.7		−5.7
A					8.0		8.0
S							
O					−11.4		−11.4

Oil Facility, we may arrive at Canada's Reserve position in the Fund. At the end of 1974, this amounted to SDR's 432.6 million or $ U.S. 529.7 million which is part of Canada's official international reserves.

(3) The third section, transactions in the General Account, is an explanation of the year-to-year changes in the General Account, both on the part of Canada and other countries which wish to use Canadian dollars. What is surprising here is that the Canadian government has been reluctant to use the IMF facilities for the purpose of stabilizing the Canadian dollar during the recent years when the value of the dollar has declined. The implication (no more than this) is that the government prefers not to subject itself to the IMF disciplinary measures which often accompany foreign currency purchases above the gold tranche.

G. The Weakness and Ultimate Collapse of the System

Effective as it may have been in the past, the International Monetary Fund is by no means the dominant feature on the international payments horizon. The original Clearing Union, as conceived by Lord Keynes, would likely have been more successful, but as outlined at Bretton Woods the IMF could not become, as hoped, the central pivot around which international trade and payments revolve. The reason is that it addressed the wrong problem. Its *raison d'etre* was to fix exchange rates, a useful enough objective during the world of the 1930s but not in a world in which flexible exchange rates are appropriate, the world of the 1960s and 70s. In attempting the impossible, it was destined to be bypassed by the real world, ultimately to become little more than an advisory agency, a useful enough function but with a minimum of influence in international finance. We can see the difficulty more clearly with the aid of the theoretical framework set forth above.

1. The Overhang

In Diagram 14-4, total international liquidity (jG) is measured on the vertical axis as before. This is G, the necessary international currency unit, multiplied by its price j in terms of the amalgam, M. Trade and payments as measured by M are represented on the horizontal axis; again it follows that Tm/jG measures velocity of circulation. Suppose an increase in the volume of reserve currency occurred. This would be a shift to R' from R. Given a specific volume of trade and payments, Tm_1, the velocity of circulation, should decrease from θ to θ'. This would be the consequence of the willingness of countries to hold additional reserves in their respective exchange fund accounts. Assuming the *contrary* were true, i.e., trading nations refused to hold the additional

Diagram 14-4

THE OVERHANG

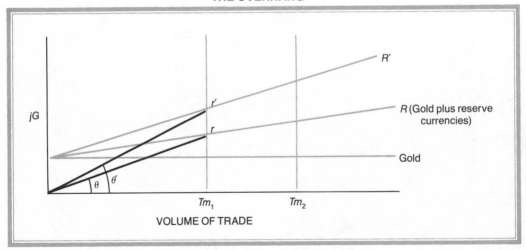

reserve funds in official accounts, an "overhang" of $r' - r$ would result and velocity of circulation would not decline. This would consist of an unwanted amount of reserve currency which would be held as foreign exchange deposits in various banks, say, in Europe. Such an "overhang" could be absorbed firstly by an expansion of trade to Tm_2, but if the volume reserve currency, R, expands *faster* than world trade and nations refuse to absorb the excess in official reserves, an overhang is inevitable. This overhang can be, and is, absorbed in the Eurocurrency market, but already this market is being satisfied, especially in the form of long-term Eurobonds, through the acquisition of deposits directly from private depositors; hence, the overhang, which consists of deposits owned by foreign banks, may be actually superfluous idle balances. Under any circumstances, during the decade of the 1960s the Eurocurrency market was not yet prepared to absorb such a large volume of overhang, and as a consequence, it became the responsibility of the foreign central banks to do so. Therein lay the difficulty.

The nature of the problem can be illustrated clearly with the aid of the analysis in Chapter 11. (See Diagram 14-5.) Under IMF rules, national central banks were obliged to purchase any excess of reserve currency (specifically U.S. dollars) which appeared on the foreign exchange markets to an amount exceeding S_2. They had to do this because of the fact that all member countries were obliged to maintain the foreign exchange value of their currencies within 1% on either side of parity as stated in terms of the U.S. dollar. The U.S. dollar, in turn, was related directly to gold at $35 = 1 oz. — the gold exchange standard. All this meant was that when the United States experienced deficits in its balance of payments it financed these with its own "U.S. claims abroad;" in other words, by simply increasing the overhang. This was, in fact, the more general rule than not, especially during the years of the Vietnam conflict. The consequence was a shift in the stock of U.S. dollars in foreign exchange markets to the right—S_2 in Diagram 14-5—and to maintain the IMF rule of 1% maximum above parity, the central banks of the member countries were required to purchase the extra U.S. dollars. This, in turn, meant that each government must either tax its subjects or borrow its own funds in order to make the purchases. In so doing, it resulted in a net transfer of wealth from the member country to the United States—the equivalent of an interest-free loan (or gift) since the U.S. was not required to send abroad equivalent exports to finance its massive payments abroad. It is small wonder that the government of France (Pres. De Gaulle) objected so strongly to the existing structure of international payments because at that time France was more often than not a creditor country with surpluses in its balance of payments. Unlike France, the Canadian government, of course, has consistently acquiesced in this prac-

Diagram 14-5

EXCHANGE RATE PEGGING, IMF

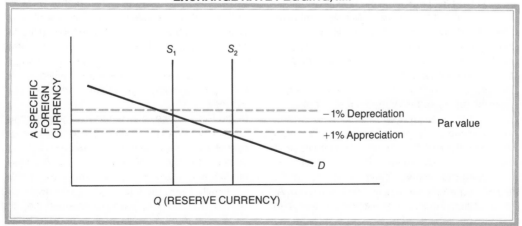

tice and has accumulated substantial amounts of U.S. dollars in the Exchange Fund Account.

At the same time, a refusal to purchase the reserve currency (U.S. dollars) is tantamount to an appreciation of the national currency in question, and this could only be done with IMF approval and would require justification that the currency is undervalued. A second alternative could exist in that the surplus U.S. dollars would never enter the foreign exchange markets in the first place. In this case the dollars would become part of the overhang as Eurodollars, but in either case the velocity of circulation would decline. It is, therefore, surprising in view of the inherent conflicts in the system that the so-called Bretton Woods System lasted as long as it did.

2. The Collapse of the System

We can describe the situation under two general headings, externally a surplus of reserve currencies or an overhang, and within the reserve countries, inflationary price increases. Under the first heading are the many problems attendant upon too much liquidity free to flow from country to country as short-term capital. This was the result of balance of payments deficits in those reserve currency countries and a consequent build-up of deposits owned by foreign residents. The necessity for supporting the value of reserve currencies meant that central banks had to put out their own currencies in exchange for the reserve currency. At the same time the speculators with their own balances were free to wager on the capacity of the central bank in question to support the values. So long as a modicum of support remained for an exchange rate there was always profit to be made on the odds that a central bank must eventually give way. These odds became greater, the greater the reserve country's balance of payments deficit or surplus.

The second heading, inflationary rising prices within the reserve country, meant that the reserve currency's purchasing power, its ultimate "worth," was declining. This proved to be the ultimate weakness of the gold exchange standard itself. It is simple enough to agree to hold a reserve currency in official reserves because at any time it may be exchanged for gold at the official price. At the same time there is an additional advantage in that the official reserves can earn interest by merely being reinvested in the reserve country

itself. But suppose domestic price levels in reserve countries rise at a faster rate than the interest being earned; it follows that a nation's reserves are declining in real value and the country in question may demand gold or some other equivalent store of value instead of the reserve currency. The situation is precisely analogous to the savings of individuals within countries which are eroded by inflationary price increases.

The first reserve currency to collapse under the strain of both these external and internal pressures was the pound sterling. In this case, the pound was a reserve currency without the prestige of the IMF par values, as in the case of the U.S. dollar, being quoted in terms of the pound. In short, central banks were not obliged to purchase the pound so as to "peg" its value in terms of their own currencies. The result was that cross rates, i.e., franc/sterling or DM/sterling rates via the U.S. dollar, had a tendency to differ in various foreign exchange markets from the agreed IMF par value, and were the direct consequence of exchange restrictions imposed during emergency periods which prevented the free flow of currencies in the process of arbitrage.

The success of the continued maintenance of par values depended upon the ability of the respective central banks (in this case the Bank of England) to acquire sufficient foreign exchange to purchase excess pounds. If the markets are all perfectly free of restrictions, stabilizing the value of the pound in the London market effectively stabilizes sterling in all markets. Should rates differ in two markets, it is a simple matter to purchase, say, French francs cheaply in London with sterling and sell them at a higher price for sterling in Paris, Brussels, etc. This is what arbitrage is all about; hence, the responsibility for maintaining the value of the pound ultimately rests with the Bank of England even though other central banks may render assistance as well by purchasing sterling with their own currencies.

In the British case, the pound had been pegged since 1949 at $ U.S. 2.80. Prior to that time the rate of $4.03 had been maintained with U.S. assistance throughout World War II and the years immediately following. During the early 1960s, especially from 1964 to 1967, it became more evident that the pound was overvalued, i.e., the prices that foreign retailers who imported British merchandise were forced to accept in a competitive market and the British factory selling prices were drawing closer together with a consequent narrowing of profit margins. Profits were no longer sufficiently great to encourage British exports, and this meant a worsening of the balance of trade.[20] In terms of the balance of payments, however, the situation was very much worse and considerable assistance from the IMF and other monetary authorities in the form of loans was required. All this was for the purpose of maintaining the value in foreign exchange of the pound at $2.80, not an easy task for the reason that already massive flights of capital from the pound were taking place in expectation of devaluation.

In the face of such an overwhelming case for devaluation, one is justified in asking the question: Why should the British government persist in what would appear to be sheer perversity? Indeed, in a vain attempt to stem rising prices at home, the government imposed a 6-month wage freeze in July, 1966. This was an eleventh hour attempt to avoid devaluation—all for naught.

The reason that the government sought to retain the value of the pound was that sterling is a reserve currency for the Sterling Area. About one-third of British exports and imports were to and from these countries; hence, it is understandable that a responsibility toward them would be felt. After all, a devaluation of the pound is a reduction in the foreign exchange value of the reserves of these countries—a sobering thought —vis-à-vis non-sterling countries.

Ultimately, a devaluation of 14% ($2.80 to $2.40) was unavoidable, forced by the inability of the British government to secure additional loans of foreign exchange to purchase the millions of pounds that were being exchanged for foreign currencies. Of course, speculators had a field day for the reason that devaluation was widely rumoured and anticipated, especially during the fortnight period prior to the actual devaluation announcement by Mr. Wilson, the Prime Minister.

What Great Britain had been experiencing during the years preceding November, 1967, was a sterling "overhang." It was made apparent itself by way of a refusal on the part of those countries and their residents outside the sterling area to accept and hold additional pounds as payments for either goods or services or as stores of value. This was particularly true of the Continental banking community (especially the Swiss bankers, the "Gnomes of Zurich") who are responsible for their clients' deposits. Hence, it is not irrational behaviour to exchange sterling for other currencies, when, and if, the exchange value of sterling is expected to decline. This is what devaluation means. Furthermore, it is rational to hold monetary assets, both official and private, in the form of gold or a currency which enjoys relatively stable domestic purchasing power. It was this latter quality which the pound lacked, for it proved to be a near impossibility for the government to maintain the necessary discipline to control both wages and prices.

The rejection of sterling as a foreign exchange asset created the overhang. Sterling investments, both short and long-term, even though earning interest, became subject to an anticipated capital loss because of an expected fall in the exchange value of the pound, and it was this which precipitated the flight from sterling. In terms of Diagram 14-4, the upward shift from R to R' was unacceptable to the international community, and sterling as a reserve currency outside the sterling area was rejected.

3. The French Solution

With an almost uncanny foresight, the French government, at the time of the sterling devaluation saw the event as " ... the beginning of an acute crisis in the international monetary system of which the pound is doubtless the weakest pillar..."[21] Actually, the French position from the beginning, during the Bretton Woods Conference, was that gold was the only international monetary reserve required. In the event of a shortage of gold to satisfy the requirements of international payments, the logical solution was simply an increase in its price. In terms of the Quantity Theory diagrams this would shift the gold base upward through an increase in the va-

---

[20]From 1962 to 1967, the balance of trade in millions of pounds was as follows:

1962	1963	1964	1965	1966	1967
+122	+124	−382	− 49	+ 84	−316

and the balance of payments:

| +192 | − 58 | −695 | −353 | −547 | −671 |

—Table 289 Annual Abstract of Statistics, 1973, Central Statistical Office, #110, HMSO.

---

[21]*The Economist*, November 25, 1967, p. 873.

Diagram 14-6

THE FRENCH SOLUTION

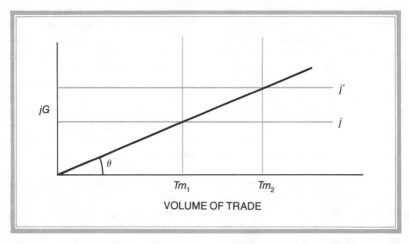

lue of the coefficient, j. (See Diagram 14-6.) Raising the price of gold would accommodate the volume of trade Tm_2 without altering velocity (the angle θ). In this way the gold exchange standard (or what came to be the dollar standard) would become superfluous, a desirable objective from the French point of view.[22]

4. The Collapse of the Dollar

But the devaluation of the pound sterling from $2.80 to $2.40 was only the beginning. During the same year, 1967, at the annual meeting of the IMF in Rio, an agreement had been reached to create the new international money, Special Drawing Rights, but neither this nor the sterling devaluation addressed the fundamental problem of overhang. In fact, an aftermath of the sterling devaluation, a massive drain of gold did occur.

During the five days following devaluation, 250 tons ($280 million worth) was sold in the London gold market. This was a flight from the U.S. dollar itself into the other store of value, gold. Though at first only temporary, it foreshadowed things to come.

It was during this post-sterling-devaluation period that the French government announced its withdrawal from the gold pool which had been formed for the purpose of stabilizing the value of the dollar in terms of gold. Consisting of eight central banks, the pool sold gold at agreed prices in the gold markets.[23] However, in selling gold, the Bank of France found that such sales to individuals (private gold holdings are not illegal in France) acted as the equivalent of central bank sales of securities in, say, Canada, for the gold was being purchased with cheques, which involved payment through bankers' deposits at the Bank of France; in this way an unwelcome contraction of bank deposits was being generated. France's action in withdrawing from the gold pool was, therefore, not simply an act of mischief but an act of self-defence under the conditions existing at the time.

---

[22]It was probably the strategic (and enviable) position of the U.S. in the scheme of things which the French found distasteful. "...What you should simply remember from looking at this table [a table showing the creation of Eurodollars to finance the U.S. deficit] is the fact that during this same period (1960-69) any other country that was faced with a balance of payments deficit of this magnitude would have been obliged to take steps to restore balance whereas the United States was not obliged to do so; the method of financing its deficit exempted it from having to restore equilibrium and it was therefore a system which caused considerable inequality in the interplay of monetary power." Valery Giscard d'Estaing, "The New World Economic Order," Address at the Ecole Polytechnique, Paris, October 28, 1975.

---

[23]These were the central banks of the U.S., U.K., Belgium, Germany, Italy, Netherlands, Switzerland, and France. The pool was formed following an earlier gold crisis in 1960 for the purpose of stabilizing the London gold price at U.S. $35/oz. through both purchases and sales of gold. By 1967, price stabilization involved only sales, not purchases, and huge drains of gold reserves resulted.

It was clear that the latter days of the gold exchange standard had arrived and its ultimate demise was rapidly approaching. Huge drains of gold took place in early 1968; in fact, *The Economist* estimated that a total of $2¾ billion (U.S. dollars) worth of gold sales took place between sterling's devaluation and mid-March 1968. This time there had been heavy borrowings in the Eurodollar market to finance gold purchases and even central banks of smaller countries were joining the rush into gold. The stampede continued until the closing of the London gold market in mid-March, to reopen on April 1, but this time without the support of the gold pool. It was no longer necessary because a two-tier price system, one for official central bank transactions and the other a free market price set in London in accordance with demand and supply, was established. This meant that the U.S. dollar was no longer freely convertible into gold.

The movement out of the U.S. dollar and into gold even had its "spillover" effect into the Canadian dollar. This was precipitated by the announcement of restrictions on U.S. direct investment abroad despite assurances by the U.S. Secretary of the Treasury, Mr. Fowler, that no restrictions of capital flows to Canada would take place. The "mini-crisis", as it had been termed, resulted in some small losses of gold, but very little foreign exchange, for it was largely psychological in origin. Mr. Sharp, then Minister of Finance, experienced little difficulty in supporting the value of the Canadian dollar but he did activate a swap line of credit with the Federal Reserve Board to an amount of $250 million so that the Canadian dollar might be protected. In addition, a purchase from the IMF of $428.1 million in U.S. dollars with Canadian dollars was made so that the Canadian reserve position with the IMF fell to practically zero—all for the purpose of shoring up the Canadian dollar if need be. Short-lived, the crisis was practically over by March, 1968, and by mid-year, the necessary repurchases back to the IMF had already begun.

But the fundamental causes of the dollar crisis remained unresolved. These were the continued U.S. balance of payments deficits which increased the dollar overhang and an overvalued U.S. dollar— overvalued in terms of gold. It was this latter which generated the next crisis which took the form of speculation against (or rather "in favour of") the D-mark. Here, the evidence supported an *undervalued* currency because the Germans had been accumulating surpluses in their balance of payments for some years, so much so that Germany was becoming a net exporter of capital. This elevated the D-mark to the position of a reserve currency.

At the same time, the French franc appeared to be *overvalued*, and the evidence for this was a considerable loss in foreign exchange reserves, about $300 million per month in 1969.[24] This, combined with domestic inflation, led to a devaluation of the French franc on August 8, 1969, from 4.93706 to 5.55419 francs per U.S. dollar, about 12½%. This was followed by a revaluation of the D-mark in September.

In the German case it was obvious to all that the D-mark could not go down in value; it must either remain constant or rise. This made it an excellent currency in which capital could find refuge, and for this reason, German bank accounts became very popular. As the rumours, and expectations, of revaluation spread (in spite of official German "denials"), short-term capital and dollar overhang moved into D-marks from francs, sterling, dollars, etc. It is interesting that the revaluation was preceded by a 4-week period of floating in order to determine a correct, free market value for the mark, suggesting that free floating does indeed have merit even during a period of fixed exchange rates. At the end of the period the government announced its new rate of DM 3.66 = $1 U.S., down from the original 4, a revaluation of 8½%. This, of course, meant a corresponding profit of 8½% for holders of DM deposits who could then seek the next likely currency for speculative profit.[25]

Of course, the significant feature of the DM revaluation was the floating period. It was significant because a chain of causation had been set up directly from the free market to a fixed rate of exchange, a concession to the efficiency of the free market in foreign exchange rate determination. Still, however, the Board of Governors at the annual meeting of the IMF in September, 1970, could conclude that " . . . the basic principles of the fixed parity system established in Bretton Woods in 1944 were sound and should be

---

[24] *The Economist*, August 16, 1969, p. 49.
[25] An estimated outflow of $100 million/day of profit taking after revaluation was occurring after two weeks of the new rate. *Economist*, November 8, 1969, p. 87.

maintained and strengthened."[26] A monument to conservatism.

By 1971, the growing balance of payments deficits of the U.S. was resulting not only in an enormous overhang of Eurodollars but also in a huge increase in official reserves as well. The SDR was finally introduced in January, 1970 and increased in amount in 1971 to a total of $6.4 billion (see Table 14-2, above); however, the U.S. dollar increase in liabilities and negative assets in 1971 amounted to $29.6 billion.[27] With such an enormous amount of liquidity, it became apparent that speculative attacks on the value of the U.S. dollar could no longer be withstood. In August of 1971, President Nixon introduced his measures to reduce the U.S. balance of payments deficits including a 10% surcharge on imports. From these emergency measures arose both the Nixon-Pompidou Conference in the Azores and the later meeting of the Group of Ten ministers in Washington, D.C. (the original ten of the General Arrangements to Borrow). In both cases the U.S. bargaining position was the 10% surcharge, and the result was a general realignment of currency values by IMF members. The "Smithsonian Agreement" central rates were, in general, up by an average of 9% against the dollar (a de facto dollar devaluation) with a range of 3% for India at the lowest to 16% for Japan at the highest. At the same time the dollar was devalued against gold with an increase in price from $35 to $38 per oz., a devaluation of $8\frac{1}{2}$%. In addition, and probably more important, was a broader band of fluctuation of rates of $2\frac{1}{4}$% on either side of the new central rate, a substantial change from the former 1% of the IMF.

Later, in April, 1972, the EEC countries agreed to take the first step toward a European Monetary Union. These countries agreed to hold the values of their currencies within a narrower range of $2\frac{1}{2}$% within the broader $4\frac{1}{2}$% of the Smithsonian band. In so doing, they agreed to settle any debts amongst themselves on a monthly basis through direct bilateral arrangements. This EMU, nicknamed the "snake," moved within the Smithsonian tunnel, in a joint float vis-à-vis all other currencies but maintaining its agreed exchange rates within the narrow $2\frac{1}{2}$% range.

5. The End of Bretton Woods

"How's the patient at your end?" said the surgeon to the overworked anaesthetist. "He's been dead for six years down mine." (The Economist, 17/2/73, p. 12.) But The Economist's corpse, the gold exchange standard on a fixed exchange rate system, was still alive, with attempts being made to return to some kind of fixed exchange rate system. But, despite meetings of finance ministers, nothing was forthcoming from either the IMF or the Group of Ten. As would be expected in such a situation, the forces of market equilibrium simply by-passed the institutional mechanism and asserted themselves independently. So it was that in February, 1973, a second devaluation of the U.S. dollar occurred. This time it was accompanied by considerable official activity, i.e. meetings, junkets, etc. of ministers, enough to indicate to speculators what was forthcoming. The consequence was that 6 billion U.S. dollars were converted into D-marks, this time for a cool 10% profit; at the same time the official price of gold was set at $42.2222 per ounce.

It was this final "assault" on the U.S. dollar which broke the system at last. In the speculation against the dollar it was the "large internationally oriented commercial banks, multinational companies with U.S. dollar budgets, and central banks" which were involved in the flight from the dollar.[28] In other words, the private sector combined with central banks had ceased to have confidence in the exchange value of the U.S. dollar, preferring instead the more stable D-mark. At the same time great movements into gold occurred as well, pushing up the free market price to over $100 per ounce.

It was the year 1973 that marked the end of the system. The great currency upheavals of early spring meant, in effect, that all currencies would be, eventually, floating. This was apparent during the turmoils of February and March, for it was clear that a lack of confidence in the U.S. dollar was the overwhelming difficulty. The further devaluation of the dollar helped to stem the movement into gold somewhat, but on the 22nd and 23rd of February, gold reached record market

---

[26]Bank of Canada, Annual Report of the Governor, 1970, p. 22.

[27]Annual Report of the Governor of the Bank of Canada, 1971, p. 21.

[28]Bank of England, Quarterly Bulletin, June, 1973, p. 129.

prices again and the dollar was once more in trouble requiring additional support from central banks. By March 1, sales of dollars were again in such large volumes that the foreign exchange markets had to close the following day.

After considerable consultations among European finance ministers in Brussels, markets were reopened on March 19, but this time *without* support for the U.S. dollar. The dollar had begun to float in the markets of Europe for the first time. The EMU "snake," on the other hand, was still floating within the 4½% Smithsonian tunnel around its central values against the U.S. dollar.

All this meant that it was no longer possible for the IMF to maintain the dollar standard. The alternative, the SDR, was agreed upon by the Committee of Twenty after lengthy discussions in 1973. It would be the new method of valuation of exchange rates based upon a "standard Basket" of currencies. The basket means that it is equal to one SDR in accordance with the currencies and amounts outlined below and which have been in effect since July 1, 1978.

The value of the SDR in terms of currencies is determined on a daily basis by applying the exchange rates of each currency in the basket to any single currency. For instance, for the U.S. dollar each of the other currencies is converted into U.S. cents, multiplied by the relative amount of each currency in the SDR and then the entire sixteen are added to arrive at the U.S. dollar equivalent. Precisely the same procedure is followed for all other currencies.

As mentioned above, the SDR was introduced into the IMF reserve system in January, 1970. At that time it was equal to one U.S. dollar or .888671 grammes of fine gold. The last official devaluation resulted in a value of one SDR = $1.20635, but with the floating dollar; the Fund itself finally agreed to institute the standard basket system on July 1, 1974, thereby completing the establishment of a new unit of international currency. All IMF accounts of members are now kept in SDR's.

Rather significant, however, are the changes outlined at the Jamaica meeting of the IMF. These "reforms" so-called, as reported in *The Economist*, January 17, 1976, include:

(1) the sale of one-sixth IMF gold holdings over a 4-year period.

(2) floating rates now "legalized" in a revised Article IV and the official gold price abolished.

(3) an increase in members' quotas and the credit tranches increased by 45%.

Such changes as these appear small beside the real world of Eurocurrencies and general increases in world liquidity. The IMF contribution of quota increases, increases in SDR's, etc. are miniscule compared to the enormous changes which have taken place in the banking systems of the world, not the least being the Bank for International Settlements.

All this led *The Economist* in its January 17, 1976 issue to ask the question, "Do we *need* an IMF?" A good question and the suggestion is made that a merger with the International Bank for Reconstruction and Development (World Bank) take place with the objective of assisting less developed countries which experience balance of payments difficulties.

The SDR basket

U.S. dollar	0.40	Belgian franc	1.6
Deutsche mark	0.32	Saudi Arabian	
Japanese yen	21	riyal	0.13
French franc	0.42	Swedish krona	0.11
Pound sterling	0.050	Iranian rial	1.7
Italian lira	52	Australian dollar	0.017
Netherlands		Spanish peseta	1.5
guilder	0.14	Norwegian krone	0.10
Canadian dollar	0.070	Austrian schilling	0.28

Source: IMF *Survey,* July 3, 1978.

Periodically the IMF revises its weighting of the 16 major world currencies. This latest revision reflects the composition of trade during the period 1972-76 and is "linked" (by means of a double SDR calculation) to both the old weights and the new on the same date. A new currency, the riyal of Saudi Arabia, has been introduced to replace the South African rand.

We can hardly avoid the conclusion that the really significant international financial organization is not the IMF at all but other organizations such as the Bank for International Settlements. This institution was founded not by governments at all but by the central banks of the West European countries (including Switzerland) in accordance with a treaty in 1930. The United States, incidentally, is not a member; but the U.S. portion of the subscription was taken over by J.P. Morgan and Co. along with two other banks. In 1969, Canada, Japan, Australia and South Africa became members.

As a central banks' "super bank" it is largely consultative and research oriented but it does, rather discreetly, participate in international affairs. It was through the BIS, for instance, that the Basle Agreements were worked out which made possible the central bank "rescue operations" for those currencies in difficulty during the recent past. In addition it has assumed the position of monitoring the Eurocurrency markets; in fact it is the *only* source of statistical information on this very important aspect of international finance.

Another institution of importance will be the European Monetary Fund, the "central bank" of EEC countries which will have the responsibility of issuance and control of the new European Currency Unit. This and the BIS appear to be closer to being the true inheritors of Keynes' original International Clearing Union than the IMF.

II. POST-BRETTON WOODS, THE SYSTEM

We can say in retrospect that the positive contribution of the Bretton Woods System was the creation of order from chaos following the Second World War. Nothing was to be gained from the hyper-inflation and depreciating exchange rates such as were characteristic of the years after World War I, and certainly the dislocations and reconstruction which were inevitable following World War II would have resulted in a replay of the 1920s was it not for the discipline of the rules and regulations of the International Monetary Fund. It is true that the free market forces of supply and demand *will* produce exchange rates which will balance payments, but we cannot readily separate, as Keynes did in his *Monetary Reform*, the

internal price level of a country from its exchange rate. The International Monetary Fund certainly did render valuable service by both requiring and furnishing the means by which exchange rates might be held constant. Once the reconstruction period was complete and production and trade were growing well beyond the expectations of the delegates at the Bretton Woods Conference, shortages of international liquidity became the problem which the Bretton Woods System was not equipped to handle.

In this section, an attempt is made—no more than an attempt—to describe in broad outline, i.e., to "model," the existing system of international payments which is the *successor* to Bretton Woods. This does not mean, by the way, that the International Monetary Fund has no part to play in the new system: only the Bretton Woods Agreements are gone. The Fund itself still has a constructive role to play, both in the structure of liquidity (the SDR's) and in rendering its service of discipline to members; after all, it still has control of drawing rights beyond the gold tranche. However, it is significant that Canada, in its recent monetary crisis, has not used the IMF facilities at all, preferring to raise its own borrowed foreign exchange from the capital markets. We can begin by considering international payments under three general headings: (1) Trade, (2) Finance of Transactions, and (3) Finance of Capital.

(1) The flow of exports/imports is, of course, the primary objective of international payments and to this end, stable prices and exchange rates are important. Historically, London was the international centre of trade and the pound sterling the international currency. As we have already seen, the U.S. dollar had assumed this function under the Bretton Woods System but currently the centre of gravity is swinging from North America back to Europe, though now it is toward an expanded EEC which promises to become a united Europe with a common currency. Thus, instead of competition between London, Paris, Germany, etc., as centres each with their own standards of banking and currency, ultimately a uniform system of banking practices will spread throughout the entire community as differences of custom and laws become minimized. A European Parliament will eventually determine what is acceptable banking procedure.

There is an important reason for this. The basic purpose of the EEC has been and is to establish free trade behind tariff barriers, and therein lies its great advantage. In order to secure the benefits of free trade, there must be two conditions — a stable domestic price level in each of the nine countries and stable exchange rates. Inflation, as it is well known, transfers existing wealth from fixed incomes to rising incomes. If one (or more) member of the EEC experiences inflation under conditions of a common currency, a transfer of wealth from non-inflationary members to the inflationary members will occur. This is because inflationary price increases cannot be confined to a single member of the economic community without some sort of "quarantine" measures (tariffs, quotas, etc.) being devised, and this violates the very principle of the economic community.

The second condition is exchange rates which are sufficiently fixed to make possible a free flow of trade and payments among the member countries. In the same way that domestic price increases transfer wealth to the inflating country, exchange rates which rise ("revaluation") also transfer wealth to the country whose rate is appreciating. Conversely, depreciating rates mean a loss of wealth to the depreciating country.

With the objective of currency stability in mind, the European Monetary Union was created in the form of mutual support for currencies in April, 1972. The central banks of the EEC countries agreed to maintain the exchange rates of their currencies within a 2½% range with all the currencies *together* floating against the U.S. dollar as well as the other world currencies. A kind of "snake" was formed consisting of member currencies' exchange rates which wriggled and writhed depending upon the relationship between some of the more powerful currencies, the DM for example, and the U.S. dollar. A rising DM would pull all other currency rates along with it. Of the nine original members, four, France, Ireland, Italy, and Great Britain, dropped out, unable to sustain the flow of funds necessary from their central banks to support their currencies which were depreciating because of high domestic inflation rates.

This is obviously unsatisfactory, and further attempts are currently being made to form a genuine union of currencies as a European Currency Unit (ECU). Such a unit, like Special Drawing Rights, would eventually add to the world's store of international liquidity with all members' currencies being represented according to a weighting system. There are, however, many practical problems to be solved and obstacles to be overcome before a full-fledged ECU will come into existence sometime in the 1980s. It is significant nevertheless that already the European currencies within the "snake" (and the Swiss franc which will always stand in isolation) are replacing the U.S. dollar as the pivotal point round which all other rates are determined. It was not so long ago that not only was a U.S. dollar devaluation thought of as unlikely but as a logical *im*possibility. (How can a currency be a numeraire and therefore, devalue against itself?) Of course it can depreciate through an appreciation of all other currencies, particularly those of western Europe. But this is not a satisfactory situation either and some other numeraire will likely be found, either the SDR or the ECU. In all probability it will be the latter, especially if it can be traded in the foreign exchange markets. It is really only a matter of reorientation of thinking toward the ECU instead of the U.S. dollar as numeraire.[29]

A European Monetary Fund will be developed eventually with the responsibility of issuing these ECU's against domestic currency and gold. At some rate of exchange, ECU's will be swapped to replace some of the U.S. dollars which member countries already have in surplus as a reserve currency. But would the ECU eventually *displace* the U.S. dollar as the world's reserve currency as well as the numeraire? This could only be true if the EEC were willing to permit its ECU to be so used; i.e., these currency units would have to be traded in the markets so that other nations outside the EEC could own them. One might imagine such a situation developing in the future so that the oil exporting countries would insist upon payment in ECU's instead of U.S. dollars. At the moment, the OPEC countries are willing to accept dollars in payment for oil because there is no other apparent currency which is reasonable. In view of the huge oil deficit in the U.S. balance of payments, the result could be a further collapse in the value of the U.S. dollar as the U.S. seeks first to purchase ECU's in the market with its own

---

[29]The situation is similar to the mental process involved in adjusting to a metric system. Instead of thinking of the Canadian dollar as $U.S. .85, we simply estimate our amount of devaluation by an exchange rate movement of, for example, 2 ECU's to 1½ ECU's.

currency with which to pay for the oil imports. Of course, the Canadian dollar would likewise sink to unheard-of levels in such a case. But all this is mere speculation at the moment, not to be taken seriously; it does serve to illustrate what can happen in the evolutionary world of trade finance. (2) The second of the general headings is the Finance of Transactions. By "transactions" is meant not simply the meeting of obligations for payments of goods but a whole range of transactions involving the world's banking systems which are themselves necessary for trade to exist. Very many of these transactions consist of "froth," i.e., bank transactions in forward and spot markets. These, as we have already seen, are necessary to "lock in" exchange rates so that a single export/import transaction may take place without the risk of exchange rate fluctuation. However, even though "froth"; they are quite real and do require foreign exchange deposits in interbank markets; Eurocurrencies are particularly suited to this purpose.

But these payments are quite harmless and have no effect on the world's structure of liquidity. They are simply short-term claims in foreign currencies which have increased in volume enormously because of the necessity to fix rates of exchange. The necessity for this has come about because of the decline of the Bretton Woods System and the exchange stability which it had provided.

With the end of the Bretton Woods System we would ordinarily expect the end of foreign exchange reserves because the purpose of reserves of foreign exchange is for intervention in the foreign exchange markets to stabilize rates. But if exchange rates are determined by the free market system alone, there is, in a real sense, no reason for either intervention or reserves of foreign exchange. The fact of the matter is that currencies have *not* been floating free in the sense that they are permitted to seek their equilibrium levels on a daily basis. While they "float" on the markets, it is a "dirty float" with intervention by central banks to influence forces of supply and demand. The Canadian dollar is typical of such intervention which consists of "maintaining orderly conditions in the market for the U.S. dollar in Canada."[30] These "orderly" conditions were maintained during the year 1977 when the Cana-

dian dollar fell from \$U.S. 1.03 in October, 1976 to U.S. .8967 in February, 1978. During that time foreign exchange reserves in the Exchange Fund Account fell by \$2.1 billion with additional borrowings in the form of standby credits of \$1.2 billion. This must be one of the most fruitless expenditures of public funds ever devised with billions of dollars being spent so that the Canadian dollar may decline in value in an orderly instead of disorderly fashion.

(3) The third heading — Finance of Capital — is considerably more serious in its implications. We have very little experience regarding the consequences of growing long-term loans in the Eurocurrency markets. All we do know is that domestic banking systems are linked together as banks to attempt to transfer domestic deposits to foreign deposits whenever the opportunities arise, when interest rates are higher in Euromarkets than in domestic markets. Consider, for example, what *could* happen if an upsurge in demand for Eurodollars should take place. U.S. domestic capital markets could become short of funds as U.S. banks transfer domestic deposits into foreign deposits. The Federal Reserve Board, therefore, would likely permit the expansion of the domestic money supply to, note carefully, finance *both* the domestic and international markets at reasonable interest rates. Similarly, Canadian banks can also switch into U.S. dollar deposits simply by offering higher rates for swapped deposits or uncovered foreign deposits. At the present time we know very little of the amounts of long-term Eurodollar lending as opposed to the short-term "froth", etc. All we know is that "deposits with banks" in foreign currencies have grown considerably and that these are "on-lent" through other banks to ultimate borrowers. Suppose there was a default in repayment of a foreign currency loan so that all the way back to the original lending bank (perhaps a Canadian bank) a corresponding default to the original deposit holder is threatened. Banks would be obligated to purchase these foreign deposits (U.S. dollars) from the foreign exchange markets and this would further weaken the Canadian dollar.

A general collapse of international finance could develop if defaults were sufficiently great in number. This would be particularly severe if a Eurocurrency multiplier does in fact exist and is reasonably large, and considerable strain could be put on existing Eurobanks as branches

---

[30]Annual Report of the Governor of the Bank of Canada, 1977, p. 27.

"scramble" for foreign deposits in the markets.[31] A collapse of international liquidity could take place as banks find that they cannot honour their obligations.

To this date there has been no threat of such "catastrophe." The only possible exception to this was the "Herstatt Affair" which shook international banks during the early years of the 1970s. Herstatt was a small bank in West Germany, a typical banking operation which had the usual foreign exchange office. It had a staff of professionals who were given the responsibility of the bank's foreign exchange operations, and, unfortunately, during a period of a declining value of the U.S. dollar they took a "long" position. In doing so they expected that the U.S. dollar would rise in value, hence, they acquired a surplus of U.S. dollars or, more accurately, made forward purchases of U.S. dollars in anticipation of a rising spot value.

Note that these forward purchases of U.S. dollars could have been covered by arranging a forward sale of U.S. dollars (or forward purchase of DM). This could have been done by means of a U.S. dollar swap into DM with the Herstatt correspondent bank in New York. But this would have negated the speculative position of selling U.S. dollars spot after the price had risen, i.e., the Herstatt foreign exchange dealers preferred to assume the risk of an open position. This, of course, was the first mistake. The second was to attempt to overcome the loss due to the decline in the U.S. dollar with additional forward purchases of larger and larger amounts. As each loss was recorded in the Accounts Department, the officials attempted to make it good by increasing their forward purchases until the amounts became staggering in volume. In doing so they failed to realize, and no one else did either, that there was a time difference between Germany and New York which was placing their entire purchase in jeopardy.

The banking day begins earlier in Germany than in New York. At the beginning of the day, Herstatt credited its correspondent bank with DM. The correspondent bank in New York had to locate depositors willing to purchase DM so that Herstatt's account could be credited with U.S. dollars six hours later. This they could not do— Herstatt was "stuck" in the middle of the transaction halfway through!

It is not likely that we shall ever see another Herstatt situation again for two reasons: the German government has increased the liquidity requirements against foreign accounts, and secondly, the right of recalling a transaction has been assured during the same day regardless of the time difference, i.e., the correspondent bank can cancel the transaction if it cannot locate sufficient DM funds.

Nevertheless, the fact still remains that the finance of long-term capital is undoubtedly the weakest aspect of international liquidity. Eurocurrency loans to less developed countries, for example, can turn out to be much more risky than originally expected. Here, it is the capacity of the international banking community to discipline itself which really matters in the end, be it exchange speculation or lending to creditworthy borrowers.

The International Monetary Fund is particularly well-suited to the function of an international "watchdog." Both for borrowers and lenders it can make valuable contributions in determining credit worthiness. Being a conservatively oriented institution it is unlikely that member countries would receive an IMF stamp of approval if domestic monetary and fiscal policies were not appropriate. In the final analysis this would appear to be the most important remaining function of the IMF, and in this it shares a similar position with the Bank for International Settlements.

---

[31]Mr. Gabriel Hauge, Chairman of the Board, Manufacturers Hanover Trust Co., speaking on the occasion of the 15th Annual Per Jacobsson Lecture, did find evidence of such a multiplier "inconclusive" and, "Even if it did exist, this would not imply, by itself, any net addition to world credit in that the Eurocurrency market was also a major alternative channel for existing credit flows." Graham Perrett, "The International Capital Market and the International Monetary System," *Finance and Development*, International Monetary Fund and World Bank, December, 1978, Vol. 15, No. 4, p. 8.

CONCLUSION

International finance is a most interesting subject because it is really never completely settled. It involves not only the banking systems of the world but also the politicians, even the heads of state in frequent consultation. This is why the "story" can never be completely, or accurately, told.

However, in sketching the broad outlines and identifying the major influences, as this chapter has attempted to do, the unavoidable conclusion is that politicians have much less influence than the current newspaper headlines might suggest. Perhaps this is a good thing because there is no individual wise enough to foresee all the consequences of decisions which are made at any time.

If there is one single area in international finance which shows the greatest promise for the future, however, it is the European Economic Community. Unlike Bretton Woods, the European Monetary Fund which will be the "central bank" of the EEC, is not springing into existence from a single conference, but is gradually evolving over many years and many conferences. From such evolutionary processes will likely come the degree of financial stability which has been characteristically absent in our international payments system in the past.

This is indeed possible especially if the EMF develops along with the already efficient and smoothly running free market system for determining exchange rates. It is quite wrong to attempt to swim against the tide in this regard because, as past events have shown, the forces of speculation are too great to withstand. Even the "dirty floats" of recent years are hardly in the best interest of all concerned in the long-run, the Canadian dollar being no exception. In the end, it is the balance of payments which determine exchange rates and any attempt to do otherwise is merely postponing the inevitable.

ADDITIONAL READINGS

Culbertson, J.M., *Money and Banking*, McGraw-Hill, New York, 1977, ch. 17, entitled "International Monetary Arrangements." A good description from an American point of view.

Friedman, Milton, *Dollars and Deficits*, Prentice-Hall, Englewood Cliffs, 1968, chs. 10, 11, and 12.

International Monetary Fund, 1945-65, IMF, Wash., D.C., 1969, Vol. III, "Documents." A history highly recommended.

Johnson, H.G., *Essays in Monetary Economics*, Unwin, London, 1969, ch. 10.

————, "The Bretton Woods System, Key Currencies and the Recent Dollar Crisis," *Three Banks Review*, June, 1972, p. 3, revised and reprinted in Readings in *Money, National Income and Stabilization* Policy, Smith, Teigen (eds.), Irwin Inc., Homewood, Ill., p. 465.

Rueff, Jacques, "Increase the Price of Gold," *The International Monetary System*, Officer & Willett (eds.), Prentice-Hall, Englewood Cliffs, 1969, p. 179. The French point of view ably stated.

PART

Policy

We are privileged to live in a period of accelerating economic change, the decade of the 1970s. This is evident not only in the process of inflation which has been with us since almost the beginning of the decade, but also in changes such as the distribution of real wealth among individuals, the allocation of shares of total output between the private and public sectors of the economy, the division of total income between consumption and investment, unemployment, etc. If we consider these within the overall context of history, never before have we experienced such an accelerated rate of economic change and simultaneously a staggering array of new problems.

Such periods of change are interesting enough for the student of economics, but even more so when the great issues of policy are being debated. Furthermore, it becomes a matter of the most vital concern when policy assumes practical dimensions with the seemingly intractable problems of inflation and unemployment. Politicians as well as economists become involved in the great debates. The last part of any book such as this should be for the purpose of tying together loose ends, identifying problem areas, looking toward the future, and considering matters of economic policy. To accomplish this task it is necessary to see how money and financial assets, or varying degrees of liquidity, fit into the complete structure of our economy. In other words, we must integrate our theory of money and assets with the rest of economics.

The principle thrust of the first three parts has been to describe institutions, particularly those which have to do with the manufacturing of money. Along with the purely descriptive sections there have been included some theoretical portions, which, hopefully, have suggested how money in its varying degrees of liquidity may affect the level of prices. There is, however, still a missing link. This has to do with reiating liquidity within the economy itself to economic activity. The classical Quantity Theorists had assumed that a "bridge" already existed between money, prices and output. Our argument has been that such a relationship cannot be taken for granted; therefore something else must exist in its place.

Chapter 15 is an attempt to fill this gap. It begins with a restatement of the theoretical principles underlying the money offer curve and the demand for liquidity curve discussed earlier. It then moves into a discussion of capital theory as developed by Professor Hayek from the great Australian tradition and as expressed by him during the great debates of the latter 1920s and 30s. Hayek's theoretical arguments as to the causes of and solutions to the Great Depression stood at that time in sharp contrast to Keynes', but, even though Keynesian principles "won the day," subsequent events have shown that, as economists, we may have committed one of the great errors of our time in failing to consider Hayekian theories in our economic policy decisions.

Chapter 16 attempts to show how and at what point in our recent Canadian history we have "erred" and what clearly must be done to restore the economic health and well-being of our country. As such, it is the most controversial of the chapters, and rightly so because different interpretations and conclusions may be drawn from the same set of circumstances. Nevertheless, the arguments presented are based on the premise that observation of events is a legitimate verification of theoretical principles, i.e., if theory fits the facts as they develop, it is likely that that particular theory is valid for the times in which we live.

In this concluding part, then, we lay out some important issues. Whereas up to this point, the emphasis has been on the development and understanding of the structure of assets, both monetary and financial, and the nature of markets for these assets, it is now time to shift our emphasis toward the study of the interrelationship between our asset structure and the real economy itself.

Of course, the relationship is immensely complicated, like so many other economic phenomena, and we can really only touch upon the nature of the problems involved. Hopefully, some concept of policy orientation may emerge as we proceed.

CHAPTER 15

Money and Economic Activity

I. A MONETARY MODEL

In this chapter we shall develop a theoretical model of the Canadian economy without the assistance of innumerable equations and sophisticated computers which are so characteristic of modern economics, particularly the so-called "quantitative economics." While it might sound presumptuous to even attempt to fit an entire economy with all its millions of independent decision-makers into such a simplified construction, it really is not, for the very reason that we are *not* constrained by sets of equations with many variables and coefficients. We have at our fingertips an analytical tool vastly more powerful than mathematics—pure reason and logic. It is a practical tool because people behave en masse in a rational way; even though individuals are unaware of the decisions taking place elsewhere, each decision tends toward a focus of rationality.

We shall develop some specific links between the liquidity of the public and the behaviour of prices, wages, etc. These links rest on hypotheses concerning the decisions and actions of Canadians, and if the hypotheses are reasonable, the conclusions follow. This first part is concerned with the monetary portion of the model and uses the concepts developed in earlier chapters. These concepts are fundamentally psychological in nature, being based on behaviour patterns of individuals which are subject to influences of time and events. Inflationary price increases which appear to be continuous certainly have their conditioning effect on individual decisions. The federal government also influences the process, the concrete example being the wage-price controls program and the guidelines. Within this environment individual decisions to save and to structure savings in particular forms of liquidity will be the consequence of the pressures and stimuli which originate from within that environment which is, of course, continuously changing. What is inflation

biased in the latter 1970s may be quite the reverse in the next decade.

A. The Money Offer Curve

1. Background

The concept of a demand for money which we have used throughout was first developed by Professor Patinkin in his great work, *Money, Interest, and Prices*. Prior to Patinkin's analysis, monetary economists had assumed that rational individuals never would require money *for the sake of having money* but for the purpose of spending it. We demand money to get rid of it. This was the assumption underlying the classical Quantity Theory of Money in its various versions, and can readily be considered a "market equilibrium" demand for money.

We can readily see this by referring once more to Pigou's demand for money (Diagram 1-5) in Chapter 1. If (other things being equal) we double the money supply we halve its value. This immediately tells us that we have a rectangular hyperbola, for only this function has this property which is, really, unit elasticity. In Diagram 15-1 let the vertical axis represent the value of money (the reciprocal of the price level) and the horizontal axis the quantity of money.

Patinkin recognized that this is not a theory of demand for money at all. Suppose we hold the quantity of money constant, *then* vary the price level of goods, what happens? We have a true demand curve for money, which, when different quantities of money are included, can describe a series of equilibrium points as shown in Diagram 15-2.[1]

On curve D_1 only, suppose the price level should double from p to $2p$ without changing the supply

---

[1]D. Patinkin, *Money, Interest, and Prices*, Harper & Row, New York, 1965, p. 47.

Diagram 15-1

"MARKET DEMAND" FOR MONEY

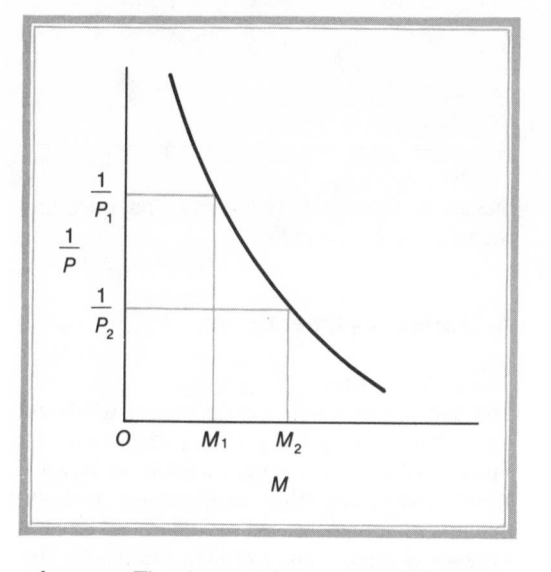

Diagram 15-2

DEMAND FOR MONEY

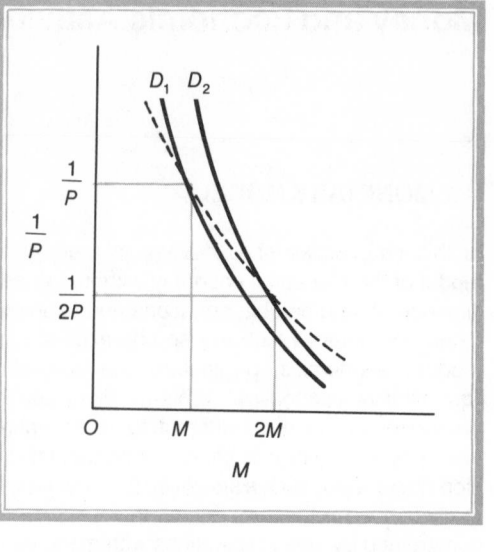

of money. The demand for money will increase. Why should anyone want to increase his demand for money under these circumstances? This is the "real balance effect" which means that people must hold on to their money balances for future expenditures, or else they will run out before the arrival of the next paycheque. It is as simple as that. The consequence of this is that surplus inventories of goods will exist until the old price level, p, re-asserts itself through a kind of "tatonnement" process in the marketplace.

Now suppose the supply of money increases to $2M$. People will feel correspondingly wealthier (their demands for money are sufficiently satisfied) so that a price of $2p$ can be accommodated on a new demand for money, D_2, and the new supply, $2M$. If we join these two intersection points, and all other similar points that we can define in the same way, and if all other conditions remain the same, we can describe a rectangular hyperbola, the classical Quantity Theory of Money as shown in Diagram 15-1.

This, then, is the background for the demand for money curves developed in Chapter 2. All that is required is to express the demand for money against the price level itself (as opposed to the reciprocal of the price level) to develop a positively sloped demand for money curve. Then, from this we develop the money "offer" curve by means of a simple subtraction (see Diagram 2-9,

Chapter 2). Further, by redefining the concept "money" as current liquidity we have avoided the many awkward problems of definition (M_1, M_2, or M_3) and at the same time recognized that purchasing power can be stored in any number of different forms which are readily transferable into current liquidity. Thus, the housewife in her weekly trip to the supermarket might first stop at her local bank to make the necessary transfer into cash or demand deposit. Or an individual, before making up his mind to make a major purchase, must first evaluate his holdings in his savings account, then decide if he can afford it. There is nothing irrational in using a savings account in this way, especially during inflationary periods when protection against rising prices is paramount.

A final "adjustment" which is appropriate to the development of the offer curve, and which will be used in our analysis, is the *ratio* of current liquidity to total liquidity on the horizontal axis and the *rate* of price change through time on the vertical. This is important, because conceptually what is likely to be happening is a concentration of liquidity toward the more liquid portion of total liquidity, as rates of inflation increase.

The rate of price change through time is an adjustment necessary to take account of the dynamic world in which we live. This rate may be zero, of course, but it need not be to have equilibrium, in the sense that sellers' demands for money can increase at the same rate as buyers' offer curves. If they do, quite simply, we have an equilibrium inflation rate as between buyers and sellers. The rate of increase in the general price level which sellers wish is precisely equal to what buyers are willing to offer. Diagram 15-3 illustrates this.

What is not shown in the diagram is market equilibrium in terms of quantity of money. An equilibrium inflation rate, such as is indicated as a constant level of L_c/L, with a certain rate of price increase must be "fed," as it were, by increasing amounts of total liquidity. This is the classical Quantity Theory of Money (double the money supply, double the price level, etc.) which asserted that money is "neutral." An increasing rate of price increases along with pure neutrality of money would be shown by an upward shift in the offer curve (O_2) and an increase in the slope of the sellers' demand for money (S_{d_2}) which would result in a new and higher rate of price increase, $(\dot{p}/p)_2$. Note that the proportion L_c/L does not change in this case. A downward shift in the money offer curve and a corresponding lowering of the slope of the sellers' demand for money can take place by means of an increase in productivity, i.e., an increase in output of goods and services without a change in money incomes which is

Diagram 15-3

AN EQUILIBRIUM RATE OF INFLATION, MONEY-NEUTRAL

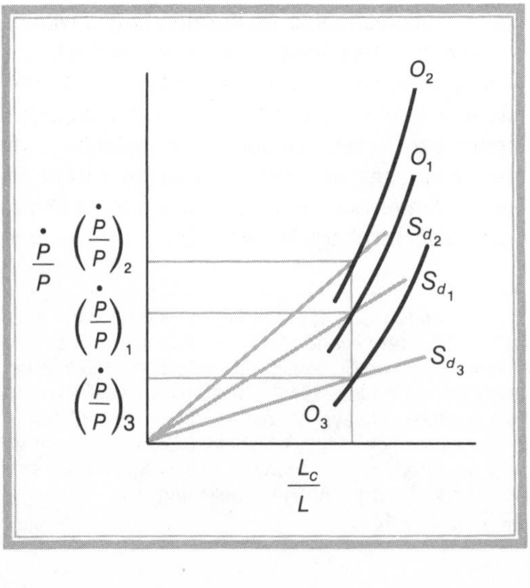

really the equivalent of a decrease in the money supply. Again there need be no change in L_c/L. This lowers the rate of inflation, of course, and, if it proceeds to the extreme, could result in a "negative inflation rate" with falling prices. Such a situation would likely result in a true "Pigou effect" because money would likely cease to be neutral. Holders of idle balances which rise in real value would probably reduce their amounts so held by spending them, thereby increasing offers of current liquidity and generating an increase in employment.[2]

2. Is Money Really Neutral?

The question of neutrality of money occupied a great deal of attention during the decade of the 1960s, particularly because of Patinkin's work. In terms of Diagram 15-1, the question resolves itself into this, Is it possible for inflation rates to increase and money to be completely neutral, i.e., for points of equilibrium between offer curves and sellers' demand curves to rise without a corresponding shift to the right? Such a rightward shift, of course, would mean a restructuring of monetary assets such that a greater proportion of current liquidity exists than before. The real balance effect alone would "reply" to this question with the caveat that it depends upon, whether money is an inferior or superior good. We can settle this by arguing that current liquidity is probably an inferior good, particularly during inflationary periods, because we are likely to take either of two actions, transfer current liquidity into future liquidity or exchange current liquidity for goods and services. If the latter, proportionately more will be offered as prices rise with increasing supplies of money and the equilibrium point will shift rightward as well as upward. Inflation, in this case, can feed upon itself in the sense that an increase in the money supply, because money is not neutral, can result ultimately in more than proportionate increases in the price level. If current liquidity is transferred to future liquidity, the opposite is true; the ratio L_c/L will decline with rising prices and thereby help to check the inflationary impact of a greater money supply.

---

[2]The Pigou effect based its premise on pure outside money. "Inside" money, money manufactured against private debt could not be so simply dealt with because (see equation 3, Chapter 10) the burden of debt would be increased, cancelling the gain in real idle balances due to the decrease in prices.

In addition to the real balance effect alone, there is the wealth effect as well which can lead to a restructuring of monetary assets. A reference once more to Chapter 10, equation 4, will serve to show that neutrality of money is a more complex issue than would appear at first sight. The left side of equation 4 consists of the various forms of primary wealth claims to real wealth, including both outside and inside money deflated by the general level of prices. We know that government debt is outside money and private debt is inside money. Suppose, then, that the general price level, P, should rise due to an expansion in the total money supply. All of the components of primary wealth (including the negative Q/P) will decline in value, but, since private debt carries a negative sign, the burden of this debt is less; hence, a redistribution in favour of the private sector as a whole will take place as private debtors find their burden of repayment easier. Of course, these "debtors" will range all the way from corporate business enterprises to consumers who borrow for purchases of durable consumer goods.

Relieving the burden of debt in this way would have an impact upon the structure of liquidity on the right side of equation 4. The "spendthrifts" of the private sector, recognizing the decline in their real debt "burden," would likely restore debt to its former level. This would increase the value of the L_c/L ratio as the private sector increased its borrowing from the banks, thereby increasing the amount of inside money.

The government, on the other hand, has no such repayment burden.[3] Any increase in the price level lowers the real value of the income it receives from taxes and borrowing; hence, it must increase the money value of its debt accordingly. There will, consequently, be a tendency for outside money to expand as a means of counteracting the increase in prices. The distribution of wealth as between the government and the private sector depends on the proportion of outside to inside money. An increase in government expenditure financed by outside money cannot only redistribute real wealth in favour of the government, but also increase monetary assets (current liquidity) on the right side of the equation. Such a situation could result, first, in an upward shift of equilibrium points (see Diagram 15-3) as inflation rates are increased, *then* a rightward shift because of more current liquidity. As noted above, this current liquidity, since it is likely to be an inferior good, can result in further price increases which are financed by the restructuring of wealth.

If all this is correct, money is clearly not neutral. Unfortunately, such a hypothesis cannot be proven, and the best we can do is either theorize or observe what transpires in the economy, and deduce either the neutrality or non-neutrality of money. It is easy enough to understand, therefore, why this particular topic has been so controversial in recent years.

Professor Johnson has argued against non-neutrality of money, pointing out that the hypothesis involves a fundamental confusion between a stock of wealth and a flow of income. As Lipsey and Archibald had shown earlier, the effect of a price increase can be countered by a one-period reduction of consumption from income so that the stock of wealth can be quickly restored in real terms to its former level. Furthermore, the tendency of interest rates to rise sufficiently to include rates of price increase suggests that the effect of price changes on the structure of wealth is minimal.[4] The criticism here rests on the basis of a short-run equilibrium analysis; hence, one has a somewhat uneasy feeling that such arguments are "forced." Suppose, for instance, that price increases are *neither* once for all *nor* at constant rates but are continuously *accelerating*, i.e., the points of equilibrium in Diagram 15-1 are

---

[3]Professor Johnson argues along with others in the Chicago tradition that the private sector will realize the increased taxes necessary to sustain the interest on higher public debt and cancel out the increase in net wealth due to an expansion of outside money. There is an assumption here that taxes are necessary to pay interest on the public debt and that everyone realizes this. Since interest is part of public expenditure and if public expenditure exceeds tax revenues, why should it be assumed that the government is not borrowing to pay the interest on the federal debt? See *Macroeconomics and Monetary Theory*, Aldine Publishing Co., Chicago, 1972, p. 113.

[4]Professor Johnson has written extensively on the subject of monetary economics and inflation. For a collection of these, see *Essays in Monetary Economics*, Allen and Unwin, London, 1969. The specific reference is to two of these essays on pages 20–21 and 82–85. A better exposition of the Archibald, Lipsey argument as well as others can be found in *Macroeconomics and Monetary Theory*, Aldine Publishing Co., Chicago, 1972, p. 110 ff.

rising to higher levels of inflation. This is the situation we have found ourselves in during the 1970s. This must mean that a continuous adjustment of stocks of wealth is necessary to maintain real values.

At the time that Johnson was writing, the mid-sixties, the stock markets were considered to be ideal "hedges against inflation" because stock prices rose along with inflationary profits and corresponding dividend distributions. But this is no longer true. Far from being effective as anti-inflation hedges, equities have themselves fallen victim to the wealth effect, i.e., a redistribution of wealth *away* from equities. This redistribution appears to have been moving in two opposite directions. The first is toward real assets, commodities, houses, property, gold, etc., which have shown tendencies to rise in money value at rates faster than prices. Some of these have likely been, in the past, underpriced and have increased in value due to market correction as well as inflation. Others are pure speculation which, in ordinary times would have a risk factor attached, but during inflationary times, this risk is substantially reduced. The second direction is toward more liquid assets which offer sufficiently high interest rates that they can result in a positive *real* rate of interest. At the same time, they offer almost complete liquidity, making possible the quick purchase of "bargains" in terms of consumer durables. Such opportunities, real or imaginary, are important for consumers during periods of inflation. (They may indeed be imaginary — a creation of the advertising industry — but nonetheless real in their effect.)

Furthermore, the fact that the inflation we have been experiencing in the 1970s seems to have gathered momentum to develop an acceleration of its own suggests that asset restructuring toward the more liquid forms of wealth (thereby financing additional price increases) is indeed taking place. Of course, there may be a considerable time lag between the initial price increase and any subsequent further finance of price increases due to a price induced wealth effect. The longer this time lag is, the greater the opportunity for other additional causes to assert themselves, and this is why proof of the wealth effect and its impact are difficult to find.

It is possible that non-neutrality of money and the wealth effect ("non-neutrality" really affects the left side of equation 4 in Chapter 10 while the

wealth effect is confined to the right side) are not significant until upper levels of inflation are reached. By then there would have been a great deal of inflationary awareness developed on the part of the public. This is often referred to as "inflationary psychology," a term which connotes an emotional overreaction to inflation on the part of the public, but which is actually very rational behaviour. For business enterprises, rising price levels which involve appropriate accounting and pricing techniques as protection against inflation, if sufficiently general, cannot only ensure survival but contribute genuine additions to real earnings. "Paper profits," for example, during early stages of inflation are likely to be incorrectly interpreted as true windfalls. Only as inflation heats up and business enterprise learns to protect itself and benefit (in real terms) from inflation, will such windfalls become real. This point will be reached when debts of all kinds are reduced in real terms and result in rising real earnings for the private sector. At that point, the non-neutrality of money shifts in favour of the private sector.

A restructuring of assets (the wealth effect) is actually a slow process. Stock markets and the investment companies through which investors deal do not take a reduction in their business activity lightly. They will make strong efforts to attract and hold clients even in the face of adverse market behaviour. Not until the investor is aware of the erosion of equity values *in real terms*, which will likely come late in the process of inflation, will he think in terms of restructuring his assets. This point will occur along with a corresponding awareness of alternatives; the hope of the gambler takes a long time to expire. In the end it is likely to be the combination of rising prices and rising interest rates which will prove to be most convincing.

B. Demand for Liquidity

A discussion of the price and interest induced wealth effects is really concerned with capital market equilibrium and how the changes in prices and interest rates affect this market equilibrium. The structure of the offer curve itself, however, is quite a different matter and involves once more the structure of another function—the "demand" for future liquidity. As usual this demand (which is really a supply function for current liquidity) is price sensitive, i.e., the higher the price offered, the greater the opportunity cost of current liquidity will be, and, other things being equal, the more liquidity the public will hold in the form of future liquidity. This was the argument in Chapter 8 in the example equations (a) through (e) which were concerned with the price of future liquidity. There it was shown that the higher the rate of return (R) the greater the opportunity cost of current liquidity held. Furthermore this cost increases with the rising rate of return in such a way that a marginal unit of current liquidity becomes more costly at higher rates than at lower rates. From this we can deduce a demand curve for current liquidity foregone which is positively sloped but with a slope which increases at higher rates as shown in Diagram 15-4. By combining the two curves, offer curve and demand for liquidity in a "two-tier" combination, we can identify the appropriate rate of inflation, given the opportunity cost of liquidity held. Note that the horizontal axis measures $1 - (L_c/L)$ in the upper portion opposed to L_c/L in the lower portion.

Suppose, for example, there is a rate, R_1, which would result in an equilibrium of sellers' demand and buyers' offer curves at $\dot{p}_1$. If it were possible

Diagram 15-4

RATES OF INFLATION AND RATES OF RETURN

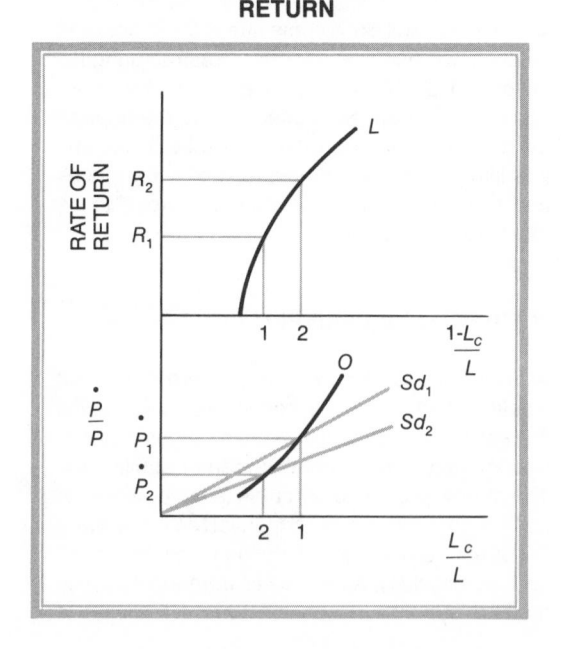

to arbitrarily set the rate of R_2, a lower rate of inflation, $\dot{p}_2$, could be achieved on the buyers' offer curve. This follows directly from the fact that buyers would only offer an amount of current liquidity equal to the proportion of total liquidity (L_c/L) at point 2 which is sufficient only for a lower inflation rate. This opens up a possibility that inflation rates might be lowered through higher rates of interest with the result that more funds would be attracted into future liquidity with less for current liquidity. There is also the possibility, however, that sellers' demands for money not being satisfied, inventories would pile up and unemployment could result.

Aside from unemployment, it would be a mistake to believe that a reduction of the rate of inflation in this fashion can be so simply achieved. Interest rates are actually only a portion of the total rates of return, R, and the interest over which the Bank of Canada has control is just a portion of this. There is, however, evidence that the influence of the Bank of Canada is growing, extending beyond the narrow range of the money market and into lending and borrowing activities of banks and financial intermediaries. This influence is partly psychological and partly the result of intense competition for funds.

There are, therefore, two distinct possibilities which should be considered: (1) raising the rates of return through a restriction of the money supply, and (2) raising rates without necessarily tight money. The first, tight money, raises the cost of money manufacture and is typical of the monetary policy measures of the past. As we have seen earlier, the competition for more savings deposits pushes up the rate structure of the chartered banks and the financial intermediaries. But there are two definite "stages" in the process. The first is a restriction of total liquidity, L, without altering the distribution of liquidity as between current and future. Money, in this "stage," is completely neutral with no change in the position of the curves in Diagram 15-4. We can imagine that the rate of interest is rising and the rate of inflation is being reduced simultaneously without any change in the relative positions of the functions.

But now we have to contend with the interest induced wealth effect because the demand for investment funds will still be just as great, and with the increasing cost of money manufacture, market interest rates must rise. But, as rates rise, these interest induced wealth effects will begin to be felt. Higher rates will reduce capital values and the public will likely either restore these values or readjust wealth holdings to compensate, i.e., shift from stocks to bonds, etc.

Rather more typical in recent years is the second of our possibilities, raising interest rates without corresponding tightness of the money supply. In this case, total liquidity is not really restricted to any great degree at all; instead the focus of Bank of Canada monetary policy has become concentrated on a money growth target. "Money," in this case, has been L_c (or M_1 as it is recorded in the statistics) the most liquid of the money supply. Interest rates, instead of being raised by the cost of money manufacture, are pushed up by, first, the Bank of Canada bank rate which affects both the money market and Treasury Bill rates, and second, by the necessity to finance the continuously growing budget deficit of the federal government. In the first instance the Bank of Canada bank rate is assuming a prestige beyond its normal money market function and is exerting an influence directly on rates of chartered banks and financial intermediaries. This is largely a psychological and expectational phenomenon. In the second, the sale of federal bonds on the market as well as Canada Savings Bonds applies an upward pressure on rates by increasing the demand for funds.

II. REAL CAPITAL INVESTMENT, A LONG-TERM ANALYSIS

A. Demand for Capital

The next part of the analysis is the relationship between actual real capital put into place and the market for funds itself. This relationship, or link, is not easy to grasp because we have not been accustomed to think in terms of long-run changes in capital requirements. But it is precisely here, in capital theory, that long-run considerations are most important.

The difference between the long-run and short-run in this analysis is that, in the short-run, real capital in place can be taken as given. One can accept, say, capital stock as a quantum, (K in the literature) and investment as net increments to capital stock, ΔK, without the bother of having to consider the nature of investment, its quantity,

why it is put into place, etc., with the full knowledge that it doesn't really matter anyway. In the short-run, capital is a mass of buildings, machinery, equipment and the like which take a long time to wear out. All this is not true in the long-run. Capital stock *is* variable, machines do wear out and are replaced with other machines (or no machines at all). The structure of the productive processes (not only *what* is produced but *how* it is produced) will change in accordance with prices and costs. And, certainly, the decision and consequences of decisions are of the greatest importance.

An analysis of capital theory is not an easy one for a second reason. It is made particularly difficult by the fact that there has been and still is no agreed methodological approach to capital theory in economics. This may sound surprising at first sight because some of our greatest theoreticians have been concerned with capital — Fisher, Frank Knight, the Austrians, etc. — yet there still is no agreed paradigm which will serve the same purpose as, for example, marginal analysis in the theory of demand and the theory of production.

A. Leijonhufvud points out this lack of a paradigm in capital and interest theory as the major contributing factor in the very many unresolved issues amongst the great economists.[5] A paradigm is very important because it is only through this that an otherwise random set of ideas and theories can develop progressively as a logical body of ideas and principles. However, of the arguments presented, the most careful, scientific and precise seems to be that of Professor Hayek, who developed from the background of the Austrian school his own analysis in his *Pure Theory of Capital*. It could be that this work will eventually emerge as the basis of the true and correct paradigm hitherto missing. At any rate, what follows is an interpretation and application of Professor Hayek's work (particularly Chapter 27) which gives us the necessary "handle" for our own analysis.

---

[5] *Keynesian Economics and the Economics of Keynes*. Oxford University Press, London, 1968, p. 219. The word "paradigm" is not encountered frequently. To save the trouble of consulting a dictionary, it means a logical system of thought based upon mutually agreed principles which everyone understands and accepts. My own way of expressing the idea to my students is a "handle."

Real capital is, of course, financed by the capital market itself. As we have already seen, the supply of funds in the market assumes a particular structure as indicated by the number and variety of financial assets in the market. The rates of return for these assets are represented by a weighted average, R, and the higher the value of R, the more the funds forthcoming into the market. The supply of funds, in other words, is positively related to the rate of return R.

Conversely, the demand for monetary capital for investment purposes is a negatively sloped function of this rate, R, i.e., the lower the cost of monetary capital the greater the demand for it. This, of course, follows from the fact that real capital, just as any other factor, is subject to the laws of diminishing marginal productivity. But there the similarity breaks down because there is something very special about capital which sets it apart from other productive factors. As was shown in Chapter 10, time is the major difference between the capitalistic, or roundabout, and the direct methods of production; furthermore, this "time" is a weighted concept, i.e., time weighted by the amount of productive factors "locked up" in the process. By producing with the roundabout method, our final output of consumer goods is greatly increased. Then why not produce *all* consumer goods in this fashion? The answer here lies in the *structure* of prices and profits.

We can show how time affects relative profits by means of the simple example developed by Professor Hayek and quoted in Chapter 1. To isolate the impact of price change, we shall assume interest rates are constant and suppose that a profit margin of 6% on all inputs exists during an equilibrium period. For a 2-year production process this would mean 12.36% and for a more direct, 1-month production process, $1/2$%. Assume a price increase which would increase all profit margins by 2%. For the 2-year process, this would mean 14.36% and for the 1-month process, $2 1/2$%. A moment's thought is all that is required to recognize that profit *rates* (on an annual basis) have changed considerably. Because of the great difference in time, entrepreneurs will realize an annual rate of 30% on the 1-month process and 6.9% on the 2-year process. Since the turnover of production is only one month (as opposed to two years) they will clearly restructure their total production toward the short-term process and this means increas-

ing the direct factor and decreasing the indirect (or roundabout) factor until the marginal products of both are equated at a new equilibrium profit rate.

This simple example which Hayek uses is particularly pertinent because it embraces three important principles. Firstly, the substitution of more direct methods of production means, generally, using more labour instead of capital and this would, therefore, mean more employment. Secondly, a fall (instead of a rise) in prices by 2% would work the arithmetic in reverse so that more roundabout methods of production must be substituted for labour. Thirdly, and most important, a rise in wage costs, and consequent reduction in shorter-term profit rates, would mean that a substitution of more roundabout methods of production for more direct, labour intensive methods would take place. This is the equivalent of a fall in prices with wages constant, and follows from the fact that it is the relationship between the cost of productive factors and prices which really matters. It is, of course, this relationship which determines the profit rates.

In an analysis of long-term influences, and these are long-term influences because it does take some time to adjust productive techniques, it is necessary to treat productive factors other than labour as "homogenous," i.e., inputs with varying time periods which produce outputs. We can see how and why this comes about. The longer the period of analysis, the more substitutable the productive factors. Entrepreneurs are free to maximize profits by varying combinations of inputs for the reason that there is sufficient time for equipment to wear out, etc. Ultimately, in the very long run, even human capital (as opposed to "labour") can be adjusted by means of education and training so that the inputs become almost indistinguishable in their homogeneity, the only difference being the time during which they must be invested to produce a final output. The finance of this input is made possible by monetary capital which comes from the capital market.

We are now ready to develop a long-term investment demand function which is crucial to our analysis. As would be expected, it is somewhat more difficult to grasp conceptually than a short-term investment demand curve because there are additional variables which must be included. Nevertheless it is well within the scope of our analysis and certainly worth the effort. Diagram

Diagram 15-5

LONG-TERM INVESTMENT DEMAND FOR REAL CAPITAL

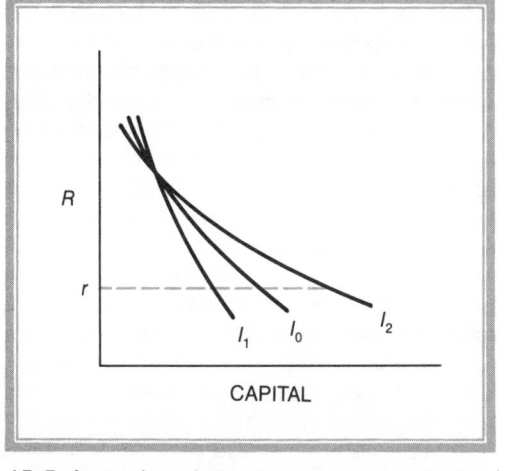

15-5 shows the relation between rates of return (referred to as Interest) and quantity of investment (in terms of real capital).

The downward sloping function reflects, of course, diminishing marginal productivity which is common to all productive factors. However, there are three positions of the investment function which must be considered as follows:

I_1, the function with the lowest elasticity, results from the increase in price of consumer goods which "tilts" investment in favour of the shorter period. At a specific rate of interest, r, less capital will be demanded by entrepreneurs for the reasons indicated in the above example, i.e., shorter period inputs are more profitable than longer period inputs. This tells us that for any given interest rate, capital requirements will be less for the same output requirement when profit margins are high than when profit margins are low.

This is very important and worth reflection. As prices rise, given the interest rate, longer-term investment requirements decline. This, again, is the "Ricardo Effect" illustrated in the example used above which Professor Hayek introduced long ago.[6] Rising prices and higher profit margins lower the real cost of labour by more than capital costs are lowered; hence, production becomes

[6]F. Hayek, *Profits, Interest and Investment*, A.M. Kelley, New York, 1939 (last printing 1969), p. 8. Actually "reintroduced" would be a better word because Ricardo first made the observation.

more labour intensive. Falling prices, on the other hand, have the opposite effect. Longer-term investment is encouraged because real costs of labour are now greater than before. Entrepreneurs will find it to their advantage to avoid direct, labour intensive production and substitute roundabout productive techniques instead. Investment demand now becomes more elastic relative to the rate of interest, and we shift toward I_2 as production becomes more capital intensive. (In all cases, only relative, or *real* prices, are the appropriate measure, not money prices. Thus, even during times of inflation, relative prices of some goods, or even prices of *all* goods, may fall relative to wages.)

The function of the interest rate, R, in all this is really a relatively minor one. It simply determines when investment will stop under the various conditions outlined. When equilibrium is reached, we can say that the marginal rate of profit is equal to the interest rate, and the marginal rate of profit, in turn, is determined by the relationship between the relative prices of consumer goods and the amount of capital goods used in their production. All this is complex enough, but there is *still* one more factor (or influence) which must be considered. As entrepreneurs proceed to use more direct input in the productive process because, we recall, the price of consumer goods has risen, the demand for non-labour inputs also increases bringing up their price. We can be more specific by considering these inputs as those which are produced by stages of production closest to the consuming stages (see Chapter 2). They will consist of the products of those stages which are most readily convertible into goods for direct consumption, or those goods which are most specific to consumption goods. Longer-term capital goods, being of a more general nature, will also be affected when investment has proceeded to a "widening" or "deepening" nature as in I_2. This has been referred to as the Accelerator Principle in business cycle theory. But the rise in price, associated with shorter-term inputs when demand is in position I_1, will cause the demand for monetary capital to shift to the right, thereby tending to force up the rate of interest.

B. Savings and Consumption

The last section requiring analysis has already been discussed in Chapter 10 and certainly in enough other works in the literature of economics to require no further elaboration here. Savings is considered at this stage only in its simplest form —non-consumption. The motives for saving that have been considered by economists are as many and varied as there are ideologies; for example, saving by "habit" or "instinct," "accumulation of wealth (power)," "saving for future consumption," etc.[7]

For our purpose, we can take for granted that saving exists, i.e., it is real and it is an important economic activity. It is important, because through savings goods for consumption need not be produced. By definition these are capital goods, which, in the case of retailers' stocks of inventory, require only time for the store to open in order to be transformed into consumer goods. Capital goods accumulate because of savings; however, for our analysis, it is not so much the savings which matter but the *route* followed by savings into investment.

It would be correct, however, to just mention in passing the existence of a type of savings which is very real and very serious — forced savings. This has long been recognized as a mechanism by which consumption may be forcefully restricted through the issue of excessive currency (in earlier years) or through the excess of investment over voluntary savings (Keynes in his *Treatise on Money*). Ricardo's *High Price of Bullion* was a classic example of an earlier forced savings analysis. Sir Dennis Robertson's "imposed lacking" is another of the same type though his approach was via the banking system. Our modern Canadian inflation is also another painfully realistic example of prices which rise faster than some money incomes and thereby force non-consumption on a certain sector of the public. As such, however, forced savings are like taxation — we have no choice — but the beneficiaries of forced savings are neither government departments nor recipients of transfer payments but incomes which rise faster than prices. As will be shown presently, such a wealth transfer is the consequence of a disequilibrium situation within our economic system.

III. MONETARY/CAPITAL EQUILIBRIUM

It is now time to fit together all the parts, each of

which has already been discussed separately, into a complete, integrated whole. The result is a "model" of the Canadian economy, which, it is hoped, offers a realistic and analytical explanation of events; furthermore, if the model is correctly constructed it should suggest a forecast of what is likely to happen in the future if the same policies and actions are continued. Being a model it is subject to the weaknesses of all economic models; it is impossible to include everything of a monetary nature which might impinge on our economic lives; other variables such as the foreign exchange value of the Canadian dollar, foreign interest rates, domestic taxation, etc., must be implicitly introduced. The function of the model is not to try to include everything which influences our economic lives but to focus attention on what appear to be the issues that are central to the operation of our economy, on the assumption that other issues, while recognized, are not sufficiently operative to warrant their introduction and the consequent increased complexity of the model which would result.

We shall begin with Diagram 15-4. Imagine that this diagram has its axes repositioned. The vertical axis is juxtaposed from left to right and the horizontal axis from the bottom to the top, the scales keeping their same values. There is, however, no change in either the offer curves or the sellers' demand curve for money; these are exactly the same, beginning, as it were, from the "origin" of the new diagram just as before.

In Diagram 15-6, Quadrant 1 may be recognized as the upper portion of Diagram 15-4, but turned over so that the R axis is on the right, and the scale, $1 - Lc/L$, runs from right to left. The consequence of this is that the L function now is also reversed, bending upward from right to left. Quadrants 1 and 3, then, are the monetary (or liquidity) quadrants of Diagram 15-6.

Quadrant 2 is the investment demand function. We do not have the difficulty of juxtaposition to form this quadrant because the diagram itself is already laid out in the normal fashion. The scale on the horizontal axis should be understood and interpreted as a quantity of capital measured in money terms by multiplying the ratio $1 - (Lc/L)$ by the total amount of liquidity. It follows that given a rate, R, the amount of investment is readily determined via the I function, and since the vertical axis is shared jointly with Quadrant 1, we can define an equilibrium of supply and demand for

---

[7]Leijonhufvud, *op. cit.*, p. 228.

Diagram 15-6

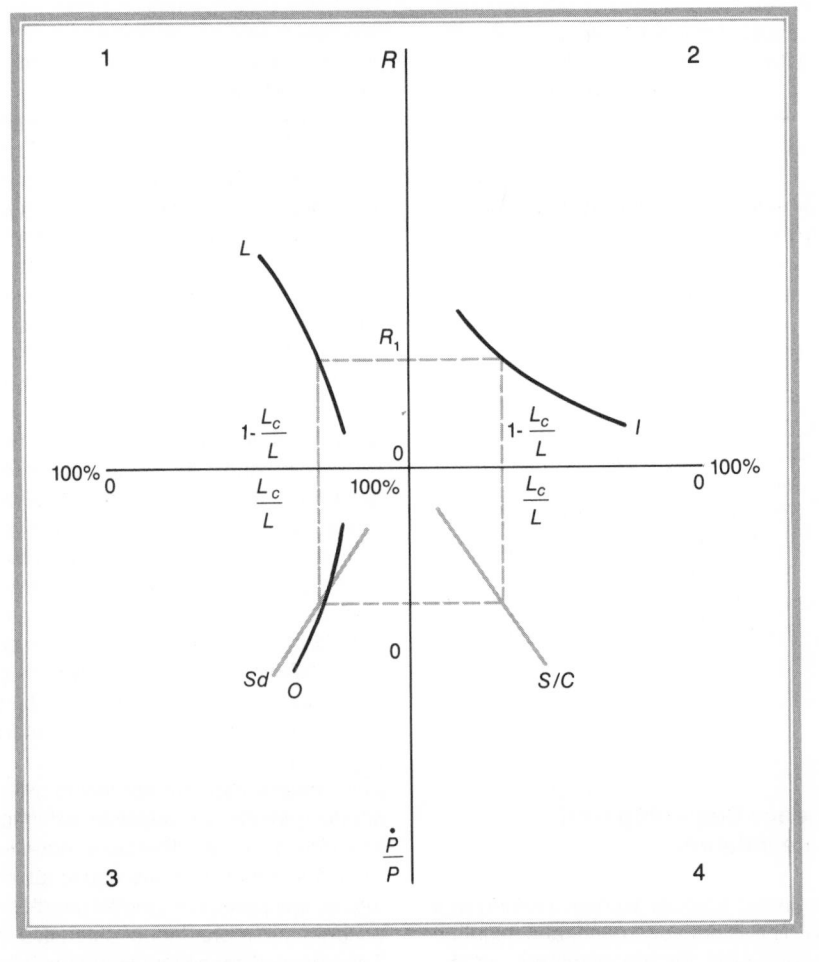

funds by imagining that the *R* axis is "hinged" such that Quadrant 1 folds over onto Quadrant 2 with the *L* function intersecting the *I* function.

Lastly, Quadrant 4 is the savings/consumption function as measured on two scales, i.e., if savings are determined on scale $1 - (Lc/L)$ it follows that consumption is automatically determined on the scale Lc/L. The vertical axis in Quadrant 4 is shared jointly with Quadrant 3 (just as the *R* axis is jointly shared by Quadrants 1 and 2). There is, in other words, an annual rate of price increase which will satisfy the equilibrium of buyers' offers and sellers' demand for current liquidity *and* the saving requirement, which is, in turn, determined by consumption.

In the complete diagram, then, the horizontal axes measure proportions of total liquidity with

scales inverted so that a single point measures $1 - (Lc/L)$ (top) at the same time that it indicates Lc/L (bottom). The vertical axis is divided at the centre to measure *R* (the weighted average rate of return for assets) and rate of price increase, $\dot{p}/p$, per unit of time. It follows that there is a "rectangle of long-run equilibrium" which can be drawn and which will have the following characteristics:

Quadrant 3: There is a specific rate of inflation (which could be zero) which will result in consumers offering a proportion of their current liquidity (L_c/L) which just satisfies sellers' demand for current liquidity. This inflation is being continuously "fed" by growing amounts of money *which must be neutral for long-run equilibrium to exist.*

Quadrant 1: The balance $(1 - L_c/L)$ of total liquidity will be structured in such a way that it will yield a rate of return R_1 which will just compensate the owners for foregone liquidity.

Quadrant 2: Given the price change for entrepreneurs (lower vertical axis) there is an investment structure which will yield a marginal rate of profit just equal to the rate of return, R_1. This will entail a quantity of investment equal to total liquidity multiplied by the ratio $(1 - L_c/L)$.

Quadrant 4: At the same time this ratio, $(1 - L_c/L)$, determines the amount of current liquidity, Lc/L, to be spent on consumption at a specific rate of inflation, $\dot{p}_1/P$.

Note carefully that the diagram requires four sets of equilibria, the savings/investment equilibrium of Quadrants 2 and 4, the equilibrium of buyers' offers and sellers' demand (Quadrant 3), the equilibrium of the rate of return on assets, and the cost of current liquidity foregone (Quadrants 1 and 3), and, finally, and very important, the equilibrium of asset structure and the corresponding investment structure laid in place by entrepreneurs (R, in Quadrants 1 and 2).

A. A Sequence Beginning with Moderate Inflation

We shall begin our analysis with an inflation rate of about 3%. This is not very much, and might be interpreted as "good for the economy" in the sense that entrepreneurs, the real debtors, appear to gain through a reduced burden of debt repayment. This is only an illusion, however, since interest rates are probably already high enough to take account of this inflation rate; nevertheless, a money illusion is generated which creates a sense of prosperity, and the money supply expands in amounts sufficient to accommodate the rate of inflation. In general, money is likely to be neutral in the sense that what redistribution of real income is taking place, is "masked" by money illusion. Money offer curves are high enough to satisfy sellers' demands for money at the 3% rate of price increase; furthermore, the ratio of funds which the public wish to hold as assets is not disturbed because sufficient augmentation of the stocks of these as-

sets is occurring along with expenditures on consumption from incomes. We shall assume further that business enterprise is also satisfied with the flow of funds into the capital market so that the structure of financial assets just coincides with the structure of businessmen's investments.

In a word, an equilibrium rate of inflation of about 3% appears to be both observed by the public and anticipated as well. Will this equilibrium be permanent in the sense that it can become a long-run equilibrium, i.e., can we be "just a little bit pregnant?" The answer is no, we cannot, as the analysis which follows proceeds to show.

The problem area lies in Quadrant 2—the investment functions. Rising prices, even low or moderate rates of price increases, must mean lower wage costs in some industries for two reasons: (1) all industrial wages do not increase at the same rate, and (2) the more progressive entrepreneurs will seek to absorb wage cost increases by improvements in productivity. The latter, productivity improvements, are much more common than might be realized and can readily be observed in published statistics for manufacturing industries. In fact, the incentive for productivity increases, and corresponding increased profit rates appear to be greater in moderate than in high inflationary periods.

This means that entrepreneurs will prefer the shorter periods of production with improvements in productivity, and therefore increase their demand for labour. This will lead to full employment and an increased demand for short-term inputs to accompany more labour intensive production. The prices of these inputs will consequently rise due to their inelasticity of supply (full employment) as the demand for long-term capital equipment declines, especially if interest rates tend to be high enough to discount the moderate inflation rate. This will cause unemployment to drop to very low levels, and the immigration rate (for Canada) will likely be high enough to satisfy shortages of specific skills. Certainly, the stock markets will tend to be "bullish" with prospects of high real profits increased by rising prices and lower real wage costs.

All this means a "tilting" of the investment function to the position of I_2 – a position of lower elasticity. Investment is now less sensitive to interest rate changes than before. But, at the same time, the increased demand for shorter-period investment necessary to accompany a growing la-

Diagram 15-7

MONETARY EQUILIBRIUM

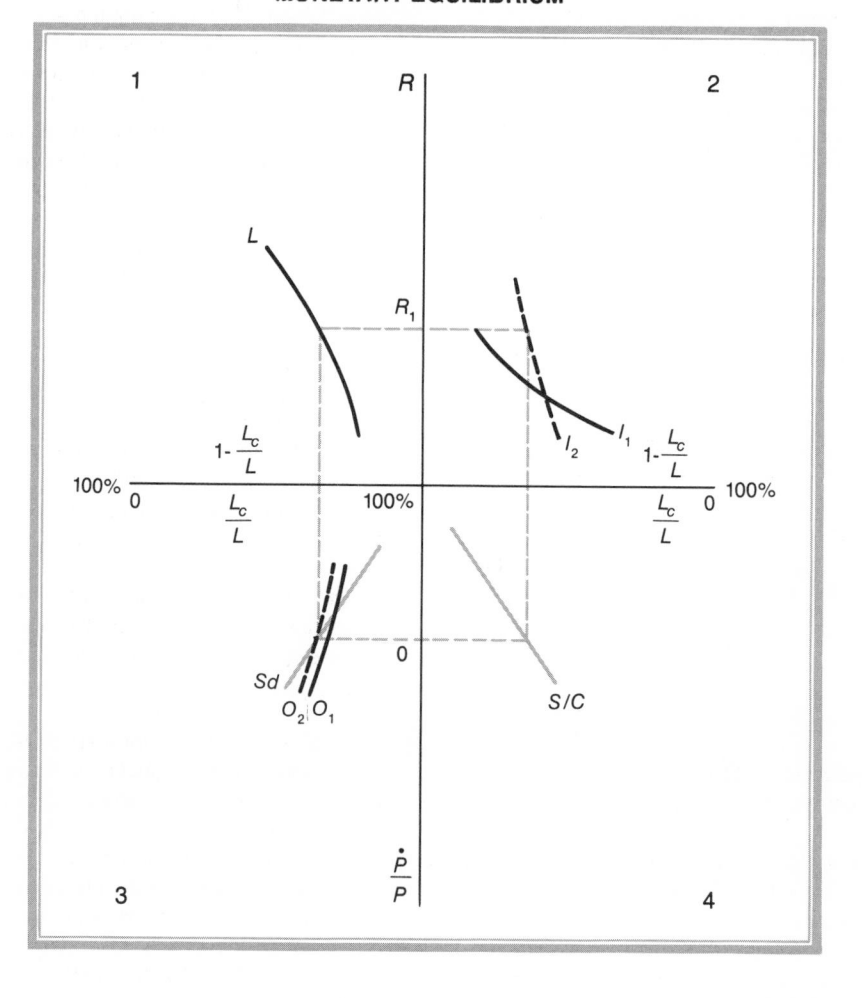

bour force means that capital equipment closer to consumer goods will also experience an increase in demand and a corresponding increase in price. This is the consequence of a lower elasticity of supply of these goods — a kind of accelerator mechanism— relative to the increased demand. This means that the investment function, I_1, will shift rightward, putting pressure on the capital market and forcing interest rates higher to I_2 (see Quadrant 2, Diagram 15-7).

Rising interest rates and consequent higher levels of less liquid assets (a higher ratio $(1 - Lc/L)$ or a lower ratio Lc/L along the L function in Quadrant 1) would result in a leftward shift in

the offer curve (Quadrant 3). (We get a shift in this case because the axis $\dot{p}/p$ is different from the axis R, i.e., the functional relationship is different for the offer curve than for the L curve in Quadrant 1.) The result *could* be (emphasize "could") a lowering of the equilibrium rate of inflation, but probably will not, because of the notorious "stickiness" of prices and wages. Instead of lowering their rates of price increases, sellers satisfy their lower demands for money by reductions in inventory.

If prices and wages were flexible downwards, it would be possible for the economic system to reach long-term equilibrium at zero inflation ra-

Diagram 15-8

MONETARY DISEQUILIBRIUM

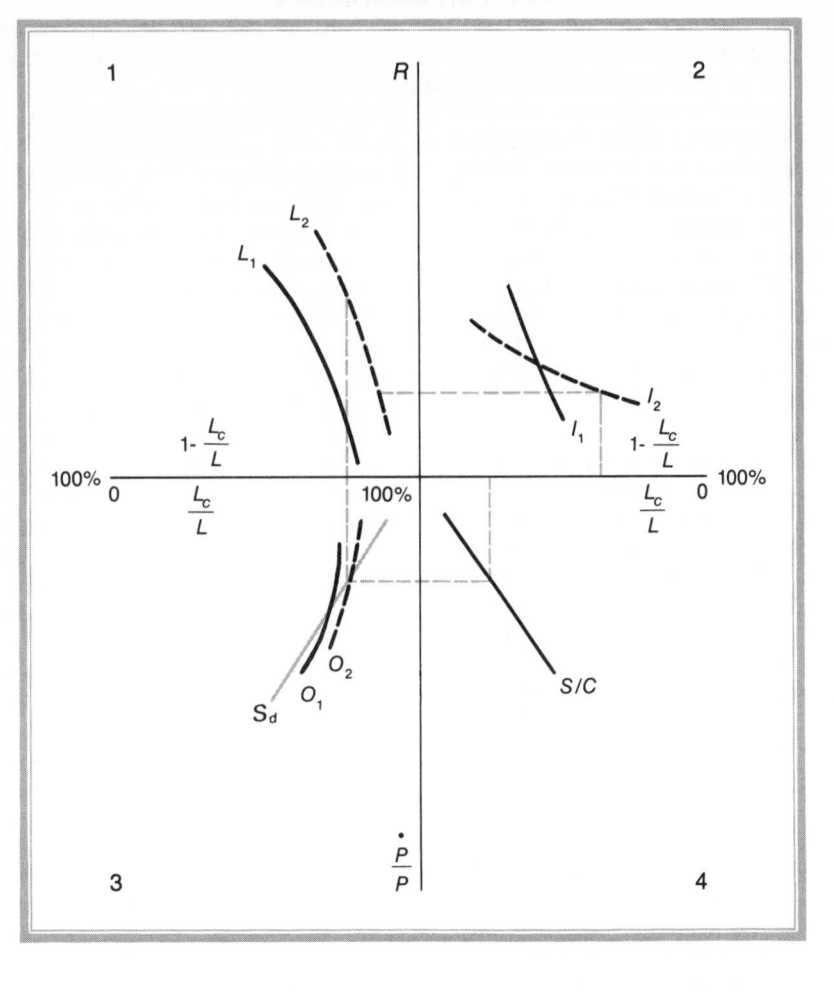

tes. This would follow from the fact that any un-employment which might result would force, through competition, a lowering of money wages in consumer goods industries and provide a new pool of labour for additional output of short-term capital goods which are the necessary inputs into production of consumer goods. To achieve this result, workers must be prepared to move from one industry to the next or even from one location to another. In this way a maldistribution of labour could be corrected.

What really happens is that the process of approaching long-run equilibrium is "short-circuited" by deliberate policies and actions taken

by government. The reason for this is a com-bination of the politicians' fear of unemployment and its consequences and the belief in the Key-nesian doctrine of aggregate demand. Unem-ployment, according to the familiar arguments of macroeconomics, is the consequence of the failure of aggregate demand. The action to be taken, therefore, is to restore aggregate demand to its former level through a stimulation of invest-ment, consumption, or, failing these, public expenditure.

To see how this "short-circuiting" operation works, we shall return to that point where the demand curve for inputs, I_1, shifts because of rising prices in these industries. (The cause of this, it will be recalled, is an inelasticity of supply due to the existence of full employment in consumer goods industries.) A time lag may exist within the banking system itself between the increased demand for loan funds for investment and the higher rate of interest. Thus, there will likely be a tendency to overshoot an equilibrium rate of interest on the part of banks as they overreact to the increased demand for funds pressing on their available supply by pushing their own rates above equilibrium levels. The Bank of Canada, in this case, may ease the pressure on existing chartered bank reserves so as to make available a greater supply of funds either to depress the interest rate or to keep it from rising (see Diagram 15-8).

Now, under the "short-circuiting" conditions, business enterprise has an alternative to the funds in short supply in the capital market. The money supply is increasing with interest rates lower than what they would otherwise be. This increased supply of funds at lower cost encourages entrepreneurs to invest in longer, more roundabout methods of production so that the investment curve (see Quadrant 2) shifts to I_2 toward greater elasticity. These more roundabout techniques of production are not only more productive but labour-saving as well.

The interesting feature of this "short-circuiting" process is the fact that the expenditure of the new funds on capital investment means an increased supply of current liquidity in the hands of the public. Offer curves will, therefore, shift to the dashed position in Quadrant 3 making possible the finance of an enhanced demand for money on the part of sellers. There is, of course, no incentive to store liquidity in the form of future liquidity because interest rates are low, maintaining a high level of wealth via the "interest induced" wealth effect.

The stage is now set, as it were, for higher rates of price increases. Current liquidity in the form of savings deposits, Canada Savings Bonds, etc., is high, ready to be transferred into demand deposits or cash. In such conditions it matters little what event (a world-wide oil price increase, for instance) furnishes the stimulus toward higher rates of price increases; the fact is that something *will* happen to act as the initial stimulus. Once begun, the process continues because all the conditions for its continuance are present. It is,

incidentally, precisely this continuation of inflation which marks the difference between Canada and Germany. The impact of oil price increases was perhaps greater in Europe than in Canada, but the ensuing inflation has been greater here than in Germany.

But there is still something of the greatest importance which is taking place in the I function of Quadrant 2. As we have seen, the I function is assuming an elastic position as in I_2. Lower interest rates mean longer, more roundabout productive methods which require less direct labour than the shorter productive techniques. Unemployment, therefore, results, but note that this unemployment is not due to a lack of aggregate demand; quite the contrary, demand is *excessive*. This is structural unemployment which means that there are not enough available jobs in industry because labour is being replaced. It is now more efficient, in economic terms, to produce with less labour because real wages are too high *relative to the lower cost of capital*.

At this particular stage in the sequence of events, it is likely that governments, recognizing that prices are rising excessively (along with unusually high rates of increase in the money supply), will attempt to curb the high rate of monetary expansion. But this is not so easily done because capital investment begun under the assumption of future interest rates at the same level as existing rates cannot be cut off in "mid-stream." The roundabout productive process is a lengthy one and requires a continuation of investment until ultimate fruition is attained. A manufacturing plant, for example, laid in place with borrowed funds which cost 5%, is useless without the installation of machinery and equipment, but if the latter must be purchased with funds costing 10%, the entire complex, averaging 7.5%, can become uneconomic. But industry has no choice; it must borrow additional funds from the capital market if the banking system is no longer able to provide the funds at low cost. The resulting pressure of demand drives the interest rate to higher levels than ever before and interest becomes, then, a genuine cost of production to be recouped in higher prices.

In terms of our diagram, the shift of the offer curve to position O_2, dashed at first, becomes realized with a higher *rate* of inflation. Correspondingly, the L curve shifts upward to L_2 with a smaller ratio of $(1 - Lc/L)$ being made available for the capital market. Similarly, in Quadrant 4, consumption will be greater and savings less. However, the most important factor in capital market equilibrium is not inadequate savings in the aggregate, but the *structure* of financial assets which no longer conforms to the *structure* of investment requirements. The liquidity which the public is willing to forego, L_2, does not equal the non-liquidity I_2 which investment requires. Interest rates, or the rates of return, indicated as R, rise to unprecedented levels, and the equity markets collapse in value, reflecting the inability of profits to keep pace with rates of inflation. These profits are "squeezed" between the double burden of rising interest costs and higher wage demands imposed by organized labour, etc., and prices which, though rising, are not rising fast enough. Rather typically, the situation is often misunderstood by the general public. Corporate profits will appear, when published, to be excessive, and, therefore, a true "cause" of rapidly rising prices, but will actually be rather small. In order to keep pace with rising rates of interest, gross profits must increase considerably because of the increased cost of the capital equipment laid down.[8]

B. A Sequence Beginning with Zero Inflation

This next sequence begins with a zero (or negligible) inflation rate which gives us complete neutrality of money without any redistributory effects whatsoever. In this case the stimulus which disturbs the equilibrium will still arise but from a different source than the price structure itself. To find such a stimulus within Canada is not difficult because there is, in the first place, the business cycle itself which generates its own momentum. The "normal" cyclical chain of events is augmented by additional exogenous stimuli which in themselves are certainly strong enough to disturb equilibrium.

---

[8]The problem can be stated as follows:

$$V = \sum_{t=0}^{N} \frac{\pi_t}{(1 + r)^t} \, dt$$

for a long-term capital project expected to last for N years. V must remain as a constant to cover the cost of investment; therefore, the value of π must approximately double as the interest rate, r, doubles.

We might consider a typical Canadian cyclical (or "endogenous") stimulus as the "Wicksell Effect" as discussed in Chapter 10. This, it will be recalled, relates the accumulation of capital as a stock to labour services which are a flow. Because of this fundamental characteristic, labour enjoys an inevitable monopoly of relative scarcity. Capital stock accumulates through time, whereas labour can increase only through natural causes or by immigration. The consequence here is that some of the capital funds must be used for the direct employment of labour. We can see this in terms of the distribution of the National Income; the share accruing to labour has tended to grow over the long-term relative to that of profits.

In countries such as Canada, rather heavily dependent upon imported capital, the tendency for capital stock to outrun labour would be greater than in countries in which capital is already in surplus, i.e., the Wicksell Effect is likely to be stronger in Canada. We require capital, yet the very act of accumulation means that it is, relative to labour, a productive factor growing in amount. We can say that in terms of population (relative to geographic size and to capital requirement) we are a small underpopulated country.

Increasing wage costs relative to the costs of capital must therefore take place. This in itself would tilt the investment function toward I_2 with a greater elasticity in response to interest rate changes. This can be counteracted, however, by improvements in productivity which have the effect of lowering wage costs for entrepreneurs. Lower wage costs will encourage the use of more direct, labour-intensive productive techniques with the result that greater employment levels can be achieved. This was particularly apparent during the middle 1960s when unemployment fell to very low levels in Canada at the same time that labour productivity gains were at their highest; hence, from the argument we may conclude that our current unemployment in Canada is primarily *structural* and results less from a lack of demand than to other countries.

In the United States, on the other hand, where labour and capital are closer to a position of relative equilibrium (a vastly greater labour force than in Canada relative to the capital stock) structural unemployment will not be so likely. Wage costs can be kept down not only through increases in productivity, but also by the greater degree of competition within labour itself. Unemployment in the U.S. will be more likely to result from cyclical causes, particularly monetary factors, which have been shown by Friedman and Schwartz, in their empirical analysis for the U.S., to be highly significant.[9] Such cyclical causes will be "exogenous" to Canada itself, but because of our high capital to labour ratio, will be felt in Canada rather strongly, not only as a decline in U.S. import demand but also as an interruption in the flow of capital to Canada necessary for the employment of labour. The observation, "when the U.S. sneezes, Canada has a cold" expresses this as a truism.

But there are other factors purely Canadian which are non-cyclical and which augment our own business cycle tendencies. We have increasingly liberal welfare benefits and arrangements which result in higher real earnings for labour. Pension plans, employee fringe benefits, etc., won by collective bargaining, tend to raise the real wage cost to employers and add further to the "tilting" effect of the Investment function toward I_2 to increase the elasticity of investment demand. Business enterprise begins to actively seek capital at the lowest cost (generally to be found in the U.S. capital market) so as to economize on the now relatively scarce and costly labour services. This imported capital serves the dual function of releasing domestic capital for other uses, on the one hand, and providing foreign exchange for additional imports of goods and services on the other. Any increase, therefore, in interest rates in the U.S., due to the U.S. business cycle or to world shortages of capital as indicated by Eurocurrency market rates, will be reflected rather quickly in the Canadian interest rate structure.

Our dependence, then, on capital imports brings us once more to the "crucial stage" in our analysis. The investment function has been tilted toward greater elasticity and a reliance upon supplies of relatively cheap capital, particularly from foreign sources. At the same time, labour costs are rising because of higher wage concessions in the collective bargaining process, benefits, etc., encouraging employers to economize

on high cost labour with labour-saving roundabout productive techniques. The result is an inability on the part of the producing sector to "create" jobs as fast as the labour force is growing.

The typical Canadian answer to this dilemma, which we shall examine in greater detail in the next chapter, is to ease the money supply so that banks can manufacture additional funds at lower interest cost. This makes possible the continued laying in place of capital equipment to complete the roundabout productive process which has already been started. Additional jobs are created in this way, to be sure, *but only on a short-term basis* because the amount of capital required to create one job is continuously growing so that ultimately a shortage of capital will be the cause of unemployment.

We truly have a "tiger by the tail." Money expansion means continuous shifts in the offer curves (Quadrant 3), and tight money means high interest costs which must be compensated for by higher prices to maintain necessary profit margins. But any slowing down of costly investment means unemployment because of an insufficiency of capital to employ labour. Yet it is the restructuring of investment toward more direct, labour-intensive techniques of production which is required to reduce unemployment *in the long run*! This it would appear, is a reasonably accurate description of the Canadian economy of the 1960s and 70s.

C. Long-term vs. Short-term Equilibrium

The analysis we have been following to this point is a long-run equilibrium process which involves adjustments of business decisions in accordance with changing data — prices, interest rates, real wage costs, etc. It is simplified, of course, to approximate a highly complex process. It is now time to grasp the nettle and identify more precisely the fundamental differences between a short-term (or Keynesian) analysis and the long-term equilibrium process which has been described in this chapter.

By now it must have become apparent to anyone brought up in the tradition of macroeconomics that something is amiss. If the argument up to now has made any sense, there will exist a funda-

---

[9]M. Friedman and A.J. Schwartz, *A Monetary History of the United States, 1867-1960*, Princeton Univ. Press, 1963.

mental conflict of principles which must be resolved. To review, once more, the main thrust of our argument: it is that the *structure* of investment adjusts in response to changes in prices of final output of consumer goods, the cost of investment (the rate of interest), and the cost of labour. But this is not all. From the financial side (i.e., Quadrants 1 and 3) the *structure* of financial assets, or the structure of liquidity, must match the structure of investment. The macroeconomic, or Keynesian argument, on the other hand, stresses only the equality of savings and investment to form the famous identity,

$$Y = \text{Consumption} + \text{Saving}$$
$$Y = \text{Consumption} + \text{Investment},$$

therefore

Investment = Saving[10]

But this is not really an identity at all because the structure of savings does not automatically equal the structure of investment, and this condition is necessary for true equality to exist. Savings deposits, for example, cannot finance long-term capital projects even though they may be equal in value terms. But to continue further, investment is, as we have argued, determined by relative prices of consumer goods and capital goods, price changes of consumer goods, the rate of interest, and the cost of labour. It follows that we cannot stimulate investment alone without having a direct impact on all other variables which make up income (Y). This means that consumption and investment (just as consumption and savings) are not additive at all. They are additive only in an *ex post* or national income sense, i.e., after the expenditures for investment and consumption have taken place.

The best that can be argued for the entire concept of aggregate demand is that it can only be a short-term approximation of what true "aggregated" demand is likely to be. It is short term because only in the immediate future will businessmen not have the time to alter their decisions. It is an approximation because the plus sign is a massive simplification of what is a very complex functional relationship. Policy measures based upon such short-term approximations alone are, therefore, wrong on two counts: (1) the

approximation itself must be inaccurate, and (2) any actions taken by governments must distort the very many independent decisions which determine the structure of productive techniques. Left to themselves, these decisions would likely approach a long-run equilibrium of full employment, but with policy measures based upon erroneous principles, the situation can be made worse. Consider, for example, a policy of lower interest rates and easy money designed to encourage investment for the purpose of increasing employment — a short-run consideration based upon the aggregate demand equation, $Y = C + I$. Lower interest rates encourage employment-saving roundabout production and the consequence is a short-run policy which defeats itself in the end. This conclusion applies with equal force to the highly complex macroeconomic model even though it is likely to be a closer approximation to reality than the simpler models of aggregate demand.

Federal fiscal policy is another of the exogenous stimuli which affects long-run equilibrium. In general a balanced budget should have little or no impact on our long-run model since the liquidity axes in Diagram 15-6 can be simply measured as net of tax. Government requirements for goods and services would similarly be excluded since the output which constitutes sellers' demand for money would be net of government requirements. This is not true of the government deficit. This will have the greatest effect on the interest rate (R) axis for Quadrants 1 and 2. The government will necessarily compete for funds from the capital market, and, being the government, will have the prestige to acquire the funds it needs against all competition at the lowest possible rate. This raises the market interest rates to higher levels than they would otherwise obtain, causing an adjustment in the I function itself as entrepreneurs revise their production planning.

The impact of government borrowing is felt when capital projects already laid down must be further financed to completion with additional borrowing. The capital market cannot accommodate such heavy demands without substantially increased interest rates. Business enterprises, therefore, have no choice but to increase their prices in order to recoup some of the increased interest costs. It is too late, in these cases, to revise investment decisions.

[10]J.M. Keynes, *The General Theory of Employment Interest and Money*, Macmillan, London, 1949, p. 63.

A similar result follows from the finance of consumer credit—interest rates are higher than they would otherwise be. However, in this case, consumer demand for durable goods, automobiles and the like, encourages the production (or import) of these goods which are frequently produced by capital intensive highly roundabout methods of production. (The day of the labour intensive automobile is long past.) Again this applies a greater pressure of demand for capital directly on the capital market.

CONCLUSION

In this chapter we have argued two basic conditions regarding equilibrium requirements: (1) An equilibrium between financial assets which are held by the public and the investment structure of business enterprise must exist for a true savings investment equality as opposed to the savings/investment identity of the Keynesian equations. Another way of suggesting this is: the liquidity foregone by savers should match the liquidity requirements of entrepreneurs who structure the capital they put into place. (2) This structure of capital must be such that it will provide employment for the existing labour force (a "Hayekian" equilibrium) within the framework of relative prices.

Both these conditions of equilibrium are "long-term" and may be violated. A violation of the first means that expenditure from savings can take place at any time. Thus, if we divide time into a series of short periods, for example four, actual expenditure from savings may not occur during the first three even though the equilibrium conditions of proposition one are continuously violated. It may not be until the fourth period that expenditure from liquid savings takes place. The buyers' offer curves, in other words, require three periods to shift to the right during which time sellers' demand for money remains sufficiently static to keep price inflation low. Not until the fourth period do sellers' demands increase.

The second condition is a Hayekian equilibrium of real values as opposed to the monetary values of the first proposition. Again it is a long-term one

and may be consistently violated for several successive short periods. Thus, even though labour-saving roundabout investment is laid in place, greater quantities of such investment can provide short-term full employment for several periods. In the long-run (say, the fourth period suggested above) capital must become too scarce to continue its growth with the inevitable result of unemployment. Quite simply, capital becomes scarce because of proposition one, the failure of savings to provide the necessary non-liquidity. We never complete the savings requirement which is called for by the investment structure which is laid down. We prefer to have the liquidity of our "savings" so as to enjoy a higher living standard for which *we have really not saved*.

Anyone familiar with neo-Keynesian macroeconomics will likely recognize that these two conditions are virtually at loggerheads with the typical macroeconomic policies and proposals of many North American economists. In the interest of academic integrity we should consider in this concluding section what these proposals are, not only to show contrast, but also to make clear the differences between long and short-term considerations. Professor James Tobin, of Yale, in a recent paper, has set forth four propositions which he considers as basic to the *General Theory* and which he considers to be relevant today.[11] These are the following:

(1) Prices of products and wages of labour respond sluggishly to excess demand and supply, i.e., there is insufficient flexibility in prices and wages to restore clearing balances in any short period of time. This was true in the years when the *General Theory* was written and is still true today.

The consequence of this inflexibility is, of course, unemployment and general recession conditions. Against this it should be made clear that Hayekian equilibrium involves *relative* wage costs and *relative* prices. That is, even though downward inflexibility of wages and prices exists, no one would argue that prices and wages are inflexible upwards. Rising prices, however, mean

---

[11]A paper presented in Calgary based upon a previous paper presented to the Western Economics Association and published in *Economic Inquiry*, the journal of that association, under the title "How Dead is Keynes?".

a fall of real wage costs. Nevertheless, it could be true that, given the economic power of organized labour and collective bargaining, wages may even be inflexible, relative to prices, downward. If this is true, it does not negate the basic truth of the Hayekian equilibrium condition but imposes an external constraint which renders it inoperative. As such it really confirms its truth.

(2) The second proposition follows directly from the first. It is that involuntary unemployment is not easily eliminated by the forces of the market alone. Of course this will be true if the first proposition is true; however, if it is relative wages and prices that matter, proposition one is not so readily acceptable and it may be that market forces could indeed work themselves out more rapidly if the "frictions" imposed by institutional factors, Unemployment Insurance Compensation, for example, were absent. No one could argue against humanitarian principles, but it is possible that UIC could be designed to assist (or "lubricate") the market forces rather than slow them down.

(3) The third proposition is particularly interesting in the light of the analysis of this chapter. Business capital formation decisions are highly psychological and subjective, and estimates of the marginal efficiency of capital, hence, investment decisions are not easily explained econometrically as simple functions of economic variables. In defense of this proposition, Tobin cites examples during the recent U.S. recession of apparent business pessimism in the light of government policy decisions. The specific danger here lay in expected anti-inflation policy measures which would likely result in unprofitability of investment projects.

This is the most intriguing of all Tobin's propositions, confirming, as it does, the futility of econometric models in view of the subjectivity of decisions on the part of businessmen. There is also another factor involved, that is the policy measures themselves which interfere with the market forces which could, through awareness on the part of businessmen of government policy, influence their decisions. This emphasizes what is perhaps the strongest point that can be made in favour of non-interference in the operation of the free market in terms of investment decisions. It is that Keynesian economics, with its emphasis upon aggregate demand and unemployment which results from a breakdown of aggregate demand, opens the door, as it were, to all kinds of interference by the government in the form of policies and actions which may result in worse consequences than the operation of the free market itself. The idea that our economy can be directed or steered in the right direction from Ottawa and still maintain freedom of action and decision-making is paradoxical enough, and Professor Tobin's third proposition, and his evidence in support of it, seems to confirm this conclusion.

(4) The last proposition which, according to Tobin, emerges from the General Theory is that the "self-correcting" mechanisms of the free market, even though strong enough in their operation, are not necessarily automatically stabilizing. Professor Tobin conceded that there is not much evidence for or against this proposition so that it must be accepted almost on faith. Certainly in recent years there has been no opportunity for the self-correcting mechanisms to prove themselves either stabilizing or destabilizing.

These four propositions illustrate very well the hiatus which stands between short and long-term analysis and the conflicts which must arise between long and short-term policy measures. It may well be true that institutions in our economic lives, governments, trade unions, and the like, have rendered long-term market forces impotent and/or certainly non-self-correcting. If so, there appear to be two obvious courses open to us: firstly, we continue on down the road toward more government controls and influence over the components of aggregate demand, ultimately to arrive at the end — complete centralized control, or secondly, we retrace our steps to disengage from the government policy measures themselves and permit the market to work out its own conclusions.

One of the more frequently heard, and absurd, truisms is "You can't turn back the clock." This is another way of saying that while we might recognize past mistakes, we can do nothing to correct them. Actually, such a fatalistic view is a concession to those segments of our society which gain from inflation (there is always a sector which stands to gain from rising prices) and which prefer to continue to gain even at the expense of others. These segments will support the continued short-term centralized economic steering which governments continuously attempt and

which are proving to be more and more important. In reply to these groups in our society we
could do no better than quote from Professor
Hayek himself.

Are we not even told that, "since in the long
run we are all dead," policy should be
guided entirely by short-run considerations? I fear that these believers in the
principle of *après nous le déluge* may get
what they have bargained for sooner than
they wish.[12]

ADDITIONAL READINGS

Friedman, M., "A Theoretical Treatment for Monetary
Analysis," *Money and Banking*, Walters (ed.),
Penguin Education, Harmondsworth, Middlesex,
England, 1973, p. 69.

---

[12]F.A. Hayek, *The Pure Theory of Capital*, Routledge &
Kegan Paul, London, 1950, p. 410.

Makinen, Gail E., *Money, The Price Level and Interest
Rates*, Prentice-Hall, Englewood Cliffs, 1977, Part
III. A good review of the controversy surrounding Monetarism vs. Keynesian economics and
policies.

Alternative Paradigms

Holbrook, Robert S., "The Interest Rate, The Price
Level, and Aggregate Output," *Readings in
Money, National Income and Stabilization Policy*,
Third Edition, Smith, Teigen (eds.), Irwin, Inc.,
Homewood, Ill., 1974, p. 38.
Laidler, David E.W., *The Demand for Money, Theories
and Evidence*, International Textbook Co., Scran-
ton, Pa., 1969, Part I.
Smith, Warren L., "A Graphical Exposition of the Com-
plete Keynesian System," *Southern Economic
Journal*, October, 1956, p. 115, reprinted in *Read-
ings in Money, National Income and Stabilization
Policy*, Third Edition, Smith, Teigen (eds.), Irwin,
Inc., Homewood, Ill., 1974, p. 61.

CHAPTER 16

The Present and the Future

INTRODUCTION

This chapter continues the process of "tying together" which was begun in Chapter 15. In the first part, a discussion of monetarist economics is continued to take up the theme of Chapter 1, which, it will be recalled, was left with some unresolved issues in the development of monetary theory. It is a difficult section to write because, during the 1960s and 1970s, there has been considerable discussion and writing on the issue of the monetarist vs. income-expenditure economics, otherwise known as macroeconomics, with its origin in Keynes' *General Theory*. Better and more detailed accounts of this great debate are available and one would be well-advised to follow up the argument of Part I with the additional readings listed at the end of this chapter. Certainly there are more objective accounts than is possible to give in these few pages which are simply not enough to do justice to one of the great debates in economic theory.

The second part of the chapter outlines Canadian experience with the hoped-for objective of identifying where we went wrong. And go wrong we did for there is hardly anyone today who would argue that Canada's economy is healthy.

I. DEMAND FOR MONEY

Chapter 1 introduced the idea of a demand for money beginning with the elementary Quantity Theory to finish with the Friedman version of a demand for money. Fundamentally, the idea underlying the principle of the Quantity Theory is that a massive "confrontation" continuously takes place between the economic activity which generates our Gross National Product and the money supply. To express the idea in slightly different terms, there is an aggregate demand for real monetary balances against an aggregate nominal supply of money furnished by the banking system. This is what

$$M = \frac{PT}{V}$$

(the original Fisherine version) states.

Our analysis has been somewhat different. Instead of a quantity of money (which implies a quantitative analysis) we have followed a structure of liquidity analysis (which implies a qualitative analysis). While the two approaches are basically different, they need not be in conflict at all; quite the contrary, it is quite possible for the two to be complementary. This is the real purpose of this chapter—to show how a reinforcement (a "synergism" in the natural sciences) may take place so that an understanding of Monetary Economics might become all the stronger. In the last analysis this is the objective in writing this book.

A. Friedman Again

When we left Friedman's version of the demand for money in the concluding section of Chapter 1, there were seven variables in the function. We can now consider these seven variables and evaluate Friedman's work as well within the context of Monetary Economics. The function can be stated as follows:

$$M = f\left(P, r_b - \frac{1}{r_b}\frac{dr_b}{dt}, r_e + \frac{1}{P}\frac{dP}{dt} - \frac{1}{r_e}\frac{dr_e}{dt}\frac{1}{P}\frac{dP}{dt}, w, \frac{Y}{r}, u\right).$$

with the numbers 1, 2, 3, 4, 5, 6, 7 marking the variables.

This happens, actually, to be a slightly earlier version of Friedman's Quantity Theory, dated 1956, and which has since been revised as we shall see presently.[1]

---

[1]"The Quantity Theory of Money — A Restatement," reprinted from *Studies in the Quantity Theory of Money*, by Milton Friedman, by permission of University of Chicago Press, Chicago, 1956, p. 9. © University of Chicago.

Though somewhat awkward looking, the terms within the functional relationship are not at all difficult to understand and interpret, once the problem of the definition of money, M, is overcome. Incidentally, it is precisely this problem of definition and quantification that the liquidity analysis avoids; we simply say that the Canadian economy is more or less liquid than before. We cannot do this in the Quantity Theory approach which requires that money be actually measured; hence, an agreed definition of money is imperative. In Friedman's function, money is taken to be demand deposits at commercial banks plus cash in circulation plus savings deposits at commercial banks.

For convenience, each of the seven variables is identified with a numbered superscript. The first of these is the general price level of goods and services. The "general price level" in this case does not suffer from the same difficulty as Fisher's price level, $P = \Sigma p_i$, because Friedman recognizes the advances made by Patinkin and others in economic theory and includes the real balance effect in his demand for money function. Fisher's demand for money, it will be recalled, was a "market demand" which rested on the functional relationship between quantity of money and price of goods and services. Money, therefore, had no price of its own (or its price was effectively by-passed). Not so in Friedman's case; the true price of money is $1/P$.[2] There should be no ambiguity, then, in interpreting the general price level which could be readily measured as an index number — the higher is this price level the greater is the money requirement.

Term 2 is the bond sector which Friedman defines in broad terms as the debt which yields a constant income stream. The term r_b is the rate which itself is constant in the case of non-marketable debt or when expectations are that the market price will remain constant (savings deposits in financial intermediaries, Canada Savings Bonds, etc.) The second part of this second term is the expected variation in market price resulting from changes

in r_b through time (hence, the time derivative). A decline in r_b (or negative change) increases the market price of a bond encouraging its sale for profit taking purposes; similarly, a rise in r_b (a positive change) means a decline in the market price of the bond, encouraging bearish purchases. Friedman later discards this second part for the sake of "streamlining" his function since the market price variations of marketable bonds simply reinforce the effect of demand for money of any changes in r_b alone. Nevertheless, a correct interpretation of his final version should definitely include this interest induced wealth effect. Of course, the functional relationship between r_b and M is inverse, i.e., the higher the value of r_b, the less the demand for money.

Term 3 is the equity portion. Friedman considers *three* sources of return here, the first being simply r_e, the equivalent of r_b in terms of dividend distributions. Term 2 is the percentage rate of change through time of the equity price which is unrelated to r_b. Here, Friedman makes an extraordinary assumption which, fortunately, he later quietly drops. The P for equities is the same P as term 1.[3] At the time of the original formulation of his version of the Quantity Theory, equities were considered to be an excellent hedge against inflation in the sense that equity prices moved with the general price level. This, as we have seen, is not at all true; therefore, if the demand for money is affected (inversely of course) by expected percentage gains in equity prices unrelated to r_b, (e.g., new oil discoveries and the like) a variable *other* than P must be used. The third part of term 3 is the equity counterpart of the market price determination for the marketable bond. Changes in expected rates of return, r_e, affect the demand for money in precisely the same fashion as bonds, i.e., falling rates (negative changes) increase equity prices and rising rates (positive changes) lower market prices of equities. Like bonds, demand for money is affected by *expected* changes in prices and rates.

Term 4 is simple enough to describe; in fact, it could have been, in the interest of neatness, included with term 1 because it is defined as the expected percentage rate of increase in the general level of prices through time. As such it is

[2]This is the conclusion one would reach from "The Quantity Theory of Money" by Milton Friedman. Reprinted by permission of the Publisher from the *International Encyclopedia of the Social Sciences*. David L. Sills, editor. Copyright © 1968 by Crowell Collier and Macmillan, Inc.

[3]Friedman, *op. cit.*, p. 6.

a measure of the return from holding physical goods, or, to express it slightly differently, the advantage of purchasing now before the price rises just as it is expected to do. Naturally, this variable affects the demand for money inversely, the stronger the expectations of rising prices (inflationary psychology) the less the demand for money.

The fifth variable is an interesting one and, as far as can be interpreted, represents Friedman's excursion into a qualitative analysis. The term w represents the value of wealth held in "non-human form." We can take this to mean the "fraction of income derived from property" (the definition in the Encyclopaedia article, footnote 2) and "the division between human and non-human wealth in the individual's portfolio of assets" (the 1956 article) — in other words, all the other possibilities of holding wealth as future liquidity alternatively to money.

Term 6 is very important; it is the stream of income, expected through time, capitalized in terms of an infinite time span by an appropriate rate of interest, r. Furthermore, this expected income stream can be taken to be a permanent income which is derived from all forms of assets, human and non-human, through time. As such it is a wealth concept which is derived from a "permanent income," and, of course, represents a rather large figure. Professor Friedman developed the permanent income hypothesis as an attempt to justify differences between consumer spending decisions which varied as between time series studies on the one hand and studies based on cross-sectional data (time constant with income as a variable) on the other. He found that empirical testing justified the permanent income hypothesis in that money held tends to vary with an estimate of permanent income (estimated by means of a weighted average of past incomes) rather than "transitory income." It was, in fact, the inclusion of this permanent income in the consumption function itself which marked an important difference between Keynesian aggregate demand and Friedman's version. We can say, then, that the greater the value of an individual's wealth, defined as capitalized permanent income, the greater the value of his consumption, and, it follows, the greater his demand for money. The last variable, u, is a "catch-all" type variable which has to do with tastes and preferences of individuals. These will vary with circumstances;

for example, uncertainties such as danger of war, a recession, etc., may encourage a greater demand for money on the part of individuals. Personal circumstances also, such as degree of mobility, type of occupation, etc., will also determine the "utility" attached to the holding of money.

Friedman then proceeds to convert his function into real terms by dividing all the terms by the price level, P. This not only eliminates term 1, P, but also renders the variables independent of the price level as indeed they should be. In the later version of his demand for money (the Encyclopaedia version) Friedman made some changes in his independent variables. He dropped the rate of capitalization of income, r, in term 6, preferring only real income as a surrogate for wealth. Also, as mentioned above, he abandoned the second part of term 2 and the second and third parts of term 3, lumping all these concepts into the terms r_b and r_e. A final adjustment was the inclusion of r_m, a term indicating the "rate of interest" or reward for holding money as cash. By this Friedman meant the advantage, measured against the rate of return from financial assets, in holding money as money ready to meet payments when they arise. The advantage rests in the avoidance not only of embarrassment but also the time and trouble necessary to transfer financial assets into cash.

The final version of Friedman's demand for money function, then, as stated in the *Encyclopaedia for the Social Sciences* is as follows:

$$\frac{M}{P} = f\left(y, w, r_m, r_b, r_e, \frac{1}{P}\frac{dP}{dt}, u\right).$$

It is the demand for money on the part of the individual wealth holder. For business enterprise the function is the same except that the variable w is excluded. There are in addition some additional interpretations required, particularly r_m, to fit the function into the behaviour patterns and requirements of businesses as opposed to wealth holders.

B. An Assessment of Friedman's Quantity Theory of Money

From the final version of the demand for money it is only a simple mathematical step to the Quantity Theory itself. All the variables within the parenthesis determine income velocity of money so that the function, f, can be represented as v, income velocity. In Quantity Theory form, Friedman's demand for money appears as follows:

$$Y = v\left(y, w, r_m, r_b, r_e, \frac{1}{P}\frac{dP}{dt}, u\right) \cdot M.$$

In this form the Quantity Equation may look complicated but it actually is not. It states, quite simply, that the money value of the national income (GNP) is equal to the income velocity of circulation of money, which is determined functionally by all the variables within the parentheses, multiplied by the quantity of money, M. But having gone this far to form a Quantity Theory, one must quantify the variables themselves within the parentheses to render this version of the Quantity Theory meaningful. This is, in fact, precisely where the difficulty lies because it is not possible to measure the variables with the existing state of our statistical knowledge.

To continue with Friedman's argument: "Broadly speaking, the total amount of money available to be held by all together is determined by the monetary structure or the monetary authorities— currently in this country, the Federal Reserve System— largely independent of the actions of the holders of money."[4] This, as we have seen in preceding chapters, is not quite correct because the public must purchase any *additions* to money stock at a price—the rate of interest. This rate could be very low indeed because the marginal cost of manufacturing new money is zero, but still the public may refuse to pay the price. Business enterprise, for example, may prefer to finance its expansion from its own funds, or, indeed, it may seek additional finance from foreign sources in which case foreign funds would be exchanged for existing Canadian dollar deposits via the Exchange Fund Account. If the public steadfastly refuses to pay the price for money, there is an alternative; the banking system could purchase government securities, thereby expanding government deposits. By increasing the national debt

in this way, deposits might be forced on the public so long as the public will acquiesce, but even here there is a possibility that confidence in both the government and the banking system could be lost.

Assuming that this is an unlikely possibility, the excess funds "forced" onto the public would, according to Friedman, "produce spirited bidding for assets and other goods which would raise their prices."[5] Unless we accept this as an exaggeration, it is contrary to fact. Aside from bull markets in the stock exchange, or speculative buying during anticipated shortages in the commodities markets, we just do not observe "spirited bidding" in the markets for goods and services. It is rather more true that any changes in the money supply require long-term periods to work themselves through the economy, i.e., shifts in offer curves do not occur at once nor do sellers' demands for money (or current liquidity) respond immediately to money supply changes. The force of competition is generally strong enough to discourage a quick response. Only during periods of generally rising prices with expectations of further price increases will the response to changes in the money supply be quick. In other words, before the price level in general will rise, the structure of liquidity must be sufficiently biased toward current liquidity and sellers must be sufficiently conscious of their opportunities for increasing their demand for money, and this may require a long time to develop.

Despite the difficulties inherent in Quantity Theory analysis, i.e., statistical measurement and time lags, there is hardly any doubt that the quantity of money (however defined) is related to the price level. The theoretical basis for this lies in the fact that long-run stability in the demand for money means that when the supply of money increases due to external factors, policies, etc., the excessive amount of money eventually results in rising prices. This relationship, as Friedman points out, is remarkably constant:

> ...there is perhaps no other empirical relation in economics that has been observed to recur so uniformly under so wide a variety of circumstances as the relation between substantial changes over short periods in the stock of money and in prices;

[4]Friedman, "The Demand for Money," *Proceedings of the American Philosophical Society*, June, 1961. Reprinted in *Monetary Theory and Policy*, Richard A. Ward, ed., International Textbook Co., Scranton, 1966, p. 208.

[5]*Ibid.*, p. 208.

the one is invariably linked with the other and is in the same direction; this uniformity is, I suspect, of the same order as many of the uniformities that form the basis of the physical sciences.[6]

Probably the greatest piece of empirical analysis of the relationship between money and the national income was the analysis of the data made available by the National Bureau of Economic Research and the Kuznets' data on U.S. national income. By means of rather ingenious econometric techniques, Friedman and Anna Schwartz were able to relate cycles of income and money cycles over a period of 90 years to show that a strong correlation did exist both in money supply and velocity of circulation, thereby proving that monetary cycles and business cycles are related.

Much less evident, however, is the *direction* of causal relationship. This is the important issue, which, in the final analysis, divides the monetarist from the non-monetarist. The Keynesian economist would argue that the line of causation runs through investment and the investment multiplier to income itself, thence to the supply of money. Fluctuations in investment, then, are responsible for changes in employment as well as income and prices. Policy should be directed toward the control of interest rates with the objective of increasing (or decreasing) investment. Friedman argues that the causal relationship runs from money to income and prices and to verify this he relies on the evidence of historical fact to show that changes in money stock have been the consequence of actual events which then have reacted upon income and prices. The causal relationship is from money to income and prices because the monetary cycle has preceded the income cycle in time; furthermore, prices also react to the increased supply of money as is indicated by the fairly steady upward trend of the price level during the entire period. The facts, Friedman says, justify two generalizations:

There is a one-to-one relationship between monetary changes and changes in money income and prices.

and

The changes in the stock of money cannot consistently be explained by the contemporary changes in money income and prices.[7]

Still, however, the sceptics, of whom Nicholas Kaldor is a chief spokesman, are not completely convinced. The causal relationship in this case, so he argues, is through investment in stocks and not the supply of money which really does not matter because velocity changes absorb any slack or tightness which may develop. It follows, therefore, that short-term interest rates which affect the cost of investment in inventory and not money are the important variables to be regulated.[8]

C. What *Is* Monetarism?

In recent years the distinction between monetarist and non-monetarist economists has become much less distinct. We find, for example, that Professor Samuelson in his *Economics* notes that monetarists prefer to "short-circuit" the process of income determination as compared to non-monetarists in the following manner:

Non-monetarist, $M \rightarrow i \rightarrow I \rightarrow NNP$
(i = interest and I = investment)
Monetarist, $M \rightarrow MV \equiv NNP$[9]

Samuelson argues that both can represent the same set of facts in a different language, "English or French," and that "reasonable men will not argue about terminology or semantics." The thrust of Samuelson's argument rests in the concept of velocity of circulation. It is velocity that makes all the difference; we recall that Friedman's conversion of the demand for money function into the Quantity Theory finished with a derivation of velocity functionally determined by seven variables. In the final analysis, according to Samuelson, the chain of causation from money to interest through investment to Net National Product is nothing more than an expression of this velocity of circulation. Thus, within the conceptual framework of

[6]Reprinted from *Studies in the Quantity Theory of Money*, by Milton Friedman, by permission of University of Chicago Press, Chicago, 1956, pp. 20-21. © University of Chicago.

[8]N. Kaldor, "The New Monetarism," Walters, *op. cit.*, p. 271.
[9]P. Samuelson and A. Scott, *Economics*, Third Canadian Edition, McGraw-Hill, 1971, p. 421.

"velocity" lies the distinction between monetarism and non-monetarism. The monetarist (Friedman) would argue that demand for money is constant except in the very long-term; therefore, an increase in the money supply means that people have more money than they wish to hold. As Professor Johnson has put it, they proceed to pass on, via the spending mechanism, their "problem" to others until the price level rises to correct the difficulty. The non-monetarist, on the other hand, would consider that an expansion in the money supply would lower the interest rate and encourage investment in stocks of inventory (the short term rate of interest) or capital equipment (the long-term rate of interest). Through the investment multiplier the national income (NNP) is raised and the money supply already exists to finance either the increased employment or higher prices.

Still, however, the essential difference between the monetarist and the non-monetarist is more fundamental than is implied by Samuelson's simplified scheme, and this, it seems, revolves around the concept of time. Keynes, as has been pointed out earlier, conceived of equilibrium in terms of the short-run, and this short-run is sufficiently short in time that price adjustments do not have time to work themselves out. This was quite clear in Keynes' world of unemployment because this was precisely his interpretation of what he saw — unemployed factors of production with apparent price/wage inflexibility.

Keynes was fundamentally a Marshallian economist in terms of his analytical approach, i.e., in terms of demand/supply relationships, and Marshall, in his *Principles*, makes quite clear that in the short period there is not sufficient time for productive processes to adjust to changes in demand. Capital equipment cannot increase readily in supply nor can skills, productive efficiency, etc.

> The supply of specialized skill and ability, of suitable machinery and other material capital, and of the appropriate industrial organization has not time to be fully adapted to demand...
> On the one hand there is not time materially to increase those appliances if the supply of them is deficient; and on the other, if the supply is excessive, some of them must remain imperfectly employed... Variations in the particular income derived from them

do not *for the time* affect perceptibly the supply; and do not directly affect the price of the commodities produced by them.[10]

One might conceive of this situation in terms of demand/supply curves as shown in Diagram 16-1. A shift leftward in demand does not necessarily mean a fall in price in the short-term but a slowing down of output with excess capacity equal to $Q_2 - Q_1$. Presumably an excessive storage of inventory of finished goods would also exist which could be reduced in either of two methods — reduction in price or reduction in output.

Storage of inventory stocks necessarily involves a cost in the form of borrowed funds which are generally short-term loans at short-term rates. When the stocks are excessive, dealers and producers will tend to reduce them, but not by lowering selling prices, which would reduce the value of their investment if demand is inelastic. By reducing the cost of inventory investment through a lower short-term interest rate, sellers and producers will find that the pressure is eased. Keynes' interpretation of the facts in his depression world led him to the conclusion that the Quantity Theory was not applicable until full employment had been reached, and, since there was not full employment, it followed that the Quantity Theory had no relevance. Until full employment, additions to the amount of money would be absorbed into a whole range of elasticities of wages, prices, outputs, and demand to changes in the supply of money.[11] Or, in terms of the Quantity Theory, a lowering of velocity of circulation would absorb the additional money before the price level would rise. This is the argument underlying Tobin's first proposition from the General Theory as set forth in Chapter 15.

The monetarist interpretation of changes in the money supply involves velocity changes as well; however, as Friedman and Schwartz have shown, velocity can *reinforce* (or counteract) the effect of changes in the money supply. But the

---

[10]A. Marshall, *Principles of Economics*, Macmillan and Co., London, 1947, p. 376. Marshall is generally thought of as indicating that prices are flexible in the short period, as he argued in his famous fish market case in Chapter 5 of his *Principles*. The passage cited suggests that he was indeed aware of price inflexibility.
[11]J.M. Keynes, *op. cit.*, ch. 21.

Diagram 16-1

PRICE ADJUSTMENT LAG

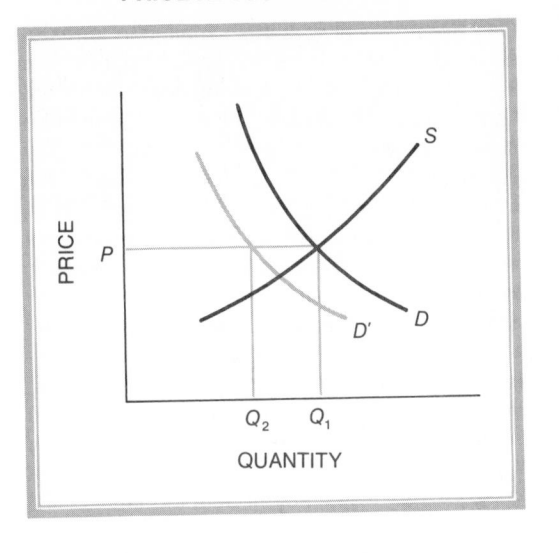

interesting feature is that both the monetarist and non-monetarist analyses come very close in the monetarist interpretation of the effect on real income. The monetarist does allow for the effect of changes in the money supply on real income as well as on prices, whereas the Keynesian considers the impact of money supply changes entirely on real income until full employment. For the monetarist, the impact of changes in the money supply splits into two "streams"; one directed toward real income (and employment) and one toward prices. The size of the impact stream "depends upon two major factors: anticipations about the behaviour of prices, . . . and the current level of output or employment compared with the full employment (permanent) level of output or employment."[12] The non-monetarist assumes no *monetary* impact on prices though modern Keynesian economists do allow for a "cost-push" effect on the price level, and this, it would seem, is the essence of the difference between the two approaches (at least as far as this writer can make out).

Though simple enough to express, this difference is nonetheless important. It means, according to

monetarists, that money matters considerably (though it is not *all* that matters) during short periods. The non-monetarist, on the other hand, would argue that money does not matter. In matters of policy, the monetarist says that any tampering with the money supply in the interest of adjusting interest rates is likely to be destabilizing; whereas the non-monetarist would assert interest rates must be suitably controlled in the interest of full employment.

This analysis of the short-run monetarist/non-monetarist controversy leads directly to the concept of the Hayekian long-run equilibrium toward which the economy progresses and which was discussed in Chapter 15. To a certain degree, we might consider the Keynesian short-period as *too* short for prices to adjust; if we do this, the Friedman monetarist might allow for price adjustments which would require a somewhat longer period— longer than the business cycle itself. If this is the case, "Hayekian time" is *very* much longer because it involves an adjustment of relative price structures which will reflect supply/demand conditions in the markets for goods as well as markets for capital inputs. At the same time, it permits a readjustment of production decisions, and these will be taken in accordance with relative costs of production including both wage costs and the costs of capital equipment. These latter costs will be broken down as appropriate for long vs. short-term debt, equity vs. bond financing, etc., depending upon the circumstances and the type of capital equipment required.

The structure of finance for this capital expenditure will, in equilibrium, correspond to the physical structure of capital. This is most important because the true saving-investment equilibrium will require that the structure of liquidity foregone by savers equate to the structure of capital investment. This is why the famous Keynesian identity, $S = I$, is really quite meaningless and is not an equation at all.

In addition, the nature of the productive process resulting, whether roundabout, time-consuming or more direct, labour intensive, will determine the long-run employment level in the economy. The failure of the saving structure to equate to the structure of investment means that the public did not continue the saving process it had begun so as to make possible the completion of the capital investment which had been laid down,

[12]Friedman, "A Theoretical Framework for Monetary Analysis," in Walters, *op. cit.*, p. 90.

and the consequence of this is a rising price level coincident with unemployment.

It will readily be seen that the Hayekian (or long-term) time period and the policy measures necessary to implement short-run objectives can be in direct conflict. As an example consider the following quotation from one of our better known textbooks in Economics:

> The Bank of Canada is our central bank, a bank for bankers and for the government. Every central bank has *one prime function*: It operates to control the economy's supply of money and credit. If business is getting worse and jobs are getting scarce, the Bank of Canada will try to expand money and credit. But if spending threatens to become excessive, so that prices are rising and there are many job vacancies, then the Bank of Canada will do all that is possible to step on the brakes and contract money and credit. The policy of the equivalent U.S. central bank, the Federal Reserve, has been aptly said to "lean against the wind" of prevailing deficient or excessive aggregate-demand spending, to promote optimal real growth and price-level stability. All mixed economies rely on such a central bank.[13]

What is most impressive about this statement (published at the beginning of this decade) is its incredibly simplistic view of the function of a central bank, i.e., to "lean against the wind" of aggregate demand. Unfortunately life is just not so simple. Policies devised for the short-run alleviation of unemployment (expansion of money and credit) will not necessarily (and probably *will* not) be appropriate for the long-term. If there is one lesson that has been learned from the experience of the 1970s it surely must be that we can no longer rely on simple Keynesian measures, adequate though they were in the days of the Great Depression, to maintain our economic well-being. Inflation and unemployment are a dear price to pay for lessons.

---

[13]P. Samuelson and A. Scott, *Economics*, Fourth Canadian Edition, McGraw-Hill Ryerson, Toronto, 1975, p. 283. This is already out of date. The central bank policy is now one of "targeting" in terms of monetary growth—a virtual agreement with the monetarist philosophy that money does matter.

The fact of the matter is that the policy of the Bank of Canada is quite different from that outlined above. The Bank has already abandoned its version of "leaning against the wind" and is now, following the lead of the German *Bundesbank*, targeting its money supply growth. This is really a victory for Professor Friedman and the monetarists, for most western central banks are now using the same approach. How and why this has come about we shall see in Part II of this chapter.

II. THE CANADIAN EXPERIENCE

A. Savings and Investment

In Part I it was argued that the well-known Savings/Investment identity does not mean that savings equal investment; in fact, it is this argument which is at the "focal point" of these chapters. Because of its significance, we would do well to expand the idea further to show in what sense an identity is really not an equation. Consider the following example:

Suppose an increment of investment is undertaken which requires a million dollars to be expended in the construction of a factory scheduled for completion in one year. Suppose further that the finance for this factory is to be a bond issue to be amortized in exactly one year. In this case, savings and investment are equal because individuals who have purchased these bonds have foregone their right to consume for one year in order that carpenters, bricklayers, etc., employed in the construction of that factory may consume instead.

Now suppose that the finance of the factory were not by means of a 1-year bond at all but through a financial intermediary which arranges a loan to be "covered" by million dollar investment certificates due for maturity in three months. This means that as fast as one issue of certificates matures, another is sold to continue the finance of the 1-year factory loan and thus maintain the solvency of the financial intermediary. In this case, savings do *not* equal investment (except in the identity sense) because the owners of these short-term investment certificates have not foregone their right to consume for one year — only three months. In short, even though a million dollars is not being spent at any one moment throughout the entire year, savings and investment are not equal because the liquidity foregone by savers is considerably less than the liquidity requirement of the investment.

This point can also be made by considering it from the consumption side. Suppose the normal annual velocity of circulation is exactly 4. The million dollars being "saved" by means of the 3-month certificates can purchase a maximum of $3 million worth of consumer goods throughout the year, whereas the million dollar bond can purchase, at the most, only $1 million of goods during the year. The difference between the two is velocity of circulation; on the average, the annual velocity of the 3-month certificates is 3 while the velocity of the bond is just 1. In both cases the savings/investment identity holds, but in only the former do savings equal investment.

In terms of liquidity, the Canadian public has foregone liquidity (in the second case) for 3 months during which time the construction of the factory has begun. But, having provided the financing for consumption by the construction workers for one-quarter of a factory, the public refuses to finish the task of saving which has already been started. Savings certificates are being converted into current liquidity for spending purposes forcing the financial intermediary to find further short-term finance for the construction workers, and the process continues in this way until the factory is completed. But such short-term financing does not reduce velocity of circulation of money sufficiently to constitute genuine savings. In short we prefer to have both the factory and the liquidity which will finance a higher real standard of living for which we have not really saved and to which we are not, therefore, entitled. Savings do not *equal* investment.

A typical Canadian solution is to locate foreign investment so that foreigners may perform the savings for us; in this case we have the factory without the sacrifice of liquidity. Our higher standard of living is made possible by means of increased imports of consumer goods using the foreign exchange which comes via the investment route. This is satisfactory until balance of payments difficulties arise due to the inevitable service requirements of foreign debt.

B. A Paradox

Another aspect of saving discussed in Macroeconomics textbooks is the famous "Paradox of Thrift." This concept, it will be recalled, was developed to show the difference between household saving and national saving; it tells us that an increase in thriftiness in general decreases the national income. This happens because consumption is reduced and each household's saving reduces the income of the next household after the manner outlined in Chapter 2.

The idea of the paradox of thrift was developed within the context of the Great Depression, a sad era of some 45 years ago. During these years the emphasis was laid upon how to increase employment within the short-term. What is surprising is that the Paradox of Thrift should remain as part of the "general theory" of macroeconomics *outside* the depression era, because, during those years, investment was conspicuous (see Chapter 3) by its absence.[14] At that time (see Chapter 4), banks had ample liquidity for lending; in fact, they found it necessary to increase their holdings of government securities because business enterprises refused (for good reason) to incur the risk of borrowing to expand their businesses. Any additional savings, therefore, could only add to this pool of excess liquidity, and since no corresponding investment was forthcoming, the national income was reduced by the simple act of not consuming.

But all this is not true in the decade of the 1970s. Capital, and savings which generate capital, are in *short* supply and businessmen pay high interest rates for their loans either to the banking system or the capital market. Far from being a "paradox," hence by implication something to be avoided, saving is precisely what is most required. Let us see what *would* happen if additional savings were made available by the public to capital markets. Interest rates, we could be sure, would drop a few points if the additional savings were sufficiently great. This would lower mortgage rates for housing, prime rates for busi-

---

[14]See, for example, Lipsey, Sparks, and Steiner, *Economics*, Harper and Row, New York, 2nd edition, pp. 542-544.

ness loans, and, generally, all rates of return for the various forms of future liquidity, precisely what business enterprises require — greater availability of funds at lower cost. Instead of being a "paradox of thrift" which would lower income, investment could be encouraged in these days of the 1970s, and we could see "boom" conditions in reasonably short order. This is why saving must be considered within the context of the time before concluding that declining income could be the result.

But there is something else which is also very important in all this business of saving. The first "act" of saving means non-consumption, but non-consumption of what? Except for depression conditions when non-consumption is forced by inadequate income, a decision not to consume a specific commodity is a signal to the producer of that commodity that profits will no longer be forthcoming and he must switch his production into something else. This is obvious enough. But when savings in general increase, this is also a signal of great importance. The public is rationally deciding that it prefers future liquidity (or future consumption from future liquidity) to present liquidity (or present consumption from present liquidity). Having received the signal through the free market system, business enterprise will respond to the public's preferences, again via the market system, by scheduling its productive process toward a more roundabout, time-consuming production technique. This means that additional capital equipment will be put into place financed by the additional savings. Employment in these industries, construction, capital goods, and the like, will increase and a "boom" can result. This is why there is nothing paradoxical about thrift at all; it is rather anachronistic that some macroeconomists persist in generalizing from the unusual depression circumstances which prevailed in western economies some 45 years ago.

There is another more serious "paradox" which we face today—the phenomena of inflation and unemployment. The typical macroeconomic interpretation of this, known as "stagflation," has been to relate the degree of resource use to the tendency for prices to rise—a kind of "J Curve" when employment is plotted against the annual rate of price increase. The discovery of this relationship has been generally attributed to A.W.

Phillips who developed the curve from British statistics, 1862 to 1958, but an earlier version of the same relation was published by A.J. Brown using data, 1881 to 1914.[15]

A more rational explanation, at least for Canada, is likely to be the coincidence of structural unemployment and excessive liquidity (or excessive aggregate demand). This arises, as has been argued in Chapter 15, from an excessive use of labour saving, roundabout production techniques which are made more profitable than the direct labour intensive techniques because of low interest rates and rising labour costs. Hardly anyone would dispute the fact that when technology replaces labour with machines, a shortage of jobs must occur unless total production of goods can increase sufficiently to employ the displaced workers.

Not *all* capital investment need be purely labour-saving, however. Quite the contrary; modern technology has not yet completely replaced the human brain in its decision-making capacity. At the unskilled level, however, the two factors of production may be competitive so that entrepreneurs may choose either of the two methods of production depending upon which is the more advantageous to him. We know that labour costs can be increased considerably by a combination of trade union pressure for higher wages and the Wicksell Effect. Labour costs, on the other hand, can be reduced by productivity gains. Thus, as output per man-hour (productivity) increases, we should expect the unemployment rate to decline because labour intensive production becomes cheaper. For example, between the years, 1961 and 1969, productivity showed a growth trend of 4.2% per year during which period unemployment averaged 4.9%. From 1970–77, productivity gains were much smaller at 2.18% per year with unemployment at an average of 6.4%.[16]

Up to this point, a somewhat artificial distinction has been made between "long" and "short"-term analysis suggesting a difference in terms of time alone. This was used to distinguish between a Keynesian argument appropriate to the period of

[15]A.J. Brown, *The Great Inflation, 1939-51*, Oxford University Press, 1955, p. 99.
[16]Growth trends were calculated from Statistics Canada data published in *Economic Review*, Ministry of Finance, April, 1978.

the 1930s and the Hayekian (or Austrian) line of reasoning which is based upon entrepreneurial decisions as to the appropriate technique of production. Simply because some time is required for this decision, it is referred to as "long-term." The Keynesian short term is characterized by economic measures designed to counteract unemployment which is "short term" because it develops before the price adjustments which influence the entrepreneur's decision take place. This is not to suggest, however, that business enterprise requires a long period of calendar time to adjust its productive process. In many cases the time may be quite short indeed.

Consider, for example, a small firm which relies on foundry castings for its raw material. These it machines to its own tolerances and specifications appropriate to its output by using lathes and lathe operators. Any increase in productivity (output per man-hour) lowers the wage cost to the entrepreneur, and, other things being equal (including interest rates), the investment structure will "tilt" toward a direct labour-intensive production technique. Employment in the firm will rise.

Now, suppose, for the sake of the argument, that wage increases, which take place through collective bargaining, result in labour's acquiring the benefits of productivity increases for itself. In addition, rising costs of living, etc., encourage further incremental wage demands. The employer may now be forced to reconsider his production process by seeking sources of castings which have already been machined to his approximate specifications but which are cheaper to him because they are produced by capital intensive techniques. The supplying company which specializes in such machining relies upon mass sales to other similar firms and can, therefore, utilize a roundabout production technique most effectively at lowest cost. In this case, the original entrepreneur can now substitute a lower cost capital intensive technique which is less expensive than his higher cost labour intensive production. A "tilting" toward capital investment has taken place and structural unemployment results. This is a "long-run" decision taken within a short span of time.

We cannot, therefore, simply divide the long-run time period into short periods of time in such a way that a series of rational short-run decisions will equal one long period. The process of long-

term decision-making actually overlaps into the short term in such a way that as time passes, the long-run decision gains in importance relative to short-term decisions. Eventually, given sufficient time, increasingly high cost labour will result in correspondingly greater capital intensive production throughout the entire productive sector with the consequence that we become "locked into" a permanent structural unemployment situation. Capital, once laid in place, cannot be removed until it is exhausted. The only way, then, to alleviate such structural unemployment is by means of an expansion of aggregate demand which, in turn, means lower interest rates to encourage more investment. So the "paradox" of macroeconomics, unemployment and inflation, is easily understood once it is seen in the light of structural unemployment; in fact, it really is not a paradox at all.

C. Canadian Policy

The Canadian experience is particularly interesting because it is an example of a conflict of economic theory within the context of actual events. There are, to put it briefly, decisions to be made by those entrusted with the responsibility of decision-making, whether elected officials or civil servants, and we, the public, must live with the consequences of these decisions.

As we saw in Chapter 5, the Bank of Canada is fairly young as central banks go, having had its origins in the extraordinary circumstances of the liquidity collapse of the 1930s. Central banks, by their nature, (the Bank of Canada is no exception) are institutions designed to replace the rigid discipline of gold as money. Thus, if we had and were content to have a gold circulating standard, the central bank would exist purely as a supplier of bank notes which are exchangeable for gold at any time. Because we have a preference for a flexibility of the money supply which gold mines cannot supply, we charge the central bank with the responsibility of acting instead of a gold mine, and more, act in such a way that the output of the "gold mine" is flexible enough to rise whenever the occasion requires it and fall when opposite conditions dictate.

This is an awesome responsibility not to be taken lightly. If an error is committed, the consequences of the error could be considerable, especially if the error is one of "commission rather than omission." To take a particular action which is wrong means that to correct the mistake, the steps must first be retraced *then* turned in the right direction. Not to take action (omission) means that the mistake can be corrected by simply taking the correct action in the first place. It is natural, therefore, that central banks, including the Bank of Canada, would tend toward conservatism, i.e., act somewhat in the same manner as the gold which they have supplanted.

This problem did not arise during the early years of the Bank's history. There was no doubt in anyone's mind as to the correct monetary action. As Governor Towers put it, a tight money policy was simply out of the question, and every encouragement was given to business enterprises to acquire the necessary credit at the lowest cost.[17]

After World War II, the removal of wartime controls and subsidies meant a release of inflationary cost pressures, on the one hand, and the freeing of ample liquid funds to finance rising prices on the other. The fiscal policy of the government at the time was one of generating a surplus of revenues for the purpose of immobilizing these surplus funds; hence, the Bank of Canada did not curtail credit and raise interest rates (tight money) believing that more harm than good would be accomplished. However, it did discourage chartered banks from financing new capital investment and the finance of inventory accumulation (historically the "correct" form of bank lending) was "not encouraged."[18]

In 1949 there were definite changes. There were production increases and the rather large annual increases in long-term investment ceased in favour of smaller increments with the consequence that the inflationary pressures of the early postwar era had largely disappeared. At the same time, there was another development which was to prove fateful for Canada as far as the future was concerned. The United States, characterized by close proximity geographically and culturally, had emerged from the War with an enormous appetite for imports, particularly raw material. Yet, there was an acute shortage of U.S. dollars

in the world because other countries, still recovering from the ravages of war, were desperately short of supplies which only the United States was capable of producing. Because of this dollar shortage and the import restrictions and exchange control regulations, Canada was turning away from its more traditional trading partners toward the obvious continuously growing market for exports which, of course, did not have a shortage of dollars. There was no foreign exchange restriction or import restriction on the part of the United States.[19]

It can be questioned that any policies such as trade preferences with Commonwealth countries could ever have been successful in orienting our trade to countries other than the U.S. in view of the obvious circumstances; nevertheless, it is significant that a public official of the stature of the Governor of the Bank of Canada should recognize and encourage what was really a short-term objective for Canadian trade policy. The long-run was over the distant horizon. No one, not even Governor Towers, could see *beyond* the dollar shortage to the day that a *dollar overhang* would be the problem. Nor, for that matter, could it have been foreseen that a free-floating Canadian dollar would be so closely tied by way of these same close trade relations to the U.S. dollar that the movement of the U.S. dollar in foreign exchange markets means an automatic movement of the Canadian dollar. In 1949, the IMF and the fixed exchange rate system was the rule which was expected to be eternal.

While it is inevitable that a central bank must evolve and develop just as any other economic institution, there is (and was) no clear indication of the direction of its growth apart from the "conservatism" inherent in the nature of its function. This "conservatism" tends toward the doctrine of the Quantity Theory of Money in its more simple Fisherine form. Still, one cannot but have enormous respect for the Bank of Canada officials who have the responsibility of steering monetary policy through business fluctuations which generally originate in the U.S. The difficulty of the task is best illustrated by a remark made by Graham Towers who said that it is extremely difficult to do better than the U.S. in matters of economic policy,

---

[17]G. Towers, Address to the Board of Trade, St. John's, Newfoundland, June 19, 1950, p. 4.
[18]*Ibid.*

[19]*Ibid.*

"hard enough" to do as well, and very easy to do worse.[20] One might have sympathy for the public servant under these conditions because of the sheer complexity of the task, i.e., it is not merely a question of developing a monetary policy for Canada, but, given the circumstances, the Bank of Canada must decide on its policy in the light of not only existing U.S. policy, but also what U.S. policy is likely to be in the future. Thus, it is really a combination of events and the Federal Reserve Board's reaction to these events— two circumstances impossible to forecast — which must be the primary input into the Governor's policy decisions.

This is why an objective on the part of the Governor of the Bank of Canada and his staff to do *better* than the U.S. seems next to impossible. It could be done, however, if the Bank could develop a longer-term view of events and orient its policy toward that view. This would mean that as the U.S. changes its policy in accordance with cyclical developments ("leaning against the wind") the Bank of Canada is already ahead in the sense that it is following a policy which the U.S. Federal Reserve Board must eventually develop itself. In other words, the Bank of Canada must be better equipped both in knowledge and input into its decision-making process than the Federal Reserve Board. This was the task Governor James E. Coyne, the successor to Graham Towers, and his staff set for themselves.

Was this task reasonable? In the light of hindsight, yes. Admittedly few recognized it at the time; there were, firstly, the problems of the business cycles of the 1950s to be overcome, but there were also some fundamental structural changes in the Canadian economy which were destined to crystallize Canada's productive system and patterns of consumption for many years in the future.

Probably the first suggestion that inflation might be a long-run possibility for the future was the investment boom following the 1954 recession. The enormous inflow of foreign capital into Canada which took place during this period was directed toward the development of resources of primary commodities for the purpose of export.

This was sparked by a general concern for the future in a world in which peace, as the Korean War had proved, was not necessarily guaranteed. The Paley Report, which stressed the importance of adequate supplies of strategic raw materials, was the official expression of this concern. The size of the inflow of foreign capital can be seen from the growth of net foreign investment from $4 billion in 1949 to $17 billion in 1960.[21]

The consequence of this enormous influx of foreign capital meant that Canadians moved toward the second stage of importing consumer goods financed by the foreign exchange which had accrued because of large imports of capital. A deficit in the balance of trade, therefore, appeared each year from the year 1956 to 1960. Most important, however, was the fact that Canada's productive capacity was being structured toward the more capital intensive types of production of export-oriented commodities. In Hayekian terms the investment function was being tilted toward more capital intensive productive processes.

The surprising feature of all this was that it was observed by the Governor of the Bank of Canada and reported as follows:

> The fact that very much larger capital investment in physical plant and equipment in Canada than in the United States did not produce a commensurately greater increase in production of goods and services in Canada illustrates a general point which I think should be taken into consideration in public discussion of these matters, which is that economic growth, in the sense of growth of total output, is not the same as, and does not necessarily accompany, "growth" in the sense of having a high level of physical capital investment. In principle there could be just as much growth in total output with a lower capital investment in the economy as a whole, although the nature of production would presumably be somewhat different.[22]

It is, of course, the last sentence which strikes us most forcefully, i.e., *the nature of production would be somewhat different*. The Governor, Mr.

---

[20]A recollection of Mr. James D. Gibson, O.B.E. in a personal interview.

[21]Annual Report of the Governor of the Bank of Canada, 1960, p. 13.
[22]*Ibid.*, p. 12.

Coyne, was already recognizing the reorientation of production toward larger amounts of capital investment which would result in unemployment. However, to be honest, he was not aware of the nature of structural employment in the Hayekian sense, rather that employment could be stimulated in Canada by means of less reliance on the part of Canadians on imports from the United States.

> I believe we will come up against insuperable obstacles to overcoming our unemployment problem in Canada if we cannot give our own producers adequate opportunities to provide goods for the Canadian market and bring about a reduction in our excessive imports from the United States.[23]

Nevertheless, there is a prophetic ring to Mr. Coyne's "insuperable obstacles." A structuring of Canadian production toward primary commodities, on the one hand, and a heavy reliance on imports on the other is a Canadian adaptation of a Hayekian tilting of the investment curve which would have likely resulted in rising prices much earlier had it not been for the inflow of imports. Once these imports are cut back, inflation follows.

At the same time, the consciousness and awareness of inflation and its dangers were always present in the mind of Governor Coyne. This was why it was so important for the Bank of Canada to maintain a control of the money supply which in turn meant restraint on the chartered banks. He abhorred the reliance on some "magic power" which could bring about additional monetary expansion combined with deficit financing which could "cure" unemployment by expanding the money supply and lowering interest rates. Quite the contrary; the banks were in a position of substantially increased liquidity adequate for all reasonable requirements for an expansion of loans to business enterprises in Canada.[24] To go beyond this would stimulate inflation which would, in turn, result in substantial deflation.

We can characterize Mr. Coyne's economic phi-losophy as more than just "conservative" in the sense that he was substituting a central bank for a gold mine in a strict application of the Quantity Theory of Money. He actually went well beyond a strictly interpreted monetary sphere, integrating the Canadian monetary system with the economic forces which determine the real economy itself. It was his, and his staff's, awareness of the importance of genuine savings, as opposed to "artifical" savings, which comes closest to the Austrian concept of capital.

> Above all, I am concerned lest Canadians should fail to appreciate or close their eyes to the implications of certain economic tendencies, in the thought that there is in monetary management some magical power or hidden hand which will relieve us of the necessity of remedying our situation by our own exertions, by not consuming more than we produce, and by prudent management of our collective affairs. Monetary expansion, low interest rates, and abundant loans not based on actual domestic savings will not counteract such trends (but if adopted will make them worse) and will be able to make little if any contribution towards alleviating the problems of large and sudden adjustments which will be necessary some day if earlier action of the appropriate character is not taken to forestall them.[25]

In this rejection of monetary action *in lieu of savings*, Mr. Coyne was showing a long-range view more far-sighted than his contemporaries. By "large and sudden adjustments" he meant the wide swings of the business cycle which are actually accentuated by "stop and go" policies of the central banks. It is in this sense that he had hoped to restore full employment and stable prices in the end.

The unfortunate circumstances which surrounded Mr. Coyne's resignation as Governor of the Bank of Canada carried with it the rejection of his economic principles which were, as will be recognized, neither new nor different because they were well within the stream of a long and

---

[23]Statement to the Senate Special Committee on Manpower and Employment, April 26, 1961.
[24]*Ibid.*

[25]Annual Report of the Governor of the Bank of Canada, 1959, p. 10.

well-respected tradition of economic theory. The fact that the Austrian school and Professor Hayek have not been so well-known in North America is not the fault of Mr. Coyne nor Professor Hayek. Neither of them were familiar with the economic principles of the other. Indeed the rather cheap pun, "Coynesian Economics" which was coined (readers may forgive another pun) by some economists to apply to the era of the 1950s is suggestive of the lack of awareness on the part of many Canadian economists of the long-standing Austrian tradition.[26] At any rate, the philosophical battle was lost to the neo-Keynesian economists and politicians, and with the appointment of the new Governor of the Bank of Canada and the new Minister of Finance, Mr. Walter Gordon, the thrust of policy was laid on measures to stimulate employment.

One must concede that these measures were successful in terms of their immediate objectives. The unemployment rate fell to 3.6% in 1966, and, as we have seen earlier, output per man-hour, or productivity, rose. The money supply increased, of course, slowly at first, but with rising rates of increase, to reach 12% per year by 1971. Thereafter, neither M_2 nor M_3 have been as low as 12%, though M_1, under the influence of "targeting," reached 8% in both 1976 and 1977. We can say then that the reign of Keynesian economics lasted some 15 years to be finally ended by the policy of targeting which was a concession to the monetarist school of Professor Friedman. It is *not*, however, a return to the ideas of Mr. Coyne by any means; for that we will likely have to wait some years yet.

It is clear, if we are to learn from the experiences of others as well as ourselves, that responsible monetary policy is essential to our economic well-being. This is the lesson of the Bundesbank which successfully controls its money supply by saying, in effect, to the banks under its jurisdiction, *this* is the amount of money expansion you may have this year and no more; do with it what you can. At the same time deposit liquidity is rigidly controlled in Germany by a system of legal ratios which further constrain the banks in their

intermediary function. At the other extreme we have the Bank of England which is attempting to control its money supply growth with varying degrees of success and experiencing an even higher inflation rate than Canada. We can learn a great deal from experiences such as these if we only take the trouble to research.

Ultimately, it is likely to be true that monetary policies of the Bank of Canada and the Minister of Finance (they are really joint policies now) must include not just short-term measures of targeting the money supply but long-term objectives designed to reduce both long-term inflation and structural unemployment. After all, the "long-term" is just as present as the short-term though its presence may not be felt quite so soon. This may be quite a task for the Bank to undertake; indeed, some might question the worth of even attempting it, preferring instead a policy of a moderate but steady annual rate of increase in the money supply or even a return to a gold standard. Successful monetary policies can be implemented, though, as other countries with both lower inflation rates and lower unemployment rates have clearly demonstrated.

CONCLUSION

Anyone who has researched the area of money and monetary policy cannot but have the greatest admiration for the professionals on the Bank of Canada staff—those who develop and administer monetary policy and those who provide the necessary information through research which makes policy decisions possible. It is a difficult task, always subject to the sharp criticism of the public with but little praise, and, except for an occasional speech by an official of the Bank, little recognition. But this is very much as it should be because it is important that the central bank always maintain a low profile. The nature of its work is such that public confidence in the Bank and the monetary system itself could be easily eroded if the administration of the monetary system were not well disciplined at all times. Most important is the fact that there must be no secrets or mysteries about the operation of either the Bank or the working of the system. This applies not only to its domestic activities but the foreign exchange

[26]See, for example, T.J. Courchene, "Recent Canadian Monetary Policy," reprinted in *Canadian Banking and Monetary Policy*, Cairns, Binhammer (eds.), McGraw-Hill Ryerson, 1972, p. 204.

markets as well. In the foreign exchange market, the paradox of the Bank's insistence upon a floating rate in the market for the Canadian dollar, with the value determined by supply and demand, at the same time that the government is borrowing to *support* its value, is an example of how *not* to inspire confidence.

The current domestic policy of the Bank of Canada is much more successful in terms of confidence. The targeting principle, combined with high interest rates,will likely prove to be successful in reducing inflation and, in the end, unemployment. The principle, in theory, is good, i.e., encourage through high interest rates sufficient savings so that additional money supply expansion required by business enterprise will find its way into M_2 or M_3 rather than M_1. This is done, of course, by means of the high bank rate established by the Bank of Canada. Should the danger arise of switching from M_2 or M_3 into M_1, to finance rising prices, there is still left the weapon of the sale of securities on the open market to restrict the money supply as rapidly as possible. Whether or not unemployment will be reduced in this way, in view of the likely existence of considerable structural unemployment, remains to be seen. Certainly the high interest cost of loans should discourage capital-intensive techniques of production if wage costs can be somehow kept sufficiently low.

Another possible policy which could be followed by the Bank of Canada would be similar to the Bundesbank of West Germany. In this case, the central bank money itself is targeted. Commercial banks, therefore, must be satisfied with these "reserves" of central bank money—there is no more —and use them as efficiently as they can. At the same time, there are the different ratios for liabilities which greatly restrict the financial intermediary function of the banks. In its latest monetary target announcement, the Bundesbank council broke with its previous practice and announced a 6 to 9% money expansion for the year 1979.[27] This flexibility permits the possibility of adjustment depending upon conditions as they develop throughout the year.

But regardless of the policy technique being followed it is certainly necessary for it to coincide with the peculiar circumstances and requirements of Canada. We are a very different country with very different conditions from any of the European countries, and the fact that Canada shares a common border with the U.S., with all the economic significance it implies, must be an equally important determining factor in whatever policy is elected.

ADDITIONAL READINGS

Courchene, Thomas J., *Money, Inflation and the Bank of Canada*, C.D. Howe Research Institute, Montreal. An important work by an authority in the field of monetary policy.

Friedman, Milton, "The Role of Monetary Policy," *American Economic Review*, March, 1968, p. 1, reprinted in *Current Issues of Economic Policy*, Reynolds, Green, Lewis (eds.), Irwin, Homewood, Ill., 1973, p. 35, also in *Readings in Money, National Income and Stabilization Policy*, Smith, Teigen (eds.), (same publisher), Third Edition, 1974, p. 412.

Kaldor, Nicholas, "Monetary Policy, Economic Stability and Growth," *Money and Banking*, Walters (ed.), Penguin Education, Harmondsworth, Middlesex, England, 1973, p. 209. An alternative view.

Reuber, Grant & R.G. Bodkin, "Stagflation: The Canadian Experience," *Issues in Canadian Economics*, Officer, Smith (eds.), McGraw-Hill Ryerson, Toronto, 1974, p. 25.

---

[27] "Monetary Growth Target for 1979," *Monthly Report of the Deutsche Bundesbank*, Vol. 31, #1, January, 1979.